Lecture Notes in Computer Science   8975

Commenced Publication in 1973
Founding and Former Series Editors:
Gerhard Goos, Juris Hartmanis, and Jan van Leeuwen

More information about this series at http://www.springer.com/series/7410

Rainer Böhme · Tatsuaki Okamoto (Eds.)

Financial Cryptography and Data Security

19th International Conference, FC 2015
San Juan, Puerto Rico, January 26–30, 2015
Revised Selected Papers

 Springer

Editors
Rainer Böhme
University of Innsbruck
Innsbruck
Austria

Tatsuaki Okamoto
NTT Laboratories
Tokyo
Japan

ISSN 0302-9743   ISSN 1611-3349   (electronic)
Lecture Notes in Computer Science
ISBN 978-3-662-47853-0   ISBN 978-3-662-47854-7   (eBook)
DOI 10.1007/978-3-662-47854-7

Library of Congress Control Number: 2015943047

LNCS Sublibrary: SL4 – Security and Cryptology

Springer Heidelberg New York Dordrecht London

Printed on acid-free paper

Springer-Verlag GmbH Berlin Heidelberg is part of Springer Science+Business Media
(www.springer.com)

Preface

FC 2015, the 19th International Conference on Financial Cryptography and Data Security, was held during January 26–30, 2015, at the Intercontinental San Juan Hotel in Puerto Rico. This edition received the highest number of participants in the history of FC.

We received 102 paper submissions, out of which 33 were accepted, 10 as short papers and 23 as full papers, resulting in a full-paper acceptance rate of 25 %. These proceedings contain revised versions of all the papers, abstracts of three posters, and an edited transcript of the keynote address. The keynote was given by Gavin Andresen, Chief Scientist of the Bitcoin Foundation, who shared with the audience his view on "What Satoshi Did Not Know."

The Program Committee consisted of 53 members with diverse research interests and experience. Papers were reviewed double-blind, with each paper assigned to at least three reviewers. Submissions by Program Committee members received at least four reviews each. During the discussion phase, additional reviews were solicited when necessary. We ensured to the extent possible that all papers received fair and objective evaluation by experts and also a broader group of Program Committee members. The final decisions were made based on the reviews and discussions. The task of paper selection was not easy, and we could not include a number of solid papers for lack of space.

We would like to sincerely thank the authors of all submissions. We, and the Program Committee as a whole, were impressed by the quality of submissions contributed from all around the world. This gave us the opportunity to compile a strong and diverse program.

Our sincere gratitude also goes to the Program Committee. We were extremely fortunate that so many brilliant people volunteered to not only write reviews, but also actively participate in discussions for a period of several weeks. A handful of Program Committee members, whom we asked to serve a shepherds, spent additional time during the holiday season in order to help the authors improving their works. We are also indebted to 88 external reviewers who significantly contributed to the comprehensive evaluation of papers. Lists of Program Committee members, external reviewers, and shepherds appear after this note.

We also thank Joseph Bonneau, the conference General Chair, in particular for working closely with us and providing outstanding support at every step. We also benefited greatly from advice and feedback from Rafael Hirschfeld, the conference Local Arrangements Chair, and from the Board of Directors of the International Financial Cryptography Association.

Finally, we are grateful to the Bitcoin Foundation, NTT, Google, Mirror, SAP, and the National Science Foundation for their generous support.

April 2015

Rainer Böhme
Tatsuaki Okamoto

Organization

Program Committee

Ross Anderson	University of Cambridge, UK
Giuseppe Ateniese	Sapienza University of Rome, Italy
Rainer Böhme	University of Innsbruck, Austria
Alvaro Cardenas	UT Dallas, USA
Sherman S.M. Chow	Chinese University of Hong Kong, SAR China
Nicolas Christin	Carnegie Mellon University, USA
Emiliano De Cristofaro	University College London, UK
Roberto Di Pietro	Bell Labs, France
Serge Egelman	UC Berkeley/ICSI, USA
William Enck	North Carolina State University, USA
Martin Gagne	Wheaton College, USA
Matthew Green	Johns Hopkins University, USA
Jens Grossklags	Pennsylvania State University, USA
Boris Hemkemeier	Commerzbank AG, Germany
Urs Hengartner	University of Waterloo, Canada
Nadia Heninger	University of Pennsylvania, USA
Nicholas Hopper	University of Minnesota, USA
Benjamin Johnson	Carnegie Mellon University, USA
Stefan Katzenbeisser	TU Darmstadt, Germany
Andrew Ker	University of Oxford, UK
Florian Kerschbaum	SAP, Germany
Aggelos Kiayias	University of Athens, Greece
Tadayoshi Kohno	University of Washington, USA
Anja Lehmann	IBM Research Zurich, Switzerland
Helger Lipmaa	University of Tartu, Estonia
Stefan Lucks	Bauhaus-Universität Weimar, Germany
David M'Raihi	Perzo, Inc., USA
Mark Manulis	University of Surrey, UK
Kanta Matsuura	University of Tokyo, Japan
Catherine Meadows	Naval Research Laboratory, USA
Sarah Meiklejohn	University College London, UK
Refik Molva	EURECOM, France
Tyler Moore	Southern Methodist University, USA
Arvind Narayanan	Princeton University, USA
Satoshi Obana	Hosei University, Japan
Tatsuaki Okamoto	NTT, Japan
Claudio Orlandi	Aarhus University, Denmark

Roberto Perdisci	University of Georgia, USA
Josef Pieprzyk	Queensland University of Technology, Australia
Bart Preneel	KU Leuven and iMinds, Belgium
Ahmad-Reza Sadeghi	TU Darmstadt, Germany
Rei Safavi-Naini	University of Calgary, Canada
Pierangela Samarati	Università degli Studi di Milano, Italy
Thomas Schneider	TU Darmstadt, Germany
Gil Segev	Hebrew University, Israel
Emin Gün Sirer	Cornell University, USA
Carmela Troncoso	Gradiant, Spain
Doug Tygar	UC Berkeley, USA
Serge Vaudenay	EPFL Lausanne, Switzerland
Huaxiong Wang	Nanyang Technological University, Singapore
Ralf-Philipp Weinmann	Comsecuris UG, Germany
Akira Yamada	KDDI, Japan
Jianying Zhou	Institute for Infocomm Research, Singapore

External Reviewers

Gilad Asharov	Christian Forler
Aaron Atwater	Julien Freudiger
Monir Azraoui	Christina Garman
Foteini Baldimtsi	Thomas Gibson-Robinson
Harry Bartlett	Vasilis Gkatzelis
Sonia Bogos	Steven Goldfeder
Leon Groot Bruinderink	Jens Hermans
Niklas Büscher	Maximilian Hils
Shaoying Cai	Rob Jansen
Seyit Camtepe	Mahavir Jhawar
Andrea Cerulli	Marc Juarez
Jie Chen	Nikolaos Karvelas
Sandy Clark	Hassan Khan
Richard Clayton	Ayumu Kubota
Shaanan Cohney	Alptekin Küpçü
Bernardo David	Russell W.F. Lai
Daniel Demmler	Hyung Tae Lee
Sabrina De Capitani Di Vimercati	Hoi Le
Ruggero Donida Labati	Su Le
Maria Dubovitskaya	Hoon Wei Lim
Alexandre Duc	Eik List
Benjamin Edelman	Shujun Li
Kaoutar Elkhiyaoui	Roel Maes
Steven Englehardt	Andrew Miller
Sebastian Faust	Simone Mutti

Khoa Nguyen
Michael Nielsen
Melek Önen
Simon Oya
Roel Peeters
Yu Pu
Kenneth Radke
Samuel Ranellucci
MichałRen
Oscar Reparaz
Reza Reyhanitabar
Markus Riek
Cédric Van Rompay
Andre Schaller
Katerina Samari
Sumanta Sarkar
Yukiko Sawaya
Matteo Signorini
Douglas Stebila

Mehdi Tibouchi
Catherine Tucker
Luke Valenta
Marie Vasek
Christian Wachsmann
Boyang Wang
Jakob Wenzel
Jia Xu
Xing-Dong Yang
Yanjiang Yang
Mandel Yu
Thomas Zacharias
Bingsheng Zhang
Liang Feng Zhang
Tao Zhang
Mingyi Zhao
Yongjun Zhao
Xifan Zheng
Michael Zohner

Shepherds

Ross Anderson	University of Cambridge, UK
Alvaro Cardenas	UT Dallas, USA
Sherman S.M. Chow	Chinese University of Hong Kong, SAR China
Roberto Di Pietro	Bell Labs, France
Jens Grossklags	Pennsylvania State University, USA
Boris Hemkemeier	Commerzbank AG, Germany
Nicholas Hopper	University of Minnesota, USA
Benjamin Johnson	Carnegie Mellon University, USA
Tyler Moore	Southern Methodist University, USA
Arvind Narayanan	Princeton University, USA
Ahmad-Reza Sadeghi	TU Darmstadt, Germany

Contents

Privacy and Incentives

Applications and Attacks

Authenticated Data Structures

Poster Abstracts

Invited Talk

What Satoshi Did Not Know

Gavin Andresen[✉]

Bitcoin Foundation, Washington, D.C., USA
gavinandresen@gmail.com

1 Introduction

When Bitcoin was invented six years ago (cf. [8]), Barack Obama had just been inaugurated president and Lady Gaga had just released her first big single. If you are 20 years old, that probably seems like forever ago. If you are 48 like me, that seems like not all that long ago. I first heard about Bitcoin in 2010, and was attracted to it because it combined economics, peer-to-peer networking and crypto in a really interesting way.

I'm going to talk about what we have learned over the last six years. Satoshi knew a lot, but he wasn't omniscient – I think there were a lot of things, both big and small, that he didn't know when he was inventing Bitcoin. I will finish by talking about some things that I think we still do not know.

2 What Satoshi Didn't Know

I think one of the things Satoshi did not know is *would it bootstrap?* Would anybody, besides geeks like me and him, be interested in this complicated piece of technology? Is there some way of creating value out of nothing? Because that's the thing that trips up most people: how can you bootstrap a currency from literally zero value? It had no worth for the first year of its life. I don't think Satoshi knew if this was possible or not. If you go back and look at some of his early writings, he was completely wrong about the ways it might bootstrap. He assumed it would be used as a spam filter device for email, something like a practical HashCash [1] system. But he was wrong about that. The way it bootstrapped was a guy buying a couple of pizzas for 10,000 bitcoins and people taking that leap of faith that it could actually be successful and might be worth a dollar or two at some point in the future.

I think something else Satoshi did not know is *was it legal?* When I first got involved in Bitcoin in 2010 we still did not know the answer and that actually worried me a lot. I was thinking: could I get arrested for working on this technology? Would I be thrown in jail? I was pretty sure I wouldn't – it was an open source project, I was not trying to rip anybody off and nobody was paying me any money. It didn't seem like there was a whole lot of room for authorities to

G. Andresen — I would like to thank Malte Möser for his help in preparing this transcript.

R. Böhme and T. Okamoto (Eds.): FC 2015, LNCS 8975, pp. 3–10, 2015.
DOI: 10.1007/978-3-662-47854-7_1

come down hard, arrest me and throw me in jail. But I am sure Satoshi thought about that and it's something he didn't know on the social side.

The situation is much better today. Last year, the SEC published an advisory about "Ponzi schemes using virtual currencies" [11]. And the important word in there is "using". They are not saying that virtual currencies are Ponzi schemes, they are just warning investors that if you see a too good to be true scheme using Bitcoin or Litecoin or Dogecoin or any of the other altcoins, then be careful. You are probably getting ripped off. That's a much better situation than we were in six years ago, where I think, if you asked the SEC, they probably would have classified Bitcoin as a Ponzi scheme.

3   Penny-Flooding

I think something else Satoshi didn't know was *how annoying people are on the Internet*. We all know this, but until you actually create a system and launch it and see all of the different ways people attack it, I don't think you really *know* it. There were some properties of the first Bitcoin releases that were subject to abuse and I think Satoshi didn't completely internalize how willing people would be to abuse this thing, even if there is absolutely no economic incentive for doing so. People will abuse your system just to be annoying if you are popular enough.

Early in Bitcoin's life we had a big problem with what we called "penny-flooding". Penny-flooding works as follows: I set up two machines and send bit-coins from one to the other all day long. If transactions are free, there is nothing stopping me from doing that. I can just flood the network with transactions that accomplish nothing, transferring them back and forth for ever and ever. Near the end of 2010 that was a pretty big problem on the Bitcoin network. Figure 1 shows the number of transactions on the Bitcoin network in 2009 and 2010. You can see this huge spike at the end of 2010, and there are a couple of other spikes which were earlier penny-flooding attacks. The vast majority of transactions were one or more annoying people doing this just because they could.

We actually found a solution to this which is now called proof-of-stake, although we didn't call it that back then. This is probably my most proud email from Satoshi, where I came up with the idea of using the age of a transaction and the size of the transaction in terms of bitcoin value to prioritize transactions and rate limit free transaction based on this scarce resource of old bitcoins. And Satoshi said "You may have finally solved one of the most challenging problems". There are a number of altcoins that have taken the same idea and use proof-of-stake for other things. We think that's a bad idea, and you can talk to Andrew Miller, Greg Maxwell, or Andrew Poelstra about why; they have looked pretty hard at proof-of-stake systems and thought about whether they can possibly work. But certainly, for supporting free transactions on the network, if we go back to that graph, it worked really well. The penny-flooding stopped as soon as we implemented this change and things got back on track.

The idea there is really pretty deep. It really is a core idea behind Bitcoin that scarcity plus utility equals value. If something is scarce and it is useful then it has

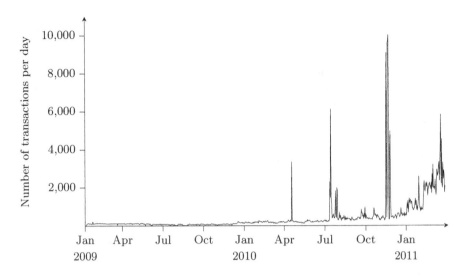

Fig. 1. Transaction volume in the early days of Bitcoin

value. In the Bitcoin system, bitcoins are the primary scarce resource: there are
only a certain number that are ever created, there are only a certain number in
circulation and the cryptography makes sure that those rules are followed. Transaction priority turns out to be another scarce resource that we can use in the Bitcoin
system, and that's what we used to prevent penny-flooding. It is not obvious that
this is a scarce resources, but if you want one bitcoin that is a year old and hasn't
been spent, then that's a scarce resource, even if you don't spend it.

I think one of the more unexplored parts of the Bitcoin system is other uses
of old unspent transaction outputs. There has been a lot of thinking that has
started to happen, there hasn't been lots of code written, there hasn't been a
lot of systems implemented, but some of the ideas might be leveraging them
for further denial-of-service attack prevention. For example, you could imagine
requiring some bitcoin deposit to merely join the network. Of course we don't
want to do that because we want the network to grow. But you could imagine
that if we had a really big problem with Sybil attacks [4], then requiring that
somebody somehow gets some bitcoins that they control, as a kind of gate to
join the network, might make sense. Another idea we have talked about for
years is bitcoin deposits as pseudonymous identity anchors: if I hold a hundred
bitcoins that are five years old and I can prove that I hold them, that might be
a useful type of anchor for a persistent identity. And as long as I hold them I
will maintain that identity. There are all sorts of issues there, but we've talked
about this and I don't think anybody has actually tried to do it yet.

It is interesting to think about whether you could spend bitcoins as denial-
of-service prevention for other systems that aren't Bitcoin-related. I would be
very interested in seeing that. So far most people think about using bitcoins as

a token that you spend to get access to some other system, but you don't have to spend them, just having them might be good enough in a lot of cases.

I will note that spent transaction outputs are not a scarce resource, those are easy to create, it is easy to spend bitcoins over and over again. So if you are thinking about this, do think about spent versus unspent, and the edge case of when bitcoins go from unspent to spent which is where all the interesting things happen.

4 Was Satoshi a Cryptographer?

When I see popular press articles about Satoshi, he is often called a cryptographer. But is he really a cryptographer? I don't think so. There is actually very little cryptography in Bitcoin. We've got ECC keys, ECDSA signatures and hashing. And thats about it. All of Bitcoin is built from those primitives. If you actually look at the code, the way Satoshi used cryptography is fairly naive. He used OpenSSL, but he didn't use it very deeply. We are using OpenSSL deeply now, and there are all sorts of nasty little edge cases down there. I think if he were a cryptographer he would have been much more careful there. There is no mentioning of Schnorr signatures [10], Lamport signatures [7], none of the stuff I would expect a real cryptographer to mention in the source code. I don't see any comments like "I didn't use Lamport signatures here because they are too big". And there is a quote from Satoshi, that I ran across when I was preparing this talk, where he said "Crypto may offer a way to do 'key blinding'. I did some research and it was obscure, but there may be something there. 'group signatures' may be related" [9]. I think that shows you that with what Satoshi knew about cryptography, he probably wasn't a cryptographer, I don't think he was up on the very latest crypto research.

5 The Difference Between Transaction Validity and Meaning

I want to talk a little bit about something else I don't think Satoshi knew. I don't think Satoshi internalized the difference between validating a transaction and understanding what that transaction was about. And I think if he did, he would have designed Bitcoin differently. Transaction *validity* asks the question: should this transaction be allowed into the block chain? And the rules for this are pretty simple. First, a transaction has to be syntactically correct, you have to be able to parse it off the wire. Second, the redemption conditions have to be correct. Today, that typically means an ECDSA signature has to be valid for the previously generated public key. Third, the sum of the input amounts has to be greater than or equal to the sum of the output amounts. You are not allowed to create new bitcoins by creating transactions (there was an integer overflow bug early on that broke that rule – that was bad). Finally, it does not double-spend any inputs, so you do not spend any bitcoins twice. Those are basically the rules for normal transactions. There are special conditions for coinbase transactions that create bitcoins, but I'm not going to talk about those here.

Transaction *meaning* is slightly different, and I think a lot of people don't understand this. In fact, I don't think I understood this and I don't think Satoshi understood this. Transaction meaning is who is being paid, how much are they being paid and who authorized the payment. Ideally, the meaning of the transaction would only be shared between the parties involved in the transaction and nobody else would have to know anything about it.

Satoshi's original wallet understood two transaction types. The first one is very simple: the person who holds the bitcoins creates a transaction that says "you need to check the signature of the public key" and the recipients, when they want to spend the bitcoins, provide a signature that satisfies those conditions. These pay-to-public-key transactions mix validation and meaning more than necessary; everybody observing the transaction knows the public key needed to redeem them.

Bitcoin transactions are expressed in a simple, Forth-like scripting language. The scriptPubKey in the funding transaction specifies how the funds are locked, and the scriptSig in the redeeming transaction satisfies the locking condition. In the simplest case, the scriptPubKey is just a public key and the OP_CHECKSIG operator, and the scriptSig is a digital signature for that private key.

Satoshi also implemented another transaction type which just moves the public key over to the redeeming side and replaces it with a hash of the public key. He did that to keep the resulting "bitcoin addresses" short enough to easily copy and paste. However, I think if Satoshi actually had understood OpenSSL a little bit better and knew that he could fit public keys into 33 bytes instead of 65 bytes, he wouldn't have bothered. He probably would have just had longer bitcoin addresses and we all would be using the first type of transactions. Almost all bitcoin transactions on the network these days are of the second type ("pay to public key hash").

So, we have this little language that the scriptSig and the scriptPubKey allow and there is an interesting question here: why did Satoshi allow opcodes in the scriptSig? The scriptSig is the part that you provide to prove that you know enough to satisfy the conditions of the transaction. So you could have a scriptPubKey that is 11 equals and you (or anybody else smart enough to work out that eleven equals eleven) satisfy it with a scriptSig that is just 11. You could also express that as 6 5 +, but there is really no reason to do that because the person who is creating the scriptSig can always just run the script, get the results and put the data on the stack instead of putting the operations on the stack. I think Satoshi probably did it this way for legacy reasons, but I think if he had been thinking about the fact that you don't need to know the meaning of a transaction I think he would have designed it differently. I don't think he would have allowed operators in the signature.

If he had been thinking ahead, I think he would have realized that you do not need to provide the redemption conditions in advance. We have actually evolved Bitcoin with another transaction type called pay-to-script-hash, where the entire redemption script is provided when the redemption happens and you just give a hash of the redemption script when you are funding the transaction. This is a step towards breaking the link between what does a transaction mean and is it valid. You can validate the funding transaction, but you don't know in advance how the locked funds will be redeemed.

The tricky bit, if you start thinking about breaking the meaning with validation, is what do you do with transaction fees. The system really wants to know what the fee is on a transaction so that it can prioritize it and reward the miner. Ideally, you'd have a system that removes the last two of the validation rules that I was talking about earlier. It would be nice if you didn't have to validate that the sum of the inputs is greater than equal to the sum of the outputs, if that was blinded somehow and you could just be assured that no bitcoins are created. It might also be nice to get rid of the condition that there are no double-spends. You could imagine a system where you just throw transactions into the block chain and as long as they are correct it's okay. If there are double spends then end-user's wallet software would throw red flags and say "somebody is trying to rip you off, they are double spending". But if you think that all the way through, that gets complicated. The system does need to know what part of a transaction is fees because those get assigned to the miner. And that is blurring meaning and validation because I am not paying a particular miner, I am paying any miner in the world who happens to mine my transaction. It exposes some knowledge about the transaction. And as we think about systems like Zerocash [2] or other systems that are trying to be completely anonymous, that's an interesting design point that I think people are going to be wrestling with for a long time.

6   Scaling

I don't think Satoshi knew how to *scale the system*. He has this quote "each transaction must be sent over the network twice". And that's just not true. There is this really neat current area of research of set reconciliation (cf. [5]). Basically, set reconciliation is a way for two machines to express differences in information they have using bandwidth proportional to the size of those differences. So, in Bitcoin's case, if I find a new block, I don't have to re-send all of the transactions that are part of that block because you probably already have 99.9 % of them from when they were originally broadcast across the network. I'm really excited about this, invertible bloom lookup tables [6] are now my current favorite data structure, and I am working with a research group at UMass on set reconciliation applied to the Bitcoin system.

7   Recent Cryptography Results

There is a number of cryptography results that have happened since 2009 that obviously Satoshi did not know about because they hadn't been invented yet. We didn't know about fully homomorphic encryption, and we didn't know any practical algorithms for non-interactive zero knowledge proofs or SNARKs (cf. [3]).

Six years is not very long, but if you look at the literature quite a lot has happened since then and we do know a lot more know than we knew back then. And I think there are lots of interesting things that will happen over the next six years, too.

8   What Gavin Doesn't Know

There are a bunch of things that I don't know right now. I don't know if the *identity* problem is going to be solved. I think a lot of what people talk about doing in Bitcoin relies on having a good, pseudonymous identity/reputation system. It seems to me that in a pseudonymous world there are completely unsolved problems. I haven't seen a good system that isn't subject to long-range attacks. And we have certainly seen those happening in the Bitcoin world. We have seen people with stellar reputations on Silk Road, apparently honest, stand-up people pushing drugs that are reliable for a while but eventually decide to steal everybody's money. I don't know if there is a solution to that problem, but it's an interesting problem.

Will there be a practical solution to the *privacy* problem? All of this neat crypto we have is fantastic, but I don't know if it will scale and I don't know if it will be low cost enough for people to actually to decide to use it. I think that's an open problem that will be very interesting to watch.

I think there is all sorts of work that can be done with probabilistic and approximating algorithms. There have been some ideas about using flaky but fast hardware to do Bitcoin mining. Because, as long as you check the work that comes out of Bitcoin mining and you just throw out the bad results, maybe its better and more power-efficient to have a really fast but at the same time really flaky piece of hardware that is running some approximations of the double-SHA algorithm. I think that's interesting and I wonder if there are other probabilistic algorithms that might be incredibly useful. An obvious one is certainly full nodes probabilistically checking transactions. If you can't afford to check every single transaction across the network then just check half of them, and as long as you do it in a random way everybody will be checking all of them several times anyway and it all works out. I have a feeling that there might be other problems where probabilistic algorithms could be really interesting.

Can streaming algorithms be applied to Bitcoin problems? I know that there is a fairly active area of computer science research on streaming algorithms that don't keep all 18 petabytes of data in memory but deals with data as it comes along. I think that might be an interesting area of research.

9   Conclusion

I have learned a lot in the last six years; experience is a great teacher. One challenge going forward will be to continue to learn by doing as the consequences of mistakes rise higher and higher. That challenge will be met by clever people like you, who are constantly thinking and researching and experimenting.

References

1. Adam Back. Hashcash A Denial of Service Counter-Measure (2002). http://www. hashcash.org/papers/hashcash.pdf. Accessed on 10 February 2015
2. Ben-Sasson, E., Chiesa, A., Garman, C., Green, M., Miers, I., Tromer, E., Virza, M.: Zerocash: decentralized anonymous payments from bitcoin. In: Proceedings of the 2014 IEEE Symposium on Security and Privacy (SP), pp. 459–474. IEEE (2014)
3. Ben-Sasson, E., Chiesa, A., Genkin, D., Tromer, E., Virza, M.: SNARKs for C: verifying program executions succinctly and in zero knowledge. In: Canetti, R., Garay, J.A. (eds.) CRYPTO 2013, Part II. LNCS, vol. 8043, pp. 90–108. Springer, Heidelberg (2013)
4. Douceur, J.R.: The sybil attack. In: Druschel, P., Kaashoek, M.F., Rowstron, A. (eds.) IPTPS 2002. LNCS, vol. 2429, pp. 251–260. Springer, Heidelberg (2002)
5. Eppstein, D., Goodrich, M.T., Uyeda, F., Varghese, G.: What's the difference? efficient set reconciliation without prior context. In: Proceedings of the ACM SIG-COMM Conference, pp. 218–229. ACM, New York (2011)
6. Goodrich, M.T., Mitzenmacher, M.: Invertible bloom lookup tables. In: 49th Annual Allerton Conference on Communication, Control, and Computing, pp. 792–799. IEEE (2011)
7. Leslie, L.: Constructing digital signatures from a one-way function. Technical report SRI International Computer Science Laboratory, October 1979
8. Satoshi Nakamoto. Bitcoin: A Peer-to-Peer Electronic Cash System (2008). https://bitcoin.org/bitcoin.pdf. Accessed on 10 February 2015
9. Nakamoto, S.: Re: Not a suggestion. https://bitcointalk.org/index.php?topic=770. msg9074#msg9074.2010. Accessed on 17 March 2015
10. Schnorr, C.-P.: Efficient signature generation by smart cards. J. Cryptol. 4(3), 161–174 (1991)
11. U.S. Securities and Exchange Commission. Ponzi Schemes Using Virtual Currencies (2014). http://www.sec.gov/investor/alerts/ia_virtualcurrencies.pdf. Accessed on 28 February 2015

Cybercrime

Are You at Risk? Profiling Organizations and Individuals Subject to Targeted Attacks

Olivier Thonnard, Leyla Bilge$^{(\boxtimes)}$, Anand Kashyap, and Martin Lee

Symantec Research Lab, Culver City, USA
{Olivier_Thonnard,Leylya_Yumer,Anand_Kashyap,Martin_Lee}@symantec.com

Abstract. Targeted attacks consist of sophisticated malware developed by attackers having the resources and motivation to research targets in depth. Although rare, such attacks are particularly difficult to defend against and can be extremely harmful. We show in this work that data relating to the *profiles* of organisations and individuals subject to targeted attacks is amenable to study using epidemiological techniques. Considering the taxonomy of Standard Industry Classification (SIC) codes, the organization sizes and the public profiles of individuals as potential risk factors, we design case-control studies to calculate *odds ratios* reflecting the degree of association between the identified risk factors and the receipt of targeted attack. We perform an experimental validation with a large corpus of targeted attacks blocked by a large security company's mail scanning service during 2013–2014, revealing that certain industry sectors and larger organizations –as well as specific individual profiles – are statistically at elevated risk compared with others. Considering targeted attacks as akin to a public health issue and adapting techniques from epidemiology may allow the proactive identification of those at increased risk of attack. Our approach is a first step towards developing a predictive framework for the analysis of targeted threats, and may be leveraged for the development of cyber insurance schemes based on accurate risk assessments.

Keywords: Targeted attacks · Epidemiology · Risk analysis · Cyber insurance

1 Introduction

In recent years, we observe a dramatic increase on targeted attacks [31]. Publicised attacks, such as Shamoon among many others, show how such attacks may cause considerable disruption and financial harm to Internet users. Unfortunately, the traditional malware defense mechanisms are not adequate to detect such attacks. Therefore, organisations need to remain vigilant for the presence of such malware within their systems. However, targeted attacks remain rare. Many organisations may not need to expend significant resources in attempting to detect threats to which they may never be exposed. Similarly, some organisations may be in imminent danger of being attacked, yet have little security infrastructure in place to detect and reorganisations [2].

© International Financial Cryptography Association 2015
R. Böhme and T. Okamoto (Eds.): FC 2015, LNCS 8975, pp. 13–31, 2015.
DOI: 10.1007/978-3-662-47854-7_2

Anecdotal evidence from publicised targeted attacks hints that certain industry sectors and certain employee profiles may be at heightened risk of attack. For instance, the Nitro campaign was associated with the chemical industry [8], Luckycat affected with the shipping and defence industries, among others [32,35]. Most infamously of all, Stuxnet [11,30] targeted a specific industrial control system operating within the energy sector.

It may be intuitive that critical industries such as defence and chemical industrial sectors are more prone to targeted attacks than other sectors. However, this is not sufficient to assess the *level of risk* a targeted cyber attack may pose to a given organization. Identifying the specific industrial sectors and the specific user profiles which may be at heightened risk requires more than intuition and assumption.

One method of identifying high risk sectors and employees is to consider targeted attacks as akin to a *public health issue*. Epidemiological science has developed various statistical techniques for discovering associations between lifestyle or genetic factors, and adverse health outcomes. Once predisposing factors for diseases have been discovered, campaigns can be instigated to educate those affected of their particular risk and how this risk can be mitigated.

Case-control studies are commonly used within health-care research to identify *risk factors* within a population that are associated with developing a disease. A risk factor is a binary variable that can be observed within members of a population to test if the risk factor is associated with a health outcome. Such factors may be lifestyle factors or the prior exposure to an environmental pollutant. An advantage of case-control studies is that they can be *retrospective* by design, and used to investigate groups already affected by an issue. In such a study the incidence of many potential risk factors within the members of a subject group known to by afflicted by a disease (the cases) are compared with those of a second similar group that does not have the disease (the controls). Risk factors can then be identified through their statistical association with the disease using a well characterised methodology.

In this paper, we show that it is possible to conduct a rigorous case-control study in which the detection of being sent a targeted attack is considered as the *outcome*. Such a study can identify the potential risk factors, such as the activity sector and size of an organisation or job characteristics of an employee, that might be associated with being subject to a cyber attack. The identification of these risk factors allows organisations to assess their risk level and take proactive measures to mitigate or at least to control this risk. Moreover, it could be also beneficial for cyber insurance systems that suffer from elaborated risk assessment methodologies for assigning accurate insurance ratings to the organizations or individuals.

By applying this approach to a large corpus of targeted attacks blocked by e-mail scanning service of a large security company, we show that larger organizations and specific industry sectors, such as *National Security and International Affairs*, or the *Energy* and *Mining* sectors, are strongly associated with the risk of receiving targeted attacks and hence can be considered of being at higher risk than other industry sectors. Furthermore, incorporating data obtained from

LinkedIn about the employees that were targeted in these companies, we have found that not only Directors or high-level executives are likely to be targeted, but other specific job roles such as Personal Assistants are even more at risk of targeted attack compared to others.

The rest of this paper is organized as follows. In Sect. 2 we discuss related works and position our contribution. Section 3 gives some background on epidemiology concepts used in this work and describes the design of our case-control study. We present and discuss our experimental results obtained with a large corpus of targeted attacks in Sect. 4. Section 5 concludes the paper.

2   Related Work

The use of epidemiology concepts in computer security is not novel. However, we note that previous work has mainly focused on malware epidemics and computer worm epidemiology, *i.e.*, developing analytical models for computer virus propagation and worm outbreaks within vulnerable populations in the Internet.

In the years 1991 to 1993, pioneering work by Kephart *et al.* extended classical epidemiological models with directed-graphs to model the behavior of computer viruses and determine the conditions under which epidemics are more likely to occur [15–17]. Follow-up work relied mostly on the classical Susceptible → Infected → Recovered (SIR) epidemiology model – developed by Kermack-McKendrick for modeling infectious disease epidemics [10,12] – to measure the total infected population over time during an Internet worm outbreak. Examples of such studies include various analyses of significant worm outbreaks such as CodeRed [22,29,39] and Slammer epidemics [21]. In [38] the authors examined other types of propagation like email worms (*e.g.*, the Witty worm, also studied by Shannon and Moore in [28]).

Another closely related research area has looked more specifically at *response* technologies for computer virus propagation and Internet worm epidemics. In early work Wang *et al.* investigated the impact of immunization defenses on worm propagation [36]. Subsequently Zou *et al.* developed a more accurate *two-factor* worm model that includes the dynamic aspects of human countermeasures and the variable infection rate. Then Moore *et al.* investigated methods for Internet quarantine and have set up in [23] requirements for containing self-propagating code. Later, Zou *et al.* proposed a dynamic quarantine defense method inspired by methods used in epidemic disease control and evaluated the approach through simulation of three Internet worm propagation models [40].

Follow-up work by Porras *et al.* studied a hybrid quarantine defense approach by looking at potential synergies of two complementary worm quarantine defense strategies under various worm attack profiles [26]. Finally, Dagon *et al.* extended the classical SIR model and created a diurnal model which incorporates the impact of time zones on botnet propagation to capture regional variations in online vulnerable populations [9].

The analysis of the current state of the art in computer epidemiology reveals clearly a lack of research in the field of developing predictive analytics for more advanced threats, such as *targeted attacks*. Our study is a first step towards considering such attacks as a public health issue amenable to epidemiological studies. However, the techniques required for modeling targeted threats are different from those used previously in computer worm epidemics. Targeted trojans differ from other common forms of malware in that the attacker researches and selects potential targets to which the attacks are directed. It is not necessarily the behavior of the individual or the vulnerable status of a system that leads to exposure to malware, but rather something specific to the individual (or the organization he belongs to) that leads them to come to the attention of attackers.

Closer to our research is the work done by Carlinet *et al.* in [7], where the authors have used epidemiological techniques to identify risk factors for ADSL users to generate malicious traffic. The study identified that the use of web and streaming applications and use of the Windows operating system were risk factors for apparent malware infection. Recently, Bossler and Holt conducted a similar study looking at factors associated with malware infection, finding that media piracy was positively correlated with infection, as was "associating with friends who view online pornography", being employed and being female [6]. In [18], the author conducted a preliminary case-control study on academic malware recipients, using the HESA JACS coding of academic subjects to investigate the relationship between research interests and the receipt of targeted attacks. While the methodology used in [18] was similar as the one used in this paper, the study was performed on a limited scale (with only academic recipients) and at the level of individuals instead of organizations. A recent study by Levesque et al. [19] analyzes the interactions between users, AV software and malware leveraging studies widely adopted in clinical experiments. Finally, in [33] the authors provided an in-depth analysis of targeted email attacks and the associated malware campaigns as orchestrated by various teams of attackers.

The main contribution of this paper is to show how statistical techniques borrowed from the public health community may be effectively used to derive putative *risk factors* associated with the profiles of organizations likely to be at an increased risk of attack because, *e.g.*, of their activity sector or organizational size. further extended to develop a predictive framework in which the degree of risk of being attacked could be evaluated even more precisely by combining an extended set of relevant factors pertaining to the profile of organisations or the individuals belonging to them.

3   Methodology

3.1   Epidemiology Concepts

In epidemiology, a commonly used method for determining if a factor is associated with a disease consists in performing a retrospective *case-control* study [20] in which a population known to be afflicted with a disease is compared to a similar population that is unafflicted. For example, the risk of tobacco use on lung cancer is assessed by comparing the volume of tobacco use of the population that is afflicted with lung cancer(1) with the disease-free (0) population [1].

Note that, while a case control study can be effective at identifying *risk factors*, it cannot impart information about the likelihood of an outcome, since we are pre-selecting an afflicted group rather than searching for the affliction in a random population [27].

If we now substitute "afflicted with a disease" with "encountered a targeted attack", we can use these same epidemiology techniques to identify risk factors that are associated with targeted attacks, and leverage this knowledge to identify the characteristics of risky organisations and individuals.

To interpret the results of a case control study, we need to calculate the *odds ratio* (OR) that is a measure of the degree of association between a putative risk factor and an outcome – the stronger the association, the higher the odds ratio [4]. Suppose that p_{11} is the probability of afflicted entities possessing the risk factor and p_{01} is the probability of afflicted entities not possessing the risk factor. Similarly, p_{10} is the probability of unafflicted individuals within the control group also possessing the risk factor, and p_{00} is the probability of unafflicted individuals in the control group not possessing the risk factor. The odds ratio (OR) is then calculated as:

$$OR = \frac{p_{11} \times p_{00}}{p_{10} \times p_{01}}$$

Empirical measurements that sample populations have an inherent rate of error. To reach the test of being in excess of 95 % certain that any risk factor that we have identified is an actual risk factor and not an artefact of our test, we need to calculate the standard error associated with our sampling using:

$$SE(\log_e OR) = \sqrt{\frac{1}{n_{11}} + \frac{1}{n_{10}} + \frac{1}{n_{01}} + \frac{1}{n_{00}}}$$

where n_{11} is the number of afflicted entities possessing the risk factor, n_{10} is the number of afflicted entities without the risk factor, n_{01} is the number of control unafflicted entities with the risk factor, and n_{00} is the number of control unafflicted entities without the risk factor. The upper and lower 95 % confidence values (W,X) for the natural logarithm of the odds ratio are then calculated as:

$$\begin{cases} W = \log_e OR - (1.96\, SE(\log_e OR)) \\ X = \log_e OR + (1.96\, SE(\log_e OR)) \end{cases}$$

The 95 % confidence interval for the odds ratio is the exponential of W and X, e^W to e^X. In order for a putative risk factor to be positively associated with an outcome with greater than 95 % probability, both e^W and e^X should be greater than 1.0. For the risk factor to be negatively correlated with the outcome, both e^W and e^X should be less than 1.0 [24].

3.2 Case-Control Study Design

As our main goal is to discover risk factors for being victims of targeted attacks, our case-control study consists in analyzing organizations and individuals that encountered e-mail based targeted attacks, and compare them with the ones that did not. Note that there exists other means of exploitation to compromise the targets. Nevertheless, the data we use for this study comprises of only attacks that spread through e-mails and therefore, we focus on finding the risk factors for e-mail based targeted attacks (also referred to as *spear-phishing* emails).

Organization Level. For this study, the *afflicted* population is composed of 3,183 organisations that was identified by a large security company's mail scanning service as being victims of at least one e-mail based targeted attacks. Note that the process of finding the victims involves careful manual effort.

In case-control studies one crucial step is to prepare the *control* group selectively. Ideally, the control group should be as large as possible, to increase the number of subjects in the study to act to reduce the calculated standard error values and increase the power of the study. However, this also acts to increase the resources necessary to conduct the study. Typically the size of the control group should be in the order of at least four times larger than the afflicted group [14]. Therefore, we constructed our control group from 15,915 organisations through *random* selection from 37,213 organisations that received traditional malware attacks during 2013. It is worth noting that random sampling is usually considered as the best sampling approach in order to avoid any bias in the representativeness of the control population [5].

We performed a case-control study with two different organization-level features to understand whether they could be one of the risk factors for targeted attacks. Motivating by the fact that a majority of notable targeted attacks seem to be launched against organizations operating in specific sectors, we chose first to investigate the industry sector of the organizations that are part of our customer base. We identify the sector of the organizations in our control group by leveraging both internal data sources (*e.g.*, marketing and customer data) as well as publicly available sources providing the Standard Industry Classification (SIC) (such as www.leadferret.com and www.companycheck.co.uk) for customers and organisations lacking such detailed information. For this study, we restrict ourselves to the primary Standard Industry Classification (SIC) *2-digit* code [25], and leave the analysis of the more detailed SIC 4-digit classification as future work.

The second feature we used in our case-control study is the size of the organization in terms of number of employees. Organisations were divided into 4 size groups according to the number of employees that used the large security company's mail scanning service. Therefore, the size we estimated for the organizations might be smaller that organization's actual size. Nevertheless, these numbers should reflect quite accurately the organisation sizes, and more importantly, the relative differences in size among different organisations.

Individual Level. In addition to the organizational-based risk factors, we conducted a case control study to investigate individual-based risk factors that are associated with targeted attacks. While the afflicted group consists of the individuals that received e-mail based targeted attacks, the control group is composed of individuals that are in the same organizations and never received targeted attacks. The individual-based features are computed from information that can be obtained from the corresponding LinkedIn profiles of the individuals.

From the 3,183 afflicted organizations that we studied in the previous section we selected organizations that allow us focus only on organizations that have enough data (at least 100 afflicted and 300 unafflicated employees) for accurate statistical inference and that have the appropriate mailing convension (`<firstname>(.|_)<lastname>@<copanydomain>` or `<lastname>(.|_)<firstname>@<copanydomain>`) for their employees such that it is possible to collect her/his LinkedIn profiles information using the LinkedIn search API. Following these two criteria, we were able to obtain LinkedIn profiles of 4150 afflicted individuals and 12031 unafflicated individuals from 82 organizations.

The most insightful features we were able to extract from the LinkedIn profiles of the users are as follows:

- *Job Level:* The job level indicates an employee's position in an organization's hierarchy. We have considered 7 job levels: *Intern, Temporary Workers, Support Staff, Individual Contributors, Managers, Directors, and Executives.*
- *Job Type:* The job type indicates the job function performed by an employee in an organization's hierarchy. We have considered 9 job types: *Operations, Engineering, IT, Sales and Marketing, HR, Finance, Legal, QA, and Research.*
- *Location:* The location field in LinkedIn is typically free form text (e.g., San Francisco Bay Area, Greater Mumbai Area, etc.), and may not contain the name of a country. We look up the name of the country by searching the location string on Google and Wikipedia.
- *Number of LinkedIn Connections:* We divide the number of LinkedIn connections into four groups: *0, 1–250, 250–500, and 500+.*

3.3 Validation with Chi-Square Test

To validate the odds ratio results, we performed a *chi-square* test, which is commonly used in statistics to test the significance of any association in a contingency table containing frequencies for different variables. More specifically, chi-square allows to test the *null hypothesis* that there is no significant association between two (or more) variables, the alternative being that there is indeed an association of any kind [5,13].

In this case, we apply the chi-square test to measure the association between the variables *afflicted* versus *unafflicted* on one hand, and *has factor 'x'* versus *don't have factor 'x'* on the other hand. For example, *SIC code'x'* versus *other sector*. The same test can be performed using any other risk factor as variable, instead of the SIC code. The test consists then in comparing the *observed* frequencies (O) with the *expected* frequencies (E) obtained by using the marginal totals for rows and columns. If the two variables are not associated, the expected and observed frequencies should be close to each other and we should not observe any significant difference between the two, any discrepancy being due to merely random variation.

The chi-square test allows us to evaluate the difference between expected and observed frequencies: we just need to calculate the sum of the squared differences between the observed and expected values (*i.e.*, $\sum(O - E)^2/E$), and then compare the final value to the distribution of the chi-square statistic with $(r - 1)(c - 1)$ degrees of freedom, where r is the number of rows and c the number of columns (*i.e.*, in this case we have only 1 degree of freedom). As a result, we obtain a probability value p that allows us to accept or reject the null hypothesis with a certain confidence level. In most cases, we consider $p < 0.05$ as a significant probability to safely reject the null hypothesis, and thus conclude that there is good evidence of a relationship between the two variables.

By repeating this statistical test for each risk factor under test, we calculate the chi-square p-value to evaluate the significance of any association between a specific factor and the fact of receiving targeted attacks within the selected population. As shown in our experimental results (Sect. 4), it enables us to validate the statistical significance of Odds Ratios for any association discovered between a risk factor and the receipt of targeted attacks. Note, however, that chi-square is not an index of the *strength* of the association between the tested variables. Also, certain categories may be excluded from the test because of a too small sample size. The conventional criterion for a chi-square test to be valid is that at least 80 % of the expected frequencies exceed 5 and all the expected frequencies exceed 1 [5, 13].

4   Experimental Results

4.1   Organization Risk Factors

The SIC 1987 taxonomy contains 83 distinct *major group* codes denoted by the first 2 digits of the SIC classification. Of these, 78 were represented in the classifications of organisations studied. Table 1 presents the results of the case-control study we performed on the sector of the organizations. Because of the space limitations, we only provide the results of the sectors that have the highest and lowest assossiation with targeted attacks. Note that to get solid statistica results higher confidence, every test was repeated five times, and we consider the median value as final outcome, excluding outliers that might result as an artefact of the random sampling.

Positive statistical significance was taken to be if the lower value of the 95 % confidence interval was greater than 1.0; negative statistical significance was taken to be if the upper value of the 95 % confidence interval was less than 1.0. Using these definitions, 37 of the major group classifications were found to be significantly associated with the set of organisations in the *afflicted* group, with the major group *National Security and International Affairs* showing the strongest association with the targeted attacks. A further 8 major group classifications, as well as the additional group of *Nonclassifiable Establishments* (99) were significantly negatively associated with the *afflicted* group. These categories, which include sectors such as Real Estate, Legal Services, Construction or Agricultural Services, seem even protected from receiving targeted cyber attacks. Yet, it does

Table 1. Odds ratios (OR) for the sectors that the highest and lowest association with targeted attacks.

SIC2	SIC2 Description	Odds ratio	Confidence interval	χ^2 p-val
97	National Security and International Affairs	22.55	4.87 − 55.56	< .001
40	Railroad Transportation	11.26	1.25 − 44.93	0.011
14	Mining and Quarrying of Nonmetallic Minerals, Except Fuels	5.01	1.51 − 24.80	0.033
96	Administration of Human Resource Programs	4.69	1.68 − 23.31	< .001
10	Metal Mining	4.10	1.69 − 9.90	0.001
44	Water Transportation	3.77	1.61 − 8.95	0.001
92	Justice, Public Order, And Safety	3.75	2.02 − 53.72	< .001
96	Administration Of Economic Programs	3.64	1.52 − 45.49	0.003
28	Chemicals and Allied Products	2.92	2.14 − 3.98	< .001
29	Petroleum Refining and Related Industries	3.12	1.62 − 9.57	0.040
13	Oil And Gas Extraction	2.87	1.55 − 6.59	0.001
60	Depository Institutions	2.74	1.98 − 3.80	< .001
37	Transportation Equipment	2.17	1.40 − 3.37	0.001
49	Electric, Gas, And Sanitary Services	2.12	1.43 − 3.24	< .001
48	Communications	1.58	1.10 − 2.27	0.019
27	Printing, Publishing, And Allied Industries	1.50	1.12 − 2.01	< .001
65	Real Estate	0.75	0.58 − 0.97	0.020
64	Insurance Agents, Brokers and Service	0.62	0.39 − 0.98	0.031
81	Legal Services	0.58	0.43 − 0.77	< .001
99	Nonclassifiable Establishments	0.34	0.31 − 0.38	< .001
17	Construction - Special Trade Contractors	0.24	0.14 − 0.41	< .001
07	Agricultural Services	0.18	0.04 − 0.75	0.007

not mean that organizations in these sectors will never see any targeted attack, however it is much less likely, and if this happens, it is unlikely to be due to their business activity but rather to some other factor.

To make it easier to further process the OR results, we have normalized them using the customary normalization method: $OR_{norm} = (OR - 1)/(OR + 1)$. By doing so, we normalize all OR values in the range $[-1, 1]$, with 0 as neutral value (corresponding to $OR = 1$). The OR_{norm} results for SIC2 sectors are visualized in Fig. 1 along with their respective confidence ranges.

As mentioned earlier, the second organization-based feature we analyze is the size of the organizations. We also wanted to evaluate whether the *organisational size* may be statistically associated with the receipt of targeted attacks. The results of this case control study is visualized in Fig. 2, which shows the normalized OR values for the various size groups along with their respective 95 % confidence range. The results indicate that as the common sense suggests the size of the organisation is highly correlated with being at risk to targeted attacks.

While certain results might look intuitive, others can be more surprising. For example, major SIC groups 73 (Business Services) and 15 (Construction) were ranked in our data among the *most frequently* targeted sectors (in terms of

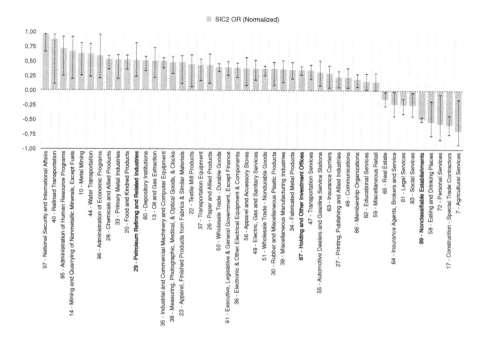

Fig. 1. Normalized Odds Ratios for the major SIC (2 digits) categories. Values above 0.0 refer to industry sectors that are at higher risk of receiving targeted attacks (the higher, the more at risk). Sectors associated with normalized OR lower than 0.0 are protected from such attacks.

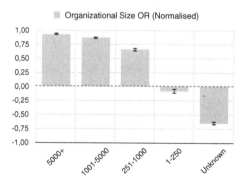

Fig. 2. Normalized Odds Ratios for organization size groups. The risk of receiving targeted attacks increases significantly with the size of the organization.

absolute numbers), however it does not appear to be significantly at higher risk of attack compared to other categories. This might be due to the size of these categories which may comprise a relatively larger proportion of organizations. Conversely, other categories corresponding to apparently *less targeted* sectors (like the Mining sector) now appear to have very high odds ratio, and may be thus at increased risk of attack. The same holds for the size groups, where smaller organizations (1–250) are by far more numerous and might thus appear as more frequently targeted, however the associated Odds Ratio shows that they are at significantly reduced risk of attack compared to very large companies (5000+).

4.2 Individual Risk Factors

The results for the case-control study of the four individual risk factors are presented in Figs. 3 and 4. Some of the results are intuitive; for example, the directors and managers in an organization are at higher risk of being targeted than individual contributors. While the results for number of LinkedIn connections is fairly interesting, the results we obtain with geographical location based features are confusing. The odds-ratio calculation of LinkedIn connections numbers feature shows that employees who have between 1 and 500 connections are at significantly higher risk of being targeted when compared to people who have

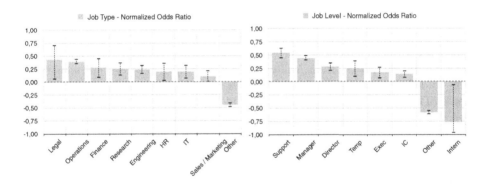

Fig. 3. Normalized Odds Ratios for individual job types and job levels.

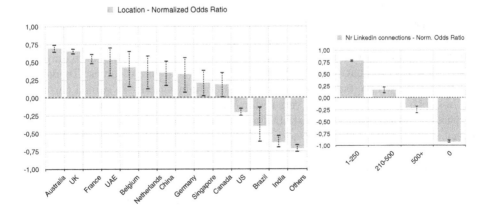

Fig. 4. Normalized Odds Ratios for individual locations and number of LinkedIn connections.

more than 500 connections. Based on the organizations that we have analyzed, employees based in US, Brazil, and India are at significantly reduced risk of being targeted, however, employees in China, Europe, and Australia are at high risk of being targeted. This is quite surprising. While it is hard to make any reasoning without deeper investigation, the reason for obtaining such results for the location-based feature might be due to the nature of our data collection methodology for the individuals. Note that the analysis we performed on individuals strongly depends on the number of LinkenIn profields we were able to find using the simple heuristic we explained earlier.

4.3 Combined Results

While individual OR and OR_{norm} results provide interesting insights into which risk factors might be associated with targeted attacks, in this Section we propose a straightforward yet powerful technique to combine all odds ratios previously found with respect to individual features.

A simple way to combine all normalized OR values would be to take their average. However, this method has many drawbacks, *e.g.*, it does not take into account the relative importance of each factor, nor their interrelationships. Hence, a smarter and more flexible way of aggregating multiple scores consists in using Multi-Criteria Decision Analysis (MCDA), which provides mathematical tools to define advanced *aggregation models* matching a set of complex requirements (The details of the methodology could be find in the Appendix). In this case, we wanted to assign relative importances to individual OR scores, as well as a fuzzy decision threshold on the amount of high scores required to obtain a global score accurately reflecting a significant high risk of becoming victim of a targeted attack in the near future. For these reasons, we decided to combine all normalized OR values using the *Weighted OWA* (WOWA) operator [34], which can aggregate an input vector by taking into account both the reliability of the information sources (as the weighted mean does), and at the same time, by weighting the values in relation to their relative ordering (as the OWA operator).

WOWA makes use of two different weighting vectors: a vector p, which quantifies the relative importances of the different features, and a vector w, which weights the values in relation to their relative *ordering* and allows us to emphasize different combinations of largest, smallest or mid-range values. To define these vectors, we use both our expertise and domain knowledge gained through an in-depth analysis of victim versus non-victim profiles, as well as the characteristics of various statistical distributions of our dataset. For w we computed for every employee the number of odds ratios higher than 1.0, and then compared the distribution of this counting measure for victims and non-victims in our population. It turns out that starting at a count of 4 odds ratio greater than 1.0, the two distributions cross each other, with the number of victims largely exceeding the number of unafflicted customers. Hence, we have set vector w such that it models an aggregation of "at least 4" high scores to obtain a high combined score.

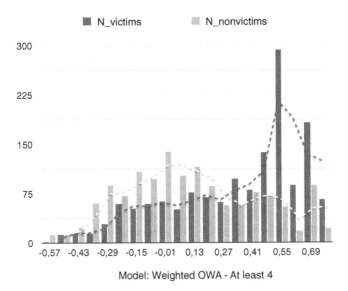

Fig. 5. Combined risk factor distribution for targeted vs non-targeted individuals (Model: Weighted OWA, with at least 4 high risk factors).

Similarly, by investigating the importance and prevalence of individual risk factors in our population, we have set the components of vector p to the following values:

$$p = [0.32, 0.08, 0.08, 0.12, 0.16, 0.24]$$

with the respective weights corresponding to the following list of features:

$$[SIC2, org\_size, job\_type, job\_level, location, nr\_linkedin\_conn]$$

The results of this combined analysis are displayed in Fig. 5, which represents the distribution of combined risk scores for victims and non-victims. We only considered here individuals having complete profiles and belonging to the SIC sectors for which we could obtain statistically significant results. Figure 5 shows interesting and very promising results, as we can see a clear difference in the distributions in particular starting at combined risk scores above 0.27. By identifying additional features that could be used as risk factors, this combined risk model would probably further improve our capability to truly assess cyber risk, and thus to proactively identify who is at increased risk of attack in the near future based on his/her intrinsic characteristics. Just like for health insurance models, our combined risk model could thus be used to design cyber insurance schemes that accurately reflect real-world risks in cyber space.

4.4   Follow-Up Study

A case-control study is not designed to test the power of the identified risk factors for predicting future attacks, as this would require instead a full *cohort* study,

Table 2. Follow-up study in 2014 (Q1) on a subset of SIC codes (2 digits)

SIC2	Category	Targeted (1 in x)	Renewal (1 in x)	Org./week (%)
97	National Security and International Affairs	2.4	12.0	‖‖ı․․‖‖ı․․․․
60	Depository Institutions	3.3	8.1	․․‖‖ı․․ı․ı․․․
13	Oil and Gas Extraction	3.4	9.8	ı․ı․․․․․․․․․․
64	Insurance Agents, Brokers and Service	6.9	20.0	․․․․․․․․․․․․․․
81	Legal Services	17.7	26.5	․․ ․․․․․․․․
65	Real Estate	18.9	54.6	․․․․ ․ ․․․․

Table 3. Follow-up study in 2014 (Q1) on the Organisation size

Org. size	Targeted (1 in x)	Renewal (1 in x)	Org./week (%)
1-250	8.2	12.8	․․․․․․․․․․․․․
251-1,000	2.8	6.6	․․․ı․․․․․․․․․
1,001-5,000	1.9	9.0	․․ı‖․․․․․․․․․
5,000+	1.4	16.8	․‖‖ı․ı‖ı․․․

which requires a significant amount of resources and is beyond the scope of this paper. However, to evaluate the predictive nature of our case-control study, we performed a limited follow-up study examining subsequent attacks in the first Quarter (Jan-Mar) of 2014 by taking the organisational size and a limited set of SIC categories as the only risk factors under consideration. In this follow-up study, we have observed the proportion of targeted organisations (expressed as "1 in x" ratios) among our sample population, the proportion of *newly targeted* organisations that previously belonged to our control group (referred to as the *renewal rate*), and the targeted organisations ratios as observed on a *weekly* basis in 2014-Q1.

In Table 3, we note that the observed incidence of targeted attack during 2014-Q1, segmented by organisational size, is consistent with the predictive model. The odds ratios calculated from 2013 data suggest the risk of attack increases with the size of the organisation, and new statistics for 2014 seem to follow the very same trend. Furthermore, the trend line showing the weekly rate of targeted organizations is well-aligned with the predictive model calculated in 2013. Only the renewal rate for size group *5000+* seems to be somehow an outlier (the number of newly targeted companies in this group seems to be significantly smaller), and may thus indicate that attackers have initiated a change in their tactics by targeting more heavily smaller organisations, instead of large multinational companies.

Finally, Table 2 shows the incidence of targeted attacks in 2014-Q1 for a subset of SIC codes (2-digits). Here too, we observe the predictive model is consistent with subsequent observations: SIC codes identified as being at higher risk of attack in 2013 exhibit much higher proportions of organizations afflicted by new waves of targeted attacks in 2014. Conversely, for SIC categories that had a strong negative statistical significance in 2013 (Table 1), these particular sectors of activity seem to have a protective effect for those organizations, as only a few of them encounter targeted attacks on a weekly basis (which may happen merely by accident, or due to other circumstances perhaps).

5   Conclusion

As demonstrated by recent high-profile and highly publicised attacks against governments and large industries, cyber criminals seem to rely increasingly on more sophisticated malware and targeted threats as an effective means for industrial espionage. While the high profile identification of those threats may be effective in raising awareness of the danger, it does not necessarily help in determining the level of risk that targeted malware may really pose to an organisation. It is thus important to develop tools for security practitioners to assess rigorously the true level of risk to which their organization might be exposed to, *e.g.*, because of the sector of activity, the profitability of the industry, its geographical location, or possibly any other profile characteristic susceptible of being a significant risk factor.

In this paper, we show that these *risk factors* can be effectively determined for different organizations by adapting appropriate techniques from epidemiology. Considering the taxonomy of standard industry classification codes and the organizational size as potential risk factors, we have designed *case-control* studies to calculate odds ratios reflecting the degree of association with the receipt of targeted attack. A validation with a large corpus of targeted attacks blocked by [company name] mail scanning service during the whole year 2013 revealed that certain industry sectors – such as *National Security* and the *Energy* sectors, among others – are statistically at elevated risk compared with others. Similarly, we found that the risk of receiving targeted attacks increases significantly with the organizational size.

The epidemiology techniques used in this study may be further extended to allow the proactive identification of those at increased risk of attack. We believe our study is a first step towards developing a predictive framework for the analysis of targeted threats, where the degree of risk of being attacked may be calculated from a more comprehensive set of relevant factors pertaining to the profile of an organisation, or of the individuals belonging to it. A precise quantification of these risk factors – and more importantly, the combination hereof – will strengthen the epidemiological model and its capability for predicting which specific individuals or companies are the most at risk of being attacked in the near future. This, in turn, will enable organizations to take proactive measures to mitigate or at least control this risk by investing the appropriate level of resources.

Appendix A: Detailed Odds Ratio (OR) Results

Table 4. OR calculated as per *Organisational size*

Organisation size	Odds ratio	Confidence interval	χ^2 p-value
5,000+	27.12	20.59–35.72	< .001
1,001–5,000	14.13	12.45–17.03	< .001
251–1,000	4.90	4.39– 5.46	< .001
1–250	0.85	0.79– 0.91	< .001
UNK	0.21	0.18– 0.23	< .001

Table 5. OR calculated as per individual *job type* and *job level*.

Job level	Odds ratio	Confidence interval	χ^2 p-value
Support Staff	3.46	2.62 - 4.56	< .001
Managers	2.63	2.35 - 2.94	< .001
Directors	1.79	1.51 - 2.13	< .001
Temporary Workers	1.74	1.27 - 2.39	0.007
Executives	1.45	1.16 - 1.82	0.013
Individual Contributors	1.29	1.13 - 1.47	0.003
Others	0.27	0.25 - 0.30	< 0.001
Interns	0.16	0.03 - 0.84	0.099

Job Type	Odds ratio	Confidence interval	χ^2 p-value
Legal	2.36	1.08 - 5.16	0.178
Operations	2.23	2.00 - 2.48	< .001
Finance	1.81	1.22 - 2.70	0.033
Research	1.66	1.27 - 2.17	0.002
Engineering	1.61	1.35 - 1.93	< .001
HR	1.69	1.19 - 2.41	0.031
IT	1.47	1.13 - 1.93	0.041
Sales & Marketing	1.25	1.01 - 1.54	0.231
Others	0.38	0.34 - 0.42	< .001

Appendix B: Combining Odds Ratios using Multi-Criteria Decision Analysis

We use *Multi-Criteria Decision Analysis* (MCDA) to design an aggregation model for the calculation of combined risk scores, taking as input all odds ratio associated with the individual features. A typical MCDA problem consists to evaluate a set of alternatives w.r.t. different criteria using an *aggregation function* [3]. The outcome of this evaluation is a global score obtained with a well-defined aggregation model that incorporates a set of constraints reflecting the preferences and expectations of the decision-maker (Table 4).

An aggregation function is defined as a monotonically increasing function of n arguments $(n > 1)$: $f_{aggr} : [0, 1]^n \longrightarrow [0, 1]$ (Table 5).

In the family of *averaging* aggregation functions, the *Ordered Weighted Average* (OWA) operator extends these functions by combining two characteristics: (i) a weighting vector (like in a classical weighted mean), and (ii) *sorting* the inputs (usually in descending order). OWA is defined as [37]:

$$OWA_{\mathbf{w}}(\mathbf{x}) = \sum_{i=1}^{n} w_i x_{(i)} = < \mathbf{w}, \mathbf{x}_{\searrow} >$$

Table 6. OR calculated as per individual *location* and *Linkedin connections.*

Location	Odds ratio	Confidence interval	χ^2 p-value
Germany	1.91	1.10 - 3.30	0.137
Netherlands	2.27	1.31 - 3.93	0.059
UAE	2.83	1.57 - 5.10	0.004
India	0.23	0.18 - 0.31	< .001
France	3.53	2.90 - 4.28	< .001
China	2.19	1.48 - 3.24	0.001
USA	0.67	0.61 - 0.75	< .001
Brazil	0.48	0.27 - 0.86	0.095
Australia	5.75	4.59 - 7.19	< 0.001
UK	4.74	4.14 - 5.43	< 0.001

Linkedin connections	Odds ratio	Confidence interval	χ^2 p-value
1-250	8.73	7.83 - 9.73	< .001
251-500	1.40	1.23 - 1.60	< .001
500+	0.62	0.53 - 0.73	< .001
0	0.05	0.04 - 0.06	< .001

where $\mathbf{x}_\searrow$ is used to represent the vector $\mathbf{x}$ arranged in decreasing order: $x_{(1)} \geq x_{(2)} \geq \ldots \geq x_{(n)}$. This allows a decision-maker to design more complex decision modeling schemes, in which we can ensure that only a portion of criteria is satisfied without any preference on which ones precisely (*e.g.*, "at least" k criteria satisfied out of n). OWA differs from a classical weighted means in that the weights are not associated with particular inputs, but rather with their *magnitude*. It can thus emphasize a subset of largest, smallest or mid-range values (Table 6).

It might be useful sometimes to also take into account the *reliability* of each information source in the aggregation model, like in Weighted Mean (WM). Torra [34] proposed thus a generalization of OWA, called *Weighted OWA* (WOWA). This aggregation function quantifies the *reliability* of the information sources with a vector $\mathbf{p}$ (as the weighted mean does), and at the same time, allows to weight the values in relation to their relative *ordering* with a second vector $\mathbf{w}$ (as the OWA operator). It is defined by [34]:

$$WOWA_{\mathbf{w},\mathbf{p}}(\mathbf{x}) = \sum_{i=1}^{n} u_i x_{(i)},$$

where $x_{(i)}$ is the ith largest component of $\mathbf{x}$ and the weights u_i are defined as

$$u_i = G\left(\sum_{j \in H_i} p_j\right) - G\left(\sum_{j \in H_{i-1}} p_j\right)$$

where the set $H_i = \{j | x_j \geq x_i\}$ is the set of indices of the i largest elements of $\mathbf{x}$, and G is a monotone non-decreasing function that interpolates the points $(i/n, \sum_{j \leq i} w_j)$ together with the point $(0,0)$. Moreover, G is required to have the two following properties:

1. $G(i/n) = \sum_{j \leq i} w_j$, $i = 0, \ldots, n$;
2. G is linear if the points $(i/n, \sum_{j \leq i} w_j)$ lie on a straight line.

References

1. Alberg, A.J., Ford, J.G., Samet, J.M.: Epidemiology of lung cancer: ACCP evidence-based clinical practice guidelines (2nd edition). Chest **132**(3 Suppl), 29S–55S (2007)
2. BBC News.: Shamoon virus targets energy sector infrastructure, August 2012. http://www.bbc.co.uk/news/technology-19293797
3. Beliakov, G., Pradera, A., Calvo, T.: Aggregation Functions: A Guide for Practitioners. Springer, Berlin (2007)
4. Bland, J.M., Altman, D.G.: Statistics notes: the odds ratio. BMJ **320**(7247), 1468 (2000)
5. Bland, M.: An Introduction to Medical Statistics (Oxford Medical Publications). Oxford University Press, USA (2000)
6. Bossler, A., Holt, T.: On-line activities, guardianship, and malware infection: an examination of routine activities theory. Int. J. Cyber Criminol. **3**(1), 400–420 (2009)
7. Carlinet, Y., Mé, L., Debar, V., Gourhant, Y.: Analysis of computer infection risk factors based on customer network usage. In: Proceedings of the 2008 Second International Conference on Emerging Security Information, Systems and Technologies, SECURWARE 2008, pp. 317–325 IEEE Computer Society, Washington, DC (2008)
8. Chien, E., O'Gorman, G.: The nitro attacks, stealing secrets from the chemical industry. symantec security response. http://bit.ly/tDd3Jo
9. Dagon, D., Zou, C., Lee, W.: Modeling botnet propagation using time zones. In: Proceedings of the 13th Network and Distributed System Security Symposium (NDSS) (2006)
10. Daley, D.J., Gani, J.M.: Epidemic Modeling: An Introduction. Cambridge University Press, Cambridge (1999)
11. Falliere, N., Murchu, L.O., Chien, E.: W32.Stuxnet Dossier, February 2011. http://www.symantec.com/security_response/whitepapers.jsp
12. Frauenthal, J.C.: Mathematical Modeling in Epidemiology. Springer, Heidelberg (1980)
13. Greenwood, P.E., Nikulin, M.S.: A Guide to Chi-Squared Testing. Wiley Series in Probability and Statistics. Wiley, New York (1996)
14. Grimes, D.A., Schulz, K.F.: Compared to what? finding controls for case-control studies. Lancet **365**(9468), 1429–1433 (2005)
15. Kephart, J., White, S., Chess, D.: Computers and epidemiology. IEEE Spectr. **30**(5), 20–26 (1993)
16. Kephart, J.O., White, S.R.: Directed-graph epidemiological models of computer viruses. In: IEEE Symposium on Security and Privacy, pp. 343–361 (1991)
17. Kephart, J.O., White, S.R.: Measuring and modeling computer virus prevalence. In: Proceedings of the 1993 IEEE Symposium on Security and Privacy, SP 1993, p. 2. IEEE Computer Society, Washington, DC (1993)
18. Lee, M.: Who's next? identifying risk factors for subjects of targeted attacks. In: 22nd Virus Bulletin International Conference, pp. 301–306, September 2012
19. Levesque, F.L., Nsiempba, J., Fernandez, J.M., Chiasson, S., Somayaji, A.: A clinical study of risk factors related to malware infections. In: Proceedings of the 2013 ACM SIGSAC Conference on Computer and communications security (CCS 2013) (2013)
20. Mann, C.J.: Observational research methods. research design II: cohort, cross sectional, and case-control studies. Emerg. Med. J. **20**(1), 54–60 (2003)
21. Moore, D., Paxson, V., Savage, S., Shannon, C., Staniford, S., Weaver, N.: Inside the slammer worm. IEEE Secur. Priv. **1**(4), 33–39 (2003)

22. Moore, D., Shannon, C., Brown, J.: Code-red: a case study on the spread and victims of an Internet worm. In: ACM SIGCOMM/USENIX Internet Measurement Workshop (IMW) 2002, pp. 273–284, Marseille, France, November 2002
23. Moore, D., Shannon, C., Voelker, G., Savage, S.: Internet quarantine: requirements for containing self-propagating code. In: wenty-Second Annual Joint Conference of the IEEE Computer and Communications INFOCOM 2003, vol. 3, pp. 1901–1910. IEEE Societies, March-April 2003
24. Morris, J.A., Gardner, M.J.: Calculating confidence intervals for relative risks (odds ratios) and standardised ratios and rates. Br. Med. J. (Clin. Res. Ed.) **296**(6632), 1313–1316 (1988)
25. Occupational Safety & Health Administration. SIC Manual. http://www.osha.gov/pls/imis/sic_manual.html
26. Porras, P., Briesemeister, L., Skinner, K., Levitt, K., Rowe, J., Y.-C. A. Ting. A hybrid quarantine defense. In: Proceedings of the 2004 ACM workshop on Rapid malcode, WORM 2004, pp. 73–82. ACM, New York (2004)
27. Schulz, K.F., Grimes, D.A.: Case-control studies: research in reverse. Lancet **359**(9304), 431–434 (2002)
28. Shannon, C., Moore, D.: The spread of the witty worm. IEEE Secur. Priv. **2**(4), 46–50 (2004)
29. Staniford, S., Paxson, V., Weaver, N.: How to own the internet in your spare time. In: Proceedings of the 11th USENIX Security Symposium, pp. 149–167. USENIX Association, Berkeley (2002)
30. Symantec.: Stuxnet 0.5: The Missing Link, February 2013. http://www.symantec.com/content/en/us/enterprise/media/security_response/whitepapers/stuxnet_0_5_the_missing_link.pdf
31. Symantec.: Internet Security Threat Report, vol. 19, April 2014. http://www.symantec.com/threatreport/
32. Symantec Security Response.: The Luckycat Hackers, White paper. http://www.symantec.com/security_response/whitepapers.jsp
33. Thonnard, O., Bilge, L., O'Gorman, G., Kiernan, S., Lee, M.: Industrial espionage and targeted attacks: understanding the characteristics of an escalating threat. In: Balzarotti, D., Stolfo, S.J., Cova, M. (eds.) RAID 2012. LNCS, vol. 7462, pp. 64–85. Springer, Heidelberg (2012)
34. Torra, V.: The weighted OWA operator. Int. J. Intell. Syst. **12**(2), 153–166 (1997)
35. Trend Micro.: Luckycat redux, Inside an APT Campaign with Multiple Targets in India and Japan. Trend Micro Research Paper (2012). http://www.trendmicro.co.uk/media/wp/luckycat-redux-whitepaper-en.pdf
36. Wang, C., Knight, J.C., Elder, M.C.: On computer viral infection and the effect of immunization. In: Proceedings of the 16th Annual Computer Security Applications Conference, ACSAC 2000, p. 246. IEEE Computer Society, Washington, DC (2000)
37. Yager, R.: On ordered weighted averaging aggregation operators in multicriteria decision-making. IEEE Trans. Syst. Man Cybern. **18**(1), 183–190 (1988)
38. Zou, C., Towsley, D., Gong, W.: Email worm modeling and defense. In: Proceedings of the 13th International Conference on Computer Communications and Networks (ICCCN 2004), pp. 409–414, October 2004
39. Zou, C.C., Gong, W., Towsley, D.: Code red worm propagation modeling and analysis. In: Proceedings of the 9th ACM conference on Computer and communications security, CCS 2002, pp. 138–147. ACM, New York (2002)
40. Zou, C.C., Gong, W., Towsley, D.: Worm propagation modeling and analysis under dynamic quarantine defense. In: Proceedings of the 2003 ACM workshop on Rapid malcode, WORM 2003, pp. 51–60. ACM, New York (2003)

Computer-Supported Cooperative Crime

Vaibhav Garg[1], Sadia Afroz[2]([⊠]), Rebekah Overdorf[1], and Rachel Greenstadt[1]

[1] Drexel University, Philadelphia, USA
[2] UC Berkeley, Berkeley, USA
sadia.afroz@berkeley.edu

Abstract. This work addresses fundamental questions about the nature of cybercriminal organization. We investigate the organization of three underground forums: BlackhatWorld, Carders and L33tCrew to understand the nature of distinct communities within a forum, the structure of organization and the impact of enforcement, in particular banning members, on the structure of these forums. We find that each forum is divided into separate competing communities. Smaller communities are limited to 100–230 members, have a two-tiered hierarchy akin to a gang, and focus on a subset of cybercrime activities. Larger communities may have thousands of members and a complex organization with a distributed multi-tiered hierarchy more akin to a mob; such communities also have a more diverse cybercrime portfolio compared to smaller cohorts. Finally, despite differences in size and cybercrime portfolios, members on a single forum have similar operational practices, for example, they use the same electronic currency.

Keywords: Cybercrime · Economics · Social network analysis · Dunbar number

1 Introduction

The notion of what it means to be 'organized' is contentious, even in traditional crime [12]. Cybercrime complicates this debate through underground forums, where the cooperation can be described both as (vertically integrated) firms [20] and cybercrime commons [2]. Understanding the organization of such criminal networks, however, can help distinguish important actors on these forums, the economic efficiency of enforcement, and the comparative impact of distinct enforcement strategies [21,28,32].

Research in economics of security establishes the incentives for cybercriminals to organize (e.g. specialization [13]), the cost to cooperation (e.g. ripper tax [15]), and cybercriminals' response in managing trust (e.g. banning misbehaving members [2,32]). However, it does not examine the resulting nature of cybercriminal organizations as shaped by these distinct and often conflicting forces, e.g. preferential attachment [30].

© International Financial Cryptography Association 2015
R. Böhme and T. Okamoto (Eds.): FC 2015, LNCS 8975, pp. 32–43, 2015.
DOI: 10.1007/978-3-662-47854-7_3

This paper addresses three questions about the nature of cybercriminal organization on underground forums. *First,* is a single underground forum comprised of distinct cybercriminal communities? If so what are the similarities and differences across communities, specifically in terms of topics of communication between participants? *Second,* we compute and correlate various measures of centrality (or importance) for individual cybercriminals on a single underground forum. Centrally located cybercriminals may receive more responses to public posts [26], be more trusted by their peers [23], have access to more quality information [7], need fewer overall transactions and thus lower associated costs [25], and enjoy leadership positions [5]. *Finally,* we investigate the impact of community (rule) enforcement on underground forums. Specifically, we examine the impact of banning members on social networks metrics that are associated with sustainable trust management in cybercriminal online forums [2]. We make four contributions:

1. **We show that there are distinct sub-communities of cybercriminals on underground forums.** Smaller communities have 100-230 members, similar to the Dunbar number, and have a two-tiered hierarchy with centralized control similar to a gang [6]. Larger communities have flatter hierarchies, distributed control, and multiple tiers, similar to a mob [6] as well as a more diverse cybercrime portfolio.
2. **We note that most communities sub-specialize in specific crimes.** Communities on a single forum, however, have similar operational practices.
3. **We find that different measures of centrality correlate on all forums.** Some cybercriminals may enjoy disproportional advantage as they may simultaneously be more popular [26], imbue more trust [23], have access to better and more information [7], have lower transaction costs [25], and be considered leaders [5].
4. **We observe that banning misbehaving nodes can have a tangible and positive impact on the structure of the network.** When members with higher closeness/betweenness centrality are removed the change in small world characteristics may be greater. Thus, individuals who can propagate information over shorter paths are better at reducing trust in the network.

2   Background

Previous work observed two kinds of organizations in traditional crime [27]: gangs and mobs. Gangs have a two-tier hierarchy with a central leader and a group of followers that adhere to central command; mobs have a more complex command and control structure and typically specialize in specific crimes. Ethnographic accounts from the 1980's noted that cybercriminal organizations lacked characteristics of a mob, as they do not specialize [22]. While there is incentive for individual market participants to specialize [24], it is unclear whether the same is true for organized cybercrime entities, e.g. to leverage comparative advantage [18]. In this paper, we begin to explore the notion of 'organization' in cybercrime as it applies to underground forums. We analyze three underground forums that were leaked anonymously and were publicly available. Our study is orthogonal to the previous studies on these forums that provided descriptions of the forums [26], analyzed cybercrime commons [2] and proposed an algorithm to identify duplicate identities of pseudonymous cybercriminals [1].

Trust: The main challenge to cybercriminal organization is the lack of trust among peers [32] and incentive to cheat [15]. Décary [7] notes the presence of small communities on IRC chat rooms; he argues that small communities allow each member to know everyone else, emphasizing the importance of direct ties. Humans may only have meaningful relationships with up to a 150 people (i.e. the Dunbar number), with a confidence interval of 100 to 230 [10], even online [9]. We examine whether or not an underground forum starts to divide into distinct communities as the size of an underground forum increases beyond the Dunbar number.

The Dunbar number should not necessarily limit cybercriminal membership in a single community, as it is possible to design mechanisms to scale trust [2]. For example, peer-produced ratings allow buyers to evaluate a seller for credibility [26]; forum members who do not comply with rules, e.g. by creating duplicate accounts, can be banned. We explore how trust and trust management strategies, e.g. banning members, shape the organization of cybercriminal networks on underground forums.

Importance of centrality measures: Individual criminals have a higher probability of pay-off depending on their ability to interpret market signals of quality (of goods, services, and individual traders) [8]. Thus, a cybercriminal's ability to succeed or make profits may depend on their location in the network, which is measured by centrality. Examination of Russian malware writers noted that individuals with higher technical skills were more centrally located [16]. Simultaneously, Dupont examined a co-offending network of 10 cybercriminals and noted that the more popular criminal did not control the most botnets [11]. From an enforcement perspective, focusing on degree central criminals is efficient in the former case but not in the latter. Examining the correlation between various centrality measures on underground forums would illuminate the structural properties of the market and thereby inform deterrence measures [29].

3   Analyses

This study investigates the nature of organization in cybercrime as it manifests on underground forums. We analyze three underground forums: BlackhatWorld (BW), Carders (CC), and L33tCrew (LC) (Table 1).

To analyze the forums, we model the private message interactions of a forum as a weighted directed graph, $G = (V, E)$, where each node, $v \in V$, is a member of the forum, each edge, $e = A \rightarrow B$, is a non-trivial and non-administrative private message from member A to member B and weight w_{AB} is the edge weight

Table 1. Summary of forums

Forum	Language	Date covered	Users	Users with private msg	Banned users
BlackhatWorld	English	08/2005-03/2008	8718	1690 (19.38%)	43
Carders	German	02/2009-12/2010	8425	4290 (50.92%)	1849
L33tCrew	German	05/2007-11/2009	18834	7687 (40.81%)	913

denotes the number of messages sent from A to B. We remove the administrative and automated messages from the private messages. If a member only had administrative messages during his entire time in the forum, that member is also removed from the network. The resulting graph is used as the social network of a forum in the following analyses.

3.1   Analysis 1: Identifying Communities

Our goal for this study is to see whether or not distinct communities exist within a forum and compare topics among these communities.

Methodology: The main challenge to cybercriminal organization is lack of trust. Trust may not scale beyond Dunbar limits; thus, as a forum gets larger it may begin to fragment into distinct communities. To find these communities we use the Louvain method which is a fast heuristic approach based on modularity optimization [4]. Modularity of a network is the fraction of the edges that fall within the given groups minus the expected fraction if edges were distributed at random. The range of values for modularity is [-1, 1]. Networks with high modularity have dense connections between the nodes within modules but sparse connections between nodes in different modules.

Distinct communities may be similar or different. For example, different communities may compete for the same cybercrime; alternatively, they may specialize to leverage comparative advantage [17]. We use topic modeling to examine whether different communities specialize. We apply Latent Dirichlet Allocation (LDA) [3] on the private messages of community members to discover topics of their discussion and rank the topics based on their occurrence.

Results: The largest forum, L33tCrew, has the smallest number of non-trivial communities, but most of the communities on L33tCrew are larger than the other two forums (Table 3). The size of the communities on BlackhatWorld is smaller than Carders and L33tCrew and the communities are well separated (high modularity score) compared to that of the other forums (Table 2). We suspect this is because BlackhatWorld was less mature than the other two forums when the data was collected. Every forum has some common topics, usually the payment method or method of communication (Table 4). For example, the members of Carders use ukash/Paysafecard whereas on BlackhatWorld members use paypal. On L33tCrew the most common media for communication are ICQ/Jabber, but on BlackhatWorld members use Aim, Yahoo! and MSN instant messaging services. Details of the results are explained in the following subsections.

Table 2. Network structure of the forums. Here, ACC = Avg. Clustering Coeff. and LCC = Largest Connected Component. The *# communities* column shows the number of communities with the number of trivial communities (that have less than 4 members) are shown within bracket. We found that as forums get larger, the number of large communities decreases.

Forum	Density	ACC	LCC	# communities	Modularity	Largest community
BlackhatWorld	0.002	0.052	943	18 (+4)	0.46	212
Carders	0.003	0.103	2923	14 (+13)	0.29	800
L33tCrew	0.003	0.108	6116	8 (+16)	0.28	2348

BlackhatWorld: On BlackhatWorld, 1620 members, out of 8718, participated in private message interaction. The Louvain method discovers 22 communities with modularity score 0.46. 18 of the communities have at least 4 members. The largest community in BlackhatWorld has 212 members. All the communities have similar structures: two-tier organization with a few central members and the majority of the members are connected to the central members. Every

Table 3. Size and special topics of the communities.

C #	BlackhatWorld		Carders		L33tCrew	
	Memb	Special topic	Memb	Special topic	Memb	Special topic
1	212	Video upload	800	Drugs	2348	Cardable shops
2	203	Blogger generator	527	Gametimecards	1696	Anonymity services
3	142	Ebook	375	WebMoney	1447	Apple devices
4	138	Account creators	352	Bots	1419	Crypter
5	104	Invites	311	Packstation	393	Tickets
6	99	Keyword stuffing	284	Fake packstation	198	Accounts
7	97	Xrumer	253	Video game	116	Perfume
8	93	Article generator	245	ATM skimmer	35	Trojans
9	90	Account creators	237	Cardable shops		
10	81	Torrents	231	VPN, WII		
11	79	Fantomaster	212	VPN		
12	77	Bulk email	197	Trojan		
13	60	Cloaking	111	Gamekeys		
14	59	Adsense	124	Jabber		
15	47	Cracked tools				
16	46	Stumblebot				
17	39	Tutorials				
18	16	Script				

Table 4. Common topics of the forums

BlackhatWorld	Carders	L33tCrew
Payment method (Paypal)	Payment method (PSC, Ukash, WMZ)	Payment (PSC, euro, WMZ)
Contact (AIM, Yahoo!)	Contact (ICQ, Jabber)	Contact (ICQ)
Blackhat seo tools	Carding, Stolen accounts	Carding, Stolen accounts
Make money online		

community has some special topics, for example, community 1 trades tools for automatic video uploading and CAPTCHA solving (Table 3).

Carders: On Carders, we found 27 communities with 0.29 modularity, out of which 14 communities have more than 100 members. Our result shows that smaller communities tend to have one central node and show a two-tier hierarchy (Appendix A). The largest community with 800 members has several central members instead of just one. The topics of this community are more varied than the other communities. These topics include selling Apple products (iPhone, iPad, macbook), crypting services and drugs, for example, MDMA. Other communities have their own specialized topics. For example, community 10 trades VPN services and handheld devices like Wii and iPod. Interestingly, although many communities sell similar types of products like drugs and accounts, there are differences in the actual product being traded, for example, community 1 sells ephedrone (ephe) and diazepam but community 5 sells Viagra.

L33tCrew: On L33tCrew, 7687 members participated in private message interactions. The Louvain method found 24 communities with modularity score 0.28, out of which 8 communities had at least 4 members. Communities in L33tCrew are much larger than BlackhatWorld and Carders. Some communities specialize in specific topics (Table 3), for example community 1 trades cardable shops list (online stores that accept stolen cards), stealer (malware for stealing accounts) and fake packstation.

3.2   Analysis 2: Identifying Central Members

Centrality measures enumerate distinct properties, i.e. each measure represents a separate notion of the node's importance in the network. The *degree centrality* of a node indicates the total number of edges that connect it to other nodes. Degree central cybercriminals exude higher trust to peers [23] and receive higher responses to public posts [26]. *Betweenness centrality* enumerates the number of shortest paths that pass through a node. On IRC chat rooms, individuals with high betweenness centrality have access to more information both quantitatively and in terms of diversity [7]. Finally, *closeness centrality* indicates how far a node is from every other node in the network. High closeness centrality may lower transaction costs by reducing the number of overall transactions for a specific cybercriminal [25]. These centrality measures examine direct connections.

Eigenvector centrality indicates the importance of indirect connections by examining both the popularity of a node and the popularity of their connections [5]. Criminals with high eigenvector centrality may indicate leadership [5]. If centrality measures correlate it would indicate that the same criminals that exude higher trust also enjoy other advantages such as lower cost and access to higher quality information.

Methodology: We use Networkx [14] to compute six centrality measures (CM) on the social networks of the forums: degree (D), in degree (ID), out degree (OD), closeness (C), betweenness (B), and eigenvector centrality (E). We calculated the correlations between the various centrality measures for all three forums using SciPy statistics package [19] and report the Spearman's ρ in Table 5.

Table 5. Intercorrelation (Spearman's ρ) between the centrality measures, ranges from -1 to 1 where 1 indicates perfect positive correlation. Here E = Eigenvector, C = Closeness, B = Betweenness, ID = In-degree, OD = Out-degree, and D = Degree centrality. On BlackhatWorld all the centrality measures are positively correlated which means that some cybercriminals were simultaneously popular (degree), closer to other nodes (closeness), connected to other popular criminals (eigenvector) and had a higher proportion of shortest path going through them (betweenness). On Carders and L33tCrew, all but closeness centrality are positively correlated.

	BlackhatWorld					Carders					L33tCrew				
Cent	C	B	ID	OD	D	C	B	ID	OD	D	C	B	ID	OD	D
E	0.08	0.66	0.81	0.50	0.71	-0.43	0.79	0.91	0.62	0.77	-0.55	0.85	0.95	0.84	0.91
C		0.33	0.18	0.51	0.37		-0.19	-0.33	-0.11	-0.21		-0.39	-0.51	-0.35	-0.41
B			0.81	0.84	0.88			0.90	0.83	0.90			0.91	0.92	0.94
ID				0.56	0.85				0.71	0.88				0.88	0.96
OD					0.87					0.94					0.96

Results: Spearman's ρ assesses how well the relationship between two variables can be described using a monotonic function. All the correlations were statistically significant for $p<0.001$; however, the degree of correlation differs, as is evident from the ρ values that range from 0.08 to 0.96. Thus, some cybercriminals were simultaneously popular (degree), had a higher proportion of shortest path going through them (betweenness), closer to other nodes (closeness), and connected to other popular criminals (eigenvector).

Centrally located criminals have competitive advantage, e.g. through better access to market signals [7]. All four centrality measures were highly correlated across all forums. In addition the distribution of centrality was highly skewed, i.e. a few nodes had high centrality, while most were peripheral. This indicates that a majority of cybercriminals may receive a lower volume of responses to their posts [26], find it difficult to collaborate with the most technically adept cybercriminals [11] and have less access to quality information [7]. Thus, they are likely to be ripped off, with a handful of centrally located individuals who enjoy high profits and low transaction costs.

3.3   Analysis 3: Impact of Enforcement

Underground forums are policed by moderators and admins who enforce forum rules by issuing warnings and banning users when these rules are violated. For example, users can be banned for spamming or having multiple accounts [26]. It is unclear if banning users has any impact on the functioning of the network, positive or negative. It has been noted that joining these forums is free [2] and cybercriminals often have duplicate accounts [1], in fact having duplicate accounts is the most frequent reason for individuals being banned [26]. After getting banned, banned users either simply rejoin the forum or use a potentially undetected duplicate account. Here we investigate the change in network topology when misbehaving nodes are removed and contrast it with the change witnessed due to the regular churn of users in the forum.

Methodology: For each banned user u_i, we calculate the corresponding node centrality, specifically betweenness, closeness, degree and eigenvector. Since the success of a network often corresponds with the *small world* characteristics [2,31], we examine the change in average clustering coefficient (ACC) and average path length (APL) respectively; for disconnected graphs we consider the APL of the largest connected component. For each user u_i we construct two graphs G_{ib} and G_{ia}: G_{ib} from all of the private messages sent between all users in the 30 days before u_i was banned and a graph G_{ia} from all of the private messages sent between all users in the 30 days after u_i was banned. When multiple users are banned in the same time period we model them as one node. Thus, all the messages to and from all banned nodes are assigned to one node entity. If one banned node sends a message to another node banned in the same period, it would manifest as a loop in our graph. We calculate the centrality scores for u_i on G_{ib}; we also compute ACC and APL on both G_{ib} and G_{ia}. ΔACC is given by ACC_{ia}-ACC_{ib} and ΔAPL by $APL_{ia} - APL_{ib}$. We compute the correlations between network metrics, ΔACC and ΔAPL, and centrality measures to examine whether removing more central offenders has a higher impact.

Finally, Δ ACC and Δ APL should be significantly different when users are banned as compared to the change observed due to periodic churn in the underground forum. We partition the graph data into 30 day snapshots for the entire duration of the dataset. We compute the change in ACC and APL for these snapshots to get a vector of ΔACC_r and ΔAPL_r. We use Wilcoxon Test, a non-parametric test to compare the difference in means, to contrast the difference between ΔACC and ΔACC_r as well as ΔAPL and ΔAPL_r. The analysis is conducted using Networkx and R.

Results: We calculated the correlations between small world metrics, ΔACC and ΔAPL, and the various centrality measures (the Spearman's ρ is reported in Table 6). In general the results for BlackhatWorld and L33tCrew are not significant. This may be the result of fewer data points for those forums compared to Carders. BlackhatWorld only banned 43 members overall, while all the banning on L33tCrew happened in the last three months of its operational lifetime.

Table 6. Intercorrelation (Spearman's ρ) of the centrality measures with ΔACC, ΔAPL.

	BlackhatWorld		Carders		L33tCrew	
CM	ΔACC	ΔAPL	ΔACC	ΔAPL	ΔACC	ΔAPL
Betweenness (B)	-0.39	0.32	-0.12***	-0.05*	-0.05	0.11
Closeness (C)	0.07	-0.12	-0.07**	-0.05*	-0.19*	0.11
Degree (D)	-0.15	0.22	-0.19***	-0.03	-0.06	0.10
Eigenvector (E)	0.07	-0.12	-0.14***	-0.04	-0.01	0.004
p-value: 0.05> * > 0.01 > ** > 0.001 > ***						

For Carders, which banned 22 % of its members, betweenness as well as closeness centrality correlated with small world characteristics (p < 0.05). Thus, banning individuals who can propagate information over shorter paths may be better for reducing trust in the network. From a deterrence perspective a potential solution for law enforcement is to hijack the accounts of cybercriminals with higher closeness/betweenness centrality to spread noise on the forum.

We compared the mean values for ΔACC and ΔAPL, for when users get banned vs. the regular churn in the network. The change in small world characteristics for all forums were the same for banned members as for the regular churn (p-value >> 0.05). Thus, it appears that individuals currently being banned are not close to other nodes.

4   Discussion and Conclusion

In this paper we examine and evaluate the 'organization' of cybercriminals as it manifests on underground forums. Research on cybercrime often presupposes organization [24]. The nature and purpose of this organization, however, is seldom examined.

We noted the presence of distinct communities despite the focused nature of the forums. We found that smaller communities organize in a two-tier hierarchy akin to a gang and are limited in size to Dunbar number; larger communities can have thousands of members, manifest a multi-tiered complex hierarchy, and specialize in a more diverse portfolio of cybercrimes compared to smaller cohorts. We observed that some cybercriminals simultaneously had lower transaction costs, access to better information, and higher visibility in the network. Then it is likely that if law enforcement targets only the central members, it would both lower the overall profits and reduce trust within the carding community. Finally, we found that the impact of banning misbehaving cybercriminals is similar that of the periodic churn of the forum.

There are obvious limitations of this research in terms of generalization. The differences noticed between BlackhatWorld and the German carding forums might be an effect of localization. Future efforts need to repeat these analyses on additional data sets of both specialized forums dedicated to specific topics and other general purpose underground forums. It is also important to examine the temporal development of trust and organization in these communities. Finally, given trust is a key element for the stability of the forums, it would be illuminating to investigate the strategic creation and positioning of fraudulent sybils to target the sustainability of these forums.

Acknowledgment. We thank the anonymous reviewers and our shepherd Jens Grossklags for their valuable feedback. We are grateful to Damon McCoy for providing us access to the dataset. This work is supported by Intel through the ISTC for Secure Computing and National Science Foundation CNS-1347151.

A   Example of Social Networks

Figures 1 and 2 show the structure of the communities in Carders. Here, nodes are scaled according to their degree centrality.

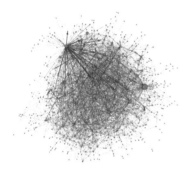

Fig. 1. The largest community of Carders does not have any one central big node.

Fig. 2. Three communities of Carders: Community 12 (purple), 13 (green), 14 (brown)(Color figure online).

References

1. Afroz, S., Caliskan-Islam, A., Stolerman, A., Greenstadt, R., McCoy, D.: Doppelgänger finder: Taking stylometry to the underground. In: IEEE Symposium on Security and Privacy. IEEE (2014)
2. Afroz, S., Garg, V., McCoy, D., Greenstadt, R.: Honor among thieves: a commons analysis of cybercrime economies. In: eCrime Researcher's Summit. APWG, IEEE (2013)
3. Blei, D.M.: Probabilistic topic models. Commun. ACM **55**(4), 77–84 (2012)
4. Blondel, V.D., Guillaume, J.L., Lambiotte, R., Lefebvre, E.: Fast unfolding of communities in large networks. J. Stat. Mech. Theory Exp. **2008**(10), P10008 (2008)

5. Bonacich, P.: Technique for analyzing overlapping memberships. Sociol. Methodol. **4**, 176–185 (1972)
6. Brenner, S.W.: Organized cybercrime-how cyberspace may affect the structure of criminal relationships. North C. J. Law Technol. **4**(1), 1–50 (2002)
7. Décary-Hétu, D.: Information exchange paths in irc chat rooms. In: Morselli, C. (ed.) Crime and Networks, pp. 218–230. Taylor & Francis Group, New York (2014)
8. Décary-Hétu, D., Leppänen, A.: Criminals and signals: An assessment of criminal performance in the carding underworld. Security Journal (2013)
9. Dunbar, R.: You've got to have (150) friends. The New York Times, The Opinion Pages (2010)
10. Dunbar, R.I.: Neocortex size as a constraint on group size in primates. J. Hum. Evol. **22**(6), 469–493 (1992)
11. Dupont, B.: Skills and trust: a tour inside the hard drives of computer hackers. In: Morselli, C. (ed.) Crime and Networks, pp. 195–217. Taylor & Francis Group, New York (2014)
12. Finckenauer, J.O.: Problems of definition: what is organized crime? Trends Organized Crime **8**(3), 63–83 (2005)
13. Franklin, J., Perrig, A., Paxson, V., Savage, S.: An inquiry into the nature and causes of the wealth of internet miscreants. In: ACM Conference on Computer and Communications Security, pp. 375–388 (2007)
14. Hagberg, A., Swart, P., S Chult, D.: Exploring network structure, dynamics, and function using networkx. Technical report, Los Alamos National Laboratory (LANL) (2008)
15. Herley, C., Florêncio, D.: Nobody sells gold for the price of silver: dishonesty, uncertainty and the underground economy. In: Moore, T., Pym, D., Ioannidis, C. (eds.) Economics of Information Security and Privacy, pp. 33–53. Springer, US (2010)
16. Holt, T.J., Strumsky, D., Smirnova, O., Kilger, M.: Examining the social networks of malware writers and hackers. Int. J. Cyber Criminol. **6**(1), 891–903 (2012)
17. Hunt, S.D., Morgan, R.M.: The comparative advantage theory of competition. J. Mark. **59**(2), 1–15 (1995)
18. Jennings, W.P.: A note on the economics of organized crime. East. Econ. J. **10**(3), 315–321 (1984)
19. Jones, E., Oliphant, T., Peterson, P.: Scipy: Open source scientific tools for python (2001). http://www.scipy.org/
20. Kanich, C., Kreibich, C., Levchenko, K., Enright, B., Voelker, G.M., Paxson, V., Savage, S.: Spamalytics: an empirical analysis of spam marketing conversion. In: Proceedings of the 15th ACM Conference on Computer and Communications Security, pp. 3–14. ACM (2008)
21. McCoy, D., Pitsillidis, A., Jordan, G., Weaver, N., Kreibich, C., Krebs, B., Voelker, G.M., Savage, S., Levchenko, K.: Pharmaleaks: understanding the business of online pharmaceutical affiliate programs. In: Proceedings of the 21st USENIX Conference on Security Symposium, pp. 1–16. USENIX Association (2012)
22. Meyer, G.R.: The social organization of the computer underground. Technical report, DTIC Document (1989)
23. Monsma, E., Buskens, V., Soudijn, M., Nieuwbeerta, P.: Partners in Cybercrime. An Online Cybercrime Forum Evaluated From a Social Network Perspective. Ph.D. thesis, Thesis in Sociology and Social Research, Universiteit Utrecht, Netherlands (2010)
24. Moore, T., Clayton, R., Anderson, R.: The economics of online crime. J. Econ. Perspect. **23**(3), 3–20 (2009)

25. Morselli, C., Giguère, C., Petit, K.: The efficiency/security trade-off in criminal networks. Soc. Netw. **29**(1), 143–153 (2007)
26. Motoyama, M., McCoy, D., Levchenko, K., Savage, S., Voelker, G.M.: An analysis of underground forums. In: Proceedings of the 2011 ACM SIGCOMM Conference on Internet Measurement Conference, pp. 71–80. ACM (2011)
27. Peretti, K.K.: Data breaches: what the underground world of carding reveals. Santa Clara Comput. High Technol. Law J. **25**(2), 375–413 (2008)
28. Sparrow, M.K.: The application of network analysis to criminal intelligence: an assessment of the prospects. Soc. Netw. **13**(3), 251–274 (1991)
29. Xu, J.J., Chen, H.: Crimenet explorer: a framework for criminal network knowledge discovery. ACM Trans. Inf. Syst. (TOIS) **23**(2), 201–226 (2005)
30. Yip, M., Shadbolt, N., Webber, C.: Structural analysis of online criminal social networks. In: IEEE International Conference on Intelligence and Security Informatics (ISI), pp. 60–65. IEEE (2012)
31. Yip, M., Shadbolt, N., Webber, C.: Why forums?: an empirical analysis into the facilitating factors of carding forums. In: Proceedings of the 5th Annual ACM Web Science Conference, pp. 453–462. ACM (2013)
32. Yip, M., Webber, C., Shadbolt, N.: Trust among cybercriminals? Carding forums, uncertainty and implications for policing. Policing Soc. **23**(4), 516–539 (2013)

There's No Free Lunch, Even Using Bitcoin: Tracking the Popularity and Profits of Virtual Currency Scams

Marie Vasek[✉] and Tyler Moore

Computer Science and Engineering Department,
Southern Methodist University, Dallas, Tx, USA
{mvasek,tylerm}@smu.edu

Abstract. We present the first empirical analysis of Bitcoin-based scams: operations established with fraudulent intent. By amalgamating reports gathered by voluntary vigilantes and tracked in online forums, we identify 192 scams and categorize them into four groups: Ponzi schemes, mining scams, scam wallets and fraudulent exchanges. In 21 % of the cases, we also found the associated Bitcoin addresses, which enables us to track payments into and out of the scams. We find that at least $11 million has been contributed to the scams from 13 000 distinct victims. Furthermore, we present evidence that the most successful scams depend on large contributions from a very small number of victims. Finally, we discuss ways in which the scams could be countered.

1 Introduction

An effective, though unfortunate, way to determine that a new technological platform has "arrived" is by observing the presence of scammers leeching off those using the system. Shortly after the advent of the telegraph, sneaky punters began placing bets on recently-completed horse races at faraway bookmakers who had not yet observed the result [1]. Once telephones became pervasive, unsolicited calls by scammers became problematic. No sooner had email become popular, then a flood of messages promising riches from Nigerian princes began filling people's inboxes.

In this paper, we investigate scams targeting the virtual currency Bitcoin, which has exploded in popularity since its introduction in 2009 [2]. As more people have been drawn to Bitcoin, frequently out of a desire to get rich quickly, more hucksters have appeared to take advantage of these eager new targets. Because Bitcoin is so new, the newly emerging scams are frequently poorly understood. The goal of this paper is to systematically investigate different types of Bitcoin scams, explain how they work, and measure their prevalence. It is hoped that by understanding how these scams work we will identify ways to arrest their rise.

To that end, we identify four types of scams currently plaguing Bitcoin: high-yield investment programs, mining investment scams, scam wallet services and scam exchanges. Using reports obtained from discussion forums and tracking

© International Financial Cryptography Association 2015
R. Böhme and T. Okamoto (Eds.): FC 2015, LNCS 8975, pp. 44–61, 2015.
DOI: 10.1007/978-3-662-47854-7_4

websites, we study 41 distinct scams operational between 2011 and 2014 where we could find the associated Bitcoin address(es). So while the study is by no means comprehensive, we are able to analyze the block chain and provide a lower bound estimate of the prevalence and criminal profits associated with these scams.

We find that $11 million worth of bitcoin has been contributed to the scams, and that at most $4 million has been returned to the victims. For the HYIPs and mining scams, we estimate that about 13 000 victims contributed funds. We also show that the most successful scams draw the vast majority of their revenue from a few victims, presenting an opportunity for law enforcement to track down and prosecute the scammers.

Section 2 describes the methodology for identifying scams, as well as how we examine the block chain to identify payments into and out of scams. Section 3 reports on high-yield investment programs (HYIPs), online Ponzi schemes where existing investors are paid lucrative returns from the contributions of new investors. Section 4 examines mining-investment scams, which is a form of advanced-fee fraud that exploits people's interest in Bitcoin mining by promising a way to profitably mine without making large up-front investments in expensive hardware. Sections 5 and 6 cover scam wallets and exchanges, respectively. Here, the scammers provide sought-after services such as mixing at a seemingly affordable price, only to steal incoming transfers from customers. Section 7 compares the different scam categories and considers what the appropriate response, if any, should be from the Bitcoin community and policymakers. Finally, we review related work in Sect. 8 and conclude in Sect. 9.

2 Methodology for Identifying Scams and Associated Transactions

We compile a list of 349 distinct candidate scams from an aggregated thread on bitcointalk.org[1], a blacklist of suspected fraudulent services maintained at http://www.badbitcoin.org/thebadlist/index.htm, and a website tracking Bitcoin-based HYIPs called cryptohyips.com[2]. We manually inspected all services on the list to identify only those operations established with fraudulent intent. For instance, we exclude Hashfast, a mining company that recently filed for Chap. 11 bankruptcy protection, as well as losses from Mt. Gox, a bitcoin exchange that failed. We also removed a number of false positives with no clear connection to cryptocurrencies, such as unclechiens.com (a Chinese restaurant in Texas). In total, this sheds 26 % of our candidate list.

We also exclude from consideration all efforts beyond the purview of this paper, such as phishing websites, malware websites, and pay-for-click websites. We are left with 192 scams to investigate further, 55 % of the candidates. We categorize each scam's type by inspecting the website through the Internet Archive

---

[1] https://bitcointalk.org/index.php?topic=576337.
[2] Data and analysis scripts are publicly available at doi:10.7910/DVN/28561.

(since many scams have since disappeared) and targeted Google searches on the domain.

We next seek out associated Bitcoin addresses for each scam using threads on bitcointalk.org, reddit.com/r/bitcoin, and named addresses and transactions on blockchain.info. We exclude any "dual-use" addresses that are also used for other purposes. In all, we find usable Bitcoin addresses for 20 % of the scams.

The next goal is to identify payments made into and out of the scam. To that end, we download the Bitcoin block chain using the Bitcoin Core client on August 25, 2014. Using znort987's Bitcoin blockparser [3] we query for all transactions involving our set of scammy addresses. This gives us traffic levels for incoming transactions to each scam. We then take a complete SQL dump of the Bitcoin block chain and query for all the transactions where the input or output address match one of our scam addresses. This gives us the Bitcoin addresses of the victims as well as the outgoing transactions from the scam. To separate out transactions made by scammers, we omit all outgoing transactions going to other addresses associated with the same scam. We also omit transactions occurring before and after the first incoming transaction to the scam.

One challenge for researchers inspecting a block chain is dealing with multiple sources and destinations in transactions. Figure 1 demonstrates the three cases where these transactions arise. We deal with multiple source–single destination transactions (Fig. 1 (left)) as follows. If the destination is a scam address and the source addresses are not also identified as being part of the scam, we group the source addresses together as a single victim.[3] In general, two addresses are assigned to the same *address group* if they ever paid into the same scam during the same transaction. For multiple-source transactions involving a scam address, we only count the scam address's contribution towards the total payout from the scam.

For transactions with a single source and multiple destinations (Fig. 1 (center)), we attribute only the source amount to the scam. For instance, suppose Fig is a victim address and Honeydew is the scam. Even though Fig pays 0.4 BTC, we tally only the 0.32 BTC transferred to Honeydew as part of the scam's total incoming payments.

With multiple sources and destinations (Fig. 1 (right)), we assign the amount paid in or out of the scam to the corresponding address group. For example, suppose Lemur is the scam address. Here, the victim group Koala–Jaguar–Iguana contributes 1.6 BTC to Lemur's scam. While in theory services such as Coin-Join [4] could account for many such transactions, in practice we do not observe very many transactions of this type.

Finally, we note that when identifying victim groups we could mistakenly identify online web wallets that pay out multiple users from the same address as a single address group. To check for this, we inspected all multiple-destination transactions whose source address appeared more than three times. In all cases, we did not find that the source addresses corresponded to web wallets. One

---

[3] Note that we deliberately make no attempt to deanonymize the actual victims beyond identifying that the addresses participated in the scam.

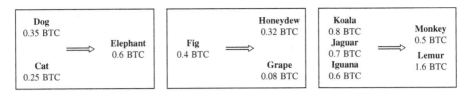

Fig. 1. Multiple-address transactions in Bitcoin.

Table 1. For each scam category, we report whether we can directly observe transactions corresponding to what victims pay into scams, what is paid out to victims, and what is paid out to the scammer (indicated by a ✓).

	Victim pay in	Payout to victim	Payout to scammer
HYIPs	✓	✓	derived
Mining scams	✓	derived	derived
Scam wallets			✓
Exchange scams			✓

potential explanation for this is that many scams prohibit using web wallets as a method of payment.

In addition to gathering data directly from the blockchain, we also analyze scams that raise funds through selling shares. We gather the share holdings from BitFunder and cross list that with cost of the shares from announcements on bitcointalk.org. For each scam, we omit the top holding who we verify is the scammer in all instances.

Ideally, we would analyze payments from victims into scams, payments back to victims, and scammer profits. For some scams, we can observe all such payments, whereas for others we can only observe certain categories. Table 1 summarizes the types of observable transactions for each scam type. Full details are given in subsequent sections.

Finally, due to high volatility of the bitcoin exchange rate, it makes sense to also report scam revenues in terms of its dollar equivalent. In order to convert BTC to USD, we gathered the daily closing USD-BTC exchange rate from the four highest-volume USD exchanges during the period of our study (Mt. Gox, Bitstamp, Bitfinex and BTC-E), as reported to http://www.bitcoincharts.com. We then converted any transactions into USD using the average exchange rate on the day of the transaction.

3   High Yield Investment Programs

Moore et al. first described high-yield investment programs (HYIPs) in [5]. HYIPs are online Ponzi schemes where people are promised outlandish interest rates on deposits (e.g., 1–2 % interest per day). Unsurprisingly, the schemes eventually collapse, and they are replaced by new programs often run by the same criminals. Moore et al. observed that these HYIP schemes relied on virtual currencies such as Liberty Reserve, Perfect Money, and EuroGoldCash for deposits and withdrawals. The centralized nature of these particular currencies has left them vulnerable to countermeasures by law enforcement. For example, Liberty Reserve was taken down by the US government in 2013 for money-laundering activities. In response, some programs have begun accepting decentralized digital currencies such as Bitcoin and Litecoin. Furthermore, most HYIPs directly advertise Bitcoin addresses in order to accept incoming payments, as opposed to using a payment processor such as BitPay or Coinbase.

We observe a number of different types of HYIPs that accept Bitcoin: HYIPs that stay in the traditional HYIP ecosystem; HYIPs that bridge the traditional HYIP ecosystem and the Bitcoin community; and HYIPs that originate in the Bitcoin ecosphere.

3.1 Traditional HYIPs

We first investigated the extent to which traditional HYIPs have begun to embrace Bitcoin. To our surprise, we found that most HYIPs do not accept bitcoin as payment. We believe the reason why is that the leading kit for developing HYIP websites, Gold Coders, does not support payments in Bitcoin or other cryptocurrencies. Neisius and Clayton analyzed the HYIP ecosystem, and they estimated that between 50–80 % of HYIP websites they observed used the Gold Coders kit [6].

When we observed several "aggregator" websites that track HYIPs, we found some traditional HYIPs that accept BTC or LTC. We then inspected HYIPs with a publicly-accessible incoming address but had never been mentioned on bitcointalk.org. All of these programs had insignificant transaction volume. Based on these findings, we do not consider traditional HYIPs further in our analysis.

3.2 Bridge HYIPs

Some scams first appear in the traditional HYIP ecosystem before being brought over to the Bitcoin world through posts on bitcointalk.org. In these cases we frequently find a high volume of BTC transactions. For example, Leancy claimed to have received over \$5 M in investments[4] from a variety of currencies. From observing payments into its Bitcoin address, we estimate \$1 674 270 came from bitcoin deposits.

Overall, we observe a total of nine such scams that brought in 12 622 BTC (\$6.5M) from September 2, 2013 through September 9, 2014. Table 2 reports key summary statistics for the nine bridge HYIPs observed. Median lifetime of

---

[4] https://web.archive.org/web/20140322111925/https://leancy.com/.

Table 2. Summary statistics for HYIPs.

	Bridge HYIPs	Bitcoin-only HYIPs
# Scams	9	23
Median lifetime (days)	125	37
# still operational	1	0
Victim pay in		
# address groups (total)	9 410	3 442
# address groups (median)	298	157
Amount paid (total)	$6 456 593	$842 909
Payout to victim		
Amount paid (total)	$3 464 476	$802 655
Payout to scammer		
Amount paid (total)	$2 992 117	$40 254

the bridge HYIPs is 125 days, with one HYIP still in operation at the time of writing.

The $6.5 M in contributions came from 9 410 distinct address groups, which provides an upper bound for the number of victims contributing to these scams. The scams in turn paid at most $3.5 M back to the victims, leaving $3 M in profit to the operators. It is likely that at least some of the $3.5 M in payouts went to addresses controlled by scammers, so we expect the actual profit rate to be much higher.

These summary statistics obscure the details of how individual scams performed over time. Figure 2 (top) plots the aggregate payments into and out of the nine bridge HYIPs. We can see that, in aggregate, the payments flowing into the scams always keep pace with the payments flowing out. We also see huge spikes in the money flowing in at different points throughout the period, with nearly all of the activity taking place in 2014. Figure 2 (bottom) breaks out the incoming payments to the associated scams. We can see that the first big spike is due to the rise of Leancy, the second Cryptory, the third Rockwell Partners and the fourth Cryptory (with a small contribution form Rockwell Partners). Hence the overall burstiness observed in the scam contributions can be attributed to different scams receiving a surge of investment before falling rapidly.

Figure 3 compares the transactions in and out for the top 8 performing bridge HYIPs. The graphs are presented in decreasing order of scam size, and the graph also includes a green dotted line indicating the day the scam first appeared on the bitcointalk.org forum.

For example, for Leancy (top right) we see the first BTC transaction on December 16, 2013, but the volume picks way up on February 4, 2014 when a user, LeancyBTC, posted an advertisement for the scheme in the Bitcoin forums[5].

---

[5] https://bitcointalk.org/index.php?topic=448250.

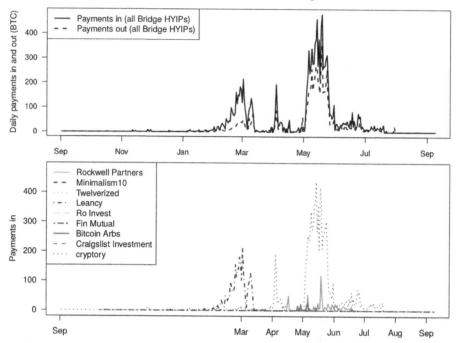

Fig. 2. Top: Daily volume of all payments into and out of Bridge HYIPs wallet incoming transactions. Bottom: daily volume of incoming payments split by HYIP.

Most reports precede spikes in investment, though the jump is not always as immediate as in the case of LeancyBTC's post.

The other key conclusion that can be drawn from these graphs is that the most successful scams manage to pay out far less than they take in, and they do so consistently over time. In theory, Ponzi schemes need not collapse until withdrawal requests overwhelm the cash reserves of the scammer. In practice, for Leancy and Cryptory, the scheme stopped paying out as soon as the funds stopped flowing in. These operators could have kept up the appearance of legitimacy by honoring withdrawal requests after new deposits stopped, but they chose not to. Instead, they found it more profitable to simply disappear once the deposits did.

For the less successful scams (bottom of graph), the outgoing payments often exceed the incoming payments. Hence, in these cases it does appear that the scammer gave up once the scam failed to take off, even after honoring withdrawal requests that exceeding available deposits.

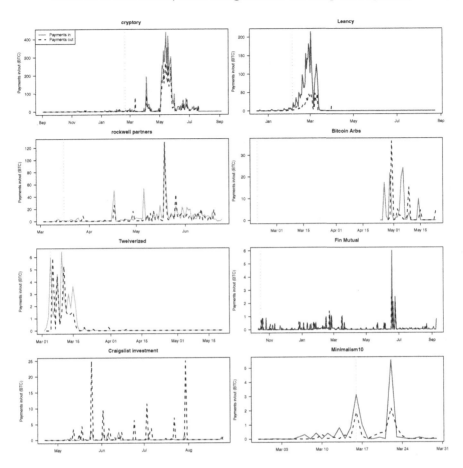

Fig. 3. Daily volume of payments into and out of Bridge HYIPs, sorted by total payments received. The green dotted line indicates when the scam is first promoted on bitcointalk.org.

3.3   Bitcoin-Only HYIPs

In addition to HYIPs that happen to accept bitcoin, many shady operators have set up Ponzi schemes using bitcoin as a method of payment. We term these frauds *Bitcoin-only HYIPs* because they operate like HYIPs even if they do not share the same heritage as traditional HYIPs.

The premise behind Bitcoin-only HYIPs varies considerably. Some purport to be legitimate investment vehicles. The biggest of these is Bitcoin Savings and Trust (first launched under the name "First Pirate Savings and Trust") which allegedly raised 4.5 million USD [7]. (Unfortunately, since the address used for this Ponzi was also used for a legitimate Bitcoin marketplace, we do not include it in our analysis. Reported estimates in volume vary greatly[6]). Others purport to be online Bitcoin wallets offering an outlandishly high daily rate of return on the money kept in the wallet. While these schemes are fraudulent by design, they lure in unsuspecting, naïve victims as well as those fully aware that they are investing in a Ponzi scheme. The rest were transparently Ponzis. Some of these offer an "hourly" rate of return and purport to deposit that return back hourly. Others offer an increased payout upon a subsequent pay in. Some schemes just offer a lump payout after a period of time.

In total, we observed 23 Bitcoin-only Ponzi schemes, which earned 1 562 BTC (843 K USD) from January 2, 2013 through September 9, 2014. Table 2 reports the key summary statistics. Compared to Bridge HYIPs, Bitcoin-only HYIPs are shorter-lived and less profitable. The schemes collapse within 37 days (median) and the scammers have collectively netted only $40 K during that time. Again, we expect that some of the payouts to victims are actually addresses controlled by scammers, so the scammer's profit is likely higher.

4 Mining Scams

Since virtually every operation that sells mining equipment has been accused of being a scam, we adopt the narrower definition of scams as those mining operations that take payments from "investors" but never deliver product. Note that "cloud mining" operations that are transparently Ponzi schemes are considered in our HYIP discussion in Sect. 3. Furthermore, we also exclude the many "cloud mining" operations that have not been shown to be Ponzi schemes but are dubious in nature.

We analyze five mining scams (Labcoin, Active Mining Corporation, Ice Drill, AsicMiningEquipment.com, Dragon-Miner.com). We consider Labcoin here instead of Sect. 3 since it did not promise outrageous returns and it did purport to deliver hashing output to some degree[7]. Similarly, Active Mining and Ice Drill are operations that raised money to purportedly make ASICs and share the profits but never delivered. AsicMiningEquipment.com and Dragon-Miner.com are fraudulent mining e-commerce websites.

Relevant summary statistics are presented in Table 3. Notably, due to the nature of the scam, none of this contributed money is returned to the victims.

5 Scam Wallets

We now consider fraudulent services that masquerade as Bitcoin wallets. Note that we categorize wallets that purport to offer a daily return on savings as Ponzi schemes and discuss them in Sect. 3. Scam wallets, by contrast, offer many of the features of online wallets, but with a key difference: the operators siphon some or all of the currency transferred to the wallet.

---

[6] https://bitcointalk.org/index.php?topic=576337#post_toc_38.

[7] https://bitcointalk.org/index.php?topic=263445.msg3417016.

The basic ruse goes as follows:

1. Victim deposits bitcoin into scam wallet.
2. If the amount of money falls below the threshold, the money stays.
3. If the amount of money is above the threshold, the scammer moves the money into her own wallet.

We identified this process by examining 15 threads on the bitcointalk.org forums and 7 threads on the Bitcoin subreddit (reddit.com/r/bitcoin) where users complained of losing money once they began depositing larger amounts. Bitcointalk users `drgonzo`[8] and `Artificial`[9] put over 10 bitcoin into their respective Easy Coin accounts in early 2013 but were each left with 0.099 bitcoin (0.1 bitcoin minus their mixing fee) immediately following. Whereas Bitcointalk user `BitcoinOnFire`[10] reports that the first Easy Coin transaction he made worked, but when he moved over a few bitcoin in early 2014, that was quickly drained. Bitcointalk user `Kazimir`[11] reports that putting in less than 0.1 bitcoin into Bitcoinwallet.in late 2013 which was fine. Reddit user `LutherForThePeople`[12] reports putting in a small amount of bitcoin into Easy Coin in 2013 which was fine and then upon putting in more bitcoin, the scammers drained his account.

We were able to analyze three of these services (Onion Wallet[13], Easy Coin[14], and Bitcoinwallet.in[15]), in which all transfers from the victims were ultimately delivered to the same address held by the scammer. These particular scams advertise themselves as offering a mixing service that enhances transaction anonymity for customers. In fact, all three services appear to be operated by the same scammer, because the siphoning transfers all go directly to the same Bitcoin address. The wallets do in fact operate a mixing service, which makes it impractical to trace back incoming transfers from victims into the service. However, since the scammer sends all stolen bitcoins to the same address, we are able to track the ill-gotten gains for these three scams collectively.

Figure 4 (top) plots the amount of Bitcoin drained out of victim accounts each week. The highly volatile trend suggests that the scam had more success in 2013 compared to 2014. However, normalizing the scammer intake against the BTC–USD exchange rate, as in Fig. 4 (bottom), tells a different story. It suggests that the scammer drains off an amount of BTC corresponding to a steady USD-denominated wage. Compared to the Bitcoin HYIPs and mining scams, these

---

[8] https://bitcointalk.org/index.php?action=profile;u=106769.
[9] https://bitcointalk.org/index.php?action=profile;u=109912.
[10] https://bitcointalk.org/index.php?action=profile;u=323407.
[11] https://bitcointalk.org/index.php?action=profile;u=58460.
[12] https://www.reddit.com/user/LutherForThePeople.
[13] http://ow24et3tetp6tvmk.onion/.
[14] http://easycoinsayj7p5l.onion/ and https://web.archive.org/web/20130905204338/
https://easycoin.net/.
[15] https://web.archive.org/web/20140213235218/https://bitcoinwallet.in/.

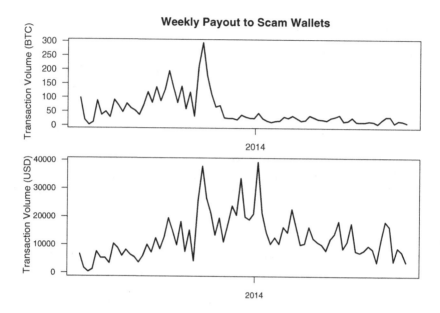

Fig. 4. Weekly payouts to scam wallets in BTC (top) and USD (bottom).

wallet scams offer a much steadier stream of between $10–40 K in ill-gotten gains each week. In total, this scammer's revenue (through 11 September 2014) was about 4 100 BTC, which corresponds to nearly $1 million. Finally, we note that the scam continues unabated at the time of this writing.

6   Bitcoin Exchange Scams

We look at four scams purporting to be Bitcoin exchanges: BTC Promo, btc-Quick, CoinOpend, and Ubitex. Most of these scams entice victims by offering features that many other exchanges do not offer such as PayPal/Credit Card processing, or a better exchange rate than established players. Unfortunately for the customer, they they never actually receive the bitcoin or cash after making payment. Ubitex purported to be an in-person exchange, but never got off the ground. Speculation exists as to whether Ubitex is a scam or just a flopped business, but we treat it as a scam here.

Table 3 reports the key figures for the scam exchanges. The longer-lived scam exchanges survived for approximately three months, but they also drew in the least amount of money from victims. CoinOpend and btcQuick each operated for less than one month, but during that time drew in hundreds of thousands of dollars from victims.

Table 3. Lifetime and payouts for scam wallets and exchanges, plus mining scam payouts.

Scam	Lifetime		Payout to scammer	
	Days	Alive?	BTC	USD
Scam wallets	535	yes	4 105	$359 902
Scam exchanges				
BTC Promo	98	yes	44	$22 112
btcQuick		no	929	$73 218
CoinOpend	29	no	575	$264 466
Ubitex	91	no	30	$ 96[a]
Mining scams	Data Source			
Labcoin	Blockchain		241	$48 562
AMC	BitFunder		18 041	$1 327 590
Ice Drill	BitFunder		14 426	$1 558 008
Asic Mining	Blockchain		12.6	$5 532
Dragon Miner	Blockchain		1.63	$1 019

[a]20.189BTC corresponding to $15 515 reported invested on GLBSE, but not trackable on block chain. Address is from `bitcointalk` forum post asking for Ubitex donations.

7 Discussion

7.1 Revisiting the Scam Categories

The scams presented differ in several key ways, as summarized in Table 4. First, we can see that Bridge HYIPs have taken in the most revenue from victims. This may reflect the more mature nature of these scams, as traditional HYIPs have been operating for years. Thus, they already have an established base of users and extensive advertising. The Bitcoin-based schemes, by contrast, are much newer and so we would expect that the scams are not as refined. A less optimistic interpretation, therefore, is that there is considerable room for growth in the magnitude of these frauds as Bitcoin increases in popularity. Furthermore, we note that true total of scammer profits could be much higher, given that we could only track revenues for 21 % of the reported scams.

The scams also differ in the way they "hook" victims. HYIPs exploit people's greed, or more precisely, their susceptibility to the narrative that it is easy to get rich quick just by using Bitcoin. Mining scams exploit this same desire, but wrap it in more measured promises of future riches. Mining scams are classic advanced-fee fraud: victims pay money in hopes of getting larger sums down the line, but that day never comes.

Wallet and exchange scams, by contrast, exploit the difficulty people have in judging the legitimacy of web services. Thus, the scammers take advantage

Table 4. Recap of Bitcoin scam categories and features.

Scam category	Scam revenue		Hook	Victim awareness	Trackability
Bridge HYIPs	$6.5 M	(in)	Greed	low–high	med
Bitcoin-only HYIPs	$840 K	(in)	Risk appetite, greed	high	high
Mining scams	$2.9 M	(in/out)	Advanced-fee fraud	low	low
Wallet scams	$360 K	(out)	Information asymmetry	low	low
Exchange scams	$455 K	(out)	Information asymmetry	low	low

of an information asymmetry that naturally exists. So long as it is difficult to distinguish between good services and bad ones, there will remain an opening for scammers to profit.

User awareness to the scams also varies considerably. Some participants in HYIPs know that they are likely investing in a Ponzi scheme, but they hope to cash out before the scheme collapses. Most Bitcoin-based HYIPs, however, are transparent about the dodgy nature of the service. For example, Bit Twin offers to double your bitcoins within 48 hours. Hence, some scams might even be considered a form of gambling. However, investors in mining, exchange and wallet scams are usually completely unaware that anything untoward is going on with the service until they have lost their money.

Finally, we can distinguish between how inherently trackable these scams are. Some bridge HYIPs can be readily tracked, since they publish a single incoming payment address online. Others use a service such as `blockchain.info` which generates a new incoming address for each visitor. Many require investors to sign up first in order to receive the incoming payment address, which could be changed for different investors. Most Bitcoin-only HYIPs can be readily tracked, since the service usually posts the address in order to signal trustworthiness in the service. Any service that attempts to hide the payment addresses would be viewed with suspicion.

Mining, exchange and wallet scams need not be trackable. The ones we observed happened to make their addresses publicly available, but there is no reason that this should always be. Hence, we anticipate these frauds to remain difficult to track via the block chain moving forward.

7.2   How Are Victim Payments into Scams Distributed?

We now examine how the size of payments into scams are distributed. This is an important question, because it influences how successful scammers select targets. A relatively even distribution of payments into scams would indicate that scammers must recruit lots of victims who each contribute a small but substantial amount. By contrast, an uneven distribution suggests that scammers should focus on the small number of marks who will give away the vast majority of the money contributed to the scheme.

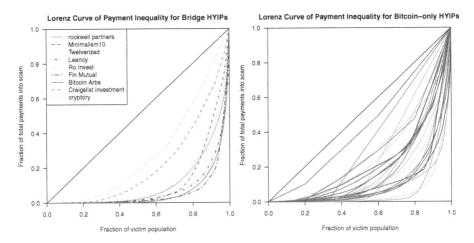

Fig. 5. Lorenz curve for Bridge HYIPs (left) and Bitcoin-only HYIPs (right).

To answer this question, we compute measurements typically used in assessing income inequality. Figure 5 plots Lorenz curves for each of the HYIP scams we identified. Perfect equality would be indicated by a diagonal line with slope equal to 1, while curves appearing further down and to the right indicate greater inequality in payments from address groups. The left graph plots Bridge HYIPs while the right plots Bitcoin-only Ponzis. We see considerable variation, but with a small number of victims contributing much of the payments in most cases. For instance, in Leancy approximately 20 % of the victim population contributed 90 % of the payments to scammers. We see even greater variation in the Bitcoin-only HYIPs.

Next, we consider variations across scam categories. Figure 6 (left) plots the Lorenz curves for all payments into the 3 scam categories. Payments into mining scams are the most skewed: nearly all of the total contributions come from less than 10 % of the victims. While still very skewed, Bridge HYIPs rely on contributions from more victims than do the Bitcoin-only HYIPs: the smallest 80 % of address groups account for around 5 % of the scammer's haul for Bitcoin-only HYIPs, compared to 15 % for Bridge HYIPs.

Figure 6 (right) examines the relationship between inequality of payments into scams and the total money drawn into the scams. The graph plots the Gini coefficient for each scam (where 0 indicates all incoming payments are equal and 1 indicates complete inequality) against the total payments paid into each scam. We can see that the least successful scams tend to be the most equal, whereas the most successful scams are more unequal. Hence, for a scam to be successful, it appears that it must catch the few "big fish" who will pay the bulk of the money into the scam.

The high concentration in payment size into scams has implications for law enforcement actions against the scammers. Most successful scams have a few

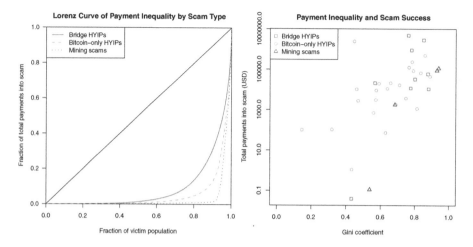

Fig. 6. Lorenz curve for total payments into scam categories (left); scatter plot comparing Gini coefficient to the amount of money stolen by scammers (right).

big contributors, who might be more willing to assist with in an investigation. Furthermore, the individual losses suffered by these victims are more likely to meet the threshold required to get the attention of high-tech crime units.

7.3 Policy Options

We have already established that different types of Bitcoin scams exist, and that many are growing in popularity. But there are many issues with Bitcoin, as well as cybercrime in general. Given that context, why might Bitcoin scams matter? Here are three plausible reasons: (i) if there are many victims, (ii) if substantial amounts of money is being lost, or (iii) if the scams undermine trust in the ecosystem.

This paper has established a lower bound on answers to the first two reasons. The number of victims and magnitude of their losses, while considerable, is substantially smaller than those afflicted by failures elsewhere in Bitcoin, such as the Mt. Gox collapse. So on the current figures alone, we cannot conclude that eradicating these scams should take priority.

However, there are two counterarguments that suggest a more robust response is warranted. First, the scams are growing substantially in popularity and profitability. Rooting out the scams at this early stage may be more feasible, and doing so we could avoid the substantial indirect costs imposed by exposing many new Bitcoin users to such a negative experience. The second counterargument is that, for the wallet and exchanges scams at least, their continued prevalence threatens to undermine trust in the overall ecosystem. If people cannot determine whether the service they are interacting with is legitimate due to an information asymmetry, then everyone in the ecosystem, even legitimate exchanges and wallets, suffers.

8 Related Work

High-yield investment programs were first documented in the research literature by Moore et al. [5]. They documented over 1 000 such scams, provided a primer on the ecosystem's operation, and established that tracking websites accurately monitor the scam's operation. Neisius and Clayton also investigated HYIPs, focusing on the profits accrued by support organizations in setting up and monitoring HYIP scams [6]. Both papers focused on traditional HYIPs that have operated with impunity for several years using centralized virtual currencies such as Liberty Reserve and Perfect Money. In this paper, we have instead focused on HYIPs that use cryptocurrencies as payment. The block chain has enabled us to accurately measure, for the first time, the amount of money transferred into HYIPs by victims and out by the scam operators.

Huang et al. consider Bitcoin mining malware and quantify the amount of bitcoin that Bitcoin mining botnets have minted using the block chain [8]. Our paper does not consider malware, but our block chain analysis techniques are similar to those of Huang et al. (as well as Meiklejohn et al. and Ron and Shamir [9–11]). Vasek et al. examine the prevalence of denial-of-service attacks against Bitcoin services [12]. These attacks are another avenue for criminals to profit as well as another threat to Bitcoin's success. Möser et al. systematically analyze Bitcoin mixing services, which some of the scams we study purport to be [13]. Christin measures transactions made on the Silk Road, a large online marketplace that was shut down by the US federal government, and finds over 1.2 million dollars in sales monthly, despite (or because of?) the purported anonymity of the marketplace [14]. While the Silk Road is not a scam (though we do not doubt that there were scammers abusing the service), it has certainly harmed Bitcoin's reputation, much like the scams we study might if they became more prevalent. Moore and Christin studied how often and why Bitcoin-currency exchanges collapsed [15]. While in this paper we investigated fraudulent exchanges set up to steal customer deposits, Moore and Christin focused on legitimate exchanges that shut down. While some label such failed exchanges as scams, particularly when they are unable to return outstanding customer deposits, we exclude them from consideration here.

The Bitcoin Foundation surveyed prominent Bitcoin participants about different hypotheticals that could affect the Bitcoin ecosystem [16]. While they did not explicitly ask about Bitcoin scams, they found that mismanaged Bitcoin businesses was a top threat to Bitcoin's success. They also found people feared Bitcoin getting a "bad reputation" for being a haven for wicked behavior. This includes a concern over Bitcoin being used for gambling (e.g., many Bitcoin-only HYIPs). The scams presented in this paper doubtless could harm Bitcoin's reputation if they are not eradicated.

9   Concluding Remarks

Scams – operations established with fraudulent intent – pose serious dangers to the Bitcoin ecosystem. First, there is the direct harm imposed on the victims who pass money to the scammers, never to see it again. Second, and perhaps more substantially, there is indirect harm imposed on all users, even those who don't fall victim to scams. This harm manifests in damage to the reputation of legitimate operations and the undermined trust of users who become more reticent to try out new services.

Fortunately, the block chain creates an opportunity in that transactions may often be tracked, which could make it easier to assess the true risk posed by scams and make it harder for scammers to hide. To that end, in this paper we have presented the first systematic, empirical analysis of Bitcoin scams. We identified four categories of scams: Ponzi schemes, mining scams, scam wallets and fraudulent exchanges. By analyzing transactions into and out of 42 such scams, we estimate that approximately \$11 million has been contributed to scams by at least 13 000 victims, much of it within the past year.

We found that Bridge HYIPs, an established scam that predates Bitcoin, take in 60 % of the total revenue. The block chain has enabled us to more accurately estimate the financial success of these scams than in previous work, by directly measuring money flowing into HYIPs for the first time. We also worry that the other scam categories may soon rise to the level of HYIPs as scammers wise up to what is possible.

To combat any future rise, continued measurement of the threat as outlined in this paper is essential. Furthermore, by investigating losses from victims contributing the largest amounts, there may be an opportunity for law enforcement to crack down on scams more effectively.

Acknowledgments. This work was partially funded by the Department of Homeland Security (DHS) Science and Technology Directorate, Cyber Security Division (DHS S&T/CSD) Broad Agency Announcement 11.02, the Government of Australia and SPAWAR Systems Center Pacific via contract number N66001-13-C-0131. This paper represents the position of the authors and not that of the aforementioned agencies.

References

1. Standage, T.: The Victorian Internet. Walker & Company, New York (1998)
2. Nakamoto, S.: Bitcoin: a peer-to-peer electronic cash system (2008). https://bitcoin.org/bitcoin.pdf
3. znort987, blockparser https://github.com/znort987/blockparser
4. Maxwell, G.: CoinJoin: Bitcoin privacy for the real world, https://bitcointalk.org/index.php?topic=279249. Accessed 29 August 2014
5. Moore, T., Han, J., Clayton, R.: The postmodern ponzi scheme: empirical analysis of high-yield investment programs. In: Keromytis, A.D. (ed.) FC 2012. LNCS, vol. 7397, pp. 41–56. Springer, Heidelberg (2012)

6. Neisius, J., Clayton, R.: Orchestrated crime: the high yield investment fraud ecosystem. In: Proceedings of the Eighth APWG eCrime Researcher's Summit, Birmingham, AL, Sep. 2014
7. Securities and Exchange Commission, SEC v. Trendon T. Shavers, et al. http://www.sec.gov/litigation/complaints/2013/comp-pr2013-132.pdf
8. Huang, D.Y., Dharmdasani, H., Meiklejohn, S., Dave, V., Grier, C., McCoy, D., Savage, S., Weaver, N., Snoeren, A.C., Levchenko, K.: Botcoin: monetizing stolen cycles. In: Proceedings of the Network and Distributed System Security Symposium (2014)
9. Meiklejohn, S., Pomarole, M., Jordan, G., Levchenko, K., McCoy, D., Voelker, G.M., Savage, S.: A fistful of Bitcoins: characterizing payments among men with no names. In: Proceedings of the Internet Measurement Conference, pp. 127–140. ACM (2013)
10. Ron, D., Shamir, A.: Quantitative analysis of the full bitcoin transaction graph. In: Sadeghi, A.-R. (ed.) FC 2013. LNCS, vol. 7859, pp. 6–24. Springer, Heidelberg (2013)
11. Ron, D., Shamir, A.: How did dread pirate roberts acquire and protect his bitcoin wealth? In: Böhme, R., Brenner, M., Moore, T., Smith, M. (eds.) FC 2014 Workshops. LNCS, vol. 8438, pp. 3–15. Springer, Heidelberg (2014)
12. Vasek, M., Thornton, M., Moore, T.: Empirical analysis of denial-of-service attacks in the Bitcoin ecosystem. In: Böhme, R., Brenner, M., Moore, T., Smith, M. (eds.) FC 2014 Workshops. LNCS, vol. 8438, pp. 57–71. Springer, Heidelberg (2014)
13. Möser, M., Böhme, R., Breuker, D.: An inquiry into money laundering tools in the Bitcoin ecosystem. In: Proceedings of the Seventh APWG eCrime Researcher's Summit. pp. 1–14. IEEE (2013)
14. Christin, N.: Traveling the Silk Road: a measurement analysis of a large anonymous online marketplace. In: Proceedings of the 22nd International Conference on World Wide Web, pp. 213–224 (2013)
15. Moore, T., Christin, N.: Beware the middleman: empirical analysis of Bitcoin-exchange risk. In: Sadeghi, A.-R. (ed.) FC 2013. LNCS, vol. 7859, pp. 25–33. Springer, Heidelberg (2013)
16. Bitcoin Foundation, Removing impediments to Bitcoin's success: A risk management study 2014. https://bitcoinfoundation.org/static/2014/04/Bitcoin-Risk-Management-Study-Spring-2014.pdf

Sidechannels

Multi-class Traffic Morphing
for Encrypted VoIP Communication

W. Brad Moore$^{(\boxtimes)}$, Henry Tan, Micah Sherr, and Marcus A. Maloof

Georgetown University, Washington, USA
{wbm,ztan,msherr,maloof}@cs.georgetown.edu

Abstract. In a *re-identification attack*, an adversary analyzes the sizes of intercepted encrypted VoIP packets to infer characteristics of the underlying audio—for example, the language or individual phrases spoken on the encrypted VoIP call. *Traffic morphing* has been proposed as a general solution for defending against such attacks. In traffic morphing, the sender pads ciphertext to obfuscate the distribution of packet sizes, impairing the adversary's ability to accurately identify features of the plaintext.

This paper makes several contributions to traffic morphing defenses. First, we argue that existing traffic morphing techniques are ineffective against certain re-identification attacks since they (i) require a priori knowledge of what information the adversary is trying to learn about the plaintext (e.g., language, the identity of the speaker, the speaker's gender, etc.), and (ii) perform poorly with a large number of classes. Second, we introduce new algorithms for traffic morphing that are more generally applicable and do not depend on assumptions about the goals of the adversary. Finally, we evaluate our defenses against re-identification attacks, and show, using a large real-world corpus of spoken audio samples, that our techniques reduce the adversary's accuracy by 94 % with low computational and bandwidth overhead.

1 Introduction

Over the last decade, the use of voice-over-IP services as an alternative to land-lines and mobile phones has dramatically increased. For instance, Skype calls accounted for just 2.9 % of the international call market in 2005 [19]; by 2012, that percentage increased by an order of magnitude to 34 % [20]. Between 2011 and 2012, the number of concurrent users online nearly doubled from 27 million to 50 million [16].

Additionally, VoIP offers the ability to more easily secure the communication content using end-to-end (e2e) encryption – either as part of the communication protocol (cf. Skype [3]) or by layering established cryptographic protocols such as SSL/TLS (cf. WebRTC). The widespread adoption of encrypted VoIP services such as Skype implies a more secure communication infrastructure that is resistant to eavesdropping.

However, existing work has shown that even when strong encryption is applied, encrypted VoIP streams often leak significant information about the

© International Financial Cryptography Association 2015
R. Böhme and T. Okamoto (Eds.): FC 2015, LNCS 8975, pp. 65–85, 2015.
DOI: 10.1007/978-3-662-47854-7_5

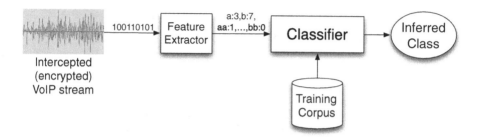

Fig. 1. Attack workflow. An adversary conducts a re-identification attack by extracting features from an intercepted, encrypted stream. In this example, each observed packet size is mapped to a symbol from the alphabet $\Sigma = \{a, b\}$. The feature extractor counts the number of occurrences of each symbol ("unigram") and adjacent pair of symbols ("bigram"). Using a corpus of labeled training data whose features have been similarly extracted, the attacker uses machine learning techniques to infer the class of the intercepted communication (e.g., the speaker is speaking German or is Groucho Marx).

plaintext audio. To conserve bandwidth, most popular VoIP systems make use of variable bit-rate (VBR) encoders in which the amount of output data per time unit varies according to the complexity of the audio sample. Importantly, although VoIP systems may encrypt audio packets, the systems' underlying use of VBR induces a side-channel through which an adversary may infer information about the plaintext by observing only the sizes of encrypted packets. In particular, Wright et al. showed that such observations are sufficient to accurately infer the language being spoken [26]. As shown in Fig. 1, an adversary can extract features from the ciphertext based on packets sizes and use machine learning techniques to infer attributes of the underlying plaintext. Followup work by many of the same authors demonstrated that machine learning techniques could additionally identify speakers [13] and phrases [24,27] with high accuracy. Throughout this paper, we use the term *class* to denote a group of audio samples that share a common attribute (e.g., speaker's gender, speaker's identity, or spoken language).

We present a novel blackbox approach that we call *Muffler* to defend against traffic analysis of encrypted VoIP streams. As with other blackbox defenses [28], we assume a closed-source VoIP client that sends encrypted packets, e.g., Skype. To maintain compatibility with existing applications, Muffler operates as an add-on security layer; we make no modifications to client software.

1.1 Strawman Defenses

An obvious and simple defense against VoIP re-identification attacks is to replace VBR codecs with CBR encoding. However, this strategy would require either degradation of call quality, or a significant increase to stream bandwidth. CBR encoding is not well-suited for networks with limited bandwidth (e.g., mobile

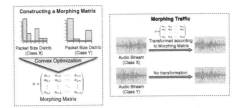

Fig. 2. Conceptual overview of the traffic morphing approach by Wright et al. [28].

data networks) – our aim is to develop defenses that incur low bandwidth over-heads.

1.2 Background: Traffic Morphing

To defeat traffic analysis while maintaining high-quality audio, Wright et al. proposed a *traffic morphing* approach in which one class of traffic is transformed to match the statistical properties of another existing class [28]. Specifically, they selectively add padding to packets to obfuscate a stream's true distribution of packet sizes and make the stream appear indistinguishable from another distribution while minimizing the amount of padding necessary. Using a comparison function such as the χ^2 statistic and convex optimization, they find the distribution closest to a target distribution that is attainable by padding (see Fig. 2, left). The result is a *morphing matrix A* where each value a_{ij} in the matrix represents the probability that an (encrypted) audio sample of size s_i is padded to s_j (see Fig. 2, right). They show that for binary classification, their traffic morphing technique significantly degrades the accuracy of the classifier from 71 % (without obfuscation) to 30 %, while incurring a communication overhead of 15.4 % [28].

In a blackbox design, packet padding can be achieved by tunneling the encrypted VoIP packets in another layer of encryption where padding may be added.

The receiver decrypts this layer and discards the padding to obtain the original encrypted VoIP stream. Importantly, while the sender can pad packets, packet sizes cannot be decreased since the VoIP client functions as a blackbox. That is, if $s_j < s_i$, then $a_{ij} = 0$ in the morphing matrix.

1.3 A New Approach to Blackbox Traffic Morphing

This paper proposes a new traffic morphing technique that we call Muffler. In contrast to existing work in which one distribution is morphed to a another 'target' distribution, we construct a new synthetic distribution to which all input audio streams are morphed. Also, as discussed in the next section, a limitation of existing techniques is that they assume that the sender knows the adversary's intent (e.g., to determine if the speaker is speaking English or German). With Muffler, we adopt a stronger threat model and assume that the sender

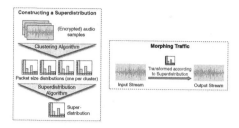

Fig. 3. Conceptual overview of Muffler.

does not know the adversary's classification task (language, speaker, gender re-identification, etc.).

Figure 3 presents a high-level overview of Muffler. Given a background corpus of encrypted audio (either labeled or unlabeled), Muffler uses clustering techniques to form groups of samples, where each group could potentially be a classification used by an adversary in a re-identification attack. For example, a cluster of samples could correspond to spoken Arabic, female speakers, et cetera. Using these clusters, Muffler creates a "superdistribution" of packet sizes to which *all* discovered clusters may be mapped. Using a large suite of classifiers, we demonstrate that Muffler effectively thwarts traffic analysis of encrypted VoIP streams with both low computation and bandwidth overheads.

2   Improved Traffic Morphing

The state-of-the-art defense against re-identification attacks is the traffic morphing approach introduced by Wright et al. [28]. (We survey other related literature in Sect. 8). In this section, we highlight some of the advantages of Muffler over this existing work.

2.1   Lightweight Traffic Morphing

The approach taken by Wright et al. uses convex optimization to find the best-matching distribution between two audio streams. Calculating the optimal stream transformation requires over an hour on their tested audio samples [28]. Muffler avoids expensive convex optimizations and is therefore able to *dynamically* adapt to the input signal: we show that our processes are sufficiently lightweight to adjust the transformation mappings in real-time.

2.2   Finding a Morphable Distribution

As described above, we consider blackbox defenses, where the traffic morphing approach may only increase packet sizes. Wright et al. study both whitebox and blackbox solutions, where packet sizes may be decreased in the former case, e.g., by temporarily using a lower bitrate. For whitebox systems, their traffic

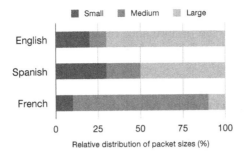

Fig. 4. A hypothetical example of packet size distributions for spoken English, French, and Spanish. Although the distribution of Spanish may be morphed (by padding) to appear as the distribution of English, the reverse is not possible. None of the three distributions is a viable target to which the other two distributions may be mapped.

morphing scheme optimally morphs one distribution into another. For clarity, we will refer to the two distributions throughout this paper as the "source" and "target", respectively.

For blackbox settings, where the only permitted operation is padding packets, it may be impossible to transform an existing distribution into another existing distribution. Consider the example distributions of packet sizes for spoken English, French, and Spanish depicted in Fig. 4. Morphing the Spanish distribution to appear as the English distribution is straightforward: a portion of Spanish small packets are padded to appear as medium packets, and a greater portion of Spanish medium packets are padded to appear as large packets. However, given the distributions shown in the figure, the converse is not possible: an English speaker's traffic cannot be morphed into a Spanish speaker's, and in fact none of these three distributions can be morphed to from both of the other two.

The key benefit of Muffler is that it calculates, based on a set of speakers' streams, the "superdistribution" *with minimal bandwidth cost* that may serve as the target distribution for any of the source distributions. Once the superdistribution is established, Muffler then uses lightweight traffic morphing techniques to map streams to the superdistribution.

2.3 Automated Class Detection

The traffic morphing technique introduced by Wright et al. requires labeled training data (e.g., audio samples that are marked as containing spoken English, French, or Spanish). To avoid this, we apply unsupervised clustering techniques to an unlabeled corpus of audio samples containing representative samples for the classes that an adversary may attempt to re-identify. An advantage of our unsupervised learning technique is that the classes need not be explicitly labeled in the corpus. Hence a large and diverse corpus of audio samples may be sufficient to construct a superdistribution that captures a large range of possible classifications.

In Sect. 4, we show that (1) simple clustering techniques are sufficient to detect classes, and (2) the performance of Muffler when clustering is used to detect classes is approximately equivalent to cases where the classes are explicitly specified.

3   System and Attacker Models

We consider two parties communicating via a stream of encrypted VoIP packets. Each packet represents a fixed-time audio sample encoded using a VBR codec. We denote the stream of audio samples recorded by the sender as an ordered list $S = \langle s_1, \ldots, s_m \rangle$. Let $v(s_i)$ be the output of sample s_i after encoding with the VBR codec and $E(v(s_i))$ be the encryption of that encoded output. Let $|E(v(s_i))|$ be the length (in bits) of that ciphertext. We define the alphabet Σ as the set of possible lengths of encrypted audio samples produced by the codec; i.e., $\cup_{s_i \in S} \{|E(v(s_i))|\} \subseteq \Sigma$, with equality usually being the case for spoken audio that is longer than a few seconds. Without loss of generality, we consider the symbols (packet sizes) in Σ to be ordered by size; that is, we set $\Sigma = \langle z_1, \ldots, z_n \rangle$ such that $z_i < z_j$ iff $i < j$. Finally, we assume that $\forall s_i \in S$, $|E(v(s_i))| - |v(s_i)| = c$, where $c \geq 0$ is a small constant. This latter assumption is necessary to allow an adversary to determine the size of the unencrypted audio sample $|v(s_i)|$ without knowledge of the sample or the decryption key. Or, equivalently, we assume that the audio samples have not been padded.

We model a passive adversary who intercepts all encrypted VoIP packets in the order in which they were sent. The adversary does not have access to the plaintext. Let $L = \langle l_1, \ldots, l_m \rangle$ be an ordered list of the lengths of ciphertexts for the stream S. That is, $l_i = |E(v(s_i))|$, $l_i \in \Sigma$. We note that the sequence L induces a distribution of packet lengths. The adversary's goal is to use the side-channel L to infer information about S.

We consider *classes* of speakers where speakers that share a particular attribute (e.g., gender) belong to the same class. Let $\mathcal{A} = \langle a_1, \ldots, a_q \rangle$ be the set of classes that are of interest to the adversary. For a given sample S, we denote the correct class as $\bar{a}_s$. As with existing work, we assume that an audio stream has exactly one class. By assumption, $\bar{a}_s \in \mathcal{A}$ and, to avoid the trivial case, $|\mathcal{A}| > 1$.

We also conservatively assume that the adversary has access to a corpus Γ of unencrypted audio samples such that (i) $S \notin \Gamma$, (ii) for all $S' \in \Gamma, \bar{a}_{S'} \in \mathcal{A}$, (iii) for all $S' \in \Gamma$, $\bar{a}_{S'}$ is known to the adversary (i.e., the corpus is labeled with the correct classes), and (iv) the adversary may compute the lengths of ciphertexts $\langle l'_1, \ldots, l'_m \rangle$ produced by encoding and encrypting the audio of each sample in Γ. The first requirement ensures that the intercepted stream does not already appear in the corpus, while the second conservatively assumes that each sample in the corpus has a class in $\mathcal{A}$. Finally, for any audio stream S whose encoded ciphertext may be intercepted by the adversary, we assume that there are samples in Γ that belong to the class $\bar{a}_s$. We say that such a corpus provides *coverage* of the class $\bar{a}_s$.

Given L and Γ, the adversary's goal is to correctly infer $\overline{a}_s$—that is, to re-identify the audio's class. The goal of Muffler is to make the adversary's probability of correctly guessing $\overline{a}_s$ similar to the probability of guessing correctly without L.

As discussed above and visualized in Fig. 1, the adversary may frame the re-identification task as a machine learning problem. For example, the approach by Wright et al. forms n-grams (overlapping segments of n-length sequences) over L, and uses a count of each n-gram as a feature for a machine learning classifier [26]. Using a background corpus to train the classifier, Wright et al. show that the adversary can reliably predict $\overline{a}_s$ when no obfuscation is applied. In Sect. 6 and in Appendix A, we formalize our security properties under the assumption that the adversary uses n-grams as features, noting that this approach is used by all re-identification attacks of which we are aware [24, 26–28].

With Muffler, we assume the speaker has access to a corpus of audio samples, Γ', that he may use to form a superdistribution to which traffic may be morphed (see Fig. 3). As with Γ, we assume that Γ' provides coverage, i.e., there are samples in Γ' of the same class as the speaker's audio streams. Unlike Γ, we do not require that the samples in Γ' be labeled with their correct classes.

We envision that Γ' could be bundled with the Muffler software or obtained by the user. We note that acquiring a large corpora of speech is not particularly difficult: we use the public domain Librivox [15] collection of audio books; George Mason University maintains a set of more than 1,800 speech samples that cover a large range of languages and accents [1]; the University of Pennsylvania's Linguistic Data Consortium hosts hundreds of language corpora [2].

In this paper, we let $\Gamma' = \Gamma$. This is a conservative assumption, as it allows the adversary to train on the exact data used by the sender to form its superdistribution. (In cases where Muffler is applied, the adversary is allowed to train on the modified packets).

Importantly, we note that a non-goal of our system is to provide *deniability*: Muffler does not attempt to conceal its use. Since Muffler morphs traffic to a superdistribution that may not resemble any non-obfuscated distribution, an adversary could use similar classification techniques to detect it. Our goal is to provide VoIP communication that resists re-identification attacks.

4   Forming the Superdistribution

In order to reduce the ability of an adversary to reliably determine any attributes of an audio stream, we aim to shape the distribution of the packet sizes within the streams such that classification (re-identification) is as difficult as possible. One method to make streams indistinguishable would be to pad each packet to the maximum size, which, while effective in preventing classification of speakers, negates the bandwidth savings achieved by using VBR in the first place. Another method is to attempt to pad a stream's packets in order to 'morph' the packet distribution to resemble that of other known streams. As discussed above, such an approach was explored by Wright et al. [28], and Muffler can also be categorized as a traffic morphing system. However, the approach by Wright et al.

Algorithm 1. Given an array of distributions from a training corpus, calculate the superdistribution to which each input distribution may be mapped

```
 1: proc calcSuperdistribution(arrayOfDistributions)
 2:   packetSizes ← ⟨zₙ, ..., z₂, z₁⟩, n ← |packetSizes|
      {iterate through packet sizes, starting with the largest}
 3:   for all p₁ in packetSizes do
 4:       Max ← largest frequency of packetsize p₁
          {given the maximum, create a superdistribution to which all other distributions may be morphed:}
 5:       for all dist in arrayOfDistributions do
 6:           deficit ← Max
 7:           for all p₂ in packetSizes[packetSizes.index(p₁):n] do
 8:               deficit ← deficit − dist[p₂]
 9:               if deficit < 0 then
10:                   dist[p₂] ← −1 × deficit
11:                   break
12:               end if
13:               if p₁ == p₂ then
14:                   dist[p₂] ← −1 × Max
15:               else
16:                   dist[p₂] ← 0
17:               end if
18:           end for
19:       end for
20:   end for
21:   return ArrayOfDistributions[0]
      {After the last iteration, each distribution in arrayOfDistributions will be identical, and equal to the smallest
      possible (bandwidth-wise) distribution to which any of the distributions could be transformed.}
```

is not well-suited for disguising multiple classes, since not all streams are easily morphable to all other streams.

Muffler considers the distributions of all speakers in a training corpus, and then calculates the least bandwidth-intensive distribution to which *all* speakers in the corpus could be padded to. Specifically, letting $L_s = \langle l_{1_s}, \ldots, l_{m_s} \rangle$ be an ascending list of the m different posssible lengths of ciphertexts for a stream s: Muffler calculates superdistribution L_{super} such that for all $1 \leq n \leq m$, $\sum(l_{n_{super}} + \cdots + l_{m_{super}}) = \max_s(\sum(l_{n_s} + \cdots + l_{m_s}))$ over all streams s in the corpus.

The process used to calculate this superdistribution is presented as Algorithm 1. The algorithm is given an array of distributions such as that visualized in Fig. 4. Each of the three bars in the figure reflects a different speaker class, the distinction between which our superdistribution will seek to eliminate. Note that Algorithm 1 creates a superdistribution from unigrams. (Sect. 4.1 presents the algorithm for n-grams).

The algorithm works as follows: in line 4, the algorithm finds, amongst the input distributions, the largest count for the largest packet-size (z_n). In our example, the largest proportion of z_3 packets (where z_3 is the largest packet size) occurs in Spanish, and this maximum value is 30 %.

Lines 5–20 describe the formation of the superdistribution. Conceptually, the superdistribution considers the relative frequencies of the packet sizes, in order of decreasing packet size. The superdistribution uses the largest relative frequency amongst the input distributions.

4.1 n-Gram Superdistributions

Algorithm 1 calculates a superdistribution based on the distributions of packet sizes in a set of streams. However, morphing only unigrams may be insufficient if the adversary is using n-grams to classify streams. (In Sect. 7, we evaluate the effectiveness of a unigram-based superdistribution against an adversary who uses trigrams).

To defend against n-gram adversaries, we construct multiple superdistributions. Muffler computes a superdistribution for each unique sequence of $n - 1$ packet lengths. That is, if Muffler is considering trigrams and a packet length z_q in a sample is proceded by packet sizes z_a and z_b, then Muffler increments the counter for z_q in the distribution corresponding to the sequence $\langle z_a, z_b \rangle$. There will be $|\Sigma|^{n-1}$ such superdistributions.

Muffler uses this set of superdistributions, once built, to dynamically morph packets. Given the $(n - 1)$ packets that were most recently output, Muffler uses the corresponding superdistribution (i.e., the one that matches the $(n-1)$-length sequence) to determine how the next packet should be morphed. The morphing operation is explained in more detail in Sect. 5.

4.2 Dynamic Clustering

Algorithm 1 takes as input an array of distributions of packet sizes, where each distribution within the array corresponds to a class (e.g., Spanish, English, and French, in the case of language re-identification). However, it may be the case that the classes are not known a priori—either because the corpus is unlabeled or the sender does not know the type of re-identification that the adversary will attempt (e.g., language vs. speaker re-identification). We expect that this latter case will be the norm in most deployment scenarios.

In light of this, we explored an alternate method of superdistribution generation in which the algorithm, given the set of streams as a whole, first creates its own classifications of the streams using an unsupervised clustering algorithm. In what follows, we will refer to this data preprocessing step as *dynamic clustering*.

We find that k-means clustering is sufficient to automatically generate the input distributions for Algorithm 1, given an unlabeled collection of audio samples. In Sect. 7, we show that Muffler is similarly able to mitigate re-identification attacks when the speaker's training corpus is (i) labeled or (ii) unlabeled and k-means clustering is applied. We discuss finding an appropriate value of k in Sect. 9.

5   Mapping to the Superdistribution

Algorithm 2 describes how Muffler transforms an input stream to resemble a predetermined superdistribution. For clarity, we focus on the particular case in which the sender wishes to morph his traffic at the level of trigrams; we note that the algorithm works for any size n-gram.

Algorithm 2. Given a calculated superdistribution array, pad the packets of an input stream as necessary to map its distribution to the superdistribution

```
 1: proc morphStream(packetInStream, targetDistro, numPossibleSizes, gramSize)
 2:   currentDistro ← an array of numPossibleSizes^{gramSize} empty distribution arrays
 3:   precedingNPackets← an empty queue of packet sizes
 4:   maxSizePacket ← a maximally-sized packet
 5:   for all x in range(0,gramSize) do
 6:       currentPacket ←packetInStream.dequeue()
 7:       packetOutStream.enqueue(maxSizePacket)
 8:       precedingNPackets.enqueue(currentPacket.size())
 9:   end for
10:   while currentPacket ← packetInStream.dequeue() do
11:       distributionDisparities ← an array noting the current distribution's disparity from the target distribution.

12:       for all possibleSize in range(currentPacket.size(),maxPossibleSize) do
13:           if currentDistro[precedingNPackets][possibleSize]/currentDistro[precedingNPackets][totalPackets] <
             targetDistro[precedingNPackets][possibleSize] then
14:               probabilitiesOfChoosing[possibleSize] ← (targetDistro[precedingNPackets][possibleSize] - current-
                 Distro[precedingNPackets][possibleSize]) x maxPossibleSize / (1 + possibleSize)
15:           else
16:               probabilitiesOfChoosing[possibleSize] ← 0
17:           end if
18:       end for
19:       chosenPacketSize ← WEIGHTEDCHOOSER(distributionDisparities)
20:       currentDistro[precedingNPackets][chosenPacketSize]++
21:       currentDistro[precedingNPackets][totalPackets]++  //totalPackets being the sum of all packet sizes
22:       precedingNPackets.enqueue(chosenPacketSize)
23:       precedingNPackets.dequeue()
24:       padAndSendPacket(currentPacket,chosenPacketSize)
25:   end while
```

In lines 5–8, we pad the initial $n - 1$ packets to the maximum packet size. (Since packets usually convey $20\,\mathrm{ms}$ of audio, this initial maximal padding is quickly amortized away).

After this initial special case, the algorithm proceeds as follows: based on the previous $n - 1$ outputted packet sizes (i.e., the packets that were transmitted after being morphed), we compare the target distribution of what should come next to the actual distribution of what has followed these two packet sizes in the current, obfuscated, output stream so far. In lines 13–17, the algorithm assigns probabilities to the possible choices for the packet size to output, based on which sizes are most underrepresented. These probabilities are skewed slightly toward smaller packets in line 14. On line 19, we use the WeightedChooser subroutine, which chooses a random packet size from those with disparities (i.e., distances from the superdistribution) greater than zero, weighted by the value of the disparity; or, if there are no such probabilities greater than zero, it returns the largest packet size. In lines 20–22, the current distribution is updated with the packet size we have chosen, and the precedingNPackets window is shifted forward to include this packet. In line 23, the current packet is sent, after being padded to the chosen packet size.

6   Security Analysis

Theorem 1. *Our scheme is IND-CGA (Indistinguishability against Chosen Generator Attack) secure.*

The IND-CGA game allows an adversary A to select a pair of *generators* g_0 and g_1, where generators are algorithmic models of speakers. Specifically, a generator outputs packet streams which share characteristics similar to those that would be produced by a particular speaker. From the pair of generators provided by the adversary, one such generator is chosen at random, with the choice being invisible to A. The randomly chosen generator is then used to produce a packet sequence, which is then morphed (using Muffler) and returned to A. Given g_0, g_1, the Muffler algorithms, and the morphed stream, the adversary's goal is to decide whether the randomly chosen generator was g_0 or g_1. Intuitively, if the adversary cannot make this determination *for any set of generators g_0 and g_1*, then the morphing provides a form of indistinguishability, which is exactly the goal of Muffler.

We remark that in the standard indistinguishability under chosen-plaintext attack (IND-CPA) game used to evaluate cryptosystems, the adversary there is allowed to choose arbitrary packet streams, as opposed to generators. As such, any reasonable blackbox morphing technique must morph all packets to the maximum size to be secure under IND-CPA, since the adversary could choose a sequence of all smallest-size packets and a sequence of all largest-size packets as his inputs. The adversary could then trivially identify that the smallest-size sequence was the one randomly chosen if the morphed sequence contains a single packet that is not the largest size. This applies to less extreme packet streams. As such, in our IND-CGA game, we restrict the adversary to choosing randomized generators whose output reflect real speech distributions.

In our analysis, we assume that the adversary performs classification by using n-grams as features. As explained in more detail in Appendix A, we believe that this is a realistic assumption, at least given currently known re-identification attacks, all of which (to the best of our knowledge) perform classification using n-grams (cf. [24, 26–28]). In Appendix A, we show that Muffler achieves IND-CGA under assumptions that existing work and our empirical results indicate hold true in practice.

7   Evaluation

Dataset. We gather public-domain audio from Librivox [15], a collection of literature read aloud by volunteers. This source of data is especially good for our purposes, as the variance in background noise as well as the quality and frequency response of the microphones being used are all factors that affect the ability of a codec to compress the audio stream; this makes traffic morphing more difficult, since the streams are more easily distinguishable than if they were all recorded in a controlled environment with identical equipment. From the Librivox dataset, we extract 100 samples of 200 s of audio from each of 158 different speakers, totaling nearly 878 h of audio.

We encode the audio samples from the Librivox dataset using the Silk codec [21] (the same codec used by Skype until late last year, and the basis for the current codec). The output of this encoding step is a series of discrete audio packets. Using Silk's default parameters, there are eight possible sizes for the encoded audio; i.e., $|\Sigma| = 8$. Since we assume that the adversary is not able to decipher the traffic, we consider only the sizes, and not the content, of these packets.

Methodology. In order to measure the efficacy of Muffler, we compare an adversary's ability to classify VoIP streams without any obfuscation beyond basic encryption, to an adversary's ability to classify streams that have been morphed with Muffler. The adversary's goal is to identify the speaker of an intercepted stream, from amongst the 158 speakers in our dataset.

Each sample in the Librivox dataset is an ordered sequence of packet sizes, $L = \langle l_1, \ldots, l_m \rangle$. From this sequence, we count the occurrences of unigrams, bigrams, and trigrams, where a unigram is a symbol, a bigram is a subsequence of two contiguous symbols, etc. The counts for each unigram, bigram, etc. are used as features for a machine learning classifier. For supervised learning, each sample is labeled with its correct class (as specified in the Librivox data). In this paper, we present results for adversaries using (i) unigrams and (ii) unigrams, bigrams, and trigrams.

The adversary uses a battery of classifiers: three variations of k-Nearest-Neighbor and Naïve Bayes, the J48 decision tree algorithm (based on C4.5), and a support vector machine (SVM) [25]. For the adversary who examines only unigrams, the training corpus contains only unigram counts; the stronger adversary has counts for unigrams, bigrams, and trigrams as training features.

To evaluate the efficacy of Muffler to mitigate re-identification attacks, we compare the adversary's ability to correctly classify streams with Muffler and without any attempted traffic morphing. For each configuration, we report the *mean classification accuracy* amongst all the machine learning classifiers and the *worst case accuracy*—i.e., the classification accuracy of the best performing classifier (and the worst-case accuracy from the perspective of the communicants).

For the results presented below, we use five-fold cross-validation. We conservatively assume that the adversary has access to the same corpus used by Muffler to form the superdistribution; that is, $\Gamma = \Gamma'$. However, the adversary always has access to a labeled training corpus; when Muffler uses dynamic clustering, we assume that the speaker does not know the class that interests the adversary (language, speaker identity, etc.) and consequently remove the labels from Γ'. For dynamic clustering, we use k-means clustering with $k = 32$.

For all cases where Muffler has been applied, the adversary allowed to train on the morphed versions of the packet streams.

7.1   Baseline Classification

Without any obfuscation (other than the encryption of packets), each of these classifiers is extremely adept at classifying speakers. The adversary's unigram classifiers average 26.3 % accuracy in identifying the speaker, among 158 possible speakers, with the best classifier being able to correctly classify the speaker 28.1 % of the time. Trigram classifiers average 43.3 % accuracy in identifying the speaker, with a worst case accuracy of 72.4 %, provided by SVM.

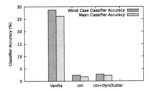 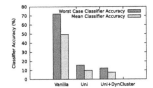 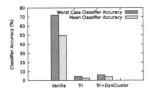

Fig. 5. Unigram-based adversary accuracy, with no morphing (Vanilla), Muffler using a labeled training corpus (Uni), and Muffler with k-means clustering ($k = 32$) applied to an unlabeled training corpus (Uni+DynCluster).

Fig. 6. Accuracy of re-identification when adversary considers the frequencies of trigrams. *Left:* No morphing. *Center:* Labeled training corpus, considers only unigrams. *Right:* Unlabeled corpus, considers only unigrams.

Fig. 7. Accuracy of re-identification when adversary considers the frequencies of trigrams. *Left:* No morphing. *Center:* Labeled corpus, and considers trigrams. *Right:* Unlabeled corpus, and considers trigrams.

7.2   Obfuscation Against Unigram Classifiers

Using our method for unigram distribution obfuscation, we are able to significantly reduce the average and worst case accuracies of the unigram classifier battery: Fig. 5 illustrates the accuracy of the classifiers before and after Muffler has been applied. Applying our unigram obfuscation technique reduces the average accuracy of the classifiers from 26.2 % to 1.8 %, and the worst case accuracy from 28.6 % to 2.4 % when Muffler has access to a labeled training corpus.

The bars marked "Uni+DynCluster" in Fig. 5 show Muffler's accuracy when provided an unlabeled training corpus. (The corpus used by the adversary to train his classifiers remains labeled). Here, k-means clustering is used on the entire set of audio streams in the training corpus Γ', and the resulting clusters are used as speaker classes by Muffler. The superdistribution is calculated by combining these 32 distributions.

The high comparative efficacy of our algorithm when using dynamic clustering is important to note. The similar performance of our algorithm when using dynamic clustering versus using a priori knowledge of class divisions means that deployment of Muffler would have very few technical hurdles: concealing speakers within a network could be achieved by simply placing Muffler at the edge of that network.

7.3   Obfuscation Against Trigram Classifiers

Unigram-based traffic morphing is less effective when the adversary classifies streams based on longer n-grams.[1] Figure 6 shows the accuracy of classification

---

[1] There is, of course, decreasing returns when n is large. As n increases, there are more unique n-length sequences and each are less likely to occur in the test data; hence, they provide less predictive value.

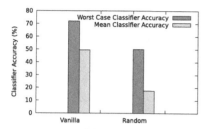

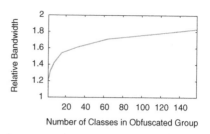

Fig. 8. Accuracy of re-identification when the adversary considers the frequencies of unigrams, bigrams, and trigrams for streams without obfuscation *(left)* and streams with random padding *(right)*.

Fig. 9. Relative bandwidth overhead (w.r.t. unmorphed streams) of Muffler when considering uni-, bi-, and trigrams to build the superdistribution, as a function of the number of classes in the Librivox training data.

based on trigrams on our audio streams. These "trigram classifiers" achieve very high accuracy on unobfuscated streams, with a worst-case accuracy of 72%, and an average-case accuracy of 49.6%, as can be observed from the first pair of bars. Muffler significantly degrades the accuracy of re-identification, providing mean and worst-case classification rates of 9.8% and 15.8% respectively.

When we use our trigram-based superdistribution, the adversary's classifier accuracy drops even more. As seen in the middle bars of Fig. 7, the worst- and average-case accuracies drop to 4.6% and 2.8%, respectively. This represents a reduction in accuracy of 94%, for the worst-case, when compared to unmorphed traffic.

7.4   Random Padding

We wish to show that the decreased accuracy of re-identification is not merely due to padding the streams away from their original form, but rather is attributable to morphing traffic to the superdistribution. We implement a simpler traffic morphing algorithm that randomly pads each packet in a stream by an amount adjusted such that the bandwidth cost of this random padding was similar to that of Muffler. As expected, while the padding did slightly decrease the adversary's ability to classify speakers, its efficacy at this task was far below that of our trigram superdistribution obfuscation technique, as shown in Fig. 8. While the average classifier accuracy dropped to 17.5%, worst-case accuracy stood at 50.0%. As mentioned in Sect. 7.3, the equivalent worst-case accuracy for Muffler is 4.4%.

7.5   The Cost of Privacy

Figure 9 shows the relative cost of Muffler using a unigram superdistribution on the Librivox dataset, compared to the unmodified stream's bandwidth, for various numbers of speakers (classes) from which superdistributions are created.

Because the cost of creating a superdistribution from a set of speakers depends on which speakers are included in that set, for each set size, we take a random sample of 16 possible combinations, and average the results to arrive at the data in the figure. Creating a superdistribution between two speakers in the set has a 20 % bandwidth cost, while a superdistribution from 128 speakers incurs a 79 % increase in bandwidth, on average. By comparison, the cost of full padding to the largest packet size (roughly analogous to using a constant bitrate audio codec) is a 171 % increase over the original stream's size.

7.6   CPU Overhead

In comparison to existing traffic morphing techniques, Muffler avoids expensive operations and has a low CPU overhead. To build the superdistribution and morph the entire 878-hour corpus of audio from Librivox takes Muffler just under 30 min on a 3.1 GHz Xeon E31220 with 8 GB of DDR3 memory. This factor of 1,765 between the CPU time and amount of audio processed in that time means that it is entirely possible to have a Muffler implementation that dynamically updates the superdistribution being mapped to regularly, even while obfuscating several audio streams at once.

8   Related Work

Website fingerprinting. Much of the early work in packet- and stream-based traffic analysis focused on identifying the webpages conveyed in intercepted HTTPS streams. Sun et al. showed that the web page being visited by a user over an SSL-encrypted connection can often be identified based solely on the sizes of the objects being accessed. They additionally showed that this attack was resilient against padding object sizes as an obfuscation technique [18]. Later, Hintz introduced website fingerprinting techniques that infer the identity of a requested website by examining the size of an observed HTTPS stream [10]. In addition to inferring content, website fingerprinting has also been proposed as a method to defeat anonymity systems (most notably, Tor [6]) by identifying the webpages that have been requested by an observed client [5,9,22,23]. Kadianakis [12] has suggested applying a variant of Wright et al.'s traffic morphing technique [28] to protect Tor against fingerprinting attacks.

Voice-over-IP. A series of papers including the work of Wright et al. discussed earlier have examined traffic analysis as a means to infer attributes about the audio signal embedded in an encrypted VoIP stream, and explored morphing techniques to disguise one class of speaker as another [26,28]. However, when there are more than two possible classifications, they do not explore *which* distribution should be chosen as the target distribution. Subsequent work by many of the same authors showed that particular phrases can be identified by observing only the sizes of encrypted packets [24,27]. Similarly, Khan et al. demonstrated that the adversary can identify the speaker of a conversation given a set of potential speakers, a corpus of their speech, and the encrypted VoIP stream [13].

Defenses. Developing defenses against traffic analysis is a growing area of research. Liberatore and Levine proposed padding packets up to the network MTU as a defense against web fingerprinting attacks [14]. However, recent work by Dyer et al. showed that such a strategy is ineffective against an adversary who employs a Naïve Bayes or a support vector machine classifier [7]. Folga et al. [8] explored the use of polymorphic blending to evade detection by intrustion detection systems. Their polymorphic blending approach included altering payload characteristics such as the byte frequency to resemble normal traffic. Iacovazzi and Baiocchi explored finding optimally efficient (with respect to bandwidth) algorithms to mask traffic against traffic classification tools [11], but their technique allows packet fragmentation, and is not applicable to our model.

9   Discussion and Limitations

Improved Dynamic Clustering. When implementing Muffler using dynamic clustering, there remains a choice of how many classes should be derived from the audio corpus. For our testing purposes, we found $k = 32$ to be sufficient for k-means clustering. It may be useful to adjust k given any available background knowledge of the audio streams being combined into a superdistribution. Additionally, other clustering approaches that automate the process of discovering the *number* of clusters (for example, X-means clustering [17]) may serve as a drop-in replacement for k-means clustering.

The Inviability of Pairs. As previously argued, a traffic morphing system that morphs one speaker class to resemble another specific class is not well-suited for masking the identities of a large set of speakers (since it is unlikely that any one speaker in the set will have a distribution to which all other speakers can be padded). However, it could be argued that such approaches are sufficient, when applied in a pairwise fashion. Even if such a method were able to make pairs of speakers indistinguishable, an obfuscation scheme that results in the adversary knowing that a stream comes from one of two speaker classes still leaks considerable information. Additionally, we know that the packet size distributions of the speakers in the pair can very easily be such that one speaker cannot be padded to resemble the other, nor vice versa. This paper argues for a more versatile technique that morphs potentially many input distributions to a single, synthetic target distribution.

Muffler beyond VoIP. This paper shows the effectiveness of Muffler in the context of protecting against VoIP re-identification attacks. The general traffic analysis attack framework applies to other situations in which variations in packet sizes may reveal attributes of the plaintext. For example, similar traffic analysis attacks are applicable to streaming video (which also uses VBR codecs), remote database access, and anonymous web browsing. Although we do not evaluate it in this paper, Muffler can be straightforwardly applied to protect against re-identification attacks on encrypted streaming video. For applications where packets are sent at irregular time intervals—in particular, web browsing—Muffler would also need to consider the *timing* of packets.

10   Conclusion

This paper proposes an efficient blackbox defense called Muffler that protects against encrypted VoIP re-identification attacks. Our approach is based on the fabrication of a *superdistribution* to which all of the streams in a population can be morphed. Experimental results using a large corpus of audio show that even against an adversary who applies a battery of machine learning techniques, Muffler reduces the adversary's accuracy by 94 %, while maintaining half of the bandwidth savings provided by using a variable-bitrate codec.

Acknowledgements. We thank the anonymous reviewers for their helpful feedback. This work is partially supported by the National Science Foundation (NSF) through grants CNS-1064986, CNS-1149832, CNS-1445967, and CNS-1223825.

A   Security Analysis

We do not attempt to strengthen the security of VBR encoding to traditional IND-CPA but argue that under certain assumptions, our scheme is able to provide information theoretic indistinguishability against the best known speaker re-identifying attacker.

Definition 1. *A scheme is IND-CGA (Indistinguishability against Chosen Generator Attack) secure if, for all pairs of probabilistic polynomial-time adversaries A_1, A_2, their advantage in the following game is negligible.*

Algorithm 3. Security Experiment

$b \xleftarrow{\$} \{0, 1\}$

$sd \xleftarrow{\$} calcSuperdistribution(trainingData)$

$(g_0, g_1, state) \xleftarrow{\$} A_1(sd, trainingData)$

$stream \xleftarrow{\$} g_b()$

$c \xleftarrow{\$} morphStream(stream, sd, trainingData, state, c)$

$b' \xleftarrow{\$} A_2(sd, trainingData, state, c)$

Return $(b == b')$

The $\xleftarrow{\$}$ notation implies that the function on the right is randomized. In this game, the adversary (the pair of algorithms A_1, A_2) has access to the training data and the superdistribution sd. For simplicity, we consider $numPossibleSizes$ and $gramSize$ fixed and public. The adversary selects two stream generators g_0, g_1, where the generators produce packet streams under some restrictions detailed below. The game selects one at random, generates an actual packet stream from it, morphs it to c using our morphing (Algorithm 2) and returns it to the adversary. The adversary's goal is to determine which generator was selected.

We first define generators.

Definition 2. *Generators model speakers whose audio is processed into packets as a VBR codec encryption layer would. A stream of packets output by a specific generator shares n-gram characteristics with all other streams output by that generator. A generator's output is always randomized in the same way that the audio streams by the same speaker having 2 different conversations will be encoded differently.*

Since we perform a black-box modification of the packet stream by padding it, allowing the adversary to define, and therefore know, the input packet stream will allow it to win the game trivially. By allowing the adversary to define a generator, the adversary is still able to select the stream characteristics which will give it the best probability of winning the game.

While not a rigorous definition, this allows a generator to be implemented as a human speaker who is generating packets by using an encrypted VoIP service, or even a text-to-speech program with a large set of words, where generating output corresponds to selecting a random string of words, running them through the text-to-speech program and then running the produced audio through an encrypted VoIP service.

We also make the following assumptions and restrictions, with justification, to complete our security argument.

Assumption A1. *The adversary is only allowed to choose generators whose output characteristics are covered by the training data.*

A generator with output that does not sufficiently match any of the training data corresponds to a speaker whose speech patterns are not represented in the training data. Unfortunately, our system is not designed to protect such users.

Assumption A2. *Our probabilistic morphing technique maps a valid packet stream (one which follows Assumption A1) to one which is negligibly close to the superdistribution.*

Additionally, the output packet stream distribution does not vary over time.

Our morphing algorithm is designed such that the output stream converges to the superdistribution quickly and stays there. To evaluate whether this holds in practice, we compared morphed distributions to the expected output of the superdistribution. We used the Bhattacharyya distance measure [4] which is used to measure the similarity between two discrete (or continuous) probability distributions. This measure has been used in feature extraction and speaker recognition among other areas of research.

To construct the expected trigram distribution of the superdsitribution, we generated packet streams using the superdistribution as a transition matrix. Recall that the superdistribution, on trigrams, is defined as 64 probability distributions, one for each bigram prefix. As such, we generated streams with each

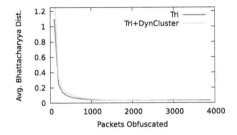

Fig. 10. The Bhattacharyya Distance between morphed distributions and the expected perfect output of the superdistribution

of the possible bigrams as an initial state, repeated this process 1000 times, and calculated the expected distribution over all the runs.

Figure 10 shows, for both our labeled and unlabeled techniques, the mean Bhattacharyya distance, over all morphed streams in our corpus against the superdistribution described above, as the number of packets in the stream increases. As the figure shows, the distance quickly converges to 0 as the number of packets obfuscated increases, indicating that the distributions are very similar.

Assumption A3. *In a realistic stream of packets, any long subsequence of packets carries very little, if any, additional information.*

The efficiency of our unigram obfuscator against a tri-gram adversary in Sect. 7.3 lends support to the assumption that any n-gram characteristics for large n are removed or reduced after morphing.

Under these assumptions, it is straightforward to show that our scheme is IND-CGA (Indistinguishability against Chosen Generator Attack) secure.

Proof. From Assumptions A1 and A2, the stream returned to A_2 will have n-gram characteristics of the superdistribution.

We remark that classification with n-grams is the basis for all re-identification attacks with which we are familiar [24, 26–28], and is regularly used in informational retrieval and natural language processing for similar identification tasks. That is, we believe our adversary model reflects best-known attack techniques.

From Assumption A3, the returned packet stream is effectively indistinguishable against such an adversary.

The other thing the adversary can do is to attempt to first reverse the morphing before deciding which stream was used. Consider its attempt to revert the ith packet. From Assumption A2 and the way the morphing probabilities are calculated, we note that his probabilistic inference on the source packet, based on the what the packet is and all preceeding packets, is always the same (no matter what the source packet actually was) since the n-gram distribution of packets prior to i is the superdistribution. Therefore, the best the adversary can do is guess.

What remains to be shown is how the security argument is affected by relaxing Assumption A2. Since the algorithm works as a black box with actual packet streams, it isn't always able to output the packet that would keep the actual output n-gram distribution close to the superdistribution.

We postulate that for short packet streams, where our algorithms works the poorest, the adversary does poorly due to lack of information. On long packet streams the output distribution is very close to the superdistribution, as shown by the bhattacharyya distance tests in Fig. 10. As the source streams embed more difficult patterns of n-grams which prevent us from outputting the superdistribution, the adversary's advantage, and the extent of his ability to reverse the morphing, increases.

References

1. The Speech Accent Archives. http://accent.gmu.edu/
2. Linguistic Data Consortium (LDC). https://www.ldc.upenn.edu/
3. Berson, T.: Skype Security Evaluation, October 2005. http://www.anagram.com/berson/abskyeval.html
4. Bhattacharyya, A.: On a measure of divergence between two statistical populations defined by their probability distribution. Bull. Calcutta Math. Soc. **35**, 99–110 (1943)
5. Cai, X., Zhang, X.C., Joshi, B., Johnson, R.: Touching from a distance, : website fingerprinting attacks and defenses. In: ACM Conference on Computer and Communications Security (CCS) (2012)
6. Dingledine, R., Mathewson, N., Syverson, P.: Tor: the second-generation onion router. In: USENIX Security Symposium (USENIX) (2004)
7. Dyer, K.P., Coull, S.E., Ristenpart, T., Shrimpton, T.: Peek-a-boo, i still see you: why efficient traffic analysis countermeasures fail. In: IEEE Symposium on Security and Privacy, Oakland (2012)
8. Folga, P., Sharif, M., Perdisci, R., Kolesnikov, O., Lee, W.: Polymorphic blending attacks. In: USENIX Security Symposium (2006)
9. Herrmann, D., Wendolsky, H., Federrath, R.: Website fingerprinting: attacking popular privacy enhancing technologies with the multinomial Naïve-bayes classifier. In: ACM Workshop on Cloud Computing Security (CCSW) (2009)
10. Hintz, A.: Fingerprinting websites using traffic analysis. In: Dingledine, R., Syverson, P.F. (eds.) PET 2002. LNCS, vol. 2482, pp. 171–178. Springer, Heidelberg (2003)
11. Iacovazzi, A., Baiocchi, A.: Padding and fragmentation for masking packet length statistics. In: Pescapè, A., Salgarelli, L., Dimitropoulos, X. (eds.) TMA 2012. LNCS, vol. 7189, pp. 85–88. Springer, Heidelberg (2012)
12. Kadianakis, G.: Packet size pluggable transport and trafcmorphing. Technical report 2012-03-004, Tor Project, Inc. (2012)
13. Khan, L.A., Baig, M.S., Youssef, A.M.: Speaker recognition from encrypted VoIP communications. Digital Invest. **7**(1–2), 65–73 (2010)
14. Liberatore, M., Levine, B.N.: Inferring the source of encrypted HTTP connections. In: ACM Conference on Computer and Communications Security (CCS) (2006)
15. Librivox: Librivox: Free Public Domain Audiobooks. http://librivox.org/
16. Mercler, J.: 50 Million Concurrent Users Online. http://skypenumerology.blogspot.se/2013/01/50-million-concurrent-users-online.html

17. Pelleg, D., Moore, A.W.: X-means: extending k-means with efficient estimation of the number of clusters. In: International Conference on Machine Learning (2000)
18. Sun, Q., Simon, D.R., Wang, Y.-M., Russell, W., Padmanabhan, V.N., Qiu, L.: Statistical identification of encrypted Web browsing traffic. In: IEEE Symposium on Security and Privacy, Oakland (2002)
19. TeleGeography: International Carriers' Traffic Grows Despite Skype Popularity (2006). http://www.telegeography.com/products/commsupdate/articles/2006/12/01/telegeography-update-international-carriers-traffic-grows-despite-skype-popularity/
20. TeleGeography: Telegeography Report Executive Summary (2013). http://www.telegeography.com/page_attachments/products/website/research-services/telegeography-report-database/0003/6770/TG_executive_summary.pdf
21. Vos, K., Jensen, S., Soerensen, K.: SILK Speech Codec. Internet-Draft draft-vos-silk-02, Internet Engineering Task Force, September 2010
22. Tao Wang and Ian Goldberg. Improved Website Fingerprinting on Tor. In Workshop on Privacy in the Electronic Society (WPES), 2013
23. Wang, T., Cai, X., Nithyanand, R., Johnson, R., Goldberg, I.: Effective attacks and provable defenses for website fingerprinting. In: USENIX Security Symposium (USENIX) (2014)
24. White, A.M., Snow, K., Matthews, A., Monrose, F.: Phonotactic reconstruction of encrypted VoIP conversations: hookt on fon-iks. In: IEEE Symposium on Security and Privacy, Oakland (2011)
25. Witten, I.H., Frank, E., Hall, M.A.: Data Mining: Practical Machine Learning Tools and Techniques, 3rd edn. Morgan Kaufmann, Burlington (2011)
26. Wright, C.V., Ballard, L., Monrose, F., Masson, G.M.: Language identification of encrypted VoIP traffic: Alejandra y Roberto or Alice and Bob? In: USENIX Security Symposium (USENIX) (2007)
27. Wright, C.V., Ballard, L., Coull, S.E., Monrose, F., Masson, G.M.: Spot me if you can: uncovering spoken phrases in encrypted VoIP conversations. In: IEEE Symposium on Security and Privacy, Oakland (2008)
28. Wright, C.V., Coull, S.E., Monrose, F.: Traffic morphing: an efficient defense against statistical traffic analysis. In: Network and Distributed System Security Symposium (NDSS) (2009)

Protecting Encrypted Cookies from Compression Side-Channel Attacks

Janaka Alawatugoda[1]([⊠]), Douglas Stebila[1,2], and Colin Boyd[3]

[1] School of Electrical Engineering and Computer Science,
Queensland University of Technology, Brisbane, Australia
janaka.alawatugoda@qut.edu.au
[2] School of Mathematical Sciences, Queensland University of Technology,
Brisbane, Australia
stebila@qut.edu.au
[3] Department of Telematics, Norwegian University of Science and Technology,
Trondheim, Norway
colin.boyd@item.ntnu.no

Abstract. Compression is desirable for network applications as it saves bandwidth; however, when data is compressed before being encrypted, the amount of compression leaks information about the amount of redundancy in the plaintext. This side channel has led to successful CRIME and BREACH attacks on web traffic protected by the Transport Layer Security (TLS) protocol. The general guidance in light of these attacks has been to disable compression, preserving confidentiality but sacrificing bandwidth. In this paper, we examine two techniques—heuristic separation of secrets and fixed-dictionary compression—for enabling compression while protecting high-value secrets, such as cookies, from attack. We model the security offered by these techniques and report on the amount of compressibility that they can achieve.

1 Introduction

To save communication costs, network applications often compress data before transmitting it; for example, the Hypertext Transport Protocol (HTTP) [1, Sect. 4.2] has an optional mechanism in which a server compresses the body of an HTTP response, most commonly using the gzip algorithm. When encryption is used to protect communication, compression must be applied before encryption (since ciphertexts should look random, they should have little apparent redundancy that can be compressed). In fact, to facilitate this, the Transport Layer Security (TLS) protocol [2, Sect. 6.2.2] has an optional compression mode that will compress all application data before encrypting it.

While compression is useful for reducing the size of transmitted data, it has had a negative impact when combined with encryption, because the amount of compression acts as a *side channel*. Most research considers side-channels such as timing [3,4] or power consumption [5], which can reveal information about cryptographic operations and secret parameters.

© International Financial Cryptography Association 2015
R. Böhme and T. Okamoto (Eds.): FC 2015, LNCS 8975, pp. 86–106, 2015.
DOI: 10.1007/978-3-662-47854-7_6

Compression-Based Leakage. In 2002, Kelsey [6] showed how compression can act as a form of side-channel leakage. If plaintext data is compressed before being encrypted, the length of the ciphertext reveals information about the amount of compression, which in turn can reveal information about the plaintext. Kelsey notes that this side channel differs from other types of side channels in two key ways: "it reveals information about the plaintext, rather than key material", and "it is a property of the algorithm, not the implementation".

Kelsey's most powerful attack is an *adaptive chosen input attack*: if an attacker is allowed to choose inputs x that are combined with a target secret s and the concatenation $x\|s$ is compressed and encrypted, observing the length of the outputs can eventually allow the attacker to extract the secret s. For example, to determine the first character of s, the attacker could ask to have the string $x = $ prefix*prefix combined with s, then compressed and encrypted, for every possible character $*$; in one case, when $* = s_1$, the amount of redundancy is higher and the ciphertext should be shorter. Once each character of s is found, the attack can be carried out on the next character. The attack is somewhat noisy, but succeeds reasonably often.

Key to this attack is the fact that most compression algorithms (such as the DEFLATE algorithm underlying gzip) are *adaptive*: they adaptively build and maintain a *dictionary* of recently observed strings, and replace subsequent occurrences of that string with a code.

The CRIME and BREACH Attacks. In 2012, Rizzo and Duong [7] showed how to apply Kelsey's adaptive chosen input attack against gzip compression as used in TLS, in what they called the *Compression Ratio Info-leak Mass Exploitation (CRIME)* attack. The primary target of the CRIME attack was the user's cookie in the HTTP header. If the victim visited an attacker-controlled web page, the attacker could use Javascript to cause the victim to send HTTP requests to URLs of the attacker's choice on a specified server. The attacker could adaptively choose those URLs to include a prefix to carry out Kelsey's adaptive chosen input attack. Some care is required to ensure the padding does not hide the length with block ciphers, but this can be dealt with. The CRIME attack also applies to compression as used in the SPDY protocol [8].

As a result of the CRIME attack, it was recommended that TLS compression be disabled, and the Trustworthy Internet Movement's SSL Pulse report for December 2014 finds that just 7.2 % of websites have TLS compression enabled [9]; moreover, all major browsers have disabled it.

However, compression is also built into the HTTP protocol: servers can optionally compress the body of HTTP responses. While this excludes the cookie in the header, this attack can still succeed against secret values in the HTTP body, such as anti-cross-site request forgery (CSRF) tokens. Suggested by Rizzo and Duong, this was demonstrated by Gluck et al. [10] in the *Browser Reconnaissance and Exfiltration via Adaptive Compression of Hypertext (BREACH)* attack.

Mitigation Techniques. Gluck et al. [10] discussed several possible mitigation techniques against the BREACH attack, listed in decreasing order of effectiveness:

1. Disabling HTTP compression.
2. Separating secrets from user input.
3. Randomizing secrets per request.
4. Masking secrets (effectively randomizing by XORing with a random nonce).
5. Length hiding (by adding a random number of bytes to the responses).
6. Rate-limiting the requests.

Despite the demonstrated practicality of the BREACH attack, support for and use of HTTP compression remains widespread, due in large part to the value of decreasing communication costs and time. In fact, compression is even more tightly integrated into the proposed HTTP version 2 [11]. Techniques 2–4 generally require changes to both browsers and web servers. For example, masking secrets such as anti-CSRF tokens requires new mark-up for secrets to apply the randomized masking technique. Techniques 5–6 can be unilaterally applied by web servers, though length hiding can be defeated with statistical averaging, and rate-limiting must balance legitimate requests and information leakage.

Current drafts of HTTP/2 [11] include a new technique for header compression called HPACK [19], in which header fields independently are compressed from other inputs, and after each header field the compression algorithm resets the dictionary; thus, each header is compressed in its own context. Assuming user input and secrets never end up in the same header, this can be considered an instance of technique 2, separating secrets from user inputs.

Related Work. There has been little academic study of compression and encryption. Besides Kelsey's adaptive chosen input attack and the related CRIME and BREACH attacks, the only relevant work we are aware of is that of Kelley and Tamassia [12]. They give a new security notion called *entropy-restricted semantic security* (ER-IND-CPA) for *keyed compression functions* which combine both encryption and compression: compared with the normal indistinguishability under chosen plaintext attack (IND-CPA) security notion, in ER-IND-CPA the adversary should not be able to distinguish between the encryption of two messages that *compress* to the same length. Kelley and Tamassia then show how to construct a cipher based on the LZW compression algorithm by rerandomizing the compression dictionary. Unfortunately, the ER-IND-CPA notion does not capture the CRIME and BREACH attacks, which depend on observing messages that compress to different lengths. Klinc et al. [18] showed how block ciphers operating in various chaining modes can be compressed to some extent without compromising the security of encryption. However, that work is limited to block ciphers with chaining modes, and does not address compression before encryption.

In leakage-resilient security definitions [13,14], leakage of the secret key is addressed. This differs from the setting in compression-based side-channel attacks, which addresses leakage of the plaintext. Thus, previous leakage-resilient approaches are not suitable to model compression-based side-channel attacks.

Our Contributions. In this work, we study symmetric-key compression-encryption schemes, characterizing the security properties that can be achieved by various mitigation techniques in the face of CRIME- and BREACH-like attacks.

To some extent, the side channel exposed by compression is fundamentally unavoidable: if transmission of data is decreased, nothing can hide the fact that some redundancy existed in the plaintext. Hence, we focus our study on the ability of the attacker to learn specific "high value" secrets embedded in a plaintext, such as cookies or anti-CSRF tokens. In our models, we imagine there is a secret value ck, and the adversary can adaptively obtain encryptions

$$\mathrm{Enc}_k(m'\|ck\|m'') \tag{1}$$

for prefix m' and suffix m'' of its choice; the attacker's goal is to learn about ck.

The first mitigation technique we consider is that of *separating secrets*. During compression/encryption, an application-aware filter is applied to the plaintext to separate out any potential secret values from the data, the remaining plaintext is compressed, then the secrets and compressed plaintext are encrypted; after decryption, the inverse of the filter is used to reinsert the secret values in the decompressed plaintext. Assuming the filter fully separates out all secret values, we show that the separating secrets technique is able to achieve a strong notion of protection, which we call *chosen cookie indistinguishability* (CCI): the adversary cannot determine which of two cookies ck_0 and ck_1 of the adversary's choice was encrypted with messages of the adversary's choice given ciphertexts as in (1).

The second mitigation technique we consider is the use of a *fixed-dictionary compression scheme*, where the dictionary used for compression does not adapt to the plaintext being compressed, but instead is preselected in advance based on the expected distribution of plaintext messages, for example including common English words like "the" and "and". We show that, if the secret values are sufficiently high entropy, then fixed-dictionary compression is able to achieve *cookie recovery* (CR) security: if the secret cookie is chosen uniformly at random, the adversary cannot recover the entire secret cookie even given an adaptive message attack as in (1). While cookie recovery security does not meet the "gold standard" of indistinguishability notions for encryption, it may be sufficient for some settings, for example protecting compressed HTTP traffic from CRIME and BREACH attacks that try to recover cookies and anti-CSRF tokens.

We also characterize the relationship among the CCI and CR security notions, as well as an intermediate notion called *random cookie indistinguishability* (RCI) and the ER-IND-CPA notion of Kelley and Tamassia [12].

In the separating secrets technique, if the number of secrets extracted by the separating filter is relatively small, then the compressibility generally remains close to that of normal compression of the full plaintext. In the fixed-dictionary compression technique, compressibility suffers quite a bit compared to adaptive techniques on the full plaintext, although if the dictionary is constructed from a corpus of text similar to the plaintext, then some compression can be achieved.

Figure 1 summarizes experimental results comparing compression ratios for these two techniques on the HTML, CSS, and Javascript source code of the

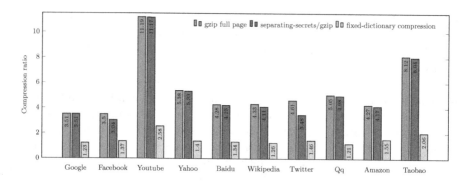

Fig. 1. Compression ratios of full page compression versus mitigation techniques

top 10 global websites as reported by Alexa Top Sites (http://www.alexa.com/topsites). On average, the compression ratio (uncompressed : compressed size) of gzip applied to the full source code was 5.42×; applying a separation filter that extracted all values following `value=` in the HTML source code yielded an average compression ratio of 5.20×; compression of each page using a fixed dictionary trained on all 10 pages yielded an average compression ratio of 1.55×.

2 Definitions

Notation. If x is a string, then x_i denotes the ith character of x; $x_{i:\ell}$ denotes the length-ℓ substring of x starting at position i: $x_{i:\ell} = x_i\|\ldots\|x_{i+\ell-1}$. If x and y are strings, then $x \preceq y$ denotes that x is a substring of y. The *index* of x in y is the smallest i such that $y_{i:|x|} = x$ and is denoted by $\mathrm{ind}_y(x)$; if $x \npreceq y$, we denote $\mathrm{ind}_y(x) = \bot$. The empty string is denoted by ϵ.

2.1 Encryption and Compression Schemes

Definition 1 (Symmetric-Key Encryption). *A symmetric-key encryption scheme Π for message space $\mathcal{M}$ and ciphertext space $\mathcal{C}$ is a tuple of algorithms:*

- KeyGen() $\xrightarrow{\$}$ k: *A probabilistic key generation algorithm that generates a random key k in the keyspace $\mathcal{K}$.*
- $\mathrm{Enc}_k(m) \xrightarrow{\$} c$: *A possibly probabilistic encryption algorithm that takes as input a key $k \in \mathcal{K}$ and a message $m \in \mathcal{M}$ and outputs a ciphertext $c \in \mathcal{C}$.*
- $\mathrm{Dec}_k(c) \to m'$ or $\bot$: *A deterministic decryption algorithm that takes as input a key $k \in \mathcal{K}$ and a ciphertext $c \in \mathcal{C}$, and outputs either a message $m' \in \mathcal{M}$ or an error symbol $\bot$.*

Correctness of symmetric-key encryption is defined in the obvious way: for all $k \xleftarrow{\$} \mathrm{KeyGen}()$ and all $m \in \mathcal{M}$, we require that $\mathrm{Dec}_k(\mathrm{Enc}_k(m)) = m$.

Definition 2 (Compression Scheme). *A compression scheme Γ for message space $\mathcal{M}$ with output space $\mathcal{O}$ is a pair of algorithms:*

- *$\text{Comp}(m) \overset{\$}{\to} o$: A possibly probabilistic compression algorithm that takes as input a message $m \in \mathcal{M}$ and outputs an encoded value $o \in \mathcal{O}$.*
- *$\text{Decomp}(o) \to m'$ or $\bot$: A decompression algorithm that takes as input an encoded value $o \in \mathcal{O}$ and outputs a message $m' \in \mathcal{M}$ or an error symbol $\bot$.*

Note that $|\text{Comp}(m)|$ may not necessarily be less than $|m|$; Shannon's coding theorem implies that no algorithm can encode every message with shorter length, so not all messages may actually be "compressed": some may increase in lenth.

Correctness of a compression scheme is again defined in the obvious way: for all $m \in \mathcal{M}$, we require that $\text{Decomp}(\text{Comp}(m)) = m$.

In this paper, we are interested in *symmetric-key compression-encryption schemes*, which formally are just symmetric-key encryption schemes as in Definition 1, but usually have the goal of outputting shorter ciphertexts via some form of compression. Of course, every symmetric-key encryption scheme is also a symmetric-key compression-encryption scheme, with "compression" being the identity function. We will often deal with the following specific, natural composition of compression and symmetric-key encryption:

Definition 3 (Composition of Compression and Encryption). *Let $\Gamma = (\text{Comp}, \text{Decomp})$ be a compression scheme with message space $\mathcal{M}$ and output space $\mathcal{O}$. Let $\Pi = (\text{KeyGen}, \text{Enc}, \text{Dec})$ be a symmetric-key encryption scheme with message space $\mathcal{O}$ and ciphertext space $\mathcal{C}$. The symmetric-key compression-encryption scheme $\Pi \circ \Gamma$ constructed from Γ and Π is the following tuple:*

$$(\Pi \circ \Gamma).\text{KeyGen}() = \Pi.\text{KeyGen}()$$
$$(\Pi \circ \Gamma).\text{Enc}_k(m) = \Pi.\text{Enc}_k(\Gamma.\text{Comp}(m))$$
$$(\Pi \circ \Gamma).\text{Dec}_k(c) = \Gamma.\text{Decomp}(\Pi.\text{Dec}_k(c))$$

Note that $\Pi \circ \Gamma$ is itself a symmetric-key encryption scheme with message space $\mathcal{M}$ and ciphertext space $\mathcal{C}$. If Γ and Π are both correct, then so is $\Pi \circ \Gamma$.

2.2   Existing Security Notions

The standard security notion for symmetric-key encryption is indistinguishability of encrypted messages. In this paper, we focus on chosen plaintext attack. The security experiment $\text{Exp}_\Pi^{\text{IND-CPA}}(\mathcal{A})$ for indistinguishability under chosen plaintext attack (IND-CPA) of a symmetric-key encryption scheme Π against a stateful adversary $\mathcal{A}$ is given in Fig. 2. The *advantage* of $\mathcal{A}$ in breaking the IND-CPA experiment for Π is $\text{Adv}_\Pi^{\text{IND-CPA}}(\mathcal{A}) = \left| 2\Pr\left(\text{Exp}_\Pi^{\text{IND-CPA}}(\mathcal{A}) = 1\right) - 1 \right|$.

Kelley and Tamassia [12] give a definition of *entropy-restricted* IND-CPA *security* which applies to keyed compression schemes Π, and demands indistinguishability of encryptions of messages from the same class $\mathcal{L} \subseteq \mathcal{M}$; typically,

$\mathrm{Exp}_{\Pi}^{\mathsf{IND\text{-}CPA}}(\mathcal{A})$

> 1: $k \stackrel{\$}{\leftarrow} \Pi.\mathrm{KeyGen}()$
> 2: $b \stackrel{\$}{\leftarrow} \{0,1\}$
> 3: $(m_0, m_1, st) \stackrel{\$}{\leftarrow} \mathcal{A}^E()$
> 4: **if** $|m_0| \neq |m_1|$, **then return** $\perp$
> 5: $c \leftarrow \Pi.\mathrm{Enc}_k(m_b)$
> 6: $b' \stackrel{\$}{\leftarrow} \mathcal{A}^E(c, st)$
> 7: **return** $(b' = b)$

$E(m)$

> 1: **return** $\Pi.\mathrm{Enc}_k(m)$

$\mathrm{Exp}_{\Pi,\mathcal{L}}^{\mathsf{ER\text{-}IND\text{-}CPA}}(\mathcal{A})$

> 1: $k \stackrel{\$}{\leftarrow} \Pi.\mathrm{KeyGen}()$
> 2: $b \stackrel{\$}{\leftarrow} \{0,1\}$
> 3: $(m_0, m_1, st) \stackrel{\$}{\leftarrow} \mathcal{A}^E()$
> 4: **if** $m_0 \notin \mathcal{L}$ or $m_1 \notin \mathcal{L}$, **then return** $\perp$
> 5: $c \leftarrow \Pi.\mathrm{Enc}_k(m_b)$
> 6: $b' \stackrel{\$}{\leftarrow} \mathcal{A}^E(c, st)$
> 7: **return** $(b' = b)$

$E(m)$

> 1: **return** $\Pi.\mathrm{Enc}_k(m)$

Fig. 2. Security experiments for indistinguishability under chosen plaintext attack (IND-CPA, left) and entropy-restricted IND-CPA (ER-IND-CPA, right)

$\mathcal{L}$ is the class of messages that encrypt (compress) to the same length under $\Pi.\mathrm{Enc}$, such as:

$$\mathcal{L}_\ell = \{m \in \mathcal{M} : |\Pi.\mathrm{Enc}(m)| = \ell\}.$$

The ER-IND-CPA security experiment is given in Fig. 2; the corresponding advantage is defined similarly. Kelley and Tamassia note that any IND-CPA-secure symmetric-key encryption scheme Π, combined with any compression scheme Γ, is immediately ER-IND-CPA-secure. As well, it is easily seen that if a symmetric-key encryption scheme is ER-IND-CPA-secure for the class $\mathcal{L}_\ell = \{m \in \mathcal{M} : |m| = \ell\}$, then that scheme is also an IND-CPA-secure symmetric-key encryption.

2.3   New Security Notions

In this paper, we focus on the ability of an attacker to learn about a secret piece of data inside a larger piece of data, where the attacker controls everything except the secret data. We use the term *cookie* to refer to the secret data; in practice, this could be an HTTP cookie in a header, an anti-CSRF token, or some piece of personal information. We will allow the attacker to adaptively obtain encryptions of compressions of data of the form $m'\|ck\|m''$ for a secret cookie ck and adversary-chosen message prefix m' and suffix m''.

We now present three notions for the security of cookies in the context of compression-encryption schemes:

- *Cookie recovery* (CR) *security:* A simple, but relatively weak, security notion for symmetric-key compression-encryption schemes: it should be hard for the attacker to *fully recover* a secret value, even given adaptive access to an oracle that encrypts plaintexts of its choosing with the target cookie embedded.
- *Random cookie indistinguishability* (RCI) *security:* The adversary has to decide which of two randomly chosen cookies was embedded in the encrypted plaintext, given adaptive access to an oracle that encrypts plaintexts of its choosing with the target cookie embedded.

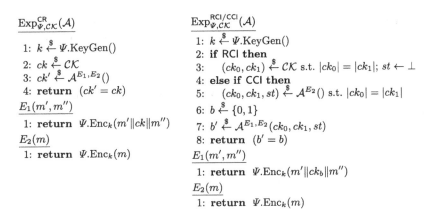

Fig. 3. Security experiments for cookie recovery (left) and random cookie indistinguishability and chosen cookie indistinguishability (right) attacks

– *Chosen cookie indistinguishability* (CCI) *security:* Here, the adversary has to decide which of two cookies of the adversary's choice was embedded in the encrypted plaintext, given adaptive access to an oracle that encrypts plaintexts of its choosing with the target cookie embedded.

These security notions are formalized in the following definition, which refers to the security experiments shown in Fig. 3.

Definition 4 (CR, RCI, CCI Security). *Let Ψ be a symmetric-key compression-encryption scheme. Let $\mathcal{A}$ denote an algorithm. Let $\mathcal{CK}$ denote the cookie space. Let $\mathsf{xxx} \in \{\mathsf{CR}, \mathsf{RCI}, \mathsf{CCI}\}$ be a security notion. Consider the security experiment $\mathrm{Exp}_{\Psi,\mathcal{CK}}^{\mathsf{xxx}}(\mathcal{A})$ in Fig. 3. Define $\mathrm{Adv}_{\Psi,\mathcal{CK}}^{\mathsf{CR}}(\mathcal{A}) = \Pr\left(\mathrm{Exp}_{\Psi,\mathcal{CK}}^{\mathsf{CR}}(\mathcal{A}) = 1\right)$ as the probability that $\mathcal{A}$ wins the cookie recovery experiment for Ψ and $\mathcal{CK}$. Similarly, define $\mathrm{Adv}_{\Psi,\mathcal{CK}}^{\mathsf{xxx}}(\mathcal{A}) = \left|2\Pr\left(\mathrm{Exp}_{\Psi,\mathcal{CK}}^{\mathsf{xxx}}(\mathcal{A}) = 1\right) - 1\right|, \mathsf{xxx} \in \{\mathsf{RCI}, \mathsf{CCI}\}$, as the advantage that $\mathcal{A}$ has in winning the random cookie and chosen cookie indistinguishability experiments.*

Remark 1. The CR, RCI, and CCI security notions intentionally include only the confidentiality of the cookie as a security goal, and not the confidentiality of any non-cookie data in the rest of the message. In most applications it would be desirable to obtain confidentiality of non-cookie data as well, and in many real-world situations, the application layer's cookie and non-cookie data are jointly sent to the security layer (such as SSL/TLS) for encryption. Our notions do not preclude the scheme from encrypting the non-cookie data as well (and in fact our constructions in Sects. 3 and 4 do so). However, it is not possible in general to require confidentiality of the non-cookie data while still allowing it to be compressed, as that brings us back around to the original problem that motivated the work—compression of adversary-provided data can lead to ciphertexts of different lengths that break indistinguishability. This cycle can be broken by demanding some length restriction on the separated non-cookie data, such as in the ER-IND-CPA notion described in Sect. 2.2, but we omit that complication to focus solely on the security of the high-value secret cookies.

2.4   Relations and Separations Between Security Notions

Cookie recovery, being a computational problem rather than a decisional problem, is a weaker security notion. Keeping CR as an initial step, the RCI and CCI notions gradually increase the security afforded to the cookie.

The following relations exist between security notions for symmetric-key compression-encryption schemes:

$$CCI \implies RCI \implies CR.$$

In other words, every scheme that provides chosen cookie indistinguishability provides random cookie indistinguishability, and so on. Moreover, these notions are distinct, and we can show separations between them:

$$CR \implies\!\!\!\!\!/\ \ RCI \implies\!\!\!\!\!/\ \ CCI.$$

Additionally, we can connect our new notions with existing notions:

$$ER\text{-}IND\text{-}CPA \implies IND\text{-}CPA \implies CCI \quad \text{and} \quad CCI \implies\!\!\!\!\!/\ \ IND\text{-}CPA.$$

These last relations should be interpreted as follows. A standard (non-compressing) IND-CPA-secure symmetric-key encryption scheme is also CCI-secure. This is not to say, however, that an IND-CPA-secure symmetric-key encryption scheme combined with a compression scheme, such as $\Pi \circ \Gamma$ in Definition 3, is CCI-secure.

The proofs of these relations and counterexamples for the separations appear in the full version of the paper [15]. A brief discussion of the intuition for each appears in Appendix A.

3   Technique 1: Separating Secrets from User Inputs

In this section we analyze a mitigation technique against attacks that recover secrets from compressed data: separating secrets from user inputs. The basic idea of separating secrets from user inputs is: given an input, use a filter to separate all the secrets from the rest of the content, including user inputs. Then the rest of the content is compressed, while the secrets are kept uncompressed. This mitigation technique is a generic mitigation technique against a whole class of compression-based side-channel attacks.

3.1   The Scheme

Definition 5 (Filter). *A filter is an invertible (efficient) function* $f : \{0,1\}^* \to \{0,1\}^* \times \{0,1\}^*$.

Given a filter f and a compression scheme Γ, the separating-secrets scheme $SS_{f,\Gamma}$ is given in Fig. 4.

Our results will make use of the following two conditions on filters. Intuitively, a filter is *effective* if it removes cookies from an input string, and is *safe* if no prefix/suffix can fool the filter into separating out one cookie but not another.

Definition 6 (Effective Filter). *Let* $\mathcal{CK}$ *be a cookie space, and let* f *be a filter. We say that* f *is* effective *at separating out* $\mathcal{CK}$ *if, for all* $ck \in \mathcal{CK}$ *and all* m', m'', *we have that* $ck \not\preceq y$, *where* $(x, y) = f(m'\|ck\|m'')$.

Definition 7 (Safe Filter). *Let* $\mathcal{CK}$ *be a cookie space, and let* f *be a filter. We say that* f *is* safe *for* $\mathcal{CK}$ *if, for all* $ck_0, ck_1 \in \mathcal{CK}$ *such that* $|ck_0| = |ck_1|$ *and all* m', m'', *we have that* $|x_0| = |x_1|$ *and* $y_0 = y_1$, *where* $(x_0, y_0) = f(m'\|ck_0\|m'')$ *and* $(x_1, y_1) = f(m'\|ck_1\|m'')$.

Example Cookie Space and Filter. Let $\lambda \in \mathbb{N}$ and let $\mathcal{CK}$ be the set of alphanumeric strings starting with the literal "secret" and starting and ending with a space (denoted by ␣), i.e., strings matched by the regular expression

$$\text{␣secret[A-Za-z0-9]}^\lambda\text{␣}$$

Let f be a filter that uses the above regular expression to separate out secrets. Consider a string of the form $m = m_0\text{␣}ck_1\text{␣}m_1\text{␣}ck_2\text{␣}m_2\text{␣}\ldots\text{␣}ck_n\text{␣}m_n$, where m_i contains no substring matching the above regular expression and ck_i is a string completely matching the above regular expression (excluding the initial and terminal space ␣). Then $f(m) = (pt_s, pt_{ns})$, where $pt_s = ck_1\|\ldots\|ck_n$ and $pt_{ns} = m_0\|\tau\|m_1\|\tau\|\ldots\|m_n$, and τ represents a fixed replacement token that can not appear as a substring of any $m \in \mathcal{M}$. The above filter f is effective at separating out and safe for the above $\mathcal{CK}$. The intuitive reason for this is that, since each cookie begins and ends with a character ␣ which does not appear within the cookie, no prefix or suffix can cause the filter to not separate a cookie.

$SS_{f,\Gamma}.\text{Comp}(m)$

1: $(pt_s, pt_{ns}) \leftarrow f(m)$
2: $\widetilde{pt_{ns}} \leftarrow \Gamma.\text{Comp}(pt_{ns})$
3: **return** $pt_s\|\widetilde{pt_{ns}}$

$SS_{f,\Gamma}.\text{Decomp}(pt)$

1: Parse $pt_s\|\widetilde{pt_{ns}} \leftarrow pt$
2: $pt_{ns} \leftarrow \Gamma.\text{Decomp}(\widetilde{pt_{ns}})$
3: $m \leftarrow f^{-1}(pt_s, pt_{ns})$
4: **return** m

Fig. 4. Abstract separating-secrets compression scheme SS

3.2   CCI Security of Basic Separating-Secrets Technique

In this section we analyze the security of separating-secrets mitigation technique according to CCI notion. Let $\Pi = (\text{KeyGen}, \text{Enc}, \text{Dec})$ be an IND-CPA-secure symmetric-key encryption scheme and $\text{SS}_{f,\Gamma}$ be the separating-secrets compression scheme given in Fig. 4. We consider the security of the resulting symmetric-key compression-encryption scheme $\Pi \circ \text{SS}_{f,\Gamma}$, showing that, if the filter f safely separates out cookies, then breaking chosen cookie indistinguishability of $\Pi \circ \text{SS}_{f,\Gamma}$ is as hard as breaking indistinguishability (IND-CPA) of encryption scheme Π. The proof of Theorem 1 appears in Appendix B.

Theorem 1. *Let Π be a symmetric-key encryption scheme and let Γ be a compression scheme. Let $\mathcal{CK}$ be a cookie space, and let f be a filter that is safe for $\mathcal{CK}$. Let $\mathcal{A}$ be any adversary against the CCI security of the separating-secrets symmetric-key compression-encryption scheme $\Pi \circ \text{SS}_{f,\Gamma}$, and let q denote the number of queries that $\mathcal{A}$ makes to its E_1 oracle. Then $\text{Adv}_{\Pi \circ \text{SS}_{f,\Gamma}, \mathcal{CK}}^{\text{CCI}}(\mathcal{A}) \leq q \cdot \text{Adv}_{\Pi}^{\text{IND-CPA}}(\mathcal{B}^{\mathcal{A}})$, where $\mathcal{B}$ is an algorithm, constructed using the adversary $\mathcal{A}$ as described in the proof, against the IND-CPA security of the symmetric-key encryption scheme Π.*

3.3   Separating Secrets in HTML

Separating secrets from user inputs is a realistic mitigation technique against the BREACH attack: in the application layer, some fields which contain secrets (such as anti-CSRF tokens) can be identified and separated from the HTTP response body. In order to implement separating secrets from user inputs in HTML we need to describe a filter f_{HTML}.

One possible method to separate secrets in HTML is to separate the content assigned to the `value` attribute of HTML elements. Among other uses, the `value` attribute defines the value of a specific field in a form. The HTML code segment of Fig. 5 shows inclusion of a secret anti-CSRF token as a hidden `input` field in a web form, which will appear in a HTML response body. By separating the content in the `value` attribute, we separate the anti-CSRF token.

The following (case-insensitive) regular expression can be used to separate out quoted anti-CSRF tokens in the `value` attribute of HTML elements:

```
value\s*=\s*"[A-Za-z0-9]+"|value\s*=\s*'[A-Za-z0-9]+'
```

```
<form action="/money_transfer" method="post">
<input type="hidden" name="csrftoken"
       value="OWT4NmQlODE4ODRjN2Q1NT1hMmZlYWE...">
...
</form>
```

Fig. 5. HTML code segment showing inclusion of anti-CSRF token in a web form

Table 1. Compression performance (file size in bytes and compression ratio) for separating secrets (Sect. 3) and fixed dictionary (Sect. 4) techniques

Website	Uncompressed	gzip full page		Separating secrets		Fixed dictionary	
Google.com	145 599	41 455	(3.51×)	41 502	(3.51×)	117 794	(1.23×)
Facebook.com	48 226	13 785	(3.50×)	15 863	(3.04×)	35 036	(1.37×)
Youtube.com	467 928	41 813	(11.19×)	41 893	(11.17×)	181 676	(2.58×)
Yahoo.com	444 408	82 572	(5.38×)	83 342	(5.33×)	318 386	(1.40×)
Baidu.com	74 979	17 519	(4.28×)	17 727	(4.23×)	55 950	(1.34×)
Wikipedia.org	48 548	11 217	(4.33×)	11 809	(4.11×)	38 406	(1.26×)
Twitter.com	57 777	12 520	(4.61×)	16 618	(3.48×)	39 712	(1.46×)
Qq.com	626 297	124 108	(5.05×)	125 747	(4.98×)	519 830	(1.21×)
Amazon.com	234 609	54 922	(4.27×)	56 278	(4.17×)	150 924	(1.55×)
Taobao.com	192 068	23 658	(8.12×)	23 898	(8.04×)	93 410	(2.06×)

This filter is effective at separating out and safe for the implied set of cookies, in the sense of Definitions 6 and 7.

However, the above regular expression is not perfect, highlighting the challenges of using heuristic techniques to separate out secrets.

First, the above regular expression will also capture the `value` attribute of HTML elements other than hidden `input` elements, such as `option`, which may not need to be treated as secret, so it is not as efficient as it could be.

Second, the above regular expression does not capture anti-CSRF tokens in unquoted `value` attributes, such as `value=OWT4NmQ1`, which are allowed by the HTML specification. While it is easy to add an additional term such as `|value\s*=\s*[A-Za-z0-9]+` to the regular expression to capture unquoted attributes, this filter would no longer be effective in the sense of Definition 6: if a cookie is `value=OWT4NmQ1`, and the adversary constructs $m' = $ `value=`, then $m'\|ck = $ `value=value=OWT4NmQ1`, and the filter applied to $m'\|ck$ would separate out `value=value` as the cookie and leave `=OWT4NmQ1` unprotected.

3.4 Experimental Results on Separating-Secrets in HTML

Table 1 shows the result of applying the above regular expression to separate secrets on the top 10 global websites of Alexa Top Sites. As most pages contain little data in `value` attributes, the total amount of space required to transmit the separated secrets plus the remaining data is not much more than when the full page is compressed. (Table 1 also contains performance results of the fixed dictionary technique, to be discussed in Sect. 4).

3.5 Discussion

The main drawback of the separating secrets technique is that the separation filter must be application-dependent. We noted already the challenges in using the heuristic regular expression above to capture anti-CSRF tokens: it may separate out non-secrets as well as secrets (which yields suboptimal compression) and it does not capture unquoted tokens (which is a problem for security).

Moreover, this HTML filter also only captures secrets in a `value` attribute, which does not necessarily capture all values that might be considered sensitive. For example, should the titles of books in a search results page on an shopping site be considered secret? If so, an alternative separation filter would have to be developed. To provide complete certainty, secret separation would require additional markup with which the developer clearly identifies which data should be treated as secret. Otherwise, any sensitive values which are not separated may be compressed together with user inputs and other application data, and hence remain open to the compression-based side-channel.

4   Technique 2: Fixed-Dictionary Compression

The CRIME and BREACH attacks work because the dictionary constructed by the DEFLATE compression algorithm is adaptive: if the attacker injects a substring of the target secret into the plaintext nearby the secret itself, then the plaintext will compress more because of the repeated substring. Some early compression algorithms were non-adaptive, using a fixed dictionary mechanism. For example, Pike [16] used a fixed dictionary of 205 popular English words and a variable length coding mechanism to compress typical English text at a rate of less than 4 bits per character. Another recent algorithm, Smaz [17], similarly uses a fixed dictionary consisting of common digrams and trigrams from English and HTML source code, allowing it to compress even very short strings. Because the CRIME and BREACH attacks rely on the adaptivity of the compression dictionary, fixed-dictionary algorithms can offer resistance to such attacks while still providing some compression, albeit not as good as adaptive compression.

In this section, we investigate the use of fixed-dictionary compression in the context of encryption. We describe the basic idea of fixed-dictionary compression. We show that fixed-dictionary compression-encryption schemes can satisfy cookie recovery security for sufficiently large cookies. We then present an example of a modern fixed-dictionary compression algorithm and report on the compression ratios achieved by our algorithm.

4.1   The Scheme

In general, fixed-dictionary compression schemes work by advancing through the string x and looking to see if the current substring appears in the dictionary $\mathcal{D}$: if it does, then an encoding of the index of the substring is recorded, otherwise an encoding of the current substring is recorded. The compression scheme must specify the encoding rules in a way that unambiguously discriminates between the two cases to allow for correct decompression.

An abstract version of a fixed-dictionary fixed-width compression algorithm FD is given in Fig. 6. FD checks if the current substring of length w appears

$FD_{\mathcal{D},w,\ell}.\mathrm{Comp}(x)$	$FD_{\mathcal{D},w,\ell}.\mathrm{Decomp}(y)$
1: $y \leftarrow \epsilon$	1: $x \leftarrow \epsilon$
2: $i \leftarrow 1$	2: $i \leftarrow 1$
3: **while** $i \leq \|x\| - w + 1$ **do**	3: **while** $i \leq \|y\|$ **do**
4: **if** $x_{i:w} \preceq \mathcal{D}$ **then**	4: **if** y_i encodes an index **then**
5: $y \leftarrow y \parallel$ encoding of $\mathrm{ind}_{\mathcal{D}}(x_{i:w})$	5: $x \leftarrow x \parallel \mathcal{D}_{y_i:w}$
6: $i \leftarrow i + w$	6: $i \leftarrow i + 1$
7: **else**	7: **else**
8: $y \leftarrow y \parallel$ encoding of $x_{i:\ell}$	8: $x \leftarrow x \parallel$ decoding of $y_{i:\ell'}$
9: $i \leftarrow i + \ell$	9: $i \leftarrow i + \ell'$
10: **return** y	10: **return** x

Fig. 6. Abstract fixed-dictionary fixed-width compression scheme FD. Note the simplification that ℓ characters of x are encoded as ℓ' characters of y.

in the dictionary $\mathcal{D}$. If it does, it records the index of the substring in $\mathcal{D}$ and advances w characters. If it does not, it records the next ℓ characters directly, then advances. (Using $\ell > 1$ but $\ell < w$ may be more efficient when it comes to encodings). One could treat $\mathcal{D}$ either as a set of strings (recording which element is matched) or a long string (recording the starting and ending position of the matching substring); we will use the latter in the rest of this section.

For example, if $\mathcal{D}$ = "cookierecoveryattack", then $FD_{\mathcal{D},4,2}.\mathrm{Comp}$ ("recover the cookie") yields 7ver_the_1ie.

4.2 CR Security of Basic Fixed-Dictionary Technique

Let Π be a symmetric-key encryption scheme. Let $\mathcal{D}$ be a dictionary of length d and $FD_{\mathcal{D},w,\ell}$ be the abstract fixed-dictionary compression scheme in Fig. 6.

Suppose the cookie space is binary strings of length 8λ, or equivalently byte strings of length λ: $\mathcal{CK} = \{\texttt{0x00}, \ldots, \texttt{0xFF}\}^{\lambda}$.

If Π is a secure encryption scheme, then, intuitively, the only way the adversary can learn information about the cookie from seeing ciphertexts $\mathrm{Enc}_k(\cdot \| ck \| \cdot)$ and $\mathrm{Enc}_k(\cdot)$ is from the length of the ciphertext: if some substring of ck appears in the dictionary $\mathcal{D}$, then ck will compress, and that length difference tells the adversary that the secret cookie is restricted to some subset of $\mathcal{CK}$ matching $\mathcal{D}$.

The situation is subtler in the full CR experiment: the attacker can provide m' and m'' and get $\mathrm{Enc}_k(\mathrm{Comp}(m'\|ck\|m''))$. If the last few bytes of m' followed by the first few bytes of ck appear in $\mathcal{D}$, then the string will compress more. This allows the attacker to carry out a CRIME-like attack on the first few bytes of ck.

For example, let $w = 4$ and suppose $\mathcal{D}$ = 1234567890ABCDEFGHIJKLMNOP QRSTUVWXYZ and $\mathcal{CK} = [\text{0-9A-F}]^{\lambda}$. The attacker can query $m' = 890$, $m' = 90A$, $m' = \text{0AB}, \ldots$. In exactly one case, the adversary's m' combined with the cookie's first byte will be in the dictionary, telling the adversary ck_1. For example, if $ck_1 = \text{B}$, then when the adversary queries $m' = 90A$, the value that is compressed and then encrypted is $m'\|ck\|m'' = \text{90AB} \ldots$, which is a substring of $\mathcal{D}$.

While this allows the attacker to recover the first byte or two of the secret cookie with decent probability, it drops off exponentially; a similar argument applies to the last few bytes of the secret cookie. Theorem 2 captures this issue. Theorem 2 only provides quantifiable security when the cookie length n is significantly bigger than the compression window w. Additionally, this type of attack on the first/last few bytes of the cookie precludes *indistinguishable* security, which is why we focus on cookie *recovery* here. (Admittedly, in some settings recovering the first/last few cookie bytes may still be quite damaging).

Theorem 2. *Let Π be a symmetric-key encryption scheme. Let $\mathcal{D}$ be a dictionary of d words, each of length ℓ. Let w be positive integer. Let $\mathcal{CK} = \Omega^n$. Let $\mathcal{A}$ be any adversary against the cookie recovery security of the fixed-dictionary symmetric-key compression-encryption scheme $\Pi \circ \mathrm{FD}_{\mathcal{D},w,\ell}$. Then $\mathrm{Adv}^{\mathsf{CR}}_{\Pi \circ \mathrm{FD}_{\mathcal{D},w,\ell}}(\mathcal{A}) \leq \mathrm{Adv}^{\mathsf{IND\text{-}CPA}}_{\Pi}(\mathcal{B}) + 2^{-\Delta}$, where $\mathcal{B}$ is an algorithm, constructed using adversary $\mathcal{A}$, against the $\mathsf{IND\text{-}CPA}$ security of the symmetric-key encryption scheme Π, and*

$$\Delta \geq \left(1 - d\left(1 - \left(1 - \frac{1}{|\Omega|^w}\right)^{n-3w+1}\right)\right)$$

$$\cdot \log_2\left(|\Omega|^{n-2w} - |\Omega|^{n-2w} \cdot d\left(1 - \left(1 - \frac{1}{|\Omega|^w}\right)^{n-3w+1}\right)\right).$$

For example, for cookies of $n = 16$ bytes, with a dictionary of $d = 4000$ words each of length $w = 4$, we have $\Delta \geq 63.999695$. Doubling d gives $\Delta \geq 63.999391$. The derivation of the formula in Theorem 2 appears in Appendix C.

4.3 Experimental Results on Fixed-Dictionary Technique

Table 1 shows the result of applying a fixed-dictionary based compression algorithm to the top 10 global websites of Alexa Top Sites. The 4000-byte dictionary was built from the most common 8-, 16-, and 32-character substrings of the pages. The compression algorithm was based in part on the Smaz [17] algorithm and was adapted slightly from Fig. 6, to allow for variable-length words to be matched. Specifically, when attempting to encode the substring at the current position at line 4 in Fig. 6, we first try variable length words in order of decreasing length, checking to see if $w = 18$, then $w = 16$, then ..., then $w = 4$ characters can be found in the dictionary. This requires the encoding to include both index and length of the dictionary substring.

- To encode a dictionary word at index $0 \leq j < 4096$ of length $w = 2w' + 4, 0 \leq w' \leq 7$, store 16 bits: 1 || [12-bit encoding of j] || [3-bit encoding of w'].
- To encode 2 lower-ASCII characters $z_1 z_2$, store 16 bits: 00 || [7-bit encoding of z_1] || [7-bit encoding of z_2].
- To encode 1 byte z, store 16 bits: 01000000 || [8-bit encoding of z].

4.4   Discussion

The main drawback of the fixed dictionary mitigation technique is that in practice it achieves relatively poor—albeit non-zero—compression compared with adaptive compression techniques. However, it does not rely on application-dependent or heuristic techniques for separating secrets.

Acknowledgements. The authors acknowledge support by Australian Research Council (ARC) Discovery Project DP130104304.

A   Relations and Separations Between Security Notions

This section briefly gives the intuition for the proofs of the relations and separations of the security notions; details appear in the full version [15].

- IND-CPA $\implies$ CCI: A (non-compressing) IND-CPA-secure symmetric-key encryption scheme provides indistinguishability of any pair of equal-length chosen messages, including messages involving a cookie. The proof proceeds by a hybrid argument, making the cookie used in each query made by the adversary to its E_1 oracle independent of the secret bit b.
- CCI $\;\not\!\!\!\implies$ IND-CPA: A degenerate scheme that uses a separating-secrets filter to extract secret cookies then encrypt the cookies but not the non-cookie data is CCI-secure but not IND-CPA-secure for the whole message.
- CCI $\implies$ RCI: A straightforward simulation: an adversary who cannot distinguish between encryptions of equal-length cookies of its choosing can also not distinguish between encryptions of randomly chosen equal-length cookies.
- RCI $\;\not\!\!\!\implies$ CCI: A counterexample is constructed that uses a separating-secrets filter: an extra ciphertext component c_2 is added, consisting of a point function applied to the separated secrets, where the point function is 1 on a single, publicly known cookie value z. With high probability, two randomly chosen cookies will not match z, so c_2 carries no useful information and the scheme is RCI-secure, but a CCI adversary can choose one cookie that matches z and one that does not, so c_2 allows distinguishing of the chosen cookies.
- RCI $\implies$ CR: A straightforward simulation: an adversary who recovers a cookie given only ciphertexts easily distinguishes encryptions of cookies.
- CR $\;\not\!\!\!\implies$ RCI: A counterexample is constructed: an extra ciphertext component c_2 is added, consisting of a random oracle applied to the message. The adversary gets encryptions of $m'\|ck\|m''$ for m', m'' of its choice; without querying the random oracle on exactly $m'\|ck\|m''$, c_2 provides no information to the adversary, so the scheme is CR-secure. However, an RCI adversary can check the random oracle on the two given random cookies, so c_2 allows distinguishing of the given random cookies.

B   Proof of CCI Security of Separating-Secrets Technique

Proof of Theorem 1. The proof proceeds in a sequence of games, using a hybrid approach. Each Game i proceeds as in the original CCI security experiment, except that the queries to E_1 are answered as in Fig. 7. Let Adv^i denote the probability that game i outputs 1.

$E_1(m', m'')$
1: **if** query $\# \leq i$ **then**
2:     **return** $\Pi.\text{Enc}_k(\text{SS}_{f,\Gamma}(m' \| ck_0 \| m''))$
3: **else if** query $\# > i$ **then**
4:     **return** $\Pi.\text{Enc}_k(\text{SS}_{f,\Gamma}(m' \| ck_b \| m''))$

Fig. 7. Oracle E_1 used in Game i in proof of Theorem 1.

Game 0. This is the original CCI security game for Π. By definition, $\text{Adv}^{\text{CCI}}_{\Pi \circ \text{SS}_{f,\Gamma}, \mathcal{CK}}(\mathcal{A}) = \text{Adv}^0$.

Transition from Game $(i-1)$ to Game i, $1 \leq i \leq q$. Each hybrid transition changes how one query is answered; if the adversary's behaviour differs because of the change in answering the query, we can construct a simulator $\mathcal{B}_i$ that wins the IND-CPA game for Ψ, as shown in Fig. 8. When the IND-CPA challenger uses $b = 0$, c^* is the encryption of the separating-secrets compression of $m' \| ck_i \| m''$, so $\mathcal{B}_i$ is playing game $(i-1)$ with $\mathcal{A}$. When the IND-CPA challenger uses $b = 1$, c^* is the encryption of the separating-secrets compression of $m' \| ck_0 \| m''$, so $\mathcal{B}_i$ is playing game i with $\mathcal{A}$. Since f is safe for $\mathcal{CK}$, the separating-secrets compressions of $m' \| ck_0 \| m''$ and $m' \| ck_1 \| m''$ have the same length, and thus the pair of chosen messages given from the simulator in E_1 to the IND-CPA challenger is valid according to the IND-CPA experiment. Thus, $\left| \text{Adv}^{i-1} - \text{Adv}^i \right| \leq \text{Adv}^{\text{IND-CPA}}_{\Psi}(\mathcal{B}^{\mathcal{A}}_i)$.

Analysis of Game q. Since the adversary's view is independent of b in Game q, we have $\text{Adv}^q = 0$.

Conclusion. Combining the above results, we have $\text{Adv}^{\text{CCI}}_{\Psi,\mathcal{CK}}(\mathcal{A}) \leq \sum_{i=1}^{q} \text{Adv}^{\text{IND-CPA}}_{\Psi}(\mathcal{B}^{\mathcal{A}}_i) = q \cdot \text{Adv}^{\text{IND-CPA}}_{\Psi}(\mathcal{B}^{\mathcal{A}})$ (with a small abuse of notation in creating a single $\mathcal{B}$ from the disparate $\mathcal{B}_i$). $\qquad \square$

C   Analysis of Security of Fixed-Dictionary Technique

C.1   Probability Bounds, No Prefix/Suffix

In this section, we compute the amount of information given to the adversary from knowing the length of the compressed cookie, without any adversarially

$\underline{\mathcal{B}_i^{A,E}()}$

1: $(ck_0, ck_1, st) \xleftarrow{\$} \mathcal{A}^{E_2}()$
   s.t. $|ck_0| = |ck_1|$
2: $\hat{b} \xleftarrow{\$} \{0,1\}$
3: $b' \xleftarrow{\$} \mathcal{A}^{E_1,E_2}(ck_0, ck_1, st)$
4: **return** b'

$\underline{E_2(m)}$

1: **return**
   $E(SS_{f,\Gamma}.\text{Comp}(m))$

$\underline{E_1(m', m'')}$

1: **if** query $\# < i$ **then**
2:    **return** $E(SS_{f,\Gamma}.\text{Comp}(m' \| ck_0 \| m''))$
3: **else if** query $\# = i$ **then**
4:    $pt \| \widetilde{pt_{ns}} \leftarrow SS_{f,\Gamma}.\text{Comp}(m' \| ck_{\hat{b}} \| m'')$
5:    $pt' \| \widetilde{pt_{ns}}' \leftarrow SS_{f,\Gamma}.\text{Comp}(m' \| ck_0 \| m'')$
6:    Give $(pt \| \widetilde{pt_{ns}}, pt' \| \widetilde{pt_{ns}}')$ to IND-CPA challenger
7:    Receive c^* from IND-CPA challenger
8:    **return** c^*
9: **else if** query $\# > i$ **then**
10:    **return** $E(SS_{f,\Gamma}.\text{Comp}(m' \| ck_{\hat{b}} \| m''))$

Fig. 8. Simulator $\mathcal{B}_i$ used in the proof of Theorem 1

chosen prefix or suffix. This can be computed by calculating the amount of information given by knowing how many substrings of the cookie appear in the dictionary. For the analysis, we treat $\mathcal{D}$ as a set of strings. Proofs for results in this section appear in the full version of the paper [15].

First we calculate the probability that a given string is a substring of a randomly chosen cookie.

Lemma 1. *Let $x \in \Omega^w$ be a word, and let $ck \xleftarrow{\$} \Omega^n = \mathcal{CK}$ be a random string of n characters. Then $\Pr(x \preceq ck) \leq 1 - \left(1 - \frac{1}{|\Omega|^w}\right)^{n-w+1}$.*

We now compute that probability that one of a set of given strings is a substring of a randomly chosen cookie:

Lemma 2. *Let $\mathcal{D} \subseteq \Omega^w$ with $|\mathcal{D}| = d$ be a dictionary of d words of w characters. Let $ck \xleftarrow{\$} \Omega^n = \mathcal{CK}$ be a random string of n characters. Then*

$$\Pr(\exists x \in \mathcal{D} : x \preceq ck) \leq d \left(1 - \left(1 - \frac{1}{|\Omega|^w}\right)^{n-w+1}\right).$$

Recall the definition of conditional entropy for random variables X and Y:

$$H(Y \mid X) = \sum_{x \in \text{supp}(X)} \Pr(X = x) H(Y \mid X = x)$$

$$= - \sum_{x \in \text{supp}(X)} \Pr(X = x)$$

$$\cdot \sum_{y \in \text{supp}(Y)} \Pr(Y = y \mid X = x) \log_2 \Pr(Y = y \mid X = x).$$

We now compute the amount of entropy about the cookie given knowledge about the number of substrings of the cookie that appear in the dictionary:

Lemma 3. *Fix $\mathcal{D}$. Let #SUB(ck) denote the number of substrings of ck that appear in $\mathcal{D}$. Suppose CK is a uniform random variable on $\mathcal{CK}$. Then*

$$H(CK \mid \#\mathrm{SUB}(CK)) \geq \left(1 - d\left(1 - \left(1 - \frac{1}{|\Omega|^w}\right)^{n-w+1}\right)\right)$$

$$\cdot \log_2\left(|\mathcal{CK}| - |\mathcal{CK}| \cdot d\left(1 - \left(1 - \frac{1}{|\Omega|^w}\right)^{n-w+1}\right)\right).$$

For example, if we have 16-byte cookies ($\mathcal{CK} = \{\mathtt{0x00}, \ldots, \mathtt{0xFF}\}^{16}$), and the dictionary $\mathcal{D}$ is a set of $d = 4096$ words of length $w = 4\,\mathrm{bytes}$, then

$$H(CK \mid \#\mathrm{SUB}(CK)) \geq 127.998395.$$

Concluding our analysis of the information learned given to the adversary without any adversarially chosen prefix or suffix, we give a bound on the amount of entropy about the cookie given the length of the compressed cookie:

Lemma 4. *Fix $\mathcal{D}$ with d words of length w over character set Ω. Denote the length of a cookie ck compressed with dictionary $\mathcal{D}$ by $\mathrm{COMPLEN}(ck) = |\mathrm{FD}_{\mathcal{D},w,\ell}.\mathrm{Comp}(ck)|$. Suppose CK is a uniform random variable on $\mathcal{CK}$. Then*

$$H(CK \mid \mathrm{COMPLEN}(CK)) \geq H(CK \mid \#\mathrm{SUB}(CK))$$

$$\geq \left(1 - d\left(1 - \left(1 - \frac{1}{|\Omega|^w}\right)^{n-w+1}\right)\right)$$

$$\cdot \log_2\left(|\mathcal{CK}| - |\mathcal{CK}| \cdot d\left(1 - \left(1 - \frac{1}{|\Omega|^w}\right)^{n-w+1}\right)\right).$$

Lemma 4 follows from the data processing inequality and Lemma 3.

C.2   Probability Bounds, Prefix/Suffix

Suppose CK is a uniform random variable on $\mathcal{CK} = \Omega^n$. We know that $H(CK) = n \log_2(|\Omega|)$. Trivially, $H(CK \mid CK_1) = (n-1)\log_2(|\Omega|)$, where CK_1 is the first character of CK. Similarly, $H(CK \mid CK_{1:a}) = (n-a)\log_2(|\Omega|)$ and finally $H(CK \mid CK_{1:a}, CK_{n-b:b}) = (n-a-b)\log_2(|\Omega|)$.

Consider the following CRIME-like attack on the beginning of the cookie. Let $\mathcal{D}$ be a dictionary with d words of length w over character set Ω. Let $ck \in \Omega^n$. Let $O(\cdot)$ be an oracle that, upon input a of length $w - m$, with $1 \leq m \leq w - 1$, returns 1 if and only if $a\|ck_{1:m} \in \mathcal{D}$.

The CRIME-like attack works as follows:

1. For each $x \in \mathcal{D}$, query $x_{1:w-1}$ to the oracle. If a query for $x_{1:w-1}$ returns 1, then it is known that $ck_{1:1} \in Z_1 = \{z : x_{1:w-1}\|z \in \mathcal{D}\}$. If no query returns 1, then return $\emptyset$.

2. For $m = 2, \ldots, w - 1$: For each $x \in \mathcal{D}$ such that $x_{w-m} \in Z_{m-1}$, query $x_{1:w-m}$ to the oracle. If a query for $x_{1:w-m}$ returns 1, then it is known that $ck_{1:m} \in Z_m = \{z_1 z_2 \ldots z_m : x_{1:w-m} \| z_1 z_2 \ldots z_m \in \mathcal{D}\}$. If no query returns 1, then return $Z_1, \ldots, Z_{m-1}$.
3. Return $Z_1, \ldots, Z_{w-1}$.

A corresponding attack on the suffix is obvious.

Let CRIMEpre(ck) denote the output obtained from running the above prefix CRIME attacks on ck, CRIMEsuf(ck) denote the output from the corresponding suffix attack. Let CRIME(ck) = (CRIMEpre(ck), CRIMEsuf(ck)).

Noting that in the best case the CRIME attack allows the attacker to learn the first $w - 1$ and the last $w - 1$ characters of the cookie, some trivial lower bounds are:

$$H(CK_{1:w-1} \mid \text{CRIME}(CK)) \geq 0$$

$$H(CK_{n-w+1:w-1} \mid \text{CRIME}(CK)) \geq 0$$

However, the CRIME attack provides no information about the remaining characters, so $I(CK_{1:w-1}, CK_{w:n-w+1}) = 0$ and $I(CK_{1:n-w+1}, CK_{n-w+1:w-1}) = 0$, and thus $H(CK_{w:n-w+2} \mid \text{CRIME}(CK), \text{COMPLEN}(CK)) = H(CK_{w:n-w+2} \mid \text{COMPLEN}(CK))$.

Finally, we have that

$$
\begin{aligned}
&H(CK \mid \text{CRIME}(CK), \text{COMPLEN}(CK)) \\
&\quad \geq H(CK_{1:w-1} \mid \text{CRIMEpre}(CK)) + H(CK_{w:n-w+2} \mid \text{COMPLEN}(CK)) \\
&\qquad + H(CK_{n-w+1:w-1} \mid \text{CRIMEsuf}(CK)) \\
&\quad \geq 0 + H(CK_{w:n-w+2} \mid \text{COMPLEN}(CK)) + 0
\end{aligned}
$$

and we can obtain a lower bound on $H(CK_{w:n-w} \mid \text{COMPLEN}(CK))$ using Lemma 4.

References

1. Fielding, R., Reschke, J.: Hypertext Transfer Protocol (HTTP/1.1): Message Syntax and Routing. RFC 7230 (Proposed Standard) (2014)
2. Dierks, T., Rescorla, E.: The Transport Layer Security (TLS) Protocol Version 1.2. RFC 5246 (Proposed Standard) (2008). Updated by RFCs 5746, 5878, 6176
3. Kocher, P.C.: Timing attacks on implementations of Diffie-Hellman, RSA, DSS, and other systems. In: Koblitz, N. (ed.) CRYPTO 1996. LNCS, vol. 1109, pp. 104–113. Springer, Heidelberg (1996)
4. Kelsey, J., Schneier, B., Wagner, D., Hall, C.: Side channel cryptanalysis of product ciphers. In: Quisquater, J.-J., Deswarte, Y., Meadows, C., Gollmann, D. (eds.) ESORICS 1998. LNCS, vol. 1485, pp. 97–110. Springer, Heidelberg (1998)
5. Hutter, M., Mangard, S., Feldhofer, M.: Power and EM attacks on passive 13.56 mhz RFID devices. In: Paillier, P., Verbauwhede, I. (eds.) CHES 2007. LNCS, vol. 4727, pp. 320–333. Springer, Heidelberg (2007)

6. Kelsey, J.: Compression and information leakage of plaintext. In: Daemen, J., Rijmen, V. (eds.) FSE 2002. LNCS, vol. 2365, pp. 263–276. Springer, Heidelberg (2002)

7. Rizzo, J., Duong, T.: The CRIME attack. Presented at ekoparty 2012 (2012). http://goo.gl/mlw1X1

8. The Chromium Projects: (SPDY). http://dev.chromium.org/spdy

9. Trustworthy Internet Movement: SSL Pulse (2014). https://www.trustworthy internet.org/ssl-pulse/

10. Gluck, Y., Harris, N., Prado, A.: SSL, gone in 30 s: A BREACH beyond CRIME. In: Black Hat USA 2013 (2013)

11. Belshe, M., Peon, R., Thomson, M.: Hypertext Transfer Protocol version 2. Internet-Draft (2014). http://tools.ietf.org/html/draft-ietf-httpbis-http2-16

12. Kelley, J., Tamassia, R.: Secure compression: theory & practice. Cryptology ePrint Archive, Report 2014/113 (2014). http://eprint.iacr.org/2014/113

13. Akavia, A., Goldwasser, S., Vaikuntanathan, V.: Simultaneous hardcore bits and cryptography against memory attacks. In: Reingold, O. (ed.) TCC 2009. LNCS, vol. 5444, pp. 474–495. Springer, Heidelberg (2009)

14. Naor, M., Segev, G.: Public-key cryptosystems resilient to key leakage. In: Halevi, S. (ed.) CRYPTO 2009. LNCS, vol. 5677, pp. 18–35. Springer, Heidelberg (2009)

15. Alawatugoda, J., Stebila, D., Boyd, C.: Protecting encrypted cookies from compression side-channel attacks (full version). Cryptology ePrint Archive, Report 2014/724 (2014). http://eprint.iacr.org/2014/724

16. Pike, J.: Text compression using a 4 bit coding scheme. Comput. J. **24**, 324–330 (1980)

17. Sanfilippo, S.: Smaz: small strings compression library (2009). https://github.com/antirez/smaz

18. Klinc, D., Hazay, C., Jagmohan, A., Krawczyk, H., Rabin, T.: On Compression of Data Encrypted with Block Ciphers Cryptology ePrint Archive, Report 2010/477. http://eprint.iacr.org/2010/477

19. Peon, R., Ruellan, H.: HPACK-Header Compression for HTTP/2. http://http2.github.io/http2-spec/compression.html

Fingerprinting Web Users Through Font Metrics

David Fifield[1][(✉)] and Serge Egelman[1,2]

[1] University of California, Berkeley, USA
{fifield,egelman}@cs.berkeley.edu
[2] International Computer Science Institute, Berkeley, USA

Abstract. We describe a web browser fingerprinting technique based on measuring the onscreen dimensions of font glyphs. Font rendering in web browsers is affected by many factors—browser version, what fonts are installed, and hinting and antialiasing settings, to name a few—that are sources of fingerprintable variation in end-user systems. We show that even the relatively crude tool of measuring glyph bounding boxes can yield a strong fingerprint, and is a threat to users' privacy. Through a user experiment involving over 1,000 web browsers and an exhaustive survey of the allocated space of Unicode, we find that font metrics are more diverse than User-Agent strings, uniquely identifying 34 % of participants, and putting others into smaller anonymity sets. Fingerprinting is easy and takes only milliseconds. We show that of the over 125,000 code points examined, it suffices to test only 43 in order to account for all the variation seen in our experiment. Font metrics, being orthogonal to many other fingerprinting techniques, can augment and sharpen those other techniques.

We seek ways for privacy-oriented web browsers to reduce the effectiveness of font metric–based fingerprinting, without unduly harming usability. As part of the same user experiment of 1,000 web browsers, we find that whitelisting a set of standard font files has the potential to more than quadruple the size of anonymity sets on average, and reduce the fraction of users with a unique font fingerprint below 10 %. We discuss other potential countermeasures.

1 Introduction

Web browser fingerprinting exploits measurable characteristics of browsers to build an identifier that can be used to track the same browser over time. Fingerprinting works even when cookies are disabled, and can be hard for users to defend themselves against. A fingerprint is composed of a variety of measurements of the browser environment, typically acquired through client-side JavaScript. Previous studies have identified many sources of fingerprintable variation, including the User-Agent string, the list of system fonts, and the list of installed browser plugins [5,8].

© International Financial Cryptography Association 2015
R. Böhme and T. Okamoto (Eds.): FC 2015, LNCS 8975, pp. 107–124, 2015.
DOI: 10.1007/978-3-662-47854-7_7

Fig. 1. The Unicode code point U+00C6 LATIN CAPITAL LETTER AE rendered at `font-size: 1000%` in various styles in Firefox 24 (top) and Chromium 35 (bottom). Even when JavaScript is forbidden from reading the pixel data, it can tell the difference between browsers by measuring the dimensions of rendered glyphs. Notice that Firefox has chosen a sans-serif and Chromium a serif font for the CSS cursive and fantasy families. The browsers chose different serif fonts from among those available, and even the same font in the same style appears at different sizes.

In this work, we examine another facet of font-based device fingerprinting, the measurement of individual glyphs. Figure 1 shows how the same character in the same style may be rendered with different bounding boxes in different browsers. The same effect can serve to distinguish between instances of even the same browser on the same OS, when there are differences in configuration that affect font rendering—and we find that such differences are surprisingly common. By rendering glyphs at a large size, we magnify even small differences so they become detectable. The test is invisible—the glyphs are drawn on the background and never actually appear onscreen—and fast, taking less than a second when the code points tested come from a carefully chosen small set.

At the most basic level, font metrics can tell when there is no installed font with a glyph for a particular code point, by comparing its dimensions to those of a placeholder "glyph not found" glyph. But even further, font metrics can distinguish different fonts, different versions of the same font, different default font sizes, and different rendering settings such as those that govern hinting and antialiasing. Even the "glyph not found" glyph differs across configurations.

Font metric–based fingerprinting is weaker than some other known fingerprinting techniques. For example, it is probably strictly inferior to canvas fingerprinting [16], which gets not only bounding boxes but also pixel data. However, it is relevant because it is as yet effective against Tor Browser, a browser whose threat model includes tracking by fingerprinting [23, Sect. 4.6], and which already defends against easier, more powerful attacks. For instance, Tor Browser was highlighted in a recent study [4] as being the only browser to resist canvas fingerprinting.

We performed an experiment with more than 1,000 web users that tested the effectiveness of font fingerprinting across more than 125,000 code points of Unicode. 34 % of users were uniquely identified; the others were in various anonymity sets of size up to 61. We found that the same fingerprinting power, with this user population, can be achieved by testing only 43 code points. We tested a proposed anti-fingerprinting defense of using standard fonts in the web browser, and found it to be effective, more than quadrupling the size of anonymity sets on average.

2   Related Work

Eckersley [8] investigated the potential of fingerprinting in the absence of usual tracking technologies like cookies. The well-known Panopticlick experiment collected hundreds of thousands of submissions and is still ongoing. Fingerprints are derived from a variety of features: User-Agent string, HTTP request headers, whether cookies are enabled, time zone, screen size, browser plugins and their versions, whether certain long-term state storage ("evercookies") are blocked, and the list of system fonts. These limited features uniquely identified 84 % of participants. Fingerprints that had changed slightly between visits were found to be nevertheless linkable to previous fingerprints.

Previous studies [5, 8] have considered fingerprinting using the list of installed fonts; that is, a list of names like "Courier" and "Lucida." An ordered list of font names is available from the Java and Flash plugins. Nikiforakis et al. [19] describe how to get an unordered list of font names from JavaScript when Java and Flash are not available. For each of a long list of known font names, render a reference string using that font, and—using the same APIs that we use in this work to measure individual glyphs—compare its rendered dimensions against a database of known fonts. The technique has been known since at least 2007 [20] and was found to be in use by a large fingerprinting company.

Mowery and Shacham [16] found the HTML canvas element [18, Sect. 4.11.4] to be a rich source of variation. They measured an entropy of 5.73 bits, with 116 unique fingerprints in a population of 294. Their technique is to ask the browser to draw shapes and text to a pixel buffer, and then read back the resulting bitmap. Variations in how browsers draw antialiased lines, for example, are fingerprintable characteristics. They tested font rendering using both system and web fonts, and found, as we do, that the appearance of nominally identical fonts differs across systems. Like us, they recruited users for their experiment from Mechanical Turk and had a similar sample size. Canvas fingerprinting is more powerful than what we describe in this work; however our technique works even when HTML canvas is absent or disabled.

Mowery et al. [15] fingerprinted JavaScript implementations using performance benchmarks. A web browser's JavaScript implementation is an integral part of the browser, and optimization techniques such as just-in-time compilation mean that timing characteristics of even the underlying physical processor may be exposed. They were able to correctly identify a browser family 98 % of the time. They also show how the use of a privacy technology, in this case NoScript, can paradoxically make a user more identifiable, by leaking individualized blocking preferences. Mulazzani et al. [17] used the success and failure of standard JavaScript test suites to identify different JavaScript engines.

Acar et al. [5] in 2013 tested the prevalence of fingerprinting in the wild, scanning the top million Alexa sites with a focus on font probing. Their system, FPDetective, found 404 of the top million sites using JavaScript font probing, and discovered some previously unknown commercial fingerprinting providers. They also found fingerprinting scripts that disguised themselves, for example by removing themselves from the DOM after execution.

A further study by Acar et al. [4] in 2014 measured the prevalence of canvas fingerprinting, evercookies, and "cookie syncing" in the wild. They found canvas fingerprinting in use by 5 % of the top 100,000 Alexa sites, mostly because of third-party advertisement code. They found instances of evercookies restoring ordinary HTTP cookies and vice versa, and discovered a new evercookie vector used by trackers. They quantified the effect of cookie syncing, the sharing of identifying tokens across domain in circumvention of the same-origin policy.

Previous work has used the measurement of bounding boxes as a means of detecting what fonts are installed, and in turn using the list of installed fonts as a fingerprint feature. The technique we describe in this work is different: its output is not a list of font names, but a list of individual glyph dimensions. It does not require a list of candidate font names known in advance. While it may be possible to infer some characteristics of the target system, such as the list of installed fonts, from a font-metric fingerprint, that is not the main goal. The goal is only to hash as much variation as possible into some kind of unique identifier. Glyph dimensions have the potential to be more sensitive than font names (as the "same" named font may in fact be different on different systems), but they also may miss obscure fonts that are never selected by the browser unless asked for by name. Of course, there is no reason for a tracker to limit itself to one kind of fingerprinting. In this study we consider font metric fingerprinting in isolation, with the understanding that it can be combined with other techniques for better performance.

3   Methodology

We collected measurements through a web page with a JavaScript program that inserts code points into the DOM and measures the dimensions of their corresponding glyphs. The program renders in turn 125,776 Unicode code points over the course of a few minutes. The list consists of every code point in every assigned block of Unicode 7.0.0 [25], with the exception that only the first 256 code points are included from the two Supplementary Private Use Area blocks (U+F0000–U+FFFFF and U+100000–U+10FFFF), which would otherwise contain 65,536 code points each. The code points cover every writing system known to Unicode.

Each code point is drawn six times, once with no font specified (default), then once in each of the five generic CSS families (sans-serif, serif, monospace, cursive, fantasy) [14, Sect. 15.3.1]. Generic font family names are usually used in a CSS rule to express a rough idea of how text should look, when no specific matching named font is found. These generic CSS family names are mapped to concrete fonts at the browser's discretion, depending in part on user preferences and what fonts are available. Fonts were rendered very large, with CSS style `font-size: 10000 %`, in order to better distinguish small differences in dimensions. At this size, typical dimensions for the letter 'A' in the default style are 1155×1900 pixels. The size of each code point is measured indirectly, by placing it in a box and measuring the size of the box. The box is emptied before refreshing the browser UI, so the user does not actually see anything appear onscreen. Thus, fingerprinting can occur without the user's awareness.

We recruited users from Amazon Mechanical Turk and did not impose any restrictions on participation (e.g., geographic region, completion rate, etc.) in order to yield a diverse sample. For each submission, we recorded only the browser's User-Agent string, the elapsed time, and the height and width in pixels of every code point in every font style. Participants were paid $0.25 each. In order to detect duplicate submissions by the same user, the web page set a cookie with a randomly generated token and a lifetime of 30 days.

Following Eckersley [8], we use entropy as the measure of variation. For a vector of categorical values S, the probability of observing a particular value v is $P_S(v) = \frac{|x \in S : x = v|}{|S|}$; that is, the number of observations of that value divided by the length of the vector. The entropy of S is the sum of the entropies of all the distinct values it comprises:

$$H(S) = - \sum_{v \in S} P_S(v) \log_2 P_S(v).$$

We will be considering the case where the entries of S are the observed dimensions of a certain code point across all experiment submissions. If we think of the data set as a matrix with one row for every user submission and one column for every code point, an individual S is one of the columns.

In order to compute conditional entropy given a set of code points already measured, we will partition the submissions (rows of the matrix) into equivalence sets according to equality in the already-measured code points, so that two submissions are in the same equivalence set if and only if all their corresponding measured code points have the same dimensions. We consider a column of the partitioned matrix not as a single vector, but a set $\mathcal{S}$ of vectors, one for each partition. The entropy of $\mathcal{S}$ is the sum of the entropies of each of its constituent vectors, each scaled by its length.

$$H(\mathcal{S}) = - \sum_{S \in \mathcal{S}} \frac{|S|}{\sum_{T \in \mathcal{S}} |T|} H(S).$$

Such partitions may be further subdivided along additional code points, until all partitions contain elements that are equal in every code point not already measured, at which point the remaining conditional entropy is zero and no further distinctions can be made.

4   Results

We received 1,022 submissions. After removing 6 that had a duplicate cookie, there remained 1,016. The maximum entropy possible, if every submission were distinct, is therefore $\log_2(1016) = 9.989$ bits. Table 1 shows how the submissions broke down with respect to operating system and web browser. Our user sample was drawn from Mechanical Turk users and its composition is not representative of that of the web as a whole.

Table 1. Operating systems and web browsers parsed from user-agent strings.

523	51%	Windows 7	504	50%	Chrome 36
245	24%	Windows 8	241	24%	Firefox 31
80	8%	other Windows (XP or Vista)	155	15%	Chrome 37
72	7%	OS X 10.9	41	4%	other Chrome (6–35 or 38–39)
40	4%	other OS X (10.5–10.8 or 10.10)	31	3%	other Firefox (9–30 or 32–34)
39	4%	GNU/Linux other than Android	27	3%	Safari (4–8)
10	1%	Android	17	2%	Internet Explorer (9–11)
7	1%	iOS			

Considering 4-tuples (OS, OS version, browser, browser version), there were 94 distinct OS+browser combinations, having an entropy of 4.151 bits. There were 48 (5 %) unique combinations, and 28 (3 %) were in a set of size 2. The largest set of identical OS+browser combinations, Chrome 36 on Windows 7, contained 281 elements.

The User-Agent string is more variable than OS+browser, as it may contain additional information such as the browser's minor release number. The User-Agent is also useful as a trivial baseline of fingerprintability. Within the input set of 1,016, there were 175 distinct User-Agent strings, having an entropy of 5.148 bits. There were 116 submissions (11 %) with a unique User-Agent, and another 42 (4 %) that were in a set of size 2. The most common User-Agent appeared 220 times, and was "Mozilla/5.0 (Windows NT 6.1; WOW64) AppleWebKit/537.36 (KHTML, like Gecko) Chrome/36.0.1985.143 Safari/537.36"; i.e., Chrome 36 on 64-bit Windows 7.

Now, on to the fingerprinting attack. There were 444 distinct complete font metric measurements, having an entropy of 7.599 bits. There were 349 submissions (34 %) that were identified uniquely by font metrics, and another 84 (8 %) that were in a set of size 2. The largest anonymity set contained 61 submissions, 50 of which also shared the most common User-Agent (the others were slight variations: 32-bit Windows instead of 64-bit, or a different micro-release of Chrome). The most common User-Agent appeared 220 times; we observed 46 different font fingerprints for it, 29 of them unique.

Two or more fingerprinting techniques may be combined in order to extract more variation. The combination of font metrics and User-Agent, where two fingerprints are considered equal only if their User-Agents are equal and all their corresponding font metrics are equal, leads to 531 distinct submissions and an entropy of 8.058 bits. 440 of those (43 %) are identified uniquely, and another 76 are in a set of size 2. The largest anonymity set contained 51 elements, which happened to be Chrome 36 on Windows 8.1.

Table 2. Code points with the most and least individual entropy.

rank	individual entropy (bits)	code point	name
#1	4.908178	U+20B9	INDIAN RUPEE SIGN
2	4.798824	U+20B8	TENGE SIGN
3	4.698577	U+FBEE	ARABIC LIGATURE YEH WITH HAMZA ABOVE WITH WAW ISOLATED FORM
4	4.698577	U+FBF0	ARABIC LIGATURE YEH WITH HAMZA ABOVE WITH U ISOLATED FORM
5	4.698577	U+FBF2	ARABIC LIGATURE YEH WITH HAMZA ABOVE WITH OE ISOLATED FORM
6	4.698577	U+FBF4	ARABIC LIGATURE YEH WITH HAMZA ABOVE WITH YU ISOLATED FORM
7	4.657576	U+F002	*Private Use Area*
8	4.652798	U+F001	*Private Use Area*
9	4.646632	U+FD3D	ARABIC LIGATURE ALEF WITH FATHATAN ISOLATED FORM
10	4.640043	U+FBF8	ARABIC LIGATURE YEH WITH HAMZA ABOVE WITH E INITIAL FORM
11	4.640043	U+FBFB	ARABIC LIGATURE UIGHUR KIRGHIZ YEH WITH HAMZA ABOVE WITH ALEF MAKSURA INITIAL FORM
⋮	⋮	⋮	
125,766	2.573742	U+202A	LEFT-TO-RIGHT EMBEDDING
125,767	2.573742	U+202B	RIGHT-TO-LEFT EMBEDDING
125,768	2.573742	U+202D	LEFT-TO-RIGHT OVERRIDE
125,769	2.573742	U+202E	RIGHT-TO-LEFT OVERRIDE
125,770	2.481283	U+202C	POP DIRECTIONAL FORMATTING
125,771	2.462760	U+000C	FORM FEED (FF)
125,772	2.462760	U+000D	CARRIAGE RETURN (CR)
125,773	0.156341	U+00AD	SOFT HYPHEN
125,774	0.000000	U+0009	CHARACTER TABULATION
125,775	0.000000	U+000A	LINE FEED (LF)
125,776	0.000000	U+0020	SPACE

Table 2 shows the code points with the greatest and least individual entropy across all submissions. The top of the list includes many code points from the Currency Symbols, Private Use Area, Arabic, and Georgian blocks of Unicode. The Private Use Area block is one in which font designers are free to do what they like; the meanings of the code points is left unspecified. The bottom of the list has mostly whitespace and control characters. Only three code points were identical in every submission, always having a size of 0×0: U+0009 CHARACTER TABULATION, U+000A LINE FEED, and U+0020 SPACE. All three are considered "inter-element whitespace" in HTML [18, Sect. 3.2.4] and do not count as text when they are the only thing appearing in an element. There are two other inter-element whitespace characters, U+000C FORM FEED and U+000D CARRIAGE RETURN; all submissions had them with zero width (except for one oddball Chrome 36 with a width of 1), and some browsers give them zero height while others give them the line height. The only code point with less entropy than a whitespace character was U+00AD SOFT HYPHEN, with 0.156 bits, which apparently renders at 0×0 in all browsers but Internet Explorer, where it has nonzero height.

The full suite of 125,776 code points took a mean time to test of 570 seconds with a standard deviation of 394. The shortest test took 70 seconds and the longest 50 min. Figure 2 shows the distribution of elapsed times. Part of the variance is definitely attributable to differing CPU speeds, and disk latency as seldom-used font files are dredged off of disk. The test likely took longer for users who moved the tab it was running in to the background. The spike at around 500 s is probably explained by the throttling that browsers apply to timers running in background tabs [24, 27]: the program tests 256 code points

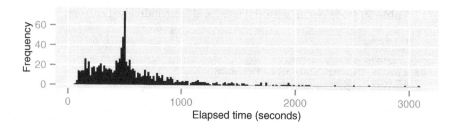

Fig. 2. Time taken to measure all code points in all styles.

in a batch, and if the browser throttles to one batch per second, it takes about $125776/256 = 491.3125$ s to test all batches.

Though our data collection experiment took many minutes, fingerprinting requires only milliseconds. We found a subset of 43 code points that suffices to account for all the variation found in the complete set. The reduced subset is shown in Table 3 and a sample fingerprint using it is in Appendix A. We constructed the subset using a greedy algorithm that first selected the code point having the highest individual entropy, then the one with the highest conditional entropy given that the first code point had already been measured, and so on until only uniform, zero-entropy subsets remained.

It is important to remember that entropy measurement is limited by sample size. For example, we measured 5.148 bits of entropy for the User-Agent from our population of 1,016 browsers, while the Panopticlick experiment [8] measured 10.0 bits from a population of about 470,000. We have measured 7.599 bits of entropy in font metric measurements, out of a theoretical maximum 9.989. Before running this experiment, we had done a preliminary test of 496 browsers (under slightly different conditions: Unicode 6.3.0 and `font-size: 2000 %`) and measured 7.080 bits of entropy out of a theoretical maximum of 8.954. We expect the entropy to continue to grow, though from the limited sample size it is not possible to say whether or where variability will hit a plateau. Figures 4 and 5 in Sect. 6 give a rough idea of how entropy may be expected to increase with sample size.

5   Sources of Variation

We have seen that the dimensions of individual glyphs can vary widely, and that some code points are more variable than others. Figure 3 compares the variation observed in two selected code points. There is variation even within the same browser on the same operating system. In this section we explore the causes of these phenomena.

Text rendering is a subtle and complex part of a web browser. Even in the Latin alphabet, layout is more than simply stacking boxes together: considerations such as ligatures, kerning, and combining characters come into play. Some other writing systems are even more complex, causing browsers to rely on OS-provided libraries for text layout. These libraries, including Pango on

Table 3. Code points with the greatest conditional information gain. These 43 code points suffice to capture all the variation of the full set of 125,776. The conditional entropy on each line measures the variation remaining conditioned on the code points on preceding lines already having been measured. Note that the selected code points do not simply appear in order of increasing rank; at each step the algorithm chooses one, the measurement of which gives the most additional information. Slanted type indicates a Unicode block name when a code point is not individually named. There is nothing magic about the set shown here; many others would do just as well. A sample fingerprint using this code point set appears in Appendix A.

rank	individual entropy (bits)	conditional entropy (bits)	code point	name
#1	4.908178	4.908178	U+20B9	INDIAN RUPEE SIGN
190	4.223916	0.843608	U+2581	LOWER ONE EIGHTH BLOCK
18	4.607439	0.496079	U+20BA	TURKISH LIRA SIGN
933	4.008738	0.264101	U+A73D	LATIN SMALL LETTER AY
6,715	3.794592	0.217025	U+FFFD	REPLACEMENT CHARACTER
2	4.798824	0.173474	U+20B8	TENGE SIGN
194	4.215221	0.120687	U+05C6	HEBREW PUNCTUATION NUN HAFUKHA
676	4.063433	0.075592	U+1E9E	LATIN CAPITAL LETTER SHARP S
5,876	3.892304	0.067049	U+097F	DEVANAGARI LETTER BBA
367	4.137402	0.060762	U+F003	*Private Use Area*
100,605	3.440790	0.045069	U+1CDA	VEDIC TONE DOUBLE SVARITA
90,538	3.517391	0.035899	U+17DD	KHMER SIGN ATTHACAN
6,029	3.879878	0.028690	U+23AE	INTEGRAL EXTENSION
7,176	3.763447	0.028359	U+0D02	MALAYALAM SIGN ANUSVARA
62,371	3.549727	0.025836	U+0B82	TAMIL SIGN ANUSVARA
55,549	3.603737	0.022298	U+115A	HANGUL CHOSEONG KIYEOK-TIKEUT
101,598	3.429199	0.020307	U+2425	SYMBOL FOR DELETE FORM TWO
683	4.063107	0.015840	U+302E	HANGUL SINGLE DOT TONE MARK
55,755	3.598234	0.015405	U+A830	NORTH INDIC FRACTION ONE QUARTER
5,872	3.894021	0.014138	U+2B06	UPWARDS BLACK ARROW
122,695	3.894021	0.012554	U+21E4	LEFTWARDS ARROW TO BAR
297	4.163269	0.011433	U+20BD	RUBLE SIGN
806	4.028184	0.010647	U+2C7B	LATIN LETTER SMALL CAPITAL TURNED E
7,967	3.702500	0.010586	U+20B0	GERMAN PENNY SIGN
3	4.698577	0.010389	U+FBEE	ARABIC LIGATURE YEH WITH HAMZA ABOVE WITH WAW ISOLATED FORM
55,358	3.616671	0.007269	U+F810	*Private Use Area*
56,251	3.583220	0.006550	U+FFFF	*Specials*
102,938	3.382354	0.005807	U+007F	DELETE
33	4.593589	0.005638	U+10A0	GEORGIAN CAPITAL LETTER AN
73,091	3.523493	0.005521	U+1D790	MATHEMATICAL SANS-SERIF BOLD ITALIC CAPITAL ALPHA
96,023	3.486238	0.003839	U+0700	SYRIAC END OF PARAGRAPH
99,164	3.449583	0.003839	U+1950	TAI LE LETTER KA
55,116	3.618169	0.003553	U+3095	HIRAGANA LETTER SMALL KA
54,880	3.620506	0.003194	U+532D	*CJK Unified Ideographs*
125,759	2.831178	0.002712	U+061C	ARABIC LETTER MARK
869	4.020008	0.002712	U+20E3	COMBINING ENCLOSING KEYCAP
6,702	3.796600	0.002712	U+FFF9	INTERLINEAR ANNOTATION ANCHOR
7,849	3.708330	0.001969	U+0218	LATIN CAPITAL LETTER S WITH COMMA BELOW
872	4.018562	0.001969	U+058F	ARMENIAN DRAM SIGN
962	4.004011	0.001969	U+08E4	ARABIC CURLY FATHA
99,577	3.445643	0.001969	U+09B3	*Bengali*
55,774	3.596681	0.001969	U+1C50	OL CHIKI DIGIT ZERO
102,439	3.404409	0.001969	U+2619	REVERSED ROTATED FLORAL HEART BULLET

7.599160 bits total entropy

GNU/Linux, Graphics Device Interface (GDI) or DirectWrite on Windows, and Core Text on Mac OS X, are independent code bases and do not behave identically. Browsers additionally impose their own customizations atop the base text rendering.

The fonts that are installed by default are different on different operating systems. This fact, combined with the differences in layout engines, contribute to a strong per-OS fingerprinting effect. To disguise this effect completely would be difficult, and in Sect. 6 we assume that OS and browser are inherently fingerprintable, and only seek to reduce further fingerprintability.

Even systems having the "same" named fonts installed may be fingerprintable because they have different revisions of the same font. For example, both Debian 7.6 and Ubuntu 14.04 include the DejaVu fonts, but Debian has version 2.33 of the font and Ubuntu has version 2.34. We found that there are detectable differences in some code points rendered using DejaVu, including some which are listed in the DejaVu changelog [1] as having been added or modified in version 2.34.

Different font rendering settings can distinguish end-user systems. We tracked down one-pixel differences in the width of 134 code points, on two systems that were configured very similarly (Tor Browser 4.0-alpha-1 on Debian "jessie", with the same font files and libraries), to different font hinting settings.

Six of the 43 points selected by our distinguishing algorithm and shown in Table 3 are currency symbols. Here they are shown along with their unconditional entropies and ranks:

rank	individual entropy (bits)	code point	name
#1	4.908178	U+20B9	INDIAN RUPEE SIGN
2	4.798824	U+20B8	TENGE SIGN
18	4.607439	U+20BA	TURKISH LIRA SIGN
297	4.163269	U+20BD	RUBLE SIGN
872	4.018562	U+058F	ARMENIAN DRAM SIGN
7,967	3.702500	U+20B0	GERMAN PENNY SIGN

The code points corresponding to the rupee and tenge signs are the two most entropic overall, and other currency symbols form a hotspot of high entropy. Five of those listed (all but U+20B0) are in the top 1 % overall. It may be that relative newness of the glyphs which these code points represent contributes to their variability. The sign for the Kazakhstani tenge was approved by the National Bank of Kazakhstan in 2007 and added to Unicode 5.2 in 2009 [26]. The Indian rupee sign was presented by the Government of India and added to Unicode 6.0 in 2010. The Armenian dram sign was added to Unicode 6.1 in 2012; the Turkish lira sign to Unicode 6.2 in 2012; and the ruble sign to Unicode 7.0 in June, 2014. All these glyphs were newly created symbols, the results of various public design competitions. For comparison, a much older currency symbol, U+20AC EURO SIGN, introduced in Unicode 2.1.2 in 1998, is in the bottom 4 % of variability, at rank #123,190 with 3.301 bits.

The Private Use Area block, U+E000–U+F8FF, has high variability. Font designers are free to give their own meaning to code points in this block, so what glyphs are shown depends heavily on what fonts are available.

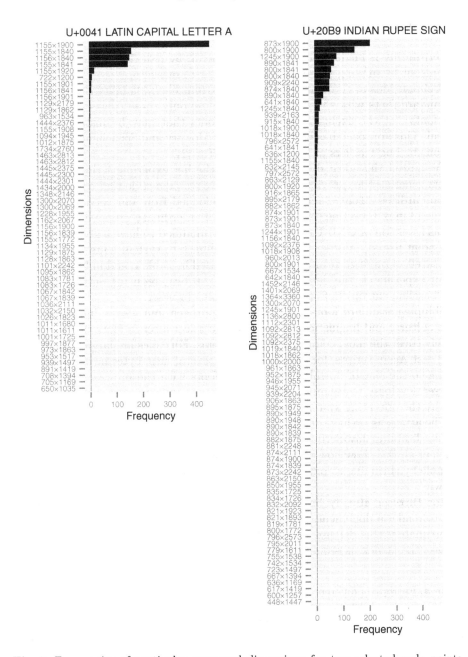

Fig. 3. Frequencies of particular measured dimensions for two selected code points in the default style. Measurements of U+0041 (the letter 'A') had 54 distinct values, 38 of them unique, with an entropy of 2.575 bits. U+20B9 (the currency symbol '₹') took on 87 distinct values, 50 of them unique, with an entropy of 4.288 bits. Note the several occurrences of dimensions that differ by one pixel, for example 1155×1840 and 1156×1840, and a "long tail" of infrequently seen dimensions.

6   Defenses Against Fingerprinting

Fingerprinting is made more difficult, in general, by reducing differences across systems; or by making those differences harder to measure.

A simple idea to eliminate variation due to font file availability is to ship a set of standard fonts with the web browser, and use only those (plus downloadable web fonts), at the exclusion of any other fonts that may be installed on the system. This approach has been suggested by Mowery and Schacham [16, Sect. 5] and on the bug trackers of Mozilla [22] and Tor [21].

We tested this idea: during our data-gathering experiment, in addition to the six generic styles previously mentioned, we tested a style that consisted only of standardized `@font-face` web fonts downloaded from our server. The style included Linux Libertine [13] as an example of an ordinary proportional font, as well as a version of GNU Unifont [6] specially modified to have a glyph for every code point tested, in order to prevent any fallback to system fonts.

The effect on fingerprintability is summarized in Table 4, and in Figs. 4 and 5. In our experiment, the defense saved about 2.6 bits, reducing entropy to near the "baseline entropy" of operating system plus browser.

Shipping standard fonts is a promising approach, but also a difficult one. It takes cultural and linguistic understanding to select a set of fonts that will adequately cover the most common writing systems. Font files are large—those covering east Asian scripts, for example, can be several megabytes uncompressed— adding to the size of downloads. Including fonts with the browser requires the browser developer to assume ongoing maintenance and expertise costs previously held by the operating system developer.

The attack as we have designed it relies on client-side execution of JavaScript. Simply disabling JavaScript is unlikely to be an effective defense, however. Heiderich et al. [11] show how to use CSS to measure the size of DOM elements, for example by shrinking a container through animation and causing its contents to reflow.

Tor Browser already imposes a limit on the number of fonts that can be used to render a document, in order to defend against font enumeration attacks. Unfortunately this defense is ineffective against the attack we have described, because the attack uses only generic font names.

Table 4. Entropy of different variables across the 1,016 submissions. "Standard fonts" uses the simulated defense discussed in Sect. 6. "OS+browser" is the 4-tuple (OS, OS version, browser, browser version) extracted from the User-Agent string, without any other User-Agent information. Lower numbers are better in all columns except "largest set."

Variable	entropy	# distinct	# unique	largest set
System fonts and User-Agent	8.058 bits	531	440	51
System fonts	7.599 bits	444	349	61
Standard fonts and User-Agent	6.128 bits	270	197	181
User-Agent	5.148 bits	175	116	220
Standard fonts	4.957 bits	150	99	203
OS+browser	4.151 bits	94	48	281

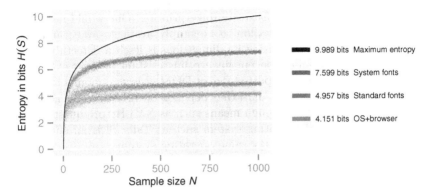

Fig. 4. How entropy in different variables changes for different sample sizes. The black line is $\log_2(N)$, the maximum entropy possible if all browsers were measurably different. For each N, we formed a vector S composed of N individual submissions sampled with replacement from the overall population of 1,016, and computed the entropy of S in different variables. We repeated the sampling ten times for each N. The red line "System fonts" shows the effectiveness of font metric fingerprinting with no countermeasures. The blue line "Standard fonts" shows a simulation of the standard-font defense described in Sect. 6. The difference between the red and blue lines, $7.599 - 4.957 = 2.642$ bits, is the reduction in entropy achieved through the simulation of standardized fonts. The green line "OS+browser" is the entropy of only the OS and browser components of the User-Agent, with other information stripped away; it represents a lower bound on entropy achievable if we assume that different OSes and browsers are intrinsically distinguishable by some means. The entropy of User-Agent is not shown but would be slightly above "Standard fonts," 5.148 bits at the right side (Color figure online).

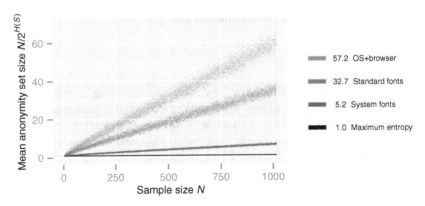

Fig. 5. Another view of the same data. This plot shows $N/2^{H(S)}$, where H is the entropy function. This quantity is the (geometric) mean size of the anonymity set that a random element finds itself a part of. (See Appendix B for a proof.) With maximum entropy, every element would be the sole member of its own anonymity set.

Randomizing the size of onscreen glyphs, or just randomizing the sizes reported to JavaScript, would frustrate fingerprinting. One would need to take care not to allow the randomization to be simply averaged away, and keep in mind that a browser's randomizing its dimensions is itself a detectable feature. FireGloves [2] was a proof-of-concept fingerprint-resistant browser extension for Firefox that randomized the reported size of DOM objects, among other things. FPBlock [12] proposes to track data that depends on HTML element elements, and prevent its exfiltration through means such as XMLHttpRequest.

Using a standardized operating system such as Tails [3] is an effective way to blend in with other users of the same operating system.

7 Future Work

We hope to collaborate with the maintainers of Tor Browser to develop and deploy a patch along the lines of the standard-font defense described in Sect. 6. The Tor Browser maintainers have indicated a willingness to work with us and a ticket tracks development progress [9]. Tor Browser is a good target for deployment of a defense, because it already defends against other, more direct and powerful attacks that are still effective in other browsers, even in private browsing mode.

Canvas fingerprinting could be strengthened using the information gain–based selection technique we have used to refine the set of code points tested. Rather than testing only the 26 letters of the English alphabet, canvas fingerprinting could test carefully selected code points from Unicode.

Our technique could perhaps be strengthened by testing more than one code point at a time, using combinations designed to reveal differences in the handling of ligatures, kerning, combining characters, right-to-left text, and other font features. Font technologies such as OpenType [10] support a large number of features that are being made available to CSS [7].

8 Conclusion

We have presented and evaluated a new web fingerprinting attack based on measuring the onscreen size of font glyphs. We conducted a user experiment to test nearly the entire repertoire of Unicode in various CSS font styles, and then developed a narrow set of code points that can quickly and effectively fingerprint web users. We simulated a standard-font defense against fingerprinting. Font metric–based fingerprinting can supplement other techniques in order to increase their effectiveness.

9 Source Code

Source code for the web experiment and analysis programs is available in a Git repository at https://repo.eecs.berkeley.edu/git-anon/users/fifield/fontfp.git.

Acknowledgments. We thank Mike Perry for suggesting the idea of testing what code points lack font coverage as a means of fingerprinting, and for guidance during development of the test code; Gunes Acar for extensive conversation on this technique and fingerprinting in general; Georg Koppen for comments on a draft of this paper and on the history of font measurement; Alex Kantchelian for advice regarding information gain measurements; Kamil Jozwiak, Benjamin Smedberg, and John Daggett for help regarding fonts in Firefox; and the tor-assistants mailing list for help testing Tor Browser.

A Sample Fingerprint

This is a sample font metric fingerprint using the fast code point testing set of Table 3. The system represented is Tor Browser (Firefox 24.8.0) in Tails 1.1.1 [3]. The fingerprint can be hashed into a single short identifier rather than being stored in the long form shown here.

	default	sans-serif	serif	monospace	cursive	fantasy
U+20B9	636×1200	636×1200	636×1200	602×1200	636×1200	636×1200
U+2581	769×1200	769×1200	769×1200	602×1200	769×1200	769×1200
U+20BA	636×1200	636×1200	636×1200	602×1200	636×1200	636×1200
U+A73D	824×1200	818×1200	824×1200	818×1200	818×1200	818×1200
U+FFFD	1025×1200	1025×1200	1025×1200	602×1200	1025×1200	1025×1200
U+20B8	636×1200	636×1200	636×1200	602×1200	636×1200	636×1200
U+05C6	307×1200	441×1200	307×1200	441×1200	441×1200	441×1200
U+1E9E	829×1200	769×1200	829×1200	769×1200	769×1200	769×1200
U+097F	524×1598	524×1598	524×1598	524×1598	524×1598	524×1598
U+F003	1000×1226	977×1200	1000×1226	1000×1219	977×1200	977×1200
U+1CDA	636×1200	636×1200	636×1200	602×1200	636×1200	636×1200
U+17DD	0×2002	0×2002	0×2002	0×1856	0×2002	0×2002
U+23AE	521×1200	521×1200	521×1200	602×1200	521×1200	521×1200
U+0D02	886×1472	886×1472	886×1472	886×1472	886×1472	886×1472
U+0B82	763×2000	763×2000	763×2000	763×2000	763×2000	763×2000
U+115A	1000×1226	1000×1219	1000×1226	1000×1219	1000×1219	1000×1219
U+2425	500×1200	500×1200	500×1200	500×1200	500×1200	500×1200
U+302E	0×1226	0×1219	0×1226	0×1219	0×1219	0×1219
U+A830	636×1200	636×1200	636×1200	602×1200	636×1200	636×1200
U+2B06	838×1200	838×1200	838×1200	838×1200	838×1200	838×1200
U+21E4	838×1200	838×1200	838×1200	602×1200	838×1200	838×1200
U+20BD	636×1200	636×1200	636×1200	602×1200	636×1200	636×1200
U+2C7B	491×1200	491×1200	491×1200	491×1200	491×1200	491×1200
U+20B0	636×1200	636×1200	636×1200	602×1200	636×1200	636×1200
U+FBEE	500×1200	500×1200	500×1200	500×1200	500×1200	500×1200
U+F810	16×1200	16×1200	16×1200	1000×1230	16×1200	16×1200
U+FFFF	636×1200	636×1200	636×1200	602×1200	636×1200	636×1200
U+007F	600×1200	600×1200	600×1200	602×1200	600×1200	600×1200
U+10A0	723×1200	840×1200	723×1200	840×1200	840×1200	840×1200
U+1D790	774×1200	774×1200	774×1200	774×1200	774×1200	774×1200
U+0700	1000×1200	1000×1200	1000×1200	1000×1200	1000×1200	1000×1200
U+1950	500×1200	500×1200	500×1200	500×1200	500×1200	500×1200
U+3095	1000×1200	1000×1200	1000×1200	1000×1200	1000×1200	1000×1200
U+532D	16×1200	16×1200	16×1200	1000×1230	16×1200	16×1200
U+061C	636×1200	636×1200	636×1200	602×1200	636×1200	636×1200
U+20E3	0×1200	0×1200	0×1200	0×1200	0×1200	0×1200
U+FFF9	0×1200	0×1200	0×1200	602×1200	0×1200	0×1200
U+0218	685×1200	635×1200	685×1200	602×1200	635×1200	635×1200
U+058F	636×1200	636×1200	636×1200	602×1200	636×1200	636×1200
U+08E4	636×1200	636×1200	636×1200	602×1200	636×1200	636×1200
U+09B3	636×1200	636×1200	636×1200	602×1200	636×1200	636×1200
U+1C50	500×1200	500×1200	500×1200	500×1200	500×1200	500×1200
U+2619	896×1200	896×1200	896×1200	602×1200	896×1200	896×1200

B   Mean Anonymity Set Size from Entropy

This appendix contains a proof of the claim in Fig. 5, that an entropy measurement implies a mean anonymity set size. Refer to Sect. 3 for notation.

Claim. Let S be a vector of categorical values with N elements and k distinct values $v_1, \ldots, v_k$. For $i \in 1, \ldots, k$, let c_i signify the number of times v_i appears in S: $P_S(v_i) = c_i/N$. Then the quantity $N/2^{H(S)}$, shown in Fig. 5, is $\left(\prod_{i=1}^{k} c_i^{c_i}\right)^{\frac{1}{N}}$; that is, the geometric mean of the vector that results from replacing each element of S with the number of times that element appears (a vector where each c_i appears c_i times).

Proof.

$$N/2^{H(S)}$$

$$= N/2^{\left(-\sum_{i=1}^{k} P_S(v_i) \log_2 P_S(v_i)\right)}$$

$$= N \cdot 2^{\left(\sum_{i=1}^{k} \frac{c_i}{N} \log_2 \frac{c_i}{N}\right)}$$

$$= N \prod_{i=1}^{k} 2^{\left(\frac{c_i}{N} \log_2 \frac{c_i}{N}\right)}$$

$$= N \prod_{i=1}^{k} \left(\frac{c_i}{N}\right)^{\frac{c_i}{N}} = N \left(\prod_{i=1}^{k} \frac{c_i^{c_i}}{N^{c_i}}\right)^{\frac{1}{N}}$$

Because $\sum_{i=1}^{k} c_i = N$, $\prod_{i=1}^{k} N^{c_i} = N^N$, and so

$$N \left(\prod_{i=1}^{k} \frac{c_i^{c_i}}{N^{c_i}}\right)^{\frac{1}{N}} = N \left(\frac{\prod_{i=1}^{k} c_i^{c_i}}{N^N}\right)^{\frac{1}{N}}$$

$$= N \frac{\left(\prod_{i=1}^{k} c_i^{c_i}\right)^{\frac{1}{N}}}{N} = \left(\prod_{i=1}^{k} c_i^{c_i}\right)^{\frac{1}{N}}.$$

$\square$

References

1. DejaVu fonts full changelog (version 2.34). http://dejavu-fonts.org/wiki/Full_changelog
2. FireGloves. http://fingerprint.pet-portal.eu/?menu=6
3. Tails. https://tails.boum.org/
4. Acar, G., Eubank, C., Englehardt, S., Juarez, M., Narayanan, A., Diaz, C.: The Web never forgets: persistent tracking mechanisms in the wild. In: Proceedings of the 21st ACM conference on Computer and Communications Security (CCS 2014), November 2014. https://securehomes.esat.kuleuven.be/gacar/persistent/the_web_never_forgets.pdf

5. Acar, G., Juarez, M., Nikiforakis, N., Diaz, C., Gürses, S., Piessens, F., Preneel, B.: FPDetective: dusting the web for fingerprinters. In: Proceedings of the 20th ACM conference on Computer and Communications Security (CCS 2013), November 2013. https://www.cosic.esat.kuleuven.be/publications/article-2334.pdf
6. Czyborra, R.: GNU Unifont. http://unifoundry.com/unifont.html
7. Daggett, J.: CSS fonts module level 3. Candidate recommendation, W3C, October 2013. http://www.w3.org/TR/2013/CR-css-fonts-3-20131003/
8. Eckersley, P.: How unique is your web browser? In: Proceedings of the 10th Privacy Enhancing Technologies Symposium, pp. 1–18, July 2010. https://panopticlick.eff.org/browser-uniqueness.pdf
9. Fifield, D.: #13313: Enable bundled fonts in Tor Browser, October 2014. https://trac.torproject.org/projects/tor/ticket/13313
10. FontShop International: OpenType user guide, April 2012. https://www.fontfont.com/staticcontent/downloads/FF_OT_User_Guide.pdf
11. Heiderich, M., Niemietz, M., Schuster, F., Holz, T., Schwenk, J.: Scriptless attacks: Stealing the pie without touching the sill. In: Proceedings of the 2012 ACM Conference on Computer and Communications Security, CCS 2012, pp. 760–771. ACM, New York, NY, USA (2012). http://www.nds.rub.de/media/emma/veroeffentlichungen/2012/08/16/scriptlessAttacks-ccs2012.pdf
12. Kim, D.: Detection and prevention of web-based device fingerprinting. In: 2014 IEEE Symposium on Security and Privacy, May 2014. http://www.cs.utexas.edu/dkim/papers/webfingerprint-poster_sp14.pdf
13. Libertine Open Fonts Project: Linux Libertine. http://www.linuxlibertine.org/
14. Lie, H.W., Çelik, T., Bos, B., Hickson, I.: Cascading style sheets level 2 revision 1 (CSS 2.1) specification. W3C recommendation, W3C, June 2011. http://www.w3.org/TR/2011/REC-CSS2-20110607
15. Mowery, K., Bogenreif, D., Yilek, S., Shacham, H.: Fingerprinting information in JavaScript implementations. In: Wang, H. (ed.) Proceedings of W2SP 2011. IEEE Computer Society, May 2011. https://cseweb.ucsd.edu/hovav/dist/jspriv.pdf
16. Mowery, K., Shacham, H.: Pixel perfect: Fingerprinting canvas in HTML5. In: Fredrikson, M. (ed.) Proceedings of W2SP 2012. IEEE Computer Society, May 2012. https://cseweb.ucsd.edu/hovav/dist/canvas.pdf
17. Mulazzani, M., Reschl, P., Huber, M., Leithner, M., Schrittwieser, S., Weippl, E.: Fast and reliable browser identification with javascript engine fingerprinting. In: Web 2.0 Workshop on Security and Privacy (W2SP), May 2013. http://www.sba-research.org/wp-content/uploads/publications/jsfingerprinting.pdf
18. Navara, E.D., Berjon, R., Leithead, T., O'Connor, E., Pfeiffer, S., Faulkner, S.: HTML5. Candidate recommendation, W3C, February 2014. http://www.w3.org/TR/2014/CR-html5-20140731/
19. Nikiforakis, N., Kapravelos, A., Joosen, W., Kruegel, C., Piessens, F., Vigna, G.: Cookieless monster: exploring the ecosystem of web-based device fingerprinting. In: Proceedings of the 2013 IEEE Symposium on Security and Privacy, pp. 541–555. SP 2013, IEEE Computer Society, Washington, DC, USA (2013). https://seclab.cs.ucsb.edu/media/uploads/papers/sp2013_cookieless.pdf
20. Patel, L.: JavaScript/CSS font detector, March 2007. http://www.lalit.org/lab/javascript-css-font-detect/
21. Perry, M.: #2872: Limit the fonts available in TorBrowser, April 2011. https://trac.torproject.org/projects/tor/ticket/2872
22. Perry, M.: Bug 732096 - Add a preference to prevent local font enumeration, comment 18, March 2012. https://bugzilla.mozilla.org/show_bug.cgi?id=732096#c18

23. Perry, M., Clark, E., Murdoch, S.: The design and implementation of the Tor Browser. Technocal report, Mar 2013. https://www.torproject.org/projects/torbrowser/design/

24. Russell, K.: Issue 66078: Background tabs with webgl slow down browser due to missing flow control, December 2010. https://code.google.com/p/chromium/issues/detail?id=66078

25. Unicode Inc: Blocks (Unicode character database), April 2014. http://www.unicode.org/Public/7.0.0/ucd/Blocks.txt

26. Unicode Inc: DerivedAge (Unicode character database), May 2014. http://www.unicode.org/Public/7.0.0/ucd/DerivedAge.txt

27. Zbarsky, B.: Bug 633421 - Clamp setTimeout/setInterval to something higher than 10ms in inactive tabs, February 2011. https://bugzilla.mozilla.org/show_bug.cgi?id=633421

Cryptography in the Cloud

Sorting and Searching Behind the Curtain

Foteini Baldimtsi[1,2] and Olga Ohrimenko[3(✉)]

[1] Boston University, Boston, USA
foteini@bu.edu
[2] University of Athens, Athens, Greece
[3] Microsoft Research, Cambridge, UK
oohrim@microsoft.com

Abstract. We propose a framework where a user can outsource his data to a cloud server in an encrypted form and then request the server to perform computations on this data and sort the result. Sorting is achieved via a novel protocol where the server is assisted by a secure coprocessor that is required to have only minimal computational and memory resources. The server and the coprocessor are assumed to be honest but curious, i.e., they honestly follow the protocol but are interested in learning more about the user data. We refer to the new protocol as *private outsourced sorting* since it guarantees that neither the server nor the coprocessor learn anything about user data as long as they are non-colluding. We formally define private outsourced sorting and present an efficient construction that is based on an encryption scheme with semi-homomorphic properties.

As an application of our private sort we present MRSE: the first scheme for outsourced search over encrypted data that efficiently answers multi-term queries with the result ranked using frequency of query terms in the data, while maintaining data privacy.

Keywords: Private sort · Privacy in the cloud · Ranked search on encrypted data

1 Introduction

Consider the following scenario: Mr. Smith owns an array of data elements A that he outsources to an honest-but-curious untrusted party, Brad. Mr. Smith then asks Brad to perform various linear operations on the elements of A resulting in an array B and then, sort B and return the sorted result, B_{sorted}, back to him. However, Mr. Smith does not trust Brad and wishes to keep A, B and B_{sorted} secret. Thus, he decides to encrypt every element of A using a public key semantically secure cryptosystem. To let Brad perform computations on the encrypted array A, Mr. Smith can simply use a semi-homomorphic cryptosystem that supports addition of ciphertexts. Hence, the remaining question is: how is Brad going to sort the encrypted B?

© International Financial Cryptography Association 2015
R. Böhme and T. Okamoto (Eds.): FC 2015, LNCS 8975, pp. 127–146, 2015.
DOI: 10.1007/978-3-662-47854-7_8

If the array A was encrypted under a fully homomorphic encryption scheme (FHE) [14,28], then Brad could perform sorting himself. FHE allows one to perform both homomorphic addition and multiplication, thus, Brad could simply translate a sorting network into a circuit and apply it to B. Unfortunately, all known FHE schemes are still too far away from being practical for real life applications and cannot be implemented by Brad. Hence, Brad suggests to Mr. Smith to use order preserving encryption (OPE) [7] for A since this makes sorting a trivial task for him. Mr. Smith gets excited but soon realizes that an encryption scheme that supports homomorphic addition and comparison of ciphertexts is not secure even against a ciphertext attack (as shown by Rivest *et al.* [26]). If Mr. Smith just wanted Brad to sort A, then OPE would be sufficient but it is crucial to Mr. Smith that Brad can also perform certain operations on A. Moreover, allowing Brad to learn the relative order of elements in A violates owner's privacy requirements.

Mr. Smith is determined to design a protocol for *private outsourced sorting* that will be efficient, preserve his data privacy and allow Brad to perform certain computations on his data. Thus he decides to encrypt his data with a semi-homomorphic cryptosystem and add another party to the model: Angelina. Angelina is given the decryption key and her sole role is to help Brad with sorting. Mr. Smith assumes that Brad and Angelina are not colluding with each other but both are interested in learning more about his data. Hence, he extends his privacy requirements as follows: after Brad's and Angelina's interaction Brad receives B_{sorted} which is the sorting of an encrypted B, while neither of them learns anything about the plaintext values of B nor B_{sorted}. It follows from the privacy requirement that Angelina never sees an encryption of neither B nor B_{sorted}, otherwise she could trivially decrypt them.

The Brad and Angelina model is often encountered in reality. We can see Brad as the provider of cloud storage and computation (i.e., cloud server) who is trusted to perform operations on clients' data but at the same time may be curious to learn something about them. Angelina models a *secure coprocessor* (e.g., the IBM PCIe[1] or the Freescale C29x[2]) that resides in the cloud server and is invoked only to perform relatively small computations. Secure coprocessors provide isolated execution environments, which is important for our model since it ensures that the two parties are separated. We note that the assumption of non-collusion is justified since the cloud provider and secure coprocessor usually are supplied by different companies and, hence, have also commercial interests not to collude.

In this paper, **we present *private outsourced sort* executed by two parties such that neither of them learns anything about the data involved**. This setting is perfect for letting one use not only storage but also computing services of the cloud environment without sacrificing privacy. We give the formal definition and present an efficient construction that implements private outsourced sort by relying only on additive homomorphic properties of an

---

[1] http://www-03.ibm.com/security/cryptocards/pciecc/overview.shtml.

[2] http://www.freescale.com/webapp/sps/site/prod_summary.jsp?code=C29x.

encryption scheme. Sorting is, arguably, one of the most common and well studied computations [18] over data in the "before cloud era" which indicates that it will be of interest as an outsourced computation to the cloud. Our model is of particular interest since it does not only allow the cloud server to privately and efficiently sort encrypted data, but also allows certain computations on the data. Hence, it can be a useful tool for answering sophisticated queries on an encrypted database and, for example, returning top results satisfying the query.

The main component of most of the sorting algorithms is the pairwise comparison of elements. A few methods for comparison of encrypted data have been proposed in the literature, where the most well known ones either depend on homomorphic encryption or on garbled circuits. The protocol by Veugen [29] depends on homomorphic encryption and presents a private comparison protocol where the cloud server learns the result of the comparison, while the coprocessor learns nothing. To use a garbled circuits solution, as Bost *et al.* [8] suggest, one could use the comparison circuit by Kolesnikov *et al.* [19] in combination with the efficient garbled circuit implementation of Bellare *et al.* [6] and an oblivious transfer protocol like the one due to Asharov *et al.* [3]. However, this solution requires the parties to generate a fresh circuit for each pairwise comparison. For our construction we choose to use homomorphic encryption techniques due to its simplicity and efficiency.

Outsourced Ranked Text Search. We give a concrete application of our new sorting framework through the problem of outsourcing *ranked search* over encrypted data to the cloud. The goal is to rank the result according to its relevance to the query by using the standard frequency (tf) and inverse document frequency (idf) method [30]. In order to perform a ranked search of this type efficiently, a *search index* is created in advance where an idf of every term in every document in the collection is stored. In the cloud based information retrieval setting, where the cloud server is not trusted, the client outsources the search index to the server in an encrypted format and then submits keyword search queries to the server. If we only allow *single term* queries then a solution is relatively easy: the client creates the search index where each term is stored with a list of documents sorted by relevance. Then, he encrypts the index using some symmetric searchable encryption scheme (SSE) and outsources it to the server. When the client wants to search for a term, he submits a *trapdoor* to the server, who locates the term in the index and returns the encrypted list of documents to the user.

However, precomputing sorted results becomes infeasible and not scalable when the system is required to handle *multi-term* queries, since the result depends on all the keywords in the query which is not known in advance. Hence, the client has to upload the search index where frequencies (idfs) for every term are ordered according to document identifiers. When querying the system, the client creates a trapdoor for every term in the query and submits them to the server. The server then locates the corresponding rows in the SSE encrypted search index and is left with two tasks: (a) add the located rows of encrypted

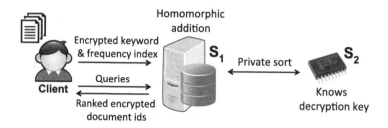

Fig. 1. Ranked multi-keyword searchable encryption (MRSE) model.

frequencies together in order to compute the score of every document w.r.t. the query, and (b) sort the resulting list of encrypted scores.

It is easy to see that our *private outsourced sorting* is the perfect tool for the scenario described above. The client can encrypt the keyword frequencies using a semi-homomorphic encryption scheme (e.g., Paillier [25]) and then outsource them to the cloud server, S_1. S_1 is equipped with a secure coprocessor, S_2, who stores the decryption key. Our mechanism allows the cloud server to first add the encrypted frequencies of the keywords in the query and then sort them with the help of S_2. We refer to our proposed construction as Multi-keyword Ranked Searchable Encryption (MRSE) and give its overview in Fig. 1.

Our contributions are summarized below:

- Formally define *private outsourced sorting* (Definition 1) and present a simulation based privacy definition (Definition 2).
- We present an efficient implementation of private outsourced sorting in Sect. 3.2 that requires $O(N(\log N)^2)$ time for sorting, where N is the total number of elements to be sorted.
- In Sect. 4.1 we present MRSE, the first system that efficiently supports multi-keyword search and computes a ranked result based on word frequencies in a secure and private way.

2   Preliminaries

In Table 1 we summarize the notation used throughout the paper. Then, we present the building blocks used for our construction.

2.1   Homomorphic Cryptosystem Protocols

Paillier Cryptosystem. The Paillier cryptosystem [25] is a semantically secure public key encryption scheme based on the Decisional Composite Residuosity assumption. We use $[m]$ to denote an encryption of a message under Paillier cryptosystem with a public, secret key pair $K_P = (PK_P, SK_P)$. Paillier cryptosystem is homomorphically additive, that is, $[m_1] \cdot [m_2] = [m_1 + m_2]$.

Table 1. Notation.

Symbol	Meaning
k	Security parameter
$K_P = (PK_P, SK_P)$	Paillier public/secret keys
$K_{QR} = (PK_{QR}, SK_{QR})$	QR public/secret keys
$[m], [[m]], \|m\|$	m encrypted using first and second layers of Paillier, and QR
$Gen_{StE}, E_{StE}, SK_{StE}$	StE keygen, encr. and secret key
$\mathbf{D} = \{D_1, \ldots, D_N\}$	Document collection of size N
M	Number of unique terms/keywords in $\mathbf{D}$
t, T	Term/keyword and its StE trapdoor
$q = (t_1, \ldots, t_{l_q})$	Query of l_q terms
F	Frequency table
I	Secure search index

Generalized Paillier. Our construction relies on the generalization of the Paillier cryptosystem introduced by Damgård and Jurik [13] along with its special property that allows to doubly encrypt messages and use the additive homomorphism of the inner encryption layer under the same secret key [1,20]. By $[m]$ we denote an encryption of m using the first layer (basic Paillier encryption) and by $[[m]]$ we denote encryption of m using the second layer.

The extension allows a ciphertext of the first layer to be treated as a plaintext at the second layer. Moreover, the nested encryption preserves the structure over inner ciphertexts and allows one to manipulate it as follows [1]:

$$[[m_1]]^{[m_2]} = [[m_1][m_2]] = [[m_1 + m_2]].$$

We note that this is the only homomorphic property that our protocols rely on (i.e., we do not require support for ciphertext multiplication).

Private Selection of Encrypted Data. Additive homomorphism and generalized Paillier encryption can be used to select one of two plaintexts without revealing which one was picked. We adopt this operation from [1] (with several modifications) and define $[[c]] \leftarrow \mathsf{EncSelect}(PK_P, SK_P, [a], [b], [[v]]^3)$ where (PK_P, SK_P) is a pair of Paillier public, secret keys as before, a and b are the two plaintext values and v is a bit that indicates whether a or b should be returned. If v is 0, $\mathsf{EncSelect}$ returns a re-encryption of a, otherwise it returns a re-encryption of b. Hence, $\mathsf{EncSelect}$ imitates the computation $c = (1 - v) \times a + v \times b$ but over ciphertexts as follows:

$$\mathsf{EncSelect}\,([a], [b], [[v]]) = ([[1]][[v]]^{-1})^{[a]}[[v]]^{[b]} = [[(1 - v)[a] + v[b]]] = [[c]].$$

---

[3] We note that v has to be encrypted using the second layer of Paillier in order to use the homomorphic properties of the cryptosystem.

Table 2. $[x] \leftarrow \mathsf{StripEnc}(\mathsf{PK_P}, \mathsf{SK_P}, [\![x]\!])$: Interactive protocol between S_1 and S_2 for stripping off one layer of Paillier encryption.

$S_1(\mathsf{PK_P}, [\![x]\!])$		$S_2(\mathsf{PK_P}, \mathsf{SK_P})$
pick $r \in \{0,1\}^{\ell+1}$		
$[\![x+r]\!] := [\![x]\!]^{[r]}$	$\xrightarrow{[\![x+r]\!]}$	
		decrypt $[\![x+r]\!]$
	$\xleftarrow{[x+r]}$	encrypt $[x+r]$
$[x] := [x+r][r]^{-1}$		

Note that the result c is doubly encrypted. For our purposes we require the output values to be encrypted using the first layer of Paillier encryption only. Simply sending $[\![c]\!]$ for re-encryption would be insecure since S_2 would learn the value of c. Instead, we propose a protocol StripEnc, where S_1 randomizes the encryption of the value x he wants S_2 to re-encrypt, receives the re-encryption and removes the randomization. Hence, when S_2 decrypts the element he receives a random value and learns nothing about x. The complete protocol StripEnc is presented in Table 2 where we rely on the homomorphic properties of layered Paillier encryption.

We analyze the privacy guarantees of StripEnc and EncSelect in the full version of the paper [4] and show that each primitive can be simulated due to semantic properties of Paillier encryption.

Private Comparison of Encrypted Data. In this work, we are interested in the following private comparison setting: the first server S_1 owns two encrypted numbers $[a]$ and $[b]$ and the second server S_2 owns the secret key $\mathsf{SK_P}$. The goal of the protocol is for S_1 to obtain the encryption of the relation between a and b without learning neither the actual numbers nor the comparison result v, where $v = 1$ if $a \geq b$ and $v = 0$, otherwise. We also require S_2 to learn nothing about the relation between a and b but just help S_1 to obtain an encryption of the comparison result. For this purpose, we adapt the protocol of Bost et al. [8] and define $[\![v]\!] \leftarrow \mathsf{EncCompare}(\mathsf{PK_P}, \mathsf{SK_P}, \mathsf{PK_{QR}}, \mathsf{SK_{QR}}, [a], [b])$, an interactive comparison protocol between S_1 and S_2 that gives the above security guarantees.

The protocol is given in Table 3 and it proceeds as follows. S_2 knows the encryption and decryption keys for both Paillier and QR, $(\mathsf{PK_P}, \mathsf{SK_P}, \mathsf{PK_{QR}}, \mathsf{SK_{QR}})$, while S_1 knows the corresponding public keys $(\mathsf{PK_P}, \mathsf{PK_{QR}})$ and two values a and b encrypted under Paillier's scheme. S_1 first computes $[z] = [a] \cdot [b]^{-1} \cdot [2^\ell] \bmod n^2$ and blinds it with a random value r before sending it to S_2 (or else S_2 would learn the comparison result). S_2 computes $\tilde{d} = d \bmod 2^\ell$, S_1 similarly computes $\tilde{r} = r \bmod 2^\ell$ and they engage in a private input comparison protocol (we can use the DGK protocol [12] as suggested by Bost et al. [8]) that compares $\tilde{d}$ and $\tilde{r}$. At the end of this protocol, S_1 receives an encrypted bit λ that shows the relation between $\tilde{d}$ and $\tilde{r}$

Table 3. $\llbracket v \rrbracket \leftarrow$ EncCompare($PK_P, SK_P, PK_{QR}, SK_{QR}, [a], [b]$): Interactive Private Comparison between two parties S_1 and S_2 such that only S_1 learns an encryption of the comparison bit $\llbracket v \rrbracket$. For simplicity, QR keys are omitted when EncCompare is called from private sort protocol in Table 5. This protocol is an adaptation of the comparison protocol from [8].

$S_1(PK_P, PK_{QR}, [a], [b])$	$S_2(PK_P, SK_P, PK_{QR}, SK_{QR})$

$[z] := [2^\ell] \cdot [a] \cdot [b]^{-1} \bmod n^2$
pick $r \in \{0, 1\}^{\ell+k}$.
$[d] := [z] \cdot [r] \bmod n^2$ $\qquad \xrightarrow{[d]}$

$\qquad\qquad\qquad\qquad\qquad\qquad$ decrypt $[d]$
$\tilde{r} := r \bmod 2^\ell$ $\qquad\qquad\qquad\qquad\quad$ $\tilde{d} := d \bmod 2^\ell$

$\qquad\qquad \xrightarrow{\ \|\lambda\| \ \leftarrow\ \text{Compare } \tilde{r}, \tilde{d}\ }$

$\qquad\qquad \xleftarrow{\ \|d_\ell\| \ }$ $\qquad\qquad$ encrypt d_ℓ

encrypt r_ℓ
$\|v\| := \|d_\ell\| \cdot \|r_\ell\| \cdot \|\lambda\|$
$\qquad \xleftarrow{\ \llbracket v \rrbracket \ \leftarrow\ \text{ReEncryptBit}(PK_P, SK_P, PK_{QR}, SK_{QR}, \|v\|)\ }$

$(\lambda = 1 \Leftrightarrow \tilde{d} < \tilde{r})$. The output λ from the private input comparison protocol is encrypted using QR scheme. Finally, S_1 computes the most significant bit of z, denoted by v, by computing $\|v\| = \|d_\ell\| \cdot \|r_\ell\| \cdot \|\lambda\|$. The important security property of this protocol is that S_1 never sees the comparison result in the clear and S_2 never receives an encryption of it.

The above protocol returns as a result bit v encrypted using QR cryptosystem, $\|v\|$, for which only S_2 knows the secret key SK_{QR}. However, for the purpose of our sorting task (where we require private comparison and a call to EncSelect) S_1 needs to know this bit encrypted using second layer of generalized Paillier cryptosystem, that is, $\llbracket v \rrbracket$. Below we introduce $\llbracket v \rrbracket \leftarrow$ ReEncryptBit($PK_P, SK_P,$ $PK_{QR}, SK_{QR}, \|v\|$) protocol to securely re-encrypt the bit v such that neither S_1 nor S_2 learns its value. The privacy guarantees of the complete EncCompare can be found in the full version of the paper [4].

The ReEncryptBit protocol consists of the following steps:

- S_1 picks a random bit r.
- S_1 computes two values $\|s_r\| := \|v\| \cdot \|0\|$ and $\|s_{1-r}\| := \|v\| \cdot \|1\|$ which are equal to $v \oplus 0$ and $v \oplus 1$, respectively.
- S_1 sends $\|s_0\|$ and $\|s_1\|$ to S_2 (i.e., using r as a secret permutation).
- S_2 decrypts them (always gets a "0" and a "1" in an order that is independent of v), re-encrypts them using second layer of Paillier scheme and sends them back to S_1 in the same order as he received them.
- Given that S_1 knows the permutation bit r, he outputs $\llbracket s_r \rrbracket$ which corresponds to the relation between a and b.

2.2 Searchable Encryption

Symmetric searchable encryption (SSE) allows a user that has in his possession a collection of documents $\mathbf{D} = \{D_1, \ldots, D_N\}$ to compute a "secure search
index", I, over these documents and then outsource the index to the server. The
server should be able to search on I without learning anything about the actual
collection $\mathbf{D}$. In traditional definitions of searchable encryption the user gives as
input the actual document collection and his SSE secret key and receives back
a secure index I and a set of ciphertexts [11]. Here we consider a generalized
notion of SSE called: *structured encryption* (StE), that was given by Chase and
Kamara [10] and allows SSE for arbitrarily-structured data. In particular, a data
type $\mathcal{T}$ is defined by a universe $\mathcal{U} = \{\mathcal{U}_k\}_{k \in \mathbb{Z}}$ and an operation $\mathtt{Query}: \mathcal{U} \times \mathcal{Q} \to \mathcal{R}$
with $\mathcal{Q} = \{\mathcal{Q}_k\}_{k \in \mathbb{N}}$ being the query space and $\mathcal{R} = \{\mathcal{R}_k\}_{k \in \mathbb{N}}$ being the response
space, where k is the security parameter. The StE scheme then consists of the
following algorithms:

$\mathsf{SK_{StE}} \leftarrow Gen_{\mathsf{StE}}(1^k)$ run by the owner of the data. The output is owner's secret
    key $\mathsf{SK_{StE}}$ for the security parameter k.
$I \leftarrow E_{\mathsf{StE}}(\mathsf{SK_{StE}}, \delta)$ run by the owner to encrypt a data structure δ of type $\mathcal{T}$,
    under his secret key $\mathsf{SK_{StE}}$. The output is the secure index (encrypted data
    structure) I sent to the server.
$T \leftarrow Trpdr(\mathsf{SK_{StE}}, t)$ is a deterministic algorithm run by the owner to generate
    a trapdoor T for a query $t \in \mathcal{Q}$. It outputs either T or the failure symbol $\perp$.
$a \leftarrow Search(I, T)$ is run by the server to perform a search for a trapdoor T and
    outputs an answer $a \in \mathcal{R}$.

The construction of ranked search discussed in Sect. 4.2 uses a dictionary data
type for StE. In particular, the keys (or queries) of a dictionary are keywords
of the document collection $\mathbf{D}$. The value (or a response) that corresponds to a
particular keyword in the dictionary is a sequence of pairs of document ids and
encrypted frequency scores.

2.3 Text Search and Ranking

We represent a document collection using an inverted index [30]. Each unique
term, or keyword, t appearing in the collection is associated with a set of document ids J_t, where each document id $d \in J_t$ corresponds to a document containing t. We refer to J_t as a posting list of term t.

We consider free text queries [21]. A free text query q is a set of terms and
the result to q is a set of documents J_q that contain at least one of the terms in
q. We can define J_q in terms of posting lists as $J_q = \bigcup_{\forall t \in q} J_t$.

In this paper we use a common ranking of search results based on frequency
of query terms in each document and the collection, namely tf-idf [30]. Let N be
the number of documents in the collection and cf_t be the frequency of term t in
the collection then inverse document frequency, idf, is defined as: $\mathrm{idf}_t = \log \frac{N}{\mathrm{cf}_t}$.
Document frequency of term t in document d is defined as: $\mathrm{tf\text{-}idf}_{t,d} = \mathrm{tf}_{t,d} \times \mathrm{idf}_t$,

where $\text{tf}_{t,d}$ is frequency of term t in document d. If a document d does not contain t, $\text{tf-idf}_{t,d} = 0$.

Given a free text query q for each document $d \in J_q$ a score based on frequencies is computed as $\text{score}(q, d) = \sum_{t \in q} \text{tf-idf}_{t,d}$. Documents in J_q can then be sorted according to the output of the score function. We use F to denote the frequency table of all $\text{tf-idf}_{t,d}$ entries including zero entries.

3 Private Sort

In this section we define a new tool for secure outsourced computation: a *private sort*, or private outsourced sort, protocol and present its efficient construction.

3.1 Model

Private sort[4] is executed between two parties S_1 and S_2 as follows. S_1 has an array A encrypted using a secret key SK that is known to S_2 but not S_1. The goal of private sort is for S_1 to obtain B, a re-encryption of a sorted array A, such that neither S_1 nor S_2 learn anything about the plaintext values of A (e.g., their initial order, frequency of the values) while running the protocol. We consider the honest-but-curious model: our servers honestly follow the protocol but might try to analyze the protocol transcript to infer more information about the data in the array. We formally capture the definition of private sort below.

Definition 1 *(EncSort). An encrypted sorting functionality* $\mathsf{EncSort}(\mathsf{PK}, \mathsf{SK}, A)$ *takes as input a public/secret key pair* (PK,SK) *of a semantically secure cryptosystem* $\{Gen_{\mathsf{SS}}, E_{\mathsf{SS}}, D_{\mathsf{SS}}\}$, *and an array* $A = [E_{\mathsf{SS}}(v_i)]_{i \in \{1,N\}}$ *of* N *elements where each element is encrypted individually using* PK. *Let* π *be a permutation of indices 1 to* N *that corresponds to the indices of* A's *elements sorted using its unencrypted values* v_i. *Then, the output of* EncSort *is an array* $B = [E_{\mathsf{SS}}(v'_j)]_{j \in \{1,N\}}$ *where* $v'_j = v_{\pi(i)}$ *and* $i \in \{1, N\}$.

In the definition above, though $v'_j = v_{\pi(i)}$, it holds with very high probability that $E_{\mathsf{SS}}(v'_j) \neq E_{\mathsf{SS}}(v_{\pi(i)})$ since fresh randomness is used during re-encryption. We note that Definition 1 can be easily expanded to take as input an array A that stores (key, value) pairs and the output is required to be sorted using values.

We describe the privacy property of the encrypted sorting functionality stated above using the paradigm for defining privacy in the semi-honest model given by Goldreich [15].

Definition 2 *(EncSort Privacy). Let* Π_{EncSort} *be a two party protocol for computing* EncSort *functionality.* S_1 *takes as input* (PK, A) *and* S_2 *takes as input* (PK, SK). *When* Π_{EncSort} *terminates* S_1 *receives the output* B *of* EncSort. *Let*

---

[4] We note that one should not confuse our problem with Multi-Party Computation protocols for sorting [16,17], where every party has an input array and the goal is to output to every participating party the sorting of all inputs combined.

$\text{VIEW}_{S_i}^{\Pi_{\text{EncSort}}}$ (PK, SK, A) *be all the messages that S_i receives while running the protocol on inputs* PK, SK, A *and* $\text{OUTPUT}^{\Pi_{\text{EncSort}}}$ *be the output of the protocol received by S_1.*

We say that Π_{EncSort} privately computes EncSort, *i.e.,* Π_{EncSort} *is a private outsourced sort, if there exists a pair of probabilistic polynomial time (PPT) simulators* $(\text{Sim}_{S_1}, \text{Sim}_{S_2})$ *such that*

(1) $(\text{Sim}_{S_2}(\text{PK}, A), \text{EncSort}(\text{PK}, \text{SK}, A)) \approx$

$$(\text{VIEW}_{S_1}^{\Pi_{\text{EncSort}}}(\text{PK}, \text{SK}, A), \text{OUTPUT}^{\Pi_{\text{EncSort}}}(\text{PK}, \text{SK}, A));$$

(2) $\text{Sim}_{S_1}(\text{PK}, \text{SK}, N) \approx \text{VIEW}_{S_2}^{\Pi_{\text{EncSort}}}(\text{PK}, \text{SK}, A),$

where N is the size of the array A and $\approx$ denotes computational indistinguishability for all tuples PK, SK, A.

The intuition behind the privacy definition of EncSort is as follows. S_1 has an array A encrypted using a semantically secure encryption and by the end of the protocol he receives an array B which contains the values of A sorted and encrypted using fresh randomness, i.e., a property of semantic security. S_2 has the corresponding secret key SK and receives nothing as an output. VIEW_{S_i} captures messages that S_i receives while participating in Π^{EncSort}. In order to capture that S_1 does not learn anything about SK, and plaintext of A or B as a consequence, one has to show that there exists a simulator of S_2, Sim_{S_2}. Sim_{S_2} knows exactly what is known to S_1 and nothing more. The main property of Sim_{S_2} is that S_1 should not be able to distinguish if he is interacting with Sim_{S_2} or with S_2 who knows the secret key of the encryption scheme. Hence, S_1 learns nothing more than he knew already. The privacy guarantee for S_1 is similar. One shows that there is a simulator Sim_{S_1} that knows the key pair of the cryptosystem and only the size of A.

3.2 Construction

In this section we develop a construction for the *private sort* functionality EncSort(PK, SK, A) presented in Definition 1. From now on we assume that the array A is encrypted using the first layer of Paillier cryptosystem (Sect. 2.1), however, the system can be adapted to higher levels with corresponding adjustment to the protocols.

Our private sort protocol relies on (a) homomorphic properties of the generalized Paillier cryptosystem from Sect. 2.1 to allow S_1 and S_2 to privately compare and swap pairs of ciphertexts, and (b) a data independent sorting network, Batcher's sort [5], which allows to sort the data such that comparisons alone do not reveal the order of the encrypted elements. We first describe a protocol for sorting just two elements and then use it as a blackbox for general sorting. Finally, we show how to extend the protocol to sort an array where an element is not a single ciphertext value but a (key, value) pair where key and value are individually encrypted and sorting has to be performed on value.

Table 4. $([c], [d]) \leftarrow \mathsf{EncPairSort}(\mathsf{PK_P}, \mathsf{SK_P}, [a], [b])$: Interactive protocol between S_1 and S_2 for sorting two encrypted elements such that only S_1 receives the result. The key pair for Paillier cryptosystem is denoted as $K_P = (\mathsf{PK_P}, \mathsf{SK_P})$.

$S_1(\mathsf{PK_P}, [a], [b])$ $S_2(\mathsf{PK_P}, \mathsf{SK_P})$	
$[\![v]\!] \leftarrow \mathsf{EncCompare}(K_P, [a], [b])$	% Compare a, b: $v := a \geq b$.
$[\![[c]]\!] \leftarrow \mathsf{EncSelect}(K_P, [a], [b], [\![v]\!])$	% $c := (1 - v)a + vb$.
$[\![[d]]\!] \leftarrow \mathsf{EncSelect}(K_P, [a], [b], [\![1]\!][\![v]\!]^{-1})$	% $d := va + (1 - v)b$.
$[c] \leftarrow \mathsf{StripEnc}(K_P, [\![[c]]\!])$	% Strip a layer of encryption
$[d] \leftarrow \mathsf{StripEnc}(K_P, [\![[d]]\!])$	% for c and d.

Two Element Sort. We develop a protocol between two parties S_1 and S_2 to blindly sort two encrypted values. In particular, S_1 possesses encryptions of a and b, $[a]$ and $[b]$, while S_2 has the corresponding decryption key $\mathsf{SK_P}$. S_1 and S_2 engage in an interactive protocol, $\mathsf{EncPairSort}$, by the end of which S_1 has a pair of values $([c], [d])$ such that $(c, d) = (a, b)$ if $a \leq b$ and $(c, d) = (b, a)$, otherwise. Informally, $\mathsf{EncPairSort}$ has the following privacy guarantees. S_1 and S_2 should learn nothing about values a and b nor their sorted order. The formal definition of $\mathsf{EncPairSort}$ is a special case of $\mathsf{EncSort}$ in Definition 1 with $N = 2$.

The $\mathsf{EncPairSort}$ makes use of the comparison protocol $\mathsf{EncCompare}$ from Sect. 2.1 to help S_1 to acquire an encryption of the bit v that denotes whether $a \geq b$ or not. Given a Paillier encryption of v we can then use a ciphertext selection $\mathsf{EncSelect}$ from Sect. 2.1 to blindly swap a and b according to v, i.e., their sorted order. The last step of the protocol brings the encryption of swapped a and b back to the first layer of Paillier. The complete protocol $\mathsf{EncPairSort}$ is shown in Table 4.

Theorem 1. *The* $\mathsf{EncPairSort}$ *protocol in Table 4 is a private outsourced sorting protocol according to Definition 2 for the case* $N = 2$.

Proof (Sketch). In order to show that $\mathsf{EncPairSort}$ in Table 4 is secure according to Definition 2 we need to construct two simulators Sim_{S_1} and Sim_{S_2} that show that behavior of S_1 and S_2 can be simulated without their corresponding private inputs and hence cannot reveal any information about these inputs to S_2 and S_1, correspondingly.

We construct Sim_{S_2} as follows. Sim_{S_2} has access to private inputs of S_1 in the protocol. The VIEW of S_1 consists of VIEW's from $\mathsf{EncCompare}$ and two invocations of $\mathsf{EncSelect}$ and $\mathsf{StripEnc}$ protocols. In the full version [4] we show that there exist simulators for each of these functionalities. Then Sim_{S_2} for $\mathsf{EncPairSort}$ simply invokes $\mathsf{EncCompare}$ simulator once, and $\mathsf{EncSelect}$ and $\mathsf{StripEnc}$ simulators twice each. The construction of Sim_{S_1} is symmetrical.

General Sort. In the previous section we developed an interactive method $\mathsf{EncPairSort}$ for blindly sorting two elements (Table 4). In this section, we use $\mathsf{EncPairSort}$ as a blackbox to build a protocol $\mathsf{EncSort}$ for privately sorting N

Table 5. $B \leftarrow \mathsf{EncSort}(\mathsf{PK_P}, \mathsf{SK_P}, A)$: Interactive protocol between S_1 and S_2 for privately sorting an array A of N elements encrypted using Paillier encryption such that only S_1 acquires the sorted result B (see Definition 2). Paillier key pair is denoted using $K_\mathsf{P} = (\mathsf{PK_P}, \mathsf{SK_P})$. See Fig. 2 for an illustration for the case when $N = 4$.

$S_1(\mathsf{PK_P}, [a], [b])$	$S_2(\mathsf{PK_P}, \mathsf{SK_P})$	
$[v] \leftarrow \mathsf{EncCompare}(K_\mathsf{P}, [a], [b])$		% Compare a, b: $v := a \geq b$.
$[[c]] \leftarrow \mathsf{EncSelect}(K_\mathsf{P}, [a], [b], [v])$		% $c := (1 - v)a + vb$.
$[[d]] \leftarrow \mathsf{EncSelect}(K_\mathsf{P}, [a], [b], [1][v]^{-1})$		% $d := va + (1 - v)b$.
$[c] \leftarrow \mathsf{StripEnc}(K_\mathsf{P}, [[c]])$		% Strip a layer of encryption
$[d] \leftarrow \mathsf{StripEnc}(K_\mathsf{P}, [[d]])$		% for c and d.

elements according to Definition 2. Recall that $\mathsf{EncSort}$ is an interactive protocol between S_1 and S_2. S_1 has an encrypted array A that he wishes to sort and S_2 has a secret key of the underlying encryption scheme. In the end of the protocol, S_1 obtains a re-encryption of his array A with S_2's help while neither of them learn anything about A nor its sorting.

Privacy properties of two element sorting $\mathsf{EncPairSort}$ guarantee that S_1 does not learn the result of the comparison of two encrypted elements nor anything about the elements being compared. Hence, sorting algorithms that make calls to a comparison function depending on the data are not applicable in our scheme (e.g., quick sort performs a different sequence of comparisons depending on the layout of the data it is sorting, giving $O(N \log N)$ comparisons on average). For our purposes we require a sorting network that performs comparisons in a data-independent manner and guarantees that after performing a deterministic sequence of comparisons the result is sorted. We pick Batcher's sorting [5] for our purposes. Even though asymptotically AKS [2] is more efficient, it has high hidden constants that in practice make it inferior to Batcher's sorting network.

Batcher's sorting network sorts an array of N elements using $O(N(\log N)^2)$ data independent calls to a comparator function (i.e., the number of rounds is the same for a fixed N independent of the data). One can view the network in $O((\log N)^2)$ consecutive levels where $O(N)$ pairs of elements are compared and swapped at every level. In particular, let A_i be an array of elements at ith level such that A_1 is the input array, where $A_i\{j\}$ denotes the jth element of array A_i. Each level i takes as input array A_i and produces A_{i+1} where the pairs scheduled to be sorted at level i are in sorted order in A_{i+1}. For example, $A_2\{0\}$ and $A_2\{1\}$ contain $A_1\{0\}$, $A_1\{1\}$ in sorted order, $A_2\{2\}$ and $A_2\{3\}$ contain $A_1\{2\}$, $A_1\{3\}$ in sorted order and so on. We use pairs_i to denote an iterator over pairs that need to be sorted in the ith level and $\mathsf{pairs}_i.\mathsf{next}$ returns the next pair to be sorted.

In Table 5 we present our protocol $\mathsf{EncSort}$ where S_1 performs Batcher's sorting network using S_2 to help him sort the elements of pairs at every level of the network. To sort every pair, S_1 and S_2 run $\mathsf{EncPairSort}$. Recall that the output of $\mathsf{EncPairSort}$ is encrypted using the first layer of Paillier cryptosystem, hence, the result of pairwise sorting at level i can be used as input for calls to $\mathsf{EncPairSort}$ in the next level $i + 1$. (See Fig. 2 for an illustration of $\mathsf{EncSort}$ on an example array of size 4.) Recall that S_1 and S_2 are two non-colluding honest but curious adversaries and hence will execute their side of the protocol faithfully.

Theorem 2 (EncSort **Privacy**). *The EncSort protocol in Table 5 is a private outsourced sorting protocol according to Definition 2.*

Proof (Sketch). The protocol EncSort in Table 5 makes $O(N(\log N)^2)$ calls to EncPairSort protocol in Table 4. In Theorem 1 we showed that there exist simulators Sim_{S_1} and Sim_{S_2} for EncPairSort. Hence, the simulators for EncSort can be trivially constructed by calling corresponding simulators of EncPairSort.

Theorem 3 (EncSort **Performance**). *The EncSort protocol in Table 5 has the following performance guarantees:*

- *The storage requirement of S_1 is $O(N)$;*
- *The total computation required by S_1 and S_2 is $O(N(\log N)^2)$;*
- *The communication complexity between S_1 and S_2 consists of $O(N(\log N)^2)$ rounds;*
- *If S_2 has $O(1)$ storage, the time overhead of the protocol is $O(N(\log N)^2)$;*
- *If S_2 has $O(N)$ storage, the time overhead of the protocol is $O((\log N)^2)$.*

Proof (Sketch). S_1 needs to have $O(N)$ storage space in order to store the original array A of size N along with the intermediate sorting results. The intermediate storage is at most two arrays A_i and A_{i+1} since after finishing the ith level of sorting S_1 can safely discard array A_i. S_2, on the other hand, is only required to store the keys of the encryption schemes used and perform field arithmetic to run encryption and decryption algorithms on constant number of elements.

The protocol requires $O(N(\log N)^2)$ roundtrips between S_1 and S_2 where S_1 and S_2 perform a constant computation after every round. If S_2 has $O(N)$ memory then a highly parallelizable nature of the Batcher's sorting network can be exploited. It allows all invocations of EncPairSort during a single round i to be run in parallel since they operate on different pairs of the array A_i.

Key-Value Sort. In the previous section we described how to sort an array where every element of an array is an encrypted plaintext used for comparison. However, the protocol is easily expandable to work on arrays where every element is a pair of ciphertexts representing a (key, value) pair and value is used to sort the array. The main alternations happen in EncPairSort protocol where the input is not two ciphertexts as in Table 4 but two pairs of ciphertexts: $([k_1], [v_1])$ and $([k_2], [v_2])$, and similarly in the output. Since comparison is performed only on values EncCompare is called only on $[v_1]$ and $[v_2]$. Once the bit representing the result of the comparison is computed, EncSelect is used not only on the ciphertexts of the values but also on the keys. That is, if values have to be swapped so do their corresponding keys. This functionality is used in Sect. 4.2 when sorting document identifiers using their query score. There, the key is an encrypted document id and value is an encryption of the corresponding score.

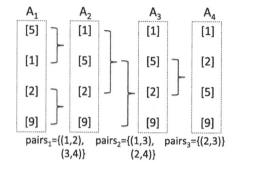

pairs$_1$={(1,2), (3,4)}   pairs$_2$={(1,3), (2,4)}   pairs$_3$={(2,3)}

Invocation of EncPairSort protocol between S$_1$ and S$_2$ that returns two re-encrypted sorted values to S$_1$.

Fig. 2. Example of EncSort protocol in Table 5 for sorting an encrypted array of four elements $5, 1, 2, 9$ where $[m]$ denotes a Paillier encryption of message m and pairs$_i$ denotes a pair of elements to be sorted. Note that only S_1 stores values in the arrays A_i while S_2 blindly assists S_1 in sorting the values.

4 Private Ranked Search (MRSE)

We now give an overview our Multi-keyword Ranked Searchable Encryption (MRSE) framework that allows an owner of a data collection to outsource his documents to a server S_1 and then search on them and receive ranked results, using our *private sort* protocol.

4.1 MRSE Security Model

MRSE builds on the SSE model [11] where a server, given an encrypted document collection and the corresponding secure search index, while answering multiple search queries, should not be able to deduct anything regarding the data collection or the corresponding search index apart from the *access* and *search* patterns. By the term *access pattern* we denote the identifiers of the documents that contain a query keyword, while the *search pattern* refers to any connection between queries that the server may derive (e.g., if specific query terms have been queried before and how many times). The MRSE model assumes that it is sufficient to return to the client only document identifiers and not the actual document. This is consistent with related work on searchable encryption with ranking, e.g., [9].

Our setting consists of two servers S_1 and S_2, where the user queries only S_1. S_1 is required to return the document id's that match the search query *sorted* by relevance criteria (i.e., tf-idf) by running *private sort* with S_2. We examine the privacy of the client against S_1 and S_2 separately. This is sufficient for the overall privacy given that S_1 and S_2 are non-colluding and the privacy of the interaction between them is limited to using private sort as specified in Definition 2.

Informally, MRSE privacy definitions capture the following: S_1 learns the number of documents and unique keywords in the collection (he can infer this from the size of the encrypted index), as well as the search pattern of client queries since he observes the "encrypted" queries of the user. However, S_1 learns nothing about the access pattern. S_2, on the other hand, only learns the number of documents in the collection and knows when the client is querying the system. However, S_2 learns nothing about the access and search patterns, and hence does not know anything about the content of the queries. We note that S_1's capabilities are similar to those of the server in the original SSE definition [11] while S_2 learns much less. The formal definitions can be found in [4].

4.2   MRSE Construction

We are now ready to present the details of our MRSE construction. We split our description into two phases: the *setup* phase and the *query* phase.

Setup and Initialization. The client sets up the system by generating a secret key for StE, $\mathsf{SK_{StE}}$, and a public/secret key pair for Paillier cryptosystem ($\mathsf{PK_P}$, $\mathsf{SK_P}$). Then, shares $\mathsf{PK_P}$ with S_1 and ($\mathsf{PK_P}, \mathsf{SK_P}$) with S_2. We omit exact details of how the client sends the secret key to S_2 but any efficient key wrapping algorithm suffices for our purposes. S_1 and S_2 are honest but curious and interact with each other faithfully only using the private sort protocol from Sect. 3.2.

The client first extracts all M unique terms[5] from his collection of documents **D** and associates every unique term t with an array F_t of size N. An element in position d of list F_t corresponds to the frequency of term t in document with id d, i.e., tf-idf$_{t,d}$ as defined in Sect. 2.3. Note that tf-idf$_{t,d}$ is zero if the term t does not appear in document d. Given all tf-idf$_{t,d}$ entries the client obtains the frequency table F where the number of rows is M (number of unique terms in **D**) and the number of columns is N (number of documents in **D**). The client then maps every frequency score tf-idf$_{t,d}$ to an integer and encrypts it using the first layer of Paillier encryption (Sect. 2.1). The mapping to integers ensures that we can use Paillier cryptosystem whose plaintext space is defined over $\mathbb{Z}_n$. Note that, once encrypted, the table representing frequencies of terms does not reveal the number of documents that every term appears in, i.e., the length of the posting list. We overload the notation and define $[F_t] = \{[\text{tf-idf}_{t,d}] \mid \forall d \in \{1, N\}\}$.

The client then wishes to upload encrypted term and frequency index to S_1 and query it later. For this purpose, he uses a structured encryption scheme as defined in Sect. 2.2. Since the frequencies are already in an encrypted form, it is sufficient to create a searchable index for all the terms and allow S_1 to find the corresponding frequency array $[F_t]$ only if he is given a trapdoor for t. To do so, we consider a simplified version of the labeled data structured encryption scheme described in [10]. Let $\mathsf{SK_{StE}}$ consist of two random k-bit strings K_1, K_2 and let G_{K_1} and G'_{K_2} be two different pseudo-random functions (PRF) with keys K_1 and K_2, respectively.

The client first sorts the terms using the lexicographic order and numbers each term in this order as $\{t_1, t_2, \ldots, t_M\}$. Then, he picks a pseudo-random

---

[5] Stemming and removal of stop words is outside of the scope of our paper.

permutation π and creates an auxiliary index of pairs $(t_i, \pi(i))$ $\forall i \in \{1, M\}$. He also appends $\pi(i)$ to the corresponding $[F_{t_i}]$ and permutes the pairs $(\pi(i), [F_{t_i}])$, i.e., creates a dictionary that maps a keyword t_i to a list of encrypted scores for all the documents in the collection (not only the documents in which the keyword appears at).

Then, the encryption algorithm of StE, E_{StE}, works as follows. For every $i \in \{1, M\}$, the *search key* $k_{t_i} = G'_{K_2}(t_i)$ and the value $(\pi(i), [F_{t_i}]) \oplus G_{K_1}(t_i)$ are computed. Both are stored together in the secure index I which is sent as an input to S_1. We do not give to S_1 the encryption of the document collection since this is outside of our model.

Query Phase. During the query phase, the client computes the trapdoor $T \leftarrow Trpdr(\mathsf{SK}_{\mathsf{StE}}, t)$ for each keyword t in the query q. In our scheme, $Trpdr$ sets T to $(G_{K_1}(t), G'_{K_2}(t))$. The client then sends the trapdoors of all the query terms (i.e., an "encrypted" representation of the query) $\mathbf{T} = \{T \mid \forall t \in q\}$ to S_1. Server S_1, upon receiving client's query $\mathbf{T}$, can locate each encrypted keyword $t \in q$ using the corresponding trapdoors by running $Search(I, T)$ $\forall T \in \mathbf{T}$. The *Search* algorithm parses T as (α, β) and computes the answer as $I(\beta) \oplus \alpha$, where $I(\beta)$ is the value stored in I under the *search key* β. The answer is a vector $[F_t] = \{[\text{tf-idf}_{t,d}] \mid \forall d \in \{1, N\}\}$ for every term t in the query.

Computing Document Scores: Recall that $[F_t]$ is an array of individually encrypted tf-idf$_{t,d}$ scores for $d \in \{1, N\}$. In order to compute the document scores, S_1 uses the additive property of the homomorphic encryption scheme and for every document d computes an encrypted score $e_d = [\text{score}(q, d)] = \sum_{t \in q}[\text{tf-idf}_{t,d}]$. Note that e_d is simply an encryption of $\text{score}(q, d)$. S_1 then creates an array A of (key, value) pairs where a key is an encryption of a document id and value is the corresponding encrypted score: $A = \{([1], e_1), ([2], e_2), \ldots, ([N], e_N)\}$.

Sorting Document Scores: The server S_1 has acquired the final scores for every document identifier, however, these scores are encrypted which prohibits S_1 from sorting them and returning the document identifiers sorted by their relevance to the query q. To sort the documents, S_1 engages with S_2 in the private sorting protocol EncSort defined in Table 5 and its extension to (key,value) pairs in Sect. 3.2. The protocol returns to S_1 an array $B = \{([d_1], e_{d_1}), ([d_2], e_{d_2}), \ldots, ([d_N], e_{d_N})\}$ which corresponds to a re-encryption of array A sorted using document scores, that is $D(e_{d_1}) \leq D(e_{d_2}) \leq \ldots \leq D(e_{d_N})$ where D is a decryption algorithm of Paillier cryptosystem and d_i are document identifiers.

Finally, S_1 sends to the client array B. According to client preference, S_1 can send document identifiers with scores, omit scores, or send only the top k results. The client has the Paillier decryption key and can easily decrypt the ordered sequence of document identifiers (and scores) received from S_1.

4.3 MRSE Analysis

Here, we give an informal analysis of why MRSE is secure against S_1 and S_2 and refer the reader to [4] for a proof. The client's document collection $\mathbf{D}$ and the scores are represented as the encrypted index I which is stored semantically encrypted with S_1 only. The client encrypts frequency scores for all documents and unique terms in F, including zeroes, hence, S_1 does not learn anything about the collection except the number of documents N and the number of unique terms M in $\mathbf{D}$. The client sends his queries to S_1 and, hence, S_1 learns the search pattern, i.e., if the keywords were queried before or not. Note that the search pattern is also leaked in the original StE scheme since StE generates a deterministic trapdoor for the same term.

The security properties of private sort in Definition 2 guarantee that as long as S_1 and S_2 behave honestly neither one learns anything about the array of document scores they are sorting. Since S_2 is invoked to participate in private sort he learns N, the number of documents in the collection, and that a client has queried S_1 but learns nothing more about query keywords or query length. The performance of MRSE is summarized in the following theorem.

Theorem 4 (MRSE Performance). *MRSE protocol presented in Sect. 4.2 gives the following performance guarantees:*

- *The client takes $O(N \times M)$ time and space to setup the system, and $O(|q|)$ time to generate a query;*
- *The communication cost between the client and S_1 during the query phase is $O(|q| + N)$;*
- *The space requirements for S_1 and S_2 are $O(N \times M)$ and $O(1)$, respectively;*
- *The query phase takes $O(N(\log N)^2)$ for both S_1 and S_2;*

where N is the number of documents and M is the number of unique terms in the collection, and $|q|$ is the query size.

A proof of Theorem 4 can be found in the full version [4].

4.4   Comparison with Related Work

In this section we compare MRSE with other multi-keyword searchable encryption schemes with ranked results. Cao *et al.* [9] provide one of the first schemes that allow ranked *multi-keyword* search. The scheme sorts documents using the score based on "inner product similarity" (ips) where a document score is simply the number of matches of query keywords in each document. This ranking is not as standard in information retrieval as tf-idf since it loses information about keyword importance to the document collection w.r.t. document lengths and other keywords (e.g., documents which contain all query keywords are ranked equally). The scheme of [9] also proposes a heuristic to hide the search and access patterns by adding dummy keywords and noise. As a result, the returned document list may contain false negatives and false positives. Query phase of the scheme is expensive for the client since query generation time is $O(M^2)$, i.e., quadratic in the number of unique keywords in the original collection, M, and the length of the trapdoor for every query is $O(M)$. To answer the query, the server has to perform $O(N \times M^2)$ computation, where N is the number of documents in the

Table 6. Comparison of MRSE with multi-keyword searchable encryption schemes returning ranked results in terms of **sound**ness of the result, the **ranking** technique, the **client** query generation time, **server(s)** time to compute the result and the **privacy** guarantees. We note that schemes [9] and [27] are single server solutions. Inner product similarity is denoted as ips, N is the number of documents and M is the number of unique terms in the collection, $|q|$ is the query length, * denotes the use of FHE techniques, CCA-2 is security against chosen ciphertext attack for SSE schemes [11]. All the time complexities are asymptotic.

$S_1(\mathsf{PK_P}, A)$ $\qquad\qquad\qquad\qquad\qquad\qquad$ $S_2(\mathsf{PK_P}, \mathsf{SK_P})$	
$A_1 \leftarrow A$	
for $i \in \{1, \ldots, k-1\}$	% $k = O((\log N)^2), N = |A|$.
$\quad (x, y) \leftarrow \mathsf{pairs}_i.\mathsf{next}$	% ith level of Batcher's sort.
$\quad \mathsf{while}((x, y) \neq \bot)$	
$\quad\quad (A_{i+1}\{x\}, A_{i+1}\{y\}) \leftarrow \mathsf{EncPairSort}(K_P, A_i\{x\}, A_i\{y\})$	% Sort x, y entries of A_i.
$\quad\quad (x, y) \leftarrow \mathsf{pairs}_i.\mathsf{next}$	% Next pair of A_i to sort.
$B \leftarrow A_k$	

collection. In comparison, the client of our scheme is required to generate only a constant size trapdoor for every term in the query which is likely to be much smaller than M. Also, the work for the server in MRSE is $O(N(\log N)^2)$.

Örencik and Savaş [23,24] also propose protocols for ranked multi-keyword search. Their ranking is loosely based on frequency of a word in the document where fake keywords and documents are added, hence, their scheme also may return false negatives and positives. Recent proposal by Örencik et al. [22] is a solution with two non-colluding servers. Their first server works similar to our S_1, however, the interaction between the two servers is very different and gives much weaker privacy guarantees than our system. In particular, the second server has access to the result of every query in the clear, revealing information about user's data collection as well as the search and access patterns. Recall that in our scheme S_2 is merely assisting S_1 during sorting and never sees neither the queries nor the data. Finally, storage requirement of the second server is linear in the size of the collection, while it is constant for S_2 in MRSE.

Another recent work that uses tf-idf and inner product similarity based ranking is the one due to Strizhov and Ray [27]. Their model assumes a single server that performs only the search functionality and not the sorting of the results. In particular, the client generates N trapdoors for every term in the query, the server finds the required encrypted documents and scores, returns them to the client who performs the sorting based on tf-idf himself. Moreover, the frequency table has to be encrypted under a fully homomorphic encryption (FHE) scheme in order for the server to be able to perform ranking. Using FHE in such a setting is a direct solution but unfortunately is very inefficient.

In Table 6 we present a comparison of our MRSE scheme with the schemes discussed above. We compare them in terms of soundness of the returned result (e.g., if the result contains false positives), ranking method, client query generation time and search complexity for the server(s). The last column of the table presents privacy guarantees of the schemes. We note that privacy of [9] is harder to compare with since a heuristic is used to hide access and search patterns.

Acknowledgments. The authors would like to thank Seny Kamara, Markulf Kohlweiss and Roberto Tamassia for useful discussions and suggestions on how to improve the results and the write-up in hand. Olga Ohrimenko worked on this project in part while at Brown University, where her research was supported in part by the National Science Foundation under grants CNS–1012060 and CNS–1228485. Foteini Baldimtsi was supported by the Center for Reliable Information Systems and Cyber Security (RISCS) and grant CNS–1012910 (Boston University), and also in part by the FINER project by Greek Secretariat of Research Technology (University of Athens) and CNS–0964379 (Brown University).

References

1. Adida, B., Wikström, D.: How to shuffle in public. In: Vadhan, S.P. (ed.) TCC 2007. LNCS, vol. 4392, pp. 555–574. Springer, Heidelberg (2007)
2. Ajtai, M., Komlós, J., Szemerédi, E.: An O(n log n) sorting network. In: ACM Symposium on Theory of Computing, STOC 1983, pp. 1–9. ACM (1983)
3. Asharov, G., Lindell, Y., Schneider, T., Zohner, M.: More efficient oblivious transfer and extensions for faster secure computation. In: ACM Conference on Computer and Communications Security, CCS 2013, pp. 535–548. ACM (2013)
4. Baldimtsi, F., Ohrimenko, O.: Sorting and searching behind the curtain: private outsourced sort and frequency-based ranking of search results over encrypted data. Cryptology ePrint Archive, Report 2014/1017 (2014)
5. Batcher, K.E.: Sorting networks and their applications. In: AFIPS Spring Joint Computing Conference (1968)
6. Bellare, M., Hoang, V.T., Keelveedhi, S., Rogaway, P.: Efficient garbling from a fixed-key blockcipher. In: IEEE Symposium on Security and Privacy, SP 2013, pp. 478–492. IEEE (2013)
7. Boldyreva, A., Chenette, N., O'Neill, A.: Order-preserving encryption revisited: improved security analysis and alternative solutions. In: Rogaway, P. (ed.) CRYPTO 2011. LNCS, vol. 6841, pp. 578–595. Springer, Heidelberg (2011)
8. Bost, R., Popa, R.A., Tu, S., Goldwasser, S.: Machine learning classification over encrypted data. Cryptology ePrint Archive, Report 2014/331 (2014)
9. Cao, N., Wang, C., Li, M., Ren, K., Lou, W.: Privacy-preserving multi-keyword ranked search over encrypted cloud data. In: Conference on Information Communications, INFOCOM 2011, pp. 829–837. IEEE (2011)
10. Chase, M., Kamara, S.: Structured encryption and controlled disclosure. In: Abe, M. (ed.) ASIACRYPT 2010. LNCS, vol. 6477, pp. 577–594. Springer, Heidelberg (2010)
11. Curtmola, R., Garay, J., Kamara, S., Ostrovsky, R.: Searchable symmetric encryption: improved definitions and efficient constructions. In: ACM Conference on Computer and Communications Security, CCS 2006, pp. 79–88. ACM (2006)
12. Damgard, I., Geisler, M., Kroigard, M.: A correction to efficient and secure comparison for on-line auctions. Int. J. Appl. Cryptol. **1**(4), 323–324 (2009)

13. Damgård, I., Jurik, M.: A generalisation, a simplification and some applications of Paillier's probabilistic public-key system. In: Kim, K. (ed.) PKC 2001. LNCS, vol. 1992, pp. 119–136. Springer, Heidelberg (2001)
14. Gentry, C.: A fully homomorphic encryption scheme. Ph.D. thesis, Stanford University (2009). http://crypto.stanford.edu/craig
15. Goldreich, O.: Foundations of Cryptography, vol. 2. Cambridge University Press, Cambridge (2001)
16. Huang, Y., Evans, D., Katz, J.: Private set intersection: are garbled circuits better than custom protocols? In: NDSS (2012)
17. Jónsson, K.V., Kreitz, G., Uddin, M.: Secure multi-party sorting and applications. In: Applied Cryptography and Network Security, ACNS 2011 (2011)
18. Knuth, D.E.: The Art of Computer Programming: Sorting and Searching, vol. 3, 2nd edn. Addison Wesley Longman Publishing Co., Inc., Redwood City (1998)
19. Kolesnikov, V., Sadeghi, A.-R., Schneider, T.: Improved garbled circuit building blocks and applications to auctions and computing minima. In: Garay, J.A., Miyaji, A., Otsuka, A. (eds.) CANS 2009. LNCS, vol. 5888, pp. 1–20. Springer, Heidelberg (2009)
20. Lipmaa, H.: An oblivious transfer protocol with log-squared communication. In: Zhou, J., López, J., Deng, R.H., Bao, F. (eds.) ISC 2005. LNCS, vol. 3650, pp. 314–328. Springer, Heidelberg (2005)
21. Manning, C.D., Raghavan, P., Schütze, H.: Introduction to Information Retrieval. Cambridge University Press, Cambridge (2008)
22. Örencik, C., Kantarcioglu, M., Savaş, E.: A practical and secure multi-keyword search method over encrypted cloud data. In: International Conference on Cloud Computing, CLOUD 2013, pp. 390–397. IEEE (2013)
23. Örencik, C., Savaş, E.: Efficient and secure ranked multi-keyword search on encrypted cloud data. In: Proceedings of the 2012 Joint EDBT/ICDT Workshops, EDBT-ICDT 2012, pp. 186–195. ACM (2012)
24. Örencik, C., Savaş, E.: An efficient privacy-preserving multi-keyword search over encrypted cloud data with ranking. Distribut. Parallel Databases $32(1)$, 119–160 (2014)
25. Paillier, P.: Public-key cryptosystems based on composite degree residuosity classes. In: Stern, J. (ed.) EUROCRYPT 1999. LNCS, vol. 1592, p. 223. Springer, Heidelberg (1999)
26. Rivest, R.L., Adleman, L., Dertouzos, M.L.: On data banks and privacy homomorphisms. In: Foundations of Secure Computation, pp. 169–177. Academic Press (1978)
27. Strizhov, M., Ray, I.: Multi-keyword similarity search over encrypted cloud data. In: Cuppens-Boulahia, N., Cuppens, F., Jajodia, S., Abou El Kalam, A., Sans, T. (eds.) SEC 2014. IFIP AICT, vol. 428, pp. 52–65. Springer, Heidelberg (2014)
28. van Dijk, M., Gentry, C., Halevi, S., Vaikuntanathan, V.: Fully homomorphic encryption over the integers. In: Gilbert, H. (ed.) EUROCRYPT 2010. LNCS, vol. 6110, pp. 24–43. Springer, Heidelberg (2010)
29. Veugen, T.: Comparing encrypted data. Manuscript (2010). http://isplab.tudelft.nl/sites/default/files/Comparingencrypteddata.pdf
30. Zobel, J., Moffat, A.: Inverted files for text search engines. ACM Comput. Surv. $38(2)$, 6 (2006)

Resizable Tree-Based Oblivious RAM

Tarik Moataz[1,2]([✉]), Travis Mayberry[3], Erik-Oliver Blass[4],
and Agnes Hui Chan[3]

[1] Department of Computer Science, Colorado State University,
Fort Collins, CO, USA
`tmoataz@cs.colostate.edu`
[2] IMT, Telecom Bretagne, Plouzané, France
[3] College of Computer and Information Science,
Northeastern University, Boston, MA, USA
{`travism,ahchan`}`@ccs.neu.edu`
[4] Airbus Group Innovations, 81663 Munich, Germany
`erik-oliver.blass@airbus.com`

Abstract. Although newly proposed, tree-based Oblivious RAM schemes are drastically more efficient than older techniques, they come with a significant drawback: an inherent dependence on a fixed-size database. Yet, a flexible storage is vital for real-world use of Oblivious RAM since one of its most promising deployment scenarios is for cloud storage, where scalability and elasticity are crucial. We revisit the original construction by Shi et al. [17] and propose several ways to support both increasing and decreasing the ORAM's size with sublinear communication. We show that increasing the capacity can be accomplished by adding leaf nodes to the tree, but that it must be done carefully in order to preserve the probabilistic integrity of data structures. We also provide new, tighter bounds for the size of interior and leaf nodes in the scheme, saving bandwidth and storage over previous constructions. Finally, we define an oblivious pruning technique for removing leaf nodes and decreasing the size of the tree. We show that this pruning method is both secure and efficient.

1 Introduction

Oblivious RAM has been a perennial research topic since it was first introduced by Goldreich [8]. ORAM allows for an access pattern to an adversarially controlled RAM to be effectively obfuscated. Conceptually, a client's data is stored in an encrypted and shuffled form in the ORAM, such that accessing pieces of data will not produce any recognizable pattern to an adversary which observes these accesses. Being a powerful cryptographic primitive, many additional uses besides storage can be envisioned for ORAM, such as an aid for homomorphic circuit evaluation, secure multi-party computation, and privacy-preserving data

---

T. Moataz—Work done while at Northeastern University.
T. Moataz and T. Mayberry—Both are first authors.

© International Financial Cryptography Association 2015
R. Böhme and T. Okamoto (Eds.): FC 2015, LNCS 8975, pp. 147–167, 2015.
DOI: 10.1007/978-3-662-47854-7_9

outsourcing. Given the advent of cloud computing and storage, and all their potential for abuse and violation of privacy, ORAM schemes are important for the real-world today.

A crucial aspect of ORAM schemes is their implied overhead. In today's cloud settings, the choice to use the cloud is chiefly motivated by cost savings. If the overhead is enough that it negates any monetary advantages the cloud can offer, the use of ORAM will be impractical. Previous ORAM schemes have had a common, major drawback that has hindered real-world use: due to eventually necessary "reshuffling" operations, their worst-case communication complexity was linear in the size of the ORAM. Recent works on ORAM, e.g., by Shi et al. [17], Stefanov et al. [18], and many derivatives, have proposed new ORAM schemes that are tree-based and have only poly-logarithmic worst-case communication complexity.

However, new tree-based approaches have exposed another barrier to the real-world adoption of ORAMs: the maximum size of the data structure must be determined during initialization, and it cannot be changed. This is not an issue in previous linear schemes, because the client always had the option of picking a new size during the "reshuffling", being effectively a "reinitialization" of the ORAM. In tree-based ORAMs, though, a reinitialization ruins the sublinear worst-case communication complexity.

Resizability is a vital property of any ORAM to be used for cloud storage. One of the selling points of cloud services is elasticity, the ability to start with a particular footprint and seamlessly scale resources up or down to match demand. Imagine a startup company that wants to securely store their information in the cloud using ORAM. At launch, they might have only a handful of users, but they expect sometime in the long-term to increase to 10,000. With current solutions, they would have to either pay for the 10,000 users worth of *storage* starting on day one, even though most of it would be empty, or pay for the *communication* to repeatedly reinitialize their database with new sizes as they become more popular. Reinitializing the ORAM would negate any benefit from the new worst-case constructions. Additionally, one can imagine a company that is seasonal in nature (e.g., a tax accounting service) and would like the ability to downsize their storage during off-peak times of the year to save costs.

Consequently, the problem of resizing these new tree-based ORAMs is important for practical adoption in real-world settings. In light of that, we present several techniques for both increasing and decreasing the size of recent tree-based ORAMs to reduce both communication and storage complexity. We focus on constant client memory ORAM (the Shi et al. [17] ORAM) since it is an interesting setting, especially for hardware-constrained devices and large block sizes or situations where multiple parties want to share the same ORAM so need to exchange the state. We are able to show that, although the resizing techniques themselves are intuitive, careful analysis is required to ensure security and integrity of ORAMs. In addition, we show that it is nontrivial to both allow for sublinear resizing and maintain the constant client memory property of Shi et al. [17] ORAM.

The technical highlights of this paper are as follows:

1. Three provably secure strategies for increasing the size of tree-based ORAMs, along with a rigorous analysis showing the impact on communication and storage complexity and security.
2. A provably secure method for pruning the trees to decrease the size of a tree-based ORAM, again including rigorous analysis showing that security and integrity of the data structures is preserved.
3. A new, tighter analysis for the Shi et al. [17] ORAM which allows for smaller storage requirements and less communication per query than previous work.

2   Building Blocks

We will briefly revisit the constant-client memory tree-based ORAM of Shi et al. [17], focusing on the relevant details which are necessary to understand our resizing techniques.

2.1   Preliminaries

An Oblivious RAM is a cryptographic data structure storing blocks of data in such a way that a client's pattern of accesses to those blocks is hidden from the party which holds them. ORAMs offer block reads and writes. That is, they provide Read(a) and Write(d, a) operations, where a is the address of a block, and d notes some data. Let N be the total number of blocks the ORAM can store. Each ORAM block is uniquely addressable by $a \in \{0, 1\}^{\log N}$, and the size of each block is ℓ bits.

Data in the ORAM [17] is stored as a binary tree with N leaves. Each node in the tree represents a smaller ORAM *bucket* [7] which holds k (encrypted) blocks. When clear from the context, we will use the terms node and bucket interchangeably. Each leaf in the tree is uniquely identified by a *tag* $t \in \{0, 1\}^{\log N}$. With $\mathcal{P}(t)$, we denote the path which starts at the root of the tree and ends at the leaf node tagged t.

Blocks in the ORAM are associated with leaves in the tree. The association between blocks and their addresses is a lookup table with size equal to $N \cdot \log N$. This table is called the *position map*, and in order to maintain efficiency it is recursively stored in series of smaller ORAMs [17]. The central invariant of tree-based ORAMs is that a block tagged with tag t will always be found in a bucket somewhere on the path $\mathcal{P}(t)$. Blocks will enter the tree at the root and propagate toward the leaves depending on their tag.

2.2   Tree-Based Construction

Shi et al. [17]'s ORAM implements Read and Write operations by applying, first, ReadAndRemove(a) operation, followed by an Add(d, a). A ReadAndRemove(a) will first fetch the tag t from the position map, thereby determining the path

$\mathcal{P}(t)$ in the ORAM tree on which that block exists. The client will download all $\log N$ nodes in $\mathcal{P}(t)$, and decrypt all blocks. For each block $a' \neq a$ on path $\mathcal{P}(t)$, the client will upload back to the server a re-encrypted version of that block. For block a, the client will upload an encrypted *dummy* block, which is a special value signifying that the block is empty. The client does this in a bucket-by-bucket, block-by-block decrypt and encrypt manner, to keep client memory constant in N. As long as the encryption is secure, the server will not learn which block the client was interested in, because all they will see is fresh encryptions replacing every block in the path. For the Add operation, the client uniformly chooses a new tag $t \xleftarrow{\$} \{0, \dots, N-1\}$ that associates block a to a new leaf, encrypts d and inserts the resulting ciphertext block into the root.

After every access, an *eviction* is performed to percolate blocks towards the leaves, freeing up space for new blocks to enter at the root. The eviction is a random process that chooses, in every level, ν buckets and evacuates randomly one real element to the corresponding child (as determined by its tag). To stay oblivious, the eviction accesses both child buckets in turn, thereby (re-)encrypting both buckets. Again, this is done in a block-by-block manner to keep client memory constant.

3   Resizable ORAM

3.1   Technical Challenges

The challenge behind resizing tree-based ORAMs is threefold:

1. Increasing the size of the tree will have an impact on the bucket size. A leaf node may become an interior node while increasing the ORAM, and vice versa in the decreasing case. The original analysis by Shi et al. [17] differentiates between interior and leaf nodes, while for resizing we will have to generalize the analysis to consider both cases at once.
2. For $n > N$ elements, we must determine the most effective strategy of increasing the number of nodes to optimize storage and communication costs for the client.
3. Reducing the size of the tree is non-trivial, especially when targeting low communication complexity and constant client memory. A mechanism is required for moving elements from pruned nodes into other buckets in an oblivious, yet efficient way while still maintaining overflow probabilities.

3.2   Resizing Operations

To allow for resizing, we introduce two new basic operations by which a client can resize an ORAM, namely Alloc and Free:

- Alloc: Increase the size of the ORAM so that it can hold one additional element of size ℓ.
- Free: Decrease the size of the ORAM so that it can hold one element fewer.

3.3   Security Definition

Resizing an ORAM should not leak any information besides the current number of elements. Thus, we need to augment the standard ORAM security definition by our resizing operations.

Definition 31. *Let* $\overrightarrow{y} = \{(op_1, d_1, a_1), (op_2, d_2, a_2), \ldots, (op_M, d_M, a_M)\}$ *be a sequence of M operations (op_i, d_i, a_i), where op_i denotes a* Read, Write, Alloc *or* Free *operation, a_i equals the address of the block if $op_i \in \{$Add, ReadAndRemove$\}$ and d_i the data to be written if $op_i =$ Add.*

Let $A(\overrightarrow{y})$ be the access pattern induced by sequence $\overrightarrow{y}$. A resizable ORAM is secure iff, for any PPT adversary $\mathcal{D}$ and any two same-length sequences $\overrightarrow{y}$ and $\overrightarrow{z}$ where $\forall i \in [M] : \overrightarrow{y}(i) =$ Alloc $\Leftrightarrow \overrightarrow{z}(i) =$ Alloc $\wedge \overrightarrow{y}(i) =$ Free $\Leftrightarrow \overrightarrow{z}(i) =$ Free,

$$|Pr[\mathcal{D}(1^\lambda, A(\overrightarrow{y})) = 1] - Pr[\mathcal{D}(1^\lambda, A(\overrightarrow{z})) = 1]| \leq \epsilon(\lambda),$$

where λ is a security parameter, and $\epsilon(\lambda)$ a negligible function in λ.

For sake of completeness, considering buckets in resizable ORAM as trivial ORAMs [7], all blocks are IND-CPA encrypted. Also, whenever a block is accessed by any type of operation, its bucket is re-encrypted block-by-block.

4   Adding

We begin by describing a *naïve* solution that will add a new level of leaves when $n > N$. However, this already leads to a problem: when n is only slightly larger than N, we are using twice as much storage as we should need. The second strategy, *lazy expansion*, will postpone creation of an entire new level until we have enough elements to really need it. In both the naïve and second solution, there are thresholds causing large "jumps" in storage space. As this can be expensive, we present a third solution dubbed *dynamic expansion*. This strategy progressively adds leaf nodes to the tree, thereby gradually increasing the tree's capacity. This last strategy is particularly interesting, because it results in an unbalanced tree, requiring careful analysis to ensure low overall failure probability of the ORAM.

4.1   Tightening the Bounds

Communication and storage complexities represent the core comparative factor between strategies, and both are dependent primarily on bucket sizes. Consequently, it is important to get a tight analysis for both interior and leaf bucket sizes. The original bounds for bucket sizes given by Shi et al. [17] are substantially larger than necessary. Therefore, as a first contribution, we give new, tighter bounds for interior and leaf node sizes.

Interior Nodes. We first address the size of interior nodes by using standard queuing theory. Let I_i denote the random variable for the size of interior nodes of the ith level in the tree. For eviction rate ν, we compute the probability of a bucket on levels $i > \log \nu$ having a load of at least k (i.e., a size k bucket overflows) to:

$$\Pr(I_i \geq k) = \nu^{-k}. \tag{1}$$

In [17], the eviction rate was chosen to be equal to 2 with an overflow probability equal to 2^{-k}. However, if we adjust the bucket size to be $\frac{k}{\log(\nu)}$, the overflow probability is still 2^{-k}, namely $\Pr(I_i \geq \frac{k}{\log(\nu)}) = 2^{-k}$.

This follows from Eq. 1 by replacing k by $\frac{k}{\log(\nu)}$. Also, we can investigate the optimal value for the eviction rate ν in terms of communication cost. For $\nu = 4$, we obtain the same overflow probability as with $\nu = 2$ with buckets of half the size. The communication complexity does not change, as we are evicting twice as much, but with buckets of half the size. For larger eviction rates $\nu > 4$ the communication complexity becomes larger. Note that this also reduces the storage by a factor of 2. For N elements stored in the ORAM, the probability that an interior node overflows during eviction computes to

$$\Pr(\exists i \in [\nu \cdot \log N] : I_i \geq \frac{k}{\log(\nu)}) = 1 - \Pr(\forall i \in [\nu \cdot \log N] : I_i < \frac{k}{\log(\nu)}) \tag{2}$$

$$= 1 - \prod_{i=1}^{\nu \cdot \log N} (1 - \Pr(I_i \geq \frac{k}{\log(\nu)})) \tag{3}$$

$$= 1 - (1 - 2^{-k})^{\nu \cdot \log N}.$$

In particular for $\nu = 4$, the optimal choice of the eviction rate,

$$\Pr(\exists i \in [4 \cdot \log N] : I_i \geq \frac{k}{2}) = 1 - (1 - 2^{-k})^{4 \cdot \log N}.$$

The buckets that can overflow during an access are limited to those in the paths accessed during the eviction, i.e., $\nu \cdot \log N$ buckets accessed. Also, the number of buckets taken into account is actually $\nu \cdot \log N$ instead of $2\nu \cdot \log N$. This follows from the fact that for every parent, we write only one real element to one child. Consequently, per eviction and per level, only one child can overflow. For Eq. 3, an equality still holds since the buckets can be considered independent in steady state [12].

Given security parameter λ, to compute the size of interior buckets, we solve the equation $2^{-\lambda} = 1 - (1 - 2^{-k})^{\nu \cdot \log N}$ to $k = -\log(1 - (1 - 2^{-\lambda})^{\frac{1}{\nu \cdot \log N}})$.

For example, to have an overflow probability equal to 2^{-64}, $\lambda = 64$, $N = 2^{30}$, $\nu = 4$, the bucket size needs to be only 36 while Shi et al. [17] determined the bucket size be equal 72 for the same overflow probability. Moreover, since N, the number of elements in the ORAM, has a logarithmic effect on the overflow probability, the size of interior nodes will not change for large fluctuations of the number of elements N. For example, for $N = 2^{80}$, the interior node still has size 36 with overflow probability 2^{-64}.

Leaf Nodes. Let B_i denote the random variable describing the size of the ith leaf node. Thinking of a leaf node as a bin, a standard balls and bins game argument provides us the following upper bound

$$\Pr(B_i \geq k) \leq \binom{N}{k} \cdot \frac{1}{N^k} \leq \frac{e^k}{k^k}.$$

The second inequality follows from an upper bound of the binomial coefficient using Stirling's approximation. For N leaves, we have

$$\Pr(\exists i \in [N] : B_i \geq k) = \Pr(\bigcup_{i=1}^{N} B_i \geq k)$$

$$\leq \sum_{i=1}^{N} \Pr(B_i \geq k) \tag{4}$$

$$\leq \frac{N}{e^{k \cdot (\ln(k) - 1)}}.$$

Note that in Eq. 4, we have used the union bound. Based on the same parameters as in the previous example, the size of a leaf node has to be set only to 28 to have an overflow probability equal to 2^{-64}. To compute this result, one solves the equation $k = e^{W(\frac{\log 2^\lambda \cdot N}{e}) + 1}$, where $W(.)$ is the product log function. While the size of the interior node can be considered constant for large fluctuations of N, the size of a leaf node should be carefully chosen depending on N. Every time the number of elements increases by a multiplicative factor of 32, we have to increase the size of the leaf node by 1 to keep the same overflow probability.

Note that for both interior and leaf node size computations, we do not take into account the number of operations (accesses) performed by the client. As with related work, the number of ORAM operations is typically considered part of security parameter λ. The larger the number of operations performed, the larger the security parameter has to be.

4.2   1st Strategy: Naïve Expansion

Let N and n respectively denote the number of leaf nodes and elements in the ORAM. The naïve solution is simply adding a new leaf level, as soon as the condition $n > N$ occurs. The main drawback of this first naïve solution is the waste of storage which can be explained from two different perspectives. The first storage waste consists on creating, in average, more leaf nodes than elements in the ORAM. The second storage waste in the under-usage of the leaf nodes while they can hold more elements with a slight size increase. Our second strategy will try to get rid of this drawback.

4.3   2nd Strategy: Lazy Expansion

This technique consists of creating a new tree level when the number of elements added is equal to α times the number of leaf nodes in the tree. For a N leaves tree, the client is allowed to store up to $\alpha \cdot N$ elements in the ORAM without increasing the size of the tree. As soon as $n > \alpha \cdot N$, the client asks the server to create a new level of leaves with $2 \cdot N$ leaf nodes.

This lazy increase strategy is performed recursively. For example, if the size of the ORAM tree is now equal to $2 \cdot N$, then the client will work with the same structure as long as $\alpha \cdot N < n \leq \alpha \cdot 2 \cdot N$. Once $n > \alpha \cdot 2 \cdot N$, a new level of leaves with now $4N$ leaf buckets is created.

To be able to store more elements, our idea is to slightly increase the leaf bucket size. Therewith, we can keep the same overflow probability. Note the tradeoff between increasing the size of leaf nodes and the communication complexity of the ORAM. To read or write an element in the ORAM, the client downloads the path starting from the root to the leaf node. If the size of this path (when increasing the size of the bucket) is larger than a regular ORAM tree with the same number of elements, then this technique would not be worth applying.

Gentry et al. [6] have shown that by increasing the leaf node size from k to $\alpha + k$, we can reduce the storage overhead while handling more elements than leaf nodes. For N leaf nodes, we can have up to $\alpha \cdot N$ elements. While Gentry et al. [6] chose α to optimize the storage cost for a given overflow probability, we instead target the computation of the value α for the optimal communication complexity. In our subsequent analysis, the previous bounds for interior and leaf node sizes as computed in Sect. 4.1 are used.

First, we determine a relation between the size x of a leaf bucket and factor α for our 2nd strategy. Then, we compute the optimal value of α as a function of the security parameter λ, the size of the interior nodes, and the current number of leaves. To calculate the overflow probability, we focus on the worst case occurring when there are $\alpha \cdot N$ elements in an ORAM with N leaves.

Lemma 41. *Let x denote the optimal leaf bucket size for the* 2nd *strategy. Then,*

$$\alpha = \frac{x}{e} \cdot \left(\frac{2^{-\lambda}}{N}\right)^{\frac{1}{x}} \tag{5}$$

holds, where λ is the security parameter and N the number of leaf nodes.

Proof. By a balls-and-bins argument, we are in a scenario where we insert uniformly at random $\alpha \cdot N$ balls into N bins. The ith bin overflows if there are x balls from $\alpha \cdot N$ that went to the same i^{th} bin. The possible number of combinations equals $\binom{\alpha \cdot N}{x}$. By applying the upper bound inequality to the probability of the union of events (possible combinations), we obtain

$$\Pr(B_i \geq x) \leq \binom{\alpha \cdot N}{x} \cdot \frac{1}{N^x}$$
$$\leq \left(\frac{e \cdot \alpha \cdot N}{x}\right)^x \cdot \frac{1}{N^x}$$
$$= \left(\frac{e \cdot \alpha}{x}\right)^x.$$

Computing the union bound over all leaf nodes results in

$$\Pr(\exists i \in [N] : B_i \geq x) \leq N \cdot (\frac{e \cdot \alpha}{x})^x.$$

In order to have overflow probability equal $2^{-\lambda}$ as previous work, we must verify that $N \cdot (\frac{e \cdot \alpha}{x})^x = 2^{-\lambda}$ which is equivalent to $\alpha = \frac{x}{e} \cdot (\frac{2^{-\lambda}}{N})^{\frac{1}{x}}$. $\qquad \square$

Corollary 41. *Let k denote the size of the interior node. The best communication complexity for the 2nd strategy is achieved iff the leaf bucket size x equals*

$$x = \frac{\frac{k}{\ln 2} + \sqrt{k - 4 \cdot k \cdot \log \frac{2^{-\lambda}}{N}}}{2}$$

Proof. First, note that if N leaf nodes can handle $\alpha \cdot N$ elements, the tree is flatter compared to the naïve solution where the tree will have height $\log N$ instead of $\log \alpha \cdot N$. However, the downside of the 2nd strategy is the leaf bucket size increase. In order to take the maximal advantage of this height reduction, we define the optimal leaf buck size x that can have the best communication complexity compared to the naïve solution. Let C_1 and C_2 denote, respectively, the communication complexity needed to download one path for the first and second strategy. For an interior node with size k and a leaf bucket for the naïve strategy with size y, the communication complexities C_1 and C_2 compute to

$$C_1 = (\log \alpha \cdot N - 1) \cdot k + y \text{ and } C_2 = (\log N - 1) \cdot k + x.$$

The best value of x for a fixed value of y, k and λ is the maximum value of the function f defined as

$$f(x) = C_1 - C_2 = y - x + k \cdot \log \alpha.$$

The first derivative of f is $\frac{df}{dx}(x) = x^2 - \frac{k}{\ln(2)} \cdot x + k \cdot \log \frac{2^{-\lambda}}{N}$. This quadratic equation has only one valid solution for a non-negative leaf buckets size and $2^\lambda \gg N$. The only valid root for the first derivative is

$x = \frac{\frac{k}{\ln 2} + \sqrt{k - 4 \cdot k \cdot \log \frac{2^{-\lambda}}{N}}}{2}$. $\qquad \square$

Once we have computed the optimal leaf node size, we can plug the result into Eq. 5 to compute the optimal value α. For example, for $N = 2^{30}$ leaves, the size of the leaf bucket in the naïve strategy is $y = 28$, the size of the interior node $k = 36$. Applying the result of Corollary 41 outputs the size of the leaf bucket for an optimal communication complexity which is equal to $x \approx 85$. Applying the result of Lemma 41, we obtain $\alpha \approx 15$. The communication complexity saving compared to the naïve strategy is around 7% while the storage savings is a significant 87%.

One disadvantage of the 2nd strategy is the possibility of storage underutilization. Imagine the client stores $\alpha \cdot N$ elements in the ORAM tree. When adding a new element, it will trigger the creation of a new leaf level, which is a waste of storage. For example, the client can have $\alpha \cdot N + 1$ elements in his ORAM tree, then performs a loop which respectively adds and deletes two elements. This loop will imply the allocation of an unused large amount of storage (in $O(N)$). Also, this loop implies leaf node pruning which is more expensive (in term of communication complexity) compared to leaf increasing as we will see in Sect. 5.

4.4   3rd Strategy: Dynamic Expansion

Our dynamic solution tackles the underutilization of storage described in the previous section. Instead of adding entire new levels to the tree, we will progressively add pairs of leaf nodes to gradually increase the capacity of the tree. This has the advantage of matching a user's storage cost expectation: every time the ORAM capacity is increased, storage requirements increase proportionally. However, unlike our previous techniques, we are now no longer guaranteed to have a full binary tree. This implies a overflow probability recalculation of two different levels of leaf nodes.

Let us assume that we start with a full binary tree containing $N = 2^l$ leaf nodes. Dynamic insertion results in the creation of two different levels of leaves. The first one is on the lth level while the other one in on the $(l + 1)^{th}$ level. In general, after adding $\eta \cdot \alpha$ elements, the number of leaves in the lth level is equal to $N - \eta$ while the number of leaves in the $(l + 1)^{th}$ level is equal to 2η.

At this point, we must carefully consider how to tag new elements that are added to the tree. If we choose tags following a uniform distribution over all the $N - \eta + 2 \cdot \eta = N + \eta$ leaves, we will violate ORAM security. An adversary will be able to distinguish with non-negligible advantage between two elements added before and after increasing the number of leaf nodes in the ORAM, as the assignment probabilities to (leaf) nodes will be different at varying points in the tree's lifecycle.

An efficient solution to this problem is to keep the probability assignment of leaf nodes equally likely for all subtrees with a common root. We implement this approach by setting a leaf's assignment probability in the lth level to $\frac{1}{2^l}$ and to $\frac{1}{2^{l+1}}$ in the $(l + 1)^{th}$ level. We now analyze the size of leaf buckets with an overflow probability of $2^{-\lambda}$. We consider the general case where we add $\eta < N$ leaf nodes to the ORAM.

Lemma 42. *Let B_i denote the random variable describing the size of the ith leaf node, $1 \leq i \leq N + \eta$. For the 3rd strategy and a bucket of size B_i, the overflow probability computes to*

$$\Pr(\exists i \in [N + \eta] : \ B_i \geq k) \leq \frac{2 \cdot N}{k + 1} \cdot (\frac{2 \cdot e \cdot \alpha}{k})^k.$$

Proof. After adding η leaf nodes to the structure, the ORAM contains $N + \eta$ leaves. The probability that at least one leaf node has size larger than k is

$$\Pr(\exists i \in [N + \eta] : \ B_i \geq k) = \Pr(\bigcup_{i=1}^{N+\eta} B_i \geq k)$$

$$\leq \sum_{i=1}^{2 \cdot \eta} \Pr(B_i \geq k) + \sum_{i=2 \cdot \eta+1}^{N+\eta} \Pr(B_i \geq k) \qquad (6)$$

Note that the leaf nodes ranging from 1 to $2 \cdot \eta$ are in the $(l+1)^{th}$ level with an assignment probability equal to $\frac{1}{2 \cdot N}$ while leaves ranging from $2 \cdot \eta + 1$ to

$N + \eta$ belongs to the upper level and have an assignment probability equal to $\frac{1}{N}$. We obtain

$$\text{for } 1 \leq i \leq 2 \cdot \eta : \Pr(B_i \geq k) \leq \binom{\alpha \cdot (N + \eta)}{k} \cdot (\frac{1}{2 \cdot N})^k$$

$$\text{for } 2 \cdot \eta + 1 \leq i \leq N + \eta : \Pr(B_i \geq k) \leq \binom{\alpha \cdot (N + \eta)}{k} \cdot (\frac{1}{N})^k.$$

Note that $\alpha \cdot (N + \eta)$ is the current number of elements in the ORAM. We plug both inequalities in to Eq. 6 and get

$$\Pr(\exists i \in [N + \eta] : B_i \geq k) \leq 2 \cdot \eta \cdot \binom{\alpha \cdot (N + \eta)}{k} \cdot (\frac{1}{2 \cdot N})^k + (N - \eta) \cdot \binom{\alpha \cdot (N + \eta)}{k} \cdot (\frac{1}{N})^k$$

$$\leq (\frac{2 \cdot \eta}{2^k} + N - \eta) \cdot (1 + \frac{\eta}{N})^k \cdot (\frac{e \cdot \alpha}{k})^k.$$

The bound above is depending on η. Thus, we now compute the value of $\eta < N$ maximizing the bound. This leads us to the function $g(\eta) = (\frac{2 \cdot \eta}{2^k} + N - \eta) \cdot (1 + \frac{\eta}{N})^k$. Function g has a local maximum value for any $\eta, 1 \leq \eta \leq N$ such that $\eta_{max} = \frac{N}{A} \cdot \frac{k - A}{A(k+1)}$ where $A = 1 - \frac{1}{2^{k-1}}$. We replace η_{max} in g to get an upper bound for any any η and $k \geq 2$,

$$\Pr(\exists i \in [N + n] : B_i \geq k) \leq g(n_{max}) \cdot (\frac{e \cdot \alpha}{k})^k$$

$$\leq N \cdot \frac{A + 1}{k + 1} \cdot (\frac{k(A + 1)}{A(k + 1)})^k \cdot (\frac{e \cdot \alpha}{k})^k$$

$$\leq \frac{2 \cdot N}{k + 1} \cdot (\frac{2 \cdot e \cdot \alpha}{k})^k.$$

As $k \geq 2$, we conclude with $(\frac{k(A+1)}{A(k+1)})^k \leq 2^k$ and $\frac{A+1}{k+1} \leq \frac{2}{k+1}$.   □

So, the overflow probability decreases exponentially when increasing bucket size k. Note that, in the proof, we have maximized the overflow probability independently of the number of nodes added (which is a function of η). In practice, k could be smaller for some intervals of insertions, but we have chosen a maximal value to avoid issues related to changing the leaves' size during insertions.

4.5   Comparison of Strategies

We present a comparison between our three strategies in terms of storage complexity (Fig. 2) and communication complexity per access (Fig. 1). We perform our comparison on a block level, thereby remaining independent of the actual block size.

Communication complexity: The 2nd strategy offers best communication complexity. This is due to shorter paths, a result of flatter trees – compared to the naïve 1st solution. Also, compared to the 3rd strategy, the leaf buckets have

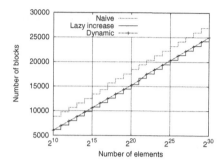

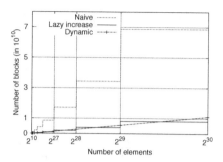

Fig. 1. Communication, blocks per access

Fig. 2. Storage cost, blocks

smaller size. For a number of elements $N = 2^{30}$ and 2^{-64} overflow probability, the interior node size equals 36 which is appropriate for all three strategies. The difference consists on the size of the leaf buckets as well as the height of the resulting tree. The bucket size for the naïve (1st), lazy (2nd) and dynamic (3rd) strategy respectively equals 28, 85 and 130 blocks. The tree's height for the naïve solution equals 30 while for the lazy and dynamic solution the tree height is 26 since $\alpha \approx 2^4$. In Fig. 1, for an eviction rate used equals 4, the entire communication complexity (upload/download) on the main ORAM respectively equals 26928, 24210 and 25020 blocks for the naïve, lazy and dynamic solution. Note that per access, we save around 7 % in communication cost. Recall that our main purpose is to reduce the storage overhead while maintaining the same communication complexity. However, our results show that storage optimization has a direct consequence on reducing the communication complexity as well.

Storage complexity: There is no "clear winner". Depending on the client's usage strategy, the dynamic (3rd) strategy can be considered best, as it provides more intuitive and fine grained control over storage size. However, if the insertion of elements follows a well defined pattern where the client is always expanding their capacity by a factor of α, the 2nd strategy will result in cheaper cost. The cost reduction is significant, around 87 % fewer blocks compared to the naïve solutions.

Independently of the blocks size, this represents 87 % of storage cost savings. Consider the following example: we fix the block size to 4096 Byte and the number of elements to $N = 2^{30}$, resulting in a dataset size equal to 4 TByte. Based on Amazon S3 pricing [1] where the price is equal to 0.029 USD per GByte per month, the client has to store, for the naïve solution, $\sim 2.8.10^{14} \approx 262$ TByte, implying ~ 7600 (USD) per month. With the lazy solution, the client has to store only ~ 31 TBytes, which is only 900 (USD) per month (almost 10 times cheaper than the naïve solution).

In general, both the 2nd and 3rd strategies outperform the naïve one in terms of communication and storage complexities.

4.6   Position Map

To maintain constant client memory, it is important to recursively store the mapping between tags and elements in a position map on the server. This position map is stored in a logarithm number of ORAMs with a number of leaves increasing exponentially from one ORAM to the other. With a position map factor τ, $N = \tau^l$, the position map is composed of $l - 1$ small ORAMs where $ORAM_i$ has a number of leaves equal to τ^i, $1 \leq i \leq l - 1$.

Surprisingly, resizing the position map is trivial, e.g., following one of the two subsequent strategies: (1) use the same strategy of resizing (adding/pruning) that we apply on $ORAM_{l-1}$, or (2) create a new level of recursion in the case of adding, or deleting the last level of recursion in the case of pruning. Assume N elements; each element is associated to a leaf tag that has size $\log N$ bits. We describe each solution for the case of the naïve adding strategy.

(1) When we add a new line to the main ORAM ($ORAM_l$), we have $2 \cdot N$ leaves instead of N leaves. Similarly, we increase the size of the last ORAM of the position map ($ORAM_{l-1}$) to have a new level of leaves. The only issue with this solution is that we should increase the block size. Instead of having $O(\tau \cdot \log N)$ bits, it will have now $O(\tau^2 \cdot \log N)$ bits. Every time an element is accessed, the corresponding block is modified to have the new size. Note that when we add a new level of leaves, we can always access all elements of the ORAM using the previous mapping. For this, we just append at the end of the tag fetched an additional bit 0 or 1 to access a random child (to stay oblivious and access the entire path). After accessing any "old" elements (old denotes elements with a previous mapping), the mapping is updated to have $\log N + 1$ bits instead of $\log N$.

(2) The second solution is straightforward and based on creating a new level of recursion when a new level of leaves is created. Note that blocks in this level will have $O(\tau \cdot \log N + 1)$ bits instead $O(\tau \cdot \log N)$. To access an "old" element, we use the same method described above.

5   Pruning

Assume an ORAM storing N elements. Now, the client deletes η elements from the ORAM. Consequently, the naïve ORAM construction now contains $N - \eta$ elements, but still has N leaves. Consequently, the client tries saving unnecessary storage costs and frees a number of nodes from the ORAM. Similar to adding element to the ORAM tree, we tackle pruning by presenting two different strategies. The first one, a *lazy pruning*, prunes the entire set of leaves of the lowest level l and merges content with level $l - 1$. Our second strategy consists of a *dynamic pruning* that deletes two leaf nodes for a specific number of elements removed from the ORAM. Again, we will analyze overflow probabilities induced by such pruning as well as complexities.

5.1 Lazy Pruning

In Sect. 4.3, we have demonstrated that leaves can store significantly more elements while only slightly increasing their size. We will use this observation to construct a new algorithm for lazy pruning. Assume that the leaf level contains N leaves for $\alpha \cdot N$ elements stored. Let η denote the number of elements deleted by the client. For sake of simplicity, assume that, at the beginning, we have $\eta = 0$ and N leaf nodes. Our pruning technique is similar to the "lazy" insertion described previously. Whenever $\alpha \cdot \frac{N}{2} < \eta \leq \alpha \cdot N$, we keep the same number of leaves. Within this interval, the client can add or delete elements without applying any change to the structure, as long as the number of elements remains within the defined interval. If the number of deletion equals $\alpha \cdot \frac{N}{2}$, the client proceeds to remove an entire level of leaf nodes. The client proceeds to read every leaf node, along with its sibling, and merges them with their parent node. While this appears to be straightforward, an oblivious merging of siblings into their parent is more complex under our constant-client memory constraint. We will discuss this in great detail below.

Besides, the major problem of this technique is its unfortunate behavior in case of a pattern oscillating around the pruning value. For example, the if the client deletes $\alpha \cdot \frac{N}{2}$ elements, prunes the entire level, then adds a new element back. Now the ORAM structure has more than $\alpha \cdot \frac{N}{2}$ elements in $\frac{N}{2}$ leaves, so the client has to again double the number of leaves. This pattern will result in high communication costs.

5.2 Dynamic Pruning

Given that pruning an entire level at once is very inefficient, we now investigate how pruning can be done in a more gradual way. For every α elements we delete, we will prune two children and merge their contents into their parent node. The pruning will *fail* if the number of elements in both children and parent is more than k. This can only occur if there are more than k elements associated (tagged) to these children. The following lemma states the upper bound of the overflow probability for the parent node after a merging. Recall that we begin with a full binary tree of N leaves and $\alpha \cdot N$ elements. Assume that we have already deleted $\alpha(\eta - 1)$ elements, and we want to delete an additional α elements.

Lemma 51. *Let P_η denote the random variable of the size of the ηth parent node. For dynamic pruning, the probability that pruning will fail equals*

$$\Pr(P_\eta > k) \leq \left(\frac{2e \cdot \alpha}{k}\right)^k$$

Proof. The pruning will fail *iff* there are more than a total of k elements in the parent and the children. Any element in these three buckets must be tagged for either the left or the right child. In order to compute the overflow probability of the parent, we compute the probability that more than k elements are tagged to both children.

$$\Pr(P_\eta > k) = \binom{\alpha \cdot (N - \eta)}{k} \cdot (\frac{2}{N})^k$$

$$\leq (\frac{e \cdot \alpha \cdot (N - \eta)}{k})^k \cdot (\frac{2}{N})^k$$

$$\leq (1 - \frac{\eta}{N})^k \cdot (\frac{2e \cdot \alpha}{k})^k$$

$$\leq (\frac{2e \cdot \alpha}{k})^k$$

In conclusion, the probability decreases exponentially with bucket size k. The upper bound is independent of the number of pruned nodes η. In practice, the bounds are tighter, especially for larger values of η.

Complexity of Oblivious Merging. The cost of dynamic pruning boils down to the cost of obliviously merging three buckets of size k. We can achieve this with $O(k)$ communication and constant memory complexity. First, note that we do not have to merge all three buckets at once. All that is required is an algorithm which obliviously merges two buckets. We can then apply it to successively merge three buckets into one. Since the adversary already knows that the two buckets being merged have no more than k elements in them (as shown above), the idea will be to retrieve the elements from each bucket in a more efficient way that takes advantage of this property.

Input: Configuration of buckets A and B
Output: A permutation which randomly "lines up" bucket B to bucket A
// Slots in A and B start either empty or full; mark slots in A as
   ''assigned'' if block from B is assigned in π
$x \leftarrow$ number of empty slots in A ;
$y \leftarrow$ number of full slots in B ;
$d \leftarrow x - y$;
for i *from 1 to k* **do**

    if $B[i]$ *is full* **then**

        $z \xleftarrow{\$}$ all empty slots in A;

    else

        if $d > 0$ **then**

            $z \xleftarrow{\$}$ all non-assigned slots in A;

            $d \leftarrow d - 1$;

        else

            $z \xleftarrow{\$}$ all full slots in A;

        end

    end

    $\pi[i] \leftarrow z$;

    $A[z] \leftarrow$ assigned ;

end
return π ;

Algorithm 1. GeneratePermutation(A, B)

In Algorithm 1, the client randomly permutes the order of the elements in one bucket, subject to the constraint that, for all indices, at most one of the elements between both buckets is real. That is, the permutation "lines up" the two buckets so that they can be merged efficiently. Special care must be given to generate this permutation using only constant memory. The client makes use of "configuration maps" which simply indicate, for every slot in a bucket, whether that slot is currently full or empty. These maps can be stored encrypted on the server and take up $O(1)$ space each in terms of blocks (because the buckets contain $O(\log N)$ elements and a single block is at least $\log N$ bits [17,18]). Then, the client iterates through the slots in one bucket, randomly pairing them with compatible slots in the other (i.e., a full slot cannot be lined up with another full slot). An additional twist is that an empty slot can be lined up with either a full or empty slot in the other bucket, but not at the expense of "using up" an empty slot that might be needed later since we cannot match full with full. Therefore, we have to also keep a counter of the difference between empty slots in the target bucket and full slots in the source bucket.

As seen in Fig. 3, once the client generates the permutation, they can retrieves the elements pairwise from both buckets (i.e., slot i from one bucket and the slot which is mapped to i via the permutation from the other bucket), writing back the single real one to the merged bucket.

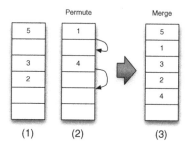

Fig. 3. Illustration of permute-and-merge process. Bucket (2) is permuted and then merged with bucket (1) to create a new, combined bucket (3).

It remains to show that this permutation does not reveal any information to the adversary. If it was a completely random permutation, it would certainly contain no information. However, we are choosing from a reduced set: all permutations which cause the bucket to "line up" with its sibling.

Fortunately, we can formally prove that our permutation does not reveal any information beyond what the adversary already knows. This is because there are no permutations which are inherently "special" and are more likely to occur, over all possible initial configurations of the bucket. For every permutation and load of a bucket, there are an equal number of bucket configurations (i.e., which slots contain real elements and which do not) for which that permutation is valid.

To make this approach work, we need to slightly modify the behavior of the bucket ORAMs. Previously, when a new element was added to a bucket, it did not matter which slot it went into in that bucket. It was possible, for instance, that all the real elements would be kept at the top of the bucket and, when adding a new one, the client would simply insert that element into the first empty slot that it could find. However, to use this permutation method equalwe require that the buckets be in a random "configuration" in terms of which slots are empty and which are filled. Therefore, when inserting an element, the client should choose randomly amongst the free slots. Again, this is possible with constant client memory using our configuration maps. With this behavior, applying the above logic leads to the conclusion that the adversary learns nothing about the load of the bucket from seeing the permutation.

Refer to Appendix A for the full security proof.

5.3   Privacy Analysis

Theorem 51. *Resizable ORAM is a secure ORAM following Definition 31, if every node is a secure trivial ORAM.*

Proof (Sketch). Given that ORAM buckets are secure trivial ORAMs, we have to show that two access patterns induced by $\vec{y}$ and $\vec{z}$ of the same length are indistinguishable. Compared to traditional ORAM, resizable ORAM includes two new operations, Alloc and Free. Note that those operations should be in the same positions for both sequences, otherwise, distinguishing between the access pattern will be straightforward. Furthermore, we have already shown that, for increasing the size of the ORAM, Alloc for the 2nd and 3rd strategies will not induce any leakage. Also, lazy or dynamic pruning strategies will not leak any information about the load of the buckets. That is, the Free operation is oblivious. So, these additional operations do not leak any other information besides the actual number of elements (or a window that bounds the current number of elements for strategies 1 and 2). Also, the access patterns induced by other operations in both sequences $\vec{y}$ and $\vec{z}$ are indistinguishable (see the proof by Shi et al. [17]). We can conclude that resizable ORAM is a secure ORAM following Definition 31.   □

6   Related Work

We are the first to rigorously investigate the topic of resizing current tree-based ORAMs [5,6,14,17,18] and tackle the challenges that can arise from resizing these ORAMs. Our work especially focuses on tree-based ORAM constructions [5,6,14,17,18] for the *constant client memory* setting.

Oblivious RAM was introduced by Goldreich and Ostrovsky [7]. Much work [2–11,13–20] has been published to reduce the communication complexity between client and storage. Early schemes were able to optimize *amortized* cost to be poly-logarithmic, but still maintained linear worst-case cost [9,16,19,20], due to the fact that they all eventually require an expensive reshuffling. Yet, resizing these types of ORAM is straightforward. Adjusting the size can be done at the same time as reshuffling, for no cost. The only leakage in this case will be the information about the total number of elements stored in the ORAM.

Avoiding the expensive reshuffling, Shi et al. [17] presented the first tree-based construction that involves *partial* reshuffling of the ORAM structure for every access. Thus, the amortized cost equals the worst-case cost with communication complexity of $O(\log^3 N)$ blocks. An additional advantage of this construction is its constant client memory requirement (in term of blocks). Constant client memory ORAM constructions are especially attractive in scenarios with, for example, embedded devices or otherwise constrained hardware.

Further results show that you can improve communication complexity if poly-logarithmic client memory is acceptable [5,6,18]. Gentry et al. [6] optimize Shi et al. [17] by introducing a k-ary structure with a new deterministic eviction algorithm. This results in $O(\frac{\log^3 N}{\log \log N})$ for a branching factor equal to $O(\log N)$, but the client must have $O(\log^2 N)$ client memory available. Inspired by [17], for a client memory equal to $\Theta(\log N)$, Stefanov et al. [18] presented Path ORAM, a construction with communication complexity in $O(\log^2 N)$. A subsequent work by Fletcher et al. [5] reduces communication complexity by a factor of 2 by reducing the size of the buckets. We leave the problem of resizing these non-constant memory ORAMs to future work.

7   Conclusion

We are the first to show how to dynamically resize constant-client memory tree-based Oblivious RAM. This allows for use cases where clients do not know in advance exactly how much storage they will need and/or wishes to scale their storage needs efficiently and cheaply. We have shown that the naïve solution of adding leaf nodes induces a significant, unnecessary overhead. Instead, more advanced strategies, lazy insertion and dynamic insertion, can save dramatically on communication and storage cost compared to the naïve solution, although neither strategy is clearly superior to the other. Furthermore, we have demonstrate that the size of a tree-based ORAM can be decreased efficiently using an oblivious pruning technique. Throughout the paper, we have rigorously analyzed the overflow probability for each technique and presented a tight analysis of both interior and leaf node sizes.

Acknowledgments. This work was partially supported by NSF grant 1218197.

A   Proof: Oblivious Permute-and-Merge

Lemma A1. *Given two buckets with maximum size k and load m and n respectively, over the random configurations of those buckets, Algorithm 1 will output a uniformly random permutation which is independent of m and n.*

Proof. We can determine the probability of a particular permutation π being chosen, given m and n, with a counting argument. It will be equal to

$$\frac{\text{\# of configurations for which } \pi \text{ is a valid permutation}}{\text{total \#of configurations } \times \text{ \# of valid permutations for a given configuration}}$$

The number of configurations for which π is a valid permutation depends on m and n, but not on π itself. This can be seen if you consider that applying the permutation to a fixed configuration of the bucket simply creates another, equally likely configuration. The number of configurations for the sibling bucket that will "match" with that bucket are exactly the same no matter what the actual configuration of the first bucket is. Knowing this, combined with the fact that the probabilities must sum to one, tells us immediately that every permutation is equally likely. However, we can continue and express the total quantity for our first expression as

$$\binom{k}{m}\binom{k-m}{n}$$

This can be thought of as choosing the m full slots for one bucket freely and then choosing the n full slots in the second bucket to line up with the free slots in the already chosen first bucket. The number of valid permutations per configuration can equally be determined via a counting argument as

$$\binom{k-m}{n} \cdot (k-n)! \cdot n!$$

That is, choosing free slots for the n elements in the second bucket and then all permutations of those elements times the permutations of the free blocks. That gives us a final expression for the probability of choosing permutation π of

$$\frac{\binom{k}{m}\binom{k-m}{n}}{\binom{k}{m}\binom{k}{n}\binom{k-m}{n} \cdot (k-n)! \cdot n!} \tag{7}$$

With some algebraic computations, we can show that the Eq. 7 can be simplified to $\frac{1}{k!}$. That is, this shows that the number of permutations, for any random distribution of load in a bucket, is independent of the current load. Again, since this does not depend on π (but only on the size of the bucket), every permutation must be equally likely over the random configurations of the buckets. □

Corollary A1. *A permutation π chosen by Algorithm 1 gives no information about the load of the buckets being merged.*

Proof. By our above lemma, independent of the load each permutation is chosen uniformly over the configurations of the two buckets. Therefore the permutation cannot reveal any information about the load. □

References

1. Amazon: Amazon s3 pricing (2014). http://aws.amazon.com/s3/pricing/
2. Boneh, D., Mazieres, D., Popa, R.A.: Remote oblivious storage: Making oblivious RAM practical, March 2011. http://dspace.mit.edu/bitstream/handle/1721.1/62006/MIT-CSAIL-TR-2011-018.pdf
3. Chung, K.-M., Pass, R.: A Simple ORAM. IACR Cryptology ePrint Archive, Report 2013/243 (2013)
4. Damgård, I., Meldgaard, S., Nielsen, J.B.: Perfectly secure oblivious RAM without random oracles. In: Ishai, Y. (ed.) TCC 2011. LNCS, vol. 6597, pp. 144–163. Springer, Heidelberg (2011)
5. Fletcher, C.W., Ren, L., Kwon, A., van Dijk, M., Stefanov, E., Devadas, S.: RAW Path ORAM: A Low-Latency, Low-Area Hardware ORAM Controller with Integrity Verification. IACR Cryptology ePrint Archive, Report 2014/431 (2014)
6. Gentry, C., Goldman, K.A., Halevi, S., Julta, C., Raykova, M., Wichs, D.: Optimizing ORAM and using it efficiently for secure computation. In: De Cristofaro, E., Wright, M. (eds.) PETS 2013. LNCS, vol. 7981, pp. 1–18. Springer, Heidelberg (2013)
7. Goldreich, O., Ostrovsky, R.: Software protection and simulation on oblivious RAMs. J. ACM 43(3), 431–473 (1996)
8. Goldreich, O.: Towards a theory of software protection and simulation by oblivious RAMs. In: Proceedings of Symposium on Theory of Computing, New York, USA, pp. 182–194 (1987)
9. Goodrich, M.T., Mitzenmacher, M.: Privacy-preserving access of outsourced data via oblivious RAM simulation. In: Aceto, L., Henzinger, M., Sgall, J. (eds.) ICALP 2011, Part II. LNCS, vol. 6756, pp. 576–587. Springer, Heidelberg (2011)
10. Goodrich, M.T., Mitzenmacher, M., Ohrimenko, O., Tamassia, R.: Oblivious RAM simulation with efficient worst-case access overhead. In: Proceedings of Cloud Computing Security Workshop, Chicago, USA, pp. 95–100 (2011)
11. Goodrich, M.T., Mitzenmacher, M., Ohrimenko, O., Tamassia, R.: Privacy-preserving group data access via stateless oblivious RAM simulation. In: Proceedings of the Symposium on Discrete Algorithms, Kyoto, Japan, pp. 157–167 (2012)
12. Hsu, J., Burke, P.: Behavior of tandem buffers with geometric input and Markovian output. IEEE Trans. Commun. 24(3), 358–361 (1976)
13. Kushilevitz, E., Lu, S., Ostrovsky, R.: On the (in)security of hash-based oblivious RAM and a new balancing scheme. In: Proceedings of Symposium on Discrete Algorithms, Kyoto, Japan, pp. 143–156 (2012)
14. Mayberry, T., Blass, E.-O., Chan, A.H.: Path-PIR: lower worst-case bounds by combining ORAM and PIR. In: Proceedings of the Network and Distributed System Security Symposium, San Diego, USA (2014)
15. Ostrovsky, R., Shoup, V.: Private information storage (extended abstract). In: Proceedings of the Symposium on Theory of Computing, El Paso, USA, pp. 294–303 (1997)
16. Pinkas, B., Reinman, T.: Oblivious RAM revisited. In: Rabin, T. (ed.) CRYPTO 2010. LNCS, vol. 6223, pp. 502–519. Springer, Heidelberg (2010)
17. Shi, E., Chan, T.-H.H., Stefanov, E., Li, M.: Oblivious RAM with $O((\log N)^3)$ worst-case cost. In: Lee, D.H., Wang, X. (eds.) ASIACRYPT 2011. LNCS, vol. 7073, pp. 197–214. Springer, Heidelberg (2011)

18. Stefanov, E., van Dijk, M., Shi, E., Fletcher, C.W., Ren, L., Yu, X., Devadas, S.: Path ORAM: an extremely simple oblivious RAM protocol. In: Conference on Computer and Communications Security, pp. 299–310 (2013)
19. Williams, P., Sion, R.: Usable PIR. In: Proceedings of Network and Distributed System Security Symposium, San Diego, USA (2008)
20. Williams, P., Sion, R., Carbunar, B.: Building castles out of mud: practical access pattern privacy and correctness on untrusted storage. In: Conference on Computer and Communications Security, Alexandra, USA, pp. 139–148 (2008)

Sublinear Scaling for Multi-Client
Private Information Retrieval

Wouter Lueks[1] and Ian Goldberg[2]([⊠])

[1] Institute for Computing and Information Sciences (iCIS),
Radboud University Nijmegen, Nijmegen, The Netherlands
`lueks@cs.ru.nl`
[2] Cheriton School of Computer Science,
University of Waterloo, Waterloo, ON, Canada
`iang@cs.uwaterloo.ca`

Abstract. Private information retrieval (PIR) allows clients to retrieve records from online database servers without revealing to the servers any information about what records are being retrieved. To achieve this, the servers must typically do a computation involving the entire database for each query. Previous work by Ishai et al. has suggested using batch codes to allow a single client (or collaborating clients) to retrieve multiple records simultaneously while allowing the server computation to scale sublinearly with the number of records fetched.

In this work, we observe a useful mathematical relationship between batch codes and efficient matrix multiplication algorithms, and use this to design a PIR server algorithm that achieves sublinear scaling in the number of records fetched, even when they are requested by *distinct, non-collaborating* clients; indeed, the clients can be completely unaware that the servers are implementing our optimization. Our multi-client server algorithm is several times faster, when enough records are fetched, than existing optimized PIR severs.

As an application of our work, we show how retrieving proofs of inclusion of certificates in a Certificate Transparency log server can be made privacy friendly using multi-client PIR.

1   Introduction

Private Information Retrieval, or PIR, was introduced in the seminal work of Chor et al. in 1995 [3]. In PIR, a client wishes to retrieve information from online database servers while revealing to the database operators *no information* about what data she seeks. That this is even possible is counterintuitive, but consider the *trivial download* scheme: the database server sends the entirety of the database to the client, who searches it herself. This is clearly private, but comes at a high communication cost for large databases. Non-trivial PIR schemes aim to achieve the same level of privacy while transmitting far less data. The simplest PIR schemes assume that the database consists of an array of equal-sized blocks, and that the client knows the index of the block she wishes to retrieve. However, previous work showed that this simple query mechanism can

© International Financial Cryptography Association 2015
R. Böhme and T. Okamoto (Eds.): FC 2015, LNCS 8975, pp. 168–185, 2015.
DOI: 10.1007/978-3-662-47854-7_10

be used as a black box to realize more expressive database search functionality, including search by keywords [4] and private SQL queries [16].

Chor et al.'s original 1995 work showed one cannot have both information-theoretic privacy (i.e., privacy even when the server is computationally unbounded) and a sublinear (in the size of the database) communication cost if only one server is employed. However, information-theoretic PIR (IT-PIR) schemes circumvent this impossibility result by using multiple database servers and a *noncollusion* assumption—that at most a bounded number of servers (less than the total number) will collude against the client. They achieve a communication cost much smaller than the size of the database, and modern ones additionally achieve *robustness*—even if some of the servers are unresponsive, buggy, or actively malicious, the client can nonetheless retrieve her information (and identify the misbehaving servers) [2,7,9].

If information-theoretic privacy is not required, computational PIR (CPIR) schemes can be used. These schemes rely on computational or cryptographic assumptions to guarantee privacy against a single database server at low communication cost [14]. Devet and Goldberg [6] also recently proposed a hybrid PIR scheme that combines a CPIR scheme with an IT-PIR scheme to achieve some of the desirable properties of both, while hedging against violations of either the computational or noncollusion assumptions.

While much effort has gone into reducing the communication costs of PIR protocols, it is also important to consider the computational cost. A PIR server typically must process the entirety (or at least a significant fraction) of the database when handling each query, lest it learn information about what the client is likely *not* seeking.

Not all PIR schemes can beat the trivial download approach. Sion and Carbunar [20] found that it would always be faster to simply download the entire database than to use Kushilevitz and Ostrovsky's CPIR scheme [14]. Later, Olumofin and Goldberg [17] noted that a more modern CPIR scheme by Aguilar Melchor and Gaborit [1], as well as a number of IT-PIR schemes, are orders of magnitude faster than the trivial download scheme. However, the computation costs are still nontrivial, requiring on the order of 1 s of CPU time[1] per gigabyte of database size, for each IT-PIR query.

In order to reduce the per-query CPU cost, a number of authors have proposed *batch* techniques, in which a PIR server performs a computation over the database and a batch of simultaneous queries, resulting in less work than computing over the database once for each query separately. Henry et al. [12] propose a batching method based on *ramp schemes* particular to Goldberg's IT-PIR scheme [9], while Ishai et al. [13] use *batch codes* (discussed in more detail below) to provide multi-query computational speedups for any PIR scheme.

Both of these proposals, however, require that the *clients* construct their queries in a special way to achieve the batching speedups. This means that these approaches help only in those scenarios where single clients (or closely cooperating groups of clients) are fetching large batches of queries at the same time.

---

[1] However, this CPU time is almost completely parallelizable if multiple cores or servers are available.

Our Contributions. In this work, we address the more general case in which a PIR server wishes to process a batch of queries simultaneously, whether they were received all from the same client, each query from a unique client, or anything in between. We approach this problem by first observing a mathematical relationship between Ishai et al.'s method of applying batch codes to speed up IT-PIR and a special case of matrix multiplication where the left matrix has a specific structure (Sect. 3). We then generalize this observation to the case of general matrix multiplication. In doing so, we remove all restrictions on the structure of the queries to be batched. We accept a more modest batching speedup to remove the single (or coordinated) client restriction and the potentially large amount of communication induced by Ishai et al.'s method.

We apply our new technique to the setting of Certificate Transparency (Sect. 4), in which web clients fetch information about TLS certificates from log servers, but should hide from the log servers which certificate's information it fetches. This appears to be a perfect opportunity to employ PIR, but the large number of *non-cooperating* clients expected to use the system makes multi-client batching imperative. We note that while batching queries reduces the total computation time at the cost of increasing the latency for individual queries, this extra latency is not an issue in this particular application. We implement and measure our new technique on top of the open-source Percy++ PIR library [10] (Sect. 5).

While our practical improvements—a little more than a 4-fold speedup—are modest, we do offer *sublinear* scaling in the number of queries for *independent* clients, something simpler improvements cannot offer. Additionally, any other system-level optimizations can easily be used on top of our algorithmic ones.

2   Background

Our construction combines Goldberg's robust IT-PIR scheme [9] with fast matrix multiplication techniques inspired by batch codes. Therefore, we first review and compare these notions.

2.1   Goldberg's Robust IT-PIR Scheme

Goldberg models the database as an $r \times s$ matrix $\mathbf{D}$ over a finite field $\mathbb{F}$. Every row in $\mathbf{D}$ corresponds to a single *block* in the database; every block consists of s field elements. To request block j (non-privately) the client could simply send j to the server. However, as a first step, we express the PIR operation as a vector-matrix multiplication before producing a true privacy-friendly scheme. The client constructs the jth standard basis vector e_j of $\mathbb{F}^r$ (i.e., the vector of length r with all zeros except for a 1 in the jth position) and sends it to the server. The requested block j is then obtained by calculating the vector-matrix product $e_j \cdot \mathbf{D}$.

To make the query privacy friendly, the client in Goldberg's scheme creates a $(t + 1)$-out-of-ℓ Shamir secret sharing [19] of this standard basis vector e_j. It sends one share to each of the ℓ database servers, which compute the vector-matrix product with the database and return the result. Lagrange interpolation of the shared vectors gives the standard basis vector; since matrix multiplication and Lagrange interpolation are linear, interpolation of the results yields the jth block of the database. The secret sharing scheme guarantees that as long as at most t servers collude, they learn nothing about the target block.

Goldberg's scheme is robust [7,9]. It permits some of the servers to misbehave, while still enabling the client to recover her record and identify the misbehavers.

Communication cost. To read a single block, the client sends r field elements to, and receives s field elements from, each server. For a fixed database size of n field elements, it is best to select $r = s = \sqrt{n}$. Henry et al. [12] show how to build on this simple fixed-block-size PIR primitive to handle more realistic databases with variable-sized records.

Serving multiple simultaneous queries. Suppose a server receives multiple queries $v_1, \ldots, v_q$ simultaneously. It could answer them by computing the q vector-matrix products $v_i \cdot \mathbf{D}$ individually. However, it can also first group the queries into one matrix $\mathbf{Q}$ where row i consists of query v_i. Then the server computes the matrix-matrix product $\mathbf{Q} \cdot \mathbf{D}$. Row i of the result is the response to the ith query.

With a naive matrix multiplication algorithm the work the server needs to do is the same in both cases: about $2qrs$ operations (qrs multiplications, and about the same number of additions). However, as we will see, using better matrix-multiplication techniques will significantly improve the situation.

Ramp scheme. Henry et al. [12] replace the Shamir secret sharing in Goldberg's PIR scheme with a *ramp scheme*. In this way, a single client can encode more information in each server request, and can retrieve q blocks instead of just 1 *without* increasing the per-server computation or communication cost at all. The large drawback to this scheme (in addition to being useful only for single clients making multiple queries, and not for multiple clients making single queries) is that it must trade some of the robustness of Goldberg's scheme for extra parallel queries, or conversely, that it requires $q - 1$ extra servers in order to maintain the same level of robustness.

2.2 Batch Codes

Batch codes can be used to answer multiple queries efficiently. The idea, proposed by Ishai et al. [13], is to encode the database in a special way, so that a single client can efficiently make multiple queries. This idea is best illustrated using an example. As in the rest of this paper, we apply the batch codes to Goldberg's IT-PIR scheme.

Suppose we want to prepare a database with r rows for two simultaneous queries. We create three separate databases: $\mathbf{D}_1$, containing the first $r/2$ rows; $\mathbf{D}_2$, containing the last $r/2$ rows; and $\mathbf{D}_3 = \mathbf{D}_1 \oplus \mathbf{D}_2$. Any two queries, say for blocks i_1 and i_2, can be answered by making at most one PIR query to each of the $\mathbf{D}_i$: if blocks i_1 and i_2 are not in the same half of the database, the queries can be answered by making one PIR query to $\mathbf{D}_1$ and one to $\mathbf{D}_2$. Suppose, on the other hand, that i_1 and i_2 are both in the first half. Then block i_1 can be retrieved directly, while block i_2 is obtained by making one query to $\mathbf{D}_2$ and one to $\mathbf{D}_3$. Taking the XOR of the latter two results yields the desired row in the first half. Two queries for the second half are handled similarly.

This procedure reduces the computational cost for the server. As we saw in the previous section, a naive method requires $4rs$ field operations; in contrast, the batch code solution requires only $3rs$ field operations (again, half multiplications and half additions).

Note that to hide which indices the client is querying she needs to make a query to each of the three parts, even if two would suffice to get the answer. This means that the client sends $\frac{3}{2}r$ elements to, and receives $3s$ elements from, each server. In the naive case she sends $2r$ elements and receives only $2s$ elements.

In general, an (r, N, q, m) batch code will take a database of r blocks and create m subdatabases, such that the total number of blocks in the subdatabases is N. The code can be used to answer q queries by making one request to each of the m subdatabases. The example we sketched before gives an $(r, \frac{3}{2}r, 2, 3)$ batch code.

Suppose we use an (r, N, q, m) batch code to speed up PIR queries to a database with r blocks, each consisting of s field elements. Let $N_1, \ldots, N_m$ be the number of blocks in the m subdatabases (so that $\sum_i N_i = N$). To make q queries a client needs to make one PIR query to each of the m subdatabases with respectively $N_1, \ldots, N_m$ blocks. The query to subdatabase i costs $2N_i s$ field operations. Therefore the total computational load on the server is $2Ns$. The client sends N group elements, and receives ms elements.

Subcube Batch Code. Ishai et al. [13] generalize the sketch above as follows. First, instead of splitting the database into 2 parts, it can be split into ℓ parts. A final $\ell + 1^{\text{th}}$ part is added, being the XOR of all the previous parts. Again, any two items can be obtained using $\ell + 1$ queries, one to each of the subdatabases— if the two items happen to be in the same part it is necessary to retrieve and calculate the XOR of all the other items. This gives rise to an $(r, \frac{\ell+1}{\ell}r, 2, \ell+1)$ batch code. Obviously, this is good for computation, as the server needs to do only $2\frac{\ell+1}{\ell}rs$ field operations. While the sending cost drops to $\frac{\ell+1}{\ell}r$ elements, the receiving cost rises to $(\ell + 1)s$ elements. (Note that the client always needs to retrieve the $\ell + 1$ records to protect her privacy.)

For simplicity, let us return to the case where $\ell = 2$. The scheme can be applied recursively to answer more queries. Suppose the client makes $q = 4$ queries. Group these into two pairs. Each pair can be answered by making only one query to each of the three parts $\mathbf{D}_1, \mathbf{D}_2, \mathbf{D}_3$. In total, two queries are made to each $\mathbf{D}_i$, so we can apply the above scheme again, but now on the smaller databases.

Recursively applying this scheme gives a system that can handle $q = 2^k$ queries. Table 1 summarizes the important parameters of this scheme. By taking ℓ large, this scheme gets arbitrarily close to the optimal processing time for

Table 1. Summary of batch codes with parameters [13]. The subcube code is parametrized by k and $\ell \geq 2$, while the subset code is parametrized by ℓ, r' and $0 < \alpha < \frac{1}{2}$, where $w = \alpha\ell$. The parameters r and r' scale the codes to support more blocks, without essentially changing their structure.

	Subcube	Subset
Number of blocks (r)	r	$r'\binom{\ell}{w}$
Sum of subdatabase sizes (N)	$\left(\frac{\ell+1}{\ell}\right)^k r$	$r'\sum_{j=0}^{w}\binom{\ell}{j}$
Number of queries (q)	2^k	$\geq 2^w$
Number of subdatabases (m)	$(\ell+1)^k$	$\sum_{j=0}^{w}\binom{\ell}{j}$

the server: it can answer 2^k queries with only slightly more processing than is required for a single query. However, the price is a higher communication cost for the client.

The Subset Batch Code. Ishai et al. also describe another batch code that has more favourable properties: the subset batch code. It is, however, also more complex. We only summarize the results in Table 1, and refer to their paper [13] for a full description of this scheme. The scheme is parametrized by ℓ, r', and $0 < \alpha < \frac{1}{2}$. The value w is then given by $\alpha\ell$.

It can be shown that for this code doing q queries is approximately $(1 - \alpha)/(1 - 2\alpha)$ times more expensive than doing a single query. Thus, picking a small α brings the computational overhead for the server arbitrarily close to optimal. Contrary to the subcube codes the communication overhead is also polynomial in q, however, in practice the overhead turns out to be rather high, especially when α is small.

Consider the following example. We want α to be somewhat small, so we take $\ell = 20$ so that with $\alpha = 0.2$ we get $w = 4$. Suppose we make $q = 16$ queries, Then, $N/r = 1.279$ so the computation cost for 16 queries is only 27.9% more than for 1 query. However, we need to receive $m/q = 387$ times more data than the naive approach for $q = 16$ queries. So, using this code at low computational cost can incur extremely high communication costs.

Challenges. The two main drawbacks of using batch codes for PIR are: (1) the requirement that all of the queries be generated by a single client (or by closely cooperating clients); and (2) the increased communication cost, which becomes especially prohibitive for large databases.

We will address both of these issues in this work. See Table 2 for a comparison of multi-query PIR schemes. Although we only list the subcube batch code and not the subset batch code in the table for conciseness, the two salient challenges listed above are the same for both types.

2.3 Matrix Multiplication Algorithms

Naive matrix multiplication of a matrix $\mathbf{Q}$ of size $q \times r$ with a database $\mathbf{D}$ of size $r \times s$ requires qrs multiplications and at least $q(r-1)s$ additions (although

Table 2. Comparison of multi-query PIR schemes. We show counts of per-server field operations, as well as the number of field elements sent to and received from each server, the number of extra servers the scheme requires to maintain the same robustness level as for a single query, and an indication of whether independent clients can use the method, or whether all queries must be sent by a single client (or coordinated clients). The database consists of r blocks, each containing s field elements. The number of simultaneous queries, q, is assumed to be a power of 2, and much smaller than either r or s. Note that our work achieves sublinear scaling of computation in the number of queries q, while also admitting independent clients.

	Naive	Ramp [12]	Subcube Batch Codes [13]	Our work
$\mathbb{F}$ multiplications	qrs	rs	$q^{\lg((\ell+1)/\ell)}rs$	$q^{0.80735}rs$
$\mathbb{F}$ additions	$q(r-1)s$	$(r-1)s$	$\frac{(\ell^2-1)}{\ell}q^{\lg((\ell+1)/\ell)}rs$	$\frac{8}{3}q^{0.80735}rs$
Send	qr	r	$q^{\lg((\ell+1)/\ell)}r$	qr
Receive	qs	s	$q^{\lg(\ell+1)}s$	qs
Extra servers	0	$q-1$	0	0
Independent clients	✓	×	×	✓

most implementations will actually use qrs additions). For two square matrices of size $n \times n$ this boils down to an $O(n^3)$ complexity.

Faster matrix multiplication algorithms exist that have an asymptotic complexity with a better exponent. In this paper we focus on Strassen's algorithm [21] because of its relative simplicity. This algorithm achieves a time complexity of $O(n^{\lg 7}) = O(n^{2.8074})$. Faster algorithms exist, such as that of Coppersmith and Winograd [5], which achieves an even better bound of $O(n^{2.3729})$. However, this comes at the cost of a much larger multiplicative constant.

Strassen's algorithm is extremely simple. It splits each matrix into four, equal-sized submatrices. A naive block-matrix multiplication of these would require 8 multiplications of the smaller sized matrices. However, using Strassen's algorithm, only 7 are needed. This technique is then applied recursively to the multiplications of the smaller matrices. (See Appendix A for more detail.)

3 Batch Codes as Matrix Multiplication

We have seen that answering multiple PIR queries in Goldberg's protocol requires calculating the matrix-matrix product $\mathbf{Q} \cdot \mathbf{D}$, as the rows of the resulting product are exactly the responses to the given queries. At the same time, batch codes speed up this computation. Hence, batch codes are in some way implementing fast matrix multiplication. In this section we identify this relation, explain the limitations of batch codes in this application, and demonstrate the similarities with Strassen's algorithm. For simplicity of exposition (and because this is the typical case in practice), we will use $\mathbb{F}$ of characteristic 2, so that additions are just XORs.

3.1   An Example

In Sect. 2.2 we showed how a batch code can be used to reduce two queries for the full database to three half-sized queries. In terms of matrix multiplication, the client constructs its three half-sized queries q_1, q_2, q_3 and sends them to the server. The server expresses the database $\mathbf{D}$ as a concatenation of two parts, $\mathbf{D} = \begin{pmatrix} \mathbf{D}_1 \\ \mathbf{D}_2 \end{pmatrix}$, and constructs the matrices

$$\overline{\mathbf{Q}} = \begin{pmatrix} q_1 & 0 & 0 \\ 0 & q_2 & 0 \\ 0 & 0 & q_3 \end{pmatrix}_{3 \times \frac{3}{2}r} \quad \text{and } \mathbf{M} = \begin{pmatrix} \mathbf{I} & 0 \\ 0 & \mathbf{I} \\ \mathbf{I} & \mathbf{I} \end{pmatrix}_{\frac{3}{2}r \times r}, \quad \text{so that } \mathbf{M} \cdot \mathbf{D} = \begin{pmatrix} \mathbf{D}_1 \\ \mathbf{D}_2 \\ \mathbf{D}_1 \oplus \mathbf{D}_2 \end{pmatrix}_{\frac{3}{2}r \times s},$$

where $\overline{\mathbf{Q}}$ is the block-diagonal matrix of the queries, $\mathbf{I}$ is the identity matrix, and $\mathbf{M}$ is the matrix form of the batch code (representing the linear combinations of the parts that make up the resulting subdatabases). (Note that we annotate the matrices with their dimensions.) The server now computes the linear combinations of the parts, $\mathbf{M} \cdot \mathbf{D}$, and multiplies queries $\overline{\mathbf{Q}}$ by them. This results in the familiar response structure

$$\overline{\mathbf{Q}}_{3 \times \frac{3}{2}r} \cdot \mathbf{M}_{\frac{3}{2}r \times r} \cdot \mathbf{D}_{r \times s} = \overline{\mathbf{Q}}_{3 \times \frac{3}{2}r} \cdot \begin{pmatrix} \mathbf{D}_1 \\ \mathbf{D}_2 \\ \mathbf{D}_1 \oplus \mathbf{D}_2 \end{pmatrix}_{\frac{3}{2}r \times s} = \begin{pmatrix} q_1 \cdot \mathbf{D}_1 \\ q_2 \cdot \mathbf{D}_2 \\ q_3 \cdot (\mathbf{D}_1 \oplus \mathbf{D}_2) \end{pmatrix}_{3 \times s}.$$

After receiving the results, the client combines the three rows as appropriate to recover the answers to her two original queries.

3.2   General Batch Codes as Matrix Multiplication

When using general batch codes to speed up PIR we see a similar structure. Recall that an (r, N, q, m) batch code can answer q queries to a database of r rows by splitting the computation across m subdatabases $\mathbf{K}_1, \ldots, \mathbf{K}_m$ containing a total of N rows. In the preceding example—an $(r, \frac{3}{2}r, 2, 3)$ batch code—these subdatabases were $\mathbf{K}_1 = \mathbf{D}_1$, $\mathbf{K}_2 = \mathbf{D}_2$ and $\mathbf{K}_3 = \mathbf{D}_1 \oplus \mathbf{D}_2$. For general batch codes these subdatabases will be more complicated linear combinations of the parts $\mathbf{D}_i$. The $N \times r$ matrix $\mathbf{M}$ represents these linear combinations.

Again, the client first uses the batch code to convert her q queries into m subqueries $q_1, \ldots, q_m$, where each q_i is a row vector of length equal to the number of rows in $\mathbf{K}_i$. She sends these to the server. The server constructs the linear combinations of the parts, $\mathbf{M} \cdot \mathbf{D}$, and applies the queries to them

$$\overline{\mathbf{Q}}_{m \times N} \cdot (\mathbf{M}_{N \times r} \cdot \mathbf{D}_{r \times s}) = \begin{pmatrix} q_1 & & 0 \\ & \ddots & \\ 0 & & q_m \end{pmatrix}_{m \times N} \cdot (\mathbf{M}_{N \times r} \cdot \mathbf{D}_{r \times s}).$$

The server can quickly compute this product using the block-diagonal structure of $\overline{\mathbf{Q}}$. The result is an m-row response. The client can combine those m rows to produce her desired q blocks.

Note that it is the special structure of $\mathbf{Q} = \overline{\mathbf{Q}} \cdot \mathbf{M}$ that enables the server to speed up the matrix multiplication $\mathbf{Q} \cdot \mathbf{D}$. In the PIR setting, this necessitates that $\mathbf{Q}$ be produced by a single client, or by cooperating clients.

3.3   Comparison with Strassen's Algorithm

Strassen's algorithm is similar to the matrix multiplication form of the batch codes above. In particular it also

1. partitions the database into parts $\mathbf{D}_i$,
2. forms linear combinations of the $\mathbf{D}_i$ to construct the subdatabases $\mathbf{K}_i$,
3. multiplies parts of the queries with the subdatabases, and
4. computes linear combinations of the products to produce the final result.

However, there are also differences. First, batch codes require the queries to be preprocessed by the client, or alternatively that the query matrix $\mathbf{Q}$ is given by $\overline{\mathbf{Q}} \cdot \mathbf{M}$ as above. Strassen's algorithm, on the other hand, works with any matrix $\mathbf{Q}$. Second, batch codes are essentially one-dimensional; as a result, steps 1, 2 and 3 above for batch codes operate only on complete rows, while Strassen's algorithm *subdivides* and takes *linear combinations* of rows in addition to taking *subsets* of rows (in both $\mathbf{Q}$ and $\mathbf{D}$).

While Strassen's algorithm has a higher server computational cost than batch codes, the fact that Strassen's algorithm can deal with *any* matrix $\mathbf{Q}$ is of tremendous benefit. In our PIR setting, this means that clients do not need to coordinate their queries. Indeed, they do not need to be aware that the server is implementing this optimization at all.

4   Application of Multi-client PIR: Certificate Transparency

We now examine an application where multi-client PIR is particularly useful: Certificate Transparency. Websites use digital certificates to tie possession of a particular private key to their domain name. These certificates are signed by certificate authorities (CAs). To verify the validity of a website the user's browser checks that a CA it trusts signed the certificate (or that there is a certificate chain from a trusted CA leading to the certificate). Events in recent years, like the hack of the Dutch CA DigiNotar [8], have shown that CAs cannot be trusted unconditionally. When a CA is compromised it can be used to issue false certificates that allow third parties to eavesdrop on the communication between a user and a website. The browser will not detect this as long as the compromised CA is still trusted. Certificate Transparency, as described in RFC 6962 [15], aims to detect wrongly issued certificates in a timely manner without introducing extra trust assumptions. It roughly works as follows.

1. Before a certificate is issued it is recorded by one or more *log servers*. Each of these log servers creates a signed certificate timestamp (SCT) for this certificate and will eventually add the certificate to an append-only data structure.

2. When presenting a certificate the website will also send along the SCTs from the log servers. The browser will verify that at least one trusted log server signed the certificate description.
3. The following consistency checks are done asynchronously:
   (a) An auditor, usually the browser, will check that the log server signed certificates do indeed appear in the append-only log of the log server.
   (b) Auditors and monitors check that the logs are consistent; i.e., that no certificates have been changed or retroactively inserted into the log.
   (c) CAs and webservers monitor the log to detect inconsistencies such as two certificates, by different CAs, for the same domain.

It is essential that the first check is done, because monitors can only detect falsely issued certificates when they appear in the log. However, the first check also reveals to the log server which websites the user is visiting. We will use multi-client PIR to allow many independent clients to query a log server for the proofs of inclusion of certificates.

4.1 Proving that a Certificate Is Included in the Log

The certificates are recorded in a Merkle hash tree. A Merkle hash tree is a binary tree, in which every leaf contains the hash of a certificate, while every internal node contains the hash of its children. The root then captures information about all the children. Periodically, log servers will add all the newly logged certificates to the tree and sign the new root.

The number of leaves, n, determines the structure of the Merkle hash tree. Let k be the largest power of 2 smaller than n, so that $k < n \leq 2k$. Then the left subtree of the Merkle hash tree of n nodes is the full binary tree with k leaves, while the right subtree is the Merkle hash tree of the remaining $n - k$ nodes. See Fig. 1 for an example.

This format allows log servers to construct a proof of inclusion of a certificate for an auditor. The auditor already has the certificate, and thus also the leaf corresponding to the certificate. The log server gives the auditor those node hashes needed to recalculate the root of the tree starting with the certificate. The extra nodes needed for this proof are all the siblings on the path from the leaf to the root; see Fig. 1. Finally, the auditor compares the calculated root with the signed root from the server.

The length of the proof is no larger than the height of the tree. Therefore, the size of the proof grows only logarithmically in the number of leaves. The specification requires SHA256 as the hash function for the internal nodes, so a node contains 32 bytes of data.

4.2 The Number of SSL Certificates

To determine the feasibility of retrieving the proofs of inclusion using PIR, we need to estimate the number of active and valid SSL certificates—it does not make much sense to retrieve proofs for expired certificates. We estimate the number of SSL certificates based on the following sources.

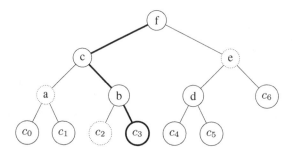

Fig. 1. An example Merkle hash tree for 7 certificates $c_0, \ldots, c_6$ encoded into the leaves. For certificate c_3 the proof of inclusion consists of all the dotted nodes: c_2, a and e. This proof can be checked as follows. First, calculate the hash of the certificate to get c_3. Then, b is the hash of c_2 and c_3; c is the hash of a and b; and, finally, f is the hash of c and e. If the calculated root f matched the signed root the auditor is convinced that the tree contains c_3.

EFF SSL Observatory. The EFF SSL observatory[2] observed about 1.4 million valid certificates in 2010.

Public Netcraft Data. In their public sample of May 2013,[3] Netcraft claimed that Symantec at that time had produced more than one third of all certificates. In their April, 2012 press release[4] Symantec quotes $811,511$ installed certificates. This gives an estimate of approximately 2.4 million certificates in 2012.

Pilot CT Server. As of early July 2014, Google's pilot certificate transparency server had logged about 4.5 million certificates.[5] It is not clear how reliable this number is, since currently there is no incentive to add all certificates to this list. Also, the log is append-only, so this number is probably higher than it should be.

Given these data points, we estimate that the number of valid SSL certificates is currently around 2^{22} or approximately 4 million.

4.3   Retrieving Proofs of Inclusion Using PIR

To make privacy-friendly retrieval of the proofs of inclusion possible, we store the proofs as records in a database and use PIR to retrieve them. To retrieve the proof, the client needs to know in which record the proof is stored. In the original system, the proof is usually retrieved from the log server by using the

---

[2] https://www.eff.org/observatory.

[3] http://www.netcraft.com/internet-data-mining/ssl-survey/, accessed July 2014.

[4] http://investor.symantec.com/investor-relations/press-releases/press-release-details/2012/Symantec-Achieves-Highest-Number-of-SSL-Certificates-Issued-Globally/default.aspx.

[5] Obtained by querying the server's API: https://ct.googleapis.com/pilot/ct/v1/get-sth.

hash of the certificate itself, but that would violate our privacy requirements. Instead, we propose that webserver provides the record indices to the clients (it is not possible to include these in the X.509 certificate as the index is not yet known when the certificate is created). Alternatively, an index structure such as a B+ tree could be used in the typical way that PIR lookups by keywords are done [4,16].

To check a proof, the auditor needs three things: the certificate itself, the list of sibling hashes, and the signed root. We assume that the auditor has already retrieved the certificate in question. The signed root can be directly retrieved as it does not give any information about the specific certificate. Therefore, the proofs that are stored in the database consist solely of the hashes that help in reconstructing the signed root. We will next consider how these proofs are stored in the database.

Storing Proofs in the PIR Database. We first count the number of proofs that need to be stored. The log is append-only, and will therefore keep growing. However, expired certificates can safely be removed from the database of proofs. Regular clients will not query for expired certificates, so a fallback to identifying methods is not a problem. Therefore, we assume that the database only contains proofs for valid certificates. We estimated this to be about 2^{22} proofs.

In the following we consider a tree containing $2^{\ell-1} < n \leq 2^\ell$ items. The length of the inclusion proofs in such a Merkle tree is at most ℓ hashes. However, it can be less; for example, the inclusion proof of c_6 in Fig. 1 consists only of the nodes d and c. For simplicity, we allocate the full ℓ hashes for every proof in the database, resulting in proofs of $32\,\ell$ bytes.

Goldberg's PIR scheme is most efficient when the number of blocks equals the number of field elements per block [12]. It thus makes sense to bundle multiple proofs into a single block (as the number of proofs is exponential in ℓ, while the length of a proof is only linear in ℓ). The location of a proof is then given by its block, and its index within the block (the size of the tree fixes the length of the proofs). When this location is provided by the webserver it should remain fixed while the certificate is valid.

Given the size of a proof and the estimated number of valid SSL certificates we get a storage requirement of $32 \cdot 22 \cdot 2^{22} \approx 0.7 \cdot 2^{32}$ bytes, or about 3 GiB. Therefore, in the following section, we evaluate our algorithm on databases of sizes 1–4 GiB.

We also note that, if the client is willing to reveal a subset of the database that contains the certificate she seeks, she can reduce the server's computational load at the cost of revealing some information about her query [18]. While trivially downloading the entire subset is one approach, PIR offers a lower communication cost—only about one *block* of information is sent to and from each PIR server—without leaking information about which certificate within the entire subset the client is querying for.

5   Implementation and Evaluation

We implemented fast matrix multiplication using Strassen's algorithm as an extension to the Percy++ open-source PIR library [10]. We implemented Strassen for the small fields $GF(2^8)$ and $GF(2^{16})$ as well as the integers modulo p. All measurements were taken in Ubuntu 12.04.4 LTS running on a machine with eight Intel(R) Xeon(R) E7-8870 CPUs, but each PIR server, which used only one core, was assigned to a different CPU.

5.1   Implementation

Strassen's algorithm works perfectly when multiplying matrices where all the dimensions are powers of two. In the PIR setting, however, this need not hold. Whenever one or more of the three matrix dimensions (q, r, or s) is odd, we split off the single excess row(s) and/or column(s) and use the naive matrix multiplication algorithm for those products. The resulting dimensions are all even, so that we can do another Strassen recursive step.

Dealing with dimensions that are non-powers of two can be costly. For example, a dimension of $2^k - 1$ will incur extra calculations at every step, resulting in a larger computation time than if the dimension were 2^k instead. Hence, our algorithm is designed to dynamically increase the number of queries (by inserting a dummy all-zeroes query) if this yields better performance.

Every recursion step yields a small overhead. Part of this is mitigated by not allocating memory every time, but at small sizes the overhead still trumps the

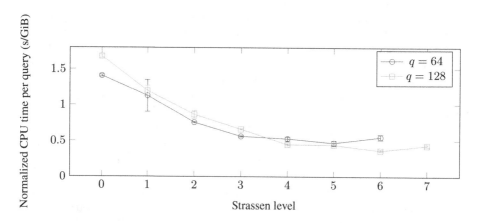

Fig. 2. Normalized CPU time per query (seconds per GiB of database size) for a 1 GiB database consisting of 32768 32768-byte records over $GF(2^8)$. We plot different Strassen levels (i.e., depth of recursion in the Strassen algorithm) and two numbers of queries, 64 and 128. Consider the $q = 64$ case. After 6 Strassen steps, the problem size has been reduced to a 1×512 matrix times a 512×512 matrix, and the algorithm bottoms out. In both cases it is better to skip this final reduction step. Error bars are shown, but most are small, and may be difficult to see.

Timings for database of size 32768×32768 over $GF(2^8)$

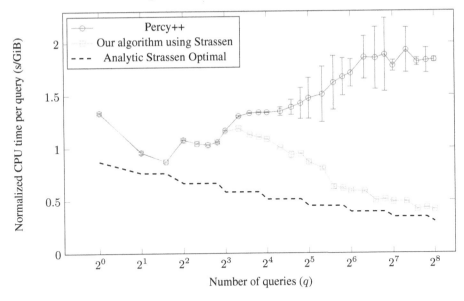

Fig. 3. Comparison between the original $GF(2^8)$ PIR implementation in Percy++ and our new version using Strassen. For the first part of the graph, the new and original algorithms give the same results, as the Strassen code is not invoked for small problem sizes. We can also easily see the effect of the hand-optimized loop in Percy++ for handling $q \leq 3$. We also compare our algorithm to the best theoretical improvements that using Strassen's algorithm can provide, using the fastest per-query time of the original Percy++ code ($q = 3$) as a reference point. Error bars are shown, but most are small, and may be difficult to see. The peak memory usage of our algorithm (for $q = 256$) was 1422 MiB, whereas Percy++ used 1060 MiB.

gain possible. We have analyzed when this happens; see Fig. 2 for an example. We then tuned our implementation to stop recursing at the optimal depth.

5.2 Experiments

For q less than about 165, the number of additions in Strassen's algorithm is slightly larger than for the naive algorithm due to the multiplicative constant of $\frac{8}{3}$ (see Table 2). However, as explained above, every recursive Strassen step reduces the number of multiplications by a factor of 7/8 or 12.5 %, starting with the very first. The small fields and the integers modulo p have in common that multiplication is a lot more expensive than addition; therefore, we expect that even one or two recursive steps of Strassen's algorithm would have a measurable effect on the performance, and the measurements in Fig. 2 bear this out. The initial dimensions of the problem dictate how many recursive steps of Strassen's algorithm can be applied, as each dimension is cut in half at each step. In

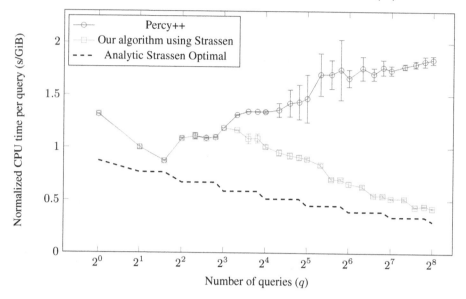

Fig. 4. We repeat the experiment of Fig. 3, but with a 4 GiB database consisting of 65536 65536-byte records. The peak memory usage of our algorithm (for $q = 256$) was 5556 MiB, whereas Percy++ used 4148 MiB.

practice, we expect that it is the number of queries that is the limiting factor (that is, q will be much smaller than either r or s), so that is what we focus on.

Figure 3 compares the performance of our new algorithm with the one in the 0.9.0 release of Percy++. All measurements are done over $GF(2^8)$, as that is the most efficient field supported by Percy++. We notice that Percy++ slows down considerably when more queries are used (we suspect cache issues may be to blame for this, but it was a completely repeatable effect). Our scheme does not suffer from this problem, and indeed produces the desired *decrease* in per-query cost as the number of queries increases. We observe a 4.4-fold performance improvement over Percy++ for $q = 256$ simultaneous queries.

We have also drawn the analytical improvements we expect from using Strassen's algorithm. Figure 3 shows the theoretical bound of the optimal Strassen gain that would be possible, measured against the *fastest* per-query time (obtained at $q = 3$) measured for the original Percy++ code. For example, for 256 queries, this gain would be $(\frac{7}{8})^8 \approx 0.344$. We see that we are quite close to this value, even though we always skip the final Strassen step.

For each Strassen recursion step, our algorithm incurs an extra subproblem of $1/4$ the size, which needs to be stored in memory. The extra memory consumption as a result of this is at most a factor of $\frac{1}{4} + (\frac{1}{4})^2 + \cdots = \frac{1}{3}$. This is confirmed by the memory usage given in Figs. 3 and 4.

Certificate Transparency. Figure 4 shows performance measures for a 4 GiB database, a size that nicely matches up with a log server's database of inclusions proofs. Again we see that using Strassen's algorithm gives a significant performance gain over just using single queries.

While batching queries results in a significantly lower processing time per query, the latency does increase. However, this is not a problem for auditing proofs of inclusion, as they are performed asynchronously. In particular, the goal is to detect misbehaving log servers, and not to protect users against falsely issued certificates directly. Some latency is therefore acceptable.

If a lower latency is required, the algorithm can easily be parallelized. Each of the seven Strassen subproblems is completely independent from the others, and creating these and recombining the result is very cheap. While we did not implement parallelization, we expect the overhead of doing so to be extremely small.

6   Conclusions

In this paper we showed how we can significantly speed up PIR queries if we allow the server to batch queries, and answer them simultaneously. Such an idea was proposed earlier in the setting of batch codes, but that proposal required coordination among the clients, which is not desirable in the PIR setting.

We analyzed batch codes in the setting of Goldberg's PIR scheme and have shown that essentially they provide a fast method for doing matrix multiplication under specific constraints on the matrices. However, since multi-client PIR in Goldberg's scheme is essentially a matrix multiplication, we can use our method to obtain sublinear scaling in the number of queries *without* requiring the queries to have been created by a single client or cooperating clients.

We described how multi-client PIR can be used to make certificate transparency more privacy friendly. We implemented Strassen's algorithm as part of Percy++ and have shown that we indeed manage to get a significant speedup when batching multi-client queries. While further system-level optimizations to Percy++ (which is already heavily optimized) might conceivably give comparable speedups in absolute terms, these will almost surely be a constant factor, whereas our algorithmic improvements *increase* with the number of simultaneous queries. Furthermore, any such system-level optimizations are likely to be able to be combined with our algorithmic improvements to yield compounded benefits.

Our implementation is open source and has been incorporated into the 1.0 release of Percy++ [11].

Acknowledgements. We thank the anonymous reviewers and Ben Laurie for their helpful feedback. This research is supported by the Natural Sciences and Engineering Research Council of Canada (NSERC) and by the research program Sentinels as project 'Revocable Privacy' (10532). Wouter Lueks is a member of the Privacy and Identity Lab (PI.lab). Sentinels is being financed by Technology Foundation STW, the Netherlands

Organization for Scientific Research (NWO), and the Dutch Ministry of Economic Affairs. The PI.lab is funded by SIDN.nl (http://www.sidn.nl). This work benefitted from the use of the CrySP RIPPLE Facility at the University of Waterloo.

References

1. Aguilar Melchor, C., Gaborit, P.: A lattice-based computationally-efficient private information retrieval protocol. In: Western European Workshop on Research in Cryptology (2007)
2. Beimel, A., Stahl, Y.: Robust information-theoretic private information retrieval. J. Cryptology **20**(3), 295–321 (2007)
3. Chor, B., Goldreich, O., Kushilevitz, E., Sudan, M.: Private information retrieval. In: 36th Annual IEEE Symposium on Foundations of Computer Science, pp. 41–50 (1995)
4. Chor, B., Gilboa, N., Naor, M.: Private Information Retrieval by Keywords. Technical report TR CS0917, Department of Computer Science, Technion, Israel (1997)
5. Coppersmith, D., Winograd, S.: Matrix multiplication via arithmetic progressions. J. Symbolic Comput. **9**(3), 251–280 (1990)
6. Devet, C., Goldberg, I.: The best of both worlds: combining information-theoretic and computational PIR for communication efficiency. In: De Cristofaro, E., Murdoch, S.J. (eds.) PETS 2014. LNCS, vol. 8555, pp. 63–82. Springer, Heidelberg (2014)
7. Devet, C., Goldberg, I., Heninger, N.: Optimally robust private information retrieval. In: 21st USENIX Security Symposium (2012)
8. Fox-IT BV: Black Tulip: Report of the investigation into the DigiNotar Certificate Authority breach, August 2012
9. Goldberg, I.: Improving the robustness of private information retrieval. In: 28th IEEE Symposium on Security and Privacy, pp. 131–148 (2007)
10. Goldberg, I., Devet, C., Hendry, P., Henry, R.: Percy++ project on SourceForge, version 0.9.0 (2013). http://percy.sourceforge.net. Accessed September 2014
11. Goldberg, I., Devet, C., Lueks, W., Yang, A., Hendry, P., Henry, R.: Percy++ project on SourceForge, version 1.0 (2014). http://percy.sourceforge.net/. Accessed November 2014
12. Henry, R., Huang, Y., Goldberg, I.: One (block) size fits all: PIR and SPIR with variable-length records via multi-block queries. In: 20th Annual Network and Distributed System Security Symposium (2013)
13. Ishai, Y., Kushilevitz, E., Ostrovsky, R., Sahai, A.: Batch codes and their applications. In: 36th ACM Symposium on Theory of Computing, pp. 262–271 (2004)
14. Kushilevitz, E., Ostrovsky, R.: Replication is not needed: single database, computationally-private information retrieval. In: 38th Annual IEEE Symposium on Foundations of Computer Science, pp. 364–373 (1997)
15. Laurie, B., Langley, A., Kasper, E.: Certificate Transparency. RFC 6962 (Experimental), June 2013. http://www.ietf.org/rfc/rfc6962.txt
16. Olumofin, F., Goldberg, I.: Privacy-preserving queries over relational databases. In: Atallah, M.J., Hopper, N.J. (eds.) PETS 2010. LNCS, vol. 6205, pp. 75–92. Springer, Heidelberg (2010)
17. Olumofin, Femi, Goldberg, Ian: Revisiting the Computational Practicality of Private Information Retrieval. In: Danezis, George (ed.) FC 2011. LNCS, vol. 7035, pp. 158–172. Springer, Heidelberg (2012)

18. Olumofin, F., Tysowski, P.K., Goldberg, I., Hengartner, U.: Achieving efficient query privacy for location based services. In: Atallah, M.J., Hopper, N.J. (eds.) PETS 2010. LNCS, vol. 6205, pp. 93–110. Springer, Heidelberg (2010)
19. Shamir, A.: How to share a secret. Commun. ACM **22**(11), 612–613 (1979)
20. Sion, R., Carbunar, B.: On the computational practicality of private information retrieval. In: 14th Network and Distributed Systems Security Symposium (2007)
21. Strassen, V.: Gaussian elimination is not optimal. Numer. Math. **13**(4), 354–356 (1969)

A Strassen's Algorithm

Strassen's algorithm is best explained by looking at matrix multiplication from a block-matrix perspective. For simplicity, assume that all matrices have size $n \times n$ where n is even. If

$$\mathbf{Q} = \begin{pmatrix} \mathbf{Q}_{11} & \mathbf{Q}_{12} \\ \mathbf{Q}_{21} & \mathbf{Q}_{22} \end{pmatrix} \quad \text{and} \quad \mathbf{D} = \begin{pmatrix} \mathbf{D}_{11} & \mathbf{D}_{12} \\ \mathbf{D}_{21} & \mathbf{D}_{22} \end{pmatrix},$$

then the matrix product $\mathbf{R} = \mathbf{Q} \cdot \mathbf{D}$ is given by

$$\mathbf{R} = \begin{pmatrix} \mathbf{R}_{11} & \mathbf{R}_{12} \\ \mathbf{R}_{21} & \mathbf{R}_{22} \end{pmatrix},$$

where

$$\mathbf{R}_{11} = \mathbf{Q}_{11} \cdot \mathbf{D}_{11} + \mathbf{Q}_{12} \cdot \mathbf{D}_{21}$$
$$\mathbf{R}_{12} = \mathbf{Q}_{11} \cdot \mathbf{D}_{12} + \mathbf{Q}_{12} \cdot \mathbf{D}_{22}$$
$$\mathbf{R}_{21} = \mathbf{Q}_{21} \cdot \mathbf{D}_{11} + \mathbf{Q}_{22} \cdot \mathbf{D}_{21}$$
$$\mathbf{R}_{22} = \mathbf{Q}_{21} \cdot \mathbf{D}_{12} + \mathbf{Q}_{22} \cdot \mathbf{D}_{22}.$$

It thus reduces to 8 matrix multiplications of size $n/2$. In Strassen's algorithm the following 7 matrix products are calculated first (note that in fields of characteristic 2, the $+$ and $-$ operations are of course the same):

$$\mathbf{M}_1 = (\mathbf{Q}_{11} + \mathbf{Q}_{22}) \cdot (\mathbf{D}_{11} + \mathbf{D}_{22})$$
$$\mathbf{M}_2 = (\mathbf{Q}_{21} + \mathbf{Q}_{22}) \cdot \mathbf{D}_{11}$$
$$\mathbf{M}_3 = \mathbf{Q}_{11} \cdot (\mathbf{D}_{12} - \mathbf{D}_{22})$$
$$\mathbf{M}_4 = \mathbf{Q}_{22} \cdot (\mathbf{D}_{21} - \mathbf{D}_{11})$$
$$\mathbf{M}_5 = (\mathbf{Q}_{11} + \mathbf{Q}_{12}) \cdot \mathbf{D}_{22}$$
$$\mathbf{M}_6 = (\mathbf{Q}_{21} - \mathbf{Q}_{11}) \cdot (\mathbf{D}_{11} + \mathbf{D}_{12})$$
$$\mathbf{M}_7 = (\mathbf{Q}_{12} - \mathbf{Q}_{22}) \cdot (\mathbf{D}_{21} + \mathbf{D}_{22}).$$

The matrix product is then given by:

$$\mathbf{R}_{11} = \mathbf{M}_1 + \mathbf{M}_4 - \mathbf{M}_5 + \mathbf{M}_7$$
$$\mathbf{R}_{12} = \mathbf{M}_3 + \mathbf{M}_5$$
$$\mathbf{R}_{21} = \mathbf{M}_2 + \mathbf{M}_4$$
$$\mathbf{R}_{22} = \mathbf{M}_1 - \mathbf{M}_2 + \mathbf{M}_3 + \mathbf{M}_6.$$

Using this algorithm, only 7 matrix multiplications of size $n/2$ are necessary. Applying this trick recursively gives a complexity of $O(n^{\lg 7})$.

Payment and Fraud Detection

Relay Cost Bounding for Contactless EMV Payments

Tom Chothia[1]([✉]), Flavio D. Garcia[1], Joeri de Ruiter[2], Jordi van den Breekel[3], and Matthew Thompson[1]

[1] School of Computer Science, University of Birmingham, Birmingham, UK
tom.chothia@gmail.com
[2] Institute for Computing and Information Sciences, Radboud University Nijmegen, Nijmegen, The Netherlands
[3] Department of Mathematics and Computer Science, Technical University Eindhoven, Eindhoven, The Netherlands

Abstract. This paper looks at relay attacks against contactless payment cards, which could be used to wirelessly pickpocket money from victims. We discuss the two leading contactless EMV payment protocols (Visa's payWave and MasterCard's PayPass). Stopping a relay attack against cards using these protocols is hard: either the overhead of the communication is low compared to the (cryptographic) computation by the card or the messages can be cached before they are requested by the terminal. We propose a solution that fits within the EMV Contactless specification to make a payment protocol that is resistant to relay attacks from commercial off-the-shelf devices, such as mobile phones. This solution does not require significant changes to the cards and can easily be added to existing terminals. To prove that our protocol really does stop relay attacks, we develop a new method of automatically checking defences against relay attacks using the applied pi-calculus and the tool ProVerif.

1 Introduction

EMV is the most widely used standard for payments using smart cards [13]. The EMV Contactless specification has been introduced to support contactless smart cards [14]. For every payment provider a different variation of the specification exists. MasterCard and Visa market their solutions as PayPass and payWave (primarily the qVSDC protocol) respectively.

A typical attack against smart cards are so-called relay attacks, as demonstrated for EMV in [10]. Here an attacker uses a reader and card emulator to relay communication between a victim's card and a genuine terminal. This way it would, for example, be possible to pay for an expensive item in a different shop while the victim thinks the payment is only for an inexpensive item. With contact based smart cards the opportunity to use this attack is limited, as the victim knows when the card is being used: namely when it is inserted into a reader. For a contactless card this protection is lost, as the transaction does not

© International Financial Cryptography Association 2015
R. Böhme and T. Okamoto (Eds.): FC 2015, LNCS 8975, pp. 189–206, 2015.
DOI: 10.1007/978-3-662-47854-7_11

require the users PIN number, it is enough to hold a reader close to a card to be able to communicate with it, even if it is inside a wallet or handbag. Therefore the attacker will have more opportunities to perform the attack and it will be less clear for the user that anything is going on. That such attacks are possible using cheap hardware, namely mobile phones, has been demonstrated in, for example, [11,12,17,20].

A typical solution to counter relay attacks are distance bounding protocols. Classic distance bounding protocols have been widely studied in the literature and elegant solutions have been proposed [6,8,10,18]. These protocols assume that card and reader share a secret and then measure the time it takes to exchange a number of bits. Based on accurate time measurements at the level of nano seconds, knowledge of the clock speeds on both sides and the speed of light, an estimate can be made of the distance to the other party with an accuracy of a few meters. This assumes an attacker that is capable of relaying messages at close to the speed of light. While this is possible with specialised hardware we considered this attacker model to be an overkill for contactless EMV [15]. As contactless transactions can only be used for small amounts without a PIN, and the use of specialised equipment may raise suspicion (and so the chance of getting caught) such an attack offers a poor risk/reward ratio. A much better risk/reward ratio will come from using inconspicuous hardware that attackers may already own, such as NFC enabled smartphones. Another practical obstacle for classic distance bounding is that currently there is no shared secret between reader and card and incorporating such (complex) protocol would require a complete redesign of the existing infrastructure.

In this paper, we propose a protocol for contactless EMV payments, which will stop relay attacks using mobile phones, or off-the-shelf USB NFC readers. The protocol we propose is simpler than existing distance bounding protocols and is based on restricting the response time of a single message to the level of milliseconds. The solution is software based and does not require additional hardware to be added to existing terminals. It will not detect messages relayed at close to the speed of light, but we show that it will stop relay attacks that use inexpensive, easily available hardware.

We observe that in the current contactless protocols there are two types of message that need to be relayed from the reader to the card. The first type of message is used in payWave to retrieve a nonce used in the previous cryptographic operation. This nonce can already be retrieved while the terminal is still requesting other commands. The second type is one that requires the card to carry out some complex cryptographic computation. This is used in both payWave and PayPass. We have found that the variation in the time it takes different cards to carry out the cryptographic calculation is larger than the time needed for smartphones to relay the message. Therefore, imposing a time bound on the reply to either of these messages cannot be used to stop relay attacks. On the other hand, the time it takes cards to reply to messages that do not require cryptographic operations is low and uniform across all the cards we looked at. However, in the current protocols, these messages can all be cached by an attacker, and therefore cannot be time bound either.

The protocol we propose fits within the current EMV Contactless specification. A message exchange is introduced that must be relayed between the reader and the card, but does not require any cryptographic computation from the card and cannot be cached. Without the cryptographic operations the timing of this message will be more uniform for different cards, so we may use this message to add a timing bound and stop relay attacks.

To formally verify the correctness of the protocol we propose a new technique for modelling relay attacks using the applied pi-calculus [1] and using the tool ProVerif [3]. It would be possible to build a formal model which includes the time of each action and detect when a message takes too long, but such models would be complex and tool support is limited. Instead we assume that the designer of a system has identified a message and a reply that the attacker will not be able to relay fast enough. Then, given this assumption, the formal verification checks if there are any messages that an attacker could pre-play, replay, or invent to break the protocol.

The contribution of this paper is:

– Showing that relay attacks are possible against MasterCard's PayPass protocol, (as well as Visa's payWave) using mobile phones that cache static messages.
– Proposing a contactless EMV protocol, which is a combination of the payWave and PayPass protocols, and which defends against relay attacks.
– Showing how these defences against relay attacks can be formally verified in the applied pi-calculus and automatically checked with the tool ProVerif.

Structure of the Paper: we review the EMV and EMV Contactless protocol specifications in Sect. 2 and we look at the practicalities of a relay attacks in Sect. 3. We present our new protocol in Sect. 4. We formally verify this in Sect. 5 and discuss its implementation in Sect. 6. We conclude in Sect. 7. Our website[1] provides additional information, such as our timing measurements from cards, complete protocol traces, ProVerif models and a video of our relay in action.

2   EMV and the PayWave/PayPass Protocols

The original contact-based EMV standard consists of four books, containing over 700 pages [13] and the EMV contactless specification [14] builds on this. Additionally, every payment provider has their own variation of the payment protocol (Book C, Kernel Specification). Currently there are 7 different variations, the most widely used of which are from MasterCard (PayPass) and by Visa (payWave). The protocols are not directly compatible with each other (although they do use the same set of basic commands), therefore a shop reader must start a transaction by querying a card to see which protocols it supports.

---

[1] http://www.cs.bham.ac.uk/~tpc/Relay/.

The aim of the payment protocols is to provide evidence to the shop reader that the card is genuine and to give the shop reader a cryptogram (referred to as the AC), which it can send to the bank as proof that a payment is due. To achieve this cards have a public key pair (PubC,PrivC), and a certificate for the public key, signed by the bank, which includes all of the card's static information, $(Cert_{PrivB}(PubC, SSAD))$ the card also includes a certificate for the banks public key $(Cert_{PrivCA}(PubB))$ and the reader has the public key for this certificate (PubCA). To form the cryptogram the card also contains a symmetric key K_M, which is only known by the card and the bank.

The steps of Mastercard's PayPass protocol are shown in Fig. 1. The first four steps initialise the protocol: the shop reader selects the payment application and the card replies with a list of application identities (AIDs) for the protocols it supports. The reader will then select the protocol it wishes to run. Next, the reader sends a "GET PROCESSING OPTIONS" (GPO) command and the card replies with the Application Interchange Profile (AIP), which indicates the specific functions the card supports, and the location of the records on the card (AFL). The card will read these records, which include all the information printed on the card (except for the CVV, but including the credit card number, referred to as the PAN), the card's public key and the card's public key certificate. The reader also reads the Card Risk Management Data Object List (CDOL) which lists the information that the reader must provide to the card so that it can make the cryptogram for the bank. The number of read actions needed varies between cards and is specified by the AFL message.

Once the data has been read from the card, the reader generates a nonce UN, and requests the cryptogram with the GENERATE AC command. This command includes all of the information requested by the card, which will include the nonce, the amount of the transaction and the currency, among other things. The card then generates a session key (K_S), based on the key it shares with the bank and the application transaction counter (ATC), which equals the number of times the card has been used. The session key is then used to calculate a MAC on the transaction details (the AC), which is what the shop sends to the bank as proof of the transaction. With no access to the symmetric key the shop cannot check the AC, so to provide evidence to the shop that the card is genuine it signs AC along with the reader's nonce and the transaction details, which is referred to as the Signed Dynamic Application Data (SDAD).

The reader checks the card's public key certificate using the copy of the bank's verification key, uses this to check the SDAD, and if all of the data is correct the shop accepts the transaction. Complete transaction traces, with all information fields parsed and explained are available on our website (apart from the credit card numbers which have been removed).

Visa's payWave qVSDC protocol is shown in Fig. 2. This protocol is a slightly compressed version of Mastercard's PayPass protocol. The main differences are that the card provides the list of the information it requires (the PDOL) in response to the protocol being selected, and this information is provided to the card as part of the GPO message. The card will calculate the AC and sign the

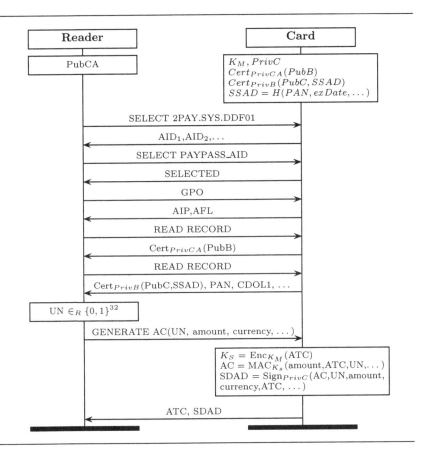

Fig. 1. The PayPass protocol

data in response to the GPO message. The GENERATE AC command is no longer used, because all of it's functionality is merged with the GPO message. After this command the terminal reads the files indicated in the AFL and can then authenticate the data after the card has left the field.

The data authentication mechanism (referred to as fDDA) generates a signature that includes a nonce from the card, and it is returned together with the cryptogram in the response to the GPO command, however, unlike PayPass, the signed data does not include the cryptogram. Therefore, it would be possible for an attacker to send a shop reader a valid SDAD and an invalid AC, which the shop would not discover until it send the AC to the bank for payment, this is known as the DDA wedge attack [19]. For a more detailed description of the EMV protocol we refer the reader to [9].

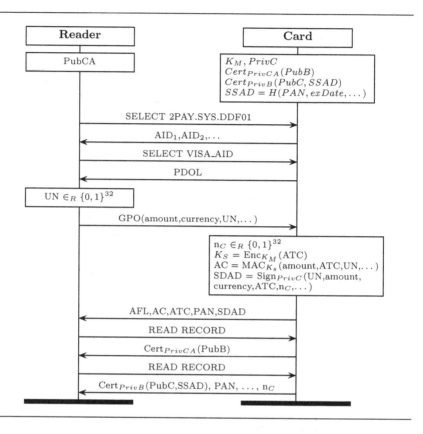

Fig. 2. Visa's payWave qVSDC protocol

3 Relay Attacks Against EMV Contactless Smart Cards

Existing implementations of Contactless EMV provide little or no protection against relay attacks. One of the most popular payment terminals in the UK imposes a limit on the total transaction time of 10 s. Such an ample time window allows an adversary to relay a transaction to everywhere in the planet (or even the moon).

A number of generic NFC relay attacks have been proposed in the literature [16,17]. Furthermore, successful relay attacks on payWave have been reported in, for example, [11]. Their average time for a relayed transaction is 1.6 s, which is an overhead of about 1.1 s compared to a regular transaction.

Our Setup. We have conducted experiments with both MasterCard's PayPass and Visa's payWave, and were able to relay transactions with both systems. Our setup consists of an NFC mobile phone to emulate the bank card and we use another NFC phone or an off-the-shelf USB reader for the terminal side.

Our implementation is multi-threaded and the data is relayed over Wifi. The relay is performed in two stages, first the reader or phone that is communicating with the card runs the protocol and records all of the static data, which is sent to the phone that will emulate the card. In the second phase, for payWave cards, the phone relays the cached data to the reader, while the card is simultaneously selected so that it is ready to reply to the relayed GPO message. The card is also asked for its nonce, which is relayed while the shop reader is reading the records, so this relay doesn't affect the overall time taken. Figure 3 gives an overview of the second stage of our payWave relay attack.

For PayPass we also cache the static messages and relay the GENERATE AC command, rather than the GPO. Additionally, we found that Android phones would put the Wifi adapter to sleep after about 100 ms of inactivity, so to avoid this slowing down the relay we send a heartbeat signal over Wifi every 80 ms. Our average transaction times for relayed payments are 623 ms for PayPass and 550 ms for payWave, much faster than times previously reported.

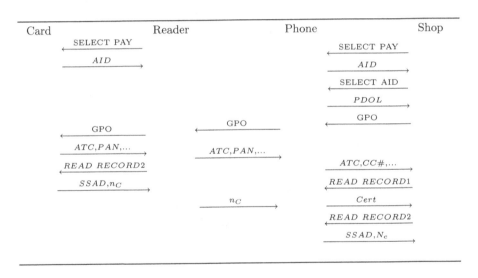

Fig. 3. The communications made by our payWave relay after pre-caching

Relay and Timing. A first attempt to prevent such relay attacks would be to set an over all time bound on the protocol. The Contactless EMV specification [14] states that the complete transaction should take less than 500 ms, however we found that shop readers did not enforce this. Furthermore, we could complete a relayed session with some cards faster than this; the fastest card was from the Dutch bank Knab and we could complete a relayed session with this card in 485 ms. The slowest card we found was one from ABN-AMRO which took on average 637 ms to complete a transaction (when not being relayed). This card was so slow that, thanks to the caching of static messages, our relay setup is able to complete a transaction with a shop reader using this card in 627 ms, i.e., 10 ms *faster* than when the card is directly communicating with the terminal. Hence, an overall time limit on the protocol cannot be used to stop relay attacks.

A second attempt to prevent relay attacks could be to set a (tighter) time bound on the dynamic messages of the protocol, i.e., the messages that need to be relayed. For PayPass this would be the GENERATE AC command, and for payWave the GPO command. These are also the commands that require the card to do some cryptographic computations which we have found leads to a large variance in the response times. For PayPass we observed average timings to GENERATE AC messages from 154 ms to 332 ms for different cards, where the overhead introduced by our relay for this message is only 161 ms on average.

Another factor that increases the time variance for computationally intensive operations is the positioning of the card within the electromagnetic field of the reader. Experiments on a payWave card (from TSB bank) show that it takes on average 108 ms to respond to the GPO command when the card is placed directly on top of the reader. Although, the same card takes on average 184 ms to respond to the GPO command when the card is placed farther away from the reader (but still within range). The fastest response to the GPO message we received from a payWave card took 105 ms, whereas the slowest took 364 ms while the shortest time we observed when relaying this message was only 208 ms. Hence, in some cases, the observed time variance between various cards was actually larger than the overhead introduced by the relay, so bounding the GPO and GENERATE AC message response times does not seem to be a practical way to stop relay attacks.

For the payWave protocol, an additional message needs to be relayed, namely the card nonce N_c. The cards do not need to perform any computation to reply to this message, and we found the time taken to reply was much more consistent. Experimenting with a number of different cards in different positions on the reader, we found that the fastest response took 20 ms and the slowest took 68 ms. So the time taken to relay this message would be noticeable to the shop terminal, however this message only contains dynamic data from the card and the command by the terminal is static, so this can be read and cached before it is requested by the shop reader (as our relay does). This means that it is also infeasible to detect relay attacks on this message using time bounds.

For our card timing experiments we used an Omnikey 5321 v2 USB reader. We note that different readers may produce different times, due to the power they provide to the card and the speed of the drivers, however the variances between the timings due to the card will be consistent. For instance, we found that the Nexus 5 phones we used where typically 15 ms–30 ms slower than the USB reader. Another factor that affects the times is the length of the messages. For example, requesting the number of PIN tries is the shortest message that the card can produce and when asked for this the card takes approximately 8 ms to reply and relaying such a short message (a couple of bytes) over Wifi takes at least 30 ms.

Below, we propose a lightweight distance bounding protocol that prevents relay attacks using off-the-shelf devices such as mobile phones. Our protocol is able to prevent such attacks while tolerating the large computing-time variance of the cards. It is worth mentioning that our protocol does not attempt to stop powerful adversaries with custom made hardware (e.g. [15], which cost more than US\$ 100K [7]). Considering that contactless payments are limited to small amounts, the cost of the hardware would be a disincentive for criminals. A video of our relay in action, and details of all our time measurements as well as a full trace of our relay are available on our website.

4   A Payment Protocol that Defends Against Relay Attacks

In the previous section, we saw that a relay based on mobile phones or USB NFC readers adds a delay to the response. This delay is small when compared to the variance of the time it takes for the card to reply to a request that requires encryption, but it is large, and detectable, when compared to the time it takes the card to reply to messages that do not require any computation. Below we will discuss a protocol that can be used to prevent relay attacks using mobile phones or USB NFC readers. This hardware is cheap and easy to get and using it in a store does not raise any suspicion, as companies such as Apple are introducing their own NFC apps to perform payments.

The problem with using the small delay caused by the relay to detect attacks is that this cannot reliably be used for commands that carry out cryptographic computations or return data that can be cached. The time of the cryptographic computations will vary due to for instance, the card's hardware or placement in the field, and so cannot be reliably bound. We fix this problem by splitting the challenge and response command from the generation of the signed authentication and cryptogram. To do this we provide the reader's nonce to the card with the GPO command (as in the payWave protocol), but we delay the generation of the signed authentication and cryptogram until the reader issues the GENERATE AC command (as in the PayPass protocol).

Our protocol, which we call the PaySafe protocol, is shown in Fig. 4. In reply to the GPO command, the reader will provide its own nonce that was generated at a previous step in the protocol (i.e. when receiving the SELECT command). As the reply to the GPO command now does not require any computation, it can be timed by the reader to detect relay attacks. To detect an attempt by an attacker to defeat the timing bound by generating their own nonce to replace the reader's or card's nonce, both the reader's and the card's nonce are included in the signed data, as is the AC, so fixing VISA's problem of allowing an attacker to inject an invalid AC.

We use existing fields within EMV to exchange the nonces, namely the Unpredictable Number and the ICC Dynamic Number for the reader and card respectively. This means the cards are still EMV compliant and additionally, since both values are included in signed data, we do not need to add an additional signature to the protocol.

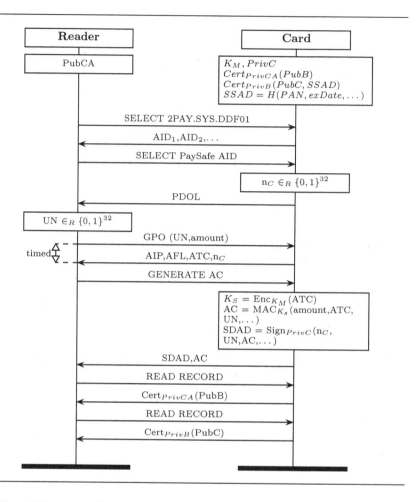

Fig. 4. The protocol PaySafe which defends against simple relay attacks

Our new proposed protocol will start in the same way as the existing EMV Contactless protocols with the selection of the payment application. After the application is selected, and before the card sends its request for data to the reader (the PDOL) the card will generates a nonce. This nonce is not sent to the reader at this point but just stored on the card.

The next step is a timed GPO command, that gives the card the data it needs and the reader's nonce. The card will immediately reply to this message with the stored nonce. As this does not require any computation the card will reply quickly and without much variance in the time taken. If this message was relayed, additional overhead would be introduced by the network communication between the phones and the communication between a phone and the genuine terminal. The exact timing will depend on the hardware used; with our hardware the reply to the PayPass GPO message took 36 ms and the PaySafe message is slightly longer. Therefore, we would suggest a time out of 80 ms, as being long enough to make sure all cards are accepted, but still quick enough to make sure the message cannot be relayed using NFC phones.

To get the cryptogram and Signed Dynamic Application Data (SDAD) from the card, the reader issues the GENERATE AC command. The card then computes the SDAD and the cryptogram and sends these to the reader. Attackers can get to this point in the protocol by sending their own nonce to either the card or the reader, so avoiding the need to relay both nonces and meeting the time restriction. To detect this both the reader's and the card's nonces are included in the signed data (SDAD). The reader will check these and terminate the transaction if they do not match the nonces that were part of the timed challenge.

After running this protocol the reader can be sure that fast nonce exchange took place with an entity that was not being relayed using mobile phones or USB NFC reader links, and, due to the SDAD, the reader can be sure that this entity was the bank card. Variations of this protocol are also possible, for instance the PDOL could be replaced with a CDOL in one of the records and the GENERATE AC message could be moved to the end, to make it much closer to the current PayPass protocol. It would also be possible to move the AIP,AFL and ATC data from the reply to the GPO into the reply to the SELECT AID, so making the reply to the GPO quicker and easier to time, however this should not be necessary and would be a further deviation from the current EMV protocols.

5   Formal Verification of PaySafe

The Applied Pi-calculus and ProVerif. To formally verify the correctness of our protocol we use the applied pi-calculus [2] and the tool ProVerif [4]. The applied pi-calculus is a formal language for describing protocols using the syntax given in Fig. 5. This language allows us to specify processes that perform inputs and outputs, run in parallel and replicate. The calculus also allows processes to declare new, private names which can be used as private channels or nonces [4]. Functions in the applied pi-calculus can be used to model a range of cryptographic primitives, e.g. MACs, signing and key generation. The "let" statement can be used to check that two terms that used these equations are equal and branch on the result. This can be used to encode "if" statements, and conditional inputs $c(=a).P$ which inputs a value and proceeds only if the value received equals a (see e.g. [4]). ProVerif is an automatic theorem proving tool that can be used to check applied pi-calculus models. It can be used to check secrecy of, for example, a key or, as we do below, it can be used to check if a process can reach a certain point. ProVerif introduces phase statements, written as $n:P$ where n is an integer. Processes will be run in the order of the numbers they are tagged with, which enforces an ordering on the commands, e.g. an output in phase 2 cannot be received by an input in phase 1.

$M, N ::=$	terms
x, y, z	variables
a, b, c, k, s	names
$f(M_1, \ldots, M_n)$	constructor application
$D ::= g(M_1, \ldots, M_n)$	destructor application
$P, Q ::=$	processes
0	nil
$\overline{M}\langle N \rangle.P$	output
$M(x).P$	input
$P \mid Q$	parallel composition
$!P$	replication
$\nu\, a.P$	create new name
let $x = D$ in P else Q	term evaluation
$n : P$	phase

Fig. 5. Syntax of the applied pi calculus

Modelling PaySafe. The applied pi-calculus model of our new protocol is given in Fig. 6. The first two communications between the card and the reader are the SELECT commands. The card listens first for the selection of the payment environment and then the selection of the particular payment application, but before replying to the second SELECT command it declares a new name n_C. The reader also generates a new name n_R and passes that to the card using the GPO command and requests the cryptogram, by sending the GENERATE AC command. The encryption is done using "let" statements and the reader checks the card's signature using an "if" statement before accepting it. The *System* process includes an arbitrary number of readers and cards, sets the card information and makes the bank's public key available to the attacker.

Verifying the Defence Against Relay Attacks. Based on our observations in Sect. 3, an attacker cannot use a mobile phone or USB equipment to relay the GPO message in our new protocol quickly enough to make the reader accept the reply. However, this alone is not enough to guarantee that our protocol stops relay attacks; it may still be possible for attackers to pre-play messages to the card, or make up their own response to the GPO message and trick the reader into believing that it came from the card.

As the attackers cannot relay the timed message to the card and get the answer back to the reader quickly enough, the attackers cannot have a meaningful interaction with the card while the reader is waiting for the reply. I.e., the attackers can perform a relay attack if, and only if, they can do so without communicating with the card between when the reader broadcasts its timed message and when it receives a reply.

$Reader = \bar{c}\langle\text{SELECT,PAYSYSDDF}\rangle.$
  $c(=\text{AID}).$
  $\bar{c}\langle\text{SELECT,aid}\rangle.$
  $c(=\text{PDOL}).$
  $\nu\, n_R.\bar{c}\langle\text{GPO,amt}, n_R\rangle.$
  $c(n'_C, \text{atc}', \text{PAN}').$
  $\bar{c}\langle\text{GENERATE AC}\rangle.$
  $c(\text{sdad}', \text{ac}').$
  $\bar{c}\langle\text{READ RECORD}\rangle.c(ssad').$
  $\bar{c}\langle\text{READ RECORD}\rangle.c(\text{cert}').$
  let $\text{cardPub}'_K =$
    $check(\text{cert}', pk(\text{bank}_K))$
  if $check(\text{sdad}', \text{cardPub}'_K) =$
    $(n_R, n'_C, \text{amt}, \text{atc}', \text{ac}')$
  $\bar{c}\langle\text{readerAccepts}\rangle$

$Card = c(=\text{SELECT},=\text{PAYSYSDDF}).$
  $\bar{c}\langle\text{AID}\rangle.$
  $c(=\text{SELECT},=\text{AID}).$
  $\nu\, n_C.\bar{c}\langle\text{PDOL}\rangle.$
  $c(=\text{GPO,amt}', n'_R).$
  $\bar{c}\langle n_C, \text{atc,PAN}\rangle.$
  $c(=\text{GENERATE AC}).$
  let $\text{mac}_K = genkey(\text{atc,bank}_K)$ in
  let $\text{ac} = mac((\text{amt}', n'_R, \text{atc}), \text{mac}_K)$ in
  let $\text{sdad} =$
    $sign((n_R, n_C, \text{amt,atc,ac}), \text{card}_K)$ in
  $\bar{c}\langle\text{sdad}\rangle.$
  $c(=\text{READ RECORD}).$
  $\bar{c}\langle sign((\text{PAN,expDate}), \text{bank}_K)\rangle.$
  $c(=\text{READ RECORD}).\bar{c}\langle\text{cert}\rangle$

$System = \nu\, \text{bank}_K.(\bar{c}\langle pk(\text{bank}_K)\rangle) \mid !\nu\, amount.!Reader$
  $\mid !(\nu\, \text{PAN}.\nu\, \text{expDate}.\nu\, \text{card}_K.\text{let cert} = sign(pk(\text{card}_K), \text{bank}_K) \text{ in } !\nu\, \text{atc}.!Card))$

Fig. 6. Applied pi-calculus model of PaySafe

Our formal modelling of relay attacks is based on this observation. Between when the reader broadcasts its timed message and when it receives the reply we lock the card process so that it cannot communicate with anyone. We also lock the other readers in the system as the attacker will not have time to relay messages to them, as well as the card. Given these locks, if the attacker can find a sequence of actions that still allows a reader to finish the protocol then a relay attack is possible. On the other hand, if the locks stop the reader from terminating then there is no sequence of relayed actions that the reader will accept from the attacker, and we can be sure that the protocol is safe from relay attacks.

We could encode a lockable process in the applied pi-calculus by adding a single 'heartbeat' output on a private name. The lockable process must acquire this before performing any input or output, and releases it again afterwards. To lock this process another process only needs to acquire the lock. A model like this could be checked by hand in the applied pi-calculus, and so provides a useful analysis method, however it cannot be checked automatically using the ProVerif tool. ProVerif can prove correctness for a protocol with an arbitrary number of runs, and an arbitrary number of concurrent processes. To make this possible ProVerif makes some compromises: the tool may not terminate and it may report false attacks. Using a heartbeat lock, as described before, results in ProVerif finding a false attack because the tool wrongly allows more than one process to acquire the lock at the same time.

Encoding a Process Lock Using Phases. To create a model that can be checked in ProVerif, and so automatically prove our protocol correct, we can use ProVerif's phase statements. To model relay attacks we use three phases $(0, 1, 2)$ and we allow the card and reader to be interacted with in phases 0 and 2. The attacker can act in all of the phases and the reader will broadcasts its request for the timed message and receive the reply in phase 1. This stops the attacker from relaying the timed message to the card and forwarding the response to the reader, but it still allows the attacker to try to replay or pre-play messages to the card, and make up its own responses to the challenge.

We make the assumption that there may be concurrent sessions of cards and readers (although the readers and cards we looked at didn't support this, future devices may). Therefore, we need to allow the reader and card process to span phases 0 and 2, but not act in phase 1, i.e. the processes must be able to jump from phase 0 to phase 2 before input actions (output actions can be forward from one phase to the next by the attacker). For the process P the following function gives us the set of processes produced by placing a phase 2 jump in front of each of the possible inputs:

$$phasesSet(P) = \{C[2\!:\!M(x).P'] \mid P = C[M(x).P']\}$$

Here $C[\_]$ ranges over all possible contexts, so the right hand side of this set comprehension matches all inputs in P, and the left hand side adds a phase command in front of the input.

We can then build a process that allows the attacker an arbitrary number of interactions with the process P, in either phase, by replicating each member of this set and placing them in parallel:

$$phases(P) = !P_1 \,|\, !P_2 \,|\, \cdots \,|\, !P_n \quad where \quad \{P_1, \ldots, P_n\} = phasesSet(P)$$

We also note that if the attacker can perform a relay attack against our system process, then there is a single distinct reader process that the attacker can get to terminate, while relaying messages. This means that it is sufficient to test if just a single reader process can terminate, and only this reader process needs to enforce the timing restrictions.

We use the *phases* function to give the attacker an arbitrary number of copies of the card and the reader they can interact with in both phases 0 and 2, and we add a single copy of the reader process that outputs its GPO message and must receive the timed relay in phase 1. This is shown in Fig. 7, where *Reader* and *Card* are as defined in Fig. 6.

Checking the *System* process with ProVerif, we find that the reader process cannot reach the *readerAccepts* action. Therefore, given the timing assumptions, we may conclude that the attacker cannot cause the reader to accept a session of the protocol, and that our protocol will stop relay attacks using cheap hardware, such as mobile phone and USB NFC readers.

Examples of Finding Attacks. To test our framework's ability to find attacks we look at what happens if the readers or the cards did not use a nonce. First we

$TestReader = \ldots$
 $c(=\text{PDOL}).\nu\, n_R.$
 $1 : \overline{c}\langle\text{GPO},\text{amt}, n_R\rangle.$
 $c(n'_C, \text{atc}', \text{PAN}').$
 $2 : \overline{c}\langle\text{GENERATE AC}\rangle.$
 $c(\text{sdad}', \text{ac}').$

 $\ldots$
 if $check(\text{scad}', \text{cardPub}'_K) =$
  $(n_R, n'_C, \text{amt}, \text{atc}', \text{ac}')$
 $\overline{c}\langle\text{phaseReaderAccepts}\rangle$

$SystemP = \nu\, \text{bank}_K.(\overline{c}\langle pk(\text{bank}_K)\rangle)$
 $|\ \nu\, \text{amount}.TestReader$
 $|\ !\nu\, \text{amount}.Readers$
 $|\ !(\nu\, \text{PAN}.\nu\, \text{expDate}.\nu\, \text{card}_K.$
  let cert $= sign(pk(\text{card}_K), \text{bank}_K)$
  in $!\nu\, \text{atc}.Cards))$

where:
 $Cards\ \ = phases(Card)$
 $Readers = phases(Reader)$

Fig. 7. Our protocol modelled using ProVerif's phase statements

removed the card's nonce from the protocol, both in the reply to the GPO message and in the check made by the reader, however we keep the timing constraints on the GPO message as imposed by the phase statements. When given this protocol model, ProVerif finds the attack illustrated in Fig. 8. In this attack, the attacker first interacts with the card to learn the current counter value and the PAN. After this, the attacker relays messages from the reader, until the reader issues its GPO message which the attacker can now reply to directly, so meeting the timing constraint. The attacker then forwards these messages to the card and continues to relay the remaining messages from the reader.

The points at which the ProVerif model changes phase are also shown in Fig. 8, and this illustrates how our method locks the card during the readers timed message. We also tested our protocol with a card nonce, but without the reader's nonce; in this case ProVerif finds a simple replay attack: the attacker interacts with the card and records a whole session, which can then be replayed to the reader's GPO message directly, so meeting the timing requirements. All of our ProVerif models are available on our website.

6 Implementing PaySafe

The protocol we propose has the advantage of only using existing EMV commands and data fields. As it is similar to the existing contactless EMV protocols, it is simple to implement. The changes from the payWave qVDSC protocol are the removal of the Signed Dynamic Application Data from the response to the GPO message, moving the card's nonce data field into the response to the GPO message and the addition of the standard EMV GENERATE AC command. The changes from the PayPass protocol are even smaller, requiring only the moving of the reader's nonce data field to the GPO message and the card's nonce data field into the response to the GPO message.

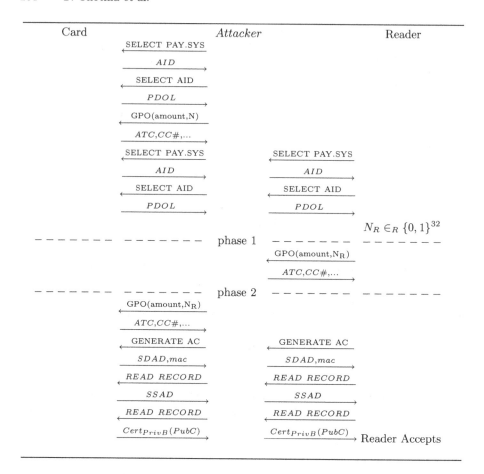

Fig. 8. Attack found by ProVerif if there is no card nonce

The EMV framework allows for multiple applications to be offered by a card. So our new protocol could be assigned a new AID and if both reader and card support the protocol it would be used. The AIDs supported will be included in the signed card information, so attackers cannot trick a reader into using a less secure protocol.

Care must be taken to ensure that deviations from the specified protocol do not make attacks possible. For instance, if cards would accept a second GPO message with a different reader nonce, an attacker could discover the card nonce with the first GPO message and then relay the readers nonce with the second GPO message. So, for PaySafe we must stop a single run of the protocol from accepting multiple GPO messages with different nonces. Clearly, our protocol only works if the nonces are actually unpredictable, unfortunately some EMV terminals have been shown to use predictable numbers [5].

7   Conclusion

Our goal in this paper was to propose a defence against relay attacks using easily available hardware on the EMV Contactless protocol, and to prove it correct. Our solution relies on the quick exchange of (previously generated) random nonces. This solution fits within the EMV Contactless specification, but is applicable to smart card protocols in general. We also have presented a new technique to model relay attacks based on a simple observation: if the reply to the timed message is received by the reader quickly enough, then the attacker cannot have interacted with the card. We have shown how this can be used to model relay attacks in the applied pi-calculus and in the automatic tool ProVerif using phase statements. As further work, we could extend our formal models to include all error handling for the protocols, as well as developing our method of modelling relay attacks into a general framework for any protocol.

Acknowledgement. We would like to thank Chris Smith, Ben Smyth, Alexander Darer, Mandeep Daroch and a number of helpful shop staff for their assistance with developing the relay.

References

1. Abadi, M., Blanchet, B.: Analyzing security protocols with secrecy types and logic programs. J. ACM **52**(1), 102–146 (2005)
2. Abadi, M., Fournet, C.: Mobile values, new names, and secure communication. In: Symposium on Principles of Programming Languages (POPL) (2001)
3. Blanchet, B.: An efficient cryptographic protocol verifier based on prolog rules. In: Computer Security Foundations Workshop (CSFW), pp. 82–96. IEEE (2001)
4. Blanchet, B., Smyth, B., Cheval, V.: ProVerif 1.88: automatic cryptographic protocol verifier, user manual and tutorial (2013)
5. Bond, M., Choudary, O., Murdoch, S.J., Skorobogatov, S., Anderson, R.: Chip and skim: cloning EMV cards with the pre-play attack. In: 35th IEEE Symposium on Security and Privacy (2014)
6. Boureanu, I., Mitrokotsa, A., Vaudenay, S.: Towards secure distance bounding. In: Moriai, S. (ed.) FSE 2013. LNCS, vol. 8424, pp. 55–68. Springer, Heidelberg (2014)
7. Capkun, S.: Personal communication (2012)
8. Cremers, C., Rasmussen, K.B., Schmidt, B., Capkun, S.: Distance hijacking attacks on distance bounding protocols. In: 2012 IEEE Symposium on Security and Privacy (SP), pp. 113–127. IEEE (2012)
9. de Ruiter, J., Poll, E.: Formal analysis of the EMV protocol suite. In: Mödersheim, S., Palamidessi, C. (eds.) TOSCA 2011. LNCS, vol. 6993, pp. 113–129. Springer, Heidelberg (2012)
10. Drimer, S., Murdoch, S.J.: Keep your enemies close: distance bounding against smartcard relay attacks. In: USENIX Security Symposium, pp. 87–102, August 2007
11. Emms, M., Arief, B., Defty, T., Hannon, J., Hao, F., van Moorsel, A.: The dangers of verify PIN on contactless cards. Technical report. CS-TR-1332

12. Emms, M., Arief, B., Freitas, L., Hannon, J., van Moorsel, A.: Harvesting high value foreign currency transactions from emv contactless credit cards without the pin. In: 21st Conference on Computer and Communications Security (CCS) (2014)
13. EMVCo: EMV - Integrated Circuit Card Specifications for Payment Systems, version 4.3 (2011)
14. EMVCo: EMV Contactless Specifications for Payment Systems, version 2.4 (2014)
15. Francillon, A., Danev, B., Capkun, S.: Relay attacks on passive keyless entry and start systems in modern cars. In: Proceedings of the Network and Distributed System Security Symposium, NDSS 2011. The Internet Society (2011)
16. Francis, L., Hancke, G., Mayes, K.: A practical generic relay attack on contactless transactions by using NFC mobile phones. Int. J. RFID Secur. Cryprography (IJRFIDSC) **2**(1–4), 92–106 (2013)
17. Francis, L., Hancke, G., Mayes, K., Markantonakis, K.: Practical NFC peer-to-peer relay attack using mobile phones. In: Ors Yalcin, S.B. (ed.) RFIDSec 2010. LNCS, vol. 6370, pp. 35–49. Springer, Heidelberg (2010)
18. Hancke, G., Kuhn, M.: An RFID distance bounding protocol. In: 2005 First International Conference on Security and Privacy for Emerging Areas in Communications Networks, SecureComm 2005, pp. 67–73. IEEE (2005)
19. Murdoch, S.J.: Defending against wedge attacks in Chip and PIN. https://www.lightbluetouchpaper.org/2009/08/25/defending-against-wedge-attacks/
20. Sportiello, L., Ciardulli, A.: Long distance relay attack. In: Hutter, M., Schmidt, J.-M. (eds.) RFIDsec 2013. LNCS, vol. 8262, pp. 69–85. Springer, Heidelberg (2013)

Private and Secure Public-Key Distance Bounding

Application to NFC Payment

Serge Vaudenay[✉]

EPFL, 1015 Lausanne, Switzerland
Serge.Vaudenay@epfl.ch
http://lasec.epfl.ch

Abstract. Distance-Bounding is used to defeat relay attacks. For wireless payment systems, the payment terminal is not always online. So, the protocol must rely on a public key for the prover (payer). We propose a generic transformation of a (weakly secure) symmetric distance bounding protocol which has no post-verification into wide-strong-private and secure public-key distance bounding.

1 Introduction

Several wireless payment systems such as toll payment systems and NFC credit cards have recently been spread. These methods allow to pay small amounts without any action from the holder (no confirmation, no PIN code) other than approaching their device to the payment terminal.

In relay attacks, a man-in-the-middle $\mathcal{A}$ passively relays messages between two participants: a *prover* P and a *verifier* V [9,10]. The prover P is a credit card (of the payer) and the verifier V is a payment terminal (of the vendor). $\mathcal{A}$ can be run by two players: a malicious customer $\mathcal{A}_1$ mimicking a payment in a shop to buy some service to V, and a malicious neighbor $\mathcal{A}_2$ to the victim P. $\mathcal{A}_1$ and $\mathcal{A}_2$ relay messages between P and V. The payer may remain clueless.

So far, the most promising technique to defeat relay attacks is distance-bounding (DB) [5]. A DB protocol has several fast challenge/response rounds during which the verifier/vendor sends a challenge bit and expects to receive a response bit within a very short time from the prover/payer. The protocol fails if some response arrives too late or is incorrect. Due to the time of flight, if P is too far from V, his time to compute the response is already over when the challenge reaches him. Here are the traditional threat models for DB.

- Honest-prover security: *man-in-the-middle attacks* (MiM) (including *impersonation fraud* [1] and the so-called *mafia fraud* [8] including *relay attacks*).
- Malicious-prover security: *distance fraud* (DF) [5], in which a far-away malicious prover pretends that he is close; *distance hijacking* (DH) [7], in which the malicious prover relies on *honest* close-by participants; *collusion frauds* (CF) [3] (including the so-called *terrorist fraud* [8]), in which a malicious prover colludes with close-by participants (but without leaking credentials).

© International Financial Cryptography Association 2015
R. Böhme and T. Okamoto (Eds.): FC 2015, LNCS 8975, pp. 207–216, 2015.
DOI: 10.1007/978-3-662-47854-7_12

– *Privacy*, where we want that no man-in-the-middle adversary can learn the identity of the prover. Wide/narrow privacy refers to whether the adversary can see if a protocol succeeds on the verifier side. Strong/weak privacy refers to whether the adversary can corrupt provers and get their secret.

For payment systems, we cannot assume an online connection to a trusted server nor a shared secret between the payer and the vendor: we must have a public-key based protocol. We can further wonder which threat models are relevant. Clearly, the man-in-the-middle attacks are the main concern. Privacy is also important as payers want to remain anonymous to observers. For undeniability, a malicious payer shall not do a distance fraud then deny having made a payment on the basis that he was too far. Distance fraud shall also be prevented to be able to catch red handed people who pay with a stolen credit card.

Table 1. Existing public-key distance bounding protocols

protocol	MiM	DF	DH	CF	Privacy	Strong privacy
Brands-Chaum [5]	Secure	Secure	Insecure	Insecure	Insecure	Insecure
DBPK-Log [6]		Insecure		Insecure	Insecure	Insecure
HPO [13]	Secure	Secure		Insecure	Secure	Insecure
GOR [11]	Secure	Secure	Insecure	Insecure	Insecure	Insecure
ProProx [18]	Secure	Secure	Secure	Secure	Insecure	Insecure
privDB	Secure	Secure	Secure	Insecure	Secure	Secure

(Missing entries correspond to absence of proof in either direction.)

Not many public-key DB protocols exist: the Brands-Chaum protocol [5], the DBPK-Log protocol [6], the protocol by Hermans, Peeters, and Onete [13] (herein called the HPO protocol), its recent extension by Gambs, Onete, and Robert [11] (the GOR protocol, herein)[1], and ProProx [18] (see Table 1). None except ProProx resist to collusion frauds. The Brands-Chaum protocol does not resist to distance hijacking [7]. In [2], Bay *et al.* have broken DBPK-Log. Neither the Brands-Chaum protocol nor ProProx protect privacy but the HPO and GOR protocols were designed for this. However, HPO does not offer strong privacy and privacy in GOR can be broken, as this will be proven in a subsequent paper.

In this paper, we transform a symmetric DB protocol symDB with no post-verification into a public-key DB protocol privDB. Assuming some weak form of DF, MiM, and DH security for symDB, we prove that privDB is DF, MiM, DH secure, and strong-private. It is the first to be provably DH-secure and the first to be strong private. We propose a suitable symDB protocol called OTDB.

---

[1] The GOR protocol is a bit different from others as it provides *anonymous authentication*. The verifier does not identify the prover in the protocol.

2   Definitions

We recall and adapt the framework of [4,18]. We assume a multiparty setting in which participants have a *location* and information travels at the speed of light. Participants receive inputs and produce outputs. Honest participants run their purported algorithm. Malicious participants may run an arbitrary probabilistic polynomial-time (PPT) algorithm. The definition below is adapted from [4,18] to accommodate identification protocols and also to bridge public-key and symmetric distance bounding.

Definition 1. *A* distance-bounding *protocol (DB) consists of what follows.*
1. B: a distance bound. 2. K_P and K_V: two PPT key generation algorithms depending on a security parameter λ. For a public-key DB identification protocol, "setting up the keys" for P and V means running $K_P \rightarrow (\mathsf{sk}_P, \mathsf{pk}_P)$ and $K_V \rightarrow (\mathsf{sk}_V, \mathsf{pk}_V)$. For Symmetric DB, provers/verifiers are paired and "setting up the keys" for a pair (P, V) means running $K_P \rightarrow \mathsf{sk}_P$ then setting $\mathsf{sk}_V = \mathsf{sk}_P$ and $\mathsf{pk}_P = \mathsf{pk}_V = \perp$. 3. $(P(\mathsf{sk}_P, \mathsf{pk}_V), V(\mathsf{sk}_V))$: a two-party PPT protocol where $P(\mathsf{sk}_P, \mathsf{pk}_V)$ is the proving algorithm and $V(\mathsf{sk}_V)$ is the verifying algorithm. At the end of the protocol, $V(\mathsf{sk}_V)$ has a private output and sends a final message Out_V. He accepts ($\mathsf{Out}_V = 1$) or rejects ($\mathsf{Out}_V = 0$).

The protocol must be complete. *I.e., such that "setting up the keys" for (P, V) then making $P(\mathsf{sk}_P, \mathsf{pk}_V)$ and $V(\mathsf{sk}_V)$ interact together, at locations within a distance up to B always makes $V(\mathsf{sk}_V)$ accept ($\mathsf{Out}_V = 1$) and output pk_P.*

Moving to noisy settings [16] follows standard techniques which are omitted herein. Verifiers are assumed to be able to validate pk_P (e.g., by means of a PKI). In what follows, $\mathsf{Validate}(\mathsf{pk}_P)$ denotes this operation.

Security of DB. Like in [4,18], all security notions are formalized by a game with three types of participants: provers, verifiers, and actors. Each participant can have several instances at different location or time. Without loss of generality, actors are malicious. The purported algorithm is P for provers and V for verifiers. There is a distinguished instance of the verifier denoted by $\mathcal{V}$. Instances of participants within a distance to $\mathcal{V}$ up to B are called *close-by*. Others are called *far-away*. We say that the adversary *wins* if $\mathcal{V}$ accepts. In security models, we only consider without loss of generality (several instances of) one verifier who is honest. In Definition 2 and 3, we consider without loss of generality (several instances of) one prover with an identity corresponding to the key pk_P.

Definition 2 ([18]). *We consider the following honest-prover security notion. At the beginning of the game, we set up the keys (following Definition 1) and give pk_V as input to all participants, sk_P as input to the prover instances, and pk_P as input to all malicious participants. The prover is honest. The DB protocol is* MiM-secure *(man-in-the-middle) if for all such settings in which there is no close-by prover, the probability that $\mathcal{V}$ accepts and outputs pk_P is negligible.[2]*

---

[2] The key generation algorithms accepts as input a security parameter λ which is omitted for simplicity reasons. Hence, $\Pr[\mathcal{V}\text{ accepts}]$ is a function of λ. We say that $f(\lambda)$ is *negligible* if for every integer d we have $f(\lambda) = \mathcal{O}(\lambda^{-d})$ for $\lambda \rightarrow +\infty$.

The DB protocol is one-time MiM-secure (OT-MiM) *if the above is satisfied in settings where there is a single verifier instance and a single prover instance.*

Definition 3 ([18]). *We consider the following malicious-prover security notion. At the beginning of the game, we use an arbitrary PPT algorithm $K(\mathsf{pk}_V)$ instead of K_P in the key setup. The DB protocol is* DF-secure *(distance fraud) if for all such settings where there is no close-by participant except V, the probability that V accepts and outputs pk_P is negligible.*

Note that the key of the malicious prover is set up maliciously (even depending on pk_V) using an algorithm K which can differ from K_P.

Privacy. The most general and prominent model for privacy is the simulation-based privacy notion in [17] which was enriched in [15]. Hermans et al. [14] presented a simpler privacy model which we call the HPVP model.

Definition 4 (HPVP Privacy [14]). *We consider an adversary playing with the following oracles: 1.* Create $\rightarrow (i, \mathsf{pk}_P)$ *runs K_P and sets pk_P as a valid key for a new prover whose number is i; 2.* Corrupt$(i) \rightarrow$ state *returns the current state (in permanent memory) of the ith prover; 3.* Draw$(i, j) \rightarrow$ vtag *draws either the ith prover (if in the left game) or the jth prover (if in the right game) and returns a pseudonym* vtag *(if the prover is already drawn, $\perp$ is returned); 4.* Free(vtag) *releases* vtag *so that it can be drawn again; 5.* SendP(vtag, m) $\rightarrow m'$ *sends a message m to a drawn tag* vtag *and gets a response m' (if* vtag *was released, $\perp$ is returned instead); 6.* Launch $\rightarrow k$ *runs a new verifier whose number is k; 7.* SendV$(k, m) \rightarrow m'$ *sends a message m to the kth verifier and gets a response m'; 8.* Result$(k) \rightarrow$ Out$_V$ *gives the final result (whether the protocol succeeded or not) of the protocol on the kth verifier side. In the privacy game, the adversary interacts with these oracles and guesses if it is left or right. The game is formalized as follows: 1. run $K_V \rightarrow (\mathsf{sk}_V, \mathsf{pk}_V)$ and initialize all verifiers with sk_V and all provers and $\mathcal{A}$ with pk_V; 2. pick $b \in \{0, 1\}$; 3. let $\mathcal{A}$ interact with the oracles (in the left game for $b = 0$ or the right game for $b = 1$) and make a guess β; 4. $\mathcal{A}$ wins if $\beta = b$. We have privacy if for every PPT adversary $\mathcal{A}$, $\Pr[\mathcal{A} \text{ wins}] - \frac{1}{2}$ is negligible. For* narrow *privacy, the adversary does not use the* Result *oracle. For* weak *privacy, he does not use the* Corrupt *oracle. Otherwise, the adversary is* wide, *respectively* strong.

Distance Hijacking. In distance hijacking [7], the prover is malicious, running an algorithm $\mathcal{A}$ and we add a honest prover $P(\mathsf{sk}_{P'}, \mathsf{pk}_V)$ with another identity P' associated to $\mathsf{pk}_{P'}$. The malicious prover runs $\mathcal{A}(\mathsf{sk}_P, \mathsf{pk}_P, \mathsf{pk}_{P'}, \mathsf{pk}_V)$. We formalize distance hijacking for DB protocols consisting of a regular (i.e., time-insensitive) initialization phase, a time-critical challenge phase, and a regular verification phase. $\mathcal{A}$ is playing a man-in-the-middle between $P(\mathsf{sk}_{P'}, \mathsf{pk}_V)$ and $V(\mathsf{sk}_V)$ except during the challenge phase when he remains passive. (See Fig. 1.)

Definition 5. *A DB protocol (B, K_P, K_V, P, V) is* DH-secure *if for all PPT algorithms K and $\mathcal{A}$, the following game makes V output pk_P with negligible probability:*

1: for public-key DB: $K_P \rightarrow (\mathsf{sk}_{P'}, \mathsf{pk}_{P'})$, $K_V \rightarrow (\mathsf{sk}_V, \mathsf{pk}_V)$, $K(\mathsf{pk}_{P'}, \mathsf{pk}_V) \rightarrow$
   $(\mathsf{sk}_P, \mathsf{pk}_P)$; if $\mathsf{pk}_P = \mathsf{pk}_{P'}$, the game aborts
   for symmetric DB: $K_P \rightarrow \mathsf{sk}_{P'}$, $K \rightarrow \mathsf{sk}_P$, set $\mathsf{sk}_V = \mathsf{sk}_P$, $\mathsf{pk}_P = \mathsf{pk}_{P'} =$
   $\mathsf{pk}_V = \perp$;
2: let $\mathcal{A}$ run $\mathcal{A}(\mathsf{sk}_P, \mathsf{pk}_P, \mathsf{pk}_{P'}, \mathsf{pk}_V)$, let V, $V_1, V_2, \ldots$ run $V(\mathsf{sk}_V)$, and let P',
   $P'_1, P'_2, \ldots$ run $P(\mathsf{sk}_{P'}, \mathsf{pk}_V)$
3: let $\mathcal{A}$ interact with $P', P'_1, P'_2 \ldots$ and $V, V_1, V_2, \ldots$ concurrently until the ini-
   tialization phase ends for V
4: let P' and V continue interacting with each other until the challenge phase
   ends for V; $\mathcal{A}$ receives the exchanged messages but remains passive
5: let $\mathcal{A}$ continue interacting with $P', P'_1, P'_2 \ldots$ and $V, V_1, V_2, \ldots$ concurrently
   during the verification phase

A DB protocol is one-time DH-secure (OT-DH) *if the above holds when there are no P'_i and V_i.*

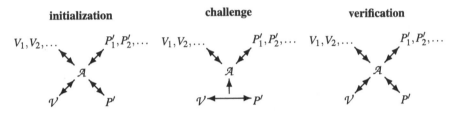

Fig. 1. Distance hijacking

3 From Symmetric to Asymmetric Distance Bounding

3.1 The OTDB Protocol

We propose a one-time DB protocol OTDB based on the Hancke-Kuhn proto-col [12]. It is represented on Fig. 2. We use a $2n$-bit secret s. It is XORed to a random mask m selected by the verifier. The answer to a challenge in iteration i is just the bit of $s \oplus m$ at position $2i - 1$ or $2i$, depending on the challenge.

We define a sub-category of simple DB protocols.

Definition 6. *A symmetric DB protocol (B, K, P, V) follows the* canonical *structure if there exist 5 PPT algorithms P_{init}, P_{chall}, V_{init}, V_{chall}, V_{ver} such that $P(s)$ and $V(s)$ are defined as follows:*

1. *$P(s)$ and $V(s)$ run the initialization phase by running P_{init} and V_{init}. These algorithms do not use s. They produce a final state σ_P and σ_V.*
2. *$P(s)$ and $V(s)$ run the challenge phase by running $P_{\mathsf{chall}}(s, \sigma_P)$ and $V_{\mathsf{chall}}(\sigma_V)$, where V_{chall} does not depend on s and produces a final state σ'_V.*
3. *$V(s)$ computes $\mathsf{Out}_V = V_{\mathsf{ver}}(s, \sigma'_V)$.*

The canonical point is that there is no interactive verification and the secret is used by P only in the challenge phase and by V only in the final verification.

Theorem 7. OTDB *follows the canonical structure. It is DF-secure, OT-MiM-secure, and OT-DH-secure.*

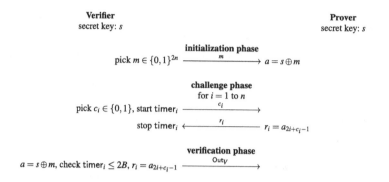

Fig. 2. The OTDB protocol.

Proof. The canonical structure of OTDB is clear.

For DF-security, we observe that whatever the adversary is doing, the distribution of a on the verifier side is uniform in $\{0,1\}^{2n}$. Since there is no close-by participant, a response can be received on time only if it was sent before the challenge was known. If $a_{2i-1} = a_{2i}$, this can be done with probability 1. Otherwise, this can only be done with probability $\frac{1}{2}$. So, the optimal probability that all responses are correct is $\sum_{w=0}^{n} \binom{n}{w} 2^{-n-w} = \left(\frac{3}{4}\right)^n$ which is negligible.

For OT-MiM-security, we consider a distant $\mathcal{V} = V(s)$ and $P(s)$ with several actors. By playing with $P(s)$, the adversary can deduce for each i either s_{2i-1} or s_{2i} but not both. To answer to $\mathcal{V}$, he must know precisely which of these two bits is needed but when he learns it, it is too late to play with $P(s)$ to get it. So, the probability to pass one round is limited to $\frac{3}{4}$. So, the probability of success is also $\left(\frac{3}{4}\right)^n$, which is negligible.

For OT-DH-security, we consider P' who is set up with a random s' and V who is maliciously set up with an independent s. In the initialization part (which can be corrupted), we let m be the value sent by $\mathcal{V}$ and m' be the value received by P'. When they start the challenge phase, $\mathcal{V}$ uses $a = s \oplus m$ and P' uses $a' = s' \oplus m'$, where m' only depends on m and s. So, a' is uniformly distributed and independent from a. The challenge part between P' and V cannot be corrupted, by definition of the OT-DH-security. Hence, $\mathcal{V}$ accepts with probability 2^{-n}, which is negligible. □

As concrete parameters, we can use $n = 49$ for a 2^{-20} online security.

3.2 The privDB Protocol

We adapt the RFID protocol from [15,17] for DB. We assume that K_V generates a key pair for a public-key cryptosystem Enc/Dec and that K_P generates a key pair for a digital signature scheme Sign/Verify. The protocol runs as follows (see Fig. 3): 1. V sends a nonce N to P; 2. P picks a random s and sends $\mathsf{Enc}_{\mathsf{pk}_V}(s \| \mathsf{pk}_P \| \mathsf{Sign}_{\mathsf{sk}_P}(N))$ to V; 3. V decrypts, verifies the signature on N, and validates pk_P (if this step fails, V sends $\mathsf{Out}_V = 0$ and aborts);[3] 4. P and V run a symmetric DB symDB based on the secret s (if this step fails, V sends $\mathsf{Out}_V = 0$ and aborts); 5. the private output of V is set to pk_P and the public one is set to $\mathsf{Out}_V = 1$. Compared to HPO [13], the encrypted channel can also be used to transmit a certificate in a private way.

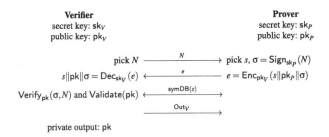

Fig. 3. privDB: strong private public-key DB from symmetric DB.

Theorem 8. *If* symDB *is DF-secure then* privDB *is DF-secure.*

The reduction is quite trivial.

Definition 9. *We say the signature scheme is* Known-Key-UF-1CMA-secure *(KK-UF-1CMA) if for any PPT algorithm* $\mathcal{A}$, *the probability to win the following game is negligible: generate a key pair* $(\mathsf{sk}_P, \mathsf{pk}_P)$ *and pick a challenge* N'; *set the chosen message* $N = \mathcal{A}(\mathsf{sk}_P, \mathsf{pk}_P, N')$ *and sign it by* $\sigma = \mathsf{Sign}_{\mathsf{sk}_P}(N)$. $\mathcal{A}$ *wins if* $N \neq N'$ *and* $\mathsf{Verify}_{\mathsf{pk}_P}(\sigma, N')$ *accepts. We say the signature scheme is* simple-UF-1CMA-secure *(S-UF-1CMA) if the same holds but for* $N = \mathcal{A}(\mathsf{pk}_P, N')$.

Clearly, the standard UF-CMA security implies S-UF-1CMA security.

Theorem 10. *If* symDB *is OT-MiM-secure, the signature scheme is S-UF-1CMA-secure, the cryptosystem resists chosen-ciphertext attacks (IND-CCA secure), then* privDB *is MiM-secure.*

Proof. We let Γ_0 denote the MiM security game. In what follows, Γ_i is a game and p_i denotes the probability that Γ_i succeeds. We want to show that p_0 is negligible. We first reduce Γ_0 to a game Γ_1 in which no two verifiers select the same nonce and no two provers select the same s (so, their e are unique as well). Clearly, $p_1 - p_0$ is negligible. In Γ_2, we simulate every verifier V who is given a e produced by a prover P. We let $N, s, \mathsf{pk}_P, \sigma$ be the values from the viewpoint of P. In the simulation, if V produced N himself, the decryption and verifications are skipped and V proceeds with $\mathsf{symDB}(s)$ directly. We say that P and V are matching instances. Otherwise, only the decryption is skipped and V

---

[3] In a previous version, N was part of the plaintext. At the conference, Erik-Oliver Blass suggested to remove it. This required to adapt the proofs.

proceeds with s, pk_P, σ. Clearly, $p_2 = p_1$. In Γ_2, no e produced by any P needs to be decrypted. In Γ_3, we sequentially replace every $e = \mathsf{Enc}_{\mathsf{pk}_V}(s, \mathsf{pk}_P, \sigma)$ by some $e = \mathsf{Enc}_{\mathsf{pk}_V}(\mathsf{rand})$ and use the IND-CCA security to deduce that $p_3 - p_2$ is negligible. In Γ_3, no information about s or σ leaks from e.

To go from Γ_3 to Γ_4, we eliminate all signatures by repeating the following transformation: let $\sigma = \mathsf{Sign}_{\mathsf{sk}_P}(N)$ be the very first signature computation. We note that σ can only be used later by a $\mathsf{Verify}_{\mathsf{pk}_P}(\sigma, N')$ computation, for $N \neq N'$. If it is not immediately followed by a this verification, we postpone the signature computation to the very first moment when σ is used. Clearly, this does not affect the probability of success. If instead it is followed by $\mathsf{Verify}_{\mathsf{pk}_P}(\sigma, N')$, we replace $\mathsf{Verify}_{\mathsf{pk}_P}(\sigma, N')$ by 0 (rejection). (So, the next transformation continues to postpone the signature.) By replacing the generation of a random N' by a S-UF-1CMA challenge (and aborting if it is not the right N'), we use the S-UF-1CMA security to deduce that the probability of success is negligibly affected. After repeating this process, we eliminate the signing operations. We obtain a game Γ_4 in which a verifier instance has up to one matching prover instance and each prover instance has up to one matching verifier instance.

In Γ_4, either $\mathcal{V}$ uses a forged signature (but we eliminate this case with the S-UF-1CMA security), or $\mathcal{V}$ has a unique matching P and they both run $\mathsf{symDB}(s)$ on a random s. By simulating everything else but this instance of symDB, we obtain the OT-MiM-security game of symDB. Due to the OT-MiM-security of symDB, we conclude that p_4 must be negligible.   □

Theorem 11. *If* symDB *follows the canonical structure and is OT-MiM and OT-DH secure; the signature scheme is S-UF-1CMA-secure; the cryptosystem resists chosen-ciphertext attacks (IND-CCA secure); then* privDB *is DH-secure.*

Proof. We let Γ_0 denote the DH security game. In what follows, Γ_i is a game and p_i denotes the probability that Γ_i succeeds. We want to show that p_0 is negligible. Since symDB has no interactive verification, Γ_0 consists of two phases after the key set up: the initialization phase and the challenge phase. The last phase matches the challenge phase of symDB between $\mathcal{V}$ and P' alone. For Γ_0 to succeed, $\mathcal{V}$ must identify P. So, we assume that $\mathcal{V}$ receives pk_P during the initialization. The main point is to realize that $\mathcal{V}$ and P' must then start with two independent keys s and s' with s' uniform. We conclude using the OT-DH-security of symDB.

We do the same reduction as in the proof of Theroem 10 to the games $\Gamma_1, \Gamma_2, \Gamma_3, \Gamma_4$ (with P' replacing P). Since $\mathcal{V}$ receives pk_P, he cannot match P'. Let s' be the randomly distributed value selected by P'. We first treat the case where there is no V_i matching P'. So, s' is never used before the challenge phase due to the canonical structure of symDB. Therefore, $\mathcal{V}$ is set up with some s which is independent from s'. Hence, we are in the situation of the OT-DH game of symDB. By using the OT-DH-security of symDB, p_3 is negligible.

Let now assume that one verifier instance matches P'. We know that it is unique and we assume that it is V_1 without loss of generality. If V_1 does not compute his Out_{V_1} before the challenge phase of the game, none of his messages depend on s' due to the canonical structure of symDB, so we can proceed as in the previous case.

Now, if V_1 sends out his Out_{V_1} before the challenge phase of the game, we define a new game Γ_5 in which Out_{V_1} is replaced by 0. In Γ_5, we can conclude as in the previous case that p_5 is negligible. So, what is left to be shown is that $p_5 - p_4$ is negligible, or equivalently that $\mathsf{Out}_{V_1} = 1$ with negligible probability in Γ_4. For that, we observe that P' is only running the initialization of symDB (which does not depend on s' by assumption on symDB) until Out_{V_1} is released. Since V_1 is set up with a random s' and that no other algorithm depends on s' in this phase, we are in an impersonation attack case. We conclude using the OT-MiM security of symDB. $\qquad\square$

Theorem 12. *If the signature scheme is KK-UF-1CMA-secure and the cryptosystem resists chosen-ciphertext attacks (IND-CCA secure),* privDB *is wide-strong private in the HPVP model.*[4]

Proof. We let Γ_0 denote the wide-strong HPVP privacy game. In what follows, Γ_i is a game and p_i denotes the probability that Γ_i succeeds. We want to show that $p_0 - \frac{1}{2}$ is negligible. We do the same reduction as in the proof of Theroem 10 to the games $\Gamma_1, \Gamma_2, \Gamma_3, \Gamma_4$ (but with KK-UF-1CMA security) and obtain that $p_4 - p_0$ is negligible. We observe that in Γ_4, the pk_P and σ by a drawn prover is never used. The public key is only important during Corrupt queries, but this does not apply on drawn provers in the HPVP model. So, drawn provers use no proper identity in Γ_4. It does not matter which prover is drawn (the left or the right), the simulation of the prover is the same. So the probability of correctly winning $\beta = b$ must be exactly $p_4 = \frac{1}{2}$. $\qquad\square$

Acknowledgements. The author would like to thank Erik-Oliver Blass, Tom Chothia, and Yvo Desmedt for valuable remarks. This work is part of the ICT COST Action IC1403 (*Cryptacus*).

References

1. Avoine, G., Tchamkerten, A.: An efficient distance bounding RFID authentication protocol: balancing false-acceptance rate and memory requirement. In: Samarati, P., Yung, M., Martinelli, F., Ardagna, C.A. (eds.) ISC 2009. LNCS, vol. 5735, pp. 250–261. Springer, Heidelberg (2009)
2. Bay, A., Boureanu, I., Mitrokotsa, A., Spulber, I., Vaudenay, S.: The Bussard-Bagga and other distance-bounding protocols under attacks. In: Kutyłowski, M., Yung, M. (eds.) Inscrypt 2012. LNCS, vol. 7763, pp. 371–391. Springer, Heidelberg (2013)
3. Boureanu, I., Mitrokotsa, A., Vaudenay, S.: Towards secure distance bounding. In: Moriai, S. (ed.) FSE 2013. LNCS, vol. 8424, pp. 55–68. Springer, Heidelberg (2014)

---

[4] KK-UF-1CMA was added in the final version of this paper after having removed N from the plaintext. It was necessary due to the adversary getting sk_P by corruption.

4. Boureanu, I., Vaudenay, S.: Optimal proximity proofs. In: Lin, D., Yung, M., Zhou, J. (eds.) Inscrypt 2014. LNCS, vol. 8957, pp. 170–190. Springer, Heidelberg (2015)
5. Brands, S., Chaum, D.: Distance bounding protocols. In: Helleseth, T. (ed.) EURO-CRYPT 1993. LNCS, vol. 765, pp. 344–359. Springer, Heidelberg (1994)
6. Bussard, L., Bagga, W.: Distance-bounding proof of knowledge to avoid real-time attacks. In: Sasaki, R., Qing, S., Okamoto, E., Yoshiura, H. (eds.) Security and Privacy in the Age of Ubiquitous Computing. IFIP Advances in Information and Communication Technology, vol. 181, pp. 223–238. Springer, New York (2005)
7. Cremers, C.J. F., Rasmussen, K.B., Schmidt, B., Capkun, S.: Distance hijacking attacks on distance bounding protocols. In: IEEE Symposium on Security and Privacy S&P 2012, San Francisco, California, USA, pp. 113–127. IEEE Computer Society (2012)
8. Desmedt, Y.: Major security problems with the "unforgeable" (Feige-)Fiat-Shamir proofs of identity and how to overcome them. In: Congress on Computer and Communication Security and Protection Securicom 1988, Paris, France, pp. 147–159. SEDEP, Paris (1988)
9. Francillon, A., Danev, B., Čapkun, S.: Relay attacks on passive keyless entry and start systems in modern cars. In: Network and Distributed System Security Symposium (NDSS 2011), San Diego, CA, USA. The Internet Society (2011)
10. Francis, L., Hancke, G., Mayes, K., Markantonakis, K.: On the security issues of NFC enabled mobile phones. Int. J. Internet Technol. Secured Trans. (IJITST) **2**, 336–356 (2010)
11. Gambs, S., Onete, C., Robert, J.-M.: Prover anonymous and deniable distance-bounding authentication. In: ACM Symposium on Information, Computer and Communications Security (ASIACCS 2014), Kyoto, Japan, pp. 501–506. ACM Press (2014)
12. Hancke, G.P., Kuhn, M.G.: An RFID distance bounding protocol. In: Conference on Security and Privacy for Emerging Areas in Communications Networks SecureComm 2005, Athens, Greece, pp. 67–73. IEEE (2005)
13. Hermans, J., Peeters, R., Onete, C.: Efficient, secure, private distance bounding without keyupdates. In: ACM Conference on Security and Privacy in Wireless and Mobile Networks, WISEC 2013, Budapest, Hungary, pp. 195–206. ACM (2013)
14. Hermans, J., Pashalidis, A., Vercauteren, F., Preneel, B.: A new RFID privacy model. In: Atluri, V., Diaz, C. (eds.) ESORICS 2011. LNCS, vol. 6879, pp. 568–587. Springer, Heidelberg (2011)
15. Ouafi, K., Vaudenay, S.: Strong privacy for RFID systems from plaintext-aware encryption. In: Pieprzyk, J., Sadeghi, A.-R., Manulis, M. (eds.) CANS 2012. LNCS, vol. 7712, pp. 247–262. Springer, Heidelberg (2012)
16. Singelée, D., Preneel, B.: Distance bounding in noisy environments. In: Stajano, F., Meadows, C., Capkun, S., Moore, T. (eds.) ESAS 2007. LNCS, vol. 4572, pp. 101–115. Springer, Heidelberg (2007)
17. Vaudenay, S.: On privacy models for RFID. In: Kurosawa, K. (ed.) ASIACRYPT 2007. LNCS, vol. 4833, pp. 68–87. Springer, Heidelberg (2007)
18. Vaudenay, S.: Proof of Proximity of Knowledge. IACR Eprint 2014/695 report (2014)

Purchase Details Leaked to PayPal

Sören Preibusch[1]([⊠]), Thomas Peetz[2], Gunes Acar[2],
and Bettina Berendt[2]

[1] Formerly Microsoft Research, Cambridge, UK
mail@soeren-preibusch.de
http://www.preibusch.de
[2] KU Leuven, Leuven, Belgium
http://www.kuleuven.be

Abstract. We describe a new form of online tracking: explicit, yet unnecessary leakage of personal information and detailed shopping habits from online merchants to payment providers. In contrast to Web tracking, online shops make it impossible for their customers to avoid this proliferation of their data. We record and analyse leakage patterns for $N = 881$ US Web shops sampled from Web users' actual online purchase sessions. More than half of the sites shared product names and details with PayPal, allowing the payment provider to build up comprehensive consumption profiles across the sites consumers buy from, subscribe to, or donate to. In addition, PayPal forwards customers' shopping details to Omniture, a third-party data aggregator with an even larger tracking reach. Leakage to PayPal is commonplace across product categories and includes details of medication or sex toys. We provide recommendations for merchants.

1 Introduction

1.1 Online Payment Providers Process Rich Transaction Data

Online payment handling is a key enabler for electronic and mobile retailing, and a growing business opportunity. Payment providers are intermediaries between merchants and their customers who buy and then pay for goods and services. As intermediaries, payment providers necessarily gain insight into the transaction, as they process personal information, just like the delivery company will need the customer's postal address. The minimum data requirements for payment handling are the order total, the receiving merchant and an authenticated payment method. This corresponds to data items traditionally collected during credit card transactions. However, a much richer set of data items becomes available for online purchases, including an itemised bill or information about the buyer, allowing for value-added services. These data are valuable for payment providers and merchants who can benefit from lower fees.

Online companion at: http://preibusch.de/publ/paypal_privacy.

© International Financial Cryptography Association 2015
R. Böhme and T. Okamoto (Eds.): FC 2015, LNCS 8975, pp. 217–226, 2015.
DOI: 10.1007/978-3-662-47854-7_13

1.2   Privacy Concerns and the Principle of Data Minimisation

The large-scale collection and processing of personal details causes privacy concerns. Concern is no longer limited to traditional items of personal information like address or demographics, but increasingly about consumption behaviour. Of particular interest is shopping data, whose value is demonstrated through myriads of loyalty card schemes. Purchase tracking now happens across channels (online / offline) and even if users are not enrolled in a loyalty scheme [1, 2].

Our research motivation is the ability of payment providers to collect purchase details at scale. Similar to Web tracking and analytics, a small number of providers cover multiple Websites (merchants) and can link transactions across those. Compared to cookie-like tracking, the privacy issues are exacerbated:

- Embedded tracking code is—in principle—ancillary to the core functionality of the Web page and can safely be filtered out (e.g., with ad-blockers). Payment handling is however essential to shopping, and users cannot complete the transaction without interacting with the payment provider.
- Unlike browsing patterns linked to a cookie identifier, consumption patterns linked to a payment method are not pseudonymous but identifiable through offline details such as credit card numbers or bank account details, which often include full name.
- Payment cards or account information serve as persistent identifiers, allowing the linkage of multiple transactions even across different logins or accounts.
- Consumers are typically unable to evade such data collection unless they refrain from shopping with the given merchant. The collection of shoppers' details is a negative externality of the contract between the merchant and the payment provider.
- Payment handling is universal across merchants and sectors. Consumer details are collected and merged across transactions even for sensitive products and merchants. This includes pharmacies or adult entertainment, for instance, where shoppers deliberately moved out of the high street and onto the Web in a pursuit of privacy.

Privacy threats arise from detailed purchase patterns when more than the minimum data required are collected. Although the principle of data minimisation has long been codified in national law and international privacy guidelines (e.g., by the OECD [3]), it is only with the European Union's upcoming General Data Protection Regulation, that data minimisation is becoming an enforceable principle [4].

1.3   Research Questions and Our Contribution

Ahead of tightening regulation regarding data minimisation, recognising that online payment handling is a growing market, we set out to explore the tracking capabilities of online payment providers.

We conducted the first industry-wide, empirical survey that quantifies the flows of customer data from $N = 881$ merchants to PayPal. We describe current practices of data proliferation which can soon be deemed privacy leaks. PayPal is chosen as the most pervasive online payment provider, covering Websites across strata of popularity [5]. We investigate which personal and transactions details merchants are sharing with PayPal above pure order totals (Fig. 1). Our survey of the ecosystem also looks for

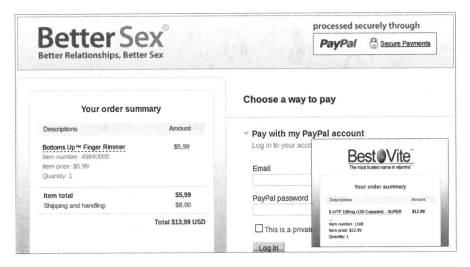

Fig. 1. Sites selling sensitive products also leak product details to PayPal: adult toys and medication (5-HTP addresses depression, anxiety, sleep disorders). Also see the online companion

per-sector differences in data sharing with payment providers or whether more popular Websites leak more or less personal details.

2 Related Work

Our investigation complements and expands an existing body of literature that has empirically examined privacy and tracking practices at large. Bonneau and Preibusch studied privacy practices across the entire online social networking ecosystem and found unsatisfactory privacy practices across the industry [6]. They also investigated data protection practices across different industries [7] and found that poor practices were commonplace regarding password security, although merchant sites did better than newspaper sites. Specifically for Web shops, more expensive shops were found to collect significantly more personal details than their cheaper competitors [8].

A number of Web privacy surveys studied the private information leakage, different tracking mechanisms and their prevalence on the Web. Krishnamurthy and Wills show how personally identifiable information leaks via online social networks, including the leakage by HTTP Referer header [9]. Other researchers surveyed the use of more advanced and resilient tracking mechanisms such as evercookies [10–12], browser fingerprinting [12–14] and cookie syncing [12], commonly reporting on questionable practices and unexpected prevalence of such technologies.

Finally, researchers looked into consumers' privacy choices in online shopping. Buyers of sensitive products (vibrators) were found to pay a premium to shop with a retailer whose privacy practices were labelled as superior by a product search engine [15]. In the largest ever lab and field experiment in privacy economics, almost one in three Web shoppers paid one euro extra for keeping their mobile phone number private

[16]. When privacy comes for free, more than 80 % of consumers choose the company that collects less personal information [16]. Earlier results indicated that price discounts override online shoppers' privacy preferences [17].

3 Methodology

3.1 Background: PayPal Integration, Information Flows, Privacy Agreements

PayPal has been a pioneer to offer payment acceptance to electronic retailers, although its product range now covers a plenitude of card and card-less payment and identity services for online, offline, and mobile transactions. Similarly to a cloud service, PayPal's offerings are characterised by their ease of set-up, pay per use, and self-service.

PayPal offers multiple ways to be embedded in the shopping workflow, traditionally depending on the type of payment [18]. On a technical level, there are two different integration routes depending on how the session data is transmitted from the merchant to PayPal: (1) server-to-server integration, where SOAP Web services or REST APIs are used to communicate transaction details from the merchant to PayPal; (2) integration via the client, where transaction parameters are passed exclusively through the query string (GET) by means of buyers' browsers.

Integration via GET is simple and readily available for hosted Websites, as no server-side communication is required ("buttons" in PayPal parlance). More sophisticated methods use server-to-server communication between the application server and the payment provider: the merchant creates a session with the payment provider when submitting all relevant transaction data. This session is then referenced through a session identifier or token ("EC token"), which is the only information that the client needs to pass on [19]. This method requires more technical expertise, but is less susceptible to manipulation by the client. However, server-to-server communication cannot be observed in a study like ours, where the client is instrumented.

Payment sessions referenced via an EC token are very common. The unobservable flow of personal information between servers is a challenge for our research. We therefore use personal data that PayPal displays back to the user to establish a lower bound for the privacy invasion by the data that is transmitted (Sect. 3.3).

The "Legal Agreements for PayPal Services" [20] outline a number of requirements for merchants. All information submitted to the API must be "true, correct, and complete" [21]. Whereas all fields containing personal information are optional [22], a "description field to identify the goods" and a URL linking back to the original product page must be provided for the popular Express Checkout method [22].

3.2 Sampling

We sample online shops that target US consumers and provide checkout in US Dollar via PayPal. The US market is chosen for its size and for being the home market of PayPal. We sample popular Web shops from real online shopping sessions, seeded from Internet Explorer users who opted in to share their browsing history. Practices at these popular online destinations impact a large consumer population. Stores are identified by their URL, as occurring before the PayPal checkout page in browser sessions. For each URL, we selected a single product for purchase, following a strict procedure.

We excluded Websites offering business services (B2B such as email marketing campaigns), banks and insurances, and restricted Websites which required a prior customer relationship such as utility companies. Airline Websites were often excluded for we were unable to complete the purchase according to our data collection protocol. EBay, PayPal internal and duplicate Websites were excluded.

Hosting sites (e.g., Yahoo! shops or Google Sites) were excluded and separated from the sample for future analysis. Such sites host multiple shops with differing implementation practices under a single domain. A few representative sub-shops were chosen for affiliate shops (e.g., spreadshirt.com) and shop-in-shop solutions (e.g., atgstores.com).

3.3   Experimental Protocol

For reliable results, a strict data collection protocol was followed during the main data collection, after a pilot study on 40 Websites. The details of the experimental setup and procedures are laid out in the Online Companion. To avoid contamination of the results by residual cookies or other re-identification methods, a virtual machine was used and reset for every recording anew. Transaction data were recorded while navigating from the product page to PayPal's checkout screen. Browsing was done in Firefox and all HTTP and HTTPS traffic was captured by mitmproxy [23] and stored. This includes GET and POST requests and the parameters submitted with them. Web forms were completed by using the same fictitious profile data on every site, a woman in her 40 s living in a major US city. A unique email address was used for each Website. Although data collection was tool-supported, there was always a human in the loop.

4   Data Analysis

4.1   Data Description

Dataset. From an initial list of 1200 extracted from browsing sessions, we successfully collected data for $N = 881$ merchant Websites: HTTP(S) traffic traces until reaching the PayPal login page, and screenshot upon arrival. The parsed logs and transcribed screenshots constitute all evidence of personal identifiable information (PII) leakage a customer can capture. More than 86 % of all Websites use a token implementation; we rely on the screenshots for those as PII leakage cannot be inferred from the client logs.

To verify our screenshot-based approach, we checked whether the PayPal screen always displays all PII received over the GET query-string. We were able to confirm that whenever customer or product data was leaked via GET, it showed up on the PayPal login screen. The only exception was for shipping costs of USD 0.00, which was forwarded but hidden in 36 cases.

Table 1. Leaked data by clusters ranked from good to bad privacy practices. The common leakage of product details is more worrying than the seeming absence of customer data: PayPal collects identity details directly during payment. Leaked: □ = sometimes, ■ = always, blank = never

	Site count	Name	Address	Email	Phone	Shipping	Quantity	Prices	Description	Prod. Name	Leak min	Leak max
C_1☺	391 (44%)										0	0
	Leaks nothing.											
C_2☺	34 (4%)	□	□				□	□	□	□	1	3
	Usually leaks two of names, item numbers, and prices.											
C_3☺	292 (33%)						□	□	□	□	3	4
	Leaks at least names, item numbers, and prices.											
C_4☹	155 (18%)					■	□	■	□	□	4	5
	Leaks at least most product details and always shipping costs.											
C_5☹	9 (1%)	■	■	□		□	□	■	□	□	6	7
	Leaks name and address in addition to product details.											

Clustering of leakage patterns. The leakage patterns form the backbone of our work. To analyse the data more deeply, we reduce the number of distinct patterns by clustering all 881 URLs into only few classes (Table 1). We use EM clustering [24], which automatically determines the appropriate number of clusters.

A natural question is whether a particular combination of endpoint and token usage enforces or prevents leakage. Analysing the clusters with association rule mining indicates no such relationship: None of the clusters are homogeneous with respect to endpoints and tokens, except for C_2, which does not contain any token implementations.

Privacy-friendly Websites tend to use a token more often: 98 % of all Websites in Cluster C_1 were using a token, compared to 86 % and 85 % for C_3 and C_4, respectively ($p < 0.0001$, two-tailed Fisher's exact test). We observe that no Websites leaking customer addresses rely on a token implementation. With a sample size of nine this holds little statistical significance, but we found no indication in the API documentation that this is a requirement on PayPal's side. We conclude that PayPal's available API methods do not bias Web shops to treat customers' privacy in a specific way.

4.2   Adding Alexa Metadata: Website Popularity and Quality

We investigated whether Website popularity and technical quality had an influence on privacy-friendliness. We use the Alexa Web Information Service (AWIS) features 'speed percentile' and 'traffic rank' as proxies. Speed percentile has no immediate bearing on cluster membership. Rather, we see that the number of sites from a certain cluster scale with the overall number of sites in the speed percentile. We further see that the distribution of sites from the clusters over the percentile bins follow no specific pattern. It can thus not be said that the speed of a Website has a positive correlation with its privacy-friendliness.

Less popular sites are found significantly more often in clusters that exhibit more leakage. More popular sites tend to leak less. For illustrative purposes, the average traffic rank is 0.4 million for C_1, 1.0 million for C_3 and 1.4 million for C_4. A Mann-Whitney U test indicates a highly significant difference in the traffic ranks per cluster ($p = 0.001$ for both pairwise comparisons). Sites in the worst leakage cluster C_5 do not appear among the 50 highest ranked in our sample.

4.3 Third-Party Tracking Facilitated by PayPal, and Internal Persistent Cookies

Analysis of the HTTP traffic observed during the experiments revealed the use of Adobe's Omniture tracking software on PayPal checkout pages. When a user lands on the PayPal checkout page, two HTTP requests were sent to paypal.d1.sc.omtrdc.net and paypal.112.2o7.net, which both belong to Omniture [25]. The requests contain metadata about the payment to be made, such as currency and transaction token, along with the user's browser characteristics such as plugins, screen dimensions and software versions [26]. Remarkably, PayPal also shares the Referer URL of the checkout page, which reveals the URL of the Web shop, and potentially the product to be purchased. The transfer of these details enables Adobe to build a better profile of 152 million PayPal users [5], by combining payment details with other online activities recorded on more than 300,000 Omniture-tracked Websites [27], which notably includes 50 of the Web shops analysed in this study.

Note that the leakage described here is different from the indirect information leakage via Referer headers as studied in [28], since the PayPal checkout page actively collects and sends the Referer of the checkout page, which would not be shared otherwise with the Omniture domains. Furthermore, by sending high-entropy browser properties such as plugins and screen dimensions, PayPal make it possible for Omniture to track users by their browser fingerprints even if they block cookies or use private browsing mode [13].

According to its privacy policy, PayPal may share customers' personal information with third-party service providers [29] who are limited to use PayPal customers' information "in connection with the services they perform for [PayPal]." Assuming the information shared with Omniture is subject to a similar agreement, it is hard to make sure whether payment information, product URL or browser characteristics are interpreted as personal information or not, given the possible interpretations of the policy and lack of transparency around PayPal's contracts with third-parties.

As of September 14th, 2014, long after we finished with the experiments, the PayPal checkout page no longer references a third-party tracker, though Omniture is still used on the PayPal homepage.

PayPal still deploys two questionable, internal tracking mechanisms: evercookies and browser fingerprinting. Although these techniques may be helpful in preventing account hijacking or similar fraudulent activities, their use is not mentioned explicitly in PayPal's privacy policy. These tracking techniques are difficult to avoid for users and have led to lawsuits and multi-million dollar settlements in the past [30].

5   Limitations

As outlined in Sect. 2, our sampling strategy combined Web shop URLs from different sources to cover both larger and smaller merchants. We expect our dataset to contain an equal distribution over more and less professional Websites, as well as more and less frequented ones.

This comes at the price of diversity of goods that are sold. It easily observed that there are more Web shops selling physical goods than there are commercial dating Websites, for instance. This makes statistically significant statements about differing privacy practices hard, if not impossible.

For obvious reasons, our data collection setup could not cover server-to-server communication, which, according to PayPal documentation [18], can be used by merchants to communicate with PayPal. Also, in our experiments we did not go beyond the PayPal checkout page to complete the payments. As a result, the data collected and leaked after the PayPal checkout page is not covered in our analysis.

6   Conclusion and Discussion

We presented a new species in the zoo of online tracking systems: explicit leakage of personal information and detailed shopping habits from online merchants to payment providers. In contrast to the widely debated tracking of Web browsing, online shops make it impossible for their customers to avoid this proliferation of their data.

By mediating online payments between merchants and buyers, payment providers are in a position to access sensitive payment details that can be used to build a detailed profile of shopping habits. Being the most popular payment provider, PayPal learns how much money its 152 million customers are spending and where. These customers are identified by name, email and postal address and through their bank details. We have demonstrated that merchant Websites are unnecessarily forwarding product details to PayPal that give a detailed view on consumers' purchases.

According to our analysis, 52 % of the Web shops in our study shared product names, item numbers and descriptions with PayPal. On the other hand, the remaining 388 sites did not share any purchase details except the amount to be paid, confirming that sharing sensitive details is not necessary for electronic retailers.

Further, we reported on the PayPal's use of the tracking service Omniture, which amplifies the privacy concerns by exposing transaction details to a widely deployed third-party tracker. A third-party tracker that has access to general Web tracking information, as well as to the details of successfully completed transactions, is in a particularly privileged situation to monitor consumption choices at large.

Web shops that use the technically more advanced token-based integration are often more privacy-friendly. Also, less popular sites are significantly more often among those that leak more personal information. There are no systematic differences across product categories, meaning that all kinds of shoppers are exposed.

By exploring the alternative privacy preserving practices that can be followed by Web shops, we distilled the following suggestions: (1) apply data minimization principle—do not leak information that is not required for processing the transaction; (2) inform customers about the data sharing in your privacy policy; (3) offer alternative, privacy-friendly payment methods; (4) use a payment gateway to prevent leakage of product URL via Referer header.

Better privacy practices for handling online payments is not only desirable for end users, but also for the merchants and payment providers whose bussinesses depend on the users' trust. At a time when personal information is said to be new currency on the Web, it seems unfair that consumers are charged twice during checkout.

Acknowledgements . We thank the Fonds Wetenschappelijk Onderzoek–Vlaanderen (FWO) for support through the project Data Mining for Privacy in Social Networks (grant number G068611N).

References

1. Valentino-DeVries, J., Singer-Vine, J.: They Know What You're Shopping For, 7 Dec 2012. http://on.wsj.com/TQ8Dbi
2. Duhigg, C.: How Companies Learn Your Secrets 16 Feb 2012. http://nyti.ms/QbbTyS
3. OECD: The OECD Privacy Framework (2013)
4. European Commission: Proposal for a Regulation of the European Parliament and of the Council on the protection of individuals with regard to the processing of personal data and on the free movement of such data (General Data Protection Regulation) (2012)
5. PayPal, About PayPal (2014). www.paypal-media.com/about
6. Bonneau, J., Preibusch, S.: The privacy jungle: on the market for data protection in social networks. In: Eighth Workshop on the Economics of Information Security (WEIS) (2009)
7. Bonneau, J., Preibusch, S.: The password thicket: technical and market failures in human authentication on the web. In: Ninth Workshop on the Economics of Information Security (WEIS) (2010)
8. Preibusch, S., Bonneau, J.: The privacy landscape: product differentiation on data collection. In: Schneier, B. (ed.) Economics of Information Security and Privacy III, pp. 263–283. Springer, New York (2013)
9. Krishnamurthy, B., Wills, C. E.: On the leakage of personally identifiable information via online social networks. In: Proceedings of the 2nd ACM Workshop on Online Social Networks (WOSN) (2009)
10. Soltani, A., Canty, S., Mayo, Q., Thomas, L., Hoofnagle, C.J.: Flash Cookies and Privacy. In: Intelligent Information Privacy Management, Papers from the 2010 AAAI Spring Symposium, Technical report SS-10–05 (2010)
11. Ayenson, M., Wambach, D.J., Soltani, A., Good, N., Hoofnagle, C.J.: Flash cookies and privacy II: now with HTML5 and ETag respawning, SSRN (2011)
12. Acar, G., Eubank, C., Englehardt, S., Juarez, M., Narayanan, A., Diaz, C.: The web never forgets: persistent tracking mechanisms in the wild. In: Proceedings of CCS 2014 (2014)
13. Eckersley, P.: How unique is your web browser? In: Atallah, M.J., Hopper, N.J. (eds.) PETS 2010. LNCS, vol. 6205, pp. 1–18. Springer, Heidelberg (2010)

14. Acar, G., Juarez, M., Nikiforakis, N., Diaz, C., Gürses, S., Piessens, F., P, B.: FPDetective: Dusting the web for fingerprinters. In: Proceedings of the 2013 ACM SIGSAC Conference on Computer and Communications Security (2013)

15. Tsai, J.Y., Egelman, S., Cranor, L., Acquisti, A.: The effect of online privacy information on purchasing behavior: an experimental study. Inf. Syst. Res. **22**(2), 254–268 (2011)

16. Jentzsch, N., Preibusch S., Harasser, A.: Study on monetising privacy. An economic model for pricing personal information European Network and information Security Agency (ENISA) (2012)

17. Preibusch, S., Kübler, D., Beresford, A.R.: Price versus privacy: an experiment into the competitive advantage of collecting less personal information. Electron. Commer. Res. **13**(4), 423–455 (2013)

18. PayPal, How would you like to integrate with PayPal? (2013). www.developer.paypal.com/webapps/developer/docs/

19. PayPal, Getting Started With Express Checkout (2013). www.developer.paypal.com/webapps/developer/docs/classic/express-checkout/integration-guide/ECGettingStarted/

20. PayPal, "Legal Agreements for PayPal Services," 2014. [Online]. Available: www.paypal.com/us/webapps/mpp/ua/legalhub-full

21. PayPal, PayPal Developer Agreement (2013). www.paypal.com/us/webapps/mpp/ua/xdeveloper-full

22. PayPal, SetExpress Checkout API Operation (NVP) (2014). www.developer.paypal.com/docs/classic/api/merchant/SetExpressCheckout_API_Operation_NVP

23. Mitmproxy project, mitmproxy 0.9 Introduction (2013). http://mitmproxy.org/doc/index.html

24. Dempster, A.P., Laird, N.M., Rubin, D.B.: Maximum likelihood from incomplete data via the EM algorithm. J. Roy. Stat. Soc.: Ser. B (Methodol.) **39**(1), 1–38 (1977)

25. Adobe Systems Incorporated, Digital marketing Adobe Marketing Cloud (2014). http://www.adobe.com/solutions/digital-marketing.html

26. Adobe Systems Incorporated, SiteCatalyst variables and query string parameters (2014). http://helpx.adobe.com/analytics/using/digitalpulse-debugger.html#id_1298

27. BuiltWith Pty Ltd. Websites using Omniture SiteCatalyst (2014). http://trends.builtwith.com/websitelist/Omniture-SiteCatalyst

28. Krishnamurthy, B., Wills, C.: Privacy diffusion on the web: a longitudinal perspective. In: Proceedings of the 18th International Conference on World Wide Web (WWW) (2009)

29. PayPal, Privacy Policy: 20 Feb 2013. www.paypal.com/webapps/mpp/ua/privacy-full

30. Singel, R.: Online Tracking Firm Settles Suit Over Undeletable Cookies, 12 May 2010. http://www.wired.com/2010/12/zombie-cookie-settlement/

How the Estonian Tax and Customs Board Evaluated a Tax Fraud Detection System Based on Secure Multi-party Computation

Dan Bogdanov[1]([⊠]), Marko Jõemets[1], Sander Siim[1,2], and Meril Vaht[1]

[1] Cybernetica, Mäealuse 2/1, Tallinn, Estonia
{dan,markoj,sanders,meril}@cyber.ee
[2] Institute of Computer Science, University of Tartu, Liivi 2, Tartu, Estonia

Abstract. The Estonian Tax and Customs Board (MTA) has identified that Estonia is losing over 220 million euros a year due to avoidance of value-added tax (VAT). The parliament proposed legislation that makes companies declare their purchase and sales invoices for automated risk analysis and fraud detection. The law was vetoed by the Estonian President on the grounds of confidentiality breach and unnecessary burden to companies. In this paper, we report on our collaboration with MTA to build a tax fraud detection system prototype that uses secure multi-party computation (SMC) to remove the companies' concerns over confidentiality. We estimate that the prototype could process a month of Estonian VAT data in ten days running on 20 000 euros worth of hardware.

Keywords: Tax fraud detection · Risk analysis · Secure multi-party computation · Case study

1 Battling Value-Added Tax Fraud in a Modern Economy

Value-added tax (VAT) is a consumption tax on the value added to a sold product or service. To simplify, when a company sells a product, it will pay a tax on the difference of the sales price of the product and the price of materials and tools acquired to create it.

According to an estimation by the Estonian Tax and Customs Board (MTA) in 2013, Estonia has 72 000 registered taxable persons, a third of whom apply for a refund of overpaid VAT every month. Among them, there are about 9 700 enterprises with a suspicion of VAT fraud. The estimated total loss in unpaid VAT exceeds 220 million euros per year [1].

One of the main ways for avoiding VAT is to not declare sales to other companies, thus reducing the VAT liability. MTA detects such fraud by analyzing the financial records of the suspect company and its partners to determine the

---

This work has received funding from the Estonian Research Council through grant IUT27-1, ERDF through EXCS, and European Union Seventh Framework Programme (FP7/2007–2013) under grant agreement n 609611 (PRACTICE).

R. Böhme and T. Okamoto (Eds.): FC 2015, LNCS 8975, pp. 227–234, 2015.
DOI: 10.1007/978-3-662-47854-7_14

actual taxable sum. MTA estimated that using the existing process, it would take 11 years to check a year's worth of transaction data that has a fraud risk. The problem is amplified by the practice of forming shadow companies with no notable economic activities and the sole purpose of enabling VAT fraud.

The government reacted in 2013 by publishing updated drafts for the Value-Added Tax Act and the Accounting Act Amendment Act. These drafts describe a mandatory annex to the monthly VAT declaration form in the online tax information system deployed by MTA. According to the new law, companies must report transactions with each partner with whom the monthly sum of transactions exceeds 1000 euros. To keep automated accounting systems simpler, taxpayers can also declare all of their invoices with all partners.

For each transaction, the company has to report the registry code of the partner, date, identifier and value of the invoice. Depending on whether the transaction was a sale or purchase, it will also include the tax value, tax rate and the taxable supply for the current period of taxation. Once MTA has the VAT declarations for a month, it can match the declared sales and purchase invoices of companies with each other using the enterprise registry codes. It can then run risk analysis algorithms to find cases where a company has incorrectly declared transactions (or not declared them at all).

The government supported the acts and adjusted the budget with the prediction that the first year of activity will increase the amount of collected VAT by at least 27.5 million euros (Table 15, page 89 of the State Budget Strategy 2015–2018 [2]). Initially, the amendments would be enforced from July 1, 2014. However, opposition quickly arose from companies whose two main concerns were the administrative burden and the significant privacy risk.

The Estonian Traders Association claimed that, for large enterprises, the changes to accounting systems will require investments and time. They also conjectured that such data collection will not eliminate VAT fraud, but will force MTA employees to waste time on fixing human errors. The association was also concerned about the security of the "super database" of financial transactions. MTA has a significant employee turnover and a tax officer could copy the database to support his or her future business ambitions in the private sector.

In a controversial move, the President of Estonia blocked the legislation with the justification that "Burdening all businesses with additional costs and obligations and creating a database containing almost all of Estonia's business secrets cannot be justified with a hypothetical, unproven conjecture that the tax hole would diminish [4]". The legislation was sent back to the parliament.

2   A Solution Based on Secure Multi-party Computation

2.1   Requirements and the Choice of the Cryptographic Platform

Examining the problem, we saw secure multi-party computation (SMC) as a solution. The companies are the input parties who have confidential data to protect. MTA is the result party, who wants to analyse the confidential inputs and learn the risk scores associated with companies. However, process-wise, MTA may not need access to the detailed records of a company before the risk analysis has deemed that the company has a high risk score.

Therefore, we can design a system that collects VAT declaration annexes from the companies in a protected form and conducts the risk analysis while the transactions are in the encrypted domain. Only the risk scores will be published to the tax officer who can then request the detailed records for the at-risk companies. This protects the information and rights of the honest taxpayers, as their declaration annexes remain encrypted in the process.

We contacted MTA and explained our intentions of building a research prototype that would perform privacy-preserving VAT fraud detection. Fortunately, they were very supportive of our goals and ready to cooperate. We were able to work together with the developers of the new VAT declaration annex in MTA's online system. We had access to the architecture and system analysis documents and held regular meetings with the analysts and architects of the system to determine the following requirements.

1. **Privacy for companies.** To reassure the private sector in Estonia, the processing of VAT declarations must guarantee the secrecy of their contents.
2. **Data utility for investigators.** MTA must conduct automated risk analysis on VAT declarations and investigate suspicious companies in detail.
3. **Transparency.** To convince the companies in the security guarantees, they could retain some degree of control over the data and its processing.
4. **Performance.** MTA collects VAT declarations on a monthly basis and needs to complete the processing of one month of data before the next month.

2.2   Application and Trust Model

Figure 1 shows a proposed deployment model for the SMC-based tax fraud detection model designed based on the requirements. In the proposed system, a company would use a special tool that loads the XML file containing the invoices, applies secret sharing to each input value and uploads the shares of each value to the SMC servers. This tool can be audited by the company to ensure that good randomness is used and the correct servers are being connected to. If all shares are sent to parties with clearly non-collusive relations, the direct perception of security for data owners is greatly improved.

MTA and the Estonian Traders Association are good host candidates for the secure multi-party system, as both are motivated to keep the privacy of the data—MTA has a legal obligation and companies own the data. Both also have the capability to run IT systems—MTA will run one anyway and companies will participate if it provides them with better privacy. The latter is achieved as currently efficient SMC systems assume that all parties know the function being computed. This means that MTA will have to agree with companies on the kinds of analyses it wants to perform and all computing parties have to deploy them.

Some efficient SMC protocols also need a third party, so we need an organization that is independent from MTA as well as other companies and has the necessary motivation and resources. In Estonia, the Information Systems and

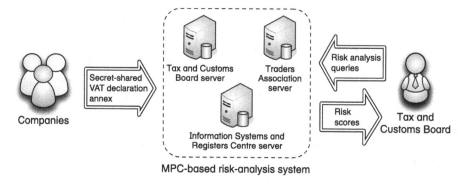

Fig. 1. Proposed deployment model for a secure tax fraud prototype

Registers Centre is a governmental agency under the Ministry of Justice tasked with maintaining security-critical registries so it is perfect for the job.

Once secret-shared inputs are stored by the computing parties, MTA can request parties to run the agreed-to risk analysis algorithms. These algorithms will run on secret-shared data and produce secret-shared results. The shares of these results will be published to the MTA. If the results show that a company has a risk, MTA needs to acquire transaction data from the secure multi-party system (in agreement with other computing parties) or the company directly.

3   Description of the Prototype

3.1   Implementation Platform

We chose the Sharemind secure multi-party computation system as our implementation platform [3]. While Sharemind supports protocols that are secure against an active adversary, we decided to use a passively secure protocol suite with three parties for its range of operations and performance. We solve the deficiencies of the passive model by deploying additional technical controls.

First, MTA can check the consistency of input data by comparing privately computed aggregate statistics of transactions to the public part of the VAT declaration. In our prototype, only MTA receives outputs from the computation, so actively tampering with the protocol to leak something from the outputs is not a feasible attack. This would need many queries, but MTA can not perform a multiple query attack undetected, because other parties involved in the computation can block them. The correctness of the computation can be checked with SMC auditing techniques.

The algorithms themselves are implemented in Sharemind's programming language SecreC. We also developed a web-based interface for secret-sharing, uploading transaction files and running queries in a web browser.

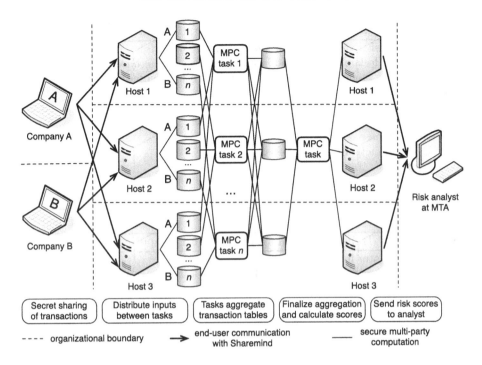

Fig. 2. Example data flow within the secure risk analysis system

3.2   The Privacy-Preserving Risk Analysis Process

Figure 2 shows the flow of private data during the risk analysis process. Algorithm 1 shows how sales and purchases are split into n tables that are aggregated by separate SMC processes. In the first part of the aggregation, n parallel SMC processes run Algorithm 2 on the sales and (with minor changes) purchase transactions. The results are gathered in the sales_aggr and purchases_aggr tables. The results of parallel computations are combined with Algorithm 3.

In the prototype, we implemented three risk analysis algorithms. First, to find high differences between partners' transactions, the values of a company's sales invoices per partner are added together and totals of the partners' purchase invoices connected to this company are added together. If the difference between sales and purchases is negative, the purchasing partner has the risk. Algorithm 4 shows how we calculate the risk based on aggregation results.

For the second risk, we find the proportion of the sum of all taxpayers' declared sales invoices from the sales total declared in the declaration main part (this is calculated as Pr_X in Algorithm 2). If the percentage is smaller than some estimated fixed amount (for example 30 %) it is counted as a risk, implying that some invoices have been left out of the declaration.

Finally, our prototype performs one pass of risk propagation so that if a partner of a company has a risk, we also mark the company as potentially risky.

Algorithm 1. Processing a secret-shared declaration at a computing party.

Data: Secret-shared VAT declaration of company with registry code X
Result: The declaration is stored in tables $sales_i$ and $purchases_i$
1 Choose a joint random value $i \in 1, 2, \ldots, n$ with other computing parties
2 **foreach** sales transaction in declaration **do**
3 | $Y \leftarrow$ transaction partner's registry code
4 | Save $[X, Y,$ transaction amount$]$ in table $sales_i$
5 **foreach** purchase transaction in declaration **do**
6 | $Y \leftarrow$ transaction partner's registry code
7 | Save $[X, Y,$ transaction amount$]$ in table $purchases_i$
8 Add X to the aggregation queue of aggregator i
9 **return**

Algorithm 2. Transaction data aggregation at a computing party.

Data: Aggregator index i, table $sales_i$
Result: Aggregated sales data stored in table sales_aggr
1 **foreach** non-aggregated X in the queue of aggregator i **do**
2 | $D_X \leftarrow$ transaction data of X from $sales_i$
3 | $Pr_X \leftarrow \dfrac{\text{sum(sales transactions in } D_X)}{\text{sum of sales transactions declared by company } X}$
4 | **foreach** transaction partner Y appearing in D_X **do**
5 | | $S_{X,Y} \leftarrow$ sum(sales transactions with Y in D_X)
6 | | Save $[X, Y, S_{X,Y}, Pr_X]$ in sales_aggr
7 | Mark X as aggregated and add it to the finalization queue
8 **return**

The analysis and implementation took 3.5 man-months of work from developers with some experience with Sharemind (but no special cryptographic training). Their main challenge was to find a suitable and efficient algorithm.

3.3 Performance of the Prototype

We generated test datasets with realistic distributions to measure the performance of our prototype on three servers with 3 GHz 12-core processors connected to a 1 Gb local network. Figure 3a shows the total running times of aggregation with up to 8 parallel tasks. We see that parallel tasks improve the efficiency by a constant factor. This is explained by Fig. 3b that shows the running time of different phases in the computation when using 4 aggregators. The performance of the finalization phase does not improve with parallel aggregations.

We believe we can speed up the final combination of aggregated tables significantly by using more efficient merging techniques. The bottleneck of our prototype seems to be the network channels, as the CPUs are not fully used. Thus, an increase in network bandwidth will also improve performance.

Algorithm 3. Aggregation finalization of sales at a computing party.

Data: Non-finalized aggregation tables sales_aggr, purchases_aggr
Result: Finalized aggregation table sales_summary
1   $Pr_X \leftarrow$ sales_aggr
2   **foreach** X in the finalization queue **do**
3   **foreach** transaction partner Y **do**
4         $S_{X,Y} \leftarrow$ sales_aggr ;   // sum(X's sales to Y)
5   **if** Y *in purchases_aggr* **then**
6            $P_{Y,X} \leftarrow$ purchases_aggr ;   // sum(Y's purchases from X)
7   **else**
8            $P_{Y,X} \leftarrow 0$
9   Save $[X,Y,S_{X,Y},P_{Y,X},Pr_X]$ in sales_summary
10 **return**

Algorithm 4. Discrepancies between declared sales and purchases.

Data: Table sales_summary
Result: Registry codes of companies with risk 1 confirmed.
1   RiskCompanies $\leftarrow \emptyset$
2   **foreach** pair of transaction partners (X,Y) in sales_summary **do**
3      $S_{X,Y}, P_{Y,X} \leftarrow$ sales_summary
4   **if** $S_{X,Y} < P_{Y,X}$ **then**
5   add Y to RiskCompanies
6   **return** RiskCompanies

---

4   Evaluation by the Estonian Tax and Customs Board

We gave a presentation and a technical report to MTA's management and experts from the risk analysis and IT departments. We focused on differences in processes, architecture and deployment that result from using SMC.

MTA representatives understood the security guarantees provided by SMC and accepted them as superior to what can be achieved with current technologies. However, the risk analysts were concerned with the required transparency. Today, MTA can perform risk analyses autonomously so that unauthorized parties have no knowledge of the kind of algorithms that are used. SMC would change this and MTA would have to agree on the algorithms with other hosts.

We argued that transparency will also improve the acceptance of the system. In response, the Director General admitted that his philosophy is to develop taxation so that taxpayers feel more responsibility on the grassroots level and consider paying taxes to be a social obligation. He agreed, that the SMC-based solution we described is a step in this direction, but stated that significant change would be needed in the processes of risk analysis to enable the sharing of related algorithms with other parties. Alternatively, SMC technology should become significantly more efficient at hiding the algorithm being evaluated or we should find ways to hide the class of algorithms used in risk analysis.

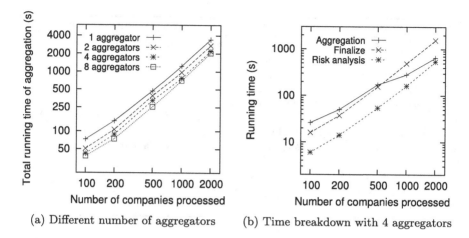

(a) Different number of aggregators   (b) Time breakdown with 4 aggregators

Fig. 3. Running times for secure tax fraud detection

Based on the calculations from MTA, 80 000 companies will upload 50 million economic transactions every month. We estimate that our prototype can process one month of Estonian economy in ten days, using about 20 000 euros worth of hardware. This was met with some concern, as today, MTA processes VAT returns in three days. The hardware cost, however, was not of much concern. With algorithmic improvements and clever hardware usage we can make the prototype an order of magnitude faster and make the running time sufficiently low for practical use.

The President of Estonia did not block an updated version of the tax legislation that granted a longer transition time to companies and solved other concerns. Thus, MTA continued to develop a non-encrypted version of the VAT declaration system for deployment in late 2014. However, MTA agreed to consider SMC as a technology for confidential data collection and analysis in future application, inspired by our prediction that the cost of deploying SMC will be further reduced in the coming years.

References

1. The transaction information system for 1000-euro purchases will be completed in November. *Ärileht*, 22 October 2013. http://arileht.delfi.ee/news/uudised/mta-1000-euroste-arvete-tehinguinfo-susteem-saab-valmis-novembris.d?id=66955998 (in Estonian). Accessed 5 September 2014
2. State Budget Strategy of Estonia 2015–2018. http://www.fin.ee/doc.php?110953. Accessed 5 September 2014
3. The Sharemind secure database and application server. http://sharemind.cyber.ee/. Accessed 5 September 2014
4. Ilves Blocks Amendment for Sweeping Disclosures in Tax Filing. National Public Broadcasting News, 19 December 2013. http://news.err.ee/v/politics/5b358dbd-8836-43ca-992c-973d206a3ec6. Accessed 5 September 2014

Authentication and Access Control

Tactile One-Time Pad: Leakage-Resilient Authentication for Smartphones

Sebastian Uellenbeck[(✉)], Thomas Hupperich, Christopher Wolf,
and Thorsten Holz

Ruhr-University Bochum, Bochum, Germany
{sebastian.uellenbeck,thomas.hupperich,christopher.wolf,
thorsten.holz}@rub.de

Abstract. Nowadays, Smartphones are widely used and they have a growing market share of already more than 55 % according to recent studies. They often contain sensitive or private data that can easily be accessed by an attacker if the device is unlocked. Since smartphones are mobile and used as everyday gadgets, they are susceptible to get lost or stolen. To prevent the data from being accessed by an attacker, access control mechanisms like user authentication are needed. However, commonly used authentication mechanisms like PINs, passwords, and patterns suffer from the same weakness: They are vulnerable against different kinds of attacks, most notably shoulder surfing. In order to prevent shoulder surfing, a secure channel between the smartphone and the user must be established that cannot be eavesdropped by an adversary.

In this paper, we concentrate on the smartphone's tactile feedback to add a new security layer to the plain PIN-based authentication mechanism. The key idea is to use vibrations as an additional channel to complement PINs with a tactile one-time pattern. To calibrate the usability of our approach, we developed a game that more than 220 participants played to determine the shortest vibration duration most people can sense. In a security evaluation, we recorded the acoustical signal of the vibration motor of five different smartphones at four different locations with a high-end microphone to cross-correlate a login scenario with a pre-recorded acoustical fingerprint of the devices. Our evaluation results demonstrate that it is not possible for an attacker to spot the user's secret under normal conditions, e. g., in a restaurant or during a conversation, even with professional equipment. Finally, we show that the required overhead of our approach is reasonable in practice and outperforms prior work.

Keywords: Authentication · Computer security · Smartphone security · Human computer interaction · Tactile feedback

1 Introduction

Smartphones are among the most popular gadgets available on the market today. According to a study by Gartner, smartphones had a market share of 55 % in the

© International Financial Cryptography Association 2015
R. Böhme and T. Okamoto (Eds.): FC 2015, LNCS 8975, pp. 237–253, 2015.
DOI: 10.1007/978-3-662-47854-7_15

third quarter of 2013 and they are expected to grow even more in the future [12]. Such devices are not only used for taking pictures, sending text messages, or surfing the Web, but also to assist sensitive applications such as online banking by receiving *mobile Transaction Authentication Numbers* (mTANs), as electronic replacement for a purse, or as key to the office door. Hence, smartphones typically contain lots of private data like contact information, personal messages, and passwords. Obviously, they become an interesting target for attackers, who can easily access the sensitive information if the device is unlocked.

Access control mechanisms, especially user authentication, can be used to protect the data if the device is lost or stolen. Typical authentication mechanisms for smartphones include PINs, passwords, and pattern-based login mechanisms that are adapted to the screen size of mobile devices. Unfortunately, all these authentication mechanisms are cumbersome. Simultaneously users think that authentication is often required for features that should not require authentication [13,17]. In general, it is difficult to attain a usable and secure authentication approach [8]. Aviv et al. [2] show that it is feasible to utilize the accelerometer as a side channel to predict PINs and patterns, making these authentication mechanism susceptible to attacks. A related threat are so called *smudge attacks* [1] on smartphones. Furthermore, a major hurdle of all existing mechanisms is that they suffer from the same weakness: They are not resistant to *shoulder surfing attacks* [21]. Here, the adversary visually observes the login and can then easily replay the observed successful authentication.

In this paper, we introduce a novel authentication method resistant to shoulder surfing attacks. To this end, we study all available channels between a user and a smartphone without additional hardware (e. g., headsets) to determine which channels can be utilized for a secure communication. It turns out that tactile feedback suits our needs best: We demonstrate that vibrations can be used as an additional channel to complement existing, PIN-based authentication mechanisms. The key insight is that we can take advantage of vibrations to establish some kind of *one-time pad* (OTP) to generate pseudo-random numbers that can be added to an existing PIN. The combination of this tactile feedback with a PIN enables an authentication mechanism that is resistant to shoulder surfing since an attacker cannot easily intercept the vibrations. In addition, smudge attacks are dwarfed as the digits entered are now randomly distributed.

We implemented a prototype of this concept in a tool called TACTILE ONE-TIME PAD (short: TACO) for the Android operating system. In a security evaluation, we analyzed how resistant the mechanism is in practice: We recorded the acoustical signal generated by vibrations for five different smartphones at four different locations with a high-end microphone. This allows us to cross-correlate a login scenario with a pre-recorded acoustical fingerprint of the devices. It turns out that an adversary cannot perform such an acoustic attack on our authentication scheme under normal conditions, e. g., during a conversation or a modestly busy place like a restaurant. Experimental results suggest that such attacks are only feasible in a very quiet place (i. e., in an anechoic room), an attack scenario beyond our threat model.

A crucial aspect of our system is the time span of a vibration (i. e., how long we let the smartphone vibrate). To determine the optimal length, we designed a game to identify the shortest vibration duration most people can perceive. In a user study with more than 220 participants, we found that 90 % of all participants were able to notice a vibration duration of 150 ms. Combined with other insights obtained during the study, we adjust the parameters of our prototype to obtain an authentication mechanism that is usable in practice.

In summary, we make the following four contributions in this paper:

1. We introduce a novel authentication scheme that utilizes the tactile feedback available on smartphones to enhance existing, PIN-based authentication mechanisms. Vibrations are used to generate pseudo-random numbers perceivable only by a user and this channel is used as an additional input during the authentication phase.
2. We present our prototype implemented for the Android platform in a tool called TACO. Our scheme does not need special/additional hardware but only the vibration mechanism available on common smartphones.
3. For a security evaluation, we recorded a pre-defined pattern from five different smartphones at four different locations to analyze the data by means of a cross-correlation and demonstrate that the scheme is resistant to acoustic attacks. We also discuss and empirically evaluate other attack scenarios.
4. We conducted a user study with 227 participants to evaluate the usability of our approach and found that the required overhead is feasible in practice.

Note that a longer version of this paper with more technical details is available as a technical report [22].

2   Related Work

In recent years, several methods for *leakage resilient* user authentication have been proposed. In the following, we provide a brief overview of the most prominent of these methods and discuss how TACO relates to them.

Yan et al. focus on the visual channel and propose *CoverPad* [24]. Here the user has to shield the screen with the palm of his hand to hinder attackers from eavesdropping a secret. The user has to consider this secret to do simple calculations and finally he has to enter the result into the device. Although the login duration seems comparable to TACO, there is no security evaluation of *CoverPad*. Therefore, we cannot know how secure *CoverPad* performs in reality. However, we evaluate what attacks TACO resists against in Sect. 4.

In the same manner, Perkovic et al. use the visual channel to transfer a secret between the user and the device, but also propose a headset as alternative [16]. Having retrieved the secret, the user can apply two methods that are based on lookup tables, or utilize simple modulo 10 calculation [23] to authenticate. In contrast to our approach, they use additional hardware to establish a secure channel between the user and the device, while we only leverage tactile feedback.

De Luca et al. evaluated three different approaches for eye-gaze interaction to enhance PIN authentication [10]. *Cued Gaze-Points* is a system presented by Forget et al. that uses a cued-recall graphical password scheme for user authentication [11]. The user has to select points on a sequence of images with his eye-gaze as secret and later look at the desired points and hold the space bar for a few seconds. In contrast to our scheme, both approaches are only resistant to shoulder surfing if the attacker only observes the user's display. In case the attacker simultaneously tracks the eyes of the user, she can obtain the secret.

Bianchi et al. proposed *Secure Haptic Keypad* (SHK) [5] as well as PHONE LOCK [4]. Both approaches make use of tactile feedback for authentication. For the first one, the user has to touch three haptic buttons that vibrate with different frequencies to authenticate. In a round-based fashion, he has to press the button that represents his partial secret. Since no visual feedback is given to a shoulder surfer, the optical channel is secured. However, as we show in Sect. 4.2, acoustic attacks on tactile feedback are feasible so the complete secret can be obtained if only one channel is eavesdropped. As opposed to this, an attacker has to eavesdrop two channels to obtain the user's screen when using TACO. For the second approach, they implemented a virtual wheel on the smartphone's touchscreen with ten segments of the same size and a selection button in the middle of the segments. Again the login process is round-based and the user has to find his own vibration pattern. To do so, he touches the segments and tries to find his tactile pattern. Having found his pattern, he has to use the selection button. The segment's allocation to vibration patterns changes randomly so shoulder surfing is not possible. Contrary to our approach, the full secret is always transfered between the user and the device meaning that an attacker only has to eavesdrop the secure channel to retrieve the secret. In Sect. 4.2, we show that eavesdropping the tactile feedback of the smartphone is possible under some conditions.

3   Tactile One-Time Pad

In this section, we describe our approach to obtain an authentication mechanism on smartphones resilient to shoulder surfing attacks.

3.1   Potential Communication Channels

Leakage resilient authentication can be implemented by using a secure channel between the user and the device. In a nutshell, we need to make the protocol interactive, so there needs to be an information flow from the user to the device (*input*), but also in the reverse direction (*helper data*). Focusing on the reverse direction, humans only have five traditional senses to obtain stimuli: sight, hearing, touch, taste, and smell. As long as smartphones are not able to change their taste or smell controlled by an application, we cannot use taste or smell to transfer information. As a consequence, sight, hearing, and touch remain as possible candidates. Restricting our setting further to smartphones without any additional hardware, there are only three potential channels to transfer information: the display, the speaker, and the vibration motor.

The first channel—the *display*—can show arbitrary graphical information. While this channel can transport a lot of information from the smartphone to a user, an adversary can also easily eavesdrop such a channel by utilizing a camera [3]. We therefore cannot assume that it is a secure channel, but need to treat this as an untrusted communication medium.

The second possibility is the smartphone's *speaker*, more precisely the audio output that can also transport a lot of information. However, the same drawback that holds for the display is also valid for the audio output: it can easily be eavesdropped with a normal microphone; for example, every smartphone is equipped with such a microphone. Note that this does not apply if head phones are allowed. However, they qualify as "additional hardware" and are hence excluded from our list of possible channels.

The third and most interesting channel from the smartphone to the user is the *vibration motor*. All smartphones offer it to provide tactile feedback to the user (e. g., for silent notification). Furthermore, a vibration unit is commonly available in many kinds of mobile devices, even in older ones such as feature phones. Tactile feedback has three main advantages over the display and the speaker. First, it is hard to eavesdrop by an attacker as it has only a limited visual and acoustic range. More precisely, the vibration of the smartphone can only be seen with a high-speed, high-resolution video camera that is placed near the smartphone [9]. The acoustic feedback depends on the resonating body the smartphone is fixed in. In case of a (wooden) table, the latter acts as resonating body and amplifies the oscillation. As a result, the vibration can be easily heard by an attacker. However, in the more likely case that a human holds his smartphone in his hand when entering a PIN, the game is very different: Here the hand absorbs the oscillation so the vibration can barely be heard anymore, even within a very small distance from the smartphone. Empirical measurements in different settings confirm this observation (see Sect. 4.2 for details). Second, tactile feedback is easy to identify by the user even in dark or noisy environments. Third, humans do not need special training to correctly recognize vibration. This hugely adds to the overall usability of our solution.

Despite its advantages, there is also the low bandwidth of the channel that needs to be considered. In a first feasibility study we found that it is hard to detect more than 10 events per second and for none of the participants it was possible to detect more than 15 events per second. Based on an empirical user study with 227 participants, we estimate that 90 % of all users can recognize at least four events per second (see Sect. 5.2). Even such a low bandwidth is enough since we only utilize tactical feedback during the authentication process.

In summary, we conclude that a leakage resilient authentication method suitable for mobile devices can be accomplished using the built-in vibration motor. In a nutshell, we combine a one-time pad that is information theoretically secure [19] (based on addition modulo 10) with a computer generated secret.

3.2 Attacker Model

For the rest of the paper, we assume an attacker that can eavesdrop on the screen/keypad (cf., [3]). More specifically, we assume the classical model of an eavesdropper that performs a shoulder surfing attack and, in addition, is able to observe the vibrations of the smartphone. An attacker may obtain a smartphone of the same model she wants to attack and measure the vibration unit in advance. Empirical evaluation results in several different settings demonstrate that this is actually hard in practice (see Sect. 4 for a more detailed justification that this rational is sound). Furthermore, the adversary can take notes and observe multiple rounds of the authentication process; an assumption that is stronger compared to previous work in this area [18].

3.3 Methodology and Implementation

A *Personal Identification Number* (PIN) typically consists of four to eight decimal digits—the secret—that has to be entered correctly to authenticate. PINs have the advantage that they are simple to create, to recall, to verify, and to change. The main drawback when using a plain PIN authentication schema is the relative ease to eavesdrop the secret. A prominent attack in this area is shoulder surfing, another one consists of analyzing the residue on the touch screen [1]. To use TACO, the user chooses a four to eight digit decimal PIN. As for plain PIN authentication, he needs to remember and enter it. In addition, the user needs to choose a vibration duration between 40 ms and 350 ms. This is used to establish a secret channel between the smartphone and the user. Note that users will choose larger values for the vibration duration in the beginning, but likely reduce this time span when they feel more comfortable with the scheme. We have captured and confirmed this behavior in a simple game-like user-study (see Sect. 5 for details).

To perform authentication, the user holds the smartphone in the palm of his hand and starts the authentication process by pressing the AUTHENTICATION button. After the button is pressed, the smartphone vibrates between zero and nine times (one digit of the one-time pad). The user has to count the number of vibrations. Having determined the number of vibrations, the user adds the first digit of his PIN. If the result is larger than 9, he subtracts 10 (i.e., only the last digit is used). This digit is now entered as the response to the actual challenge given by the phone. If the user was not able to sense the number of vibrations (e.g., as a result of disturbance or a lack of attention), he can press the REPEAT button to feel the same number of vibrations again. After the result is entered, the phone again starts the same cycle for all consecutive digits of the PIN.

If all digits have been entered correctly, the user is granted access to his smartphone. While the login is performed, the user can either shorten or extend the vibration duration; this allows to either speed up the authentication process or to increase the likelihood of recognizing the correct number of vibrations.

At this point, one can think that this might lead to a security-relevant side channel because an attacker could clock the time between two entered digits to obtain the number of vibrations or at least a hint to calculate the secret. However, this is not possible because for a given vibration duration, the full time period is always equal no matter if the smartphone vibrates zero or nine times. This is accomplished by aligning the pauses between the single vibrations, so that the complete pattern always fits the same period of time. Therefore, for a given single duration of a vibration, the length of a round is always the same.

In summary, TACO is an additional security layer for the PIN authentication scheme. In case the user is sure that no shoulder surfing occurs, he can switch it off for fast authentication. In case he suspects a possible attack, he can switch it on; the price to pay is a small additional overhead in time to perform the authentication. To test our approach and verify both its efficiency and usability, we implemented a prototype in Java for the Android platform. We also developed a game to estimate a reasonable vibration duration a user can recognize.

3.4   Extensions and Discussion

There are several potential extension of our current prototype. For example, other mathematical operations like subtraction, multiplication, or integer division could be added as part of the scheme. For some people it might be easier to perform subtractions instead of additions particularly when using PINs with large numbers. When dropping the requirement of using an OTP, this could result in a more efficient scheme. Further, we need to keep the benefit that *both* channels need to be eavesdropped by an attacker to obtain the secret key.

As a potential way to increase speed, we may want to encode the digits $0 \ldots 9$ differently. This could be done by using a binary encoding, e.g., with short and long vibrations. By using this mode, we consider a short vibration as binary zero and a long vibration as binary one. Treating the concatenation of zeros and ones as a binary number, one can transform this into a decimal number. In this mode, only four binary vibrations are required to encode ten decimal digits. Albeit, switching to this mode can act like a double-edged sword: On the one hand, it leads to a decreasing overhead. On the other hand, it also leads to an increasing difficulty since users also have to do a binary to decimal transformation before entering the result of the addition modulo ten. We may envision this as the "expert mode" for TACO—where most people start with $0 \ldots 9$ vibrations and then migrate to the faster communication pattern if needed. In summary, this requires a more extensive user study to determine if this kind of encoding allows an increase of speed while still being usable and secure.

4   Security Evaluation

We now consider different attack vectors regarding their ability to attack TACO.

4.1   Timing Attacks

In our attacker model, the attacker knows the methodology of TACO including the duration of a single vibration because she might have measured it before.

To counter timing attacks, the overall length of one round is the same, no matter which number is transmitted by vibrations (cf., Sect. 3.3). If the pattern lengths would vary, an attacker could time the duration of the vibration pattern—namely the time between two keystrokes—and guess the number of vibrations. But as the pattern duration is the same for each OTP digit, an attacker cannot obtain any information by measuring the time between two keystrokes. In addition, humans do react individually on stimuli, so we can assume that the additional time a user needs to add the OTP digit to his PIN digit and enter the sum will shadow any useful information an attacker might obtain by measuring this time. To confirm this claim, we analyzed the data obtained by a usability study we describe in Sect. 5. Since we knew the number of vibrations during this study, the secret PIN, the user's input, and all timings with a granularity of milliseconds for each user, we computed the average time and the standard deviation that elapsed between two keystrokes for all users. Figure 1 shows that users on average need more time to enter the result if the number of vibrations is greater than six. However, while the differences are less than two seconds, the standard deviation is on average larger than ± 2.5 s. In the end, this can lead to a timing side channel [14] if the attacker is able to measure this many times *and* the user's skill in adding two digits mod 10 does not improve. We argue that if the user's skill does not improve—what we can measure in an automatic fashion—, we can force him to change his PINs on a regular basis. Otherwise, no countermeasures against timing side channels are required.

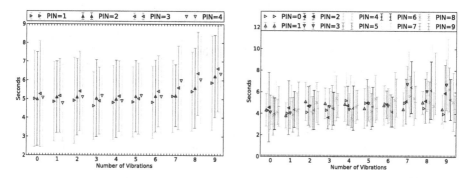

Fig. 1. Timing attacks on TACO. We analyzed the timing data from our experiments (cf., Sect. 5) to obtain the average time a user needs to enter a digit. The left figure shows the first part of our experiment, the right figure the second part of our experiment. The points are grouped by the number of vibrations.

4.2 Acoustic Attacks

In contrast to timing attacks, acoustic attacks are more severe against our scheme. If a smartphone is placed on a wooden table in a silent room, one is able to hear vibrations and most likely also to count them without any technical equipment. In this case, the secret key of the one-time pad would be broken and in combination with classical shoulder surfing it is possible to obtain the secret. At this point, the PIN can be calculated and the authentication process can be reproduced by an attacker.

Fortunately, the mobile phone is usually held in a person's hand while entering the PIN. In addition, the human body effectively shields vibrations rather than acting as a resonator compared to a wooden table. Furthermore, environmental background noise effectively disguises any sound TACO creates. Therefore, it is likely hard to count the number of vibrations when standing next to a person using TACO as it is hard to hear the vibration signals under these circumstances. To actually gather vibration signals in a room with background noise or even outside, an attacker would need rather expensive audio recording tools which would attract too much attention. In short: In a crowded room shoulder surfing is possible, but there is too much background noise to eavesdrop the vibration channel. In a deserted room, shoulder surfing becomes suspicious and an attacker cannot read the digits entered into the device, while it might be possible to eavesdrop the OTP vibrations. Hence, using two different channels with different vulnerabilities actually leads to an authentication method that is *strengthened* against the individual attack.

To quantify this attack vector in more detail, we conducted an experiment with five different smartphones at four different locations. As smartphones we used a Google Nexus S, a Google Galaxy Nexus, a LG L7 P700, a HTC Nexus One, and a Sony Xperia S. To show that it is possible to detect vibrations from further distances, we first chose a special prepared anechoic room. In our experiments, we used a large-diaphragm capacitor microphone (Rode NT2000) with a frequency spectrum between 20 Hz and 20 000 Hz, a signal-to-noise ratio of 84 dB (1 kHz rel 1 Pa, per IEC651, IEC268-15), configured with kidney directionality.

One might think that the speaker is the ideal solution to fool the attacker by creating false sounds. To prove this assumption, we conducted a short experiment by playing-back white noise with different smartphone speakers and recoding this noise with a high-end microphone. By analyzing the obtained data, we found that the small speakers of smartphones are not capable of creating noise with a high amplitude at low frequencies. Therefore, we cannot utilize the smartphone's speaker to disturb or prevent recordings of the vibrations.

For each smartphone we recorded a self-generated, 33 s long vibration pattern containing different vibration signals at each location. On the one hand, we put a long vibration (2 s) into the pattern to find a hint of the alignment of the vibrations in noisy data. On the other hand, we also added very short vibrations (50 ms to 120 ms) to have data that matches real vibration durations in the login procedure. The cross-correlation was conducted in three steps:

1. We used a Fast Fourier Transformation (FFT) to obtain the frequency-amplitude-spectrum from the clean pattern.
2. In a loop we calculated the FFT from a slice of the recorded signal that has the same length as the clean pattern. For each iteration, we moved the starting point of this slice a predefined frame window ahead.

3. We cross-correlated frequency-amplitude-spectra of the clean pattern and the slice of the recorded signal over time to get the similarity of both patterns.

The result of the cross-correlation should aim at finding similarities in different audio signals to calculate the number of vibrations. This is a difficult task when the duration is short. On the one hand, the Nyquist-Shannon sampling theorem [20] concludes that a sampling rate of $2xs^{-1}$ with x as samples leads to a detection of x samples per seconds as maximum. So with a sampling rate of 44 100 Hz, we are only able to detect frequencies between 0 Hz and 22 050 Hz. On the other hand, the duration of the signal controls the resolution of the frequency-amplitude-spectrum obtained by the FFT. The shorter the duration of the signal is, the coarser-grained the result is. For a signal duration of one second, we obtain a resolution of 1 Hz. Since we can show that 90 % of all participants in our usability study can sense vibration durations of approximately 150 ms (cf., Sect. 5.2), we have to work with a resolution of 10 Hz. This coarse-grained resolution leads to a inaccurate cross-correlation especially because it is more difficult to filter out background noise. All in all, our self-generated signal should be easy to align by means of the single long vibration (2 s) and also practice-oriented because of the different short vibrations.

To compare different recordings, we conduct a cross-correlation between the two signals. As pattern we used a clean and clear vibration recorded in an anechoic room within a distance of 0.5 m. By amplifying the signal it could be easily eavesdropped by a human attacker.

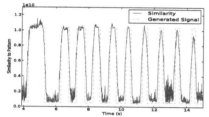

(a) Using a window of 441 frames to visualize long vibrations.

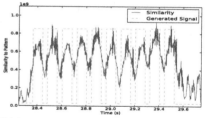

(b) Using a window of 110 frames to visualize short vibrations.

Fig. 2. Cross-correlation (solid line) between a clean vibration pattern (dashed line) of a Google Nexus S and a signal recorded in an anechoic room in a distance of 0.5 m while taking only frequencies between 150 Hz and 250 Hz into account.

As first experiment, we correlated a pattern from a Samsung Nexus S to a signal also generated in the anechoic room with the same smartphone. To visualize long vibrations we used a window of 441 frames or 10 ms to move across the signal (Fig. 2(a)). On the contrary, we used a window of 110 frames approximately 2.5 ms to obtain short vibrations (Fig. 2(b)). Note that the dashed lines delineate the clean vibration pattern while the solid lines trace the similarity we calculated. In conclusion, Fig. 2 shows that it is possible to use the acoustic side channel the vibration motor produces to obtain the number of vibrations. In this experiment, we intentionally chose the anechoic room as location to show that this side channel can be exploited. We also evaluated other smartphones, namely a Google Galaxy Nexus, a LG L7 P700, a HTC Nexus One, and a Sony Xperia S with distances of 0.5 m, 2 m and 4 m with similar results.

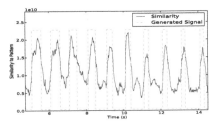

(a) Using a window of 441 frames to visualize long vibrations.

(b) Using a window of 100 frames to visualize short vibrations.

Fig. 3. Cross-correlation (solid line) between a clean vibration pattern (dashed line) of a Google Nexus S and a signal recorded on a corridor in front of an office environment in a distance of 0.5 m while taking only frequencies between 150 Hz and 250 Hz into account (Color figure online).

For the second experiment, we chose the corridor in front of an office environment as different location to record the generated signal. We started with a distance of 0.5 m between smartphone and microphone. In this setting, silent background noise was recognizable as well as keyboard noise coming from other offices and sometimes footsteps. Just like the first experiment, we were able to eavesdrop long vibrations (cf., Fig. 3(a)). Albeit, we were not able to fully reveal the generated signal for short vibrations. As one can see in Fig. 3(b), the correlation between the clean pattern and the recorded signal is not as significant as it should be to disclose the secret. Without the red bar we manually added afterwards to visualize our self generated pattern, the last two vibrations are not distinguishable from background noise. Due to the fact that the user would notice the recording of his authentication session when it is done in a distance of only 0.5 m and would be suspicious, we also recorded the self-generated pattern from a distance of 2 m and 4 m. As one can see in Fig. 4 for both correlations, no significance can be found for neither long nor short vibrations throughout to whole correlation. At this point—since we cannot even align the long vibration of 2 s—we are also not able to count the number of vibrations and are stuck. In a real attacker scenario, the attacker does not have a long vibration to align the login process. Hence, she needs to find short vibrations in the recorded signal which we were not able to find, despite the fact that we perfectly know the generated signal, but only had to align it in a range of some seconds. We repeated this experiment with all other smartphones and came to the same results for this location.

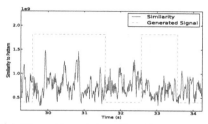 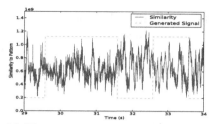

(a) The attempt to align the pattern to the generated signal with a distance of 2 m between smartphone and microphone.

(b) The attempt to align the pattern to the generated signal with a distance of 4 m between smartphone and microphone.

Fig. 4. Cross-correlation (solid line) between a clean vibration pattern (dashed line) of a Google Nexus S and a signal recorded on a corridor in front of an office environment while taking only frequencies between and 150 Hz and 250 Hz into account.

To make it even more difficult, we found another location that fits more to reality when authenticating against the smartphone being in front of our office building near a sparsely trafficked road. Outdoors, a user has to fear that attackers are shoulder surfing while walking near or behind him. Again, we generated and recorded the signals with all five smartphones having distances of 0.5 m, 2 m and 4 m. While cross-correlating the obtained signals with the clean pattern, we did not received any clue to detect the generated vibrations. Despite the highly directional kidney characteristic of the high-end microphone, the background noise in the significant frequency-range was too loud. Therefore, it was impossible to find any hints of vibrations in the signal.

In summary, we conclude that it is possible to eavesdrop the tactile feedback of TACO to attack a user's login in really silent environments. The attacker needs shoulder surfing in addition to the acoustical evaluation to obtain the user's secret. However, the requirements to gain the secrets are very high: The attacker not only needs a clean acoustic pattern of the smartphone, but also a situation where background noise is negligible *and* the distance between his microphone and the smartphone is short. We argue that an attacker with an expensive microphone trying to record the login would be suspicious for a victim.

4.3   Smudge Attacks and Shoulder Surfing

As the one-time pad effectively works as a random function in the set $\{0, \ldots, 9\}^{\ell}$ for $\ell = 4 \ldots 8$, all keys are equally alike. For this reason TACO is—in contrast to PINs, passwords, and patterns—secure against sophisticated smudge attacks [1]. Similarly, classical shoulder surfing does not reveal the secret. No matter how many cryptograms an attacker obtains, she cannot determine the underlying clear-text. Consequently, our scheme is secure as long as the attacker cannot read the secret key (i.e., the vibrations) at the same time as the cryptogram.

5 Usability Evaluation

In the following, we describe the usability evaluation of TACO.

5.1 Data Collection

Since TACO depends on the user's ability to perceive the number of vibrations, we investigated how many vibrations a user could differentiate in a given time interval. To accomplish this, we decided to develop a game as a smartphone application. Challenging authentication approaches encourage the user to practice the authentication a couple of times to learn it before actually using it. Therefore, the game should act as training the user's abilities on the one hand and observing the user's skill on the other hand.

We created two versions of the game: For the first version, we gave the player a predefined PIN $(1-2-3-4)$ he had to remember during the whole game before playing it. Letting a player choose his own PIN could result in two unsolicited situations: First, he could choose a random PIN that is hard to remember. In this case we would not evaluate the user's ability to utilize TACO, but to remember a sophisticated PIN. Second, he could choose a PIN that is too easy to remember and also too easy to work with like $(0-0-0-0)$ or $(1-1-1-1)$, which is more likely. Since recent studies have shown that user-chosen PINs as well as user-chosen passwords are far from being uniform distributed [6,15], we decided to give all players of this version a predefined PIN being easy enough to remember, but not too easy to require the execution of some basic calculations. This aspect was also important to have comparable results. We decided to give a player three "lives" in the game because three is the number of attempts real-world systems like debit or SIM cards and ATMs that use a PIN for authentication offer before the card is blocked for further usage.

To be able to compare also results for more sophisticated PINs, the second version of the game came with random but predefined PINs. Again, we gave the player the predefined PIN before playing the game, but we also added the PIN to the GUI. Displaying the random PIN on the GUI was important to receive meaningful data for the usability of TACO. Otherwise we would have challenged the players cognitive capabilities instead of evaluating the usability of TACO.

Both versions of the game are level-based and one game level equals one authentication attempt for TACO. Like for normal authentications, the user has to start the level by hitting a button. As a result, the smartphone vibrated randomly between zero and nine times. The player has to count the number of vibrations and add this to the first digit of the given PIN. Furthermore, he has to calculate the result modulo ten and enter the outcome into the smartphone in a round-based fashion. Afterwards the smartphone verifies the input. If it was incorrect, the player loses a life and stays in the same level. Otherwise the player reaches the next level having a decreased vibration duration. For three successful levels in a row the player obtains an additional life. By doing this we improved the player's immersion [7] and supported the learning phase so that

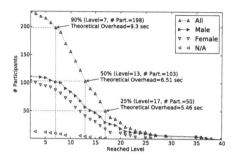
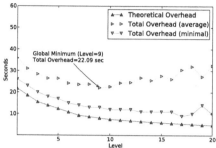

Fig. 5. Distribution of reached level grouped for male, female, n/a, and overall for both parts of the study.

Fig. 6. Overhead for the additional security layer given as theoretical overhead and the total overhead as average and mean, ordered by level.

mistakes where punished with a loss of a life and successes were rewarded by one additional life.

Participants where recruited by simply asking them to take part. We did not gave them any reward to raise their willingness to participate. Before starting the game, we explained the details by playing a guided test level. If they did not knew how to do an addition mod 10, we told them to use a (normal) addition and use only the right digit of the result in case of a two digit result. Furthermore, we tried to implement the game as similar as possible to the actual authentication method to have comparable results. To figure out what vibration interval a participant could detect, we reduced the vibration interval with increasing level. We started with a duration d of 350 ms for a single vibration. Because the complete duration for a round should always be similar (cf., Sect. 4.1), we only modified the break between two vibrations. For a round of nine vibrations, we chose $b = d \cdot \frac{13}{20}$ as break while having a break before and after the first and last vibration as well. For a single vibration we chose $b = 7.2 \cdot d$ and for two vibration we chose $b = 4.5 \cdot d$. As a result, we always get a complete duration c for one round between $2 \cdot 7.2d + d = 15.4d$ and $10 \cdot \frac{13}{20} \cdot d + 10 \cdot d = 15.5d$. Other vibration numbers match accordingly. For the first level with $d = 350$ ms a round takes at most 350 ms $\cdot 15.5 = 5.425$ s without user interaction. We therefore get $c = 4 \cdot 350$ ms $\cdot 15.5 = 21.7$ sec as complete duration for all four rounds. The duration was decreased in a stepwise fashion to exercise the player. To help the player to better detect vibrations that he had not recognized, we added a button to repeat the last vibration pattern.

5.2   Evaluation

To show the usability of our approach, we asked 187 people to play the first version of the game and 40 people the play the second version.

For TACO, the login duration takes the user's sensing capabilities into consideration. The more precise the user can feel the vibrations, the faster he can login. Figure 5 shows that all users were able to login at least once for the longest vibration duration of 350 ms. Therefore, the overhead for vibrations and pauses for a full login is 21.7 s. Note that this does not include the user's calculation time and his response. To take this into account, Fig. 6 shows the complete overhead including the users' reactions. One can see that a full login procedure can on average be performed in less than 36 s if a user choses the longest vibration duration. Hence, every participant we asked was able to authenticate in less than 36 s without prior practice and thus our scheme outperforms existing approaches in this area.

Considering Fig. 5 again, one can see that 90 % of all participants reached Level 7. Since Level 7 uses a vibration duration of 150 ms, a full login results in a duration of approximately 22 s. As one can see in Fig. 6, the theoretical overhead decreases with decreasing vibration duration, but the average login time including user interaction decreases only till level 9 and increases afterwards. This is caused by the fact that shorter vibrations are more difficult to perceive. As a consequence, users have to reflect longer about their input.

5.3 Discussion

We conducted a usability evaluation to learn whether Taco can be used in the wild. To accomplish this, we designed a game that is very similar to the actual authentication process. We showed that Taco is usable and comprehensive since all participants were able to authenticate at least once. While we found significant advantages against comparable methods, we also have to admit that the timing overhead is the main disadvantage of Taco when compared to plain PIN authentication. However, such an overhead is inevitable when adding a secure channel to a user authentication. To the best of our knowledge, Taco has the lowest time overhead of all authentication methods that are resilient against shoulder surfing, comparable secure while staying usable to an average person.

6 Conclusion and Future Work

In this paper, we showed that the tactile feedback generated by a vibration motor of a smartphone can be used as a secure channel for user authentication. We introduced Taco, an enhancement to PIN authentication which mitigates the threat of shoulder surfing. For each digit of the PIN, Taco outputs a pseudo-random number of vibration signals. The user counts these signals, adds their number to the current digit of his PIN (mod 10), and inputs the resulting digit.

On the one hand, using this secure tactile channel causes a higher duration and more user's attention to authenticate. Even though, our usability study shows that 90 % of all participants had an authentication duration of less than 22 sonds. On the other hand, this procedure protects the user's PIN from leaking and is insusceptible to several realistic attacks which need to succeed in addition to a shoulder surfing attack. Timing attacks cannot measure the number of vibrations as we implemented Taco in such way that all vibration patterns take the same time. However, we found that users need on average longer to add larger numbers having an even higher standard deviation so that there is no instant timing side channel. A long term study has to show whether users improve their skill over time when they get more familiar with TACO. Recording attacks require high-end audio recording equipment and are only feasible in a silent environment. But naturally in a silent environment shoulder surfing has a high risk to attract attention. Even if the user's input can be gathered (e. g., by camera) and high-end recording tools are available, we showed that it is hard to eavesdrop the vibration signals in real environments such as an office or outside a building.

References

1. Aviv, A.J., Gibson, K., Mossop, E., Blaze, M., Smith, J.M.: Smudge attacks on smartphone touch screens. In: WOOT (2010)
2. Aviv, A.J., Sapp, B., Blaze, M., Smith, J.M.: Practicality of accelerometer side channels on smartphones. In: ACSAC (2012)
3. Balzarotti, D., Cova, M., Vigna, G.: ClearShot: eavesdropping on keyboard input from video. In: IEEE Symposium on Security and Privacy (2008)
4. Bianchi, A., Oakley, I., Kostakos, V., Kwon, D.-S.: The phone lock: audio and haptic shoulder-surfing resistant PIN entry methods for mobile devices. In: Tangible and Embedded Interaction (2011)
5. Bianchi, A., Oakley, I., Kwon, D.S.: The secure haptic keypad: a tactile password system. In: CHI (2010)
6. Bonneau, J., Preibusch, S., Anderson, R.: A birthday present every eleven wallets? the security of customer-chosen banking PINs. In: Keromytis, A.D. (ed.) FC 2012. LNCS, vol. 7397, pp. 25–40. Springer, Heidelberg (2012)
7. Brown, E., Cairns, P.A.: A grounded investigation of game immersion. In: Extended Abstracts of Conference on Human Factors in Computing Systems (2004)
8. Cranor, L., Garfinkel, S.: Security and Usability: Designing Secure Systems That People Can Use. O'Reilly Media Inc., Sebastopol (2005)
9. Davis, A., Rubinstein, M., Wadhwa, N., Mysore, G.J., Durand, F., Freeman, W.T.: The visual microphone: passive recovery of sound from video. ACM Trans. Graph. **33**(4), 79 (2014)
10. De Luca, A., Weiss, R., Drewes, H.: Evaluation of eye-gaze interaction methods for security enhanced PIN-entry. In: Australasian Conference on Computer-Human Interaction: Entertaining User Interfaces (2007)
11. Forget, A., Chiasson, S., Biddle, R.: Shoulder-surfing resistance with eye-gaze entry in cued-recall graphical passwords. In: CHI (2010)
12. Gartner Research: Gartner Says Smartphone Sales Accounted for 55 Percent of Overall Mobile Phone Sales in Third Quarter of 2013 (2013). http://www.gartner.com/newsroom/id/2623415
13. Hayashi, E., Riva, O., Strauss, K., Brush, A.J.B., Schechter, S.E.: Goldilocks and the two mobile devices: going beyond all-or-nothing access to a device's applications. In: SOUPS (2012)
14. Kocher, P.C.: Timing attacks on implementations of Diffie-Hellman, RSA, DSS, and other systems. In: Koblitz, N. (ed.) CRYPTO 1996. LNCS, vol. 1109, pp. 104–113. Springer, Heidelberg (1996)

15. Murdoch, S.J., Drimer, S., Anderson, R.J., Bond, M.: Chip and PIN is broken. In: IEEE Symposium on Security and Privacy (2010)
16. Perković, T., Čagalj, M., Saxena, N.: Shoulder-surfing safe login in a partially observable attacker model. In: Sion, R. (ed.) FC 2010. LNCS, vol. 6052, pp. 351–358. Springer, Heidelberg (2010)
17. Riva, O., Qui, C., Strauss, K., Lymberopoulos, D.: Progressive authentication: deciding when to authenticate on mobile phones. In: USENIX Security Symposium (2012)
18. Roth, V., Richter, K., Freidinger, R.: A PIN-entry method resilient against shoulder surfing. In: CCS (2004)
19. Schneier, B.: Applied Cryptography: Protocols, Algorithms, and Source Code in C. Wiley, New York (1995)
20. Shannon, C.E.: Communication in the presence of noise. In: Proceedings of the Institute of Radio Engineers (IRE) (1949)
21. Tari, F., Ozok, A.A., Holden, S.H.: A comparison of perceived and real shoulder-surfing risks between alphanumeric and graphical passwords. In: SOUPS (2006)
22. Uellenbeck, S., Hupperich, T., Wolf, C., Holz, T.: Tactile one-time pad: smartphone authentication resilient against shoulder surfing. Technical report, Horst Görtz Institute for IT-Security (HGI), HGI-2014-003, September 2014
23. Wilfong, G.T.: Method and Apparatus for Secure PIN Entry, 08 1999. Lucent Technologies Inc, U.S. Patent, US5940511 A
24. Yan, Q., Han, J., Li, Y., Zhou, J., Deng, R.H.: Designing leakage-resilient password entry on touchscreen mobile devices. In: Chen, K., Xie, Q., Qiu, W., Li, N., Tzeng, W.-G. (eds.) ASIACCS, pp. 37–48. ACM (2013)

User Authentication Using Human Cognitive Abilities

Asadullah Al Galib[(⊠)] and Reihaneh Safavi-Naini

University of Calgary, Calgary, Canada
{aagalib,rei}@ucalgary.ca

Abstract. We present a novel approach to user authentication in which biometric data related to human cognitive processes, in particular visual search, working memory and priming effect on automatic processing, are captured and used to identify users. Our proposed system uses a carefully designed Cognitive Task (CT) that is presented to the user as a game, in order to capture a "cognitive signature" of the user. Our empirical results support the hypothesis that the captured cognitive signatures can identify users across different platforms. Our system provides a proof-of-concept for cognitive-based biometric authentication. We validate the robustness of our system against impersonation attack by experienced users, and show that it is hard to reproduce the cognitive signature by mimicking users' gameplay.

1 Introduction

The most widely used form of authentication is password system; that is, what we can remember. Password systems are attractive because they do not require any special hardware, but they are vulnerable to guessing attacks and passwords have the risk of being forgotten. Biometric authentication systems are based on *what we are* (fingerprints, iris pattern), and are immune to being lost or forgotten. However, traditional biometric systems require the use of special hardwares such as scanners or cameras. More recent biometric authentication systems are behavioral and based on *what we do*, including keyboard typing rhythm, mouse dynamics or walking gait. Behavioral biometric systems measure behavioral traits of a user to build a profile for him that will later be used to identify the user.

We present an authentication system which captures biometric data related to human cognitive processes and use that to build a profile for the user. Cognition refers to higher level brain functions (or mental processes) such as perception, learning, problem solving [1,2]. Cognitive abilities of individuals are their capacities to carry out cognitive tasks that require mental processes. Basing authentication on these processes makes our approach different from behavioral biometrics which do not attempt to invoke particular mental processes.

Our work is inspired by the reported studies on individuals differences [1] in performing cognitive tasks. We present a *cognitive task* (CT) to the user in the form of a game that will be performed by the user by interacting with

© International Financial Cryptography Association 2015
R. Böhme and T. Okamoto (Eds.): FC 2015, LNCS 8975, pp. 254–271, 2015.
DOI: 10.1007/978-3-662-47854-7_16

the computer, and using a mouse or a touchpad. The collected data during the execution of the CT will be used to extract cognitive features related to visual search ability, working memory and the effect of priming on automatic processing of the user. Visual search refers to finding a target object in a set of objects and is measured by the search time. Working memory allows individuals to hold information in their memory for later processing. Features derived from these cognitive processes in combination with other basic stimulus-response features are used to build profiles for the users that can later identify them.

The CT is presented to the user in the form of an interactive visual search game. The game starts by presenting a set of 25 different objects arranged in a 5×5 grid to the user. The task of the user is to find a particular target object in the set. The user has to drag and drop the challenge object onto the matching target object in the set. This is equivalent to performing a visual search task by the user. On performing a correct search task (or correct match), the user is rewarded with a gold coin. The user is instructed to deposit the gold coin in a "bank". On a correct deposit, the user is presented with another challenge object and a similar interaction follows. The features derived from these interactions are used to construct a cognitive signature. The signatures are then used to develop an authentication system with accuracy comparable to other established biometric approaches. A typical behavioral biometric system such as those based on mouse dynamics, measure behavioral traits that are inadvertent. Systems designed to estimate cognitive features such as ours, can be augmented to use behavioral features related to mouse dynamics to improve authentication accuracy.

Our system is based on experiments in experimental cognitive psychology and has been carefully designed to preserve the essential elements of the corresponding experiments. Attempts have also been made to ensure that the cognitive task presented to the user is intuitive and interesting. We performed experiments in controlled and non-controlled (Amazon Mechanical Turk [3]) environments. The accuracies obtained in both cases are comparable to other state-of-the-art behavioural biometric systems [4–7]. To evaluate security of the system we considered impersonation attack where an attacker attempts to mimic a target user's gameplay. Using the data collected during the target user's gameplay, we developed a simulation of their gameplay that was later provided to the attacker for the purpose of training. After that training phase, the attacker had to impersonate the target user. We considered the attack to be successful when the attacker was able to successfully authenticate himself as the target user.

Section 2 discusses the mental processes and the design of the game. Section 3 describes how the design invokes cognitive processes. We discuss feature collection and the user classification technique in Sects. 4 and 5, respectively. Section 6 provides details on experimental results and analysis. Finally, we conclude in Sect. 7.

2   Cognitive Task

We present the CT to the user in the form of a web-based game. In this Section, we first discuss cognitive processes and then the design of the CT(game). In Sect. 3 we examine how the design of the game invokes these mental processes.

2.1   Mental Processes

Visual Search. Visual search is a type of cognitive task in which the user searches through a visual field for a target [8]. Performance is generally measured by the search time. The search time depends on multiple factors such as the rate at which the user scans the alternatives. In a self-terminating search, the user stops the searching process as soon as he finds the alternative he thinks is appropriate [2,9].

Working Memory and Information Processing Speed. Working memory describes the ability of a human to hold and manipulate information in their mind over short periods of time for a cognitive task such as learning or reasoning [8]. The working memory capacity varies between individuals. The ability to reason and solve problems requires the use of information stored in working memory. However, this information is vulnerable to interruption and decay. Due to this volatility, faster processing of this information is necessary for successful completion of a cognitive task.

Automatic Processing and Priming Effect. Automatic processing, is the processing of information that guides behavior, but without being conscious of the process, and without interfering with other conscious activity that may be underway at the same time [2]. Automatic processes can be invoked by a technique called priming [2,10]. A prime is a stimulus or event that influences an ongoing action or process. Bargh et al. [10] carried out an experiment where a group of participants were exposed to words related to the concept of elderly. The participants who were primed with the elderly concept were found walking slower than the others. However, participants had no conscious awareness of the concept of the elderly or of their reaction to it.

2.2   Design of the Game

Our game provides a simple challenge-response task. In each *instance* of the challenge-response, the user is given a challenge, which is an object. The user responds by dragging the challenge object onto the matching object inside the search set. The user then receives a gold coin as a reward and deposits it in a bank. On a correct deposit, the user is challenged with a new object and the game continues as before. Our goal was to invoke the three mental processes within a minimal design space.

An image is first broken into a grid of $5 \times 5 = 25$ square cells. We refer to this partitioned image as the search set θ, $|\theta| = 25$. Each square is called a *tile*. The game starts by presenting a random challenge tile t_c at a location P_{t_c} outside the partitioned image. The tile, t_c, is a copy of a tile $t_r \in \theta$. We have divided the user's response into two actions. (1) The user drags t_c and drops it onto t_r located at position P_{t_r} within the search set, in which case t_c rests on t_r and becomes *unmovable*. We refer to this action as A_{resp}. On an incorrect match, t_c automatically moves back to position P_{t_c} signifying a *mismatch* and allowing the user to retry. (2) On a correct placement of t_c on t_r, the user is rewarded with a gold coin, g_c, which appears exactly at P_{t_r} (superimposed). The user is then instructed to deposit (*drag* and *drop*) g_c in a bank (a bounded box with the same dimensions as that of a tile) appearing at P_{t_c}. We refer to this action as A_{rew}. On depositing the coin, the user is challenged with the next tile, and the game continues as before. Therefore, one *instance* of this game is comprised of the correct placement of the target tile, A_{resp} and correct deposit of the gold coin, A_{rew} (Appendix A, Fig. 4).

From Conceptual Modeling to Implementation. In order to guarantee the invocation of the aforementioned mental processes certain constraints have been used throughout the game.

C1: At the beginning of each *instance*, a copy of a randomly chosen original tile $t_r \in \theta$ appears at P_{t_c} as the challenge tile t_c. Challenge tiles cannot be repeated. Therefore, each of the 25 partitioned portions (original tiles) of the image must appear only once as the challenge tile.

C2: On completing the action A_{resp}, t_c is superimposed on t_r and becomes *unmovable*. At this point all the *loose* tiles (tiles that have not appeared in the challenge phase till now) disappear from the grid leaving only the *unmovable* ones. This allows the user to observe the current status of the game. The user can observe the tiles that have been placed correctly till now and the remaining empty square cells on the grid. Refer to Appendix A Fig. 4(b).

C3: At the beginning of A_{resp} all current *loose* tiles in the grid are shuffled. They randomly change their positions on the grid except for the target tile t_r and the *unmovable* ones. All 25 tiles are visible during A_{resp}. Therefore the actual positions of the *loose* tiles remain unknown to the user. Refer to Appendix A Fig. 4(d).

C4: Two straight lines from P_{t_r} to P_{t_c} appear during the A_{rew} action. During this action if the gold coin touches any one of the straight lines, its color changes from green to red, without hampering the current movement (Appendix A Fig. 4(c)).

C5: The tiles consist of random-shaped black symbols on a white background. All tiles have the same opacity throughout the game. The symbols being of random shapes do not *necessarily* represent or convey any meaning to the user.

C6: We allow some tolerance on the placement of the tile and the gold. This means that the user does not need perfect accuracy when dropping t_c onto t_r or when depositing g_c at P_{t_c}. A *drop* is considered a match if t_c or g_c covers 60 % of the area of the underlying tile t_r or bank, respectively. On releasing they are automatically superimposed over their destinations. However, there are exceptions, on K random *instances* the *drop* accuracy is increased for g_c *only*, requiring 90 % overlapping area. We choose $K = k_1 \ldots k_5$ randomly from consecutive *instance* intervals $\{i_1 \ldots i_5\}$, $\{i_6 \ldots i_{10}\}$, $\ldots$, $\{i_{21} \ldots i_{25}\}$. Each time the *drop* accuracy is not met, g_c automatically moves back to P_{t_r}. The user is then allowed to re-try.

C7: Each time there is a *mismatch* t_c moves back to its original location P_{t_c}. The user is then allowed to re-try. However, as soon as the user hovers over t_c, the grid is again shuffled according to Constraint $C3$.

3   The CT Constraints and Mental Processes

Here, we illustrate the importance of the aforementioned constraints and how they aid in triggering the mental processes.

3.1   Revisiting Visual Search

Our game (CT) has been designed to invoke self-terminating searches. As soon as the user finds the target tile, further searches are not required. Due to Constraint $C1$, we refer to our search set as a (+ve) search set, meaning that the target must appear within the set. This ensures that a match always occurs and the search terminates. Constraint $C3$ aids in invoking serial search and $C5$ reduces the conspicuity of the target. If a target location is known beforehand and if a target is too conspicuous they can affect the search process [8]. If the grid was not shuffled at each instance according to $C3$ & $C7$, the user may remember certain target positions. This bias the visual search process.

3.2   Revisiting Working Memory and Information Processing Speed

Due to Constraint $C2$, the user can observe the current game status. The user can observe the empty grid cells and the already placed tiles. He can hold this information in his working memory for a short interval of time while he completes action A_{rew}. If the information is not lost, he will be able to decrease the size of the search set $|\theta|$ for the next challenge. For example, for the 11th *instance* of the game he will be able to shrink $|\theta|$ to 15, thus skipping over the already placed 10 tiles. This design concept is similar to Visual Pattern Test [11] used for measuring *pure* visual working memory. Recall that according to Constraint $C3$, after the user completes A_{rew}, all 25 tiles are visible. Therefore, if the user fails to hold the information (status of the game) in his working memory, his $|\theta|$ must be lower bounded by 15. In such case, the time elapsed on placing the target tile correctly is relatively longer. Therefore, it is necessary to investigate the working memory capacity in terms of information processing speed for each individual user.

3.3   Revisiting Automatic Processing and Priming Effect

Recall, that during A_{rew} two straight lines are drawn from P_{t_c} to P_{t_r} to guide the movement of the gold coin. Constraint $C4$ provides priming for invoking the automatic processing. We conjecture that a user who is primed with the color change of the straight lines, will drag g_c on a straighter trajectory compared to an unprimed user. We measure the effectiveness of the prime, *EOP*, as the ratio of the length of the line *not* overlapped by the gold coin to the length of the guiding line. Constraint $C6$ also has priming effect on the user, particularly on the way the gold coins are deposited in the bank, and the tiles are dropped on the grid for the subsequent *instances*. We measure the effectiveness of this priming as the ratio of the two areas. The primes are considered effective if the ratios tend to 1.

3.4 Evidence of Working Memory and Priming Effect from Experimental Data

We analyze our data to provide evidence for the underlying mental processes. Recall that after a successful match, the user can observe the game status ($C2$). If this information is not lost from the working memory, then $|\theta|$ must decrease with each *instance*, resulting in a descending series of **V**isual **S**earch **T**ime, VST. That is, VSTs must decrease with decreasing $|\theta|$'s as the game progresses. Considering information storage is likely to occur near the end of the game, since it is easiest to recall the last remaining empty cell, we find the length of sub-sequence $l = n - k + 1$ of n *instances* such that $VST_k > VST_{k+1} > \ldots > VST_n$ for $|\theta|_k > |\theta|_{k+1} > \ldots > |\theta|_n = 1$. Since the user might store partial information as well, we allow some tolerance such that v number of violations (sign changes) can happen in the sequence. Figure 1(a) shows the average sub-sequence length l (for 5 games) when v is varied from 0–3. We can observe the variations in working memory capacities among a group of users.

On the other hand, after triggering a prime, a user might, (1) receive it and get influenced (invocation of automatic processing), (2) receive it but *not* get influenced by it (no invocation of automatic processing) or, (3) *not* receive it at all; e.g. a *cautious* user dropping a gold with overlapping area $\geq 90\,\%$. Considering that the prime has been triggered in the ith *instance*, the following is a possible explanation for the three cases in the $i+1^{th}$ *instance*, for Constraint $C6$. (1) $EOP_{C6}^{i} < EOP_{C6}^{i+1}$ and g_c was misplaced at the ith *instance*. In other words, the user *drops* g_c with higher accuracy in the $i + 1^{th}$ *instance*, i.e. prime was received and was effective. (2) $EOP_{C6}^{i} \geq EOP_{C6}^{i+1}$ and g_c was misplaced in the ith *instance*, i.e. prime was received but was not effective. (3) g_c was never misplaced in the ith *instance*, i.e. prime was not received. Figure 1(b) shows the average percentage of each of these cases (for 5 games) when primes are triggered. Notice that due to slight inaccuracies in placement, all users received at least some prime. Around 30 % of the users never *missed* getting influenced (without being aware) by the prime whenever they received it.

4   Feature Estimation Process

Raw Data. The interaction data during performing the task is collected for each user: (1) The x_{ce} and y_{ce} co-ordinates of the click event e and the corresponding timestamp t_{ce}. (2) The x_{re} and y_{re} co-ordinates of the release event e and the corresponding timestamp t_{re}. (3) The horizontal co-ordinate x_{de}, $de = 1 \ldots n$

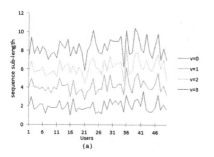
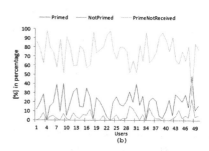

Fig. 1. We chose 50 users randomly from Experiment-1(b). (a) Average sub-sequence length with a linear relationship between VSTs and search set sizes indicating differences in working memory capacity of different users. Different curves represent varying number of violations from linear relationship. (b) Percentage of the three cases when prime is triggered (Sect. 3.4). Users are influenced in different ways.

and the vertical co-ordinates y_{de}, $de = 1 \ldots n$ of the pointing device sampled at 100 ms intervals.

4.1   Cognitive Feature Estimation

We estimate features that capture cognitive abilities from the aforementioned raw data. We also discuss other important features that are based on the users' responses to certain stimuli during the execution of an *instance*.

Drop and Pick Reaction Time, DPT (f_1, f_2). At the end of the A_{resp} action, the user picks up the gold coin, g_c, appearing at P_{t_r}. The time elapsed between the stimulus (g_c) and the user picking it up (response) is denoted by t_{DPT}^g (f_1). At the end of A_{rew}, after depositing the gold coin at P_{t_c}, the user picks t_c from location P_{t_c}. The time elapsed between the appearance of the stimulus (t_c) and the user picking it up (response) is referred to as the t_{DPT}^t (f_2). DPT might seem similar to traditional pause-and-click. However, traditional pause-and-click is highly dependent on what the user is currently reading or exploring [6]. DPT is the result of a controlled stimulus and therefore, is not content-specific.

Visual Search Time, VST & ratio(f_3, f_4). VST is the time required for the user to visually search and detect the target tile. VST is calculated by the subtraction method [2]. The subtraction method involves subtracting the amount of time information processing takes with the process from the time it takes without the process. That is the time difference between actions A_{resp} ($A_{resp}^t + t_{DPT}^t$) and A_{rew} (A_{rew}^t),

$$VST = (A_{resp}^t + t_{DPT}^t) - A_{rew}^t. \tag{1}$$

It is important to consider t_{DPT}^t in the above equation, since a t_c is exposed as soon as a g_c is deposited. So the minuend of Eq. (1) refers to the time elapsed between the exposure of t_c and its correct placement inside the grid.

The time elapsed during A_{rew} is simply the movement time and does not involve user's thinking or search time. Therefore, we are able to distill the plain visual search time for each *instance*. Moreover, note that the subtraction method allows VST to self-adjust to the user's specific environment by remaining immune to differing mouse speed or acceleration. We also consider the ratio of A_{resp}^t to $A_{resp}^t + t_{DPT}^t$, (f_4) to capture the phenomena where user searches while dragging, or searches and then drag.

Information Processing Speed, IPS (f_5). If information (game status) is not lost from the user's working memory then in the ith instance the user is left with 25 - i +1 alternatives for the search operation. We can derive the following equation for IPS from Hick-Hymen law [12,13]

$$IPS = \frac{H_i}{VST}. \tag{2}$$

The amount of information in the ith instance can be expressed as $H_i = \sum_{k=1}^{|\theta|} P_k \left(log_2 \left[\frac{1}{P_k} \right] \right)$ where P_k is the probability of the kth alternative in the ith instance with $|\theta| = 25 - i + 1$ alternatives. Due to the Constraints $C3$ & $C7$ all these alternatives are equally probable.

Pause and Search, P&S (f_6, f_7). While dragging the target tile we noticed that the user sometimes pauses and searches for the target inside the grid. If the user remains on the same pixel for more than $\alpha = 0.1$ s while dragging the tile or gold, we refer to it as a pause. We measure the ratio of tile paused time to A_{resp}^t during A_{resp} (f_6), and the ratio of gold paused time to A_{rew}^t, (f_7) during A_{rew}.

Effectiveness Of Priming, EOP (f_{8-19}). Recall that Constraint $C6$ provides the priming effect necessary to invoke an automatic processing. We measure the effectiveness of this priming through EOP_{C6}

$$EOP_{C6} = \frac{Area\ overlapped\ between\ source\ and\ destination}{Area\ of\ source\ or\ destination}. \tag{3}$$

EOP_{C6}^g (f_8) refers to the effectiveness of priming while depositing g_c (source) in the bank (destination). EOP_{C6}^t (f_9) refers to the effectiveness of priming while placing the t_c (source) on the matching tile t_r (destination). We consider related features that might capture the effectiveness of priming as well. We consider the *Drop Error Distance* for tile, $\triangle_{x_{re},\ y_{re}}^{E_t}$ (f_{10}) and gold, $\triangle_{x_{re},\ y_{re}}^{E_g}$ (f_{11}), defined as the distance from the drop point to the center of their destination. We measure the *Click Error Distance* which is the distance of the click point to the center of the tile $\triangle_{x_{ce},\ y_{ce}}^{E_t}$ (f_{12}) and the gold $\triangle_{x_{ce},\ y_{ce}}^{E_g}$ (f_{13}). We also consider the *Drop Error Angle* for tile/gold $\angle_{(x_{re},\ y_{re})}^{E_{t/g}}$ (f_{14}, f_{15}) which is the angle made from the drop point to the (+ve) x-axis with the center of the destination being the vertex, and *Click Error Angle* which is the angle made from the click point to the (+ve) x-axis with center of the tile/gold being the vertex, $\angle_{(x_{ce},\ y_{ce})}^{E_{t/g}}$ (f_{16}, f_{17}).

On the other hand, we measure the effectiveness of priming due to $C4$ as the ratio of two lengths. EOP_{C4} is the ratio of the length of the lines *not* overlapped by the gold coin to the total length of the guiding lines. EOP_{C4}^{L1} (f_{18}) and EOP_{C4}^{L2} (f_{19}) are the effectiveness of priming on the top and bottom guiding lines respectively.

5   System Design

In this Section we provide details of the classification technique used to identify the users. We then discuss the security of our system against impersonation attack. Details on how we measure the error metrics in our system are also provided.

5.1   Classification Technique

We use a statistical approach for classifying the users. We model the features as random variables $F_1, F_2, \ldots, F_n$ and assume class-conditional independence between them. In the ith *instance* of the game a row of feature values $F^i = (f_{1,i}, f_{2,i}, \ldots, f_{n,i})$ is generated. Therefore, for a sequence of k *instances* denoted by $F = (F^1, \ldots, F^k)$, the interaction information can be denoted using a matrix of size $k \times n$. During the learning stage the probability density functions of the features are estimated using a non-parametric approach. In the classification stage posterior probabilities are used to estimate the probability of a classification being correct.

Learning. The learning phase consists of the estimation of the probability density function for each of the feature vectors. A parametric approach to estimating a density, f, involves assuming that f belongs to a parametric family of distributions. We resort to using non-parametric approach, in particular, the kernel density estimator [14] to avoid making any assumption on the distribution of the underlying population and to better understand the structure of the data. The easiest non-parametric estimation of a probability distribution is the use of histogram. It is simple but has disadvantages such as discontinuity and high sensitivity to bin edges. Kernel density estimators are superior to histogram and are quite intuitive [14,15].

We estimate the unknown density function $f_j(x)$ of the jth feature vector, represented by a random variable F_j, based on its m samples (or training data) $x_1, .., x_m$. Assuming that the observations are independent realizations of F_j, the estimation of the density function, $\hat{f}_j(x)$, using a kernel density estimator, for univariate case is $\hat{f}_j(x) = \frac{1}{mh} \sum_{i=1}^{m} K\left(\frac{x-x_i}{h}\right)$. At this point, the estimation of $f_j(x)$ reduces to (1) choosing a kernel function K and, (2) selecting an appropriate bandwidth selection algorithm to determine h. Although the choice of kernel functions is not of particular importance for an experiment [14], according to our empirical results, we used Gaussian kernel among others as the kernel function K. The kernel estimate is constructed by centering the Gaussian kernel at each observation. Therefore, the value of the kernel estimated at a point x_i is simply the average of the m normal kernel ordinates at that point. Therefore, the width of the chosen kernel function determines the smoothness of the resulting density function. Oversmoothing can happen as a result of larger width whereas undersmoothing can happen due to smaller width. Therefore, selecting the appropriate width h is a crucial task while estimating the density function.

The performance of the kernel density estimator depends on how closely the estimated $\hat{f}_j(x)$ resembles the true $f_j(x)$ of the jth feature. This performance can be measured in terms of the MISE (Mean Integrated Square Error), which globally measures the distance between $\hat{f}_j(\cdot; h)$ and $f_j(x)$,

$$E[ISE(\hat{f}_j(.;h))] = E \int \hat{f}_j(x)^2 \, dx - 2E \int \hat{f}_j(x) \, f_j(x) \, dx + E \int f_j(x)^2 \, dx \quad (4)$$

We use least square cross validation (LSCV) [16,17] which is a data-driven bandwidth selector. The third term on the right hand side of Eq. (4) does not depend on h and can be ignored. The first term can be calculated from the observations. The middle term depends on h and contains an unknown quantity $f_j(x)$. In order to solve this issue, we resort to a leave-one-out LSCV. Although there are more complex bandwidth selection algorithms [18], we chose LSCV since it is simple and intuitive.

Classifying. We assume class-conditional independence between the features, modeled as random variables $F_1, F_2, \ldots, F_n$, for a user u_w, $w \in \{1, \ldots, m\}$. So for the ith *instance*, $Pr\left(F^i|u_w\right) = \prod_{j=1}^{n} Pr(f_{j,i}|u_w)$. Although the class-conditional independence between features is not true in general, the assumption works well in many complex real life systems. The posterior probability of a user u_w for an *instance*,

$$Pr\left(u_w|F^i\right) = \frac{Pr\left(u_w\right)\prod_{j=1}^{n} Pr(f_{j,i}|u_w)}{Pr(f_{1,i}, \ldots, f_{n,i})}. \quad (5)$$

We then classify a test *instance* according to the largest posterior probability. We accept a sequence of *instances* as genuine if the number of accepted *instances* exceeds some decision threshold α. The value of threshold α is set in such a way such that the false acceptance rate is close to the false rejection rate.

5.2   Security Model

Correctness and security of a biometric system is measured using False Acceptance Rate and False Rejection Rate. A biometric system should not accept a user without genuine biometric (FA), and should not reject a genuine user (FR). Therefore, both these metrics should remain close to zero. We evaluate our system performance using user u's own test sessions and other test sessions from $n - 1$ users. A positive test *session* of length l *instances* is considered misclassified for a user u, if the classifier outputs a score below the threshold α. This is referred to as a False Rejection. On the other hand, a negative test *session* is considered classified if the classifier's output score is above the threshold α. This is referred to as a False Acceptance. We calculate the FAR as the ratio of FA to TN, where FA is the number of false acceptance and TN is the number of

Table 1. Comparison with other approaches. Mouse Dynamics System (MDS), Keystroke Dyanmics System (KDS), Homogeneous Physio-Behavioral System (HBS), CBS (Cognitive based Biometric System). Session size refers to the amount of interactions during the authentication phase.

Works	FAR	FRR	Session size	System	Notes
[5]	2.46 %	2.46 %	2000 mouse actions	MDS	Free mouse movement
[4]	6.3 %	6.3 %	20 strokes	MDS	Confined within a task
[6]	1.3 %	1.3 %	20 mouse clicks	MDS	Free mouse movement
[21]	2.11 %	2.11 %	25 text characters	HBS	Confined within a task
[22]	0.01 %	4 %	683 characters	KDS	Fixed-text input
[23]	Accuracy 93.3 % – 99.5 %		200 characters	KDS	Free-text input
[Ours]	0 %, 2.3 %	0 %, 7.8 %	25 instances	CBS	Confined within a task

test *sessions* belonging to the $n - 1$ other users. The FRR is calculated as the ratio between FR and TP where FR is the number of false rejection and TP is the number of test *sessions* belonging to the user u.

Impersonation Attack. Impersonation attack in biometric systems involves an attacker generating the biometric information of a legitimate owner *somehow* without the owner being present at the scenario [19], for example by lifting latent fingerprints from objects and presenting it to the system. In our system the attacker is allowed to observe a target user's gameplay. Later on, the attacker tries to mimic that user's gameplay in order to get authenticated as the victim user. The success of the attacker is measured as the probability of success in being authenticated as the claimed user. We build a web-based program capable of simulating any user's game playing activities once fed with data collected during the data acquisition period. We then select experienced users and instruct them to observe and imitate other users' simulations (Sect. 6.3). We assume that the user's interaction data are not available to any computer programs such as spyware.

6   Experiments and Results

We formulated two questions. (1) Is it possible to verify a user based solely on the derived cognitive features with high accuracy under, (a) controlled condition and under, (b) non-laboratory condition? (2) How effective are impersonation attacks against our system when carried out by trained users?

We devised three separate experiments to answer the above questions. Since our experiments required human volunteers, we obtained approval from the Research Ethics Board of our University. The 1st experiment was carried out in a controlled environment with 23 graduate students. The 2nd experiment consisted of 129 workers from Amazon Mechanical Turk. And the 3rd one was carried out with 5 graduate students in a controlled environment and 10 Amazon Mechanical Turk workers. All experiments were divided into three phases

(1) Phase-I, where participants agreed to the consent information. (2) In Phase-II, a short video displayed how the game is played for a few *instances*. (3) In Phase-III, participants were required to fill up an exit survey consisting of the standard SUS [20] and a few other questions S_{Fun}. In all the experiments, interaction data were recorded using JavaScript and submitted passively via AJAX requests to the web server. We randomly picked a set of distinct images for each user in a *session*.

6.1   Experiment 1(a): Accuracy and Efficiency (Controlled Condition)

The goals of the 1st experiment were to figure out, (1) Accuracy and verification time of our system when users are trained in a non-distracting environment using a single platform and, (2) perform an analysis on the derived features.

Setup. Each user in a *session* is required to play the game 7 times, every time with a new random partitioned image, resulting into a dataset of $25 \times 7 = 175$ *instances*. Afterwards, they completed the exit survey. All of them used a PC with 2.10 GHz Intel i3, 4GB RAM and an wireless optical USB mouse. They used Google Chrome on a screen of resolution 1366×768 (96 DPI) in Windows 7 SP1 OS.

Intra-Session Evaluation: The dataset was divided into two parts. The first part consisting of 5 games (g_1, ..., g_5) each of 25 *instances*, is used for training purpose and the last two games g_6, g_7 are separately used for testing purpose. The average EER is 0 % suggesting that all users have consistent game playing activities in a continuous *session*. Figure 2(a) shows the variations in FAR and FRR, at $\alpha = 0.5$, as the number of *instances* are varied. Less number of *instances* e.g. 16 would have significantly decreased the enrollment and verification time but with an FRR of 8.7 %. Table 1 provides a comparison of our system with others. The verification time is the time taken to collect the verifiable biometric data and the time taken to complete the classification task [24]. It took an average 76.7 s to complete one game (25 *instances*) and an average of around 44.7 s to complete part of the game (16 *instances*), considering time intervals, ($A^t_{resp}+A^t_{rew}$). These are comparable to several recently proposed authentication technique (Table 2). Our classification time does not have any particular impact on the verification time.

Feature Analysis: We use data from the 23 users for analyzing the features. Figure 3(a) shows the correlation coefficients of pairs of features in a color-coded plot. There are a few highly correlated features. According to our observation these pairs do not have any effect on classification accuracy. We consider all 19 features, since they do not add any significant burden on the training time. We also considered the strength of each of the features in identifying the 23 users. Each feature was in turn used for learning and classifying. We found that features related to DPT, EOP_{C4}, VST and $P\&S$ are in the top 7 based on average EER.

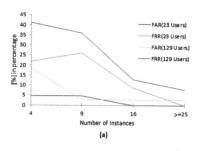
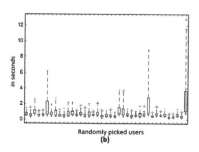

(a)

(b)

Fig. 2. (a) Avg. FAR and FRR at $\alpha = 0.5$ (Sect. 5.1) with varying number of *instances*. The first 5 games are used for training and the last 2 for testing purpose (Intra-session). (b) Box plot of Gold Pick Reaction Time (in seconds) before noise removal (whiskers set to 3) of a group of Amazon workers showing outliers.

Inter-Session Evaluation: Participants were emailed to play in three other occasions, each separated by 1-day, 2-day and 3-day intervals respectively. We consider these intervals to be congruous with real account login intervals. The training data came from the original data acquisition session $(g_1, \ldots, g_5)$. On each occasion participants were required to complete one game using any machine (except cellular device) and browser at their most suitable time. At $\alpha = 0.5$, FAR remained 0 % through all *sessions* with FRR being 0 %, 8.70 % and 4.35 % on the 1, 2 and 3-day *sessions* respectively.

6.2   Experiment 1(b): Accuracy and Efficiency (Non-Laboratory Condition)

The goal of this experiment was to evaluate the system with random users from different parts of the world who self train and later remotely authenticate. We created 4 HITs altogether. The 1st HIT was created with 130 assignments to have 130 unique workers. We gathered 129 *valid* submissions until the HIT expired. Each assignment was worth \$0.7. We refer to each HIT as a *session*. The workers were directed to the website hosting the game. After watching the video, they were required to play 7 games and then complete an exit survey. At the end workers copy-pasted a code generated on our website back to Amazon.

Intra-Session Evaluation: Similar to Experiment-I, $g_1, \ldots, g_5$ were used for training and g_6, g_7 for testing purpose. We noticed abnormal $VSTs$ in the dataset for few cases. On closer scrutiny and observing the simulations for such cases we noticed very large *Drop and Pick Reaction Time*, t^t_{DPT} and t^g_{DPT}. This shows that users are more likely to get distracted at the end of the actions (A_{resp}, A_{rew}) rather than while performing them. We detect these *extreme* outliers using interquartile range for each user u, with the upper fence $UF = f^{Q3}_u + (3 \times f^{IQR}_u)$, $f_u \in \{t^t_{DPT_u}, t^g_{DPT_u}\}$ and replacing them with UF (Fig. 2(b)). Noise removal was done separately for the training and test dataset. Figure 2(a) shows the avg. error rates for varying number of *instances* for the

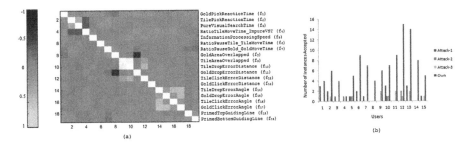

Fig. 3. (a) Correlation coefficients [-1,1] of pairs of features in a color-coded plot. (b) Results from Impersonation attack. Most *instances* are accepted as "own" rather than as the victims' (attack-1, 2 and 3) (Color figure online).

129 workers. Our classifier reaches an FAR of 2.3 % and FRR of 7.8 % with ≥ 25 *instances*. The average time it took to complete one assignment of the HIT is 24.3 min. Mouse type statistics included wireless/wired mouse (61.3 %), laptop touchpad (38.7 %) (user claimed).

Inter-Session Evaluation: We created another 3 HITs, each separated by 1, 2 and 3-day intervals respectively. We made sure participants completing the 4th HIT had already participated in the previous 3 HITs. Each assignment was worth \$0.2. We received 49, 37 and 37 valid submissions until the HIT expired. The assignment required completing only one game. As before the classifier used the initial acquired data $g_1, \ldots, g_5$ for learning. The FAR were 2.08 %, 0 %, 2.70 %, and FRR 8.16 %, 8.11 %, 5.50 % with $\alpha = 0.5$ on the 1-day, 2-days, 3-day *sessions* respectively. This suggests that even after small periods of inactivity and using the original training data, the classifier can still distinguish the users.

6.3   Experiment 2: Impersonation Attack

Impersonation attack demands trained users capable of mimicking a victim's gameplay. Therefore, participants were selected based on how fast they completed the previous *sessions*. We selected 5 participants from the 1st pool and 10 Turkers from the 2nd pool. Each assignment was worth \$0.5 (Amazon). Each participant was required to watch and mimic the simulations of 3 victims. We

Table 2. Comparison of VT, ET, test and enrollment (train + test) session size. Session size refers to the amount of interactions made during the enrollment or verification phase.

	[Ours]	[21]	[4]	[25]
Verification Time, VT (Approx.)	76.7 s, 2.5 min	39 s	25 s	5–6 min
Test session size	25 instances	25 characters	25 strokes	540 items
Enrollment Time, ET (Approx.)	9.8 min, 24.3 min	6.5 min	6.7 min	30–40 min
Enrollment session size	≥ 175 instances	250 characters	400 strokes	3780 items

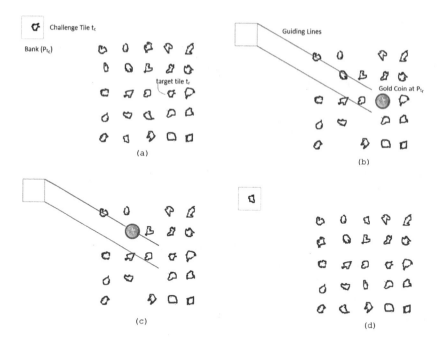

Fig. 4. (a) User is presented with a challenge tile, t_c, at the beginning of the 21st instance. (b) User performs A_{resp}, i.e. drags and drops t_c onto t_r inside the grid. On a correct match the *loose* tiles disappear showing the current game status (at 21st instance). (c) User performs A_{rew}, i.e. drags and drops gold coin, g_c, onto P_{t_c}. Top guiding line color changes from green to red as the gold coin touches it (Constraint $C4$). (d) User successfully deposits g_c and gets the next challenge tile. All 25 tiles are visible at this point. Notice that the 21 *unmovable* tiles in b and d have not changed their positions. All the *loose* tiles have changed their position (compare a and d). The target tile t_r appears at its original position in the image (Color Figure online).

considered a strong attack scenario. We, (1) displayed a clock while the simulation was playing, (2) provided the same image in the attack phase, (3) declared a bonus of $0.5 if the Turkers could mimic accurately and, (4) allowed to repeat the attacks as many times as desired. All attackers were given instructions to observe when and how tiles and gold are picked, dragged and dropped.

A successful attack would require reproducing the cognitive features of a victim. Figure 3(b) depicts the *maximum* number of *instances* (out of all attempts) that have been correctly classified to the corresponding victims. A maximum of 3 *instances* were correctly mimicked by user-1 and worker-10 and 13. None of the attackers would have successfully authenticated with the threshold set at $\alpha = 0.5$. In fact, workers 12 and 13 were identified as "themselves" in one of the games (attacks). A successful attack in this case would require mimicking almost all 19 cognitive features, which appeared to be a hard task. The challenge tiles appeared randomly, and the grid was shuffled at each instance ($C3$), and so the sequence of challenges in the simulation and actual attack differed, making it harder to recall the corresponding VSTs and other reaction times.

7   Discussion and Conclusions

Our cognitive based authentication system assumes that users play consistently and use his cognitive abilities appropriately. This is arguably a desirable property and careless treatment of security should be punished by denying access. Our proposed system, like other biometric systems cannot authenticate a user if their biometric data are damaged (e.g. a severe burn to one's finger). In cognitive based systems the damage may be long term and caused by cognitive and mental disorders, or short term when under the influence of substance. To provide user access in such cases depending on the type of the damage and the organizational policy, a different type of authentication system such as a password system, should be used as backup. Cognitive abilities can change slowly over time due to age and experience. In such cases, an adaptive enrollment mechanism is necessary to capture and represent the most current features of the user.

Analysis of user surveys shows that the game is user friendly and easy to play: 71.8 % and 85.5 % of the users agreed that the game is fun and easy respectively in S_{Fun} questions. The average SUS (System Usability Scale) [20] scores are within the user-friendly software ratings of 60–70 [26]. Our system can be used as a stand-alone system, or can be used in a multi-factor authentication system. Since well selected cognitive features cannot easily be mimicked the authentication system will be secure. Our future work will include designing systems that invoke other mental processes and extract a wider range of cognitive features.

Acknowledgments. This research is in part supported by Alberta Innovates Technology Futures and Telus Mobility Canada.

A   Related Work

The work closest to ours, although it is a combination of mouse dynamics and cognitive factors, is that of Hamdy and Traore [21]. The authors combine visual search and short-term memory effect with mouse dynamics. Their system requires the user to search for letters on a shuffled *virtual* keyboard. However, it is highly likely that the exposure of the same *virtual* keyboard and the string of letters have affected the visual search process. The work in [25] uses the concept of implicit learning from cognitive psychology whereby the user is trained on a fixed sequence which can later be used during authentication. Our system does not rely on implicit learning and uses a random challenge sequence and so the user does not repeat the same sequence of activities. Individual differences in visual search task and information processing speed are evident from recent works [27,28]. Individual differences in automatic processing due to priming are evident from [29].

References

1. Galotti, K.M.: Cognitive Psychology In and Out of the Laboratory. SAGE Publications Inc., Thousand Oaks (2013)
2. Sternberg, R.J.: Cognitive Psychology. Cengage Learning (2011)
3. Amazon mechanical turk. https://www.mturk.com/mturk/welcome. Accessed on 12/12/2014
4. Gamboa, H., Fred, A.: A behavioral biometric system based on human-computer interaction. Proc. SPIE **5404**, 381–392 (2004)
5. Ahmed, A., Traore, I.: A new biometric technology based on mouse dynamics. IEEE Trans. Dependable Secure Comput. **4**(3), 165–179 (2007)
6. Zheng, N., Paloski, A., Wang, H.: An efficient user verification system via mouse movements. In: Proceedings of the 18th ACM Conference on Computer and Communications Security CCS 2011, pp. 139–150. ACM, New York (2011)
7. Frank, M., Biedert, R., Ma, E., Martinovic, I., Song, D.: Touchalytics: on the applicability of touchscreen input as a behavioral biometric for continuous authentication. IEEE Trans. Inf. Forensics Secur. **8**(1), 136–148 (2013)
8. Wickens, C.D., Lee, J.D., Liu, Y., Gordon-Becker, S.: Introduction to Human Factors Engineering, 2nd edn. Pearson, Upper Saddle River (2003)
9. Van Zandt, T., Townsend, J.T.: Self-terminating versus exhaustive processes in rapid visual and memory search: an evaluative review. Percept. Psychophys. **53**(5), 563–580 (1993)
10. Bargh, J.A., Chen, M., Burrows, L.: Automaticity of social behavior: direct effects of trait construct and stereotype activation on action. J. Pers. Soc. Psychol. **71**(2), 230 (1996)
11. Sala Della, S., Gray, C., Baddeley, A., Allamano, N., Wilson, L.: Pattern span: a tool for unwelding visuo-spatial memory. Neuropsychologia **37**(10), 1189–1199 (1999)
12. Adams, J.A.: Human Factors Engineering. Macmillan Publishing Co Inc., New York (1989)
13. Hick, W.E.: On the rate of gain of information. Q. J. Exp. Psychol. **4**(1), 11–26 (1952)
14. Wand, M.P., Jones, M.C.: Kernel Smoothing, vol. 60. CRC Press, Boca Raton (1994)
15. Zucchini, W., Berzel, A., Nenadic, O.: Applied smoothing techniques (2003)
16. Rudemo, M.: Empirical choice of histograms and kernel density estimators. Scand. J. Stat. **9**, 65–78 (1982)
17. Bowman, A.W.: An alternative method of cross-validation for the smoothing of density estimates. Biometrika **71**(2), 353–360 (1984)
18. Jones, M.C., Marron, J.S., Sheather, S.J.: A brief survey of bandwidth selection for density estimation. J. Am. Stat. Assoc. **91**(433), 401–407 (1996)
19. Bolle, R.: Guide to Biometrics. Springer, New York (2004)
20. Brooke, J.: SUS-a quick and dirty usability scale. In: Jordan, J.W., Thomas, B., Weerdmester, B.A., McClelland, I.L. (eds.) Usability Evaluation in Industry, pp. 189–194. Taylor & Francis, London (1996)
21. Hamdy, O., Traoré, I.: Homogeneous physio-behavioral visual and mouse-based biometric. ACM Trans. Comput. -Hum. Interact. (TOCHI) **18**(3), 12 (2011)
22. Gaines, R.S., Lisowski, W., Press, S.J., Shapiro, N.: Authentication by keystroke timing: Some preliminary results. Technical report, DTIC Document (1980)

23. Villani, M., Tappert, C., Ngo, G., Simone, J., Fort, H.S., Cha, S.H.: Keystroke biometric recognition studies on long-text input under ideal and application-oriented conditions. In: Conference on Computer Vision and Pattern Recognition Workshop, 2006. CVPRW 2006, pp. 39–39. IEEE (2006)

24. Kung, S.Y., Mak, M.W., Lin, S.H.: Biometric Authentication: A Machine Learning Approach. Prentice Hall Professional Technical Reference, Upper Saddle River (2005)

25. Bojinov, H., Sanchez, D., Reber, P., Boneh, D., Lincoln, P.: Neuroscience meets cryptography: designing crypto primitives secure against rubber hose attacks. In: Proceedings of the 21st USENIX Security Symposium (2012)

26. Lewis, J.R., Sauro, J.: The factor structure of the system usability scale. In: Kurosu, M. (ed.) HCD 2009. LNCS, vol. 5619, pp. 94–103. Springer, Heidelberg (2009)

27. Chiang, A., Atkinson, R.C.: Individual differences and interrelationships among a select set of cognitive skills. Mem. Cogn. 4(6), 661–672 (1976)

28. Jensen, A.R.: Individual Differences in the Hick Paradigm. Ablex Publishing, Norwood (1987)

29. Dovidio, J.F., Gaertner, S.L.: Stereotyping, prejudice, and discrimination: Spontaneous and deliberative processes. Paper presented at the meeting of the Society of Experimental Social Psychology, Washington, DC., October 1995

Smart and Secure Cross-Device Apps for the Internet of Advanced Things

Christoph Busold[1], Stephan Heuser[1]([✉]), Jon Rios[1], Ahmad-Reza Sadeghi[2], and N. Asokan[3]

[1] Intel CRI-SC, TU Darmstadt, Darmstadt, Germany
{christoph.busold,stephan.heuser,rios.jon}trust.cased.de
[2] TU Darmstadt/CASED, Darmstadt, Germany
ahmad.sadeghi@trust.cased.de
[3] Aalto University and University of Helsinki, Espoo, Finland
asokan@acm.org

Abstract. Today, cross-device communication and intelligent resource sharing among smart devices is limited and inflexible: Typically devices cooperate using fixed interfaces provided by custom-built applications, which users need to install manually. This is tedious, time consuming, bears security and privacy risks, and contrasts the idea of Internet of Things (IoT) where intelligent devices operate in concert to enrich the overall user experience by sharing resources and capabilities.

We present Xapp, a context-aware service mobility framework for Android. Our goal is to enable users to securely distribute the functionality of applications to mutually untrusted smart devices, e.g., to enable a smartphone to use a nearby Android TV screen as a display for a video call, let a smartphone navigation app direct an autonomous vehicle, or let it use the vehicle for an object-recognition task rather than using a cloud service with the attendant privacy risks. We built a prototype for Android as the first step towards this goal. Our system is a set of extensions to the existing Remote-OSGi service platform, an emerging industry standard which unfortunately does not secure the communications between devices. This paper describes our proposal for the required security architecture. We designed and implemented an authentication protocol suite, where trust is bootstrapped using NFC for the sake of usability. On top of this we built a fine-grained access control system so that mutually mistrustful Xapp apps can be used simultaneously in the same neighborhood and even on the same devices. Hence, with Xapp users can run an Android app across multiple devices without having to install it on each of them individually. As proof of concept we present the implementation and evaluation of a video call app.

1 Introduction

Advanced embedded devices have been undergoing a dramatic development in the last decade: different classes of devices in different form factors, ranging from personal information and entertainment devices (e.g., smartphones,

© International Financial Cryptography Association 2015
R. Böhme and T. Okamoto (Eds.): FC 2015, LNCS 8975, pp. 272–290, 2015.
DOI: 10.1007/978-3-662-47854-7_17

tablets, smart TVs, wearables, automotive head units for smart cars to industrial automation systems and sensors in smart factories, are being equipped with increasing computing, storage and wireless communication capabilities. The Internet of Things (IoT) promises to intelligently interconnect these devices where applications adapt to available resources in the environment and share their capabilities to improve the user-experience and maintainability significantly: Consider for instance placing a video call from a smartphone using a nearby Android TV [2] as a display; a smartphone navigation app using the more precise GPS sensors and larger display of the head unit available in a modern vehicle; letting a navigation app direct an autonomous vehicle, or resource-constrained devices outsourcing computationally expensive tasks (e.g., object recognition) to other more powerful devices.

However, today the ability for such intelligent and adaptive device collaboration falls short. Current network discovery and media sharing protocols, like UPnP [47], DLNA [16], Apple Airplay [5] or Samsung AllShare [40], limit themselves to a set of pre-defined services. More sophisticated use-cases for advanced device collaboration, be it in the area of smart vehicles, smart buildings or personal entertainment, require custom software components that have to be installed, managed and configured individually on each device. This is tedious, time consuming, and poses security and privacy risks. Moreover, existing solutions for collaboration among devices based on migrating code from one device to another (e.g., [20,37]) do not adequately address the security and privacy risks.

Our Goal and Contributions. We present Xapp, a context-aware service mobility framework for Android, which aims at enhancing resource sharing among advanced IoT devices. Our main contributions are as follows:

1. The design of a framework that enables users to securely run an Android app across multiple devices without having to install it on each of them individually.
2. The design and implementation of an authentication protocol suite where trust is bootstrapped using NFC for the sake of usability (Sect. 3).
3. A prototype of this framework on the service-based R-OSGi [36,39] software stack, an emerging industry standard which we extended with mechanisms for fine-grained access control and secure communication (Sect. 4).
4. A proof-of-concept evaluation of a video calling application built using Xapp (Sects. 5 and 6).

Xapp differs from prior work (Sect. 7) on distributed cross-device functionality in two major aspects. First, it provides fine-grained access control on sensitive resources using a lightweight token-based authentication and authorization system. Second, it allows users to keep sensitive assets on their trusted devices. By adopting standard technologies where possible, Xapp supports multiple COTS operating systems and can be deployed either as a system-centric platform component or be installed as an app without changes to the underlying operating system.

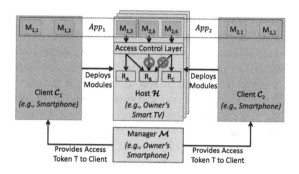

Fig. 1. System model: entities and interaction

2   System Model

2.1   Entities and Interactions

Our system model, presented in Fig. 1, involves the following entities:

- The **Host** $\mathcal{H}$ provides resources R to other devices (e.g., a smart TV sharing its screen, camera and microphone).
- The **Manager** $\mathcal{M}$ grants access to resources R on $\mathcal{H}$ to other devices (e.g., the smartphone of the smart TV's owner).
- The **Client** $\mathcal{C}$ initiates the communication and distributes parts of its application to $\mathcal{H}$ in order to use resources R.

In our model entities are devices in a network, identified by their IP addresses resolved by using service discovery (cf. Sect. 7). Applications are partitioned into a set of modules M, which represent different tasks implemented by the application and depend on a set of available resources R. This module-based approach is in line with recent component-based programming models used, for instance, Android (cf. Sect. 4.1). We use cryptographic *access tokens* T to authenticate a client $\mathcal{C}$ to a host $\mathcal{H}$ and to define $\mathcal{C}$'s privileges to access resources R on $\mathcal{H}$. Consider a video call where a user wants to access the resources of a smart TV with her smartphone. In Fig. 1 the client $\mathcal{C}_1$ (user's smartphone) requests an access token T for $\mathcal{H}$ (smart TV) as well as resources R_A and R_B (e.g., camera and microphone to place a video call) from $\mathcal{M}$ (TV owner's smartphone). The owner authorizes this request using a graphical user interface on $\mathcal{M}$. Client $\mathcal{C}_2$ similarly requests an access token T for $\mathcal{H}$ and R_C (e.g., Internet connection). They upload their respective application modules $M_{1,3}$, $M_{2,3}$ and $M_{2,4}$ to $\mathcal{H}$. After access tokens have been issued, $\mathcal{M}$ does not have to be involved at runtime anymore. The modules on the clients $\mathcal{C}_1$ and $\mathcal{C}_2$ and the modules on $\mathcal{H}$ form the distributed applications App_1 and App_2.

2.2   Threat Model

External Adversary. The main security objective of our solution is to prevent unauthorized access from one device to sensitive resources R of another device.

External attackers $\mathcal{A}_{ext}$ are classical Dolev-Yao adversaries [17]: They do not have access to any of the devices or application modules M involved, but have full control over the network and thus can eavesdrop, manipulate, inject and replay messages. Such an attack could be used, for example, to inject malicious code into an application module, which is transmitted to another device.

Internal Adversary. Each client $\mathcal{C}$, host $\mathcal{H}$ or application module can potentially be an internal attacker $\mathcal{A}_{int}$, resulting in two possible scenarios. First, a malicious $\mathcal{C}$ can send a malicious module to $\mathcal{H}$ in order to gain unauthorized access to resources R and sensitive information, or even infect the platform or other modules M on $\mathcal{H}$. Xapp should mitigate attacks from the malicious module on $\mathcal{H}$ or any other application modules M running on it.

Second, a malicious host $\mathcal{H}$, hosting application modules M, may attempt to compromise the client application, for example by tampering with modules M running on $\mathcal{H}$. Xapp should support the developer in protecting his application against such attacks by storing and processing sensitive data only on the user's trusted device (e.g., his smartphone acting as client $\mathcal{C}$).

2.3 Objectives and Assumptions

Assumptions. Every host $\mathcal{H}$ trusts its manager $\mathcal{M}$ and vice versa. This means, $\mathcal{H}$ defers to $\mathcal{M}$ as the authority who defines access control policies for local resources R, and $\mathcal{M}$ trusts $\mathcal{H}$ to enforce these access control policies correctly. Moreover, the operating system and deployed software on $\mathcal{H}$ provide sound protection against privilege escalation attacks, i.e., we assume that a module deployed by $\mathcal{A}_{int}$ cannot bypass existing access control mechanisms.

Security Objectives. Given our assumptions our main security objective is that a user's sensitive data, applications and modules M on the user's own device (client $\mathcal{C}$), are protected from the internal adversary $\mathcal{A}_{int}$ on a host $\mathcal{H}$. Furthermore, $\mathcal{A}_{int}$ can neither compromise other sensitive applications nor modules M and their data on a connected host $\mathcal{H}$. An external attacker $\mathcal{A}_{ext}$ cannot gain access to any resource R by eavesdropping on or manipulating the network channel.

Functional Objectives. The performance overhead should be low, meaning minor user interaction and the capability to automatically move modules M to a host $\mathcal{H}$. Moreover, application modules M should run independently of the underlying hardware and operating system. This requires compatibility with common operating systems. Ideally Xapp should run as a third party application.

3 Design of Xapp

In this section we present the design of our cross-device application framework Xapp. It comprises a security architecture for sandboxing modules of different applications and stakeholders (cf. Sect. 3.1) and a generic resource control

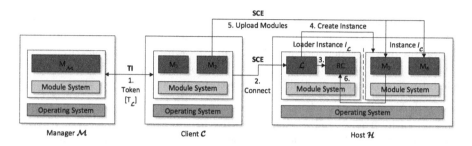

Fig. 2. Xapp Architecture

concept (cf. Sect. 3.2). Furthermore, Sect. 3.3 describes the token-based authentication and authorization system.

3.1 Architecture Overview and High-Level Idea

Our generic architecture is shown in Fig. 2. On every host $\mathcal{H}$ a component called Loader $\mathcal{L}$ manages the modules M running on $\mathcal{H}$ and their privileges to access resources R on $\mathcal{H}$. $\mathcal{L}$ is initially installed and configured on each host, either by the owner or by the device vendor. The owner takes ownership of $\mathcal{L}$ by establishing a shared symmetric key $K_{\mathcal{M}}$ between the manager $\mathcal{M}$ (e.g., his smartphone) and $\mathcal{L}$. For our implementation we use a key agreement protocol over NFC due to the required physical proximity [23]. This approach is similar to the *resurrecting duckling model* [45], where physical contact creates a binding between two entities.

Xapp enables the developer to encapsulate the functionality of an application on a client $\mathcal{C}$ into a set of modules M, which potentially use resources on a remote host $\mathcal{H}$. We implemented an adaptation of the *extended duckling model* [44] to control which clients may upload modules to $\mathcal{H}$, and which resources may be used by a client $\mathcal{C}$. When a client $\mathcal{C}$ wants to use resources R of $\mathcal{H}$, it first requests an access token $[T_{\mathcal{L}}]$ from $\mathcal{H}$'s manager $\mathcal{M}$ (Step 1) using the Token Issuing protocol (TI). $\mathcal{C}$ authenticates to $\mathcal{L}$ using the Secure Channel Establishment protocol (SCE) with this access token (Step 2), which is forwarded to the Resource Controller (RC) (Step 3). The relevant protocols will be explained later in Sect. 3.3. Next, $\mathcal{L}$ creates a restricted execution environment $I_{\mathcal{C}}$ (Step 4) for modules M uploaded by $\mathcal{C}$ (Step 5). Modules which trust each other (e.g., modules belonging to the same application) may share an instance. Modules run inside their instance $I_{\mathcal{C}}$, which provides life-cycle management. $\mathcal{L}$ is executed inside a privileged instance $I_{\mathcal{L}}$ with access to all resources.

In Xapp instances are created on demand and removed when they are no longer needed, e.g., because their modules are removed. To protect $\mathcal{H}$ from malicious modules of the internal adversary $\mathcal{A}_{int}$, instances $I_{\mathcal{C}}$ follow the principle of least privilege, meaning that direct access to resources is limited to what is basically required by their modules. When a module aims to access shared resources on $\mathcal{H}$, it queries RC located inside $I_{\mathcal{L}}$ (Step 6). RC mediates access to resources R based on a Policy $P_{\mathcal{C},\mathcal{H}}$ included in the token $[T_{\mathcal{L}}]$, as described in the following section.

3.2 Resource Control Concept

When the manager $\mathcal{M}$ creates an authentication token $[T_{\mathcal{L}}]$ for the client $\mathcal{C}$, it can bind a Policy $P_{\mathcal{C},\mathcal{H}}$ to this token. Policies are forwarded by the Loader $\mathcal{L}$ to the Resource Controller RC, which is responsible for their enforcement on $\mathcal{H}$. A Policy consists of a set of individual privileges. Each privilege Privilege(R, $\mathcal{C}$, $\mathcal{H}$, S) = $Yes \,|\, No \,|\, Ask$ describes whether the instance $I_{\mathcal{C}}$ may access resource R on $\mathcal{H}$, optionally limited to a given state S (e.g., time of day). The Ask value specifies that $\mathcal{H}$ should consult $\mathcal{M}$ at runtime when $I_{\mathcal{C}}$ tries to access this resource. Policies can further contain optional lifecycle constraints to address possible resource starvation attacks by malicious modules. For example, $\mathcal{M}$ can define that a shared resource is only accessible for a specified amount of time, or that $I_{\mathcal{C}}$ should be removed after a certain time span.

Consider the video call use case, where $\mathcal{M}$ creates a policy restricting the access of $\mathcal{C}$'s instance $I_{\mathcal{C}}$ to the camera, microphone and screen of the smart TV $\mathcal{H}$, thereby protecting the privacy of the smart TV's owner. Modules installed by $\mathcal{C}$ are denied access to other sensitive resources, such as photos accessible by the TV. Finally, $\mathcal{M}$ uses a state-aware policy to allow $I_{\mathcal{C}}$ to access the camera and microphone only when the video call module is running in the foreground on $\mathcal{H}$, and to automatically remove $I_{\mathcal{C}}$ after one hour.

3.3 Authentication and Authorization Protocols

Our design includes a flexible and secure protocol suite providing for authentication of clients, authorization for resource access and security on the communication links. This protocol suite is based on standard cryptographic primitives and due to space constraints we moved its details in Appendix A. Our protocol suite also provides offline verification, i.e., the access control token is verifiable by $\mathcal{H}$ if its manager $\mathcal{M}$ is not available. Offline verification can be achieved by token-based protocols such as Kerberos [34]. However, Kerberos requires a database with known clients, which is managed outside the protocol. Therefore we designed a custom token protocol, which can handle both ad-hoc as well as long-term clients and at the same time reduces the complexity of Kerberos.

Overview. Our protocol consists of two parts (cf. Fig. 2). During the *Token Issuing Protocol* (TI) $\mathcal{M}$ issues a Token $[T_{\mathcal{L}}]$ to $\mathcal{C}$. $[T_{\mathcal{L}}]$ is bound to a key $K_{\mathcal{C}}$, which is computed through a Diffie-Hellman key agreement scheme DH between $\mathcal{M}$ and $\mathcal{C}$. $\mathcal{C}$ uses $[T_{\mathcal{L}}]$ to authenticate itself to $\mathcal{L}$ and to establish a secure channel using the *Secure Channel Establishment Protocol* (SCE). It proceeds to request a new execution instance $I_{\mathcal{C}}$. Finally, $\mathcal{C}$ uses the SCE protocol to connect to $I_{\mathcal{C}}$ by creating a new token $[T_{I_{\mathcal{C}}}]$ encrypted by K_C and with a randomly chosen key K_I inside. The only setup requirement is a shared symmetric secret key between $\mathcal{M}$ and $\mathcal{H}$, denoted $K_{\mathcal{M}}$, which is used to authenticate and encrypt tokens with the help of an authenticated encryption scheme AE. As noted in Sect. 3.1 $K_{\mathcal{M}}$ has been established during the initial pairing between $\mathcal{M}$ and $\mathcal{H}$.

Interactive Privilege Evaluation. As described in Sect. 3.3, resources protected by an *Ask* privilege require runtime consultation of the manager $\mathcal{M}$.

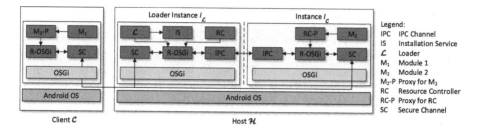

Fig. 3. Architecture of the implementation

For that purpose, the relevant host $\mathcal{H}$ sends the identity of $\mathcal{C}$ and the identifier of the requested resource R together with a nonce $\mathcal{N}$ to $\mathcal{M}$. To secure the authenticity of $\mathcal{M}$'s responses, $\mathcal{M}$ computes a message authentication code (MAC) over the decision value and the original request including the nonce $\mathcal{N}$ using the shared secret key $K_{\mathcal{M}}$. If $\mathcal{H}$ fails to verify this MAC or does not receive a response at all within a certain time frame, it defaults to deny the request.

Revocation. Since our solution focuses on time-limited deployment of cross-device applications via lifecycle constrains (cf. Sect. 3.2) we do not consider revocation in our current implementation. However, token revocation could be added to Xapp by means of revocation lists. The integrity and authenticity of revocation lists can be assured using MACs based on a key derived from $K_{\mathcal{M}}$. Alternatively, we could adopt a token status protocol comparable to OCSP [41], but since Xapp is designed for offline token validation we deem revocation lists to be better suited.

4   Implementation

Our implementation is based on the Apache Felix OSGi [3,36] framework and the R-OSGi RPC layer [39]. We run our framework on Android, which serves as an example of a modern operating system for advanced IoT devices. We highlight the technical challenges we had to tackle and describe several security extensions we developed for R-OSGi. Figure 3 shows the instantiated components.

4.1   Platform Considerations

Module System. We implemented the module system is on the OSGi platform [36], a widely-deployed platform-independent industry standard for software modularization. OSGi allows us to easily integrate existing solutions that can extend our framework with further desired functionality (such as service discovery protocols [4,29,47]), which is orthogonal to our work. OSGi divides applications into modules, called *bundles*. A bundle is a collection of self-contained Java packages, arbitrary data and a manifest file. This manifest contains meta data about the bundle along with its platform requirements, provided services and dependencies on other bundles. At runtime, bundles interact via services, which can be published to and consumed by other bundles.

Remote OSGi. The adoption of OSGi enables us to seamlessly connect modules on different devices using the remote service layer of Remote OSGi (R-OSGi) [39]. R-OSGi extends the concept of services in OSGi to remote services, which can be published to and accessed from other framework instances, possibly running on different machines. At runtime, R-OSGi can connect to other hosts running R-OSGi and search them for available remote services.

Target Operating System. The platform independence of OSGi allows us to instantiate our framework on a wide range of operating systems for advanced IoT devices with different capabilities, ranging from mobile devices and automotive head units to desktop PCs and virtual machines in cloud environments. Individual security aspects of the target operating system (most importantly application isolation and access control) must be considered when adopting our framework. For example, Android relies on process-level permissions and per-app sandboxes.[1]

For our prototype implementation we selected Android as the target platform not only because it is the most popular platform for smartphones and tablets [19], but also because it is deployed in other IoT market segments, e.g., automotive [1] and home entertainment [2]. While documentation on Android Auto is currently limited, Android TV is a standard Android distribution optimized for large screens and thus allows the deployment of Xapp without further modifications. Android is based on a Linux kernel and executes every app inside a Java virtual machine running within a separate process under its own Linux User Id (UID), which is set at installation time. Hence different applications are sandboxed at operating system level. Furthermore, Android enforces a permission framework on processes, which restricts access to system services and resources like network, file system or sensors.

4.2 Loader

The Loader $\mathcal{L}$ (see Fig. 3) is $\mathcal{H}$'s interface to an external client $\mathcal{C}$ and exposes its functionality to remote and local application modules via R-OSGi remote services. This allows clients to create, remove, start and stop their instances on a host and to deploy application modules, as explained in the following. The Loader is implemented as a set of OSGi bundles running inside a privileged instance $I_{\mathcal{L}}$.

Installer Service. The Installer Service (IS, cf. Fig. 3) is used by $\mathcal{L}$ to create and remove client instances on $\mathcal{H}$. While the implementation of IS is platform-specific,

---

[1] On PCs, IBM's Java JVM 8 provides a multi-tenancy environment [26], which efficiently isolates Java applications executed in one Java VM and uses the Java Security Manager [27] for access control. Another approach particularly interesting in the context of cloud-based environments is the GuestVM project [46], which provides isolated Java runtime environments on top of the Xen hypervisor.

it communicates using a standardized OSGi service interface with the platform-agnostic Loader component. On Android, instances are implemented as Android applications and isolated by Android's sandboxing mechanism (cf. Sect. 4.1). Our Installer Service IS for Android uses a base template application in the form of an Android Application Package (APK), which includes the OSGi framework and required bundles to communicate with C (e.g., R-OSGi). Android apps are identified by a unique package name. Accordingly, IS rewrites the package file with a new name and configures parameters specific to the new instance I_C, such as the listening port of R-OSGi.

The Loader $\mathcal{L}$ can be distributed by the device manufacturer as an Android system app or installed by the user as a standard Android app on a host $\mathcal{H}$. When app modules are deployed by a client C, the installation of the client-specific instance I_C is ideally performed silently without user interaction once $\mathcal{H}$ has validated C's access token. Due to Android-specific limitations this is only possible when $\mathcal{L}$ is an Android system app: For security reasons third-party apps cannot install or uninstall other applications silently on stock Android. Thus, if the Loader is installed as a standard third-party app on a stock Android device, our framework requires minimal user interaction, since the user has to approve the installation of I_C by clicking a button on $\mathcal{H}$.

Resource Controller. The Resource Controller (RC) exposes resources of the host $\mathcal{H}$ to a client's instance I_C using a R-OSGi service. It is executed inside the privileged Loader instance $I_{\mathcal{L}}$, which holds all permissions required to access the resources R (e.g., contacts or camera) exposed to instances I. Access to resources is mediated according to the instance-specific access control policy defined by $\mathcal{M}$ and contained in the token $[T_{\mathcal{L}}]$. The implementation of the Resource Controller is platform-specific, while its interface is the same on different operating systems.

In general, there are two possible approaches to implement access control on resources: Either the Resource Controller RC uses the existing platform-specific access control mechanisms, or RC implements the required access control hooks itself. Both approaches have advantages and disadvantages:

In the former case, RC maps privileges to operating system specific access control mechanisms. For example, Android uses *permissions* for access control on APIs as well as *discretionary* and *mandatory* access control [43] for kernel-level resources. More advanced architectures [9,24] provide interfaces to program-matically influence system-level access control decisions at runtime and could potentially be integrated with Xapp. However, such an integration would limit our solution and violate our interoperability requirements.

In the latter case, RC implements access control on resources itself, also considering fine-grained and state-aware access control policies. We opted for this approach in our implementation, since it does not require changes to the underlying operating system.

4.3   Our Extensions to Remote OSGi

Our implementation provides several security extensions to the Remote OSGi (R-OSGi) framework, as described in the following.

Secure Network Channel. The R-OSGi middleware (cf. Sect. 4.1) offers by default only TCP communication and provides no protection against an external attacker $\mathcal{A}_{ext}$. To enable secure communication between the Loader instance $I_{\mathcal{L}}$, the client $\mathcal{C}$ and his remote instance $I_{\mathcal{C}}$, we extended R-OSGi with a secure network channel (SC), which provides both confidentiality and integrity using authenticated encryption with a symmetric key (see SCE protocol in Appendix A).

Local IPC Channel. To provide efficient communication between different OSGi frameworks in separate sandboxed instances on the same host $\mathcal{H}$ (e.g., $I_{\mathcal{C}}$ and $I_{\mathcal{L}}$), we implemented an IPC communication channel using domain sockets.

Channel Filter. Since the original design of R-OSGi does not differentiate between different network channels, a service can only decide whether it wants to be published to remote hosts or not, and in that case it is always registered on *all* available channels. This is insufficient, if one wants to expose a service only via IPC to local instances executed on the same host $\mathcal{H}$. Therefore, we modified the R-OSGi implementation to include a filter on communication channels, so that services can choose the channels they are available on.

Endpoint Identification. Another challenge is that services do not know over which channel and from which endpoint they were called (i.e., remotely or locally), because this connection between the function call and the originating channel endpoint is hidden by the abstraction of R-OSGi. In our model, this information is crucial in order to decide whether access to a service should be granted or not, depending on the identity of the caller (i.e., modules M of a client $\mathcal{C}$ executed in instance $I_{\mathcal{C}}$). Thus we implemented a function to retrieve the identity of the current caller from R-OSGi. For the IPC channel we get the Linux UID of the connected process and in case of the secure network channel we extract the identity from the token that was used during the channel establishment protocol.

4.4   Xapp Development Model

To support Xapp, apps need to adhere to the (R-)OSGi programming model, since Xapp is not limited to one specific operating system. Specifically, developers need to integrate an OSGi runtime environment into their applications, such as the open-source implementation *Apache Felix* [3], on top of which the Xapp bundles (mainly R-OSGi and the Loader) as well as application-specific bundles are executed. Consequently, application modules which should migrate between hosts need to be implemented as OSGi bundles. These bundles at runtime communicate with other bundles on the local or remote host via OSGi services. OSGi services are comparable to Android services in that they adhere to the same RPC

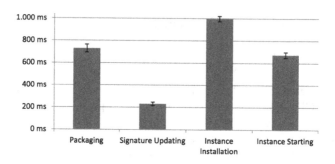

Fig. 4. Performance Evaluation (Basic Instance)

communication paradigm. To ease the work of developers who want to adopt our solution, Xapp provides a set of service definitions for common resources, such as *contacts information*, *camera* and *microphone*.

5   Evaluation

To evaluate our implementation we used two Samsung Galaxy S3 I9300 smartphones running Android 4.0.4 (client and manager) and a Nexus 10 Tablet running Android 4.2.1 (host) connected over a 802.11bgn wireless network. We use the industry standard algorithms AES-256 in EAX mode as authenticated encryption scheme AE and ECDH-256 as key exchange protocol DH.

Performance. We evaluated the performance of different components in our solution. For the Android-based implementation of the token issuing protocol we measured the elapsed time between starting the communication with the manager and receiving the token $[T_L]$. Overall the protocol takes 308.28 ± 27.73 milliseconds on average over 20 runs.

For our framework we first performed microbenchmarks to measure the time required for creating a basic instance containing no bundles. This includes all steps starting from verifying the access token $[T_L]$, creating the application package, installing and finally starting the instance I. The results are presented in Fig. 4 and show the average and the standard deviation of the time required to perform all steps over 20 runs. These numbers are reasonable considering that our implementation has not been optimized for performance yet, and we refer to our case study below for further discussion of these results. Further, we verified that the OSGi framework incurs no noticeable performance overhead at runtime using the Java Linpack benchmark [32] both in a regular Android app and in a Xapp module. The average performance over 20 runs is 143.15 ± 0.13 MFlops and 137.41 ± 0.33 MFlops respectively, which shows a small difference of 4.18 %.

We also performed microbenchmarks to measure the performance impact introduced by our access control architecture. In our Android-based implementation we query the contacts database to retrieve a single contact both in a regular Android app and in a Xapp module. The process takes on average 17.47 ± 4.41

and 65.50 ± 3.86 ms respectively over 1000 runs. The high standard deviation is caused by varying system load. The difference of around 48 ms introduced by the redirection of calls via the Resource Controller RC and the access control enforcement is partially caused by marshalling the data over the domain socket. The overhead can be reduced by mapping the memory into the process, for example using Binder IPC, instead of copying it.

Interoperability and Portability. Our design enables the isolation of modules deployed on any operating system and hardware platform which provide adequate sandboxing and privilege separation capabilities. Since our framework operates on the application level, it requires no changes to the operating system, as demonstrated by our implementation on Android. When an Android device vendor deploys Xapp, it is even possible to install new instances without user interaction by installing the Loader as a *system* app (see Sect. 4.1).

It should be noted that while we instantiated our framework on Android, our architecture only requires a standard-compliant Java Runtime Environment with an OSGi framework and a platform-dependent isolation and privilege separation mechanism (cf. Sect. 4.1). Java is used on a variety of operating systems and platforms, from smart mobile devices to mainframes, and open-source implementations of the Java Virtual Machine and a of different OSGi implementations are available.

Usability. Pairing of devices via NFC has been adopted for a wide range of consumer devices, such as printers and Bluetooth speakers. Our performance measurements (cf. Fig. 4) indicate that the time required to deploy app modules on one or more hosts (cf. Fig. 4) is reasonable considering the alternative, which is to manually search, install and later uninstall an app on each host. While the definition of access control rules in the manager app is straightforward, one possible limitation is that with a growing number of rules a user might be tempted to always allow any requests for access to privileges by a client [18]. However, since the functionality of app modules is limited and tailored to specific use cases, they only need access to a very limited set of resources, which limits the number of privileges a manager has to consider.

Proof of Concept: Video Call Application. To demonstrate the advantages and feasibility of our solution we implemented the video calling use case, where Alice uses her smartphone (Client $\mathcal{C}$) and Hector's Smart TV (Host $\mathcal{H}$) to place a video phone call to Bob. This use case highlights an advantage of app partitioning over just connecting the TV to the phone: The video stream does not have to be routed through Alice's smartphone, but can be processed and sent to the TV directly by Bob's smartphone. Furthermore, Xapp protects Alice's privacy in case the TV is untrusted, since Alice does not have to enter her login credentials on the potentially malicious smart TV. Instead, she can keep sensitive data (e.g., login credentials or contact information) on her trusted device (her smartphone).

During the implementation and evaluation of Xapp we involved a team of eight students and staff members who performed preliminary usability tests by initiating a call between two Android smartphones using a nearby smart TV (represented by a Nexus 10 tablet, see Sect. 5). Currently we are working on a more extensive and representative usability study.

Table 1. Performance Evaluation (Case Study)

Step	Average Time (ms)
Signature Updating	330.86 ± 12.86
Instance Installation	1,122.16 ± 32.47
Instance Startup	2,228.47 ± 48.49
Bundle Transmission	1,837.77 ± 49.79
Repackaging	1,271.20 ± 81.16
Total	6,790.46 ± 106.43

Table 1 presents the performance measurement results for creating an instance within this use case. In contrast to the basic instance above, these numbers contain a transmission phase, where modules with an overall size of 34.2 KByte are sent to the host and added to the installation package, which increases the startup time. The total time of our unoptimized case study implementation takes about 6.79 seconds to deploy the relevant app modules on a host $\mathcal{H}$, which is comparable to downloading and installing apps via an app market. Note that a client $\mathcal{C}$ can deploy modules on multiple hosts in parallel and in contrast to classic applications our cross-device apps do not require any further lifecycle management such as updates and configuration on the involved devices.

6   Security Considerations

In this section we discuss how Xapp achieves the previously defined security goals (cf. Sect. 2.3).

External Adversary. An external adversary $\mathcal{A}_{ext}$ needs valid access tokens to gain access to either the loader $\mathcal{L}$ on host $\mathcal{H}$ or an instance $I_{\mathcal{C}}$ deployed by a client $\mathcal{C}$. The initial pairing between $\mathcal{H}$ and the manager $\mathcal{M}$, during which a shared symmetric key $K_{\mathcal{M}}$ is established, is performed through confidential and authenticated communication. In our implementation we establish this key over NFC which is resistant against man-in-the-middle attacks due to the required physical proximity [23]. Without knowledge of the cryptographic key $K_{\mathcal{M}}$, $\mathcal{A}_{ext}$ cannot generate a valid access token $[T_{\mathcal{L}}]$ for $\mathcal{L}$. Similarly the properties of NFC also protect the authenticity of $\mathcal{M}$ and $\mathcal{C}$ when $\mathcal{M}$ issues a confidentiality-protected token $[T_{\mathcal{L}}]$ to $\mathcal{C}$. Without access to the key $K_{\mathcal{C}}$ stored in the token $[T_{\mathcal{L}}]$ $\mathcal{A}_{ext}$ is unable to deploy modules on $\mathcal{H}$. At runtime, $\mathcal{C}$ and $I_{\mathcal{C}}$ communicate through authenticated and end-to-end encrypted channel. These properties are bootstrapped from the access token $[T_{\mathcal{L}}]$ issued to $\mathcal{C}$ by $\mathcal{M}$, which prevents $\mathcal{A}_{ext}$ from communicating with the deployed instance.

Internal Adversary. As noted in Sect. 2.2 either a client $\mathcal{C}$ or a host $\mathcal{H}$ can act as an internal adversary $\mathcal{A}_{int}$. On the one hand, $\mathcal{H}$ has to be protected from a malicious module deployed by $\mathcal{C}$. To this end, we designed an access control model that mediates which modules M may access sensitive resources R on $\mathcal{H}$. To implement this model the host operating system needs to run modules M deployed in $\mathcal{C}$'s instance $I_{\mathcal{C}}$ in an isolated least-privilege container. Our Android-based implementation uses the default UID-based sandboxing mechanism (cf. Sect. 4.1), which effectively prevents modules M from accessing sensitive resources R directly. Instead, Xapp modules M use the Resource Controller RC as a deputy who enforces the access control policy defined by the manager $\mathcal{M}$. The policy is protected by our token-based authentication and access control scheme, which ensures that it cannot be forged or modified by an internal adversary $\mathcal{A}_{int}$. Dynamic access control queries evaluated by $\mathcal{M}$ at runtime are protected against impersonation, modification and replay by message authentication codes with nonces.

On the other hand, sensitive resources R of a client $\mathcal{C}$ need to be protected from a malicious host $\mathcal{H}$. Xapp's module system encourages developers to enclose sensitive operations in separate modules. A client can decide where these modules are executed. Thus Xapp allows clients to ensure that modules accessing or storing sensitive data, such as long-term credentials or contact information, remain on their trusted devices. Of course the adversary could still exploit software errors, hidden backdoors or bad application design, but this risk is not higher than for traditional applications.

Discussion. To implement our access control model we rely on the integrity and security of (system) software on the host (see Sect. 2.3). This requirement is inherent to the solutions that operate purely on the application layer. Obviously the internal adversary $\mathcal{A}_{int}$ could extend its privileges at runtime if he could compromise any privileged system services. Furthermore, access control solutions at the application layer, such as Xapp, cannot provide resilience against confused deputy [22] or collusion [42] attacks. For example, malicious modules deployed by different stakeholders could combine their privileges and use inter-process communication (IPC) to exchange sensitive assets. Reliable control on IPC would require an extension of the underlying operating system [9,24], which is possible but does not conform to our interoperability requirement. Moreover, we note that attacks using side channels (e.g., [42]) are out of scope of our framework. We stress that these limitations apply to manually deployed applications as well.

7   Related Work

Service-Based Frameworks. Related work has proposed service-based architectures to orchestrate components of distributed applications on mobile and embedded devices [6,13,14,30], which mainly focus on aspects we consider orthogonal to our work, such as context-aware service composition and discovery. While Rellermeyer et al. describe the general applicability of their R-OSGi framework [39] in IoT scenarios [38], Preuveneers et al. [37] propose a service mobility framework for mobile devices, which enables dynamic service migration. Their approach considers state transfer and synchronization, service discovery and resource constraints, while Xapp focuses on security by allowing modules to migrate between platforms in a controlled fashion subject to strict access control.

Goncalves et al. [20] propose a service mobility framework for Android, which focuses on QoS and realtime requirements for the migration of stateful services. They extend standard Android application components to be applicable in distributed systems and enable component migration between devices. While their approach is limited to the Android OS and requires developers to split apps a-priori into separate packages, Xapp assembles platform-specific instances automatically at runtime and supports fine-grained access control on resources.

Computation Offloading. Cuervo et al. [11] and Kosta et al. [31] use application partitioning to offload computational tasks from mobile devices to the cloud to speed up computations and reduce battery consumption. In both system models, the cloud is inherently trusted, and security aspects are out of scope. Haerick et al. [21] propose an OSGi-based platform designed to outsource energy-intensive computations from mobile devices to other platforms.

Xapp is a more general approach, designed to allow different devices to collaborate and use resources and services in a distributed environment, where computation offloading is only one possible use case. Xapp provides better usability by adopting ad-hoc NFC-based trust establishments. Furthermore, our solution is designed to consider the security requirements of different stakeholders by isolating application components and by controlling access to shared resources.

Fine-Grained Access Control. Our access control scheme is similar to the approach presented by Jeon et al. [28]. Their solution redirects calls to APIs via a proxy app which enforces its own fine-grained access control model, while Xapp binds capabilities to cryptographic tokens in a distributed environment.

Several system-centric security extensions have been proposed for Android, ranging from enhancements to the permission system [10,33], mocking privacy-sensitive data [7,25,48] to integrating mandatory access control [8,9,24,35]. A combination of system centric security solutions (e.g., Flaskdroid [9] or ASM [24]) with Xapp would allow developers to adhere to Android's standard permissions and APIs, but would require modifications to the underlying operating system.

8   Conclusion

Computing in personal, commercial and industrial environments is undergoing a paradigm shift. The advent of the Internet of Things (IoT) enables new use cases, in which classical computing platforms, smartphones and tablets, wearables and further electronic devices operate in concert. Application lifecycle management and secure resource sharing become increasingly important aspects in this area.

To address these new challenges, we present the design and implementation of Xapp, a framework for smart and secure cross-device IoT applications for

Android. With Xapp, Android apps can run distributed on different devices without the need to install them manually on each device. We present a proof-of-concept implementation for a video call use case, and are currently extending this work in several directions, such as prototyping other use cases, and incorporating automatic code-partitioning techniques to provide flexible tools to developers.

Acknowledgements. This work has been supported by the European Union's FP7 grant 318424 (FutureID) and by the DFG within CRC 1119 CROSSING. We would like to thank Ross Anderson for his feedback that guided the paper's final revisions.

A   Protocols

As explained in Sect. 3.3, the protocols assume a shared symmetric secret key between $\mathcal{M}$ and $\mathcal{H}$, denoted $K_\mathcal{M} \in \{0,1\}^n$, which is used to authenticate and encrypt tokens with the help of an authenticated encryption scheme $\mathsf{AE} = (\mathsf{AEnc}, \mathsf{ADec})$, where n is a security parameter.

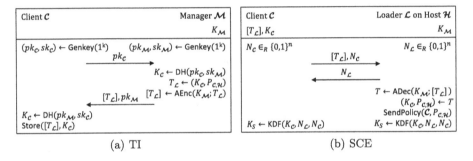

(a) TI   (b) SCE

Fig. 5. Token Issuing Protocol (TI) and Secure Channel Establishment Protocol (SCE)

Token Issuing Protocol. The Token Issuing Protocol (TI) is shown in Fig. 5(a). Both $\mathcal{M}$ and $\mathcal{C}$ generate a new asymmetric key pair. $\mathcal{C}$ sends its public key $pk_\mathcal{C}$ to $\mathcal{M}$ over an out-of-band channel. Generally we require that this channel is integrity-protected at least in one direction ($\mathcal{C}$ to $\mathcal{M}$), so that it is immune to man-in-the-middle attacks where an attacker attempts to replace $pk_\mathcal{C}$ with a different public key. We use Near-Field Communication (NFC), which directly allows $\mathcal{M}$ to verify the identity of $\mathcal{C}$ due to the physical proximity required for NFC. However, alternative implementations are also feasible, for example using QR codes. $\mathcal{M}$ creates a new Token $[T_\mathcal{L}]$, which contains the client key $K_\mathcal{C}$, as well as a description of $\mathcal{C}$'s privileges on $\mathcal{H}$, denoted by the Policy $P_{\mathcal{C},\mathcal{H}}$. $K_\mathcal{C}$ is derived using a key agreement scheme DH (e.g., Diffie-Hellmann [15]) between $\mathcal{C}$ and $\mathcal{M}$. Finally, $\mathcal{M}$ sends the token to $\mathcal{C}$ together with its public key $pk_\mathcal{M}$.

Secure Channel Establishment. The client $\mathcal{C}$ uses the Secure Channel Establishment Protocol (SCE) to connect to the Loader $\mathcal{L}$ as shown in Fig. 5(b): $\mathcal{C}$ sends

$[T_{\mathcal{L}}]$ and a randomly chosen nonce $N_{\mathcal{C}}$ to $\mathcal{L}$. $\mathcal{L}$ decrypts $[T_{\mathcal{L}}]$ using $K_{\mathcal{M}}$, thereby verifying its integrity due to the authenticated encryption. Next, $\mathcal{L}$ extracts $K_{\mathcal{C}}$ and the Policy $P_{\mathcal{C},\mathcal{H}}$, which is forwarded to the Resource Controller RC. $\mathcal{L}$ stores $K_{\mathcal{C}}$ securely in a database and later provides a decryption service to instances of $\mathcal{C}$, so that $K_{\mathcal{C}}$ cannot be exfiltrated by modules in $I_{\mathcal{C}}$. Then, $\mathcal{L}$ generates a random nonce $N_{\mathcal{L}}$, which it sends back to $\mathcal{C}$. Finally, both sides compute a shared secret session key $K_{\mathcal{S}} = \mathsf{KDF}(K_{\mathcal{C}} \,||\, N_{\mathcal{L}} \,||\, N_{\mathcal{C}})$ using a suitable key derivation function KDF [12]. In our implementation we use an HMAC/SHA1-based key derivation function. After this step, the secure channel establishment is completed and $K_{\mathcal{S}}$ will be used to protect all further communication.

$\mathcal{C}$ also uses SCE to connect to $I_{\mathcal{C}}$. Therefore $\mathcal{C}$ creates a new token $[T_{I_{\mathcal{C}}}]$ with a randomly chosen key K_I. Since no policy is established between the client and the host it attaches an empty dummy policy and encrypts the complete token $[T_{I_{\mathcal{C}}}]$ with $K_{\mathcal{C}}$. On the client side, $I_{\mathcal{C}}$ decrypts $[T_{I_{\mathcal{C}}}]$ using the decryption service provided by $\mathcal{L}$.

References

1. Android Auto. http://www.android.com/auto/
2. Android TV. http://www.android.com/tv/
3. Apache Felix. http://felix.apache.org/
4. Apache Felix UPnP. http://felix.apache.org/site/apache-felix-upnp.html
5. Apple Airplay. http://www.apple.com/de/airplay/
6. Arbanowski, S., Ballon, P., David, K., Droegehorn, O., Eertink, H., Kellerer, W., van Kranenburg, H., Raatikainen, K., Popescu-Zeletin, R.: I-centric communications: personalization, ambient awareness, and adaptability for future mobile services. Commun. Mag. IEEE **42**(9), 63–69 (2004)
7. Beresford, A.R., Rice, A., Skehin, N., Sohan, R.: MockDroid: trading privacy for application functionality on smartphones. In: HotMobile (2011)
8. Bugiel, S., Davi, L., Dmitrienko, A., Heuser, S., Sadeghi, A.-R., Shastry, B.: Practical and lightweight domain isolation on android. In: SPSM (2011)
9. Bugiel, S., Heuser, S., Sadeghi, A.-R.: Flexible and fine-grained mandatory access control on Android for diverse security and privacy policies. In: USENIX Security (2013)
10. Conti, M., Nguyen, V.T.N., Crispo, B.: CRePE: context-related policy enforcement for android. In: Burmester, M., Tsudik, G., Magliveras, S., Ilić, I. (eds.) ISC 2010. LNCS, vol. 6531, pp. 331–345. Springer, Heidelberg (2011)
11. Cuervo, E., Balasubramanian, A., Cho, D.-K., Wolman, A., Saroiu, S., Chandra, R., Bahl, P.: MAUI: making smartphones last longer with code offload. In: MobiSys (2010)
12. Dang, Q.: Recommendation for Existing Application-Specific Key Derivation Functions. NIST, 2010
13. de Deugd, S., Carroll, R., Kelly, K., Millett, B., Ricker, J.: Soda: service oriented device architecture. Pervasive Comput. IEEE **5**(3), 94–96 (2006)
14. de Souza, L.M.S., Spiess, P., Guinard, D., Köhler, M., Karnouskos, S., Savio, D.: SOCRADES: a web service based shop floor integration infrastructure. In: Floerkemeier, C., Langheinrich, M., Fleisch, E., Mattern, F., Sarma, S.E. (eds.) IOT 2008. LNCS, vol. 4952, pp. 50–67. Springer, Heidelberg (2008)

15. Diffie, W., Hellman, M.: New directions in cryptography. Inf. Theory, IEEE **22**(6), 644–654 (1976)
16. Digital Living Network Alliance. http://www.dlna.org/
17. Dolev, D., Yao, A.C.: On the security of public key protocols. Inf. Theory, IEEE **29**(2), 198–208 (1983)
18. Felt, A.P., Ha, E., Egelman, S., Haney, A., Chin, E., Wagner, D.: Android permissions: user attention, comprehension, and behavior. In: Proceedings of the Eighth Symposium on Usable Privacy and Security, SOUPS 2012, pp. 3:1–3:14. ACM, New York (2012)
19. Gartner Says Worldwide Tablet Sales Grew 68% in 2013. http://www.gartner.com/newsroom/id/2674215
20. Goncalves, J., Ferreira, L.L., Pinho, L.M., Silva, G.: Handling mobility on a QoS-Aware service-based framework for mobile systems. In: EUC (2010)
21. Haerick, W., Wauters, T., Develder, C., Turck, F.D., Dhoedt, B.: Transparent resource sharing framework for internet services on handheld devices. Annals of Telecommunications (2010)
22. Hardy, N.: The confused deputy: (or why capabilities might have been invented). SIGOPS Oper. Syst. Rev. **22**(4), 36–38 (1988)
23. Haselsteiner, E., Breitfuss, K.: Security in near field communication. In: RFIDSec (2006)
24. Heuser, S., Nadkarni, A., Enck, W., Sadeghi, A.-R.: Asm: a programmable interface for extending android security. In: USENIX Security Symposium (2014)
25. Hornyack, P., Han, S., Jung, J., Schechter, S., Wetherall, D.: These aren't the droids you're looking for: retrofitting android to protect data from imperious applications. In: ACM CCS (2011)
26. Introduction to Java multitenancy. http://www.ibm.com/developerworks/java/library/j-multitenant-java/index.html
27. SecurityManager (Java Platform SE 7). http://docs.oracle.com/javase/7/docs/api/java/lang/SecurityManager.html
28. Jeon, J., Micinski, K.K., Vaughan, J.A., Fogel, A., Reddy, N., Foster, J.S., Millstein, T.: Dr. Android and Mr. Hide: fine-grained permissions in android applications. In: SPSM (2012)
29. jSLP - Java SLP (Service Location Protocol) Implementation. http://jslp.sourceforge.net/
30. King, J., Bose, R., Yang, H.-I., Pickles, S., Helal, A.: Atlas: a service-oriented sensor platform: Hardware and middleware to enable programmable pervasive spaces. In: 2006 Proceedings of 31st IEEE Conference on Local Computer Networks, pp. 630–638. November 2006
31. Kosta, S., Aucinas, A., Hui, P., Mortier, R., Zhang, X.: ThinkAir: dynamic resource allocation and parallel execution in the cloud for mobile code offloading. In: INFOCOM (2012)
32. Linpack Benchmark - Java Version. http://www.netlib.org/benchmark/linpackjava/
33. Nauman, M., Khan, S., Zhang, X.: Apex: Extending android permission model and enforcement with user-defined runtime constraints. In: AsiaCCS (2010)
34. Neuman, B.C., Tso, T.: Kerberos: an authentication service for computer networks. Commun. Mag. IEEE **32**(9), 33–38 (1994)
35. Ongtang, M., McLaughlin, S., Enck, W., McDaniel, P.: Semantically rich application-centric security in android. In: ACSAC (2009)
36. OSGi Alliance. OSGi Service Platform Release 4. http://www.osgi.org/Main/HomePage

37. Preuveneers, D., Berbers, Y.: Context-driven migration and diffusion of pervasive services on the OSGi framework. IJAACS **3**(1), 3–22 (2010)
38. Rellermeyer, J.S., Duller, M., Gilmer, K., Maragkos, D., Papageorgiou, D., Alonso, G.: The software fabric for the internet of things. In: Floerkemeier, C., Langheinrich, M., Fleisch, E., Mattern, F., Sarma, S.E. (eds.) IOT 2008. LNCS, vol. 4952, pp. 87–104. Springer, Heidelberg (2008)
39. Rellermeyer, J.S., Alonso, G., Roscoe, T.: R-OSGi: distributed applications through software modularization. In: Cerqueira, R., Campbell, R.H. (eds.) Middleware 2007. LNCS, vol. 4834, pp. 1–20. Springer, Heidelberg (2007)
40. Samsung   Allshare.   http://developer.samsung.com/allshare-framework/technical-docs/FAQ
41. Santesson, S., Myers, M., Ankney, R., Malpani, A., Galperin, S., Adams, C.: X.509 Internet Public Key Infrastructure Online Certificate Status Protocol - OCSP. RFC 6960 (Proposed Standard) June 2013
42. Schlegel, R., Zhang, K., Zhou, X., Intwala, M., Kapadia, A., Wang, X.: Soundcomber: a stealthy and context-aware sound trojan for smartphones. In: NDSS. The Internet Society (2011)
43. Smalley, S., Craig, R.: Security Enhanced (SE) Android: bringing flexible MAC to android. In: Proceedings of NDSS (2013)
44. Stajano, F., Stajano, F.: The resurrecting duckling – what next?(transcript of discussion). In: Christianson, B., Crispo, B., Malcolm, J.A., Roe, M. (eds.) Security Protocols 2000. LNCS, vol. 2133, pp. 215–222. Springer, Heidelberg (2001)
45. Stajano, F., Anderson, R.J.: The resurrecting duckling: security issues for ad-hoc wireless networks. In: Proceedings of the 7th International Workshop on Security Protocols, pp. 172–194. Springer-Verlag, London (2000)
46. The Guest VM Project. https://kenai.com/projects/guestvm
47. Universal Plug-and-Play. http://www.upnp.org/
48. Zhou, Y., Zhang, X., Jiang, X., Freeh, V.W.: Taming information-stealing smartphone applications (on android). In: McCune, J.M., Balacheff, B., Perrig, A., Sadeghi, A.-R., Sasse, A., Beres, Y. (eds.) Trust 2011. LNCS, vol. 6740, pp. 93–107. Springer, Heidelberg (2011)

Cryptographic Primitives

Signatures and Efficient Proofs on Committed Graphs and NP-Statements

Thomas Groß[✉]

School of Computing Science, Newcastle University, Newcastle upon Tyne, UK
thomas.gross@ncl.ac.uk

Abstract. Digital signature schemes are a foundational building block enabling integrity and non-repudiation. We propose a graph signature scheme and corresponding proofs that allow a prover (1) to obtain a signature on a committed graph and (2) to subsequently prove to a verifier knowledge of such a graph signature. The graph signature scheme and proofs are a building block for certification systems that need to establish graph properties in zero-knowledge, as encentered in cloud security assurance or provenance. We extend the Camenisch-Lysyanskaya (CL) signature scheme to graphs and enable efficient zero-knowledge proofs of knowledge on graph signatures, notably supporting complex statements on graph elements. Our method is based on honest-verifier Σ-proofs and the strong RSA assumption. In addition, we explore the capabilities of graph signatures by establishing a proof system on graph 3-colorability (G3C). As G3C is NP-complete, we conclude that there exist Camenisch-Lysyanskaya proof systems for statements of NP languages.

1 Introduction

Digital signature schemes are foundational cryptographic primitives; they are useful in themselves to ensure integrity and non-repudiation and as building block of other systems. From their first construction by Rivest, Shamir and Adleman [1], digital signatures have been on bit-strings or group elements, on a committed sequence of bit-strings [2] or structure-preserved group elements [3]. In this work, we establish a signature scheme and corresponding proof system for committed graphs.

The basis for this work is the Camenisch-Lysyanskaya proof system: a collection of distributed algorithms that allow an issuer, a prover and a verifier to prove knowledge of committed values, issue a Camenisch-Lysyanskaya (CL) signature [2,4] on committed values, and prove knowledge of such a signature in zero-knowledge. It uses honest-verifier Σ-proofs (Schnorr proofs [5]) and has the advantage that it keeps all attributes in the exponent. It thereby allows us to access attributes with known discrete-logarithm-based zero-knowledge proofs of knowledge [5–10]. The attributes that could be signed are, however, limited by the message space of the CL-signature scheme: a sequence of small bit-strings.

We study how to extend the Camenisch-Lysyanskaya proof system to establish signatures on committed graphs and, by extension, on committed statements

© International Financial Cryptography Association 2015
R. Böhme and T. Okamoto (Eds.): FC 2015, LNCS 8975, pp. 293–314, 2015.
DOI: 10.1007/978-3-662-47854-7_18

from NP languages. Zero-knowledge proofs of certified or committed graphs and complex statements thereon have significant applications beyond classical graph proof techniques [11,12] or the more recent proposal of transitive signatures [13]. The key difference to earlier work is that the graph encoding is universal, enables direct access to graph elements, and allows a prover to be flexible in the statements proven after the graph is certified. Such graph proofs are instrumental in foundational techniques, such as the zero-knowledge proof of knowledge of certified Petri nets as well as in various application scenarios, such as for the certification of audited cloud topologies, for which we proposed a dedicated framework for topology proofs [14].

First, we establish a new encoding of undirected graphs into the message space of CL-Signatures. The encoding supports vertex- or edge-labeled graphs and is universal in the sense that it supports efficient proofs over arbitrary graph elements and their relations.

Second, we extend the Camenisch-Lysyanskaya proof system to graphs by integrating the graph encoding into integer commitments and the CL-Signature bootstrapping process. This allows prover and issuer to sign committed graphs with sub-graphs contributed by both parties and to prove knowledge of graph signatures in honest-verifier Σ-proofs. The obtained graph proof system in itself enables efficient zero-knowledge proofs of interesting graph properties, such as partitions, connectivity and isolation [14]. Graph proofs with a level of indirection between the authority on the graph (the issuer) and the verifier, established by a graph signature and with access to a wide range of graph properties, have not been covered by existing zero-knowledge graph proofs, such as [11,12,15], or transitive signatures [13]. While the former graph proofs are powerful constructions allowing for NP statements, e.g., graph 3-colorability or directed Hamiltonian cycle, their encoding does not cater for proving relations over graph elements in zero-knowledge. The latter is focused on the transitive closure along graph edges.

Third, we establish a proof system for graph 3-colorability (G3C) that allows us to obtain CL-Signatures on committed instances of 3-colorable graphs and to prove knowledge thereof to a verifier in zero-knowledge. Given that graph 3-colorability is NP-complete, we can lift the Camenisch-Lysyanskaya proof system to NP statements. Based on the 3-colorability proof system in a special RSA group and under the Strong RSA assumption, we show that there exists a Camenisch-Lysyanskaya proof system for any NP language, that is, the proof is capable of issuing CL-Signatures on committed statements from the NP language and to prove knowledge of such signatures in honest-verifier Σ-proofs. Whereas the G3C-reduction does not offer efficient constructions for graph proofs, it shows the expressiveness of graph signatures.

In effect, this work extends the reach of the Camenisch-Lysyanskaya proof system to signatures and proofs on structures of entire systems. To our knowledge, it is the first work to enable signatures on committed graphs. Notably, the graph elements are present in the exponents and, thereby, accessible to known discrete-logarithm-based zero-knowledge proofs on a wide range graph properties in honest-verifier proofs.

1.1 Outline

In Sect. 2, we discuss the preliminaries of our graph proof construction: Camenisch-Lysyanskaya signatures and Camenisch-Groß encoding. Based on the Camenisch-Groß encoding, we establish a canonical encoding for vertex- and edge-labeled graphs in Sect. 3. Section 4 establishes how integer commitments and CL-Signature are extended with the graph encoding. In Sect. 5 we show how graph 3-colorability can be expressed in the graph proof system as proof of the encoding's theoretical reach. Section 7 considers earlier work on zero-knowledge proofs and signatures on graphs, while Sect. 8 draws conclusions on this work.

2 Preliminaries

2.1 Assumptions

Special RSA Modulus. A *special RSA modulus* has the form $N = pq$, where $p = 2p' + 1$ and $q = 2q' + 1$ are safe primes, the corresponding group is called *special RSA group. Strong RSA Assumption* [1,7]. Given an RSA modulus N and a random element $g \in \mathbb{Z}_N^*$, it is hard to compute $h \in \mathbb{Z}_N^*$ and integer $e > 1$ such that $h^e \equiv g \bmod N$. The modulus N is of a special form pq, where $p = 2p' + 1$ and $q = 2q' + 1$ are safe primes. *Quadratic Residues.* The set QR_N is the set of Quadratic Residues of a special RSA group with modulus N.

2.2 Integer Commitments

Damgård and Fujisaki [6] showed for the Pedersen commitment scheme [16] that if it operates in a special RSA group and the committer is not privy to the factorization of the modulus, then the commitment scheme can be used to commit to *integers* of arbitrary size. The commitment scheme is information-theoretically hiding and computationally binding. The security parameter is ℓ. The public parameters are a group G with special RSA modulus N, and generators $(g_0, \ldots, g_m)$ of the cyclic subgroup QR_N. In order to commit to the values $(V_1, \ldots, V_l) \in (\mathbb{Z}_n^*)^l$, pick a random $R \in \{0,1\}^\ell$ and set $C = g_0^R \prod_{i=1}^l g_i^{v_i}$.

2.3 Known Discrete-Logarithm-Based, Zero-Knowledge Proofs

In the common parameters model, we use several previously known results for proving statements about discrete logarithms, such as (1) proof of knowledge of a discrete logarithm modulo a prime [5] or a composite [6,7], (2) proof of knowledge of equality of representation modulo two (possibly different) composite [8] moduli, (3) proof that a commitment opens to the product of two other committed values [8,17], (4) proof that a committed value lies in a given integer interval [8,9], and also (5) proof of the disjunction or conjunction of any two of the previous [18]. These protocols modulo a composite are secure under the strong RSA assumption and modulo a prime under the discrete logarithm assumption.

Proofs as described above can be expressed in the notation introduced by Camenisch and Stadler [19]. For instance,

$$PK\{(\alpha, \beta, \delta) : y = g^\alpha h^\beta \wedge \tilde{y} = \tilde{g}^\alpha \tilde{h}^\delta \wedge (u \leq \alpha \leq v)\}$$

denotes a "*zero-knowledge Proof of Knowledge of integers* α, β, *and* δ *such that* $y = g^\alpha h^\beta$ *and* $\tilde{y} = \tilde{g}^\alpha \tilde{h}^\delta$ *holds, where* $u \leq \alpha \leq v$," where $y, g, h, \tilde{y}, \tilde{g}$, and $\tilde{h}$ are elements of some groups $G = \langle g \rangle = \langle h \rangle$ and $\tilde{G} = \langle \tilde{g} \rangle = \langle \tilde{h} \rangle$. The convention is that Greek letters denote quantities of which knowledge is being proven, while all other values are known to the verifier. We apply the Fiat-Shamir heuristic [20] to turn such proofs of knowledge into signatures on some message m; denoted as, e.g., $SPK\{(\alpha) : y = g^\alpha\}(m)$. Given a protocol in this notation, it is straightforward to derive an actual protocol implementing the proof.

2.4   Camenisch-Lysyanskaya Signatures

Let us introduce Camenisch-Lysyanskaya (CL) signatures in a Strong RSA setting [2]. Let $\ell_\mathcal{M}$, ℓ_e, ℓ_N, ℓ_r and L be system parameters; ℓ_r is a security parameter, $\ell_\mathcal{M}$ the message length, ℓ_e the length of the Strong RSA problem instance prime exponent, ℓ_N the size of the special RSA modulus. The scheme operates with a ℓ_N-bit special RSA modulus. Choose, uniformly at random, $R_0, \ldots, R_{L-1}, S, Z \in QR_N$. The public key $\mathsf{pk}(\mathfrak{l})$ is $(N, R_0, \ldots, R_{L-1}, S, Z)$, the private key $\mathsf{sk}(\mathfrak{l})$ the factorization of the special RSA modulus. The *message space* is the set $\{(m_0, \ldots, m_{L-1}) : m_i \in \pm\{0, 1\}^{\ell_\mathcal{M}}\}$.

Signing hidden messages. On input $m_0, \ldots, m_{L-1}$, choose a random prime number e of length $\ell_e > \ell_\mathcal{M} + 2$, and a random number v of length $\ell_v = \ell_N + \ell_\mathcal{M} + \ell_r$. To sign hidden messages, user U commits to values V in an integer commitment C and proves knowledge of the representation of the commitment. The issuer I verifies the structure of C and signs the commitment:

$$A = \left(\frac{Z}{C R_l^{m_l} \ldots R_{L-1}^{m_{L-1}} S^{v'}}\right)^{1/e} \mod N.$$

The user completes the signature as follows: $\sigma = (e, A, v) = (e, A, (v' + R))$.

To verify that the tuple (e, A, v) is a signature on message $(m_0, \ldots, m_{L-1})$, check that the following statements hold: $Z \equiv A^e R_0^{m_0} \ldots R_{L-1}^{m_{L-1}} S^v \pmod{N}$, $m_i \in \pm\{0, 1\}^{\ell_\mathcal{M}}$, and $2^{\ell_e} > e > 2^{\ell_e - 1}$ holds.

Theorem 1. *[2] The signature scheme is secure against adaptive chosen message attacks under the strong RSA assumption.*

Proving Knowledge of a Signature. The prover randomizes A: Given a signature (A, e, v), the tuple $(A' := AS^{-r} \mod N, e, v' := v + er)$ is also a valid signature as well. Now, provided that $A \in \langle S \rangle$ and that r is chosen uniformly at random from $\{0, 1\}^{\ell_N + \ell_\varnothing}$, the value A' is distributed statistically close to uniform over

$\mathbb{Z}_N^*$. Thus, the user could compute a fresh A' each time, reveal it, and then run the protocol

$$PK\{(\varepsilon, \nu', \mu_0, \ldots, \mu_{L-1}) :$$
$$Z \equiv \pm R_0^{\mu_0} \cdots R_{L-1}^{\mu_{L-1}} A'^{\varepsilon} S^{\nu'} \pmod{N} \ \wedge$$
$$\mu_i \in \pm\{0, 1\}^{\ell_\mathcal{M}} \ \wedge \ \varepsilon \in [2^{\ell_e - 1} + 1, 2^{\ell_e} - 1]\}$$

2.5 Set Membership from CL-Signatures

Set membership proofs can be constructed from CL-Signatures following a method proposed by Camenisch, Chaabouni and shelat [21]. For a set $\mathcal{S} = \{m_0, \ldots, m_i, \ldots, m_l\}$, the issuer signs all set members m_i in CL-Signatures $\sigma_i = (A, e, v)$ and publishes the set of message-signature pairs $\{(m_i, \sigma_i)\}$ with integrity. To prove set membership of a value committed in C, the prover shows knowledge of the blinded signature σ_i' corresponding to the message m_i and equality of exponents with C. We explain this technique in detail in the extended version of this paper and denote a set membership proof $\mu[C] \in \mathcal{S}$, which reads μ encoded in commitment C is member of set $\mathcal{S}$.

2.6 Camenisch-Groß Encoding

The Camenisch-Groß (CG) Encoding [22] establishes structure on the CL message space by encoding multiple binary and finite-set values into a single message, and we will use a similar paradigm to encode graphs efficiently. We explain the key principles briefly and give more details in the extended version of this paper.

The core principle of the CG-Encoding is to represent binary and finite-set attribute values as prime numbers. It uses divisibility and coprimality to show whether an attribute value is present in or absent from a credential. The attribute values certified in a credential, say e_i, e_j, and e_l, are represented in a single message of the CL-Signature, by signing the product of their prime representative $E = e_i \cdot e_j \cdot e_l$ in an Integer attribute. The association between the value and the prime number of the encoding is certified by the credential issuer.

Divisibility/AND-Proof. To prove that a disclosed prime representative e_i is present in E, we prove that e_i divides the committed product E, we show that we know a secret μ' that completes the product:

$$PK\{(\mu', \rho) : \quad D \equiv \pm(g^{e_i})^{\mu'} h^\rho \pmod{N}\}.$$

Coprimality/NOT-Proof. We show that one or multiple prime representatives are not present in a credential, we show coprimality. To prove that two values E and F are coprime, i.e., $\gcd(E, F) = 1$, we prove there exist integers a and b such that Bézout's Identity equals 1, where a and b for this equation do not exist, if $\gcd(E, F) > 1$.

$$PK\{(\mu, \rho, \alpha, \beta, \rho') : \quad D \equiv \pm g^\mu h^\rho \pmod{N} \ \wedge \ g \equiv \pm D^\alpha (g^F)^\beta h^{\rho'} \pmod{N}\}.$$

OR-Proof. To show that a credential contains an attribute e that is contained in an OR-list, we show there exists an integer a such that $ae = \prod_i^\ell e_i$; if e is not in the list, then there is no such integer a as e does not divide the product. We use the notation $\alpha \subseteq \varXi$ for an OR-proof that α contains one or more values of $\varXi$.

3   Graph Encoding

We consider graphs over finite vertex sets, with undirected edges or directed arcs, and finite sets of vertex and edge labels. Vertices and edges may be associated with multiple labels. We leave the encoding of directed arcs to the extended version of this paper.

$$
\begin{array}{ll}
\mathcal{V} & \text{Finite set of vertices} \\
\mathcal{E} \subseteq (\mathcal{V} \times \mathcal{V}) & \text{Finite set of edges} \\
\mathcal{G} = (\mathcal{V}, \mathcal{E}, t_\mathcal{V}, t_\mathcal{E}) & \text{Graph} \\
\mathcal{L}_\mathcal{V}, \mathcal{L}_\mathcal{E} & \text{Finite sets of vertex and edge labels} \\
f_\mathcal{V} : \mathcal{V} \to \mathcal{P}(\mathcal{L}_\mathcal{V}) & \text{Labels of a given vertex} \\
f_\mathcal{E} : \mathcal{E} \to \mathcal{P}(\mathcal{L}_\mathcal{E}) & \text{Labels of a given edge} \\
n = |\mathcal{V}|, m = |\mathcal{E}| & \text{Number of vertices and edges}
\end{array}
$$

For each vertex i in $\mathcal{V}$, we introduce a vertex identifier, a prime e_i, which represents this vertex in credential and proofs. The symbol $\bot$, associated with identifier $e_\bot$ represents that a vertex is not present. All vertex identifiers are pair-wise different. We call the set of all vertex identifiers $\varXi_\mathcal{V}$, their product $\chi_\mathcal{V} = \varPi \varXi_\mathcal{V}$. For each label k in the label sets $\mathcal{L}_\mathcal{V}$ and in $\mathcal{L}_\mathcal{E}$, we introduce a prime representative e_k. All label representatives are pair-wise different. We call the set of all label representatives $\varXi_\mathcal{L}$, their product $\chi_\mathcal{L} = \varPi \varXi_\mathcal{L}$. Vertex identifiers and label representatives are disjoint:

$$
\varXi_\mathcal{V} \cap \varXi_\mathcal{L} = \emptyset \quad \Leftrightarrow \quad \gcd(\chi_\mathcal{V}, \chi_\mathcal{L}) = 1.
$$

Random Base Association. We encode vertices and edges into the exponents of integer commitments and CL-Signatures and make them therefore accessible to proofs of linear equations over exponents. We randomize the base association to vertices and edges: For a vertex index set $\mathcal{V} = 0, \ldots, i, n\text{-}1$ with vertex identifiers e_i, we choose a uniformly random permutation $\pi_\mathcal{V}$ of set $\mathcal{V}$ to determine the base $R_{\pi(i)}$ to encode vertex i. Edge bases $R_{\pi(i,j)}$ are chosen analogously with a random permutation $\pi_\mathcal{E}$.

Encoding Vertices. To encode a vertex and its associated labels into a graph commitment or CL-Signature, we encode the product of the vertex identifier $e_i \in \varXi_\mathcal{V}$ and the prime representatives $e_k \in \varXi_\mathcal{L}$ for $k \in f_\mathcal{V}(i)$ of the labels into a single of the signature message. The product of prime representatives is encoded as exponent of dedicated vertex bases $R \in G_\mathcal{V}$.

Table 1. Interface of the graph signature scheme.

Commit($\mathcal{G}; R$)	A PPT algorithm computing an Integer commitment on a graph
Keygen($1^\ell, params$)	A PPT algorithm computing the key setup
HiddenSign($C, \mathcal{V}_\mathsf{U}, \mathcal{V}_\mathsf{I}, pk_\mathsf{I}$)	An interactive PPT algorithm signing a committed graph
Private inputs:	User U: $\mathcal{G}_\mathsf{U}$, commitment randomness R; Issuer I: $\mathcal{G}_\mathsf{I}$, sk_I
Verify($pk_\mathsf{I}, C, R', \sigma$)	A verification algorithm on graph commitment C and signature σ.

Encoding Edges. To get a compact encoding and efficient proofs thereon, the encoding needs to maintain the graph structure and to allow us to access it to proof higher-level properties, such as connectivity and isolation. The proposal we make in this paper after evaluating multiple approaches is to use divisibility and coprimality similar to the CG-Encoding to afford us these efficient operations over the graph structure, while offering a compact encoding of edges.

Recall that each vertex is certified with an vertex identifier from $\Xi_\mathcal{V}$, e.g., e_i or e_j. For each edge $(i, j) \in \mathcal{E}$, we include an edge attribute as exponent of a random edge base $R_{\pi(i,j)} \in G_\mathcal{E}$, containing the product of the vertex identifiers and the associated label representatives $e_k \in \Xi_\mathcal{L}$ for $k \in f_\mathcal{E}(i,j)$ of the edge:

$$E_{(i,j)} := e_i \cdot e_j \cdot \Pi_{k \in f_\mathcal{E}(i,j)} e_k.$$

whereas we usually consider simple graphs, specialties such as multigraphs, loops (i, i) encoded as e_i^2 or half-edges encoded as $(e_j, e_\perp)$ can be included.

Definition 1 (Well-formed Graph). *We call a graph encoding* well-formed *iff 1. the encoding only contains prime representatives $e \in \Xi_\mathcal{V} \cup \Xi_\mathcal{L}$ in the exponents of designated vertex and edge bases $R \in G_\mathcal{V} \cup G_\mathcal{E}$, 2. each vertex base $R \in G_\mathcal{V}$ contains exactly one vertex identifier $e_i \in \Xi_\mathcal{V}$, pair-wise different from other vertex identifiers and zero or more label representatives $e_k \in \Xi_\mathcal{L}$, and 3. each edge base $R \in G_\mathcal{E}$ contains exactly two vertex identifiers $e_i, e_i \in \Xi_\mathcal{V}$ and zero or more label representatives $e_k \in \Xi_\mathcal{L}$.*

Theorem 2 (Unambiguous Encoding and Decoding). *A well-formed graph encoding on the integers is unambiguous modulo the base association.* *[Proof 9.1]*

4 Signatures on Committed Graphs

CL-signatures are signatures on committed messages, where messages can be contributed by issuer and user. This translates to a user committing to a hidden partial graph $\mathcal{G}_\mathsf{U}$, which is then completed by the issuer $\mathcal{G}_\mathsf{I}$ as outline in the interface in Table 1. We establish the secrecy notion of the construction first, explain the proof of representation second, and the issuing third.

As a point of reference, we give the structure of the graph signatures first. We have bases $R_{\pi(i)} \in G_{\mathcal{V}}$, which store attributes encoding vertices, and bases $R_{\pi(i,j)} \in G_{\mathcal{E}}$, which store attributes encoding edges. Observe that which base stores which vertex or edge is randomized by permutations $\pi_{\mathcal{V}}$ and $\pi_{\mathcal{E}}$.

$$Z = \cdots \underbrace{R_{\pi(i)}^{e_i \Pi_{k \in f_{\mathcal{V}}(i)} e_k}}_{\forall \text{ vertices } i} \cdots \cdots \underbrace{R_{\pi(i,j)}^{e_i e_j \Pi_{k \in f_{\mathcal{E}}(i,j)} e_k}}_{\forall \text{ edges } (i,j)} \cdots A^e S^v \bmod N$$

4.1   Secrecy Notion

In a *known-graph* proof, the structure of the graph $\mathcal{G} = (\mathcal{V}, \mathcal{E})$ is an auxiliary input to the verifier. Such a proof occurs if the prover needs to prove knowledge of a (NP-hard) property of the entire graph, e.g., a proper coloring in graph 3-colorability (cf. Sect. 2.4).

A *hidden-graph* proof keeps the structure of the graph $\mathcal{G} = (\mathcal{V}, \mathcal{E})$ secret. For instance, there are graph proofs in which a local property is proven and the graph structure itself kept secret, e.g., when proving that disclosed vertices of the graph are connected by a hidden path.

The number of bases from $\mathcal{G}_{\mathcal{V}}$ and $\mathcal{G}_{\mathcal{E}}$ in a CL-Signature reveals an upper-bound on the number of vertices n and edges m of the signed graph. A suitable padding can be introduced by encoding nil-vertices $e_\perp$ and nil-edges $(e_\perp, e_\perp)$.

Proving properties over multiple attributes reveals which bases were involved in the proof. Characteristic patterns over said bases may interfere with the CL-Signature's multi-use unlinkability. For instance, if the prover shows that vertices i and j are connected by an edge (i,j) along with properties on the vertices themselves, the verifier will learn that the bases for the vertex identifiers e_i and e_j are related to the base for the encoding of edge (i,j). To overcome this linking, the prover can obtain a collection of CL-Signatures on the same graph, each with a randomized association between bases and vertices/edges, that is, using different random permutations $\pi_{\mathcal{V}}$ and $\pi_{\mathcal{E}}$. When proving a property over the graph the prover chooses a CL-Signature from the collection uniformly at random and proves possession over that instance.

4.2   Proof of Representation

For a full proof of representation, we need to establish that the encoded graph in a graph commitment or CL-Signature is indeed well-formed (Definition 1). Given a graph commitment C the prover and verifier engage in the following proof of representation (the proof for a CL credential work analogously). We show that vertex bases contain a bi-partition of one and only one vertex identifier $e_i \in \Xi_{\mathcal{V}}$ and a set of labels $e_l \in \Xi_{\mathcal{L}}$. Edge bases contain a bi-partition of a product of exactly two vertex identifiers $(e_i \cdot e_j)$ and a set of labels $e_l \in \Xi_{\mathcal{L}}$. To prove that the representation contains exactly one vertex identifier for a vertex base and two vertex identifiers for an edge base, we establish a set membership proof.

1. Commitments. The prover computes Integer commitments on the exponents of all vertex and edge bases. For each vertex i and for each edge (i,j), the prover computes commitments on vertex attribute and identifier (all mod N):

$$C_i = R^{e_i \Pi_{k \in f_{\mathcal{V}}(i)} e_k} S^r \quad \text{and} \quad \check{C}_i = R^{e_i} S^{\check{r}};$$
$$C_{(i,j)} = R^{e_i e_j \Pi_{k \in f_{\mathcal{E}}(i,j)} e_k} S^r, \quad \check{C}_{(i,j)} = R^{e_i e_j} S^{\check{r}} \quad \text{and} \quad \dot{C}_i = R^{e_i} S^{\dot{r}}.$$

2. Proof of knowledge. We build up the proof of possession and well-formedness step by step, where it is understood the proofs will be done in one compound proof of knowledge with *referential integrity between the secret exponents*. Let us consider a proof fragment for vertices i,j and an edge (i,j) committed in a graph commitment C (the same proof structure is used for CL-Signatures).

2.1 Proof of representation. We prove that commitment C decomposes into commitments C_i, C_j, one for each vertex i,j and one commitment $C_{(i,j)}$ for each edge (i,j):

$$PK\{(\mu_i, \mu_j, \mu_{(i,j)}, \rho, \rho_i, \rho_j, \rho_{(i,j)}) :$$
$$C \equiv \pm \cdots R_{\pi(i)}^{\mu_i} \cdots R_{\pi(j)}^{\mu_j} \cdots R_{\pi(i,j)}^{\mu_{(i,j)}} \cdots S^\rho \pmod{N} \ \wedge \tag{1}$$
$$C_i \equiv \pm R^{\mu_i} S^{\rho_i} \pmod{N} \ \wedge \ C_j \equiv \pm R^{\mu_j} S^{\rho_j} \pmod{N} \ \wedge \tag{2}$$
$$C_{(i,j)} \equiv \pm R^{\mu_{(i,j)}} S^{\rho_{(i,j)}} \pmod{N}\}. \tag{3}$$

2.2 Vertex composition. Second, we need to show properties of the vertex composition, that the encoding for each vertex i contains exactly one vertex identifier $e_i \in \Xi_{\mathcal{V}}$ and zero or multiple label representatives $e_k \in \Xi_{\mathcal{L}}$. We show this structure with help of the commitments $\check{C}_i$ and set membership and prime-encoding OR proofs. This proof is executed for all vertices.

$$PK\{(\varepsilon_i, \check{\rho}_i, \gamma_i, \rho_i') :$$
$$\check{C}_i \equiv \pm R^{\varepsilon_i} S^{\check{\rho}_i} \pmod{N} \wedge C_i \equiv \pm \check{C}_i^{\gamma_i} S^{\rho_i'} \pmod{N} \wedge \tag{4}$$
$$\gamma_i[C_i] \subseteq \Xi_{\mathcal{L}} \wedge \varepsilon_i[\check{C}_i] \in \Xi_{\mathcal{V}}\}. \tag{5}$$

2.3 Edge composition. Third, we prove the structure of each edge (i,j) over the commitments $C_{(i,j)}$, showing that each commitment contains exactly two vertex identifiers $e_i, e_j \in \Xi_{\mathcal{V}}$ as well as zero or more label representative $e_k \in \Xi_{\mathcal{L}}$:

$$PK\{(\varepsilon_j, \rho_{(i,j)}, \gamma_{(i,j)}, \rho_{(i,j)}') :$$
$$\check{C}_{(i,j)} \equiv \pm \dot{C}_i^{\varepsilon_j} S^{\rho_{(i,j)}} \pmod{N} \wedge \tag{6}$$
$$C_{(i,j)} \equiv \pm \check{C}_{(i,j)}^{\gamma_{(i,j)}} S^{\rho_{(i,j)}'} \pmod{N} \wedge \tag{7}$$
$$\gamma_{i,j} \subseteq \Xi_{\mathcal{L}}\}. \tag{8}$$

2.4 Pair-wise difference. We prove pair-wise difference of vertices by showing that the vertex representatives are pair-wise co-prime over the commitments $\check{C}_i$ and $\check{C}_j$.

$$PK\{(\forall i,j : \alpha_{i,j}, \beta_{i,j}, \rho_{i,j}) : \qquad R \equiv \pm \check{C}_i^{\alpha_{i,j}} \check{C}_j^{\beta_{i,j}} S^{\rho_{i,j}} \pmod{N}\}. \qquad (9)$$

Theorem 3 (Proof of Well-formedness). *The compound proof of knowledge establishes the well-formedness of an encoded graph according to Definition 1.* [Proof 10]

4.3   Joint Graph Issuing

To jointly issue a graph CL-signature, a user commits to a hidden partial graph and the issuer adds further elements to the graph (cf. Sect. 2.4)

In the setup, the issuer establishes a user vertex space and issuer vertex space, i.e., a bi-partition on vertex and edge bases, $G_\mathcal{V}$ and $G_\mathcal{E}$ and on vertex identifiers $\Xi_\mathcal{V}$. Thus, user and issuer can encode partial graphs without interfering with each other.

In the joint graph issuing, user and issuer designate and disclose connection points (vertex identifiers) that allow the user and the issuer to connect their sub-graphs deliberately. The user constructs a graph representation by choosing two uniformly random permutation $\pi_\mathcal{V}$ and $\pi_\mathcal{E}$ for the base association on the user bases and commits to his sub-graph in a graph commitment. The user interacts with the issuer in a proof of representation of his committed sub-graph. The issuer verifies this proof, chooses uniformly random permutations for his graph elements and encodes them into his base range. The issuer creates the pre-signature of the CL-Signature scheme on the entire graph, proving that the added sub-graph is well-formed. The user completes the CL-Signature with his own randomness.

Theorem 4 (Security of Graph Signatures). *The graph signature scheme maintains confidentiality and integrity of the encoded graphs and offers existential unforgeability against adaptive chosen message attacks under the strong RSA assumption.* [Proof 9.1]

5   Graph 3-Colorability and NP Statements

5.1   Graph 3-Colorability

We adapt the following definition from Goldreich, Micali and Wigderson [11].

Definition 2 (Graph 3-Colorability). *A graph $\mathcal{G} = (\mathcal{V}, \mathcal{E})$ is said to be 3-colorable if there exists a vertex label mapping $f_\mathcal{V} : \mathcal{V} \to \{R, G, B\}$ called proper coloring such that every two adjacent vertices are assigned different color labels. This means that for each edge $(i,j) \in \mathcal{E} f_\mathcal{V}(i) \neq f_\mathcal{V}(j)$. The language graph 3-colorability, denoted G3C, consists of the set of undirected graphs that are 3-colorable. Graph 3-Colorability is known to be NP-complete.* [23]

We adapt the graph 3-colorability problem to show in honest-verifier zero-knowledge that the prover knows an CL signature on an instance of a proper coloring of a given graph $\mathcal{G}$.

Without loss of generality, we assume that graph $\mathcal{G}$ is simple and connected. The three color labels $\mathcal{L} = \{R, G, B\}$ are encoded with three primes $\Xi_{\mathcal{L}} = \{e_R, e_G, e_B\}$. The graph is encoded with vertex identifiers Ξ_V and these vertex labels. In addition to the conditions for a well-formed graph (Definition 1), we require that each vertex base contains exactly one label representative from $\Xi_{\mathcal{L}}$, which we show with a set membership proof on the secret vertex label.

The prover shows knowledge of a proper graph coloring by showing that the product of vertex identifiers and label representatives for each pair of adjacent vertices (i, j) are coprime.

Common inputs. Graph $\mathcal{G}$, public-key of the CL-issuer.
Prover input. CL-Signature on proper coloring for G3C.

1. Credential randomization and commitments. The prover computes randomizations for the graph signature as well as for all occurrences of set membership proofs. The prover computes Integer commitments on the exponents of all vertex and edge bases. For each vertex i, the prover computes two commitments on the vertex attribute and the vertex identifier:

$$C_i = R^{e_i e_{f_V(i)}} S^r \bmod N \quad \text{and} \quad \check{C}_i = R^{e_i} S^r \bmod N.$$

For each edge (i, j), the prover computes the commitment:

$$\check{C}_{i,j} = R^{e_i e_j} S^r \bmod N.$$

2. Proof of knowledge. The prover sends the commitments to the verifier. Then, prover and verifier engage in the following proof of possession over the graph signature and vertices i and j and all edges (i, j). We build upon the proof of representation and well-formedness presented in Sect. 4.2 with the following differences: Instead of proving that a vertex contains zero or multiple labels, we prove that the vertex contains *exactly one label*. Further, the proof is simplified because the edges do not contain labels. While we explain the proofs step by step, it is understood that the proofs are executed as compound proof of knowledge *with referential integrity between the secret exponents.*

2.1 Possession of CL-Signature. First, we prove of possession of the graph signature and representation of the commitments. Clause 1 proves possession of the CL-Signature on the graph. The clauses 2 and 3 prove the representation on the integer commitments on signed attributes for vertices j, j and edges (i, j), and, thereby, make the attributes accessible for the analysis of the exponents.

$$PK\{(\mu_i, \mu_j, \mu_{(i,j)}, \varepsilon, \nu', \rho_i, \rho_j, \rho_{(i,j)}) :$$

$$Z \equiv \pm \cdots R_{\pi(i)}^{\mu_i} \cdots R_{\pi(j)}^{\mu_j} \cdots R_{\pi(i,j)}^{\mu_{(i,j)}} \cdots (A')^{\varepsilon} S^{\nu'} \pmod{N} \quad \wedge \qquad (1)$$

$$C_i \equiv \pm R^{\mu_i} S^{\rho_i} \pmod{N} \quad \wedge \quad C_j \equiv \pm R^{\mu_j} S^{\rho_j} \pmod{N} \quad \wedge \qquad (2)$$

$$C_{(i,j)} \equiv \pm R^{\mu_{(i,j)}} S^{\rho_{(i,j)}} \pmod{N} \quad \wedge \qquad (3)$$

$$\mu_i, \mu_j, \mu_{((i,j))} \in \pm\{0,1\}^{\ell_{\mathcal{M}}} \quad \wedge \varepsilon \in [2^{\ell_e - 1} + 1, 2^{\ell_e} - 1]\}$$

2.2 Well-formedness. Second, we establish that the vertex attributes are well-formed: Clause 4 establishes the relation between C_i and $\breve{C}_i$ and, thereby, shows that a vertex attribute is bi-partitioned onto a vertex identifier and a label representative part. Clause 5 establishes that they contain exactly one vertex identifier and label representative of the certified sets $\Xi_{\mathcal{V}}$ and $\Xi_{\mathcal{L}}$.

$$PK\{(\varepsilon_i, \rho_i, \gamma_i, \breve{\rho}_i) :$$

$$\breve{C}_i \equiv \pm R^{\varepsilon_i} S^{\rho_i} \pmod{N} \quad \wedge \quad C_i \equiv \pm \breve{C}^{\gamma_i} S^{\breve{\rho}_i} \pmod{N} \quad \wedge \qquad (4)$$

$$\gamma_i[C_i] \in \Xi_{\mathcal{L}} \quad \wedge \quad \varepsilon_i[\breve{C}_i] \in \Xi_{\mathcal{V}}\}. \qquad (5)$$

Clause 5 is different from a proof of well-formedness as introduced in Sect. 4.2, as it enforces that vertex i contains exactly one label.

2.3 Proper coloring. Third, clauses 7 and 8 complete the statement by establishing that there is a proper coloring for the adjacent vertices i and j: Clause 7 shows that commitment $C_{(i,j)}$ is on an edge (i,j). Finally, Clause 8 establishes that the attributes for vertex i and j are coprime, by proving that Bézout's Identity equals 1. It follows that the labels of both vertices must be different.

$$PK\{(\varepsilon_i, \rho'_{(i,j)}, \alpha_{(i,j)}, \beta_{(i,j)}, \rho_{(i,j)''}) : \qquad (6)$$

$$\breve{C}_{(i,j)} \equiv \pm \breve{C}_j^{\varepsilon_i} S^{\rho'_{(i,j)}} \pmod{N} \quad \wedge \qquad (7)$$

$$R \equiv \pm C_i^{\alpha_{(i,j)}} C_j^{\beta_{(i,j)}} S^{\rho''_{(i,j)}} \pmod{N}\}. \qquad (8)$$

3. Verification. The verifier outputs *accept* if the proof of knowledge checks out; *reject* otherwise.

Lemma 1 (Knowledge of a CL-Signature of G3C). *The prover convinces the verifier in zero-knowledge that the prover knows a proper graph 3-coloring for known graph $\mathcal{G}$.* [Proof 10.1]

Lemma 2. *The proof has an asymptotic computation complexity of $O(n+m)$ exponentiations and a communication complexity of $O(n+m)$ group elements and is thereby a polynomial time proof.* [Proof 10.1]

5.2   Proofs Systems for Languages in NP

Having established a proof for certified graph 3-colorability, we can use the fact that G3C is NP-complete to establish that such Camenisch-Lysyanskaya proof systems exist for statements from other NP languages.

Definition 3. *We call a* Camenisch-Lysyanskaya *proof system a set of PPT machines Prover* P, *Verifier* V *and Issuer* I *that engage in the following protocols:*

Proof of Representation P → I : *Proof of representation on committed values* V.

Issuing I → P : *Issuing of CL-Signature σ on hidden committed values* V.

Proof of Possession P → V : *Proof of possession of CL-Signature σ.*

The issuer can act in the role of the verifier V *and thereby allow the bootstrapping of further CL-Signatures from the hidden values of existing CL-Signatures.*

Compared to a zero-knowledge proof system for an NP language, this construction offers a level of indirection: The issuer acts as auditor with authority to decide whether the statement of an NP language is fulfilled in a certain environment, and its signature binds this statement to that environment. The instance of the NP language can either be provided by the issuer or provided by the prover and verified by the issuer.

The proof follows the same strategy as one of the initial results that all languages in NP have zero-knowledge proof systems, by Goldreich, Micali and Widgerson [11]: Given a CL proof system for G3C, we use the existing poly-time NP reductions to transform any NP language statement into an instance of G3C. This instance is then encoded as a graph in a CL-Signature and knowledge of the signature proven to a verifier. Lemma 1 shows that this is a zero-knowledge proof of knowledge of a proper coloring.

Theorem 5. *Statements of languages in NP can efficiently be proven in a Camenisch-Lysyanskaya proof system based in honest-verifier zero-knowledge.*   *[Proof 10.2]*

6 Efficiency Analysis

We display the efficiency analysis for the proof predicates in Table 2, where vertex and edge composition proofs show the overhead over the basic proof of possession (cf. topology proofs [14]). We measure computational complexity in multi-base exponentiations. The communication complexity is dominated by the transmitted group elements from $\mathbb{Z}_N^*$, which is equal to the number of multi-base exponentiations (one for each Integer and Schnorr proof commitment). The most expensive proof is the complete graph representation established in the issuing, where the set membership proofs (4 MExps) and the OR-based subset proofs (6 MExps) constitute significant overhead. The square-complexity is introduced by the final disjointness proof to establish that the graph is indeed well-formed. In the down-stream proofs, the verifier trusts the issuer to only certify well-formed graphs, which allows us to reduce complexity by only the computing the proof of possession and the statement proven.

The modular exponentiations for message bases R_i are with small exponents of size of $\ell_M \ll \ell_N$, where the parameter ℓ_M can be chosen similarly small as in Direct Anonymous Attestation (DAA) [24].

Table 2. Efficiency of proofs of predicates in multi-base exponentiations (MultiExps) dependent on the number of vertices n and of edges m. For a simple graph holds $m \leq \frac{n(n-1)}{2}$.

Predicate	Basis	Commitments	MultiExps	
		#	#	O
Possession		$n + m$	$2n + 2m + 1$	$O(n + m)$
Vertex Composition	Possession	n	$3n$	$O(n)$
Edge Composition	Possession	$2m$	$4m$	$O(m)$
Total Well-formed Graph		$2n + 3m$	$n^2 + 8n + 8m + 1$	$O(n^2)$
Graph-3 Colorability (Sect. 5)		$n + m$	$6n + 4m + 1$	$O(n + m)$

In addition, the Σ-proofs employed in this work benefit from batch-proof techniques, such as [25]. The graph proofs are likely to be transformed to signature proofs of knowledge with the Fiat-Shamir heuristic [20] and can thereby be computed offline.

We have evaluated the system experimentally in [14], in computations using components of the Identity Mixer Library [26] with modulus length $\ell_n = 2048$ bits and default system parameters (ℓ_v, etc.). The performance analysis is executed on 64-bit Java JDK 1.7.13 on a Windows 7 SP 1 Thinkpad X220 Tablet, on Intel CPU i5-2520 with 2.5 GHz, 8 GB RAM, where all computations are performed on a *single processor core only*, a very conservative setup. Figure 1 contains the results of a prototypical implementation of computations of the graph signature scheme, on representative computations of commitments and a proof of knowledge thereof. Based on uniform random bit-strings of the prescribed length and number (as in the actual Schnorr proof witnesses), we compute: $C := R_0^{m_0} \cdots R_\ell^{m_\ell} S^v \bmod N$,

The simulation uses random graphs with specified number of vertices n and a derived number of edges $m := 2n$ as major independent variable (on the x-axis), the dependent variable is computation time in milliseconds (in log-scale on the y-axis).

7   Related Work

Establishing zero-knowledge proofs on graphs and their properties is a classic area of research. Such proofs were instrumental in showing that there exist zero-knowledge proof systems for all NP languages. We discuss their graph modeling: Goldreich, Micali and Wigderson [11] offered such a construction with $O(m^2)$ rounds and $O(n)$ messages each. Based on the existence of a non-uniformly secure encryption function, they explored graph isomorphism and non-isomorphism as well as graph 3-colorability (G3C). Blum's proof [12] shows directed Hamiltonian cycles (DHC) in graphs. Both proofs use a metaphor of locked boxes to formulate the proof. Goldreich et al.'s G3C proof encodes the colors of adjacent vertices in boxes. Blum's proof of Hamiltonian cycles encodes the graph's adjacency matrix

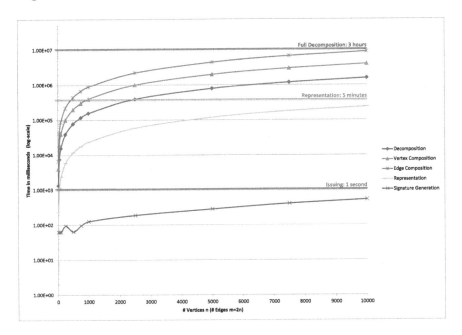

Fig. 1. Experimental performance analysis with a secure modulus length of 2048 bits, in the worst case of a non-parallelized computation on a single processor core (adapted from [14]). x-axis contains the number of vertices n and the y-axis a log-scale of computation time in milliseconds. Blue colors denote provider computations to prove properties of a committed graph, where the green line shows a proof of representation of a graph signature. Red colors denote auditing system/issuer computations to sign the graph (Color figure online).

randomly in $n + \binom{n}{2}$ such boxes, giving the verifier the choice to either verify the correct graph representation or the knowledge of the Hamiltonian cycle. Blum offers an alternative construction for G3C with a similar methodology, encoding the graph representation and the coloring of each vertex in separate yet related boxes and operating on an adjacency matrix lifted to the labeling. Goldreich and Kahan [15] offered a constant-round construction based on the existence of collections of claw-free functions, also using G3C as NP-problem. We observe that these constructions are specific to the statement to be proven and do not cater for a level of indirection through a signature scheme.

A related notion to full graph signatures is transitive signature schemes, e.g., as proposed by Micali and Rivest [13]. They are concerned with the transitive closure of signatures on graph elements, where vertices and edges are signed individually; however, they do not offer zero-knowledge proofs of knowledge on graph properties.

8   Conclusion

We have introduced a practical construction of signatures on committed graphs and zero-knowledge proofs over their structure. The scheme is special in that it enables proofs over the entire graph structure, including statements such as isolation (two vertices are not connected by any sequence of edges). The construction derives its security from the properties of the Camenisch-Lysyanskaya (CL) signature scheme under the Strong RSA assumption. The interactive proofs are honest-verifier zero-knowledge if executed with multiple rounds with small challenges. While we have established a framework for graph topology proofs separately [14], this work focuses on the foundations of graph encoding in CL-signatures itself. We show its theoretical expressiveness by proving that the scheme is capable of signing committed NP statements and proving properties thereof, via reduction to graph 3-colorability. The presented scheme is efficient and practical because once the issuer has established graph well-formedness in $O(n^2)$, the prover can resort to proofs over the graph structure in linear time. The used Σ-proofs can be handled efficiently with batch processing techniques [25]. As future work, we aim at establishing a differential graph signature scheme, which can be employed for large-scale graph topologies as found in virtualized infrastructures.

Acknowledgments. This research is supported by the EU FP7 FutureID project (http://futureid.eu) under GA n° 318424 and the EU Horizon 2020 project PrismaCloud (https://prismacloud.eu) under GA n° 644962. The author is grateful for the discussions with Jens Groth and Jan Camenisch as well as for the feedback of the anonymous reviewers considering this work.

9   Proofs

9.1   Well-Formed Encoding and Security

Proof (Unambiguous encoding and decoding: Theorem 2). We show that there is a bijection between encoding and graph.

Graph → Encoding: For each graph there exits a unique encoding modulo base association. For all vertices $i \in \mathcal{V}$ choose the vertex identifier $e_i \in \Xi_\mathcal{V}$, for the labels $k \in f_\mathcal{V}(i)$ choose the prime representative $e_k \in \Xi_\mathcal{L}$ and compute their product. As said factors are prime, it follows from the fundamental theorem of arithmetic that the $e_i \Pi_{k \in f_\mathcal{V}(i)} e_k$ represents a unique integer. Given that the user is not privy to the discrete logarithm between one base and another (guaranteed by the CL-Signature setup), the bases unambiguously separate the exponents. Thus, apart from the random permutation of the base association, the encoding is unambiguous.

Encoding → Graph: With knowledge of the elements of $\Xi_\mathcal{V}$ and $\Xi_\mathcal{L}$, an encoded product can be decoded efficiently and unambiguously into the elements of the graph. That the parties are not privy to the discrete logarithm between base and another guarantees attribute separation. The base designates unambiguously whether a vertex or an edge is encoded. Given that all representatives of the encoding are prime, the product can be decomposed into a unique factorization by the fundamental theorem of arithmetic. Each representative unambiguously represents either a vertex identifier in $\Xi_\mathcal{V}$ or a label in $\Xi_\mathcal{L}$, as both sets are disjoint.   □

Proof (Security of graph signatures: Theorem 4). The security of the scheme is directly derived from the unambiguous embedding into Integer commitments and Camenisch-Lysyanskaya signatures and their security properties. Theorem 2 establishes that the graph encoding encodes graphs unambiguously into the CL-message space. The graph structure is encoded in the exponents of the Integer commitment and CL-signature schemes. Confidentiality is derived from the information-theoretical hiding property of the Integer commitment scheme and the hiding properties of CL-signatures on committed messages. Under the condition that the adversary is not privy to the group-order of the commitment and the CL signature scheme, we obtain that integrity for both schemes holds over the integers and thereby the graph encoding (cf. [6]). We obtain existential unforgeability against chosen message attacks directly from the CL-signature scheme in Theorem 1 [2].

10   Well-Formedness Proof

The following proof is representative for the argument structure of the proofs for different predicates; others use the same tools.

Proof (Wellformedness proofs, Theorem 3). The Schnorr proofs used in the construction are honest-verifier zero-knowledge if executed repeatedly with small challenges, otherwise witness-indistinguishable. It is standard to extract from a successful prover knowledge on the secrets ranging over $\forall i, j$:

$$\mu_i, \mu_{(i,j)}, \rho, \rho_i, \rho_{(i,j)}, \varepsilon_i, \breve{\rho}_i, \gamma_i, \rho'_i, \dot{\varepsilon}_i, \gamma_{(i,j)}, \rho'_{(i,j)}, \alpha_{i,j}, \beta_{i,j}, \rho_{i,j}$$

such that all equations of the CS-notation hold for some t, where t must be ± 1 as modulus N is a product of two safe primes [6]. As CL-signatures are existentially unforgeable [2], we obtain that the messages μ_i and $\mu_{(i,j)}$ are indeed signed, and that the membership proofs for ε_i establish that $\varepsilon_i \in \Xi_\mathcal{V}$, i.e., are certified vertex identifiers (the CL multi-show unlinkability ensures that the verifier learns no other information about ε_i). The CG-OR proofs [22] yield that γ_i and $\gamma_{(i,j)}$ must encode valid vertex label identifiers (but yield no further information on the labels). Therefore, we have fixes the roots $\mu_i, \mu_{(i,j)}$ and the leaves $\varepsilon_i, \gamma_i, \gamma_{(i,j)}$ of the proof tree in the CL-notation.

It remains to show what can be derived from the equations that connect the roots to the leaves in the vertex and edge composition statements and from the pairwise difference. The technique used is a standard decomposition of certified messages in Integer commitments to make their components accessible to discrete-logarithm based proofs of knowledge; if the same secret is referenced we have an equality proof, if not there is no further information learned about the relation of the secrets. For the vertices, the equation $C_i \equiv \pm \check{C}_i^{\gamma_i} S^{\rho'_i}$ (4) establishes that $\mu_i = \varepsilon_i \gamma_i$, given that the prover does not know a multiple of the group order, $\check{C}_i$ separates out ε_i connected to the membership proof. For edges, the equation $C_{(i,j)} \equiv \pm \check{C}_{(i,j)}^{\gamma_{(i,j)}} S^{\rho'_{(i,j)}}$ (7) establishes that $\mu_{(i,j)} = \mu'_{(i,j)} \gamma_{(i,j)}$, where $\check{C}_{(i,j)}$ is shown to contain a product $\dot{\varepsilon}_i \dot{\varepsilon}_j$ in equation (3), which are in turn shown to be valid vertex identifiers (8). By that all variables are bound and the connection between the roots and the leaves established.

Finally, we claim pair-wise difference on vertices from the equation

$$R \equiv \pm \check{C}_i^{\alpha_{i,j}} \check{C}_j^{\beta_{i,j}} S^{\rho_{i,j}} \tag{9}$$

Unless the prover knows a multiple of the group order or the discrete logarithm $\log_R S$, the following equation must hold over the integers:

$$1 = \varepsilon_i \alpha_{i,j} + \varepsilon_j \beta_{i,j}.$$

It is well-known that $\alpha_{i,j}$ and $\beta_{i,j}$ only exist if ε_i and ε_j are coprime, which gives us the pair-wise difference claimed.

10.1   Graph 3-Colorability (G3C)

Proof (Graph 3-Colorability: Lemma 1).

1. Proof of Knowledge. It is standard to show that there exists a knowledge extractor for all exponents of the proof such that the equality of exponents equations are fulfilled.

We obtain from Clause 1 that the prover knows the representation of a CL-Signature of the given structure. From the existential unforgeability of CL-Signatures, we see that the issuer must have signed the secret attributes μ_i, μ_j and $\mu_{(i,j)}$. Proving equality of exponents with corresponding integer commitments is standard, by which the arguments over the commitments, such as C_i, $\check{C}_i$ and $C_{(i,j)}$ transfer to the structure of the signed messages.

The Clause 4 shows that a message μ_i consists of two factors known to the prover: $\mu_i = \varepsilon_i \gamma_i$. The following Clause 5 employs a set membership proof to show that $\varepsilon_i \in \Xi_\mathcal{V}$ and that $\gamma_i \in \Xi_\mathcal{L}$. We use that the set membership from Sect. 2.5 guarantees that ε_i and γ_i are exactly one member of the set to conclude that a message μ_i contains exactly one vertex identifier and one label identifier. Thus, μ_i is well-formed. Similarly, Clause 7 establishes the structure $\mu_{(i,j)} = \varepsilon_i \varepsilon$ for the edge (i, j), showing it to be well-formed. Because the prover is not privy to the group order, these statements hold over the integers, by the results of Damgård and Fujisaki [6]. Therefore, with the proof of representation including pair-wise difference, we conclude that the signed graph is well-formed.

Clause 8 shows that the labeling $f_\mathcal{V}$ of the signed graph is a proper coloring. Again, we employ Damgård and Fujisaki's [6] result that equations hold over the integers. We have that for each edge (i, j), the corresponding signed messages have the following structure:

$$\mu_i = \varepsilon_i \gamma_i \quad \text{and} \quad \mu_j = \varepsilon_j \gamma_j.$$

We show that the secret labels γ_i and γ_j are different by showing that μ_i and μ_j are coprime, where we use Bézout's Identity:

$$\gcd(\mu_i, \mu_j) = 1 \quad \Leftrightarrow \quad 1 = \alpha_{(i,j)} \mu_i + \beta_{(i,j)} \mu_j.$$

The equality of exponent proof of Clause 8 achieves this as follows

$$R \equiv \pm C_i^{\alpha_{(i,j)}} C_j^{\beta_{(i,j)}} S^{\rho_{(i,j)}} \pmod{N}$$

$$R^1 \equiv \pm (R_i^\mu S^{\rho_i})^{\alpha_{(i,j)}} (R_j^\mu S^{\rho_j})^{\beta_{(i,j)}} S^{\rho_{(i,j)}} \pmod{N}$$

$$R^1 \equiv \pm R^{\alpha_{(i,j)} \mu_i} S^{\alpha_{(i,j)} \rho_i} R^{\beta_{(i,j)} \mu_j} S^{\beta_{(i,j)} \rho_j} S^{\rho_{(i,j)}} \pmod{N}$$

$$R^1 \equiv \pm R^{\alpha_{(i,j)} \mu_i + \beta_{(i,j)} \mu_j} S^{\alpha_{(i,j)} \rho_i + \beta_{(i,j)} \rho_j + \rho_{(i,j)}} \pmod{N}$$

From this equation we can conclude that $\gcd(\mu_i, \mu_j) = 1$ and that, therefore, $\gamma_i \neq \gamma_j$, which implies that $f_V(i) \neq f_V(j)$ and that the CL signature indeed contains a proper coloring.   □

2. Zero-Knowledge. We claim that proof does not disclose anything else than the statement made that the prover knows a CL-Signature of a proper coloring on known graph $\mathcal{G}$.

The Σ-proofs here are zero-knowledge in an honest verifier setting if performed with multiple rounds and small challenges. It is standard to construct a simulator for all Σ-proofs of representation for the CL-Signature and the commitments as well as for their conjunction [18,19], showing that the verifier does not learn anything else than the relations on exponents shown.

It remains to be shown what the relations disclose. We will argue on the statements made on the secret messages γ_i, which contain the color. Clause 4 establishes that γ_i is part of commitment C_i, but does not disclose further information than the equality of exponents.

Clause 5 proves that γ_i is a member of the set $\Xi_{\mathcal{L}} = \{e_R, e_G, e_B\}$. This statement itself is part of the known problem definition of G3C. The set membership proof is a proof of representation for an anonymized CL-Signature and a standard proof of equality of exponents, and thereby, does not disclose further information.

Finally, Clause 8 references $\mu_i = \epsilon_i \gamma_i$ to prove that γ_i and γ_j of an adjacent edge are coprime. As the vertex identifiers are pair-wise different by definition and as all representatives are primes, this only establishes that $\gamma_i \neq \gamma_j$ as required by the G3C problem, but nothing else.   □

Proof (Polynomial Proof of G3C: Lemma 2).

Precomputation: The prover computes $2n + 1$ signature randomizations with one exponentiation each and $2n + m$ integer commitments with 2 exponentiations each. The pre-computation phase uses $6n + 2m + 1$ exponentiations, transmits $4n+m+1$ group elements, and thereby has a computation complexity of $O(n+m)$ and a communication complexity of $O(n + m)$.

Proof of Knowledge: The Schnorr proofs in the proof of knowledge are zero-knowledge if executed with small challenges over multiple rounds and can be connected with techniques from Cramer et al. [18]. The round complexity of the overall protocol is dependent on the proof mode (cf. Brands [17]).

Clause 1 is executed once yielding a Schnorr proof with $n + m + 2$ exponentiations for the prover. The clauses 2 are executed once for each vertex, such as i and j, Therefore we have n Schnorr proofs with 2 exponentiations each for the prover. The clauses 3 are executed once for each edge (i, j), making m Schnorr proofs with 2 exponentiations each for the prover. The clauses 4 are executed once for each vertex, such as i or j. We have $2n$ Schnorr proofs with 2 exponentiations each for the prover. The set membership proofs of Clauses 5 are executed once for each vertex and its label. Each set membership proof is a proof of representation of a designated CL-Signature for the set member, amounting to 3 exponentiations for the prover. In total, we have $2n$ such proofs of possessions, all done with a single Schnorr proof proving equality of exponents with the corresponding commitment. Clause 7 proves the edge structure and is executed once per edge, yielding m Schnorr proofs with 2 exponentiations each for the prover. Finally, the proper graph coloring in Clause 8 is shows once for each edge (i, j) amounting to m Schnorr proofs with 3 exponentiations for the prover.

The proof of knowledge of graph coloring thereby requires $5n + 3m + 1 = O(n + m)$ Schnorr proofs with a computational complexity for the prover of $13n + 8m + 2 = O(n + m)$ exponentiations. The total computational complexity is therefore $O(n+m)$, the communication complexity is $O(n+m)$ group elements. The G3C proof is done in polynomial time. The round complexity depends on the proof mode, where variants with multiple rounds (number of rounds depending on the error probability), with four rounds and initial commitments of the verifier on challenges, and three rounds in a Σ-proof (not zero-knowledge) are possible.□

10.2   CL Proof Systems for NP-Statements

Proof (Sketch NP-Statements: Theorem 5). Let a NP language $\mathfrak{L}$ be given. Let τ be a polynomial-time computable and invertible reduction from $\mathfrak{L}$ to Graph 3-Colorability (G3C): τ can be constructed by composing a polynomial-time reduction of $\mathfrak{L}$ to 3SAT by Cook's proof [27] and a polynomial-time reduction from 3SAT to G3C. We have that $x \in \mathfrak{L}$ iff $\tau(x)$ is 3-colorable.

On common input x, both prover and verifier compute graph $G \leftarrow \tau(x)$. In Goldreich, Micali and Widgerson's work, the proof proceeds to use any interactive zero-knowledge proof system to prove that G is 3-colorable and thereby show that $x \in \mathfrak{L}$. Our proof continues from this point to show that there exists a Camenisch-Lysyanskaya proof system.

On obtaining $\mathcal{G} = \tau(x)$, the prover constructs a graph commitment C on $\mathcal{G}$ as defined in Sect. 3, including a labeling f_V of a proper coloring of $\mathcal{G}$. The known-graph proof transmits $\mathcal{G}$ itself, yet keeps the proper coloring confidential as default.

Proof of Representation P → I: The prover interacts with an CL-Signature issuer, proving representation and well-formedness of the commitment C in a known-graph proof, disclosing information to satisfy the verification requirements of the issuer. As $\tau(x)$ is invertible, this proof of representation of G and the proper coloring serves as proof of representation for x and $x \in \mathfrak{L}$.

Issuing I → P: Upon acceptance of the proof, the issuer signs the committed graph $\mathcal{G}$ in a CL-Signature σ. Given the invertibility of τ, this signature holds for x as well. *sigma* is a CL-Signature on $\tau(x)$ and the proper coloring of $\tau(x)$ iff $x \in \mathfrak{L}$.

Proof of Possession P → V: The prover interacts with the verifier to proof knowledge of the CL-Signature σ on a proper coloring on $\mathcal{G}$ and thereby shows graph 3-colorability of $\tau(x)$, which holds iff $x \in \mathfrak{L}$. Thereby, the proof of possession of σ translates to a proof of possession of the statement $x \in \mathfrak{L}$. The proof is zero-knowledge if executed with small challenges over multiple rounds.   □

References

1. Rivest, R.L., Shamir, A., Adleman, L.: A method for obtaining digital signatures and public-key cryptosystems. Commun. ACM **21**(2), 120–126 (1978)
2. Camenisch, J.L., Lysyanskaya, A.: A signature scheme with efficient protocols. In: Cimato, S., Galdi, C., Persiano, G. (eds.) SCN 2002. LNCS, vol. 2576, pp. 268–289. Springer, Heidelberg (2003)
3. Abe, M., Fuchsbauer, G., Groth, J., Haralambiev, K., Ohkubo, M.: Structure-preserving signatures and commitments to group elements. In: Rabin, T. (ed.) CRYPTO 2010. LNCS, vol. 6223, pp. 209–236. Springer, Heidelberg (2010)
4. Camenisch, J.L., Lysyanskaya, A.: An efficient system for non-transferable anonymous credentials with optional anonymity revocation. In: Pfitzmann, B. (ed.) EUROCRYPT 2001. LNCS, vol. 2045, p. 93. Springer, Heidelberg (2001)
5. Schnorr, C.P.: Efficient signature generation for smart cards. J. Cryptology **4**(3), 239–252 (1991)
6. Damgård, I., Fujisaki, E.: An integer commitment scheme based on groups with hidden order (2001). http://eprint.iacr.org/2001
7. Fujisaki, E., Okamoto, T.: Statistical zero knowledge protocols to prove modular polynomial relations. In: Kaliski Jr., B.S. (ed.) CRYPTO 1997. LNCS, vol. 1294, pp. 16–30. Springer, Heidelberg (1997)
8. Camenisch, J.L., Michels, M.: Proving in Zero-Knowledge that a Number Is the Product of Two Safe Primes. In: Stern, J. (ed.) EUROCRYPT 1999. LNCS, vol. 1592, p. 107. Springer, Heidelberg (1999)
9. Boudot, F.: Efficient proofs that a committed number lies in an interval. In: Preneel, B. (ed.) EUROCRYPT 2000. LNCS, vol. 1807, pp. 431–444. Springer, Heidelberg (2000)
10. Chan, A.H., Frankel, Y., Tsiounis, Y.: Easy come - easy go divisible cash. In: Nyberg, K. (ed.) EUROCRYPT 1998. LNCS, vol. 1403, pp. 561–575. Springer, Heidelberg (1998)

11. Goldreich, O., Micali, S., Wigderson, A.: Proofs that yield nothing but their validity or all languages in np have zero-knowledge proof systems. J. ACM (JACM) **38**(3), 690–728 (1991)

12. Blum, M.: How to prove a theorem so no one else can claim it. In: Proceedings of the International Congress of Mathematicians. vol.e 1, p. 2 (1986) 2

13. Micali, S., Rivest, R.L.: Transitive signature schemes. In: Preneel, B. (ed.) CT-RSA 2002. LNCS, vol. 2271, pp. 236–243. Springer, Heidelberg (2002)

14. Anonymized for review: anonymized for review. In: conference proceedings to appear, November 2014

15. Goldreich, O., Kahan, A.: How to construct constant-round zero-knowledge proof systems for NP. J. Cryptology **9**(3), 167–190 (1996)

16. Pedersen, T.P.: Non-interactive and information-theoretic secure verifiable secret sharing. In: Feigenbaum, J. (ed.) CRYPTO 1991. LNCS, vol. 576, pp. 129–140. Springer, Heidelberg (1992)

17. Brands, S.: Rapid demonstration of linear relations connected by boolean operators. In: Fumy, W. (ed.) EUROCRYPT 1997. LNCS, vol. 1233, pp. 318–333. Springer, Heidelberg (1997)

18. Cramer, R., Damgård, I.B., Schoenmakers, B.: Proof of partial knowledge and simplified design of witness hiding protocols. In: Desmedt, Y.G. (ed.) CRYPTO 1994. LNCS, vol. 839, pp. 174–187. Springer, Heidelberg (1994)

19. Camenisch, J.L., Stadler, M.A.: Efficient group signature schemes for large groups. In: Kaliski Jr., B.S. (ed.) CRYPTO 1997. LNCS, vol. 1294, pp. 410–424. Springer, Heidelberg (1997)

20. Fiat, A., Shamir, A.: How to prove yourself: practical solutions to identification and signature problems. In: Odlyzko, A.M. (ed.) CRYPTO 1986. LNCS, vol. 263, pp. 186–194. Springer, Heidelberg (1987)

21. Camenisch, J.L., Chaabouni, R., Shelat, A.: Efficient protocols for set membership and range proofs. In: Pieprzyk, J. (ed.) ASIACRYPT 2008. LNCS, vol. 5350, pp. 234–252. Springer, Heidelberg (2008)

22. Camenisch, J., Groß, T.: Efficient attributes for anonymous credentials. ACM Trans. Inf. Syst. Secur. (TISSEC) **15**(1), 4 (2012)

23. Garey, M.R., Johnson, D.S., Stockmeyer, L.: Some simplified np-complete problems. In: Proceedings of the Sixth Annual ACM Symposium on Theory of Computing. pp. 47–63. ACM (1974)

24. Brickell, E., Camenisch, J., Chen, L.: Direct anonymous attestation. In: Proceedings of 11th ACM Conference on Computer and Communications Security. ACM Press, pp. 225–234 (2004)

25. Peng, K., Boyd, C., Dawson, E.: Batch zero-knowledge proof and verification and its applications. ACM Trans. Inf. Sys. Secur. (TISSEC) **10**(2), 6 (2007)

26. IBM: Specification of the Identity Mixer cryptographic library, v. 2.3.40. Specification, IBM Research, January 2013 http://prime.inf.tu-dresden.de/idemix/

27. Cook, S.A.: The complexity of theorem-proving procedures. In: Proceedings of the third annual ACM symposium on Theory of computing, pp. 151–158. ACM (1971)

Efficient Statically-Secure Large-Universe Multi-Authority Attribute-Based Encryption

Yannis Rouselakis[✉] and Brent Waters

The University of Texas at Austin, Austin, USA
yannis.rouselakis@gmail.com, bwaters@cs.utexas.edu

Abstract. We propose an efficient large-universe multi-authority ciphertext - policy attribute-based encryption system. In a large-universe ABE scheme, any string can be used as an attribute of the system, and these attributes are not necessarily enumerated during setup. In a multi-authority ABE scheme, there is no central authority that distributes the keys to users. Instead, there are several authorities, each of which is responsible for the authorized key distribution of a specific set of attributes. Prior to our work, several schemes have been presented that satisfy one of these two properties but not both.

Our construction achieves maximum versatility by allowing multiple authorities to control the key distribution for an exponential number of attributes. In addition, the ciphertext policies of our system are sufficiently expressive and overcome the restriction that "each attribute is used only once" that constrained previous constructions. Besides versatility, another goal of our work is to increase efficiency and practicality. As a result, we use the significantly faster prime order bilinear groups rather than composite order groups. The construction is non-adaptively secure in the random oracle model under a non-interactive q-type assumption, similar to one used in prior works. Our work extends existing "program-and-cancel" techniques to prove security and introduces two new techniques of independent interest for other ABE constructions. We provide an implementation and some benchmarks of our construction in Charm, a programming framework developed for rapid prototyping of cryptographic primitives.

Keywords: Attribute-based encryption · Multi-authority · Large universe · Unbounded · q-type assumption · Charm · Implementations

1 Introduction

Public key cryptography allows a sender to encrypt data such that it can only be decrypted by the owner of the corresponding secret key. Encrypting in this manner is useful for when the sender knows the specific identity of the recipient at the time the data is encrypted. However, in many scenarios the data owner might not know the exact recipients that he wishes to target, but instead wish to express sharing of the data in terms of a policy formulated over the credentials

© International Financial Cryptography Association 2015
R. Böhme and T. Okamoto (Eds.): FC 2015, LNCS 8975, pp. 315–332, 2015.
DOI: 10.1007/978-3-662-47854-7_19

or attributes of different users. Here the sender might not even know who the exact recipients are that match this policy or someone might acquire the exact credentials well after the data was encrypted and stored.

Sahai and Waters [42] put forth a different vision of encryption called Attribute-Based Encryption (ABE). In a (Ciphertext - Policy) ABE scheme the encryption algorithm takes as input the public parameters as issued by some authority as well as a boolean formula over a set of attributes. Users in the system will be issued private keys by the authority that are associated with a set of attributes. A user is able to decrypt a ciphertext if the attributes of her private key satisfy the boolean formula associated with the ciphertext.

The typical scenario presented for ABE is where a single authority issues all private keys. This works well in the setting where data is managed within one organization or trust domain. However, there are many scenarios when one will wish to describe a policy that spans multiple trust domains. For example, U.S. military and defense are several organizations that wish to manage the distribution of their own credentials. If we wished to write an access policy that referenced credentials from both of them using standard ABE, we would require one organization ceding control to another or a third party. To address this issue multi-authority or decentralized [14] ABE systems were introduced where multiple parties could play the role of an authority. Initial attempts at such systems [14,15] sacrificed a significant amount of expressiveness compared to analogs in the one authority setting. Fairly recently, though Lewko and Waters [27] provided a system that roughly matched the expressiveness. In their system a policy could be expressed as any monotonic boolean formula[1] over attributes that can be issued by any authority which publishes a public key. Their main construction technique is to use a hash over a global identifier. Upon decryption this extra component serves as a "blinding factor" that only disappears if the ciphertext is satisfied.

While the expressiveness, of the Lewko-Waters distributed ABE system is relatively strong, there are three major aspects that impact its practical performance compared to single authority systems. First, the construction is set in a group of composite order N where N is the product of three primes. This alone can make certain operations such as exponentiation over an order of magnitude slower (see Appendix D). Second, each authority in the system can "natively" support only a single attribute. If in practice we would like one party to act as an authority for up to c attributes, the party would have to create a public key consisting of c native public keys (thus blowing up the size by a factor of c). Furthermore, this only works if the attributes managed by that party can be enumerated ahead of time. This means that the attribute universe is restricted to polynomial size. Finally, the system has the native property that each authority can be used only once in each formula. In practice, if we want to get around this and let it be used up to d times we can apply a simple encoding technique due

---

[1] Actually, their system is more general in that it allows for monotone span programs.

to Lewko et al. [26].[2] This encoding however comes at the cost of blowing up both the parameters of the authority and the private key components issued by the authority by a factor of d. To make things concrete suppose that we wanted a system with an authority that managed 20 attributes each of which appeared at most 10 times in the any formula. Then the published parameters for just that one authority would need to blowup by a factor of 200 (compared to a contemporary single use CP-ABE system [11,50]) just to deal with the encoding overhead.

We will construct and implement a new decentralized ABE cryptosystem that aims to get performance close to existing single authority constructions. Our approach is to use the LW construction as a substrate from which we make two significant changes to improve performance. First, we take the existing construction and pare it down to the prime order setting. This will make it inherently faster, but incompatible with the Dual System Encryption [49] proof techniques used before. (Note we do not simulate subspaces in prime order groups [18,25,36] which itself has additional overhead.) Second, we add an additional piece to each ciphertext and private key component which allows us to use *any* string as an attribute — thus addressing the problem of an authority only supporting a single attribute and the small universe restriction. At the same time, the second change allows the system to utilize each attribute as many times as needed in each policy.

With these changes we must prove security of our scheme. As mentioned earlier, with the removal of subgroups the Dual System Encryption methodology is no longer available. We will create a proof of security in a static model of security where both the challenge ciphertexts and key queries are issued before the parameters are published. We needed the keys' queries to be non-adaptive, a property which has not been used in prior work, because the private key for a single user is issued in a piecemeal fashion. Each piece corresponds to a different authority, while in the single authority setting private key requests are naturally atomic. We extend the existing "program and cancel" techniques from two large universe constructions presented in [40] in order to adapt to the multi-authority setting and introduce two new ones. The trade-offs for our performance improvements are the use of the static model and an assumption whose size depends on the complexity of the challenge ciphertext policy.

To demonstrate the abilities of our system we implemented our algorithms in Charm and we provide timing results and comparisons to existing single-authority schemes.

1.1   Related Work

Attribute-Based Encryption was introduced by Sahai and Waters [42]. In this work, the key-policy and ciphertext-policy notions were defined and many selectively secure constructions followed [6,16,21,37,39,50]. Most of them work for

---

[2] The one use restriction is needed to make the security proof of Lewko and Waters go through, if the one use restriction were violated there is neither a known attack nor a security proof.

non monotonic access structures with the exception of the schemes by Ostrovsky, Sahai, and Waters [37], who showed how to realize negation by incorporating specific revocation schemes into the GPSW construction. Fully secure constructions in the standard model were first provided by Okamoto and Takashima [36] and Lewko et al. [26]. The first large universe KP-ABE construction in the standard model was given in [28] (composite order groups). Two large universe constructions in prime order groups were presented in [40] and both techniques, *layering* and *individual randomness*, from that paper are extended and utilized in our current construction. Okamoto and Takashima initiated the dual pairing vector space framework in various works [34–36], which lead to the first large universe KP-ABE construction in prime order group groups by Lewko [25]. Parameterized (non static) assumptions were introduced in [7] and used in several subsequent works [20,50]. The problem of an environment with multiple central authorities in ABE was considered in [14,15,27], while several authors have presented schemes that do not address the problem of collusion resistance [2–4,12,30,46].

We note that several techniques in ABE schemes have roots in Identity - Based Encryption [7–9,17,20,43,48]. Finally, we mention here the related concept of Predicate Encryption introduced by Katz et al. [23] and further refined in [10,26,35,36,44,45].

2   Preliminaries

2.1   Notation

For $n \in \mathbb{N}$, we define $[n] = \{1, 2, \ldots, n\}$. Also, for $n_1, n_2, \ldots, n_k \in \mathbb{N}$: $[n_1, n_2, \ldots, n_k] = [n_1] \times [n_2] \times \ldots \times [n_m]$. By $\{X_i\}_{i \in [n]}$ we denote a sequence of elements $X_1, X_2, \ldots, X_n$.

When S is a set, we denote by $s \xleftarrow{R} S$ the fact that the variable s is picked uniformly at random from S. We write $s_1, s_2, \ldots, s_n \xleftarrow{R} S$ as shorthand for $s_1 \xleftarrow{R} S, s_2 \xleftarrow{R} S, \ldots, s_n \xleftarrow{R} S$.

The set of matrices of size $m \times n$ with elements in $\mathbb{Z}_p$ is denoted by $\mathbb{Z}_p^{m \times n}$. Special subsets are the set of row vectors of length n: $\mathbb{Z}_p^{1 \times n}$, and column vectors of length n: $\mathbb{Z}_p^{n \times 1}$. We denote by $\langle v, w \rangle$ the inner product of vector v with w, where each vector can either be a row or a column vector. Finally, the operation $(\cdot)^\top$ denotes the transpose vector/matrix.

2.2   Access Structures and Linear Secret - Sharing Schemes

In this subsection, we present the formal definitions of access structures and linear secret-sharing schemes introduced in [5], adapted to match our setting.

Definition 1 (Access Structures [5]). *Let $\mathcal{U}$ be the attribute universe. An access structure on $\mathcal{U}$ is a collection $\mathbb{A}$ of non-empty sets of attributes, i.e. $\mathbb{A} \subseteq 2^{\mathcal{U}} \setminus \{\}$. The sets in $\mathbb{A}$ are called the* authorized sets *and the sets not in $\mathbb{A}$ are called the* unauthorized sets.

Additionally, an access structure is called monotone *if $\forall B, C \in \mathbb{A} : $ if $B \in \mathbb{A}$ and $B \subseteq C$, then $C \in \mathbb{A}$.*

In our construction, we only consider monotone access structures, which means that as a user acquires more attributes, he will not lose his possible decryption privileges. General access structures in large universe ABE can be realized by splitting the attribute universe in half and treating the attributes of one half as the negated versions of the attributes in the other half [22].

Definition 2 (Linear Secret-Sharing Schemes). *Let p be prime and $\mathcal{U}$ the attribute universe. A secret-sharing scheme Π with domain of secrets $\mathbb{Z}_p$ realizing access structures on $\mathcal{U}$ is linear over $\mathbb{Z}_p$ if*

1. *The shares of a secret $z \in \mathbb{Z}_p$ for each attribute form a vector over $\mathbb{Z}_p$.*
2. *For each access structure $\mathbb{A}$ on $\mathcal{U}$, there exists a matrix $A \in \mathbb{Z}_p^{\ell \times n}$, called the share-generating matrix, and a function δ, that labels the rows of A with attributes from $\mathcal{U}$, i.e. $\delta : [\ell] \to \mathcal{U}$, which satisfy the following:*
   During the generation of the shares, we consider the column vector $\boldsymbol{v} = (z, r_2, \ldots, r_n)^{\perp}$, where $r_2, \ldots, r_n \xleftarrow{R} \mathbb{Z}_p$. Then the vector of ℓ shares of the secret z according to Π is equal to $\lambda = A\boldsymbol{v} \in \mathbb{Z}_p^{\ell \times 1}$. The share λ_j with $j \in [\ell]$ "belongs" to attribute $\delta(j)$.

We will be referring to the pair (A, δ) as the policy of the access structure $\mathbb{A}$.

According to [5], each secret-sharing scheme (not only the linear ones) should satisfy the *reconstruction requirement* (each authorized set can reconstruct the secret) and the *security requirement* (any unauthorized set cannot reveal any partial information about the secret). More concretely, let S denote an authorized set of attributes and let I be the set of rows whose labels are in S. There exist constants $\{c_i\}_{i \in I}$ in $\mathbb{Z}_p$ such that for any valid shares $\{\lambda_i = (A\boldsymbol{v})_i\}_{i \in I}$ of a secret z according to Π, it is true that: $\sum_{i \in I} c_i \lambda_i = z$, or equivalently $\sum_{i \in I} c_i \boldsymbol{A}_i = (1, 0, \ldots, 0)$, where $\boldsymbol{A}_i$ is the i-th row of A.

On the other hand, for unauthorized sets S' no such constants exist. In this case, it is also true that if I' is the set of rows whose labels are in S', there exists a vector $\boldsymbol{d} \in \mathbb{Z}_p^{1 \times n}$, such that its first component $d_1 = 1$ and $\langle \boldsymbol{A}_i, \boldsymbol{d} \rangle = 0$ for all $i \in I'$.

Finally, we note that if the access structure is encoded as a monotonic Boolean formula over attributes there is a generic algorithm that generates the corresponding access policy in polynomial time [5,27].

Multi-Authority Attributes. In the multi-authority setting, each attribute is controlled by a specific authority $\theta \in \mathcal{U}_\Theta$, where $\mathcal{U}_\Theta$ is the set (universe) of all authorities. We assume there is a publicly computable function $\mathsf{T} : \mathcal{U} \to \mathcal{U}_\Theta$ that maps each attribute to a unique authority. Using this mapping a second labeling of rows is defined in a policy (A, δ), which maps rows to attributes via the function $\rho(\cdot) \stackrel{\mathrm{def}}{=} \mathsf{T}(\delta(\cdot))$.

In our implementation, both the attribute id's and the authority id's consist of case-sensitive alphanumeric strings. The full attributes' names are of the form "[attribute–id]@[authority–id]" and the mapping T just extracts the part after the @ of the attribute string.

2.3 Bilinear Groups and Complexity Assumption

For the following we assume familiarity of the reader with bilinear groups of prime order (see Appendix B for more information). Our construction, the complexity assumption, and the security proof are all expressed in the simpler setting of symmetric groups and can be generically transformed to the asymmetric setting by substituting roughly half of the scheme's components with the respective $\mathbb{G}_2$ terms (i.e. with the same exponents). Our implementations are all written formally in the asymmetric setting, since this is what the Charm framework dictates, although 2 out of the 5 test runs were executed with super-singular symmetric groups (see Sect. 5).

For our security proof we will use a q-type assumption on prime order bilinear groups. It is a slightly modified version of the q-Decisional Parallel Bilinear Diffie-Hellman Exponent Assumption [50]. We will be referring to our assumption as q-DPBDHE2 for short. The assumption is defined as follows:

Choose a bilinear group $\mathbb{G}$ of order p according to the security parameter κ, which admits a non-degenerate bilinear mapping $e : \mathbb{G} \times \mathbb{G} \rightarrow \mathbb{G}_T$. Pick $s, a, b_1, b_2, \ldots, b_q \xleftarrow{R} \mathbb{Z}_p$ and $R \xleftarrow{R} \mathbb{G}_T$. Let

$$D = \left(\mathbb{G}, p, e, g, g^s, \{g^{a^i}\}_{\substack{i \in [2q] \\ i \neq q+1}}, \{g^{b_j a^i}\}_{\substack{(i,j) \in [2q,q] \\ i \neq q+1}}, \right.$$

$$\left. \{g^{s/b_i}\}_{i \in [q]}, \{g^{sa^i b_j/b_{j'}}\}_{\substack{(i,j,j') \in [q+1,q,q] \\ j \neq j'}} \right)$$

The assumption states that no polynomial-time distinguisher can distinguish the distribution $\left(D, e(g,g)^{sa^{q+1}} \right)$ from the distribution (D, R) with more than negligible advantage.

The only difference between the q-DPBDHE assumption in [50] and the above assumption is that in the latter the $\{g^{sa^i b_j/b_{j'}}\}$ terms go up to $i = q+1$ instead of q. The q-DPBDHE assumption was shown generically secure in [50] and following exactly the same proof path, one can prove that the q-DPBDHE2 assumption is also generically secure. Due to lack of space and the similarity to [50], the full proof is omitted.

The assumption is closely related to the two assumptions presented in [40]. Although incomparable to both of them, it contains fewer terms, hence it is relatively weaker. This comes in contrast to the fact that our multi-authority construction supports more features than the two ABE schemes of [40]. The reason of the apparent paradox is the use of the static security and random oracle model in this work versus selective security and standard model in [40].

3   Multi-Authority Ciphertext-Policy ABE

In this section we provide the necessary background on multi-authority CP-ABE schemes and the security definition for static security.

3.1 Algorithms

A multi-authority ciphertext-policy attribute-based encryption system consists of the following five probabilistic polynomial-time algorithms:

GlobalSetup(1^κ) → GP: The global setup algorithm takes in the security parameter κ encoded in unary and outputs the public global parameters for the system. We require that descriptions of the attribute universe $\mathcal{U}$, the authority universe $\mathcal{U}_\Theta$, the global identifier universe $\mathcal{GID}$, and the mapping T are included in the global parameters.

AuthSetup(GP, θ) → {PK$_\theta$, SK$_\theta$}: The authority $\theta \in \mathcal{U}_\Theta$ calls the authority setup algorithm during its initialization with the global parameters GP as input and receives its public/secret key pair {PK$_\theta$, SK$_\theta$}.

KeyGen(GID, SK$_\theta$, u, GP) → SK$_{\text{GID},u}$: The key generation algorithm takes in the global identifier GID of a user (GID $\in \mathcal{GID}$), the secret key of an authority θ, an attribute u controlled by the authority θ, and the global parameters. It outputs a key for the identity - attribute pair (GID, u).[3]

Encrypt(M, $\mathbb{A}$, {PK$_\theta$}, GP) → CT: The encryption algorithm takes in a message M, an access structure $\mathbb{A}$, a set of public keys {PK$_\theta$} of the relevant authorities, and the global parameters. It outputs the ciphertext CT.

Decrypt(CT, {SK$_{\text{GID},u}$}, GP) → M: The decryption algorithm takes in a ciphertext CT, the set of keys of a single user GID corresponding to different attributes u, and the global parameters. It outputs either the message M when the collection of attributes satisfies the access structure of the ciphertext, or decryption fails.

We require that all schemes satisfy the following correctness property:

Definition 1. *A multi-authority CP-ABE scheme is* correct *if for any* GP *generated by the global setup algorithm, for any set of keys* {PK$_\theta$, SK$_\theta$} *generated by the authority setup algorithm, for any* CT *generated by the encryption algorithm using the relevant authorities' public keys on any message M and access structure* $\mathbb{A}$, *and for any set of keys* {K$_{\text{GID},u}$} *generated by the key generation algorithm using the relevant authorities' secret keys for one user* GID *on any* $\mathbb{A}$-authorized *set of attributes, it is true that* Decrypt(CT, {SK$_{\text{GID},u}$}, GP) = M.

3.2 Static Security

In this section we will define the static (or non-adaptive) security game between a challenger and an attacker. The difference between this security game and the adaptive one is that all queries done by the attacker are sent to the challenger immediately after seeing the public parameters. As usual, we also allow the attacker to corrupt a certain set of authorities that he can control. These authorities are chosen by the attacker after seeing the global parameters and remain the same until the end of the game.

---

[3] If a user wants a key that corresponds to multiple attributes from the same authority, the key generation algorithm is trivially extended to take in many attributes by running the "single attribute" version once for each attribute.

The game consists of the following phases:

Global Setup: The challenger calls $\mathsf{GlobalSetup}(1^\kappa) \to \mathrm{GP}$ and gives the global parameters GP to the attacker.

Attacker's Queries: Then the attacker responds with:

- A set $\mathcal{C}_\Theta \subseteq \mathcal{U}_\Theta$ of corrupt authorities and their respective public keys $\{\mathrm{PK}_\theta\}_{\theta \in \mathcal{C}_\Theta}$, which he might have created in a malicious way[4].
- A set $\mathcal{N}_\Theta \subseteq \mathcal{U}_\Theta$ of the non-corrupt authorities for which the adversary requests the public keys. Obviously, it should be disjoint from the set of corrupt authorities.
- A sequence $\mathcal{Q} = \{(\mathrm{GID}_i, S_i)\}_{i=1}^m$ of the secret key queries, where the global identities GID_i are distinct and $S_i \subseteq \mathcal{U}$ with $\mathsf{T}(S_i) \cap \mathcal{C}_\Theta = \emptyset$.
  A pair (GID_i, S_i) in this sequence denotes that the attacker requests the secret keys for the user GID_i with attributes from the set S_i. That is, the attacker gets a $\mathrm{SK}_{\mathrm{GID}_i, u} \leftarrow \mathsf{KeyGen}(\mathrm{GID}_i, \mathrm{SK}_{\mathsf{T}(u)}, u, \mathrm{GP})$ for every $u \in S_i$. According to the restriction $\mathsf{T}(S_i) \cap \mathcal{C}_\Theta = \emptyset$, none of these keys come from a corrupt authority.
- Two messages M_0, M_1 of equal length, and a challenge access structure $\mathbb{A}$ encoded in a suitable form. We require that for every $i \in [m]$ the set $S_i \cup \bigcup_{\theta \in \mathcal{C}_\Theta} \mathsf{T}^{-1}(\theta)$ is an unauthorized set of the access structure $\mathbb{A}$, where $\bigcup_{\theta \in \mathcal{C}_\Theta} \mathsf{T}^{-1}(\theta)$ is the set of all the attributes belonging to corrupt authorities. This way, the attacker will not be able to trivially win the game by decrypting the challenge ciphertext with a secret key given to him augmented with the key components from the corrupt authorities.

Challenger's Replies: The challenger flips a random coin $b \xleftarrow{R} \{0,1\}$ and replies with:

- The public keys $\mathrm{PK}_\theta \leftarrow \mathsf{AuthSetup}(\mathrm{GP}, \theta)$ for all $\theta \in \mathcal{N}_\Theta$.
- The secret keys $\mathrm{SK}_{\mathrm{GID}_i, u} \leftarrow \mathsf{KeyGen}(\mathrm{GID}_i, \mathrm{SK}_{\mathsf{T}(u)}, u, \mathrm{GP})$ for all $i \in [m]$ and for all $u \in S_i$.
- The challenge ciphertext $\mathrm{CT}^* \leftarrow \mathsf{Encrypt}(M_b, \mathbb{A}, \{\mathrm{PK}_\theta\}, \mathrm{GP})$ where $\{\mathrm{PK}_\theta\}$ is the set of all authority public keys (corrupt and non corrupt).

Guess: The attacker outputs a guess $b' \in \{0,1\}$.

Definition 2. *We say that an attacker statically breaks the scheme if it has a non negligible advantage in correctly guessing the bit b in the above security game.*

4   Our Scheme

Our scheme constitutes an augmented version of the Lewko-Waters [27] CP - ABE construction and shares several of the existing techniques. Namely, in order to allow for multiple authorities and prevent collusion between users' keys it

---

[4] The only requirement is that they have the correct type.

utilizes a hash function H that maps global identities to group elements. This hash function is modeled as a random oracle in the security proof. As noted in [27], this allows for a totally decentralized construction, since it provides all authorities with a secure way to personalize the secret key given to a specific user. To the best of our knowledge, it is still an open problem whether it is possible to create a multi-authority ABE scheme in the standard model, where no coordination is allowed between the different authorities.

Since we will be working in the random oracle model and we aim for practically deployable schemes, we combined the above technique with the technique from [50] that used a hash function F that hashes *attributes* to group elements. This way we overcame the restriction that each authority is used only once and at the same time achieved a large universe construction. This is because the random oracle usage naturally overcomes the "one-time" restriction and the policies are not any more controlled by the authorities, but by the underlying attributes. The *individual randomness technique* from [28,40] is integrated to the treatment of each attribute by choosing a fresh random exponent t.

Finally in order to "bind" the different ciphertext terms together we use the *layering* technique of [40]. For the same reason we introduce two secret sharing vectors: one that shares the secret z of the blinding factor and one that shares 0. In order to decrypt, a user has to use both of them. However, during decryption the "0-shares" are crucially entangled to the global identifier of the secret key of the user. As a result in the event that two or more users collude and try to decrypt the same ciphertext, the "0-shares" will result in a failed decryption, thus preventing collusion attacks.

4.1 Construction

Our proposed scheme consists of the following five algorithms:

GlobalSetup$(1^\kappa) \rightarrow$ GP: The global setup algorithm takes as input the security parameter κ and chooses a suitable bilinear group $\mathbb{G}$ of prime order p with generator g. It also chooses a function H mapping global identities GID $\in \mathcal{GID}$ to elements of $\mathbb{G}$,[5] and another function F mapping strings, interpreted as attributes, to elements of $\mathbb{G}$. Both of these functions will be modeled as random oracles in the security proof. Finally, it defines $\mathcal{U}$, $\mathcal{U}_\Theta$, and T as in Sect. 2.2. The global parameters are GP $= \{p, \mathbb{G}, g, H, F, \mathcal{U}, \mathcal{U}_\Theta, \mathsf{T}\}$.

AuthSetup$(\mathsf{GP}, \theta) \rightarrow \{\mathrm{PK}_\theta, \mathrm{SK}_\theta\}$: The authority setup algorithm chooses two random exponents $\alpha_\theta, y_\theta \xleftarrow{R} \mathbb{Z}_p$ and publishes PK $= \{e(g,g)^{\alpha_\theta}, g^{y_\theta}\}$ as its public key. It keeps SK $= \{\alpha_\theta, y_\theta\}$ as its secret key.

KeyGen$(\mathrm{GID}, \theta, u, \mathrm{SK}_\theta, \mathsf{GP}) \rightarrow \{\mathrm{K}_{\mathrm{GID},u}, \mathrm{K}'_{\mathrm{GID},u}\}$: The key generation algorithm takes as input the user's global identifier GID, the identifier θ of the authority, the attribute u to create a key for, as well as the authority's secret key and the

---

[5] The global identifier universe $\mathcal{GID}$ can be any set that provides a unique identifier for each user and is mapped by H.

global parameters. It should be the case that $u \in \mathsf{T}^{-1}(\theta)$, i.e. that the attribute is controlled by the specific authority.

The algorithm first chooses a random $t \xleftarrow{R} \mathbb{Z}_p$ and it outputs the secret key:

$$\mathrm{SK}_{\mathrm{GID},u} = \left\{ \mathrm{K}_{\mathrm{GID},u} = g^{\alpha_\theta} H(\mathrm{GID})^{y_\theta} F(u)^t, \mathrm{K}'_{\mathrm{GID},u} = g^t \right\}$$

$\mathsf{Encrypt}(M, (A, \delta), \{\mathrm{PK}_\theta\}, \mathrm{GP}) \to \mathrm{CT}$: The encryption algorithm takes in a message M, an access policy (A, δ) with $A \in \mathbb{Z}_p^{\ell \times n}$, the public keys of the relevant authorities, and the global parameters. As always, we define the function $\rho : [\ell] \to \mathcal{U}_\Theta$ as $\rho(\cdot) = \mathsf{T}(\delta(\cdot))$, i.e. the mapping of rows to authorities.

The algorithm first creates vectors $\boldsymbol{v} = (z, v_2, \ldots, v_n)^\top$ and $\boldsymbol{w} = (0, w_2, \ldots, w_n)^\top$, where $z, v_2, \ldots, v_n, w_2, \ldots, w_n \xleftarrow{R} \mathbb{Z}_p$. We let λ_x denote the share of z corresponding to row x, i.e. $\lambda_x = \langle \boldsymbol{A}_x, \boldsymbol{v} \rangle$, and ω_x denote the share of 0, i.e. $\omega_x = \langle \boldsymbol{A}_x, \boldsymbol{w} \rangle$, where $\boldsymbol{A}_x$ is the x-th row of A.

For each row x of A, it chooses a random $t_x \xleftarrow{R} \mathbb{Z}_p$. The ciphertext is computed as:

$$C_0 = M e(g,g)^z, \left\{ C_{1,x} = e(g,g)^{\lambda_x} e(g,g)^{\alpha_{\rho(x)} t_x}, C_{2,x} = g^{-t_x}, \right.$$

$$\left. C_{3,x} = g^{y_{\rho(x)} t_x} g^{\omega_x}, C_{4,x} = F(\delta(x))^{t_x} \right\}_{x \in [\ell]}$$

$\mathsf{Decrypt}(\mathrm{CT}, \{\mathrm{K}_{\mathrm{GID},u}, \mathrm{K}'_{\mathrm{GID},u}\}, \mathrm{GP}) \to M$: Let (A, δ) be the access policy of the ciphertext. If the decryptor has the secret keys $\{\mathrm{K}_{\mathrm{GID},\delta(x)}, \mathrm{K}'_{\mathrm{GID},\delta(x)}\}$ for a subset of rows $\boldsymbol{A}_x$ of A such that $(1, 0, \ldots, 0)$ is in the span of these rows, then for each such row x he computes:

$$C_{1,x} \cdot e(\mathrm{K}_{\mathrm{GID},\delta(x)}, C_{2,x}) \cdot e(H(\mathrm{GID}), C_{3,x}) \cdot e(\mathrm{K}'_{\mathrm{GID},\delta(x)}, C_{4,x}) =$$

$$e(g,g)^{\lambda_x} e(H(\mathrm{GID}), g)^{\omega_x}$$

The decryptor then calculates constants $c_x \in \mathbb{Z}_p$ such that $\sum_x c_x \boldsymbol{A}_x = (1, 0, \ldots, 0)$ and computes:

$$\prod_x \left(e(g,g)^{\lambda_x} e(H(\mathrm{GID}), g)^{\omega_x} \right)^{c_x} = e(g,g)^z$$

This is true because $\lambda_x = \langle \boldsymbol{A}_x, \boldsymbol{v} \rangle$ and $\omega_x = \langle \boldsymbol{A}_x, \boldsymbol{w} \rangle$, where we have $\langle (1, 0, \ldots, 0), \boldsymbol{v} \rangle = z$ and $\langle (1, 0, \ldots, 0), \boldsymbol{w} \rangle = 0$. The message can then be obtained as: $M = C_0 / e(g,g)^z$.

Re-randomizing. Due to the linearity of all exponents, re-randomizing techniques are applicable for the users' secret keys and the ciphertexts using only the public parameters. These techniques can provide properly distributed keys and ciphertexts even if originally the random choices in these algorithms are not uniform. We will use these techniques in our security reduction.

Specifically, if someone has a key $\{\mathrm{K}_{\mathrm{GID},u}, \mathrm{K}'_{\mathrm{GID},u}\}$, he can acquire a new key for (GID, u) by picking $t' \xleftarrow{R} \mathbb{Z}_p$ and constructing $\{\mathrm{K}_{\mathrm{GID},u} F(u)^{t'}, \mathrm{K}'_{\mathrm{GID},u} g^{t'}\}$.

For the ciphertext the re-randomization can be done by picking a new $z' \xleftarrow{R} \mathbb{Z}_p$, new random vectors $\boldsymbol{v}'$ and $\boldsymbol{w}'$ with the first elements z' and 0, respectively, and for each row x a new $t'_x \xleftarrow{R} \mathbb{Z}_p$. Then the re-randomized ciphertext is

$$C_0 e(g,g)^{z'}, \; \left\{ C_{1,x} e(g,g)^{\langle A_x, \boldsymbol{v}' \rangle} e(g,g)^{\alpha_{\rho(x)} t'_x}, C_{2,x} g^{-t'_x}, \right.$$

$$\left. C_{3,x} g^{y_{\rho(x)} t'_x} g^{\langle A_x, \boldsymbol{w}' \rangle}, \; C_{4,x} F(\delta(x))^{t'_x} \right\}_{x \in [\ell]}$$

5 Implementation and Evaluation

Framework. We implemented our scheme in Charm [1]; a framework developed to facilitate the rapid prototyping of cryptographic schemes and protocols. It is based on the Python language which allows the programmer to write code similar to the theoretical implementations. However, the routines that implement the dominant group operations use the PBC library [29] (written natively in C) and the time overhead imposed by the use of Python is usually less than 1%. Charm also provides routines for applying and using LSSS schemes needed for Attribute-Based systems. For more information on Charm we refer the reader to [1,13].

We tested several ABE constructions on all elliptic curve bilinear groups provided by Charm, i.e. three super-singular symmetric EC groups and two "MNT" [32] asymmetric EC groups. In Table 2 of Appendix C we present the approximate security level each group provides with respect to the discrete log problem. The source code of our implementations can be found in [47]. All our benchmarks were executed on a dual core Intel® Xeon® CPU W3503@2.40 GHz with 2.0 GB RAM running Ubuntu R10.04 and Python3.2.3.

Implementation Details. All Charm routines use formally asymmetric groups (although the underlining groups might be symmetric) and therefore we translated our schemes to the asymmetric setting. Namely, we have three groups $\mathbb{G}_1, \mathbb{G}_2$ and $\mathbb{G}_T$ and the pairing e is a function from $\mathbb{G}_1 \times \mathbb{G}_2$ to $\mathbb{G}_T$. We note here that we tried to implement our algorithms so that more operations are executed in the $\mathbb{G}_1$ group than in the $\mathbb{G}_2$ and that encryption consists mainly of operations in $\mathbb{G}_1$, compared to key generation. The reason is that the time taken to execute them in the $\mathbb{G}_1$ group is considerably smaller than $\mathbb{G}_2$ in specific asymmetric groups such as the "MNT" groups.

Regarding the comparisons to other schemes, the only fully decentralized multi-authority ABE scheme that provides expressive policies is the CP-ABE scheme of Lewko-Waters [27]. However, we decided to defer implementation and benchmarking of it for several reasons: Firstly, this scheme utilizes composite order groups, which are several orders of magnitude slower than the prime order groups that provide the same security level. We expect our scheme to be significantly faster. More information on the comparison between prime and composite groups can be found in Appendix D. Secondly, as mentioned in the introduction, the attributes utilized in the system have to be enumerated ahead of time and an

Table 1. Average running times in milliseconds of our scheme and two single authority schemes. The algorithms are denoted as GS: Global setup, AS: Authority setup, KG: Key generation for a user, EC: Encrypt, DE: Decrypt. The numbers in parentheses refer to the number of attributes in key generation, the number of rows of the policy in encryption, and the number of rows utilized during decryption. We can see the linear dependence between these numbers and the corresponding times.

Our CP-ABE [Sec. 4.1] (Multi-authority, random oracle model, statically secure)

Curve	GS	AS	KG(4)	KG(8)	KG(12)	EC(4)	EC(8)	EC(12)	DE(4)	DE(8)	DE(12)
SS512	8.4	4.1	91.5	182.9	274.6	75.0	150.4	226.4	34.5	59.2	82.3
SS1024	58.0	43.8	631.8	1263.5	1894.5	666.9	1331.2	1997.2	641.4	1275.4	1907.4
MNT159	14.4	3.7	295.9	502.7	799.7	155.9	299.4	450.1	99.3	159.8	237.5
MNT201	19.5	4.6	370.5	787.0	1205.8	191.6	401.2	592.1	133.8	237.9	321.5
MNT224	24.1	5.5	489.5	838.4	1335.2	244.1	473.0	695.9	157.0	273.2	390.3

BSW CP-ABE [6] (Single-authority, generic group model, adaptively secure)

Curve	GS	AS	KG(4)	KG(8)	KG(12)	EC(4)	EC(8)	EC(12)	DE(4)	DE(8)	DE(12)
SS512	20.1	N/A	52.9	100.1	146.9	51.0	98.5	147.6	22.5	40.3	55.3
SS1024	213.3	N/A	394.0	710.3	1026.5	360.1	681.6	997.1	482.2	909.0	1333.9
MNT159	31.2	N/A	152.8	265.2	399.4	107.5	268.2	376.9	56.4	104.7	149.1
MNT201	42.2	N/A	221.5	335.1	557.8	169.8	331.7	564.5	76.3	142.5	205.5
MNT224	52.3	N/A	192.8	447.5	566.1	209.1	329.3	595.2	94.7	175.0	253.6

Waters CP-ABE [50] (Single-authority, random oracle model, adaptively secure)

Curve	GS	AS	KG(4)	KG(8)	KG(12)	EC(4)	EC(8)	EC(12)	DE(4)	DE(8)	DE(12)
SS512	20.4	N/A	39.6	73.9	108.0	64.2	124.8	186.4	32.5	60.1	85.3
SS1024	216.3	N/A	237.7	397.5	558.6	516.4	992.9	1464.4	627.0	1200.5	1770.1
MNT159	32.7	N/A	18.3	21.8	25.7	43.4	84.5	125.2	56.3	104.5	148.8
MNT201	44.6	N/A	25.4	31.7	37.2	58.8	118.3	170.7	77.0	143.4	206.9
MNT224	55.1	N/A	31.4	38.4	45.2	71.3	137.3	205.7	95.2	177.9	258.4

one-use restriction is imposed on each attribute per policy. So even this scheme provides less flexibility than our construction. Thirdly, Charm does not support composite order groups, and finally, it is questionable the validity of the comparison between a prime order group and a composite order group, when the underlying elliptic curve is different and/or different optimizations have been applied to them.

Instead of this, we validate the claim that our system provides similar efficiency to existing single-authority ABE constructions, by providing implementation results of two single-authority ABE schemes. These are the Bethencourt-Sahai-Waters CP-ABE scheme [6] and the recent Waters CP-ABE [50]. Both of them were implemented by the Charm authors as typical examples. The former scheme is secure in the generic group model, while the implementation of the latter uses the random oracle version of it.

Timing Results. Timing results in milliseconds are shown in Table 1. We see that our scheme achieves similar operation times to the two established single-authority schemes. In general, we attempted to keep execution times for encryption and decryption relatively low, while the times for setup and key generation can be significantly higher, since they are called only once.

6   Static Security

Our main security theorem is shown below. Due to lack of space all the proofs are presented in the full version of the paper [41].

Theorem 1. *If the q-DPBDHE2 assumption holds, then all probabilistic polynomial-time adversaries with a challenge matrix of size at most $q \times q$ have a negligible advantage in statically breaking our scheme in the random oracle model.*

In our security proof we combined several techniques, which we think might be of independent interest in the study of CP-ABE systems. The first technique allows the simulator of our reduction to isolate an unauthorized set of rows and essentially ignore it for the remaining of the security reduction. In our case the simulator does that for the corrupt authorities, which are controlled by the adversary. The relevant lemma is shown in Appendix A.

Another technique utilized in the security proof is the "splitting" of the unknown parameters to two different vectors. During the generation of the authorities' public keys, the elements in the first column of the challenge policy are programmed into the $e(g,g)^{\alpha_\theta}$ component, while the remaining in the g^{y_θ}. The same technique is applied on the challenge ciphertext, where the secret sharing vector v will hold the secret $z = sa^{q+1}$ on only the first position and the zero sharing vector w will hold the unknown terms $sa^q, sa^{q-1}, \ldots, sa^2$ on all positions but the first. During the generation of the users' secret keys and the generation of the challenge ciphertext, all these terms are "recombined" to give a full series of q terms.

A   "Zero-Out" Lemma

Due to lack of space the proof of the lemma is presented in the full version of the paper [41].

Lemma 1. *Let $A \in \mathbb{Z}_p^{\ell \times n}$ be the secret sharing matrix of a linear secret sharing scheme for an access policy $\mathbb{A}$ and let $C \subseteq [\ell]$ be a non-authorized set of rows. Let $c \in \mathbb{N}$ be the dimension of the subspace spanned by the rows of C.*

Then the distribution of the shares $\{\lambda_x\}_{x \in [\ell]}$ sharing the secret $z \in \mathbb{Z}_p$ generated with the matrix A is the same as the distribution of the shares $\{\lambda'_x\}_{x \in [\ell]}$ sharing the same secret z generated with some matrix A', where $A'_{x,j} = 0$ for all $(x, j) \in C \times [n - c]$ (see Fig. 1).

$$A = \begin{bmatrix} A_{1,1} & A_{1,2} & \dots & A_{1,n} \\ A_{2,1} & A_{2,2} & \dots & A_{2,n} \\ A_{3,1} & A_{3,2} & \dots & A_{3,n} \\ \vdots & \vdots & \ddots & \vdots \\ A_{\ell,1} & A_{\ell,2} & \dots & A_{\ell,n} \end{bmatrix} \rightsquigarrow A' = \begin{bmatrix} 0 & \dots & 0 & A'_{1,n-c+1} & \dots & A'_{1,n} \\ A'_{2,1} & \dots & A'_{2,n-c} & A'_{2,n-c+1} & \dots & A'_{2,n} \\ 0 & \dots & 0 & A'_{3,n-c+1} & \dots & A'_{3,n} \\ \vdots & \ddots & \vdots & \vdots & \ddots & \vdots \\ A'_{\ell,1} & \dots & A'_{1,n-c} & A'_{1,n-c+1} & \dots & A'_{\ell,n} \end{bmatrix}$$

Fig. 1. Transformation of the policy matrix A to be used by the simulator. Rows that belong to corrupted authorities are highlighted.

B   Bilinear Groups

Our construction works with instantiations of bilinear groups of prime order. Abstractly, let $\mathbb{G}$ and $\mathbb{G}_T$ be two multiplicative cyclic groups of prime order p, where the group operation is efficiently computable in the security parameter. Let g be a generator of $\mathbb{G}$ and $e : \mathbb{G} \times \mathbb{G} \to \mathbb{G}_T$ be an efficiently computable pairing function that satisfies the following properties:

1. Bilinearity: for all $u, v \in \mathbb{G}$ and $a, b \in \mathbb{Z}_p$ it is true that $e(u^a, v^b) = e(u, v)^{ab}$.
2. Non-degeneracy: $e(g, g) \neq 1_{\mathbb{G}_T}$.

The above definition considers the so called *symmetric* groups, where the two arguments of the pairing belong to the same group. In general, there exist *asymmetric* bilinear groups, where $e : \mathbb{G}_1 \times \mathbb{G}_2 \to \mathbb{G}_T$ and $\mathbb{G}_1$, $\mathbb{G}_2$, and $\mathbb{G}_T$ are three different groups of prime order p. Several asymmetric instantiations of bilinear groups possess beneficial properties such as faster operations under the same security level and/or easier hashing to group elements.

C   Approximate Security Level of all **Charm** Elliptic Curves

In Table 2 we present the approximate security levels of all the elliptic curves supported by Charm. Although the results of the table do not necessarily translate to the security level of our assumption (or the various assumptions of the other ABE schemes), they provides an intuitive comparison between the security levels of the different instantiations. For more information on the security of discrete log and of q-type assumptions we refer the reader to [19,24,33,38].

D   Prime vs Composite Order Group Operations

In order to demonstrate the generic difference in the efficiency of prime order vs composite order implementations, we timed the group exponentiation (of a random group element with a random exponent) and pairing operations (on random group elements) in the MIRACL framework [31] for different security levels. The

Table 2. Approximate security levels of the utilized ECC groups. "SS" are super singular curves (symmetric bilinear groups), while "MNT" are the Miyaji, Nakabayashi, Takano curves (asymmetric bilinear groups). The number after the type of the curve denotes the size of the base field in bits.

Curve	Security level (Bits)
SS512	80
SS1024	112
MNT159	70
MNT201	90
MNT224	100

benchmarks were executed on a dual core Intel® Xeon® CPU W3503@2.40 GHz with 2.0 GB RAM running Ubuntu R10.04. The elliptic curve utilized for all benchmarks was the super-singular (symmetric) curve $y^2 = x^3 + 1 \mod p$ with embedding degree 2 for suitable primes p.

In Table 3 we can see the significant gap between the timings in prime and composite order groups for the same security levels. This is the main reason that we used prime order groups for our construction.

Table 3. Average timing results in milliseconds over 100 repeats of group exponentiations and pairings in MIRACL.

Group exponentiation

Security Level (Bits)	Prime	Composite(2 primes)	Composite (3 primes)
80	3.5	66.9	201.6
112	14.8	448.1	1404.3
128	34.4	1402.5	4512.5
192	273.8	20097.0	66526.0

Pairing

Security Level (Bits)	Prime	Composite(2 primes)	Composite (3 primes)
80	13.9	245.3	762.3
112	65.7	1706.8	5485.2
128	176.6	5428.2	17494.4
192	1752.3	79046.8	263538.1

References

1. Akinyele, J.A., Green, M., Rubin, A.: Charm: a framework for rapidly prototyping cryptosystems. Cryptology ePrint Archive, Report 2011/617 (2011). http://eprint.iacr.org/

2. Al-Riyami, S.S., Malone-Lee, J., Smart, N.P.: Escrow-free encryption supporting cryptographic workflow. Int. J. Inf. Sec. 5(4), 217–229 (2006)
3. Bagga, W., Molva, R., Crosta, S.: Policy-based encryption schemes from bilinear pairings. In: ASIACCS, p. 368 (2006)
4. Barbosa, M., Farshim, P.: Secure cryptographic workflow in the standard model. In: Barua, R., Lange, T. (eds.) INDOCRYPT 2006. LNCS, vol. 4329, pp. 379–393. Springer, Heidelberg (2006)
5. Beimel, A.: Secure schemes for secret sharing and key distribution. Ph.D. thesis, Dept. of Computer Science, Technion (1996)
6. Bethencourt, J., Sahai, A., Waters, B.: Ciphertext-policy attribute-based encryption. In: IEEE Symposium on Security and Privacy, pp. 321–334 (2007)
7. Boneh, D., Boyen, X.: Efficient selective-id secure identity-based encryption without random oracles. In: Cachin, C., Camenisch, J.L. (eds.) EUROCRYPT 2004. LNCS, vol. 3027, pp. 223–238. Springer, Heidelberg (2004)
8. Boneh, D., Franklin, M.K.: Identity-based encryption from the weil pairing. SIAM J. Comput. 32(3), 586–615 (2003). Extended Abstract in Crypto 2001
9. Boneh, D., Gentry, C., Hamburg, M.: Space-efficient identity based encryption without pairings. In: FOCS, pp. 647–657 (2007)
10. Boneh, D., Sahai, A., Waters, B.: Functional encryption: definitions and challenges. In: Ishai, Y. (ed.) TCC 2011. LNCS, vol. 6597, pp. 253–273. Springer, Heidelberg (2011)
11. Boneh, D., Waters, B.: Conjunctive, subset, and range queries on encrypted data. In: Vadhan, S.P. (ed.) TCC 2007. LNCS, vol. 4392, pp. 535–554. Springer, Heidelberg (2007)
12. Bradshaw, R.W., Holt, J.E., Seamons, K.E.: Concealing complex policies with hidden credentials. In: ACM Conference on Computer and Communications Security, pp. 146–157 (2004)
13. Charm. http://www.charm-crypto.com
14. Chase, M.: Multi-authority attribute based encryption. In: Vadhan, S.P. (ed.) TCC 2007. LNCS, vol. 4392, pp. 515–534. Springer, Heidelberg (2007)
15. Chase, M., Chow, S.S.M.: Improving privacy and security in multi-authority attribute-based encryption. In: ACM Conference on Computer and Communications Security, pp. 121–130 (2009)
16. Cheung, L., Newport, C.C.: Provably secure ciphertext policy abe. In: ACM Conference on Computer and Communications Security, pp. 456–465 (2007)
17. Cocks, Clifford: An identity based encryption scheme based on quadratic residues. In: Honary, Bahram (ed.) Cryptography and Coding 2001. LNCS, vol. 2260, pp. 360–363. Springer, Heidelberg (2001)
18. Freeman, D.M.: Converting pairing-based cryptosystems from composite-order groups to prime-order groups. In: Gilbert, H. (ed.) EUROCRYPT 2010. LNCS, vol. 6110, pp. 44–61. Springer, Heidelberg (2010)
19. Galbraith, S.D., Paterson, K.G., Smart, N.P., Smart, N.P.: Pairings for cryptographers. In: Discrete Applied Mathematics (2008)
20. Gentry, C.: Practical identity-based encryption without random oracles. In: Vaudenay, S. (ed.) EUROCRYPT 2006. LNCS, vol. 4004, pp. 445–464. Springer, Heidelberg (2006)
21. Goyal, V., Jain, A., Pandey, O., Sahai, A.: Bounded ciphertext policy attribute based encryption. In: Aceto, L., Damgård, I., Goldberg, L.A., Halldórsson, M.M., Ingólfsdóttir, A., Walukiewicz, I. (eds.) ICALP 2008, Part II. LNCS, vol. 5126, pp. 579–591. Springer, Heidelberg (2008)

22. Goyal, V., Pandey, O., Sahai, A., Waters, B.: Attribute-based encryption for fine-grained access control of encrypted data. In: ACM Conference on Computer and Communications Security, pp. 89–98 (2006)
23. Katz, J., Sahai, A., Waters, B.: Predicate encryption supporting disjunctions, polynomial equations, and inner products. In: Smart, N.P. (ed.) EUROCRYPT 2008. LNCS, vol. 4965, pp. 146–162. Springer, Heidelberg (2008)
24. Lenstra, A.K., Verheul, E.R.: Selecting cryptographic key sizes. In: Imai, H., Zheng, Y. (eds.) PKC 2000. LNCS, vol. 1751, pp. 446–465. Springer, Heidelberg (2000)
25. Lewko, A.: Tools for simulating features of composite order bilinear groups in the prime order setting. In: Pointcheval, D., Johansson, T. (eds.) EUROCRYPT 2012. LNCS, vol. 7237, pp. 318–335. Springer, Heidelberg (2012)
26. Lewko, A., Okamoto, T., Sahai, A., Takashima, K., Waters, B.: Fully secure functional encryption: attribute-based encryption and (hierarchical) inner product encryption. In: Gilbert, H. (ed.) EUROCRYPT 2010. LNCS, vol. 6110, pp. 62–91. Springer, Heidelberg (2010)
27. Lewko, A., Waters, B.: Decentralizing attribute-based encryption. In: Paterson, K.G. (ed.) EUROCRYPT 2011. LNCS, vol. 6632, pp. 568–588. Springer, Heidelberg (2011)
28. Lewko, A., Waters, B.: Unbounded HIBE and attribute-based encryption. In: Paterson, K.G. (ed.) EUROCRYPT 2011. LNCS, vol. 6632, pp. 547–567. Springer, Heidelberg (2011)
29. Lynn, B.: The stanford pairing based crypto library. http://crypto.stanford.edu/pbc
30. Miklau, G., Suciu, D.: Controlling access to published data using cryptography. In: VLDB, pp. 898–909 (2003)
31. Miracl crypto sdk. https://certivox.com/solutions/miracl-crypto-sdk/
32. Miyaji, A., Nakabayashi, M., Takano, S.: Characterization of elliptic curve traces under FR-reduction. In: Won, D. (ed.) ICISC 2000. LNCS, vol. 2015, pp. 90–108. Springer, Heidelberg (2001)
33. National Institute of Standards and Technology. Nist special publication 800–37 (2010)
34. Okamoto, T., Takashima, K.: Homomorphic encryption and signatures from vector decomposition. In: Galbraith, S.D., Paterson, K.G. (eds.) Pairing 2008. LNCS, vol. 5209, pp. 57–74. Springer, Heidelberg (2008)
35. Okamoto, T., Takashima, K.: Hierarchical predicate encryption for inner-products. In: Matsui, M. (ed.) ASIACRYPT 2009. LNCS, vol. 5912, pp. 214–231. Springer, Heidelberg (2009)
36. Okamoto, T., Takashima, K.: Fully secure functional encryption with general relations from the decisional linear assumption. In: Rabin, T. (ed.) CRYPTO 2010. LNCS, vol. 6223, pp. 191–208. Springer, Heidelberg (2010)
37. Ostrovsky, R., Sahai, A., Waters, B.: Attribute-based encryption with non-monotonic access structures. In: ACM Conference on Computer and Communications Security, pp. 195–203 (2007)
38. Page, D., Smart, N.P., Vercauteren, F.: A comparison of mnt curves and supersingular curves. IACR Cryptology ePrint Archive, p. 165 (2004)
39. Pirretti, M., Traynor, P., McDaniel, P., Waters, B.: Secure attribute-based systems. In: ACM Conference on Computer and Communications Security, pp. 99–112 (2006)

40. Rouselakis, Y., Waters, B.: Practical constructions and new proof methods for large universe attribute-based encryption. In: ACM Conference on Computer and Communications Security, pp. 463–474 (2013)

41. Rouselakis, Y., Waters, B.: Efficient statically-secure large-universe multi-authority attribute-based encryption. Cryptology ePrint Archive, Report 2015/016 (2015). http://eprint.iacr.org/2015/016

42. Sahai, A., Waters, B.: Fuzzy identity-based encryption. In: Cramer, R. (ed.) EURO-CRYPT 2005. LNCS, vol. 3494, pp. 457–473. Springer, Heidelberg (2005)

43. Shamir, A.: Identity-based cryptosystems and signature schemes. In: Blakely, G.R., Chaum, D. (eds.) CRYPTO 1984. LNCS, vol. 196, pp. 47–53. Springer, Heidelberg (1985)

44. Shen, E., Shi, E., Waters, B.: Predicate privacy in encryption systems. In: Reingold, O. (ed.) TCC 2009. LNCS, vol. 5444, pp. 457–473. Springer, Heidelberg (2009)

45. Shi, E., Waters, B.: Delegating capabilities in predicate encryption systems. In: Aceto, L., Damgård, I., Goldberg, L.A., Halldórsson, M.M., Ingólfsdóttir, A., Walukiewicz, I. (eds.) ICALP 2008, Part II. LNCS, vol. 5126, pp. 560–578. Springer, Heidelberg (2008)

46. Smart, N.P.: Access control using pairing based cryptography. In: Joye, M. (ed.) CT-RSA 2003. LNCS, vol. 2612, pp. 111–121. Springer, Heidelberg (2003)

47. Source code of our constructions. www.rouselakis.com\RWABE

48. Waters, B.: Efficient identity-based encryption without random oracles. In: Cramer, R. (ed.) EUROCRYPT 2005. LNCS, vol. 3494, pp. 114–127. Springer, Heidelberg (2005)

49. Waters, B.: Dual system encryption: realizing fully secure IBE and HIBE under simple assumptions. In: Halevi, S. (ed.) CRYPTO 2009. LNCS, vol. 5677, pp. 619–636. Springer, Heidelberg (2009)

50. Waters, B.: Ciphertext-policy attribute-based encryption: an expressive, efficient, and provably secure realization. In: Catalano, D., Fazio, N., Gennaro, R., Nicolosi, A. (eds.) PKC 2011. LNCS, vol. 6571, pp. 53–70. Springer, Heidelberg (2011)

Augmented Learning with Errors:
The Untapped Potential of the Error Term

Rachid El Bansarkhani[✉], Özgür Dagdelen, and Johannes Buchmann

Technische Universität Darmstadt, Fachbereich Informatik,
Kryptographie und Computeralgebra, Hochschulstraße 10,
64289 Darmstadt, Germany
{elbansarkhani,buchmann}@cdc.informatik.tu-darmstadt.de,
oezguer.dagdelen@cased.de

Abstract. The Learning with Errors (LWE) problem has gained a lot of
attention in recent years leading to a series of new cryptographic applications. Interestingly, cryptographic primitives based on LWE often do
not exploit the full potential of the error term beside of its importance
for security. To this end, we introduce a novel LWE-close assumption,
namely Augmented Learning with Errors (A-LWE), which allows one
to hide auxiliary data injected into the error term by a technique that
we call message embedding. In particular, it enables existing cryptosystems to strongly increase the message throughput per ciphertext. We
show that A-LWE is for certain instantiations at least as hard as the
LWE problem. This inherently leads to new cryptographic constructions
providing high data load encryption and customized security properties
as required, for instance, in economic environments such as stock markets resp. for financial transactions. The security of those constructions
basically stems from the hardness to solve the A-LWE problem. As an
application we introduce (among others) the first lattice-based replayable
chosen-ciphertext secure encryption scheme from A-LWE.

Keywords: Lattice-based cryptography · Encryption · Computational
assumption

1 Introduction

Lattice-based cryptography constitutes arguably one of the most promising alternatives to classical cryptography. This observation is supported by various arguments such as the conjectured resistance against quantum attacks. Moreover,
lattice-based cryptography is equipped with a rich combinatorial structure providing provable-security guarantees [1–3], while carrying out low complexity
operations and thus allowing for efficient constructions. The security of such
cryptosystems is mainly based on the hardness of either solving the Small Integer
Solution (SIS) problem or the Learning With Errors (LWE) problems. The former is widely employed for building provably secure primitives from Minicrypt,
such as collision-resistant hash functions [4,5] and signature schemes [6–10],

© International Financial Cryptography Association 2015
R. Böhme and T. Okamoto (Eds.): FC 2015, LNCS 8975, pp. 333–352, 2015.
DOI: 10.1007/978-3-662-47854-7_20

while the latter mainly serves as a hard underlying problem for the security of primitives from Cryptomania, such as key exchange [11–13] and oblivious transfer [14]. Remarkably, both problems are strongly related as SIS is considered to be the dual problem of LWE.

The LWE problem exists essentially in two variants, the decision and search version. Following this, the challenger is given $poly(n)$ number of independent samples $(\mathbf{A}_i, \mathbf{b}_i^\top) \in \mathbb{Z}_q^{n \times m} \times \mathbb{Z}_q^m$, where $\mathbf{A}_i \leftarrow_R \mathbb{Z}_q^{n \times m}$, $\mathbf{e}_i \leftarrow_R \chi$ and $\mathbf{b}_i^\top = \mathbf{s}^\top \mathbf{A}_i + \mathbf{e}_i^\top \mod q$ for $\mathbf{s} \in \mathbb{Z}_q^n$ where χ is some arbitrary distribution over $\mathbb{Z}_q^m$, typically discrete Gaussian. He is then asked to distinguish those samples from uniformly random samples in $\mathbb{Z}_q^{n \times m} \times \mathbb{Z}_q^m$. In search-LWE, however, the challenger is required to find the secret $\mathbf{s}$. Besides its presumably quantum hardness, one of the most noteworthy properties lattice-based assumptions offer is worst-case hardness of average-case instances. Starting with the works of Ajtai [1] and Micciancio and Regev [3], the hardness of some average-case instances of the SIS problem was shown to be hard as long as worst-case instances of the (decision version of the) shortest vector problem, known as GapSVP, are hard. The worst-case hardness for LWE was first stated by Regev [15]. Regev showed that if the error vector follows the discrete Gaussian distribution $\mathcal{D}_{\mathbb{Z}^m, \alpha q}$ with parameter $\alpha q \geq 2\sqrt{n}$, solving search-LWE is at least as hard as quantumly solving $\tilde{O}(n/\alpha)$-SIVP and GapSVP in n-dimensional worst-case lattices. Later, Peikert [16] and Brakerski et al. [17] gave a classical reduction from GapSVP to LWE. In [18], Döttling and Müller-Quade proved the hardness of LWE for uniformly distributed errors. Subsequently, Micciancio and Peikert [19] show that LWE remains hard even for binary errors.

Ever since the breakthrough work of Regev [15] lattice-based cryptography emerged and novel encryption schemes have been built upon LWE such as fully homomorphic encryption [20–24] and identity-based encryption [6,25–27] besides of CPA-secure [14,15,28–30] and CCA-secure encryption schemes [7,13,16,31].

Cryptographic constructions which rely on the LWE assumption usually sample an error term according to some distribution, most often Gaussian. Such a choice has many advantages over other distributions. However, many of the existing LWE-based schemes do not exploit the full potential of the error term. This observation is mainly due to three reasons, which can be summarized using the example of encryption schemes.

1. Previous LWE-based encryption schemes produce ciphertexts mainly following the idea of one-time pad encryption, where LWE samples play the role of random vectors. As a consequence, the underlying constructions heavily rely on the error term to be short in order to correctly recover the message. A major drawback of such schemes is the waste of bandwidth, i.e., all bits created for the error term are sacrificed for a few message bits.
2. There exist no proposals using the error term or other involved random variables as additional containers carrying auxiliary data, besides of its task to provide the required distributions. Once recognizing its feasibility, it fundamentally changes the way of building cryptosystems. For instance, in encryption schemes one may inject the message into the error term without necessarily changing the target distributions.

3. There is a lack of efficient trapdoor functions that recover the secret *and* the error term from an LWE instance, which is obviously a necessary condition for exploiting the error term. Only a few works such as [7,32] provide mechanisms to recover the error term. The most promising trapdoor construction is proposed by Micciancio and Peikert [7].

We make the following conclusions. The above limitations of LWE intuitively ask for an alternative LWE definition that takes account for the modifications made to the error term, while ensuring essentially the same hardness results as the traditional LWE problem. Since such an assumption already encompasses message data within the error term, one obtains, as a consequence, a generic and practically new encryption scheme secure under the new variant of the LWE assumption, where the trapdoor function is viewed as a black box recovering the secret and the error vector from a modified LWE instance. The message is subsequently extracted from the error vector. This allows one to exploit the full bandwidth of the error vector with full access to all its entries and not just its length. Remarkably, one could even combine this approach with existing methods for encryption in order to further increase the message throughput per ciphertext. In this work we address this challenge and give a detailed description of how to exploit the error vector.

Our Contribution. Based on these observations and subsequently made conclusions, we start by giving an alternative LWE definition, called Augmented LWE (A-LWE), that extends the existing one by modifying the error term in such a way that it encapsulates additional information. We further show which instantiations yield A-LWE samples that are indistinguishable from traditional LWE samples, thereby enjoying the hardness of traditional LWE. In conjunction with the high quality trapdoor candidate from [7], we have full access to the error term. This result inherently yields new cryptographic applications, which ensure security in various models while simultaneously allowing for high data load encryption that are applicable, for instance, in financial environments such as stock markets operating with huge amounts of stock information. It is even possible to encrypt lattice-based signatures much more efficiently than ordinary messages, which is an interesting technique for Internet protocols, where the acknowledgment of ip-packets represents an important measure for reliability. In this case, the whole entropy of the error term is supplied by lattice-based signatures.

Conceptually, the strategy of injecting messages into the error term allows us to derive a generic encryption scheme, where ciphertexts are represented by plain A-LWE samples. Besides of its evident security properties, that can directly be deduced from A-LWE, our construction benefits from encrypting more message bits per ciphertext and a faster decryption engine through a conceptually easier instantiation as compared to other proposals. Furthermore, we give a detailed description of how to achieve publicly-detectable replayable CCA (pd-RCCA) security [33], a slightly relaxed version of CCA2, but strictly stronger than CCA1. In fact, we propose the first lattice-based RCCA-secure encryption scheme.

Due to the versatility of the error term, this functionality does not involve ciphertext expansion. As a third application, it is possible to replace parts of the error term by signatures that are generated according to the best known and widely used lattice-based signature schemes. Specifically, we focus on the GPV signature scheme [6] in combination with the trapdoor construction [7] and the practical signature schemes presented in [8,10], and thus realize an asymmetric authenticated encryption scheme. As a nice byproduct, one can immediately transfer the proposed concepts to the CCA-secure construction provided in [7]. This allows us to increase the message throughput per ciphertext, while enjoying RCCA-security at almost no costs. Noteworthy, all the proposed concepts are also applicable to specific constructions such as the somewhat homomorphic symmetric key encryption scheme due to [34], which does not rely on the trapdoor construction from [7].

1.1   Augmented Learning with Errors

In many lattice-based cryptographic schemes, one has to sample error terms following the discrete Gaussian distribution as a requirement for the scheme to be secure. This is often due to an LWE-based security reduction. The key concept underlying our proposal is to embed further information in the error term $\mathbf{e} \in \mathbb{Z}^m$, but in such a way that the distribution of the augmented error term is indistinguishable from the discrete Gaussian distribution over $\mathbb{Z}^m$. We also show that one can embed messages in uniformly distributed error vectors using the same methodology.

The idea of our technique is the following. We employ the gadget matrix $\mathbf{G} = \mathbf{I} \otimes \mathbf{g}^\top$, firstly introduced in [7], with $\mathbf{g}^\top = (1, 2, \ldots, 2^{k-1})$ and modulus $q = 2^k$ in order to sample vectors according to the discrete Gaussian distribution $\mathcal{D}_{\Lambda_\mathbf{v}^\perp(\mathbf{G}),r}$. Vectors $\mathbf{e} \in \mathbb{Z}_q^m$ distributed according to $\mathcal{D}_{\Lambda_\mathbf{v}^\perp(\mathbf{G}),r}$ satisfy the equation $\mathbf{Ge} \equiv \mathbf{v} \bmod q$ for arbitrary $\mathbf{v} \in \mathbb{Z}_q^{m/k}$. Let $H : \{0,1\}^* \rightarrow \{0,1\}^m$ be some function and (encode, decode) a pair of algorithms which allow one to switch between the representations $\mathbb{Z}_q^{m/k}$ and $\{0,1\}^m$. We compute a random coset $\mathbf{v} = \mathsf{encode}(H(\mathsf{seed}) \oplus \mathbf{m}) \in \mathbb{Z}_q^{m/k}$, where $\mathbf{m} \in \{0,1\}^m$ denotes an arbitrary message of bit length m. We show that if H is instantiated by a cryptographic hash function modeled as a random oracle, $\mathbf{v}$ is indeed indistinguishable from uniform. We only have to take care that the input to the function H, namely the seed, has sufficient (computational) min-entropy. Whoever has access to this seed can deterministically recover the message by $\mathbf{m} = \mathsf{decode}(\mathbf{Ge} \bmod q) \oplus H(\mathsf{seed})$. This result immediately impacts all schemes that allow for error term recovery, as it enhances the compactness of the scheme.

Embedding auxiliary private information into the error term raises certain new computational problems. In addition to the secret and error vector of an LWE instance, also the new embedded message is concealed. In fact, we claim that LWE samples modified as above are indistinguishable from uniform even for adversarially chosen messages. To this end, we introduce a novel problem, namely the *Augmented* LWE (A-LWE) problem, which differs from the traditional LWE problem only in the way the error term is produced. More specifically, we split the error term $\mathbf{e} \in \mathbb{Z}_q^m$ of LWE into $\mathbf{e} = (\mathbf{e}_1, \mathbf{e}_2)$, where $\mathbf{e}_1 \in \mathbb{Z}_q^{m_1}$ and $\mathbf{e}_2 \in \mathbb{Z}_q^{m_2}$. An A-LWE sample is then distributed as follows. For a given $\mathbf{s} \in \mathbb{Z}_q^n$, first choose $\mathbf{A} \leftarrow_R \mathbb{Z}_q^{n \times m}$ uniformly at random. Then, sample $\mathbf{e}_1 \leftarrow_R \mathcal{D}_{\mathbb{Z}^{m_1}, \alpha q}$ and $\mathbf{e}_2 \leftarrow_R \mathcal{D}_{\Lambda_{\mathbf{v}}^{\perp}(\mathbf{G}), \alpha q}$, where $\mathbf{v} = \mathsf{encode}(H(\mathbf{s}, \mathbf{e}_1) \oplus \mathbf{m})$ for some function H. The tuple $(\mathbf{A}, \mathbf{b}^t = \mathbf{s}^\top \mathbf{A} + \mathbf{e}^\top)$ represents an A-LWE sample. We show that distinguishing A-LWE samples from traditional LWE samples is hard for properly chosen random function H. More formally, if H is a cryptographic hash function modeled as a random oracle, the tuple $(\mathbf{s}, \mathbf{e}_1)$ has sufficient entropy in each sample and the LWE problem for parameters m, n, α, q is hard to solve, then we obtain a negligible computational distance between LWE and A-LWE distributions. Thus, we immediately deduce the hardness of A-LWE from LWE. As an immediate consequence, the confidentiality of the message is protected as long as decision A-LWE and hence decision LWE is hard.

Based on the A-LWE hardness, we present a novel and generic encryption scheme, where ciphertexts are embodied by plain A-LWE samples. One merely employs an arbitrary suitable trapdoor construction for the function $g_{\mathbf{A}}(\mathbf{s}, \mathbf{e}) = \mathbf{s}^\top \mathbf{A} + \mathbf{e}^\top$ that allows for error term recovery. Hence, the efficiency of encryption and decryption greatly depends on the quality of the trapdoor and the inversion algorithm. The currently most efficient candidate function is known from Micciancio and Peikert [7]. Note that while some encryption schemes like [7,32] utilize such a trapdoor function, the error term is left unpacked. To the best of our knowledge, we provide the first lattice-based encryption schemes exploiting the error term as an (additional) data container in addition to its necessity for security.

1.2   Applications

CCA-Secure Encryption. Based on the A-LWE hardness, we build a conceptually new and very simple CCA1 secure encryption scheme. In previous lattice-based encryption schemes such as [7,26,29,31], ciphertexts are computed in a one-time pad manner by adding the message to a random vector coming from the LWE distribution. Thus, an adversary succeeds in the respective security game, if she is able to distinguish LWE samples from random ones with non-negligible advantage. Our scheme, however, moves apart from this approach and focuses on the error term recovery of A-LWE samples and subsequently decoding the error term. By this means, the ciphertext represents an A-LWE instance in its purest form. This implies a direct security reduction of the scheme to A-LWE. Employing the framework proposed in [7], we construct a random public key $\mathbf{A}$ that is endowed with a trapdoor. In conjunction with the corresponding inversion algorithm, we can efficiently recover the secret and the error term from the ciphertext $\mathbf{c}^\top = \mathbf{s}^\top \mathbf{A} + \mathbf{e}^\top$ with $\mathbf{e} \leftarrow_R \mathcal{D}_{\Lambda_{\mathbf{v}}^{\perp}(\mathbf{G}), \alpha q}$ for $\mathbf{v} = \mathsf{encode}(H(\mathbf{s}) \oplus \mathbf{m})$.[1] Due to $\alpha q \geq 2\sqrt{n} \geq \eta_\epsilon(\Lambda_q^{\perp}(\mathbf{G}))$, we even do not impose any further restrictions

---

[1] We show that if matrix $\mathbf{A}$ is fixed and each secret $\mathbf{s}$ is uniformly sampled from $\mathbb{Z}_q^n$, the entropy of $\mathbf{s}$ suffices to sample the entire error term from $\mathcal{D}_{\Lambda_{\mathbf{v}}^{\perp}(\mathbf{G}), \alpha q}$.

to the parameters. Such a construction is almost optimal, since we do not initiate any further transformations.

The bit size of the message is equal to the dimension of the ciphertext m resulting in a small message expansion factor, which is lower than most of the existing schemes. In fact, due to this relationship there is an incentive to increase the parameter m in order to efficiently encrypt large amounts of data involving less computations per ciphertext as compared to lower dimensions. We considered this case and can even show that decryption is essentially as fast as in lower dimensions. In particular, we provide an enhanced encryption scheme for high data load, where parts of the ciphertext and thus the error term are ignored when inverting the underlying A-LWE instance. That is, one extends any public key $\mathbf{A}_u = [\ \bar{\mathbf{A}} \mid \bar{\mathbf{A}}\mathbf{R} - h(u)\mathbf{G}_{nk}\ ] \in \mathbb{Z}^{n \times m}$ with trapdoor $[\ \mathbf{R}^\top\ \mathbf{I}\ ]^\top \in \mathbb{Z}^{nk \times m}$ to $\mathbf{A}_u^{ext} = [\ \mathbf{A}' \mid \bar{\mathbf{A}} \mid \bar{\mathbf{A}}\mathbf{R} - h(u)\mathbf{G}_{nk}\ ] \in \mathbb{Z}^{n \times (m'+m)}$ with trapdoor $[\ \mathbf{0}\quad \mathbf{R}^\top\ \mathbf{I}\ ]^\top \in \mathbb{Z}^{nk \times (m'+m)}$. When inverting a ciphertext $\mathbf{c} = (\mathbf{c}_1, \mathbf{c}_2) \in \mathbb{Z}^{m'+m}$ – that is, an A-LWE instance – only the lower part of the ciphertext $\mathbf{c}_2$ is required to recover $\mathbf{s}$ and $\mathbf{e}$. This idea does not seem to carry over to the construction of [7]. In fact, their message are fixed to nk bits and extending the public key as above cannot be applied to their scheme.

Nonetheless, we show that message injection into the error term can directly enhance the CCA-secure scheme in [7] yielding a decrease of the message expansion factor. As a result, one obtains a scheme that follows the one-time-pad approach while encapsulating further messages in the error vector. Put it differently, with message embedding one could choose smaller parameters for the scheme in [7] when encrypting the same message length. In terms of security the original proof in [7] gets through without any major modifications. Table 1 gives an overview of parameters and the corresponding sizes for various lattice-based encryption schemes where we, for simplicity, fix the ciphertext size. Note that we have $c \in \mathbb{Q}_{\geq 2}$ for a matrix statistically close to uniform, and consequently the message throughput in our scheme is at least twice as the one from [7]. The ring setting, however, allows for smaller key sizes and more efficient implementations. In Table 1 we mainly focus on the most efficient ones including the CPA-secure encryption scheme from [29]. Due to space reasons, Table 1 does not include the less efficient schemes from [16,26,31], which are characterized by large public keys or small LWE error-rates beside of high message expansion factors. For instance, in [31] the LWE error rate $\alpha = \tilde{O}(1/n^4)$ is quite small (yielding to an easier LWE instance) with public keys of size $\tilde{O}(n^2)$ bits. In [16], Peikert improved the LWE error rate to $\alpha = \tilde{O}(1/n)$ but with the cost of an increased public key of size $\tilde{O}(n^3)$. The CCA-secure encryption scheme [26] provides a trade-off of the previous proposals with an LWE error rate of $\tilde{O}(1/n^2)$ and public key size of $\tilde{O}(n^2)$ bits.

Replayable Chosen-Ciphertext Secure Encryption. The notion of replayable CCA-security, which constitutes a relaxed version of CCA2-security, was firstly introduced by Canetti et al. [33] and addresses the ability of an adversary to replay ciphertexts that decrypt to the same message. An RCCA-secure encryption scheme detects modifications carried out on the ciphertext that alter the

Table 1. Comparison of key figures among CCA1-secure encryption schemes

$m = c \cdot nk,\ k = \log q$	CCA1 [7]	CCA1 Constr. 4.1	CCA1 Constr. 4.1 + [7]	CPA [29]
Ciphertext size	$m \cdot k$	$m \cdot k$	$m \cdot k$	$m \cdot k$
Message size	nk	$c \cdot nk$	$(c+1) \cdot nk$	$cnk - n$
Message exp.	$c \cdot k$	k	$k - \frac{k}{(c+1)}$	$k + \frac{k}{ck-1}$
Error rate α	$\tilde{O}(1/n)$	$\tilde{O}(1/n)$	$\tilde{O}(1/n)$	$\tilde{O}(1/n)$
Public key size	$n \cdot m$	$n \cdot m$	$n \cdot m$	$n \cdot m$

message. Valid encryptions of the same ciphertexts, however, are allowed. Canetti et al. have shown that RCCA is sufficient for most practical applications. There exist a series of RCCA-secure encryption schemes [35–39]. However, to our knowledge, we are the first realizing an RCCA-secure encryption scheme based on lattice problems, and hence relying on the worst-case hardness of lattice problems. We show that RCCA security comes essentially through our message embedding technique with only minor modifications. Our construction resembles GPV signatures generated for the public matrix $\mathbf{G}$. Just as for standard GPV signatures, it is required to hash all sensible (random) variables such as the tag u, the secret $\mathbf{s}$ and the lower part of the error term $\mathbf{e}_2$ containing the message to $\mathbf{v} = H(u, \mathbf{s}, \mathbf{e}_2)$ using a random oracle H. Subsequently, we sample a preimage $\mathbf{e}_1 \leftarrow \mathcal{D}_{\Lambda_{\mathbf{v}}^{\perp}(\mathbf{G})}$ that serves as the upper-part of the error term. Due to the injectivity of the trapdoor function, altering the ciphertext leads to different values for the corresponding variables such that the decryption routine outputs a failure. But modifications caused to the upper part of the error term do not result in a failure as long as short vectors from $\Lambda_q^{\perp}(\mathbf{G})$ are added.

This obviously implies a publicly-detectable RCCA-secure encryption scheme (pd-RCCA), an even stronger security guarantee than plain RCCA. In fact, we have the relation CCA2 $\Rightarrow$ pd-RCCA $\Rightarrow$ secretly-detectable RCCA $\Rightarrow$ RCCA [33]. Security in the pd-RCCA model implies that a public party can check whether a modified ciphertext decrypts to the same message.

When it comes to CCA2 security, there exist many generic constructions [40–43] that ensure CCA2-security. For instance, one can use strongly unforgeable one-time signature schemes [40], commitment schemes or message authentication codes (MAC) in order to transform a CPA-secure scheme into a CCA2-secure one. However, these generic constructions typically involve high complexity and overhead resulting in a less efficient encryption scheme. Our approach works differently as it uses the error term in order to provide this feature. Once having RCCA-security one can efficiently convert the scheme into a CCA2-secure encryption scheme using generic solutions as provided in [33] or our individual approach at the expense of some small overhead.

Signature Embedding. There exist various approaches to provide message authentication of encrypted data. Many of them are generic and thus coupled to overhead and loss of efficiency. For instance, one can use MACs or digital signatures that are appended to the ciphertext. In our work we aim at providing this feature without suffering from the drawbacks of generic solutions through a thorough analysis of our encryption scheme.

Our goal is to replace parts of the error vector such as $\mathbf{e}_1$ completely by a lattice-based signature rather than appending it to the ciphertext or including it as a part of the message. This allows us to optimally exploit the full bandwidth of $\mathbf{e}_1$ due to some nice properties lattice-based signature schemes offer. One of the features is to let signatures be distributed following the discrete Gaussian distribution. For the underlying signature scheme itself, such a strategy has many advantages over other choices as it allows to decouple the distribution of the signature from the secret key, while sampling short signatures with higher probability. There exist many lattice-based proposals that have similar properties and perform very well in practice [7,8,10].

Our construction inherently relies on the capability to recover the error term from an A-LWE instance. As a result, we provide an authentication mechanism for encrypted data, since it is by construction possible to retrieve back an arbitrary discrete Gaussian vector with support $\mathbb{Z}^m$, hence also a signature, that was plugged into the error term. Therefore, we can embed signatures of size approximately $m \cdot \log(\alpha q) = O(m \log n)$ bits into the error vector, which is far more (see Table 1) than with the standard encryption schemes that are restricted to the message size. For instance, we can embed signatures of size $c \log(\alpha q) nk$ bits as compared to nk bits following [7]. Here, we denote by αq the parameter of the discrete Gaussian vector of the error term. In fact, our proposal allows for a flexible selection of parameters, because we do not impose any new constraints. However, the parameters of the signature scheme should not be too large in order to correctly invert the underlying A-LWE instances.

Remarkably, when using the encryption scheme for high data load with an extended public key $\mathbf{A}_u^{ext}$ the upper part of the error term is ignored when decrypting the ciphertext. This allows us to select the parameters in such a way that A-LWE (and LWE) is hard for arbitrarily chosen parameters of the signature scheme. Therefore, one can employ the upper-part of the error term for signatures. The resulting scheme has a CCA2-like behavior, where changes induced to the ciphertext are detected by the receiver. These ideas immediately help to improve the construction provided in [7]. In particular, we can apply the proposed techniques to the error term without changing the other ingredients. More specifically, we still build the ciphertext in a one-time pad manner, while simultaneously endowing the error vector with additional messages. The proof of security will subsequently be based on A-LWE rather than plain LWE.

Embedding Auxiliary Data in Homomorphic Encryption. As already noticed, we improve the CCA1-secure encryption scheme from [7], if we apply the proposed concepts from above to the error term. As a result, we have the first message being encrypted following the one-time pad approach and a second message injected into the error-term. However, this encryption scheme heavily relies on a trapdoor construction. But we stress that it is also possible to improve other more specific constructions that do not require trapdoors as such. For instance, if we consider the somewhat homomorphic encryption scheme due to Brakerski and Vaikuntanathan [34], we can apply essentially the same ideas without any major modifications. Indeed, it is a symmetric key encryption scheme, where a ciphertext $(\mathbf{c}_1 = \mathbf{a}, \mathbf{c}_2 = \mathbf{b} + \mathbf{m})$ is derived by adding a ring-LWE samples $\mathbf{b} = \mathbf{a}\mathbf{s} + t\mathbf{e} \in \mathcal{R}_q = \mathbb{Z}[X]/\langle f(X) \rangle$ to an arbitrary message $\mathbf{m} \in \mathcal{R}_t$ for t coprime to q and freshly sampled $\mathbf{c}_1 = \mathbf{a} \in \mathcal{R}_q$ and error vector $\mathbf{e} \in \mathcal{R}_q$. The secret key is given by the secret ring element $\mathbf{s} \in \mathcal{R}_q$. After decrypting the ciphertext, we get full access to the error-term via $\mathbf{e} = t^{-1}(\mathbf{c}_2 - \mathbf{c}_1\mathbf{s} - \mathbf{m})$. A quick view to this construction reveals, that the error term can be recovered very efficiently. Clearly, this positively impacts the performance of the different concepts, when applied to the error term.

Due to space limitations, we detail the application of our technique to obtain a CCA-secure encryption scheme and refer the reader to our full version [44] for the further aforementioned applications.

2   Preliminaries

By $\oplus$ we denote the XOR operator. We let $[\ell]$ denote the set $\{1, \ldots, \ell\}$ for any $\ell \in \mathbb{N}_{\geq 1}$. We indicate vectors by lower-case bold letters (e.g., $\mathbf{x}$) and use upper-case bold letters for matrices (e.g., $\mathbf{A}$).

A lattice is an additive subgroup of $\mathbb{R}^n$. For a basis $\mathbf{B} = \{\mathbf{b}_1, \ldots, \mathbf{b}_n\} \subset \mathbb{R}^n$ consisting of n linearly independent vectors, we define by Λ the n-dimensional lattice generated by the basis $\mathbf{B}$ where $\Lambda = \mathcal{L}(\mathbf{B}) = \{\mathbf{B} \cdot \mathbf{c} = \sum_{i=0}^{n} \mathbf{b}_i \cdot c_i \ : \ \mathbf{c} \in \mathbb{Z}^n\}$.

We define by $\rho : \mathbb{R}^n \to (0, 1]$ the n-dimensional Gaussian function $\rho_{s,\mathbf{c}}(\mathbf{x}) = e^{-\pi \cdot \frac{\|\mathbf{x}-\mathbf{c}\|_2^2}{s^2}}$, $\forall \mathbf{x}, \mathbf{c} \in \mathbb{R}^n$. The discrete Gaussian distribution $D_{\Lambda+c,s}$ is defined to have support $\Lambda + c$, where $c \in \mathbb{R}$ and $\Lambda \subset \mathbb{R}^n$ is a lattice.

Below we define the LWE distribution. For our purposes, we only focus on the error sampled by the discrete Gaussian distribution. One can easily define LWE with respect to any error distribution.

Definition 1 (LWE Distribution). *Let n, m, q be integers and $\chi_e = \mathcal{D}_{\mathbb{Z}^m, \alpha q}$ be the discrete Gaussian distribution over $\mathbb{Z}^m$. For $\mathbf{s} \in \mathbb{Z}_q^n$, define the LWE distribution $L_{n,m,\alpha q}^{\mathsf{LWE}}$ to be the distribution over $\mathbb{Z}_q^{n \times m} \times \mathbb{Z}_q^m$ obtained such that one first draws $\mathbf{A} \leftarrow_R \mathbb{Z}_q^{n \times m}$ uniformly, $\mathbf{e} \leftarrow_R \mathcal{D}_{\mathbb{Z}^m, \alpha q}$ and returns $(\mathbf{A}, \mathbf{b}^\top) \in \mathbb{Z}_q^{n \times m} \times \mathbb{Z}_q^m$ with $\mathbf{b}^\top = \mathbf{s}^\top \mathbf{A} + \mathbf{e}^\top$.*

Definition 2 (Learning with Error (LWE)). *Let $(\mathbf{A}, \mathbf{b})$ be a sample from $L_{n,m,\alpha q}^{\mathsf{LWE}}$ and $\mathbf{c}$ be uniformly sampled from $\mathbb{Z}_q^m$.*

The Decision Learning with Error (decision $\mathsf{LWE}_{n,m,\alpha q}$) problem asks to distinguish between $(\mathbf{A}, \mathbf{b}^\top)$ and $(\mathbf{A}, \mathbf{c}^\top)$ for a uniformly sampled secret $\mathbf{s} \leftarrow_R \mathbb{Z}_q^n$.

The Search Learning with Error (search $\mathsf{LWE}_{n,m,\alpha q}$) problem asks to output the vector $\mathbf{s} \in \mathbb{Z}_q^n$ given LWE sample $(\mathbf{A}, \mathbf{b})$ for a uniformly sampled secret $\mathbf{s} \leftarrow_R \mathbb{Z}_q^n$.

We say decision $\text{LWE}_{n,m,\alpha q}$ (resp. search $\text{LWE}_{n,m,\alpha q}$) is hard if all polynomial time algorithm solves decision $\text{LWE}_{n,m,\alpha q}$ (resp. search $\text{LWE}_{n,m,\alpha q}$) only with negligible probability.

Various algorithms for different tasks such as sampling from $\Lambda^{\perp}(\mathbf{G})$ or inverting LWE instances are presented in the full version [44]. In this paper we use those algorithms in a block-box way and take them as given.

3   Learning with Errors Augmented with Auxiliary Data

In this section, we show how one can augment further useful information in the error vectors of LWE samples without necessarily changing its distribution. We call this technique "message embedding" and formulate a modified LWE problem definition, namely the Augmented LWE (A-LWE) problem, where this technique is applied to LWE. We show that certain instantiations of the A-LWE problem are as hard as the original LWE problem.

3.1   Message Embedding

We start explaining the core functionality of our work leading to conceptually new cryptographic applications such as encryption schemes. In particular, we show how to generate vectors that encapsulate an arbitrary message while simultaneously following the discrete Gaussian distribution $\mathcal{D}_{\mathbb{Z}^m,r}$. This mechanism can be exploited in cryptographic applications in order to embed further information in discrete Gaussian vectors. For instance, we can apply this technique to LWE-based encryption schemes (e.g., [7]), that enable the recovery of the error term. As a result, we take advantage of an increased message throughput per ciphertext. In the full version [44] we provide a description of how to embed messages in error vectors that are uniformly distributed rather than from the discrete Gaussian distribution.

Let the very simple operations $\text{encode} : \{0,1\}^m \rightarrow \mathbb{Z}_q^{m/k}$ and $\text{decode} : \mathbb{Z}_q^{m/k} \rightarrow \{0,1\}^m$ allow to bijectively switch between the bit and vector representations. The embedding approach is realized by use of the gadget $\mathbf{G} = \mathbf{I} \otimes \mathbf{g}^{\top}$. A first idea of doing this is to sample a preimage $\mathbf{x} \leftarrow_R D_{\Lambda_v^{\perp}(\mathbf{G}),r}$ with $\mathbf{v} = \text{encode}(\mathbf{m})$ for an arbitrary message $\mathbf{m} \in \{0,1\}^m$ such that $\mathbf{Gx} \bmod q = \text{encode}(\mathbf{m})$ holds. Sampling from $D_{\Lambda_v^{\perp}(\mathbf{G}),r}$ is performed very efficiently (see [44]) and can be reduced to samples from $\mathcal{D}_{2\mathbb{Z},r}$ and $\mathcal{D}_{2\mathbb{Z}+1,r}$. However, since the target Gaussian distribution of many cryptographic schemes, such as the LWE encryption schemes, require to have support $\mathbb{Z}^m$, we modify the message to $\mathbf{m} \oplus \mathbf{r}$ prior to invoking the preimage sampler for a randomly chosen vector $\mathbf{r} \leftarrow_R \{0,1\}^m$. Below in Lemma 1 we show that given this setup we indeed obtain a sample $\mathbf{x}$ that is distributed just as $\mathcal{D}_{\mathbb{Z}^m,r}$ with overwhelming probability. To illustrate this approach exemplarily, let $\mathbf{e} \in \mathbb{Z}^m$ denote the error term with $m \in O(nk)$. We then split the error term $\mathbf{e} = (\mathbf{e}_1, \mathbf{e}_2) \in \mathbb{Z}^{m_1+m_2}$ into two subvectors, each serving for a different purpose. The second part $\mathbf{e}_2$ is used for message embedding, whereas $\mathbf{e}_1$ provides enough entropy in order to sample a random vector $\mathbf{r}$. To this end, one has to find a proper trade-off for the choice of m_1 and m_2, since a too large value for m_2 implies low entropy of $\mathbf{e}_1$. A reasonable small lower bound is given by $m_1 \geq n$, since the discrete Gaussian vector $\mathbf{e}_1$ has min-entropy of at least $n - 1$ bits as per [6, Lemma 2.10].

The message embedding functionality comes at almost no costs. Let k be a factor of m_2. One samples $\mathbf{e}_1 \leftarrow \mathcal{D}_{\mathbb{Z}^{m_1},r}$ and a preimage $\mathbf{e}_2 \leftarrow_R D_{\Lambda_{\mathbf{v}}^{\perp}(\mathbf{G}),r}$ for the syndrome $\mathbf{v} = \mathsf{encode}(\mathbf{m} \oplus H(\mathbf{e}_1))$ for some random function $H : \{0,1\}^* \to \{0,1\}^{m_2}$. Following this approach, the message is recovered by computing $\mathbf{m} = H(\mathbf{e}_1) \oplus \mathsf{decode}(\mathbf{G}_{m_2}\mathbf{e}_2 \mod q)$ where $\mathbf{G}_{m_2} = \mathbf{I}_{m_2/k} \otimes \mathbf{g}^{\top}$. In many cryptographic applications there are different random sources available, which can replace the role of $\mathbf{e}_1$ such that $\mathbf{e}$ is completely used for message embedding.

In the following theorems we prove that it is possible to simulate the discrete Gaussian distribution $\mathcal{D}_{\mathbb{Z}^m,r}$ (statistically or computationally) by use of a preimage sampler for any full-rank matrix $\mathbf{A}$. This allows for embedding messages in the error vectors of LWE without changing noticeably the LWE distribution. The proofs of the following lemmata and the case of uniformly distributed error vectors is presented in the full version [44].

Lemma 1 (statistical). *Let* $\mathbf{A} \in \mathbb{Z}_q^{n \times m}$ *be an arbitrary full-rank matrix. The statistical distance* $\Delta(\mathcal{D}_{\mathbb{Z}^m,r}, \mathcal{D}_{\Lambda_{\mathbf{v}}^{\perp}(\mathbf{A}),r})$ *for uniform* $\mathbf{v} \leftarrow_R \mathbb{Z}_q^n$ *with* $r \geq \eta_\epsilon(\Lambda^{\perp}(\mathbf{A}))$ *and* $\epsilon = \mathsf{negl}(\lambda)$ *is negligible.*

Lemma 2 (computational). *Let* $\mathbf{A} \in \mathbb{Z}_q^{n \times m}$ *be an arbitrary full-rank matrix. If the distribution of* $\mathbf{v} \in \mathbb{Z}_q^n$ *is computationally indistinguishable from the uniform distribution over* $\mathbb{Z}_q^n$, *then* $\mathcal{D}_{\Lambda_{\mathbf{v}}^{\perp}(\mathbf{A}),r}$ *is computationally indistinguishable from* $\mathcal{D}_{\mathbb{Z}^m,r}$ *for* $r \geq \eta_\epsilon(\Lambda^{\perp}(\mathbf{A}))$ *and* $\epsilon = \mathsf{negl}(\lambda)$.

3.2 Augmented LWE

Based on the message embedding approach as described above, we introduce an alternative LWE definition that extends the previous one in such a way that the error term is featured with additional information. We show how the modified error still coincides with $\mathcal{D}_{\mathbb{Z}^m,r}$ in order to allow a reduction from LWE to our new assumption. We make use of the gadget matrix $\mathbf{G} = \mathbf{I} \otimes \mathbf{g}^{\top}$ for $\mathbf{g}^{\top} = (1, \ldots, 2^{k-1})$. For simplicity, assume $q = 2^k$. For general q, the preimage sampling algorithm for $\Lambda^{\perp}(\mathbf{G})$ is more involved (see [7]).

Definition 3 (Augmented LWE Distribution). *Let* n, m, m_1, m_2, k, q *be integers with* $k = \log q$ *and* $m = m_1 + m_2$, *where* $k \mid m_2$. *Let* $H : \mathbb{Z}_q^n \times \mathbb{Z}_q^{m_1} \to \{0,1\}^{m_2}$ *be a function. Let* $\mathbf{G}_{m_2} = \mathbf{I}_{m_2/k} \otimes \mathbf{g}^{\top} \in \mathbb{Z}_q^{m_2/k \times m_2}$. *For* $\mathbf{s} \in \mathbb{Z}_q^n$, *define the A-LWE distribution* $L_{n,m_1,m_2,\alpha q}^{\mathsf{A\text{-}LWE}}(\mathbf{m})$ *with* $\mathbf{m} \in \{0,1\}^{m_2}$ *to be the distribution over* $\mathbb{Z}_q^{n \times m} \times \mathbb{Z}_q^m$ *obtained as follows:*

- *Sample* $\mathbf{A} \leftarrow_R \mathbb{Z}_q^{n \times m}$ *and* $\mathbf{e}_1 \leftarrow_R \mathcal{D}_{\mathbb{Z}^{m_1},\alpha q}$.
- *Set* $\mathbf{v} = \mathsf{encode}(H(\mathbf{s}, \mathbf{e}_1) \oplus \mathbf{m}) \in \mathbb{Z}_q^{m_2/k}$.
- *Sample* $\mathbf{e}_2 \leftarrow_R \mathcal{D}_{\Lambda_{\mathbf{v}}^{\perp}(\mathbf{G}),\alpha q}$.

– *Return* $(\mathbf{A}, \mathbf{b}^\top)$ *where* $\mathbf{b}^\top = \mathbf{s}^\top \mathbf{A} + \mathbf{e}^\top$ *with* $\mathbf{e} = (\mathbf{e}_1, \mathbf{e}_2)$.

Accordingly, we define the augmented LWE problem(s) as follows. As opposed to the traditional LWE, augmented LWE blinds, in addition to the secret vector $\mathbf{s} \in \mathbb{Z}_q^n$, also some (auxiliary) data $\mathbf{m} \in \{0, 1\}^{m_2}$. Thus, we have an additional assumption that the message $\mathbf{m}$ is hard to find given A-LWE samples. Note that the decision version requires that any polynomial bounded number of samples $(\mathbf{A}, \mathbf{b}^\top)$ from the A-LWE distribution are indistinguishable from uniform random samples in $\mathbb{Z}_q^{n \times m} \times \mathbb{Z}_q^m$. Its hardness implies that no information about $\mathbf{s}$ *and* $\mathbf{m}$ is leaked through A-LWE samples. In some scenarios, e.g., in security notions of an encryption scheme, the adversary may even choose the message $\mathbf{m}$. Hence, we require in the corresponding problems that their hardness holds with respect to A-LWE distributions with adversarially chosen message(s) $\mathbf{m}$ except for the search problem of $\mathbf{m}$.

Definition 4 (Augmented Learning with Errors (A-LWE)).
Let n, m_1, m_2, k, q *be integers with* $k = \log q$. *Let* H *be some function.*

The Decision Augmented Learning with Errors *(decision* A-LWE$_{n,m_1,m_2,\alpha q}^H$*) problem asks upon input* $\mathbf{m} \in \{0, 1\}^{m_2}$ *to distinguish in polynomial time (in* n*) between samples* $(\mathbf{A}_i, \mathbf{b}_i^\top) \leftarrow_R L_{n,m_1,m_2,\alpha q}^{\text{A-LWE}}(\mathbf{m})$ *and uniform random samples from* $\mathbb{Z}_q^{n \times m} \times \mathbb{Z}_q^n$ *for a secret* $\mathbf{s} \leftarrow_R \mathbb{Z}_q^n$.

The Search-Secret Augmented Learning with Errors *(search-s* A-LWE$_{n,m_1,m_2,\alpha q}^H$*) problem asks upon input* $\mathbf{m} \in \mathbb{Z}_q^{m_2/k}$ *to output in polynomial time (in* n*) the vector* $\mathbf{s} \in \mathbb{Z}_q^n$ *given polynomially many samples* $(\mathbf{A}_i, \mathbf{b}_i) \leftarrow_R L_{n,m_1,m_2,\alpha q}^{\text{A-LWE}}(\mathbf{m})$ *for secret* $\mathbf{s} \leftarrow_R \mathbb{Z}_q^n$.

The Search-Message Augmented Learning with Errors *(search-m* A-LWE$_{n,m_1,m_2,\alpha q}^H$*) problem asks to output in polynomial time (in* n*) the vector* $\mathbf{m}$ *given polynomially many A-LWE samples* $(\mathbf{A}_i, \mathbf{b}_i)$ *for a secret* $\mathbf{s} \leftarrow_R \mathbb{Z}_q^n$ *and* $\mathbf{m} \leftarrow_R \{0, 1\}^{m_2}$.

We say that decision/search-s/search-m A LWE$_{n,m_1,m_2,\alpha q}^H$ *is hard if all polynomial time algorithms solve the* decision/search-s/search-m A LWE$_{n,m_1,m_2,\alpha q}^H$ *problem only with negligible probability.*

Throughout the paper, the function H will be a cryptographic hash function modeled as a random oracle. For this reason we simplify the notation and denote by decision/search-s/search-m A LWE$_{n,m_1,m_2,\alpha q}$ the A-LWE problems where H is specified to be a random oracle in the A-LWE distribution.

In the following, we show that if the function H is instantiated by a random oracle, the hardness of LWE is reducible to the hardness of A-LWE. To this end, we show that the LWE and A-LWE distribution are computationally indistinguishable, if we assume that the former search problem is hard and the inputs to function H have sufficient entropy in each sample given previous samples.

Theorem 1. *Let* λ *be the security parameter. Let* n, m, m_1, m_2, k, q *be integers where* $k = \lceil \log q \rceil$, $m = m_1 + m_2$. *Let* $H : \mathbb{Z}_q^n \times \mathbb{Z}_q^{m_1} \to \{0, 1\}^{m_2}$ *be a hash function modeled as a random oracle. Let* $\alpha q \geq \eta_\epsilon(\Lambda_q^\perp(\mathbf{G}))$ *for a real* $\epsilon = \mathsf{negl}(\lambda) > 0$.

Furthermore, denote by χ_s and χ_{e_1} the distributions of the random vectors $\mathbf{s}$ and $\mathbf{e}_1$ involved in each A-LWE sample. If search $\mathsf{LWE}_{n,m,\alpha q}$ *is hard and* $\mathbb{H}_\infty(\mathbf{s}, \mathbf{e}_1) > \lambda$, *then* $L^{\text{A-LWE}}_{n,m_1,m_2,\alpha q}(\mathbf{m})$ *is computationally indistinguishable from* $L^{\text{LWE}}_{n,m,\alpha q}$ *for arbitrary* $\mathbf{m} \in \{0,1\}^{m_2}$.

Proof. We need to show that samples from $L^{\text{LWE}}_{n,m,\alpha,q}$ are indistinguishable from $L^{\text{A-LWE}}_{n,m_1,m_2,\alpha,q}(\mathbf{m})$ if we assume that the search $\mathsf{LWE}_{n,m,\alpha,q}$ problem is hard to solve in polynomial time and tuples $(\mathbf{s}, (\mathbf{e}_1)_i)$ for each sample i have sufficient entropy. That is, $L^{\text{LWE}}_{n,m,\alpha,q} \approx_c L^{\text{A-LWE}}_{n,m_1,m_2,\alpha,q}(\mathbf{m})$ for arbitrary $\mathbf{m} \in \{0,1\}^{m_2}$.

We consider a series of intermediate hybrid experiments. In the first hybrid, we modify the A-LWE samples in such a way that we replace $H(\mathbf{s}, \mathbf{e}_1)$ with a uniformly sampled value $\mathbf{u}$. Here, we use the fact, that $\mathbb{H}_\infty(\mathbf{s}, \mathbf{e}_1) > \lambda$ and the same input will be queried with negligible probability. Consequently, $\mathbf{v} = \text{encode}(H(\mathbf{s}, \mathbf{e}_1) \oplus \mathbf{m})$ becomes uniformly distributed. The next hybrid replaces $\mathbf{e}_2$ by value $\mathbf{e}_2^*$ which is sampled according to $\mathcal{D}_{\mathbb{Z}^{m_2},r}$. The final distribution is identically distributed as the original LWE. In the following we describe the hybrids more formally.

Hybrid$_1$. In the first hybrid, in each A-LWE sample we replace the value $H(\mathbf{s}, \mathbf{e}_1)$ by a uniformly sampled value $\mathbf{u} \in \{0,1\}^{m_2}$. We argue that a (polynomial-time) distinguisher notices the difference only if it queries the random oracle on input $(\mathbf{s}, \mathbf{e}_1)$. Otherwise, if $(\mathbf{s}, \mathbf{e}_1)$ has not been queried before, the distribution of $H(\mathbf{s}, \mathbf{e}_1)$ is statistically close to the uniform distribution in $\{0,1\}^{m_2}$ due to the property of a random oracle drawing elements from the output range uniformly at random. Moreover, we have $\mathbb{H}_\infty(\mathbf{s}, \mathbf{e}_1) > \lambda$ such that the same input element $(\mathbf{s}, \mathbf{e}_1)$ will not be sampled again except with negligible probability. This holds, in particular, if many samples are given to the distinguisher and all $H(\mathbf{s}, (\mathbf{e}_1)_i)$ have been replaced because by assumption we have sufficient entropy such that all pairs $(\mathbf{s}, (\mathbf{e}_1)_i)$ are distinct with overwhelming probability.

We comment on a distinguisher which queries the random oracle at a certain point on $(s, \mathbf{e}_1)$ below in the proof, and assume for now, that no such distinguisher exists.

Hybrid$_2$. In the next hybrid, we replace the error term $\mathbf{e}_2$ by value $\mathbf{e*}_2$ which is sampled according to $\mathcal{D}_{\mathbb{Z}^{m_2},r}$. Note that A-LWE samples from **Hybrid$_1$** satisfy that $\mathbf{v} = \text{encode}(\mathbf{u} \oplus \mathbf{m})$ is uniformly distributed since $\mathbf{u}$ is uniformly picked (even if $\mathbf{m}$ is chosen by the distinguisher). Now, Lemma 1 implies that $\mathcal{D}_{\Lambda_{\mathbf{v}}^\perp(\mathbf{A}),r}$ is statistically indistinguishable from $\mathcal{D}_{\mathbb{Z}^{m_2},r}$ for $r \geq \eta_\epsilon(\Lambda^\perp(\mathbf{A}))$, if H has not been queried on input $(\mathbf{s}, \mathbf{e}_1)$ before. For this reason, replacing $\mathbf{e}_2$, which is distributed according to $\mathcal{D}_{\Lambda_{\mathbf{v}}^\perp(\mathbf{A}),r}$, by vector $\mathbf{e}_2^*$ is unnoticeable to a distinguisher.

We argue that A-LWE samples from **Hybrid$_2$** are indistinguishable from LWE samples. This follows from the fact that the error term in A-LWE is now identically distributed as LWE which is the only difference between A-LWE and LWE samples. We still need to argue that it is very unlikely that a distinguisher queries the random oracle H on input $(\mathbf{s}, \mathbf{e}_1)$ for some $\mathbf{e}_1$ used in an A-LWE sample.

Suppose that there exists an algorithm $\mathcal{A}$ which distinguishes in polynomial time original A-LWE samples from A-LWE samples from $\mathbf{Hybrid}_1$ with non-negligible probability. We then construct an adversary $\mathcal{A}_{LWE}$ with black-box access to algorithm $\mathcal{A}$ that solves the search $\mathsf{LWE}_{n,m,\alpha,q}$ problem in polynomial time with non-negligible probability. This contradicts the theorem assumption that search $\mathsf{LWE}_{n,m,\alpha,q}$ is hard.

Adversary $\mathcal{A}_{LWE}$ is given samples from $L^{\mathsf{LWE}}_{n,m,\alpha,q}$ and is asked to find the secret vector $\mathbf{s}$. Let us denote by q^* the query $(\mathbf{s}, \mathbf{e}_1)$ on H made by $\mathcal{A}$, where q^* is polynomially bounded by the security parameter. Whenever algorithm $\mathcal{A}$ asks for new samples, $\mathcal{A}_{LWE}$ asks for samples in her challenge and forwards them to $\mathcal{A}$. That is, $\mathcal{A}$ obtains samples from $L^{\mathsf{LWE}}_{n,m,\alpha,q}$ instead of either version of $L^{\mathsf{A\text{-}LWE}}_{n,m_1,m_2,\alpha,q}(\mathbf{m})$. We have already shown via hybrids that $L^{\mathsf{A\text{-}LWE}}_{n,m_1,m_2,\alpha,q}(\mathbf{m})$ is indistinguishable from $L^{\mathsf{LWE}}_{n,m,\alpha,q}$, if $(\mathbf{s}, \mathbf{e}_1)$ was not sent to oracle H. This means that before $\mathcal{A}$ makes query q^* to H, those samples are indistinguishable. As a result, $\mathcal{A}$ must query H on input $(\mathbf{s}, \mathbf{e}_1)$ even if given LWE samples. We stress that after returning the hash value of $(\mathbf{s}, \mathbf{e}_1)$ to $\mathcal{A}$ it may be noticing that $\mathcal{A}_{LWE}$ has tricked her. However, eavesdropping the input to oracle H suffices to $\mathcal{A}_{LWE}$ to break her search $\mathsf{LWE}_{n,m,\alpha,q}$ problem independently whether $\mathcal{A}$ aborts at this time. Hence, if $\mathcal{A}$ queries H on input $(\mathbf{s}, \mathbf{e}_1)$ with non-negligible probability, so does $\mathcal{A}_{LWE}$ solve the search $\mathsf{LWE}_{n,m,\alpha,q}$ problem with the very same probability. By assumption there does not exist such a successful algorithm.

We conclude that the step from the original A-LWE samples to $\mathbf{Hybrid}_1$ will be unnoticeable to a distinguisher if search $\mathsf{LWE}_{n,m,\alpha,q}$ is hard, and both distributions $L^{\mathsf{LWE}}_{n,m,\alpha,q}$ and $L^{\mathsf{A\text{-}LWE}}_{n,m_1,m_2,\alpha,q}(\mathbf{m})$ are computationally indistinguishable. $\square$

Note that if the first error part $\mathbf{e}_1$ has entropy exceeding the security parameter λ, the (computational) entropy induced by $\mathbf{s}$ is not required. This is important, since a distinguisher could ask for many A-LWE samples using the same secret $\mathbf{s}$ as input to the hash function. However, as typical in encryption schemes (e.g., in [7,16,28,29] and in ours), if we fix a random matrix $\mathbf{A}$ and sample fresh secret vectors $\mathbf{s} \leftarrow \mathbb{Z}_q^n$ uniformly at random for each A-LWE sample, we can indeed choose m_1 to be zero. This corresponds to the case, where an A-LWE sample is drawn once for every fresh secret $\mathbf{s}$ resulting in essentially unrelated A-LWE instances. Hence, the secret $\mathbf{s}$ provides the sufficient randomness required as input to H.

Theorem 1 immediately entails the following statement.

Theorem 2. *Let n, m, m_1, m_2, k, q be integers with $k = \log q$ and $m = m_1 + m_2$. Let H be a random oracle as defined in Theorem 1. Let $\alpha q \geq \eta_\epsilon(\Lambda_q^\perp(\mathbf{G}))$ for a real $\epsilon = \mathsf{negl}(\lambda) > 0$. Furthermore, denote by χ_s and χ_{e_1} the distributions of the random vectors $\mathbf{s}$ and $\mathbf{e}_1$ involved in each A-LWE sample. If $\mathbb{H}_\infty(\mathbf{s}, \mathbf{e}_1) > \lambda$, then the following statements hold.*

- *If search $\mathsf{LWE}_{n,m,\alpha q}$ is hard, then search-s A-$\mathsf{LWE}_{n,m_1,m_2,\alpha q}$ is hard.*
- *If decision $\mathsf{LWE}_{n,m,\alpha q}$ is hard, then decision A-$\mathsf{LWE}_{n,m_1,m_2,\alpha q}$ resp. search-m A-$\mathsf{LWE}_{n,m_1,m_2,\alpha q}$ is hard.*

Proof. As per Theorem 1, $L_{n,m_1,m_2,\alpha q}^{\text{A-LWE}}(\mathbf{m})$ is computationally indistinguishable from $L_{n,m,\alpha q}^{\text{LWE}}$. This proves the hardness of decision A-LWE$_{n,m_1,m_2,\alpha q}$ and search-m A-LWE$_{n,m_1,m_2,\alpha q}$. And by essentially the same arguments we also deduce the hardness of search-s A-LWE$_{n,m_1,m_2,\alpha q}$, because solving the search problem implies distinguishability of A-LWE instances from uniform due to the knowledge of $(\mathbf{s},\mathbf{e})$ and by Theorem 1 we obtain distinguishability of LWE instances from uniform, hence a contradiction. $\qquad\square$

3.3 Generic Encryption Scheme from A-LWE

In what follows we provide a generic construction of an A-LWE based encryption scheme. Due to our new feature of embedding messages in the error term, we can employ any trapdoor function that allows for error-term recovery. We restrict to the case, where function H inputs only $\mathbf{s}$ (i.e., $m_1 = 0$) as discussed above. Let TDF = (KeyGen, g, g^{-1}) be a trapdoor function with $g_\mathbf{A}(\mathbf{x},\mathbf{y}) := \mathbf{x}^\top \mathbf{A} + \mathbf{y}^\top \in \mathbb{Z}^m$. The algorithm KeyGen outputs a matrix $\mathbf{A} \in \mathbb{Z}_q^{n \times m}$, that is close to uniform, with an associated trapdoor $\mathbf{T}$ used to invert $g_\mathbf{A}$. The trapdoor function satisfies $g_\mathbf{A}^{-1}(\mathbf{T}, \mathbf{c}) = (\mathbf{x},\mathbf{y})$ with $\mathbf{c} = g_\mathbf{A}(\mathbf{x},\mathbf{y})$ for arbitrary $\mathbf{x} \in \mathbb{Z}_q^n$ and properly chosen $\mathbf{y} \in \mathbb{Z}^m$.

Our generic encryption scheme from A-LWE is constructed as follows:

KGen(1^n): Generate public key pk $:= \mathbf{A} \in \mathbb{Z}_q^{n \times m}$ with trapdoor sk $:= \mathbf{T}$ where $(\mathbf{A},\mathbf{T}) \leftarrow$ TDF.KeyGen(1^n).

Enc(pk, $\mathbf{m} \in \{0,1\}^l$ with $0 \le l \le m$): Sample $\mathbf{s} \leftarrow_R \mathbb{Z}_q^n$ and compute $\mathbf{v} =$ encode($H(\mathbf{s}) \oplus \mathbf{m}) \in \mathbb{Z}_q^{m/k}$. Then, sample $\mathbf{e} \leftarrow_R \mathcal{D}_{\Lambda_\mathbf{v}^\perp(\mathbf{G}),\alpha q}$. The ciphertext is given by $\mathbf{c} = g_\mathbf{A}(\mathbf{s},\mathbf{e})$.

Dec(sk, $\mathbf{c}$) : Compute $g_\mathbf{A}^{-1}(\mathbf{T}, \mathbf{c}) = (\mathbf{s},\mathbf{e})$. Return $\mathbf{m} = $ decode($\mathbf{Ge} \bmod q) \oplus H(\mathbf{s})$.

The generic construction is mainly based on the capability of the scheme to recover the error vector. Thus, the underlying trapdoor construction acts as a black box granting full access to the secret $\mathbf{s}$ and the error term $\mathbf{e}$, when applying the secret trapdoor on a corresponding A-LWE instance. Once having revealed the error term, the message is recovered via the last step of the scheme involving the simple matrix $\mathbf{G}$ and the function $H(\cdot)$. Improving the quality of the trapdoor and its inversion algorithm directly impacts the efficiency of the encryption scheme, since decoding of the message from $\mathbf{e}$ is performed very efficiently.

Theorem 3. *The generic encryption scheme above is secure assuming the hardness of* decision A-LWE$_{n,0,m,\alpha q}$ *for* $\alpha q \ge 2\sqrt{n} \ge 2 \cdot \sqrt{\ln(2n(1+1/\epsilon))/\pi} \ge \eta_\epsilon(\Lambda_q^\perp(\mathbf{G}))$.

Proof. Ciphertexts generated according to the generic encryption scheme from above correspond to plain A-LWE samples with $m_1 = 0$. By assumption decision A-LWE$_{n,0,m,\alpha q}$ is hard, and consequently, an adversary is not able to distinguish a challenge ciphertext from uniformly chosen samples.

One can apply Theorems 1 and 2 to have a direct reduction from traditional LWE. $\qquad\square$

Remark. We like to note that one could increase the message throughput of our encryption scheme even further by embedding the message not only into the error term but also into (part of) the secret $\mathbf{s}$. This allows for an additional message of size approximately $n(k-1)$ bits. This is possible since each encryption query involves a fresh secret vector $\mathbf{s}$. One has to make sure that the hash function H is invoked on a value with sufficient entropy (e.g. the first n bits are random).

4   New Chosen-Ciphertext Secure Encryption Schemes

Due to the new functionality of embedding messages in error vectors, we are able to propose a novel encryption scheme providing full CCA security when adopting the tagging approach presented in [45,46]. In fact, we get this feature for free, if we instantiate our generic construction from Sect. 3.3 with the trapdoor provided in [7]. More specifically, the authors add a tag u to the matrix $\mathbf{A}$ such that the modified matrix $\mathbf{A}_u$ keeps changing for every encryption query.

Originally, in almost all previous encryption schemes ciphertexts are build in a one-time pad manner by adding the message to a random-looking vector coming from an LWE instance. By our modifications, we omit the way of encoding messages and the restrictions made to the parameters. Our aim is to let the ciphertexts resemble an ordinary A-LWE instance such that the hardness of the scheme can be directly reduced to the plain A-LWE problem. Indeed, the error term hides the message while following the required distribution. This allows for more flexibility, efficiency and larger messages per ciphertext at no costs. Even more, this greatly simplifies the security proof. As we show later, we can even lift up the security to publicly-detectable RCCA (pd-RCCA) with a simple trick ensuring non-malleability of ciphertexts. When applying these functionalities to the error term in the CCA1-secure scheme due to [7], the message throughput is at least twice as large while simultaneously providing pd-RCCA security instead of CCA1, as before. In addition to that, we give an intuition of how to get a CCA2-secure encryption scheme involving only minor modifications.

In this paper, we assume the reader is familiar with the various security models for encryption schemes. We refer to the full version [44] for a description of the CCA1, CCA2, and RCCA models.

4.1   CCA1-Secure Encryption Scheme

We start with a detailed description of the CCA1 secure encryption scheme and the involved algorithms. Let $H : \mathbb{Z}_q^n \rightarrow \{0,1\}^m$ be some function. Let $\mathcal{R} = \mathbb{Z}_q[x]/(f(x))$ be a ring as constructed in [7], where $f(x)$ denotes a monic irreducible polynomial of degree n. Furthermore, let $h : \mathcal{R} \rightarrow \mathbb{Z}_q^{n \times n}$ be an injective ring homomorphism mapping elements $a \in \mathcal{R}$ to the matrix $h(a)$. By $\mathcal{U} = \{u_1, \ldots, u_\ell\}$ we denote a large set with "unit differences" property. That is, for any two ring elements a_i and $a_j \in \mathcal{R}^*$ with $i \neq j$ we have $a_i - a_j \in \mathcal{R}^*$ and $h(a_i - a_j) = h(a_i) - h(a_j)$ is invertible. By $\mathbf{G}_m$ we denote the matrix $\mathbf{I}_{m/k} \otimes \mathbf{g}^\top$. Our encryption scheme works as follows.

KGen(1^n): Let $k = \log q$ and $m, \bar{m} > 0$ with $k \mid m$ and $m = \bar{m} + nk$. Invoking
  TDF.KeyGen(1^n) outputs keys $(\mathbf{A}, \mathbf{R})$, where $\mathbf{A} = [\ \bar{\mathbf{A}}\ |\bar{\mathbf{A}}\mathbf{R}\ ]$ for randomly
  selected matrix $\bar{\mathbf{A}} \in \mathbb{Z}_q^{n \times \bar{m}}$ and $\mathbf{R} \leftarrow_R \mathcal{D}$ is sampled from a desired distribution $\mathcal{D}$, typically the discrete Gaussian distribution. For instance, one
  chooses $\bar{m} = nk$ and $\mathcal{D} = D_{\mathbb{Z},t}^{\bar{m} \times nk}$ for $t \in \omega(\sqrt{\log n})$. The public and secret
  key are given by $\mathsf{pk} = \mathbf{A} \in \mathbb{Z}_q^{n \times m}$ and $\mathsf{sk} = \mathbf{R} \in \mathbb{Z}_q^{\bar{m} \times nk}$.
Enc($\mathsf{pk}, \mathbf{m} \in \{0,1\}^l$ with $0 < l < m$): Select a nonzero $u \in \mathcal{U}$. Set $\mathbf{A}_u = $
  $[\ \bar{\mathbf{A}}\ |\bar{\mathbf{A}}\mathbf{R} - h(u)\mathbf{G}_{nk}\ ]$ with $\mathbf{G}_{nk} = \mathbf{I}_n \otimes \mathbf{g}^\top$. Then, select $\mathbf{s} \leftarrow_R \mathbb{Z}_q^n$ and
  $\mathbf{e} \leftarrow_R \mathcal{D}_{\Lambda_{\mathbf{v}}^\perp(\mathbf{G}_m), \alpha q}$ where $\mathbf{v} = \mathsf{encode}(H(\mathbf{s}) \oplus \mathbf{m}) \in \mathbb{Z}_q^{m/k}$ and $\alpha q \geq 2\sqrt{n} \geq$
  $2 \cdot \sqrt{\ln(2n(1 + 1/\epsilon))/\pi}$. Output the ciphertext

$$\mathbf{c} = (u, \mathbf{b}) \in \mathcal{U} \times \mathbb{Z}_q^m \text{ with } \mathbf{b}^\top = g_{\mathbf{A}_u}(\mathbf{s}, \mathbf{e}) = \mathbf{s}^\top \mathbf{A}_u + \mathbf{e}^\top \bmod q .$$

Dec($\mathsf{sk}, \mathbf{c}$): Determine $\mathbf{A}_u = [\ \bar{\mathbf{A}}\ |\bar{\mathbf{A}}\mathbf{R} - h(u)\mathbf{G}_{nk}\ ]$.
  1. If parsing $\mathbf{c}$ causes an error or $u = 0$, output $\perp$. Otherwise invoke the
     LWE inversion algorithm as provided in [7,44] with input parameters
     $(\mathbf{R}, \mathbf{A}_u, \mathbf{b})$, which outputs a failure $\perp$ or $g_{\mathbf{A}_u}^{-1}(\mathbf{b}^\top) = (\mathbf{s}', \mathbf{e}')$.
  2. Check $\|\mathbf{e}'\| \leq \alpha q \sqrt{m}$. If it is satisfied, compute $\mathbf{r} = H(\mathbf{s}')$ and
     $\mathbf{m} = \mathbf{r} \oplus \mathsf{decode}(\mathbf{G}_m \mathbf{e}' \bmod q)$, else output $\perp$.
  3. Output $\mathbf{m}$ as the message.

Theorem 4. *The encryption scheme above is CCA1-secure assuming the hard-ness of* decision A-LWE$_{n,0,m,\alpha q}$ *for* $\alpha q \geq 2\sqrt{n} \geq \eta_\epsilon(\Lambda_q^\perp(\mathbf{G}))$.

Proof. The proof is greatly simplified as compared to [7], since we are not
required to perform any transformations to the initial A-LWE samples. In fact,
we draw samples $(\mathbf{A}, \mathbf{b}^\top) \leftarrow_R L_{n,0,m,\alpha,q}^{\text{A-LWE}}(\mathbf{m})$ from the A-LWE distribution, where
$\mathbf{b}^\top = \mathbf{s}^\top \mathbf{A} + \mathbf{e}^\top$, $\mathbf{s} \leftarrow_R \mathbb{Z}_q^n$, $\mathbf{A} \leftarrow_R \mathbb{Z}_q^{n \times m}$ and $\mathbf{e} \leftarrow_R \mathcal{D}_{\mathbb{Z}^{m_1}, \alpha q} \times \mathcal{D}_{\Lambda_{\mathbf{v}}^\perp(\mathbf{G}), \alpha q}$ with
$\mathbf{v} = \mathsf{encode}(H(\mathbf{s}) \oplus \mathbf{m})$ and $\alpha q \geq 2\sqrt{n} \geq 2 \cdot \sqrt{\ln(2n(1 + 1/\epsilon))/\pi} \geq \eta_\epsilon(\Lambda_q^\perp(\mathbf{G}))$.
Distinguishing these samples from random ones is as hard as solving decision A-
LWE$_{n,0,m,\alpha q}$ for the given parameters (see Theorem 3).
Encryption queries in our scheme are represented by ordinary A-LWE queries,
thus we can give a direct reduction. Indeed, we have $\mathbf{b}_1 = \mathbf{s}^\top \bar{\mathbf{A}} + \mathbf{e}_1 \bmod q$ and
$\mathbf{b}_2 = \mathbf{s}^\top(h(u)\mathbf{G} - \bar{\mathbf{A}}\mathbf{R}) + \mathbf{e}_2 \bmod q$, where $(\bar{\mathbf{A}}, h(u)\mathbf{G} - \bar{\mathbf{A}}\mathbf{R})$ is statistically close
to uniform by the leftover hash lemma and $h(u)\mathbf{G} - \bar{\mathbf{A}}\mathbf{R}$ is $negl(n)$-uniform for
any choice of $u \in \mathcal{U}$ following essentially the same argumentation as in [7]. All
other proof steps remain essentially the same as in [7]. Hence, the advantage
of the adversary in the CCA1 security game with our scheme from above is
negligible.   □

For instance, if one chooses $m = c \cdot nk$ corresponding to a statistical instantiation of the scheme – that is, $\mathbf{A}$ is statistically close to uniform – one can
encrypt messages of length $c \cdot nk$ bits. In combination with the one-time-pad
approach from [7] and message injection into the secret vector $\mathbf{s}$, we can embed
approximately $(c + 2)nk - n$ message bits.

Further Applications. In the full version [44] we show how to use this cryptosystem as a main building block for the first lattice-based RCCA-secure encryption scheme and provide the schemes with an optional mode for high data load encryption. Moreover, we propose an asymmetric authenticated encryption scheme (amongst others) by exploiting the full entropy of the error vector for signatures and give a more efficient variant of the somewhat homomorphic encryption scheme initially proposed by Brakerski and Vaikuntanathan [34].

Acknowledgments. The work presented in this paper was performed within the context of the Software Cluster project Sinnodium and Software Campus project *IT-GiKo* by Rachid El Bansarkhani. It was funded by the German Federal Ministry of Education and Research (BMBF). Özgür Dagdelen and Johannes Buchmann are supported by BMBF within EC-SPRIDE. The authors thank Steven Galbraith for useful comments.

References

1. Ajtai, M.: Generating hard instances of lattice problems (extended abstract). In: 28th ACM STOC, pp. 99–108. ACM Press (1996)
2. Regev, O.: New lattice-based cryptographic constructions. J. ACM **51**, 899–942 (2004)
3. Micciancio, D., Regev, O.: Worst-case to average-case reductions based on Gaussian measures. In: 45th FOCS, pp. 372–381. IEEE Computer Society Press (2004)
4. Lyubashevsky, V., Micciancio, D., Peikert, C., Rosen, A.: SWIFFT: a modest proposal for FFT hashing. In: Nyberg, K. (ed.) FSE 2008. LNCS, vol. 5086, pp. 54–72. Springer, Heidelberg (2008)
5. Arbitman, Y., Dogon, G., Lyubashevsky, V., Micciancio, D., Peikert, C., Rosen, A.: SWIFFTX: a proposal for the SHA-3 standard. In: The First SHA-3 Candidate Conference (2008)
6. Gentry, C., Peikert, C., Vaikuntanathan, V.: Trapdoors for hard lattices and new cryptographic constructions. In: Ladner, R.E., Dwork, C. (eds.) 40th ACM STOC, pp. 197–206. ACM Press (2008)
7. Micciancio, D., Peikert, C.: Trapdoors for lattices: simpler, tighter, faster, smaller. In: Pointcheval, D., Johansson, T. (eds.) EUROCRYPT 2012. LNCS, vol. 7237, pp. 700–718. Springer, Heidelberg (2012)
8. Ducas, L., Durmus, A., Lepoint, T., Lyubashevsky, V.: Lattice signatures and bimodal Gaussians. In: Canetti, R., Garay, J.A. (eds.) CRYPTO 2013, Part I. LNCS, vol. 8042, pp. 40–56. Springer, Heidelberg (2013)
9. Güneysu, T., Lyubashevsky, V., Pöppelmann, T.: Practical lattice-based cryptography: a signature scheme for embedded systems. In: Prouff, E., Schaumont, P. (eds.) CHES 2012. LNCS, vol. 7428, pp. 530–547. Springer, Heidelberg (2012)
10. Lyubashevsky, V.: Lattice signatures without trapdoors. In: Pointcheval, D., Johansson, T. (eds.) EUROCRYPT 2012. LNCS, vol. 7237, pp. 738–755. Springer, Heidelberg (2012)
11. Katz, J., Vaikuntanathan, V.: Smooth projective hashing and password-based authenticated key exchange from lattices. In: Matsui, M. (ed.) ASIACRYPT 2009. LNCS, vol. 5912, pp. 636–652. Springer, Heidelberg (2009)

12. Jintai Ding, X.L.: A simple provably secure key exchange scheme based on the learning with errors problem. Cryptology ePrint Archive, Report 2012/688 (2012). http://eprint.iacr.org/
13. Peikert, C.: Lattice cryptography for the internet. Cryptology ePrint Archive, Report 2014/070 (2014). http://eprint.iacr.org/
14. Peikert, C., Vaikuntanathan, V., Waters, B.: A framework for efficient and composable oblivious transfer. In: Wagner, D. (ed.) CRYPTO 2008. LNCS, vol. 5157, pp. 554–571. Springer, Heidelberg (2008)
15. Regev, O.: On lattices, learning with errors, random linear codes, and cryptography. In: Gabow, H.N., Fagin, R. (eds.) 37th ACM STOC, pp. 84–93. ACM Press (2005)
16. Peikert, C.: Public-key cryptosystems from the worst-case shortest vector problem: extended abstract. In: Mitzenmacher, M. (ed.) 41st ACM STOC, pp. 333–342. ACM Press (2009)
17. Brakerski, Z., Langlois, A., Peikert, C., Regev, O., Stehlé, D.: Classical hardness of learning with errors. In: STOC, pp. 575–584 (2013)
18. Döttling, N., Müller-Quade, J.: Lossy codes and a new variant of the learning-with-errors problem. In: Johansson, T., Nguyen, P.Q. (eds.) EUROCRYPT 2013. LNCS, vol. 7881, pp. 18–34. Springer, Heidelberg (2013)
19. Micciancio, D., Peikert, C.: Hardness of SIS and LWE with small parameters. In: Canetti, R., Garay, J.A. (eds.) CRYPTO 2013, Part I. LNCS, vol. 8042, pp. 21–39. Springer, Heidelberg (2013)
20. Gentry, C.: Fully homomorphic encryption using ideal lattices. In: STOC, pp. 169–178. ACM (2009)
21. Brakerski, Z., Vaikuntanathan, V.: Efficient fully homomorphic encryption from (standard) LWE. In: Ostrovsky, R. (ed.) 52nd FOCS, pp. 97–106. IEEE Computer Society Press (2011)
22. Gentry, C., Halevi, S.: Fully homomorphic encryption without squashing using depth-3 arithmetic circuits. In: Ostrovsky, R. (ed.) 52nd FOCS, pp. 107–109. IEEE Computer Society Press (2011)
23. Brakerski, Z.: Fully homomorphic encryption without modulus switching from classical GapSVP. In: Safavi-Naini, R., Canetti, R. (eds.) CRYPTO 2012. LNCS, vol. 7417, pp. 868–886. Springer, Heidelberg (2012)
24. Brakerski, Z., Gentry, C., Vaikuntanathan, V.: (leveled) fully homomorphic encryption without bootstrapping. In: ITCS, pp. 309–325 (2012)
25. Cash, D., Hofheinz, D., Kiltz, E., Peikert, C.: Bonsai trees, or how to delegate a lattice basis. In: Gilbert, H. (ed.) EUROCRYPT 2010. LNCS, vol. 6110, pp. 523–552. Springer, Heidelberg (2010)
26. Agrawal, S., Boneh, D., Boyen, X.: Efficient lattice (H)IBE in the standard model. In: Gilbert, H. (ed.) EUROCRYPT 2010. LNCS, vol. 6110, pp. 553–572. Springer, Heidelberg (2010)
27. Agrawal, S., Boneh, D., Boyen, X.: Lattice basis delegation in fixed dimension and shorter-ciphertext hierarchical IBE. In: Rabin, T. (ed.) CRYPTO 2010. LNCS, vol. 6223, pp. 98–115. Springer, Heidelberg (2010)
28. Lyubashevsky, V., Peikert, C., Regev, O.: On ideal lattices and learning with errors over rings. In: Gilbert, H. (ed.) EUROCRYPT 2010. LNCS, vol. 6110, pp. 1–23. Springer, Heidelberg (2010)
29. Lindner, R., Peikert, C.: Better key sizes (and attacks) for LWE-based encryption. In: Kiayias, A. (ed.) CT-RSA 2011. LNCS, vol. 6558, pp. 319–339. Springer, Heidelberg (2011)

30. Lyubashevsky, V., Peikert, C., Regev, O.: A toolkit for ring-LWE cryptography. In: Johansson, T., Nguyen, P.Q. (eds.) EUROCRYPT 2013. LNCS, vol. 7881, pp. 35–54. Springer, Heidelberg (2013)

31. Peikert, C., Waters, B.: Lossy trapdoor functions and their applications. In: Ladner, R.E., Dwork, C. (eds.) 40th ACM STOC, pp. 187–196. ACM Press (2008)

32. Stehlé, D., Steinfeld, R., Tanaka, K., Xagawa, K.: Efficient public key encryption based on ideal lattices. In: Matsui, M. (ed.) ASIACRYPT 2009. LNCS, vol. 5912, pp. 617–635. Springer, Heidelberg (2009)

33. Canetti, R., Krawczyk, H., Nielsen, J.B.: Relaxing chosen-ciphertext security. In: Boneh, D. (ed.) CRYPTO 2003. LNCS, vol. 2729, pp. 565–582. Springer, Heidelberg (2003)

34. Brakerski, Z., Vaikuntanathan, V.: Fully homomorphic encryption from ring-LWE and security for key dependent messages. In: Rogaway, P. (ed.) CRYPTO 2011. LNCS, vol. 6841, pp. 505–524. Springer, Heidelberg (2011)

35. Groth, J.: Rerandomizable and replayable adaptive chosen ciphertext attack secure cryptosystems. In: Naor, M. (ed.) TCC 2004. LNCS, vol. 2951, pp. 152–170. Springer, Heidelberg (2004)

36. Phan, D.H., Safavi-Naini, R., Tonien, D.: Generic construction of hybrid public key traitor tracing with full-public-traceability. In: Bugliesi, M., Preneel, B., Sassone, V., Wegener, I. (eds.) ICALP 2006, Part II. LNCS, vol. 4052, pp. 264–275. Springer, Heidelberg (2006)

37. Prabhakaran, M., Rosulek, M.: Rerandomizable RCCA encryption. In: Menezes, A. (ed.) CRYPTO 2007. LNCS, vol. 4622, pp. 517–534. Springer, Heidelberg (2007)

38. Xue, R., Feng, D.: Toward practical anonymous rerandomizable RCCA secure encryptions. In: Qing, S., Imai, H., Wang, G. (eds.) ICICS 2007. LNCS, vol. 4861, pp. 239–253. Springer, Heidelberg (2007)

39. Libert, B., Vergnaud, D.: Unidirectional chosen-ciphertext secure proxy re-encryption. In: Cramer, R. (ed.) PKC 2008. LNCS, vol. 4939, pp. 360–379. Springer, Heidelberg (2008)

40. Dolev, D., Dwork, C., Naor, M.: Nonmalleable cryptography. SIAM J. Comput. **30**, 391–437 (2000)

41. Coron, J.-S., Handschuh, H., Joye, M., Paillier, P., Pointcheval, D., Tymen, C.: GEM: a generic chosen-ciphertext secure encryption method. In: Preneel, B. (ed.) CT-RSA 2002. LNCS, vol. 2271, pp. 263–276. Springer, Heidelberg (2002)

42. Herzog, J.C., Liskov, M., Micali, S.: Plaintext awareness via key registration. In: Boneh, D. (ed.) CRYPTO 2003. LNCS, vol. 2729, pp. 548–564. Springer, Heidelberg (2003)

43. Boneh, D., Canetti, R., Halevi, S., Katz, J.: Chosen-ciphertext security from identity-based encryption. SIAM J. Comput. **36**, 1301–1328 (2007)

44. El Bansarkhani, R., Dagdelen, O., Buchmann, J.: Augmented learning with errors: the untapped potential of the error term. Cryptology ePrint Archive, Report 2014/733 (2014). http://eprint.iacr.org/

45. Kiltz, E.: Chosen-ciphertext security from tag-based encryption. In: Halevi, S., Rabin, T. (eds.) TCC 2006. LNCS, vol. 3876, pp. 581–600. Springer, Heidelberg (2006)

46. Canetti, R., Halevi, S., Katz, J.: Chosen-ciphertext security from identity-based encryption. In: Cachin, C., Camenisch, J.L. (eds.) EUROCRYPT 2004. LNCS, vol. 3027, pp. 207–222. Springer, Heidelberg (2004)

Mobile Security

BabelCrypt: The Universal Encryption Layer for Mobile Messaging Applications

Ahmet Talha Ozcan[1], Can Gemicioglu[2], Kaan Onarlioglu[3]([✉]),
Michael Weissbacher[3], Collin Mulliner[3], William Robertson[3],
and Engin Kirda[3]

[1] Middle East Technical University, Ankara, Turkey
`talha.ozcan@metu.edu.tr`
[2] Sabanci University, Istanbul, Turkey
`cgemicioglu@sabanciuniv.edu`
[3] Northeastern University, Boston, USA
`{onarliog,mw,crm,wkr,ek}@ccs.neu.edu`

Abstract. Internet-based mobile messaging applications have become a ubiquitous means of communication, and have quickly gained popularity over cellular short messages (SMS). Unfortunately, from a security point of view, free messaging services do not guarantee the privacy of users. For example, free messaging providers can record and store exchanged messages indefinitely to collect information about specific users. Moreover, these messages can be accessed by criminals who gain access to social media accounts. In this paper, we introduce BabelCrypt, a system that addresses the problem of automatically retrofitting arbitrary mobile chat applications with end-to-end encryption. Our system works by transparently interfacing with the original client applications supplied by the respective service providers. It does not require any modification to the individual applications, nor does it require any knowledge or customization for specific chat applications. BabelCrypt is able to automatically inject control messages in-band, using the underlying application's message exchange mechanism, and thus supports running arbitrarily complex encryption protocols such as OTR. We successfully used BabelCrypt with a number of popular messaging applications including Facebook Messenger, WhatsApp, and Skype. Our evaluation shows that BabelCrypt provides end-to-end security for arbitrary messaging applications while satisfactorily preserving the original user experience of the messaging application.

Keywords: Mobile messaging · Android security · Privacy

1 Introduction

Internet-based mobile messaging applications that provide services such as the discovery of other users and exchanging text messages with them have become a ubiquitous means of communication. They have quickly gained popularity over

R. Böhme and T. Okamoto (Eds.): FC 2015, LNCS 8975, pp. 355–369, 2015.
DOI: 10.1007/978-3-662-47854-7_21

cellular short messages (SMS) as such services are often free of charge, even when roaming and switching to a different cellular network operator, and are available anywhere Internet connectivity is available.

Internet-based mobile messaging has also experienced huge growth in recent years due to the availability of inexpensive smartphones and tablets. The strong ties between text communication and smartphones become even more apparent when one considers that popular services (e.g., WhatsApp and Viber) only provide client software for smartphones and tablets. Today, many online social media services such as Facebook, Microsoft, Google, and Yahoo have followed the trend and are providing their own text-based communication service. Furthermore, a large number of video and voice communication services such as Skype and Viber are also providing chat-style text messaging features.

Unfortunately, there are also significant downsides of these free and always available communication services from a security point of view; in particular, user privacy suffers. While the underlying communication can easily be secured against eavesdropping by utilizing TLS, the service provider has full, unfettered access to every message exchanged through their infrastructure. Service providers can (ab)use this power to record and store exchanged messages indefinitely; for example, to collect information about specific users and serve them targeted ads [7]. Moreover, these messages can be accessed by rogue employees of the service provider, or criminals who gain access to social media accounts. Service providers can also be subpoenaed to hand over the stored data to government and law enforcement agencies that request access to a user's communication logs.

So far, there have been several attempts to secure Internet-based mobile communication. For instance, users of certain chat clients can install and use encryption plugins such as Off-the-Record (OTR) [9] to protect their privacy. However, these chat clients support only a limited set of communication protocols. In addition, many messaging services (e.g., Skype and Viber) use custom protocols that constantly evolve, forcing the user to update the chat client frequently, thus cutting out the development of third-party clients or plugins that support message encryption. Notably, recent research has proposed Mimesis Aegis [12], a system that addresses this problem by interposing a conceptual encryption layer between software and the users interacting with them. However, this approach requires development of specific logic for each chat client supported, and does not support automatic injection of messages into the communication channel, rendering it unable to support cryptographic protocols that involve, for instance, key exchange.

In this paper, we introduce BabelCrypt, a system that addresses the problem of retrofitting arbitrary mobile chat applications with end-to-end encryption. Our system works by transparently interfacing with the original client applications supplied by the respective service providers. It does not require any modification to the individual applications, nor does it require any knowledge or customization for specific chat applications. A significant advantage of BabelCrypt over comparable solutions is that it is also able to automatically inject control messages in-band, using the underlying application's message exchange mechanism, and thus supports running arbitrarily complex encryption protocols such as OTR.

BabelCrypt consists of two core components: an encrypting keyboard that transparently secures messages typed into the application by a user, and a decrypting display overlay that automatically analyzes the GUI of the chat application in real-time and adapts its appearance to mimic that of the underlying application. As a result, users interact with BabelCrypt in the exact same way they would with the original application. We show in Sect. 6 that BabelCrypt does not have a significant detrimental impact on the user experience and is easy to use, while providing transparent end-to-end encryption for the exchanged messages.

We implemented BabelCrypt for the popular Android platform. Our prototype implementation works on any Android device that runs Android version 4.x or later, and does not require any modification to the phone or superuser access to the operating system.

The main contributions of this paper are the following:

- We introduce BabelCrypt, a system for application-independent end-to-end encryption for Internet-based mobile text messaging. Our system protects messages against access by the messaging service providers.
- We show that BabelCrypt works by interfacing with the target chat application in the same way a user would, in a transparent manner, and does not significantly detract from the original user experience. BabelCrypt supports arbitrary chat applications, and does not require modification to or previous knowledge of individual applications. When using shared passwords for encryption, BabelCrypt does not require any setup procedure.
- We propose a technique for automatically injecting messages into the underlying chat application's message exchange system, enabling BabelCrypt to run cryptographic protocols such as OTR. In this mode, BabelCrypt only requires a simple one-time initialization routine per-installed application, only requiring the user to perform two clicks on the screen.
- We evaluate BabelCrypt using a wide range of text-based communication applications to demonstrate its generic applicability, performance, and usability.

2   Threat Model and Motivation

BabelCrypt aims to protect the confidentiality of communication between users of text-based online communication services in a transparent manner, without requiring drastic changes to the user experience or additional development effort. The threat model we consider for this work is divided into four distinct scenarios described below.

In the first scenario, we assume that the communication between the messaging application on the smartphone and the service provider can be intercepted and eavesdropped on by an attacker. This scenario covers possible mistakes in the usage of cryptographic primitives, which have been documented in previous work [6]. For example, the application may fail to use transport layer encryption such as TLS for sensitive messages; otherwise, the application's use of cryptography might be implemented in an unsafe way that allows man-in-the-middle attacks.

The second scenario involves malicious communication service providers – that is, service providers that are benign, but that employ a business model based on monetizing information collected from their users. In our threat model, we assume that service providers have access to, and may record, all communication carried out through their infrastructure. They may access and use this information at any time, for example, to deliver targeted advertisements to their users. In addition, they may disclose the collected records to other entities, for instance, through company acquisitions or mergers, or to government and law enforcement agencies through subpoenas.

In the next scenario, we assume that user accounts may be compromised by an attacker. Chat services typically record conversations on the user's device or on their servers to provide conversation history and to implement a seamless hand-over between different devices owned by the same user. Therefore, an attacker can access entire conversation histories through compromised user credentials or stolen devices.

In the final scenario, we assume that third-party code embedded inside chat clients may freely intercept user communication. This might be due to malicious third-party code inclusion exploits, or implemented for benign purposes by the application developer – for example, to include advertisement libraries that scan for keywords and display targeted advertisements.

In all above scenarios, BabelCrypt aims to prevent inadvertent disclosure of users' communication records, keep their conversations confidential, and protect their privacy.

3   System Design

The design philosophy of BabelCrypt is to provide chat applications with end-to-end encryption in a completely transparent and generic manner, both from the perspective of the user and the underlying application. In particular, our system should satisfy the following design goals.

(D1) BabelCrypt must ensure that the user experience of interacting with the underlying chat application is not changed drastically.
(D2) BabelCrypt should be designed in a way that allows underlying chat application could remain oblivious to the presence of an encryption layer above it, or that it is transferring encrypted messages.
(D1) BabelCrypt must be independent of the specifics of the underlying chat application, and of the service provider infrastructure. This includes avoiding any form of modification to the underlying application's source code.

Fig. 1. The BabelCrypt system at work. The user types a message (1), when pressing send the keyboard encrypts the message and passes it to the application (2). The application sends the message (3). The application receives an encrypted message (4) and the overlay decrypts and displays the message to the user (5). Stages 3 and 4 are transparent to the user.

To this end, we designed BabelCrypt as a set of components that includes an extension to the system's software keyboard, and a GUI overlay over the chat application screen. Users of chat applications type their messages through the BabelCrypt keyboard, just like they would interact with an ordinary keyboard, which encrypts the input on the fly and feeds it into the underlying application (D1). The GUI overlay automatically mimics the display of the chat application, and shows the decrypted plaintext where the underlying application would normally display the encrypted message (D1)(D2). During this process, BabelCrypt operates as an independent layer between the user and the target application, acting as a cryptographic conduit while remaining oblivious to both (D3).

Figure 1 provides an overview of BabelCrypt. In the rest of this section, we will describe the design of the core components of BabelCrypt in more detail.

3.1   BabelCrypt Keyboard

The primary interface between BabelCrypt and the user is the BabelCrypt keyboard. This component is an enhanced software keyboard that is a substitute for the operating system's default keyboard. It functions like a typical keyboard would, but also makes it possible to encrypt user input on-the-fly when a private conversation is requested. Using an additional mode switch button added at the bottom row of the keyboard, the user is able to turn the on-the-fly encryption on or off so that the same keyboard could be used system-wide as an ordinary keyboard with applications that do not necessitate encrypted input. The current mode of operation is indicated by a distinct visual cue – in particular, by changing the background color of the keyboard so that the user does not accidentally send unencrypted messages (see Fig. 2).

When the encryption mode is on, instead of directly passing key presses to the underlying application, the BabelCrypt keyboard buffers all input, and displays it to the user in an auto-complete-bar like "plaintext field". Only when the user presses the "Return" or "Send" key is the entered text encrypted, and passed to the application. This ensures that the plaintext is never exposed to the underlying applications which may potentially leak them to the service provider without the user's knowledge. The aforementioned plaintext field makes it possible for the user to securely view and edit the text before it is sent, instead of typing blindly.

The keyboard is also tasked with encoding the ciphertext into printable characters, and splitting it into multiple messages of smaller chunks if necessary so that the underlying chat application can correctly transfer the encrypted message to the remote end.

3.2   BabelCrypt Display Overlay

The BabelCrypt display overlay is the component responsible for detecting text encrypted using BabelCrypt on the screen, and displaying it back to the user in plaintext.

This component has two main tasks. First, it continuously monitors the current foreground application window for changes to the GUI, which would indicate a new sent or received message being displayed. When such a change is triggered, this component accesses the underlying application's GUI tree, and traverses all visible nodes in it searching for encrypted text. Once ciphertext is found, BabelCrypt decodes it back to its original binary representation and decrypts it. BabelCrypt then automatically inspects the geometry of the GUI element that contains the ciphertext, overlays a textbox on top of it, and displays the decrypted text where it would originally have appeared in the chat application. In this way, we keep the original look and feel of the application, and do not change the user experience significantly.

BabelCrypt display overlay is able to perform these tasks thanks to the Android Accessibility Framework [10]. Using the accessibility API, BabelCrypt is able to access and inspect the GUI layout of the applications on the screen, without requiring modifications or the instrumentation of the application code.

Finally, similar to the keyboard component, BabelCrypt displays plaintext overlays in a distinct color to alert the user to the fact that the message has been sent encrypted (See Fig. 2).

3.3   BabelCrypt Encryption Modes

BabelCrypt is designed with two encryption modes to support different use scenarios. Each mode provides different degrees of security guarantees and usability, allowing the users of the system the flexibility to pick the one that suits their needs. In this section, we describe these modes in more detail.

Encryption with Shared Secrets. In this mode, BabelCrypt uses a basic shared secret scheme where the exchange of the cryptographic secret is delegated to the users (e.g., users share a password out of band).

The primary advantage of using this scheme is that no setup is necessary prior to running BabelCrypt; That is, users simply enter their passwords into a prompt, a key is derived from the password, and the users can immediately start exchanging messages. In addition, the communication history can be kept on the device or on the application servers in an encrypted form for future access by the user. Finally, it is relatively easy to adapt this scheme to multi-user chat rooms by simply sharing the password with all involved parties.

Of course, shared secret encryption has the significant disadvantage of providing less strict security, including no forward secrecy nor authentication. Therefore, this encryption mode is suitable for users who would like to keep their chat histories, and would like a quick conversation without any setup process.

Encryption with Key-Agreement Protocols. This second encryption mode allows users to run a cryptographic protocol over the target chat application's message exchange mechanism with the help of BabelCrypt. In this way, protocols of arbitrary complexity can be executed, for example, to perform an authenticated key exchange.

While the specific properties of such an encryption scheme depends on the actual protocol used, in general, this encryption mode makes it possible to hold a private conversation with stricter security guarantees such as authentication and perfect forward secrecy.

The primary disadvantage of this mode stems from the fact that cryptographic protocols typically require several steps of message exchanges before a session key for encryption can be established. However, performing such an exchange automatically would necessitate either establishing a separate out-of-band communication channel between two BabelCrypt endpoints, or using the in-band channel where text messages are also exchanged for this purpose. While the former is impractical, the latter is not directly possible since BabelCrypt does not have direct and automatic control over the communication channel; it can only input text into the underlying chat application through the user interacting with the keyboard.

As a result, in order to use this mode, the user needs to perform a simple one-time initialization step for every target application prior to using Babel-Crypt with them. Specifically, the user needs to register with BabelCrypt the message entry box and the "Send" button of the application, so that BabelCrypt can subsequently inject protocol messages into the application and send them automatically without user interaction.

BabelCrypt handles both the task of registering these GUI components, and injecting messages, through the Android Accessibility Framework. Upon launching a chat application for the first time, the user needs to press a new "Set" button placed in the bottom row of the BabelCrypt keyboard which activates the registration mode. Next, the user touches the message entry box and the "Send" button on the screen, BabelCrypt intercepts these touch events, translates the touch coordinates to the corresponding GUI elements, and registers the resource identifiers corresponding to the message entry box and the button. Later, when message injection is required by the running protocol, BabelCrypt automatically traverses the application's GUI tree, locates the GUI elements corresponding to the saved identifiers, injects a message into the message entry box, and programmatically presses the "Send" button. Similarly, on the receiving side, BabelCrypt

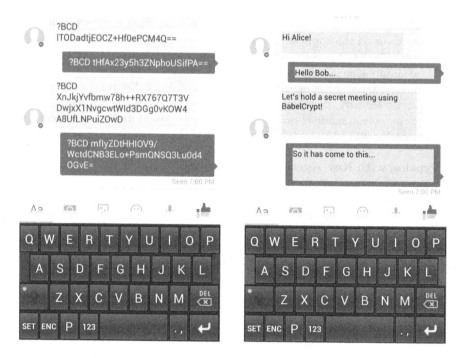

Fig. 2. An encrypted conversation displayed with BabelCrypt disabled on the left, and with BabelCrypt enabled on the right. Note that the background color of the keyboard and the overlay boxes change to indicate that a secure conversation is in progress.

overlay traverses the GUI tree to find protocol messages displayed by the chat application, and passes them to the encryption layer. In this way, after a simple initial setup, arbitrarily complex protocols can be automatically run without further user interaction.

4   Implementation

In the following, we provide details of our BabelCrypt prototype implementation and address some of the technical issues we elided in the previous sections.

4.1   Encryption Schemes

BabelCrypt currently supports one concrete encryption scheme for each of the two encryption modes it supports.

For encryption with shared secrets, we implemented a simple password-derived key scheme. Specifically, a 256-bit cryptographic key is derived from a pre-shared password using PBKDF2 with 10000 iterations. The encryption is performed using AES256 in CBC mode. IV values are transmitted along with the messages as we describe in the following sections.

For the more complex cryptographic protocol mode, we implemented the Off-the-Record Messaging (OTR) protocol, a protocol designed specifically for text-based chat applications. It provides strong security guarantees such as perfect forward secrecy and deniable authentication, and is a good fit for BabelCrypt's security goals. Note that, however, OTR uses session keys that are periodically discarded, which makes it impossible to retrieve past conversation histories. OTR also does not support multi-user chat. As such, the simpler shared secret encryption mode still remains viable in different use cases.

4.2   Message Formats

BabelCrypt employs two different types of messages, data messages and control messages. Data messages carry encrypted user input, while the control messages are used for transmitting injected protocol messages.

Data messages could either be as a 3-tuple $\{BCD, IV, CIPHERTEXT\}$ if the shared-secret encryption mode, which requires sending the IV together with the message, is being used. Or, it could be a 2-tuple $\{BCD, OTRMSG\}$ if OTR is active. Here, BCD (BabelCrypt Data) is a special sequence that indicates that the payload of this message should be decrypted and displayed. When traversing the GUI tree, the BabelCrypt overlay component identifies encrypted user input by searching for this special tag. Examples of encrypted and decrypted messages are shown in Fig. 2.

Similarly, control messages are formatted as a 3-tuple $\{BCC, ID, OTRMSG\}$, where BCC (BabelCrypt Control) is a different sequence tagging control messages. When the overlay component encounters such a message in the display, it passes the payload MSG to the encryption layer. Note that this exchange of control messages is visible in the chat application's display since control messages are transmitted through the chat application just like a normal conversation. Obviously, these messages are not human-readable, and hence, clutter the screen. Unfortunately, it is not possible for us to remove those messages from the screen as, for security reasons, the Android accessibility framework does not allow the modification of the GUI of the underlying applications. Therefore, in order not to confuse the user, BabelCrypt instead overlays a textbox on the displayed message, showing a notification informing the user that a cryptographic protocol is running and the contents of the message should be ignored.

A final issue arises from the fact that chat applications typically display both the incoming and outgoing messages on the screen. As a result, when a control message is injected by BabelCrypt into the application, it appears on the screens of both endpoints. However, control messages should only be *seen* and processed by the remote end. In order to prevent the sender from processing the control message destined for the other end, each control message also includes a randomly generated ID value. The sender inserts this to a set of IDs that should be ignored prior to sending the message and, as a result, the overlay component skips this message when searching for tagged entries on the screen. Similarly, once the control message is processed at the remote end, it is also inserted into an ignore list so that the same message is not processed multiple times, for example, when a user scrolls the screen and a previously processed message is displayed.

5   Limitations

By design, the underlying chat applications are completely oblivious of Babel-Crypt. However, this can potentially lead to unexpected consequences when delivering encrypted messages. For instance, an application that does not allow the transfer of certain characters in the text, that transforms the messages in some way, or that otherwise has similar restrictions on the message format would break the integrity of BabelCrypt messages. Hence, the decryption on the remote end would be impossible. The keyboard component of our system is responsible for simple text encoding and splitting of messages, and we did not encounter applications requiring more sophisticated message handling in our tests; however, this possibility remains.

Another potential usability disadvantage is that some of the application features such as searching in the chat history would not be possible with Babel-Crypt since the messages are stored in ciphertext. Likewise, features such as spell checking that could be performed inside an application need to be moved into the BabelCrypt keyboard as only the keyboard has access to plaintext input.

As previously noted, for secure communication protocols requiring automatic message injection, BabelCrypt necessitates a one-time setup during which the user interacts with the application's text entry box and message send button, and the system registers their GUI resource identifiers. While this approach makes BabelCrypt resonably robust against cosmetic changes to the underlying application's GUI, changes to resource identifiers may require the user to repeat the setup step, causing a minor disruption of the user experience.

Finally, BabelCrypt does not address the problem of sharing encrypted images, voice, or videos. This problem is outside the scope of this work.

6   Evaluation

In this section we describe our evaluation of BabelCrypt and show that it is compatible with prominent chat applications, that it does not incur a noticeable performance overhead, and that it does not have a significant negative impact on the user experience.

6.1   Applicability

In order to demonstrate that BabelCrypt works correctly with popular chat applications, we installed and extensively tested a set of popular applications found in the Android Marketplace. We verified that both shared password encryption and OTR modes correctly work in various applications such as the Facebook Messenger, WhatsApp, Tango, WeChat, Viber, and Skype. We note that although BabelCrypt is targeted at online messaging applications, it also works with SMS applications that display the messages as conversation flows. For instance, we verified that BabelCrypt works correctly with Go SMS [2].

Table 1. The results of a user study carried out with 40 participants, which demonstrate the usability of BabelCrypt.

Metric	Min	Q_1	Median	Mean	Q_3	Max	Lower bound on 95% confidence interval
Simplicity	75.00	75.00	100.00	**91.88**	100.00	100.0	**88.09**
Appearance	50.00	75.00	75.00	**75.62**	81.25	100.0	**70.04**
Likability	25.00	75.00	75.00	**74.38**	75.00	100.0	**70.14**

6.2 Performance

We were unable to reliably measure message round-trip times in our evaluation setup, due to factors such as network delays that lead to unpredictable latency in message delivery. Consequently, we opted to measure the performance by benchmarking the critical performance path of our system.

BabelCrypt has two execution paths that incur an overhead over the original chat application: the keyboard, and the display overlay. The keyboard is responsible for encrypting a single chunk of user input. However, the overlay component needs to traverse the entire GUI tree on each window content change, check GUI node contents for a match with the special BabelCrypt-tagged messages, and then process them, which typically includes decrypting several messages displayed on the screen at once. Thus, we chose to benchmark the overlay component since it represents the slowest path of execution in our system.

We have designed a macro benchmark that covers all of the above tasks performed by the BabelCrypt overlay. We triggered the whole process by manually sending encrypted messages to our test device from another remote device, and then measured the time for the overlay to finish detecting and processing all messages displayed on the screen. In our test setup, we used Facebook Messenger as the underlying chat application, and ran it on an off-the-shelf HTC One X smartphone. We have repeated the experiment 100 times and calculated the average runtimes. The results show that BabelCrypt incurred a performance overhead of **150.1 ms** on the average, with a standard deviation of **69.0 ms**, which indicates that the performance impact would not be detrimental to the user experience and that they would not have noticed a significant difference.

6.3 Usability

In order to evaluate the usability of the system and determine the impact of BabelCrypt on user experience, we conducted a user study with 40 participants. We confirmed that all of the participants are smartphone users, and that they are familiar with using at least one online messaging application.

We define our criteria for usability using three separate metrics. *Simplicity* is defined as the ease of interaction with the chat application, *appearance* is the perceived visual aesthetics of the application's user interface, and, finally, *likability* captures the overall subjective experience of the user when interacting with the chat application.

In our study, we provided each participant with a Samsung Galaxy S3 smartphone loaded with Facebook Messenger, and asked them to exchange messages with a remote user. An experiment observer was tasked with responding to the participant's messages using another device, so that the participant can hold a realistic conversation with a human. The participants performed this task first with the vanilla messaging application, and then repeated the process with BabelCrypt enabled. They were then given an exit survey and asked to compare their experience with the messaging application in the two experiments. Specifically, they were asked three questions to compare the BabelCrypt-enabled system to the original application for each of our usability metrics defined above, and rate their experience on a 5-point Likert scale, where a higher score indicates a positive opinion (e.g., that BabelCrypt is as easy to use as the original application) and a lower score indicates a negative response (e.g., that BabelCrypt is very hard to use). After collecting user responses, we have normalized the points to a value between 0 and 100 to calculate a score for each usability metric. Finally, we computed the average scores, and analyzed the results to calculate the lower bound on a 95 % confidence interval as to represent the worst-case scores. These results and five-number summaries of the collected data are presented in Table 1.

These results show that, BabelCrypt provides a degree of simplicity that is similar to the original messaging application. For the remaining two metrics, user feedback remains well above average, demonstrating that BabelCrypt does not have a significant negative impact on the user experience.

7   Related Work

The concept of confidential communication is not new, and solutions such as Pretty Good Privacy (PGP) [8] have been available for many years. PGP allows the encryption of arbitrary data, and it is most suitable for the encryption of email contents and attachments. Standalone systems such as PGP have good security properties, but they unfortunately suffer from poor usability. That is, users need to be familiar with the concept of public-key cryptography, and often need to install plugins that interface with the messaging application. Furthermore, if the application does not support a plugin interface, integration becomes difficult. To overcome these issues, other secure communication solutions have been developed. In the following, we discuss various systems that provide comparable solutions to BabelCrypt, and discuss the differences as well as the advantages and disadvantages.

There are several secure-messaging systems that were created specifically for smartphones, such as TextSecure [13], Threema [16], ChatSecure [15], and SilentCircle [14]. All of these services have been specifically designed to provide secure communication, but are *standalone* solutions. That is, users have to adjust to a new service and application (often with a new GUI), they have to install new software, and most importantly, they can only securely communicate with contacts that are also using this service. In comparison, BabelCrypt has been designed to integrate with existing legacy services and the corresponding mobile applications. Therefore, the user can simply install BabelCrypt on her phone and continue to use existing applications such as WhatsApp and Skype without any disruption, or the need to add new contacts from scratch. However, our solution shares the above systems' limitation that all communicating parties need to install BabelCrypt on their devices.

Some chat clients, such as Pidgin [3] and Audium [1], come with a plugin architecture that allows third parties to develop application-specific plugins. Hence, security plugins such as Off-the-Record (OTR) [9] can be used to encrypt the communication between users even if the original protocol does not provide security features. Unfortunately, however, many popular messaging applications on smartphones (e.g., Viber, WhatsApp) do not provide a plugin architecture. BabelCrypt bridges this gap on the Android platform, and is able to secure arbitrary text-based messaging applications in a generic fashion. In other words, BabelCrypt can be seen as a universal plugin that is intended to work with any existing smartphone application.

In an alternative approach, repackaging-based systems such as Aurism [17], Dr. Android [11], I-ARM [5], and Bluebox [4] modify the original application binary in order to add privacy features such as message encryption. Repackaging solutions have the advantage that they run inside the application process, and thus, in theory, can completely integrate with the target application. Unfortunately, though, in practice, such solutions are often not very effective due to the high complexity of the messaging applications. Furthermore, the repackaging process has to be redone for every update of the target application, and these applications are sometimes be protected against reverse engineering attempts using obfuscation and other anti-reversing techniques. In comparison, BabelCrypt does not require any modification to the targeted messaging applications, and thus, works independently of the complexity of the underlying application. In addition, our solution is unlikely to be affected by application updates since we interact with the target application through the system keyboard, and by accessing the application GUI through the use of standard Android platform features.

A recent, and one of the conceptually closest systems to BabelCrypt is Mimesis Aegis [12]. Mimesis Aegis also aims to provide a solution that can work with arbitrary messaging applications on smartphones. The approach provides services such as message encryption and decryption and can provide a secure communication environment. However, it has the shortcoming that application-specific code needs to be developed for each application the user wishes to use (e.g., WhatsApp is not supported in the prototype as the authors have not implemented the application-specific GUI code). In contrast, BabelCrypt aims to be more generic, and works out-of-the-box with any arbitrary text-messaging application on a smartphone without the need to develop application-specific code. Moreover, a notable advantage of BabelCrypt over comparable solutions is that it is also able to automatically inject control messages in-band, using the underlying application's message exchange mechanism, and thus, supports running arbitrarily complex encryption protocols such as OTR.

Recently, TextSecure and WhatsApp announced a collaboration to provide end-to-end security for messages exchanged using the WhatsApp mobile application and messaging service. While we laud this as a positive development for secure online communications, we also note that – to our knowledge – there are no plans to make WhatsApp's implementation of the TextSecure protocol open source or otherwise available for third party auditing. Therefore, BabelCrypt can provide an additional layer of assurance for privacy-concious users in this or similar scenarios.

8   Conclusion

Internet-based mobile messaging applications have become a ubiquitous and highly popular means of communication on mobile devices. Such services are often free-of-charge, and are available anywhere Internet connectivity is possible. Moreover, Internet-based mobile messaging has shown a significant growth in recent years due to the availability of inexpensive smartphones and tablets. Unfortunately, these messaging applications come at a cost in terms of privacy: Although the transport of the messages can be secured by the use of protocols such as TLS and are generally protected against man-in-the-middle attacks, the service provider can still (ab)use its power to record and store the exchanged messages indefinitely (e.g., to serve targeted ads to their users).

In this paper, we presented BabelCrypt, a generic, automated privacy-enhancing system that addresses the problem of retrofitting arbitrary mobile chat applications with end-to-end encryption. Our system works by transparently interfacing with the original client applications supplied by the respective service providers. BabelCrypt does not require modifications to the individual applications, nor does it require knowledge of or customization for specific chat applications. Compared to similar, existing systems, BabelCrypt has the advantage that it is able to automatically inject control messages in-band, using the underlying application's message exchange mechanism. Thus, it supports running arbitrarily complex encryption protocols such as OTR for applications that have not been designed with an open API (e.g., WhatsApp). Furthermore, BabelCrypt does not significantly alter the original user experience of the messaging applications, and thus provides a valuable and practical generic next step towards usable end-to-end security for mobile communications.

Acknowledgment. This work was supported by the Office of Naval Research (ONR) under grant N000141210165, National Science Foundation (NSF) under grant CNS-1116777, and Secure Business Austria. The authors would like to thank Erik-Oliver Blass for insightful discussions and valuable feedback.

References

1. Audium. https://www.audium.im
2. Go SMS. http://gosms.goforandroid.com/
3. Pidgin, the universal chat client. https://www.pidgin.im
4. Bluebox Security: Bluebox. https://www.bluebox.com
5. Davis, B., Sanders, B., Khodaverdian, A., Chen, H.: I-ARM-Droid: a rewriting framework for in-app reference monitors for android applications. In: IEEE Workshop on Mobile Security Technologies (2012)
6. Egele, M., Brumley, D., Fratantonio, Y., Kruegel, C.: An empirical study of cryptographic misuse in android applications. In: ACM Conference on Computer and Communications Security (2013)
7. Feloni, R.: Facebook Sued For Allegedly Using Your Private Messages To Trigger Ads, January 2014. http://www.businessinsider.com/facebook-sued-for-allegedly-using-your-private-messages-to-trigger-ads-2014-1
8. Garfinkel, S.: PGP: Pretty Good Privacy. O'Reilly Media Inc., San Francisco (1995)
9. Goldberg, I.: Off-the-Record Messaging (OTR). https://otr.cypherpunks.ca/
10. Google: Accessibility—Android Developers. https://developer.android.com/guide/topics/ui/accessibility/
11. Jeon, J., Micinski, K.K., Vaughan, J.A., Fogel, A., Reddy, N., Foster, J.S., Millstein, T.: Dr. Android and Mr. Hide: fine-grained permissions in android applications. In: ACM Workshop on Security and Privacy in Smartphones and Mobile Devices (2012)
12. Lau, B., Chung, S., Song, C., Jang, Y., Lee, W., Boldyreva, A.: Mimesis aegis: a mimicry privacy shield. In: USENIX Security Symposium (2014)
13. Open Whisper Systems: TextSecure. https://whispersystems.org
14. Silent Circle: Silent Text. https://www.silentcircle.com
15. The Guardian Project: ChatSecure. https://guardianproject.info/apps/chatsecure
16. Threema GmbH: Threema. https://www.threema.ch
17. Xu, R., Saïdi, H., Anderson, R.: Aurasium: practical policy enforcement for android applications. In: USENIX Security Symposium (2012)

METDS - A Self-contained, Context-Based Detection System for Evil Twin Access Points

Christian Szongott[1]([✉]), Michael Brenner[1], and Matthew Smith[2]

[1] Distributed Computing and Security Group,
Leibniz Universität Hannover, Hannover, Germany
{szongott,brenner}@dcsec.uni-hannover.de
[2] Department of Computer Science,
Rheinische Friedrich-Wilhelms-Universität Bonn, Bonn, Germany
smith@cs.uni-bonn.de

Abstract. Mobile Evil Twin attacks stem from the missing authentication of open WiFi access points. Attackers can trick users into connecting to their malicious networks and thereby gain the capability to mount further attacks. Although some recognition and prevention techniques have been proposed, they have been impractical and thus have not seen any adoption. To quantify the scale of the threat of evil twin attacks we performed a field study with 92 participants to collect their WiFi usage patterns. With this data we show how many of our participants are potentially open to the evil twin attack. We also used the data to develop and optimize a context-based recognition algorithm, that can help mitigate such attacks. While it cannot prevent the attacks entirely it gives users the chance to detect them, raises the amount of effort for the attacker to execute such attacks and also significantly reduces the amount of vulnerable users which can be targeted by a single attack. Using simulations on real-world data, we evaluate our proposed recognition system and measure the impact on both users and attackers. Unlike most other approaches to counter evil twin attacks our system can be deployed autonomously and does not require any infrastructure changes and offers the full benefit of the system to early adopters.

Keywords: Mobile device security · Evil twin access points · Attack detection · 802.11

1 Introduction

The growing power as well as the proliferation of mobile devices is changing the way we use the Internet. While a decade ago wired Internet was the norm, now wireless Internet is used on a daily basis. Coffee shops, fast food restaurants, mobile carriers, public transport, and many other entities offer access points for both free and paywalled Internet access. While the risks of open access points (i.e. non-WPA encrypted) have received a fair amount of coverage, they are still in widespread use and the proliferation of open access points seems to be on the

© International Financial Cryptography Association 2015
R. Böhme and T. Okamoto (Eds.): FC 2015, LNCS 8975, pp. 370–386, 2015.
DOI: 10.1007/978-3-662-47854-7_22

rise. If users connect to these open access points their devices usually store the network identifiers (SSID) and will automatically connect to all future networks with the same name. Critically this can happen silently without the user even noticing it. When a device is in range of a known access point and requires a connection to the Internet, it will associate with the access point automatically.

Unfortunately the SSID on which this mechanism is based is completely unprotected and access points do not need to authenticate themselves to the user. This opens up the door to a very easy and effective attack, in which the attacker spoofs the name of open access points to capture users devices. This kind of attack is called the evil twin attack [11].

Once the attacker has devices connected to the evil twin access point, there are diverse ways to attack them. For instance with a man-in-the-middle attack an attacker can eavesdrop and modify all unencrypted information sent and received by the user's device. Recent research has shown that weaknesses in SSL encryption of mobile devices are wide spread [2] (and are not being fixed by the developers [3]) and thus encrypted connections are threatened as well. Another possible attack is the distribution of platform specific malware by injecting malicious content into web pages or emails.

Even users who try to stem the dangers of public and unencrypted WiFi networks by activating a VPN before doing sensitive tasks are still at risk. In the study we present in this paper, we found out that more than 78 % of all connections to open access points are established automatically by the device without any user interaction. Thus, users often do not even have the chance to activate their VPN to protect themselves. Unfortunately VPN-based security measures are not widespread for private smartphone usage as well.

In order to mitigate the threats from these evil twin access points we developed a Mobile Evil Twin Detection System (METDS). METDS is a self-contained and context-based detection system, which uses as much environmental data of smartphones as possible during the association process to help decide, if the access point is legitimate or the user needs to be warned of a potential attack. To quantify the scale of the threat of evil twin attacks we performed a field study with 92 participants over a period of 2, 5 months to collect their WiFi usage patterns. We evaluated the data, implemented a prototypical detection system and optimized the relevant parameters through multiple simulations on this real-world data. With our results we show that the approach of current mobile operating systems, only checking the SSID of access points is not sufficient and leaves users at risk of being attacked. Additional environmental data such as the current location of the user, nearby wireless networks and other information is needed to mitigate this threat.

The rest of the paper is organized as follows: In Sect. 2 related work in the field of evil twin detection is presented. In Sect. 3 we describe different types of attacks in an evil twin scenario and how they can be detected with the help of network information and sensors of current mobile devices. Section 4 presents the user study we performed to gain real-world WiFi usage data. In Sect. 5 we describe our proposed detection algorithm, which is evaluated and optimized with the help of simulations in Sect. 6. Section 7 concludes the paper and gives an overview of possible future work in this research area.

2   Related Work

Surprisingly not much research has been done in the area of of evil twin detection and the protection of users against this kind of attacks. Bauer et al. [1] showed in their work how users can be tricked into associating with evil twin access points with common SSIDs and present a detection strategy that is based solely on the SSIDs of nearby access points. The authors did not evaluate their algorithms and methods with real-world data and we will show in our work that their approach is insufficient to protect against evil twin attacks. In [4] Gonzales et al. extended their work by additionally verifying the signal strength of access points. Again no proper evaluation with real world data was conducted and our experiments show that the signal strength fluctuates too much to improve the detection accuracy.

Roth et al. [8] propose an authentication method for access points that uses light color sequences, displayed to the user on devices that have to be mounted near access points. Kindberg et al. [5] also propose a system that uses physical evidence and include an adaption of the Interlock protocol into the wireless association process. They also use public displays near the access point for their authentication and key agreement protocol. These solutions have two major disadvantages. First the access point has to be visible to the users. This is quite often not the case and it is also doubtful that users would be willing to invest the effort to go and look in any case. The second disadvantage of these solutions is the requirement for additional hardware and configuration. Many providers operate thousands of public access points. Most of them would shy away from the costs for hardware and its setup for each single access point.

Song et al. [9] follow two different protection approaches. The first one uses a network sniffer to detect interpacket arrival times (IAT) and compares them to previously learned statistics of the access point. The learning process is needed since the signal strength and the saturation of the wireless network directly influences the IAT. Another approach additionally involves the IAT between the client and a remote server. Since their system needs to be trained and can not detect evil twin access points before user data is being transmitted it is not feasible for mobile devices which constantly exchange sensitive data in many different locations. Also the lack of APIs to build a network sniffer and battery consumption issues make this solution suboptimal for mobile devices. In the approach of Mónica et al. [7] watermarked packets are sent out. It constantly scans other WiFi channels to detect the packet and thereby recognize an evil twin. Similar to above this method has severe drawbacks for smartphones and similar devices. The approach of Lanze et al. [6] uses clock skew to passively detect faked access points through device fingerprinting. Unfortunately their approach also requires additional infrastructure and does not raise alarms if access points are replaced entirely, since their system is focused on attacks, that spoof the BSSID of legitimate access points.

3 Types of Mobile Evil Twin Attacks

There are several ways an attacker can use evil twin attacks to gain access to the users' device. In the following we describe such attacks and discuss which technical skills are necessary to carry them out. We also show how these attacks can be circumvented by using our Mobile Evil Twin Detection System (METDS). In the following scenarios the attacker's goal always is to fake a legitimate access point as unobtrusive as possible. Due to the lack of information provided by common mobile operating systems, the user will not be able to distinguish between a legitimate and a malicious access point.

3.1 Faking an Access Point's SSID (Type A)

This first attack scenario (called type A) only requires a very basic setup. The attacker sets up an access point with a commonly used SSID like *BTOpenzone* or *tmobile* and waits for users who previously connected to these networks to come along. This approach can be optimized significantly by obtaining SSIDs from probe request frames. Many mobile device send out probe request frames to find their favorite networks as fast as possible. These probe requests contain the SSID the device is searching for. An attacker can easily receive them with common WiFi sniffer software and thus tune the attack to the current devices in the neighborhood. Since mobile operating systems only verify the SSID to check, if the present network is known, the attack is not limited to a specific location. Mobile devices will connect to this kind of access point no matter where it is located.

While this trivial attack is currently very effective, it is also easy to counter. METDS saves the MAC-address (BSSID) of the connected access point. During subsequent connections the BSSID will be verified and simply faking the SSID will throw a warning.

3.2 Faking an Access Point's BSSID (Type B)

Assuming BSSID checks become common attackers can step up their game to circumvent these checks, since they can also fake the BSSID. Just like spoofing the SSID, spoofing a BSSID can be done with freely available tools and it docs not need any additional technical skills. We call that type of attack type B. However, this attack is already more limited than attack type A. If there are two Starbucks WiFi users who have connected to different Starbucks access points, they can no longer be targeted with the same attack, since the BSSID needs to match the exact access point. However, targeted attacks are still possible.

To further degrade the attackers capability, METDS will employ additional environmental parameters to detect evil twin access points. METDS collects the surrounding visible access points and saves SSIDs, BSSIDs and supported encryption schemes and uses a combination of measures to deal with the noisy environment - as will be described in Sect. 5. With this countermeasure in place the attacker is limited to mounting the evil twin attack at the same location as the original access point or faking at least part of the original network environment as will be described in the next subsection.

3.3 Faking a Network Environment (Type C)

An attacker who is aware of context-based detection could try to simulate the whole network environment. Therefore the attacker might take a snapshot of the target wireless network environment and imitates them with additional equipment. For instance, modified versions of the open source router software DD-WRT[1] and its virtual interfaces could be used in combination with the appropriate hardware to achieve this setup. This form of attack is possible and cannot always be prevented by METDS, however since additional equipment, technical skills and prior preparations are necessary for this kind of attack, the effort is much higher than before.

To counter this attack METDS additionally takes the device's location into account when connecting to a access point. In case the distance between the current and the saved one of the access point exceeds a specific threshold, the METDS raises a warning and interrupts the connection process.[2]

3.4 Faking the Entire Environment (Type D)

The final stage of the cat and mouse game would force the attacker to fake the entire environment (including cell towers) or execute the attack very close to the legitimate access point.

Mobile devices connect to the access point with the highest signal strength. If the attacker installs a malicious access point that has a higher signal strength than the legitimate one, the user's devices will automatically connect to his access point. In this scenario the attacker has to hazard the consequences of operating two access points that open up the same network.

Attacks of this type can not be detected by the METDS. However, the attacker is forced to execute a much more targeted and sophisticated attack than it is currently necessary. The attacker also runs the risk of the legitimate access point provider detecting the attack.

4   Field Study

To gain an overview over WiFi connections in the everyday life of smartphone users and how vulnerable they are to potential evil twin attacks, we conducted a field study. To the best of our knowledge this is the first study to gather real-world data on this type of attack potential. We recruited 92 participants

---

[1] http://www.dd-wrt.com.

[2] This is not a foolproof method, since GPS location is not always available and WiFi based positioning can be fooled by an attack of type C. However cell tower ID based positioning works in many cases and raises the bar for the attacker.

through a study mailing list and social media. They installed an Android App on their own smartphones. The app collected their WiFi usage statistics for up to 74 days with an average participation time of 46.75 days. 83 of our participants additionally completed a questionnaire with demographic questions and provided details about their network usage habits. The Android app includes a background service that records data about each connection to a WiFi network. More than 220,000 connections to WiFi networks were recorded together with additional data about the network environments and other meta data.

4.1   Survey

To conclude the study and to participate in a competition, the participants had to fill out a questionnaire. The participants were at the age of 18 to 56 with an average of 28.24 years. 13 out of the 83 participants are female. With 55 % most of the participants were students followed by 32 % full-time employees. The remaining 13 % consist of pupils, part-time workers, self-employed and unemployed persons.

60 participants stated that they use their smartphones only for private use. 22 participants use their smartphone for private use as well as professional and only one participant stated that he uses his smartphone solely for his job. Half of our participants have an IT-related background.

We also asked the participants how they assess their own IT-related knowledge. We asked them how often they ask friends and how often they are asked by friends in case of IT-related problems. The combined result show that the vast majority of the participants believe to be well grounded in IT-related topics. This means our participants are skewed towards the more tech-savvy end of the population, which to a certain extent is to be expected since we could only recruit Android users. For the purpose of this study we believe this is not much of a problem, since we had enough non-tech-savvy users to study both types of participants and we found no difference between them.

4.2   Connection Statistics

We gathered data from 223,877 connections that were established to access points during the study. As a starting point, we analyzed how big the threat of open WiFi access points is in the wild. As shown in prior research work [10] the automated connection establishment to previously configured networks is an increasingly serious threat for today's smartphone users. Therefore we collected anonymous statistics about all configured networks on the participants devices. In Fig. 1 one can see the amount of configured wireless networks per user. They are differentiated by unencrypted networks like public and open access points and encrypted networks, that use encryption schemes like WPA2-PSK or WPA-Enterprise.

One can see that the participants on average have more than 10 configured networks. On the right hand side of the diagram power users can be found having more than 20 and up to 32 different configured networks. From the view point

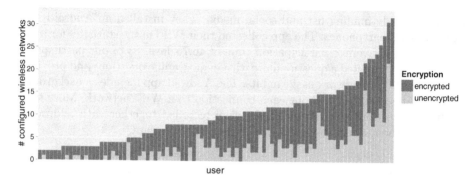

Fig. 1. Number of configured WiFi networks on participants devices, divided into unencrypted (green) and encrypted (blue) networks (Color figure online).

of evil twin attack it is critical that more than 75 % of the participants have at least one but up to 22 open WiFis configured.

Besides the number of configured networks we also collected SSIDs and encryption schemes of each configured network. Since we assume that potentially dangerous WiFi networks will have SSIDs of commonly-used public access points we analyzed which of these networks have been configured on most of the devices. We also compared the participant's believed open access point usage patterns to their actual configuration. Less than 4 % of the participants that filled out the questionnaire stated, that they use open access points more than once in a month. However more than 49 % stated that they use open access points rarely and the remaining 47 % of the participants do not use them at all.

In total we gathered data about 239 unencrypted WiFi networks from all of the 92 participant's devices. Only two of the participants stated they use open access points on a daily basis and one participant declared he uses open access points several times a month. These participants might be aware that configured unencrypted networks on their devices and that their smartphones will automatically connect to them. Of more interest are the participants who reported that they never use open WiFi access points, but have several configured on their devices. 37 participants stated not to use any open access points, but only 37.8 % of these participants did not have a single one configured on their device. The remaining 62.2 % had at least one, but up to 20 different configured open access points. With an average of 3.65 they do not have a significantly lower number of configured open WiFis than the users that stated a daily usage. From the remaining 41 participants that stated that they are using open access points rarely, only 5 had none configured. In this group the participants had an average of 4.89 configured open access points.

Another interesting piece of data collected for our proposed detection system is the device's location during the connection establishment. During the study we collected 171.532 locations which corresponds to about 79 % of all recorded connections. To determine the current position of the device we primarily use the location API of the Google Play Services if they are available on the device. The fallback to this method is the native Android location API, allowing the manual determination of the current location by cell tower triangulation and GPS. Although a GPS location has a higher accuracy the amount of time needed to obtain it is much higher than the cell tower triangulation. In our study most of the participants had Google Play Services enabled on their devices. Thereby 99.4 % of all locations have been determined through its API, which also seemed to be the most stable and reliable source for our purpose. The average accuracy of the collected locations was 115.06 m, which also seems to be sufficient for our algorithm.

As discussed above the METDS needs more environmental parameters to serve its purpose. Thus, we focused our analysis on WiFi-related environment parameters. As a first step we collected information about each WiFi network that is in communication range during the connection process to a specific network. To utilize this data for the METDS we did not only collect the SSIDs of nearby networks, but also their BSSIDs, the signal strengths, encryption schemes and the frequencies on which they operate. In our study we could observe on average 10.26 nearby WiFi networks during a connection.

To demonstrate the dangers of automatic re-connections to allegedly known networks we also investigated how often smartphones connect to WiFi networks without any kind of user interaction. For this we chose one of the major hotspot providers, T-Mobile. In our study 8 different users established a total of 476 connections to open access points of this provider. 374 of these connections have been established without any user interaction. We can rule out user interactions, since we additionally gathered data of the device's display status and lock state during the connection. Since the display was switched off we assume, that more than 78 % of these connections have been initiated by the device itself without the user even noticing it.

To gain a more detailed overview of the distribution of configured open access points we analyzed the gathered SSIDs. From a total of 238 unencrypted configured networks, we could identify 107 networks as known public hotspot networks. 30 could be assigned to personal networks and we are uncertain about the remaining 101 networks.

The above data clearly shows that evil twin attacks can affect a large number of users and that the majority of connections to popular open access points are done automatically by mobile phones without the user being aware of the connection and thus also not aware of the location of the connection.

5   METDS: Mobile Evil Twin Detection System

A detection system always has to struggle with the limited set of data that can be used for a reliable decision. The detection system we developed uses as much data from the surrounding environment as possible. As described in Sect. 3 our algorithm utilizes more parameters than any of the detection system discussed in the related work section. In the following we describe which parameters are used and how they are combined and analyzed to reach the best detection accuracy.

We start with a user's device which is in the communication range of an access point, it is about to connect to. Here our algorithm has to face two main initial situations. In the first one the user wants to connect to a wireless network for the first time and the device has never been connected to it before. In this case the METDS does not have any further knowledge of the network and can not assist the user. This is the same Trust On First Use (TOFU) decision the user always has to face in this situation. If the user has been connected to the access point before the METDS can react differently. In this case the METDS already has an appropriate dataset, that can be used to verify the current environment.

To detect malicious access points the underlying algorithm of the METDS utilizes the following parameters to describe and verify an access point's environment. Primarily the **SSID** of a wireless network is used to recognize known networks, like all current mobile operating systems do. Additionally the algorithm takes the **BSSID** of previously connected access points into account. Since a BSSID can be faked as well, the algorithm records and compares the **wireless network environment**. To characterize the environment as accurately as possible we do not only store the SSIDs of surrounding networks, but also the BSSIDs of the access points as well as their supported authentication, key management, and encryption schemes. In the course of the development of METDS we also investigated if and how the inclusion of signal strengths and frequencies could help to improve the accuracy of the detection algorithm. The signal strength is strongly dependent on the device's position and orientation, which makes it an unreliable source for the decision process. The operated frequency of the access point does not improve our results as well, since modern access points often use auto-tuning algorithms to change between WiFi channels depending on the degree of capacity utilization. Therefore both of these additional parameters lead to a higher false positive rate of the algorithm and have been excluded from the decision process. Since most of the modern smartphones and tablets are connected to a mobile communication network we additionally use **cell tower information** as an environmental parameter. As a last parameter the algorithm takes the device's **location** into account, which is determined either through the Google Play services API if present or directly through the native Android location API.

By collecting and evaluating the mentioned parameters the detection system reaches diverse states which have to be treated differently to warn the user of potentially dangerous connections to access points. However the false positive rate also needs to be kept small enough. Otherwise the acceptance and effectiveness of the system will be adversely affected.

5.1 Unknown SSID

As mentioned above, the connection to a new wireless network for which no information is stored in the METDS database will be accepted by the algorithm, since the user actively has to choose it. In this case no warning is displayed to the user, but information about the access point and the surrounding environment is stored for a later recognition of this context.

5.2 Unknown BSSID

If the algorithm detects a known SSID, but has no corresponding BSSID in its database a warning message is shown to the user, making him aware of the potentially dangerous situation. In this case the user gets two options. If the user knows that a legitimate access point is present and thereby trusts it, an access point profile is created and stored to the database. If the user is not willing to connect to it, the connection process will be canceled and no further information will be collected by the system. This basically extends the TOFU principle to new access points. This has the usability impact of asking users whether to trust a new access point of a chain of access points. For example METDS will ask the user to confirm each new Starbucks WiFi instead of blindly trusting any network with the Starbucks SSID. In our field study the average number of times a user would have to accept a new BSSID is only 8.14. This only happens when new locations are visited. Thus we believe this is an acceptable trade-off, since it significantly reduces the attack capabilities of evil twin networks.

5.3 Unknown Environment

If the tuple of SSID and BSSID can be found in the database the network environment will be verified to detect attacks in unknown environments. For this, a WiFi scan is started in the background. The result of this scan is compared to existing access point profiles of this wireless network. An access point profile consists of basic information like the BSSID and a set of different environments. These different environments are needed to consider multiple WiFi signal propagations, for instance, if an access point can be received in more than one room with highly variable sets of other receivable access points in the environment. To compare the environments the METDS calculates the Jaccard index for each combination of sets. If a combination has an Jaccard index higher than a specific threshold, the according profile is accepted as a known network environment. In multiple simulations and parameter studies we found out that a Jaccard index of 0.7 seems to be the best trade-off between the false positive and the false positive rate. However, this is a parameter which can be tuned by the user to fit their desired level of protection and their tolerance of warning messages.

Another advantage of our proposed algorithm is its ability to adapt to changing network environments. In case a known network environment is recognized, the learning algorithm adds an access point to the access point's profile, if it is found in the vicinity multiple times. The deletion of previously recorded access points is done in the same way. Using this learning algorithm METDS is able to adapt itself to environments that change over time but still detects malicious environments in unknown environments.

If the network environment of an access point is not known, cell tower information is being checked as well. The algorithm determines the location area code (LAC) and the cell ID of the current mobile network connection. These parameters are stored, verified and learned similarly to the surrounding access points. We implemented the learning here as well to take overlapping cell sites into account. If a suiting tuple of cell tower information can not be found either, a warning message is displayed and the connection process is interrupted. In our current configuration if only the cell tower is recognized but not the wireless network environment no warning message is shown, since we believe faking cell IDs is beyond most attackers. However, this is a configuration parameter and warnings can of course be shown.

5.4   Unknown Location

Since the determination of the user's current GPS position is not only time consuming but also consumes a lot of energy, this last step is only performed if the network environment as well as the cell tower information is not being recognized or if it is not available during the connection. To save energy the algorithm checks if the Google Play services are available on the device. If present, the current position can be retrieved in under 1 second and is accurate enough to meet our requirements. If they are not available, we determine the position through the native Android Location API. Fortunately more than 99 % of the users of our study that allowed us, to retrieve their location had the Google Play services installed. Hence, the usage of the native Location API can be seen as fallback solution, which will only be used very rarely.

Once the position is determined it is compared to the saved position of the stored access point. If the determined position is within a specific radius of the stored location, the position of the access point is accepted and the connection will be allowed without warnings. In a parameter study we found out, that a radius smaller than 100 m leads to many false positive warnings due to the accuracy of the determined positions. To get the most conservative detection system we chose a radius of 100 m for our simulations, we present in Sect. 6.

With the algorithm described above we try to use as much environmental data as possible to support the decision, if a malicious access point might be present. All the parameters are requested from sensors and APIs of the Android operating system. The values and profiles are stored in an on-device database. Thereby the METDS is self-contained and does not need any further communication to backend servers or additional infrastructure to work. We also take energy-efficiency seriously by preferring methods and API calls that are less power consuming.

6   Evaluation

To test our system we implemented the algorithm and simulated our detection system on the real-world data we gathered during the study.

As with all heuristic based detection systems the goal is to create a system that protects the user as much as possible while not creating too many false warnings. There will always be an area of conflict between security and usability. One caveat of our simulation and the data is that we have no way of knowing if our real world data contained evil twin attacks. However, since currently evil twin attacks would fall in category A or B with a very high probability, for the purpose of the simulation we assume the connections we gathered within our study are connections to legitimate access points. Should there have been evil twin attacks of type A or B against our subjects during the study period this does not impact our simulation results, since the evil twin would simply be viewed as another legitimate access point. This might seem unintuitive at first, however since we are only interested in finding a set of environmental parameters which are as sensitive as possible to changes in the measured environment while keeping the number of false positives as low as possible, the potential evil twin access point of type A or B do not pose a problem. We think the probability of an attack of type C or D is next to 0 since there is no motivation for attackers to invest the effort since even attack types A and B are currently undetectable to the vast majority of the population.

The simulator we developed helped us to adjust the parameters for the detection system. For a later adoption to the Android platform, we developed the detection system as well as the simulator together with all of its interfaces and libraries in Java. Thus the detection algorithm can be migrated to Android to run real-world on-device studies. The basic architecture of the simulation framework and the simulator is shown in Fig. 2.

The simulator works with data from different databases. The connection database contains all information about the connections, that have been recorded, stored and submitted to our servers during the user study. The configuration database contains all device-specific configurations, such as configured wireless networks and other meta data. In the third database all wireless networks are stored, that have been registered during the WiFi scans within the study. The data sources are connected to the simulation framework via interfaces to be easily exchangeable. The simulator itself reads input data, orchestrates components and delivers the results to the output class. The simulator component also

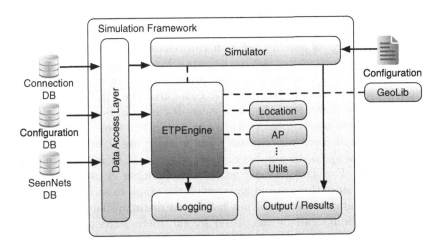

Fig. 2. Architecture of the simulation framework and its interfaces

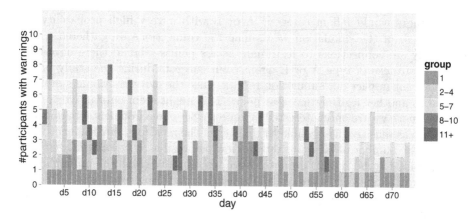

Fig. 3. Amount of BSSID and environmental warnings users saw per day. Users are grouped by how many warnings they saw per day. The huge group of users who saw no warnings is omitted for clarity (Color figure online).

reads the configuration for simulations and parameter studies. The centerpiece is the *ETPEngine*. Here the algorithm and the logic of our detection system is implemented. It utilizes several classes that assist the ETPEngine with storing and analyzing information about the wireless environments. While the logging component may help future developers to setup simulations correctly, the output component collects all results from ETPEngine and the simulator and exports them in a form that can be further processed by other programs.

6.1   Results

We simulated all participants of our study that took part in the study for 10 days or more and who connected to open access points. We left out users, that participated for a shorter period of time since the learning process of METDS needs at least a couple of days of activity before it can reliably predict the environment of access points during new connection attempts. We only simulated connections to open access points, since these are the prime targets for evil twin attacks.[3] This left us with 43 users to simulate. We configured the METDS used by the simulator with the parameters that have been discussed in Sect. 5.

In Fig. 3 one can see how many users saw how many warning messages per day. The number of users who saw only one warning are shown in dark green and the scale goes up to the number of users who saw 11 or more warning who are shown in red. For clarity we did not plot the number of users who did not see any warnings since these would have scaled the graph to such an extent that the different warning levels would not have been distinguishable. The number users with 0 warnings can be calculated by subtracting the number of users

---

[3] While it is also possible to mount evil twin attacks against Enterprise WPA networks, these would go beyond the scope of this paper.

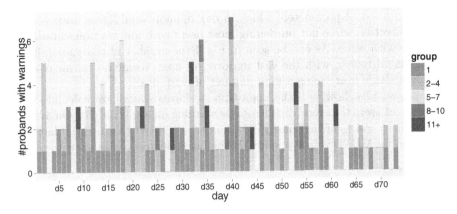

Fig. 4. All simulated warnings except new BSSID warnings during the complete study, grouped by the number of warnings. The group with 0 warnings is omitted for clarity.

shown in the diagram from 43, the total number of users in the simulation. All different types of warnings from Sect. 5 are included in this plot. As one can see the majority of users do not see any warnings and of those who do only see a small number per day and a downwards trend is visible as METDS learns. While this number may still seem high, since new BSSID warnings are included, we believe these warnings to be acceptable. The new BSSID warnings have a 0 % false positive rate and thus definitely present a new access point. We believe users should be asked before connecting to such a new network, just like when connecting to a new SSID. While our intuition says that this will be acceptable to users, we will need to deploy METDS in a full field study to test users reactions to confirm this in future work.

In Fig. 4 we removed the new BSSID warnings. The remaining warnings represent probably false positive warnings. Since our assumption is that our ground truth data contains no attacks these warnings are shown to users because the network environment changed to such an extent that the METDS decided to show it. Using our simulator we ran parameter studies to find a good configuration of METDS. The goal was to find a set of parameters that is as sensitive to potential evil twin attacks of Type B, C or D as possible, but that creates as few false positives as possible. There is no objective way to measure this since there currently are no attacks of this type. However, as soon as METDS is deployed attackers could and would upgrade their attacks from type A to type B through D. So we create a first test configuration of METDS based on a best effort estimation of parameters that would make attacks of types B through D as difficult as possible without burdening users with too many warnings. Table 1 in the appendix shows this configuration. These parameters are of course up for debate and can actually be configured on a per user basis. So if users feel they are seeing to many warnings they can tune the system down at the cost of making it easier for an attacker to fake an environment in which an evil twin attack can be mounted. This will be down to user preferences. For the rest of the paper we selected a set of parameters which in our opinion would give users a good level of protection while not burdening most users with any warnings at all and only a few with some. As can be seen in Fig. 4 the number of these undesirable warnings is fairly low, with the vast majority of users seeing no warnings at all and only a single user seeing a high number of warnings.

To get an idea how well the algorithm performs overall we calculated the percentage of users that receive at least one warning on a specific day. On average only 5.81 % ($\sigma = 4.4$) of the considered users have to react to warnings that have been raised by METDS. In Appendix B the users perspective is shown.

7   Conclusion and Outlook

In this paper we present the first study of real-world WiFi usage with respect to the susceptibility to evil twin access point attacks. We carried out a study with more than 90 participants that collected real-world WiFi usage and environmental data for more than two months. We showed that 43 of our users are susceptible to evil twin attacks since they use open access points. We introduce three types of evil twin attacks which go beyond the simple evil twin attack against current mobile devices. Furthermore we developed METDS, a prototypical detection system, that protects against the simple evil twin attacks and utilizes environmental data to mitigate the more sophisticated evil twin attacks introduced in this paper. To evaluate our detection system, we set up a variety of simulations based on the real-world data we collected from the participants of our study. Our results show, that many connections to unknown access points currently go undetected and METDS would allow users to decide whether to trust new access points or not. We also created a first test configuration of METDS to detect future sophisticated evil twin attacks and show how many false positive warnings this would entail for users. The next steps in our research are to deploy METDS and conduct a field study to both search for evil twin attacks in the wild and to evaluate the current METDS configuration with real users in their everyday life.

A   METDS Sample Configuration

In Table 1 the most important configuration parameters for our sample configuration are shown. These values have been used for the mentioned simulations from Sect. 6. As one can see the algorithm only reacts to connections to unencrypted networks. For future research other encryption schemes can be enabled to analyze similar attacks on encrypted wireless networks. The BSSID thresholds define, how often an access point needs to be detected or missed, until it is added to or removed from the according access point profile. The maximum distance threshold defines how close to each other two locations have to be at least, until the algorithm regards them as equal. The length of the learning period of an access point is defined by the next parameter. Within this period the algorithm

Table 1. Configuration parameters of the METDS

Configuration item	value
ACCOUNT_UNENCRYPTED	TRUE
ACCOUNT_WPA_PSK	FALSE
ACCOUNT_WPA_ENTERPRISE	FALSE
BSSID_DELETION_THRESHOLD	-3
BSSID_ADDITION_THRESHOLD	3
MAXIMUM_DISTANCE_THRESHOLD	100.0
LEARNING_PHASE_NEW_AP_LENGTH	604,800,000
USE_JACCARD_ALGORITHM	true
JACCARD_ENVIRONMENT_OK	0.7

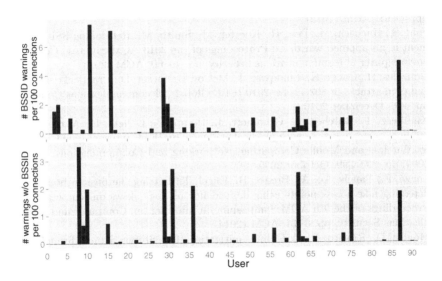

Fig. 5. Amount of warnings a user would receive per 100 connections. In the first diagram only BSSID warning are shown, in the second all remaining warnings have been plotted.

learns the access points environment and adapts itself. The current value represents one week. The last two parameter enable the Jaccard index comparison of network environments and set the threshold to 0.7 as discussed in Sect. 5.

B   User Perspective

Figure 5 shows the user's perspective. Both diagrams show the number of warnings each user (along the Y-axis) sees on average per 100 connections. In the first graph only warning messages for unknown BSSIDs are shown. As stated above we believe these warnings are necessary since they definitely present an unknown access point and a connection should not be established without the users consent. The second graph only shows the false-positives at our current configuration of METDS. Also as stated above the number of warnings shown here is configurable and is down to user preferences.

References

1. Bauer, K., Gonzales, H., McCoy, D.: Mitigating evil twin attacks in 802.11. In: 2008 IEEE International Performance, Computing and Communications Conference, pp. 513–516, December 2008
2. Fahl, S., Harbach, M., Muders, T., Baumgärtner, L., Freisleben, B., Smith, M.: Why eve and mallory love android: an analysis of android SSL (in)security. In: Proceedings of the 2012 ACM Conference on Computer and Communications Security, pp. 50–61. ACM (2012)
3. Fahl, S., Harbach, M., Perl, H., Koetter, M., Smith, M.: Rethinking SSL development in an appified world. In: Proceedings of the 2013 ACM SIGSAC Conference on Computer & Communications Security, pp. 49–60. ACM (2013)
4. Gonzales, H., Bauer, K., Lindqvist, J., McCoy, D., Sicker, D.: Practical defenses for evil twin attacks in 802.11. In: 2010 IEEE Global Telecommunications Conference, pp. 1–6, December 2010
5. Kindberg, T., Mitchell, J., Grimmett, J., Bevan, C., O'Neill, E.: Authenticating public wireless networks with physical evidence. In: IEEE International Conference on Wireless and Mobile Computing, Networking and Communications, WIMOB 2009, pp. 394–399, October 2009
6. Lanze, F., Panchenko, A., Braatz, B., Engel, T.: Letting the puss in boots sweat: detecting fake access points using dependency of clock skews on temperature. In: Proceedings of the 9th ACM Symposium on Information, Computer and Communications Security, pp. 3–14. ACM (2014)
7. Mónica, D., Ribeiro, C.: WiFiHop - mitigating the evil twin attack through multi-hop detection. In: Atluri, V., Diaz, C. (eds.) ESORICS 2011. LNCS, vol. 6879, pp. 21–39. Springer, Heidelberg (2011)
8. Roth, V., Polak, W., Rieffel, E., Turner, T.: Simple and effective defense against evil twin access points. In: Proceedings of the First ACM Conference on Wireless Network Security, WiSec 2008, p. 220, March 2008
9. Song, Y., Yang, C., Gu, G.: Who is peeping at your passwords at starbucks? - to catch an evil twin access point. In: DSN 2010, pp. 323–332 (2010)
10. Szongott, C., Henne, B., Smith, M.: Evaluating the threat of epidemic mobile malware. In: WiMob, pp. 443–450. IEEE Computer Society (2012)
11. Szongott, C., Henne, B., Smith, M.: Mobile evil twin malnets – the worst of both worlds. In: Pieprzyk, J., Sadeghi, A.-R., Manulis, M. (eds.) CANS 2012. LNCS, vol. 7712, pp. 126–141. Springer, Heidelberg (2012)

Market-Driven Code Provisioning
to Mobile Secure Hardware

Alexandra Dmitrienko[2]([✉]), Stephan Heuser[1], Thien Duc Nguyen[1],
Marcos da Silva Ramos[2], Andre Rein[2], and Ahmad-Reza Sadeghi[1]

[1] CASED/Technische Universität Darmstadt, Darmstadt, Germany
{stephan.heuser,ducthien.nguyen,ahmad.sadeghi}@trust.cased.de
[2] CASED/Fraunhofer SIT Darmstadt, Darmstadt, Germany
{alexandra.dmitrienko,andre.rein}@sit.fraunhofer.de,
marcos.dasilvaramos@trust.cased.de

Abstract. Today, most smartphones feature different kinds of secure
hardware, such as processor-based security extensions (e.g., TrustZone)
and dedicated secure co-processors (e.g., SIM-cards or embedded secure
elements). Unfortunately, secure hardware is almost never utilized by
commercial third party apps, although their usage would drastically
improve security of security critical apps. The reasons are diverse: Secure
hardware stakeholders such as phone manufacturers and mobile network
operators (MNOs) have full control over the corresponding interfaces and
expect high financial revenue; and the current code provisioning schemes
are inflexible and impractical since they require developers to collaborate
with large stakeholders.

In this paper we propose a new code provisioning paradigm for the
code intended to run within execution environments established on top
of secure hardware. It leverages market-based code distribution model
and overcomes disadvantages of existing code provisioning schemes. In
particular, it enables access of third party developers to secure hardware; allows secure hardware stakeholders to obtain revenue for usage
of hardware they control; and does not require third party developers to
collaborate with large stakeholders, such as OS and secure hardware vendors. Our scheme is compatible with Global Platform (GP) specifications
and can be easily incorporated into existing standards.

1 Introduction

Today, mobile devices have become an integral part of our life. The increasing
computing, storage and networking capabilities and the vast number and variety of mobile apps make smart devices convenient replacements for traditional
computing platforms such as laptops. As a consequence, mobile devices increasingly collect, store and process various privacy sensitive and security critical
information about users such as e-mails and SMS messages, phone call history,
location data, photos, authentication credentials (e.g., for online banking), etc.
This makes them very attractive attack targets, as the rapid growth of mobile

© International Financial Cryptography Association 2015
R. Böhme and T. Okamoto (Eds.): FC 2015, LNCS 8975, pp. 387–404, 2015.
DOI: 10.1007/978-3-662-47854-7_23

malware shows [40]. Hence, mobile security has become an important topic for industrial and academic research in recent years.

One of the major approaches to harden mobile platform security is to leverage isolated (secure) environments, where apps can execute security sensitive operations (e.g., encryption, signing, etc.) in sub-routines referred to as trusted applications, applets or trustlets. While generally isolation between the secure environment and the rest of the mobile system can be enforced in software or in hardware, hardware-supported isolation provides stronger security guaranties: It can resist software-based attacks (e.g., compromised OS-level components) and even be resilient, to a certain degree, against physical tampering.

Hardware-based isolated environments, on which we focus in this paper, can be established on top of general purpose secure hardware, such as processor-based security extensions (e.g., TrustZone [11] and M-Shield [14]) and dedicated secure co-processors, e.g., an embedded secure element available on NFC-enabled devices.

However, while such secure hardware has been available for a decade and even widely deployed on mobile platforms [20,35,41], it is owned and exclusively used by their respective stakeholders such as phone manufacturers and mobile network operators (MNOs). For instance, processor-based security extensions are normally used by phone manufacturers to securely store radio frequency parameters calibrated during manufacturing process [20], or to ensure secure boot[1], while secure elements owned by MNOs (e.g., SIM-cards) are used to protect authentication credentials of users in mobile networks. Unfortunately, they are almost never utilized by commercial apps developed by third parties. Exceptions are solutions driven by large service/OS providers like NFC payment apps Google Wallet [3] and upcoming Apple Pay [13]. Hence, many security critical apps cannot be satisfactorily implemented as long as the secure hardware interfaces remain inaccessible.

The major obstacle for utilizing hardware-based isolated environments by third party apps is the fact that underlying secure hardware is currently under full control of their stakeholders. Trusted applications, applets or tustlets must first be admitted (e.g., signed) by the respective stakeholder in order to be executed within the isolated environment. Existing code provisioning schemes either rely on a stakeholder, or require a developer to become a Service Provider (SP) and maintain code provisioning services on their own. In either case, a collaboration between developers and stakeholders is required. However, such collaboration is often infeasible in practice, as stakeholders are typically large companies whereas app developers are small or middle-size businesses. Further, regular app developers typically would not become a service provider and maintain online code provisioning services.

To overcome these obstacles, we propose to apply the app market code distribution model (as currently used by mobile platform vendors) for the distribution of code (applets, trustlets and trusted apps) for secure hardware. Mobile app

---

[1] Secure boot means a system terminates the boot process in case the integrity check of a component to be loaded fails [32].

markets have been successfully bridging the gap between app developers and large OS vendors, and thus could also serve in the same way between developers and secure hardware stakeholders. However, there are several challenges to be tackled before an app market based code submission system can be applied for the distribution of secure hardware code. We need echanisms that (i) allow the regular app to be coupled with corresponding applets, trustlets or trusted apps, given that the OS vendor and the stakeholder of secure hardware are typically different entities; (ii) provide financial incentives to secure hardware stakeholders in order to motivate them to allow third parties to leverage secure hardware; (iii) make access to secure hardware much more flexible, e.g., configurable by app developers independently from OS vendors; and, (iv) finally, address limitations of resource-constraint secure environments (e.g., Java cards), given that ability to leverage secure hardware by third party developers may result in large variety of applets exceeding resource constrains of respective secure elements.

Goals and Contributions. In this paper, we aim to tackle the challenges mentioned above and enable third party developers to leverage secure hardware widely available on commodity devices. In particular, we make the following contributions:

Market-driven code provisioning to secure hardware. We propose a new paradigm for code provisioning to secure hardware (cf. Sect. 3). The main idea is to use an app market model for distribution of secure hardware code. Our solution (i) allows developers to distribute security sensitive code (e.g., trusted apps or applets) as a part of the mobile app package. Hence, developers do not need to act as service providers (SPs) and maintain online code provisioning servers; (ii) it supports flexible and dynamic assignment of access rights to secure hardware APIs and applets by mobile app developers independently from an OS vendor and a secure hardware stakeholder; (iii) allows the secure hardware stakeholder to obtain revenue for every provisioned piece of code; (iv) allows for automated and transparent installation and deinstallation of applets on demand in order to permit arbitrary number of applets, e.g., in a constraint Java card environment. Our scheme is compatible with Global Platform (GP) specifications and can be easily incorporated into existing standards [23–25, 29].

Prototype implementation and evaluation. We prototyped our solution on Android and a Java-based secure element (SE) (cf. Sect. 4). For SE prototyping, we ported the open source JCardSim Java Card emulator [4] to Android and enhanced it with our extensions. We will make the code for JCardSim Java Card emulator on Android open source[2]. Our prototype provides a wide range of SE options: (i) Java Card emulator placed on the mobile platform, (ii) Java Card emulator resides on a separate hardware token, for instance a smartwatch, and (iii) Java Card emulator provided by a cloud-based service. We further evaluated our prototype with the NFC-based access control application [15, 18] which turns the smartphone into a key ring for electronic door (or car) keys. The security

---

[2] Please visit our project page http://jcandroid.org.

sensitive sub-routines of the app were implemented as a Java applet which was then executed within the JCardSim-based emulated environment deployed either on a smartphone, or on a smartwatch that acts as a trusted token. We then evaluated performance to confirm efficiency of our implementation.

2 Background and Problem Description

In this section, we review possible secure hardware alternatives available to developers and discuss existing code provisioning and access control mechanisms for these environments. We discuss their trade-offs and highlight disadvantages that impede use of these environments in practice.

2.1 Hardware-Based Secure Hardware Alternatives

Generally, Global Platform specifies different implementations of isolated execution environments [27]: Processor-based trusted execution environments (TEEs), and embedded or removable secure elements (SEs).

Processor-based TEEs are realized via a secure processor mode. Almost every smartphone and tablet today contains a processor-based TEE, such as TrustZone [11] and M-Shield [14]. However, their use requires third party developers to collaborate with mobile device vendors (such as Samsung and Apple) in order to get the security sensitive code admitted to run in a secure processor mode. Further, collaboration with the operating system vendor would also be required in order to enable communication between a mobile app and TEE-residing code.

Embedded SEs are distinct security sub-systems, which are available on many commercial mobile devices. They can be realized either as a standalone chip attached to the motherboard, or integrated into an NFC chip. Secure elements usually use standardized and widely supported JavaCard environment that can run Java applets. However, their interfaces are not usually exposed to third party developers. There are only a few products on the market powered by large companies, such as Google Wallet [3], Visa payWave [37] and MasterCard's PayPass [17] solutions for NFC payments, that utilize an embedded SE.

Removable SEs are security co-processors which can be attached to the device via peripheral interfaces, such as Universal Integrated Circuit Cards (UICC) (also known as SIM cards) and plug-in cards for an SD card slot (ASSD cards). UICC cards are controlled by MNOs – yet too large entities for small-size developers. Moreover, collaboration with a single MNO can only reach limited number of users. Hence, more complex business models arose that involve Trusted Service Managers (TSM) – intermediate entities that have agreements with multiple MNOs [22]. In contrast, ASSD cards (e.g., [16,39]) are not controlled by external stakeholders. On the downside, however, they are quite costly[3] and their use is limited to smartphone platforms featuring an SD card slot.

---

[3] For instance, the retail price for the cgCard [16] is 99 EUR per piece.

To summarize, all existing options have disadvantages which in fact impeded use of secure hardware by application developers in practice. This resulted in a notable shift in favor of software-based solutions compared to prior years [19], despite of general opinion that hardware-based solutions provide stronger security.

2.2 Secure Hardware APIs and Access Control Mechanisms

Currently, Android does not allow mobile apps to directly access processor-based TEEs[4]. Only embedded and removable SEs are accessible via respective APIs.

Embedded SE on Android can be accessed via an NFC API. Initially, access to this API was limited to system-level components signed with platform keys [21]. This has been changed in 4.0.4 version, which introduced a more flexible approach based on an access control list (ACL) stored in a system file. Although potentially the ACL could be updated by system apps or by the OS vendor through the over-the-air (OTA) system update, these mechanisms do not seem to be used in practice – once deployed, ACLs typically remain unmodified.

Access to removable SEs on Android is provided via a SmartCard API implemented within seek-for-Android project[5]. Access control to the SmartCard API is compliant to the Global Platform (GP) specification [29]. In particular, it uses an SE internal access control list (ACL) of which a read-only copy is fetched on system boot and enforced by an access control enforcer (ACE) – an OS side system component. ACLs on the SE can only be updated by an SE stakeholder or by a trusted (by the SE stakeholder) party.

To summarize, all existing approaches are inflexible in performing ACL updates. In either case, involvement of a trusted party is required – for instance, OS vendors are responsible for ACL updates for embedded SEs, while MNOs manage ACLs on UICC-based secure elements.

2.3 Code Provisioning

Currently, code provisioning specifications for processor-based TEEs are under development by the Global Platform Device Specification Working Group. Hence, we will discuss specifications of the code provisioning mechanisms for NFC-based and UICC-based secure elements which are already published [23,26].

Generally, there are three options for code provisioning specified: (i) Simple mode, (ii) delegated mode, and (iii) authorized mode. In a simple mode, the service provider (SP) delegates full management of its applet to an SE stakeholder. In the delegated mode, each operation for code provisioning is performed by a Trusted Service Manager (TSM) and requires a pre-authorization from the SE stakeholder for each operation. In the authorized mode, however, the SE stakeholder authorizes either TSM or SP to perform code provisioning on their own.

---

[4] Indirect access is available for certain crypto operations provided by Android's *Key-Store* https://developer.android.com/about/versions/android-4.3.html.

[5] https://code.google.com/p/seek-for-android/.

In any mode code provisioning is performed either by the SE stakeholder or by authority the SE stakeholder trusts, via over-the-air (OTA) secure channel. In this way, third party developers must either become service providers or delegate code provisioning tasks to the SE stakeholder, which raises the bar for entering market of SE-supported applications.

3   Market-Driven Code Provisioning to Secure Hardware

In this section we present our market-driven code provisioning mechanism which enables access of third party developers to secure hardware. Generally, our solution can be applied for code provisioning to secure hardware of different types. However, in the following we will concentrate on secure elements (SEs) and mechanisms for Java applet provisioning for brevity.

Our solution enables application developers to distribute applets via the app market place, e.g., packaged together with the mobile app or pulbished on a dedicated market place for applets. It relies on a developer to couple apps with corresponding applets – an approach which does not require interaction between OS vendors and SE stakeholders. Further, the scheme allows developers to define access control rules for accessing applets that are deployed during applet provisioning and independently from OS vendor. Moreover, our solution makes use of applet installation tokens issued by SE stakeholders to end users, which effectively allows SE stakeholders to enforce per-installation license fees (e.g., if obtaining the installation token requires payment). Finally, our mechanism makes use of an SE internal access control list (ACL) as defined by Global Platform (GP) Access Control Specification [29] for access control to SE APIs and is, hence, compatible with the established Global Platform mechanisms.

3.1   System Model and Assumptions

System Model. As shown in Fig. 1, our system model involves the following entities: (i) app market M, (ii) SE stakeholder S, (iii) mobile host H, (iv) secure element E, and (v) developer D. Here, D develops the mobile app A and a corresponding applet a which includes security-sensitive sub-routines. Further, H is a mobile device of the user (e.g., a smartphone or a tablet) for which the mobile app was developed, while E is a secure element of H, which is trusted to securely execute the applet a. Moreover, M is a regular market place for mobile apps managed by the (OS or device) vendor, while S is an online service managed by the SE stakeholder.

Assumptions. We assume that the SE Stakeholder S shares a symmetric key K_E with every secure element E it controls. This assumption is reasonable, as similar keys are already used by SE stakeholders to perform code management on deployed SEs[6]. Further, the mobile host H is aware of the SE identifier id_E which uniquely identifies its secure element. We also assume that all

---

[6] For instance, GP specifies [23] that Java Cards share with the card issuer (i.e., a stakeholder) the symmetric Data Encryption Key (DEK).

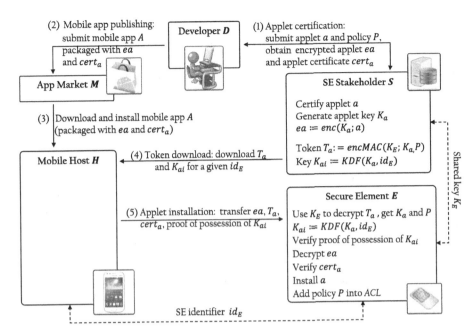

Fig. 1. Market-driven code provisioning

interactions between D and S, D and M, M and H are performed over secure (authentic and confidential) channels. For instance, the Global Platform specifications describe various standards for secure channel protocols (e.g., AES-based SCP03 [25], SCP10 [23] based on asymmetric crypto-system, and SCP81 [24] based on SSL/TLS), which can be used for secure channel establishment and communication.

3.2 Code Provisioning Scheme

The general architecture of our market-driven code provisioning scheme is depicted in Fig. 1. It shows the involved parties and their interactions in the following use cases: (1) applet certification, (2) mobile app publishing, (3) mobile app download and installation, (4) token download, and (5) applet installation. In the following we describe use cases in more details.

Applet Certification. As a first step, the developer D submits an applet a via a code submission system to SE stakeholder S for certification. The applet is accompanied with the access control policy P defining which mobile apps will be allowed to communicate with this applet (e.g., the app A). Upon receipt, S performs applet verification according to its security policy. In particular, it can perform code vetting process (as typically done by OS vendors for mobile apps). If this check passes, it creates an applet certificate $cert_a$, generates an applet-specific key K_a and encrypts the applet a under K_a. The encrypted applet ea is then returned to D together with its certificate $cert_a$.

Note, that for better efficiency one could replace applet certificate $cert_a$ with the message authentication code (MAC) of the applet generated under the key K_a. We opted for certificates in our system design due to legacy reasons, as in current systems applets are certified by means of certificates.

Mobile App Publishing. To publish a mobile app A at the app market M, the developer D includes the (encrypted) applet ea and its certificate $cert_a$ into an installation package of A and submits it to M. This step is common for a regular app development process. Whenever the mobile app A is verified by M, it will appear at the app market and will be ready for download by mobile users.

Alternatively to packaging the applet a and its certificate $cert_a$ together with a mobile app A, the developer D may opt to publish an applet on a dedicated applet market (e.g., maintained by S) and include a download link referencing the required applet, e.g., into app A's manifest (not shown in Fig. 1 for brevity).

Mobile App Download and Installation. Our solution relies on standard mechanisms for mobile app downloading and extends the app installation process with routines to detect applet-related dependencies and, if detected, to trigger a token download procedure.

Token Download. Whenever the mobile host H detects that the mobile app A requires an applet a, it connects to the SE stakeholder S and requests an applet installation token for the secure element with the identity id_E. Hence, S generates the token T_a for a given id_E and a, where T_a is an authenticated encryption (which we denote as $encMAC$) under the key K_E over the key K_a and the policy P. Further, S derives an applet installation key K_{ai} by applying a one-way key derivation function (KDF) to the key K_a and the identity id_E. The resulting token T_a and the key K_{ai} are returned to H.

As one can notice, our token download procedure requires interaction between a mobile host H and an SE stakeholder S. While potentially such a communication could be avoided using cryptographic techniques such as key derivation and oblivious hash functions, we aim to keep the SE stakeholder on the installation path in order to enable it to enforce license fees. In particular, if a license fee is required, the token download procedure can be preceded by a payment procedure, which can be realized in the same way as a mobile app purchase.

Applet Installation. To install the applet, the mobile host H sends the (encrypted) applet ea, the token T_a and the proof of possession of K_{ai} to the secure element E. Then, E extracts K_a and P from the token T_a and derives the key K_{ai} by applying a one-way key derivation function to values K_a and id_E. Next, it verifies if K_{ai} is known to the host (e.g., by means of challenge-response authentication). Further, it decrypts ea with the key K_a in order to obtain the applet a, verifies $cert_a$, installs a and adds the policy P for the applet a into ACL.

3.3   Applet Invocation

As soon as the applet a is installed, it can be invoked by user space apps residing on the mobile host H. We realized the communication between the apps and applets as defined by GP Access Control Specification [29]. In particular, a communication channel is mediated by the OS-level component access control enforcer (ACE), which fetches the access control list (ACL) from the SE-internal access rule application master (ARA-M) component. The ACL consists of data objects (DO) which contain access rules for SE access and application protocol data unit (APDU) filtering. Rules are identified by the identifier AID-REF-DO of the applet to be accessed and the hash of the application's certificate Hash-REF-DO. Further, it may include an APDU filter consisting of an APDU header and an APDU filter mask.

When the app A requests access to an applet a identified by AID-REF-DO, ACE identifies Hash-REF-DO of the app and reads the ACL rule for the specific {AID-REF-DO, Hash-REF-DO} pair. Access is granted, if such access is permitted by the ACL rule, or denied, if access is prohibited by an ACL rule or no rule is found. Further, the application can communicate with the SE applet if the command APDUs match the filter list (if given) checked by ACE.

3.4   On-demand Applet Installation

Although a secure element (SE) may host multiple applets at once, generally the space on SE is limited. As soon as a limit is reached, it may not be longer possible to install further applets. Currently, this is not yet a concern for SE environments due to the lack of available applets. Further, SE stakeholders may specify resource quota for every applet and ensure that SE resource limits are not exceeded. However, resource quota mechanisms might not be effective for our market-based code provisioning scheme, as it is not under full control of SE stakeholders. Further, our scheme is likely to stipulate development of new applets, so that a space limitation may become a concern.

To address this issue, we extended applet invocation mechanism with an SE applet manager (SEAM) component which allows for on-demand installation and deinstallation of applets in order to dynamically re-use available resources. In particular, SEAM maintains applet usage statistics in order to identify more frequently accessed applets. Whenever a currently deinstalled applet is invoked, SEAM performs dynamic applet installation and then allows the access control enforcer (ACE) to establish a communication channel between the applet and the app. Whenever the applet installation requires more resources than currently available, SEAM deinstalls a suitable (i.e., rarely used and sufficiently large) applet in order to release additional resources. Our on-demand applet installation extension is compatible to current GP specifications, i.e., it is transparent to ACE component and to mobile apps. Further, our prototype implementation and performance measurements indicate that our extension imposes low performance overhead which is well acceptable for runtime environments (cf. Sect. 4.2).

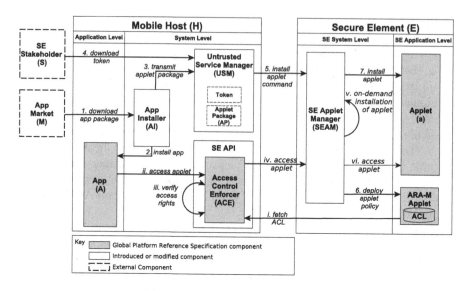

Fig. 2. Instantiated platform architecture

3.5   Platform Architecture

In Fig. 2 we depict the mobile platform architecture. It includes components we introduced to support our extensions, as well as standard components defined by Global Platform Reference Specification [29] (which we show in the figure in the dark gray color). The architecture separates the execution environment of the mobile platform into two independent worlds: Mobile host (H) and secure element (E). Apps are deployed on H via the modified app installer AI, which interacts with the untrusted service manager USM for applet deployment and token management. At runtime, apps interact with their applets via the secure element API (SE API) that embeds the GP-defined access control enforcer (ACE).

In the following, we describe component interactions for two major use cases: (i) download and installation of applet-dependent apps, and (ii) execution of applet-dependent apps.

Download and Installation of Applet-Dependent Apps. When the applet installer AI receives a request to install an applet-dependent app A (step 1), A is first extracted from the app package and installed on the mobile host H (step 2). Next, AI extracts the applet package AP (consisting of the encrypted applet ea and its certificate $cert_a$) and sends it to the untrusted service manager USM (step 3). USM stores AP in its internal storage and requests a token T_a via a secure communication channel from S using the remote application management over HTTP protocol (SCP81) [24] (step 4). Next, USM triggers applet installation process by sending the the applet package AP and token T_a to the SE applet manager SEAM (step 5). In turn, SEAM proceeds to verify the integrity and authenticity of T_a using the secret key K_E shared by the secure element E and the SE stakeholder S and decrypts T_a using K_E. Further, the encrypted applet ea is decrypted using K_a (which is embedded in T_a), and $cert_a$ is verified. If the verification process is successful, the applet a is ready for installation. Finally, SEAM deploys the new ACL rules to the ARA-M Applet (step 6) and installs the applet a on the secure element E (step 7).

Execution of Applet-Dependent Apps. Either on system boot, or just before the access rules are verified, the SE access control enforcer (ACE) fetches and caches all current ACL-rules from the ARA-M Applet (step i). When an app A requests access to an applet a (step ii), AID-REF-DO and Hash-REF-DO are retrieved by ACE and access rights for applet access are verified (step iii). If the verification was successful, ACE grants access and forwards applet access request to the SE applet manager (SEAM) (step iv), which verifies the installation status of the applet. If the applet is not yet installed, SEAM triggers the applet installation process (step v). Finally, a communication request is forwarded to the applet a (step vi) and the communication channel is successfully established between the app A and the applet a.

4 Implementation and Evaluation

In this section we briefly describe our prototype implementation and provide evaluation results.

4.1 Implementation

Our implementation is based on Java and currently targets Android devices. To prototype the secure element environment, we used the open-source JavaCard simulator jCardSim [4], which we ported on Android. As summarized in Table 1, our implementation consists of 7 software modules and includes 9558 Lines of Code (LoC) in total, of which 5651 LoC consist of ports of third party open source projects.

The JavaCard emulator is realized in the jCardSim4Android and SmartCardIO modules, consisting of 4923 and 728 LoC, respectively. The main functionality is included into a jCardSim4Android Android library – a modified version of *jCardSim* which we adapted to run on Android. The emulator provides an environment to run third-party applets, as well as the previously described ARA-M applet which stores access control rules. *jCardSim* has a dependency on the Java Remote Method Invocation (RMI) API and javax.smartcardio classes, which are not available on Android. Hence, we removed RMI functionality (which is not used in our project) and extracted the required javax.smartcardio classes from the source code of OpenJDK v7 into a SmartCardIO library.

Our secure element environment is implemented within an Android SE app which holds an instance of the JavaCard emulator and implements the functionality of the SE Applet Manager (SEAM) component. It consists of 791 LoC and depends on the jCardSim4Android module and the SpongyCastle [6] API for

Table 1. Software modules

Module	Size (LoC)	Language	Codebase	Dependencies
Android SE	791	Java/Android	-	SpongyCastle Crypto API, jCard-Sim4Android
jCardSim4Android	4923	Java/Android	jCardSim [4]	SmartCardIO
SmartCardIO	728	Java/Android	OpenJDK	-
Android Host	1124	Java/Android	-	SpongyCastle Crypto API, Communication API
Communication API	545	Java 6, Java/Android	-	-
Developer	656	Java 6	-	BouncyCastle Crypto API, Communication API
SE Stakeholder	1390	Java 6	-	BouncyCastle Crypto API, Communication API

crypto support. The functionality of the USM component is implemented within the Android Host app consisting of 1124 LoC. It depends on the SpongyCastle Crypto API and Communication API modules.

The Communication API module is responsible for the communication between different entities. In particular, it provides a unified communication framework which can be instantiated for different types of interfaces (Bluetooth, SSL/TLS, or local socket connections). It implements requests and responses and includes helper classes for data serialization, deserialization and transfer between parties. It is implemented in Java 6 and consists of 545 LoC. Further, it was ported to Java/Android to be compatible with the Android Host app.

The SE stakeholder S and developer D modules are implemented in Java 6 and consist of 1390 LoC and 656 LoC, respectively. Both modules have dependencies on the BouncyCastle [1] Crypto API and the Communication API.

External SE Deployment. As our solution strictly separates the mobile host H and the secure element E, we are able to deploy E not only on the same device as H, but also on external devices like smartwatches or even in a cloud environment. To implement such a scenario we chose to use a smartwatch emulating the secure element E and a smartphone acting as the mobile host H. The communication between the smartphone and the smartwatch is based on Bluetooth with security mode 3 (Link-Level Enforced Security) with enabled data encryption. This allows us to make use of our socket based client-server communication between H and E by simply establishing RFCOMM channels [31] and to perform the previously described applet installation and execution without any further modification to the existing code.

4.2 Evaluation

To evaluate the performance of our prototype we deployed it on an Samsung Galaxy S3 smartphone running Android 4.4 and a Samsung Galaxy Gear SM-V700 smartwatch running Android 4.2. The components that do not rely on a mobile platform (app market and SE stakeholder) were executed on a server machine (Intel i7-2600 CPU, 8 GB RAM) running Ubuntu 12.04.4 and OpenJDK 6b31. The smartphone and the server were connected via a 802.11abgn Wi-Fi network. In our evaluation we used the emulated and hardware-based secure element. Hardware-based secure element was represented by a Mobile Security Card [39] which is a representative of an ASSD card. Further, we utilized a Java applet developed for a SmartToken access control solution [15,18] (10953 Bytes). All experiments were performed 1000 times, and we present the average values and standard deviation for selected operations.

We first measured time required for the execution of the applet certification and token download protocols. Applet certification requires 173.975 ms ($\pm$ 40.517 ms) on average, while token download needs 144.235 ms ($\pm$ 26.729 ms).

The most performance-critical operations are applet installation, deinstallation and applet execution, as they are performed at runtime during execution of the mobile app. We measured their performance in two different use-cases: (i) mobile host H and secure element E deployed on the same smartphone and (ii) mobile host H deployed on smartphone while the secure element E is deployed on a smartwatch. Further, for the sake of comparison we measured the applet execution for the hardware-based SE. However, we could not measure applet installation and deinstallation operations for the hardware-based SE, as standard JavaCard environments do not support on-demand installation and deinstallation of applets.

Table 2 shows the average time (and standard deviation) required for the applet installation and deinstallation process for use-cases (i) and (ii). Furthermore, it shows how long it took to execute a simple operation (receiving 4 Bytes and sending 10 Bytes) in the applet from an app residing on H. The process starts within the app, requests the execution and ends after the result of the operation is successfully received by the app.

Overall, we deem these results reasonable and promising for a real-life deployment of our architecture, especially when considering that our implementation has not been optimized for performance yet.

5 Related Work

The most relevant work to ours is the On-board credentials (ObC) framework developed by Nokia researchers [34]. In particular, incentives behind ObC are

Table 2. Applet installation, deinstallation and execution. Average values and standard deviation

	Applet instal- lation, ms	Applet de- installation, ms	Applet execution, ms
Mobile host H and secure element E on the same smartphone	46.265 ± 19.188	15.763 ± 7.851	38.430 ± 18.464
Mobile host H on the smartphone, secure element E on the smartwatch	415.266 ± 77.998	205.356 ± 72.539	150.335 ± 50.069
Hardware-based secure element E	-	-	24.471 ± 1.863

similar to ours – to open secure hardware to third party developers. ObC enables developers to implement security sensitive subroutines of their applications in the form of ObC scripts, which can be loaded into and executed within an isolated execution environment. Put forward by Nokia, the framework is deployed on commercial Nokia devices (e.g., Nokia Lumia), on top of ARM TrustZone and TI M-Shield TEEs. However, the ObC framework does not address access control aspects to ObC APIs from mobile apps – in fact, such access is still controlled by the OS vendor. Hence, third party developers need to collaborate with the OS vendor in order to execute their ObC scripts within the isolated execution environment. Further, the framework is an intellectual property of Nokia and is limited to Nokia platforms. Moreover, ObC is primarily tailored for processor-based TEEs, while we focus on secure co-processors – Java-cards, and address Java-card specific challenges (e.g., on-demand applet installation).

Akram et al. [7–10] aim to solve similar problem by different means – they propose a new paradigm to hand over the control and management of smartcard applications to the end-user. Similarly, Global Platform specifies a consumer-centric provisioning model where the user has more control over their isolated execution environments [28]. In contrast to these works, we aim to remain compliant with the traditional SE ownership model and expose secure hardware to third party developers by means of more flexible SE code provisioning mechanisms and providing financial incentives to SE stakeholders.

Vasudevan et al. [41] proposed a challenge to the research community to present sound technical evidence that application developers and users can benefit from hardware security features. Our work aims to address challenges related to utilizing secure hardware by application developers.

Ekberg et al. [20] discussed reasons for limited use of secure hardware on mobile devices, such as security requirements and concerns of different stakeholders and absence of standardized APIs for accessing secure hardware. We believe, that our work can help to satisfy security requirements of different stakeholders.

Masti et al. [38] proposed an architecture that can provide an isolated execution environment as a cloud service. The authors focus on light-weight processor extensions (like Intel TXT) and virtualized trusted platform modules (TPMs) in order to provide concurrent dynamic root of trusts to multiple cloud-based virtual machines. Generally, this work aims to solve an orthogonal problem. However, our cloud-based architecture instantiation can largely benefit from proposed hardware-based security anchors in the cloud.

González, et al. [30] proposed an open big data platform for sensors that leverages the Open Virtualization framework – an open source implementation of the Global Platform's TEE specifications [2] for ARM TrustZone [5]. Their efforts are directed towards building an open source community around Open Virtualization, while our primary goal is to enable access to secure hardware for third parties.

Marforio et al. [36] concentrated on secure and practical bootstrapping techniques for security services on mobile devices. They particularly discussed the importance of binding user identities to underlying mobile platforms and proposed an architecture to provide secure user enrollment and migration from one platform to another in the context of mobile TEEs.

The white paper [33] describes <tBase, a commercial trusted OS by Trustonic and highlights provisioning mechanisms for trusted apps. Similarly to our approach, provisioning mechanisms of <tBase leverage symmetric keys shared between the TEE stakeholder and the TEE. However, similarly to provisioning solutions specified by Global Platform (cf. Sect. 2.3), they require a trusted third party (in a form of TSM) to manage code provisioning process, while our solution relies on untrusted service manager (USM) which can reside on untrusted mobile host.

Anwar et al. [12] proposed a new access control to secure element APIs by mobile apps on Android devices. Their concern is the fact that Access Control Enforcer (ACE) that mediates access to the secure element is an OS-level component which can be manipulated in case OS gets compromised. Authors propose to utilize trusted computing concepts in order to establish trust into OS-level components. In particular, they leverage processor-based TEE in order to ensure integrity of ACE component and lock access to SE if integrity is not preserved. On a down side, this solution requires significant modifications to system level software, as well as additional support in hardware, which is hard to achieve in practice. Hence, we opt for approach specified by Global Platform for sake of compatibility. Nevertheless, our code provisioning scheme can be combined with the access control solution proposed in this paper.

6   Conclusion

Currently, there is no flexible model for third party app developers to access and use the available secure hardware on smartphones. This is an unfortunate situation since secure hardware provides an isolated execution environment that would drastically improve the security of mobile apps. We propose a new model for flexible distribution and provisioning of secure hardware code (applets, trustlets, or trusted applications) for third party app developers. Our solution is compatible to specifications of Global Platform (GP) and allows developers to use existing app markets and couple their secure hardware code (e.g., applets in case of Java card) to mobile apps that require security critical operations to be executed in an isolated environment. The proposed ecosystem will allow the secure hardware stakeholders to generate revenue by enforcing per-installation fees for secure hardware code. We developed a prototype based on Java card and applied it to a smartphone (and a smartwatch) for an access control application that uses smartphone to open doors with NFC locks. We are planning to open source our port of JCardSim Java Card emulator to Android which will help industry and other researchers to build upon our work and deploy applet-dependent apps on smartphone platforms or even use a smartwatch as an isolated execution environment.

Acknowledgements. We thank N. Asokan for several fruitful discussions and feedback to the paper draft. Further, we thank anonymous reviewers for their helpful comments. This work was partially supported by the German ministry of education and research (Bundesministerium fr Bildung und Forschung, BMBF) within the Software Campus initiative.

References

1. BouncyCastle crypto API. https://www.bouncycastle.org/
2. GlobalPlatform - device specifications. http://www.globalplatform.org/specificationsdevice.asp
3. Google Wallet: Shop. Save. Pay. With your phone. http://www.google.com/wallet/
4. jCardSim Java card runtime environment simulator. http://jcardsim.org/
5. Sierraware. http://www.sierraware.com
6. SpongyCastle crypto API. http://rtyley.github.io/spongycastle/
7. Akram, R.N., Markantonakis, K.: Rethinking the smart card technology. In: the Second International Conference on Human Aspects of Information Security, Privacy, and Trust, pp. 221–232 (2014)
8. Akram, R.N., Markantonakis, K., Mayes, K.: A paradigm shift in smart card ownership model. In: International Conference on Computational Science and its Applications (ICCSA 2010), pp. 191–200, Washington, DC, USA. IEEE Computer Society (2010)
9. Akram, R.N., Markantonakis, K., Mayes, K.: User centric security model for tamper-resistant devices. In: IEEE International Conference on e-Business Engineering (ICEBE 2011), pp. 168–177 (2011)
10. Akram, R.N., Markantonakis, K., Mayes, K.: Trusted platform module for smart cards. In: 6th International Conference on New Technologies, Mobility and Security, NTMS 2014, pp. 1–5. IEEE (2014)
11. Alves, T., Felton, D.: TrustZone: integrated hardware and software security. Inf. Q. **3**(4), 18–24 (2004)
12. Anwar, W., Lindskog, D., Zavarsky, P., Ruhl, R.: Redesigning secure element access control for NFC enabled Android smartphones using mobile trusted computing. In: International Conference on Information Society (i-Society), June 2013

13. Apple Press. Apple Announces Apple Pay: Transforming Mobile Payments with an Easy, Secure and Private Way to Pay, September 2014. https://www.apple.com/pr/library/2014/09/09Apple-Announces-Apple-Pay.html
14. Azema, J., Fayad, G.: M-Shield mobile security technology: Making wireless secure. Texas Instruments white paper (2008). http://focus.ti.com/pdfs/wtbu/ti_mshield_whitepaper.pdf
15. Busold, C., Dmitrienko, A., Seudi, H., Taha, A., Sobhani, M., Wachsmann, C., Sadeghi, A.-R.: Smart keys for cyber-cars: secure smartphone-based NFC-enabled car immobilizer. In: ACM Conference on Data and Application Security and Privacy (CODASPY), February 2013
16. Certgate. Certgate products. cgCard (2012). http://www.certgate.com/wp-content/uploads/2012/09/20131113_cgCard_Datasheet_EN.pdf
17. Clark, S.: MasterCard and Samsung introduce embedded NFC payments (2013). http://www.nfcworld.com/2013/12/13/327343/mastercard-samsung-introduce-embedded-nfc-payments/
18. Dmitrienko, A., Sadeghi, A.-R., Tamrakar, S., Wachsmann, C.: SmartTokens: delegable access control with NFC-enabled smartphones. In: Katzenbeisser, S., Weippl, E., Camp, L.J., Volkamer, M., Reiter, M., Zhang, X. (eds.) TRUST 2012. LNCS, vol. 7344, pp. 219–238. Springer, Heidelberg (2012)
19. Edgar Dunn and Company. Advanced payments report (2014). http://www.paymentscardsandmobile.com/wp-content/uploads/2014/02/PCM_EDC_Advanced_Payments_Report_2014_MWC.pdf
20. Ekberg, J.-E., Kostiainen, K., Asokan, N.: The untapped potential of trusted execution environments on mobile devices. IEEE Secur. Priv. 99:1 (2014) (PrePrints)
21. Elenkov, N.: Accessing the embedded secure element in Android 4.x (2012). http://nelenkov.blogspot.de/2012/08/accessing-embedded-secure-element-in.html
22. European Payments Council - GSMA. Trusted Service Manager. Service management requirements and specifications. EPC 220–08. Version 1.0 (2010). http://www.europeanpaymentscouncil.eu/index.cfm/knowledge-bank/epc-documents/epc-gsma-tsm-service-management-requirements-and-specifications/epc 220-08-epc-gsma-tsm-wp-v1pdf/
23. Global Platform. Card specification. Version 2.2 (2006)
24. Global Platform. Remote application management over HTTP protocol, September 2006
25. Global Platform. Global Platform card technology: Secure channel protocol 03, September 2009
26. Global Platform. GlobalPlatform's proposition for NFC mobile: Secure element management and messaging. White paper (2009). http://www.sicherungssysteme.net/fileadmin/GlobalPlatform_NFC_Mobile_White_Paper.pdf
27. GlobalPlatform. GlobalPlatform Device Technology. TEE System Architecture. Version 1.0 (2011). http://globalplatform.org/specificationsdevice.asp
28. GlobalPlatform. A new model: The consumer-centric model and how it applies to the mobile ecosystem (2012). http://www.globalplatform.org/documents/Consumer_Centric_Model_White_PaperMar2012.pdf
29. GlobalPlatform. Secure element access control (2012). http://www.globalplatform.org/specificationsdevice.asp
30. González, J., Bonnet, P.: Towards an open framework leveraging a trusted execution environment. In: Wang, G., Ray, I., Feng, D., Rajarajan, M. (eds.) CSS 2013. LNCS, vol. 8300, pp. 458–467. Springer, Heidelberg (2013)
31. Google. Android API guide - Bluetooth (2010). http://developer.android.com/guide/topics/connectivity/bluetooth.html

32. Itoi, N., Arbaugh, W.A., Pollack, S.J., Reeves, D.M.: Personal secure booting. In: Varadharajan, V., Mu, Y. (eds.) ACISP 2001. LNCS, vol. 2119, pp. 130–144. Springer, Heidelberg (2001)

33. Ekberg, J.-E.: Trustonic. <t-base - a trusted execution environment. White paper (2014)

34. Kostiainen, K., Ekberg, J.-E., Asokan, N., Rantala, A.: On-board credentials with open provisioning. In: ACM Symposium on Information, Computer, and Communications Security (ASIACCS), pp. 104–115. ACM (2009)

35. Kostiainen, K., Reshetova, E., Ekberg, J.-E., Asokan, N.: Old, new, borrowed, blue - a perspective on the evolution of mobile platform security architectures. In: First ACM Conference on Data and Application Security and Privacy, pp. 13–24 (2011)

36. Marforio, C., Karapanos, N., Soriente, C., Kostiainen, K., Čapkun, S.: Secure enrollment and practical migration for mobile trusted execution environments. In: The Third ACM Workshop on Security and Privacy in Smartphones and Mobile Devices (SPSM), pp. 93–98. ACM, New York (2013)

37. Marlowe, C.: Intel and Visa join forces to boost mobile payments (2012). http://www.dmwmedia.com/news/2012/02/28/intel-and-visa-join-forces-to-boost-mobile-payments

38. Masti, R.J., Marforio, C., Čapkun, S.: An architecture for concurrent execution of secure environments in clouds. In: The ACM Cloud Computing Security Workshop (CCSW), pp. 11–22 (2013)

39. Press Release, Giesecke and Devrient. G&D makes mobile terminal devices even more secure with new version of smart card in microSD format. http://www.gi-de.com/en/about_g_d/press/press_releases/G%26D-Makes-Mobile-Terminal-Devices-Secure-with-New-MicroSD%E2%84%A2-Card-g3592.jsp

40. TrendLabs. 3Q 2012 security roundup. Android under siege: Popularity comes at a price (2012). http://www.trendmicro.com/cloud-content/us/pdfs/security-intelligence/reports/rpt-3q-2012-security-roundup-android-under-siege-popularity-comes-at-a-price.pdf

41. Vasudevan, A., Owusu, E., Zhou, Z., Newsome, J., McCune, J.M.: Trustworthy execution on mobile devices: what security properties can my mobile platform give *me*? In: Katzenbeisser, S., Weippl, E., Camp, L.J., Volkamer, M., Reiter, M., Zhang, X. (eds.) TRUST 2012. LNCS, vol. 7344, pp. 159–178. Springer, Heidelberg (2012)

Privacy and Incentives

On Non-cooperative Genomic Privacy

Mathias Humbert[1]([✉]), Erman Ayday[2], Jean-Pierre Hubaux[1],
and Amalio Telenti[3]

[1] Laboratory for Communications and Applications, EPFL, Lausanne, Switzerland
{mathias.Humbert,jean-pierre.hubaux}@epfl.ch
[2] Department of Computer Science, Bilkent University, Ankara, Turkey
erman@cs.bilkent.edu.tr
[3] The J. Craig Venter Institute, La Jolla, USA
atelenti@jcvi.org

Abstract. Over the last few years, the vast progress in genome sequencing has highly increased the availability of genomic data. Today, individuals can obtain their digital genomic sequences at reasonable prices from many online service providers. Individuals can store their data on personal devices, reveal it on public online databases, or share it with third parties. Yet, it has been shown that genomic data is very privacy-sensitive and highly correlated between relatives. Therefore, individuals' decisions about how to manage and secure their genomic data are crucial. People of the same family might have very different opinions about (i) how to protect and (ii) whether or not to reveal their genome. We study this tension by using a game-theoretic approach. First, we model the interplay between two purely-selfish family members. We also analyze how the game evolves when relatives behave altruistically. We define closed-form Nash equilibria in different settings. We then extend the game to N players by means of multi-agent influence diagrams that enable us to efficiently compute Nash equilibria. Our results notably demonstrate that altruism does not always lead to a more efficient outcome in genomic-privacy games. They also show that, if the discrepancy between the genome-sharing benefits that players perceive is too high, they will follow opposite sharing strategies, which has a negative impact on the familial utility.

Keywords: Genomic privacy · Interdependent privacy · Game theory · Altruism

1 Introduction

The decreasing cost in genome sequencing has dramatically increased the availability and use of genomic data in many domains such as healthcare, research, law enforcement, and recreational genomics. Any individual can obtain the sequencing of a significant part of his genome for less than $100. This availability

Erman Ayday—This work was carried out while the author was at EPFL.

R. Böhme and T. Okamoto (Eds.): FC 2015, LNCS 8975, pp. 407–426, 2015.
DOI: 10.1007/978-3-662-47854-7_24

raises many questions regarding the management (storage, sharing, etc.) and, ultimately, the privacy of genomic data. The genome contains very sensitive information about its owner such as his ethnicity, kinship, and predisposition to diseases. If this data is leaked, there could be serious consequences such as genetic discrimination, divorce [1] and blackmail (considering e.g., fatherhood issues) [9]. As genomic data is personal data, we could let individuals manage it independently of each other. However, as shown in [14], the genomic data of close relatives is highly correlated, thus leading to interdependent privacy risks. Hence, all genome-related decisions should be made by considering that genomic data is not only personal, but also *familial* data.

Nevertheless, thousands of individuals already spontaneously share their genomic data online, either anonymously[1] or with their real identity (e.g., on OpenSNP.org). Even for individuals who do not share their genomic data online, important decisions regarding the storage security of their genomes have to be made. Some will decide to store it on personal devices, others on external (potentially untrusted) servers. In both cases, guaranteeing security and privacy has a non-negligible cost. Therefore, in this work, we consider that an individual whose DNA has been sequenced must make decisions on (i) whether to share his genomic data, and (ii) how much to invest in securing the storage of this data.

We analyze the strategic behaviors of members of the same family in a genomic-privacy context by using a game-theoretic approach. Game theory has been shown to be very useful for analyzing the behavior of strategic agents in information security settings [3]. In particular, interdependent security (IDS) games have been proposed [20] for scenarios where agents make decisions that affect not only their own security risks but also those of others. Following the IDS works, we define two interdependent privacy (IDP) games between family members with different perceived benefits, costs and privacy levels. First, we study the interplay between two family members. With the two-player setting, we derive a closed-form expression to quantify genomic privacy of any individual given one of his relatives' genome, and compute different closed-form Nash equilibria for the two games we study. Furthermore, we consider some altruistic[2] behavior within a family. Then, we extend the two-player game to consider N family members who decide whether to secure or disclose their genomes. To efficiently compute the Nash equilibrium of the N-player game, we make use of multi-agent influence diagrams (MAIDs), an extension of Bayesian networks that enables us to include decision and utility variables. With this approach, we can significantly reduce computational complexity with respect to a classic extensive-form game. Note that, compared to IDS games that rely upon theoretical models of interdependence, the indirect risks in the IDP games come from the actual familial correlations evidenced by genetics. Moreover, we quantify genomic-privacy loss with real genomic data, which provides very tangible results.

---

[1] Anonymization has been proven to not be an effective technique for protecting identities of the data owners in the genomic context [12, 26].

[2] Each player takes into account the other players' utility when making a decision.

Our results show that, if the discrepancy is too high between the players' perceptions of the genome-sharing benefits, they will follow opposite strategies, creating externalities. These misaligned incentives lead to inefficient equilibria that result in a familial utility lower than when incentives are aligned. Our analysis also shows that, surprisingly, altruism does not always lead to a more efficient outcome in a genomic privacy game. Yet, such suboptimal equilibrium can be avoided if the players coordinate.

2 Model

Users: We consider a set of N users from a family whose genotypes are sequenced. We focus on the most common DNA variant, the single nucleotide polymorphism (SNP).[3] We assume that all users have the same number and set Ω of SNPs sequenced. Users have to make choices regarding the investment in securing their genomic data and the sharing of this data (e.g., to help research). A user might prefer storing his genomic data on a personal, and possibly mobile, device. For instance, as suggested in [6], there are various advantages to keeping a person's genome on a smartphone. It is portable, highly personal, and has very good computational and storage capabilities. Unfortunately, malware in smartphones has exploded over the last few years [25], and keeping a mobile device secure causes non-negligible costs. Alternatively, a user could decide to outsource the storage of his genomic data to a third party. A user might also want to publicly share his SNPs, essentially because his perceived benefits outweigh the perceived cost (loss) for his genomic privacy.[4] We assume such users typically do not invest in securing their genomes on their personal devices, as they are already publicly disclosed.

Adversary: The adversary's goal is to collect and infer genomic data. His reasons for gathering individuals' genotypes can be multiple. For instance, he could sell the collected genomic data to life or health insurance companies that would then use it to genetically discriminate against potential insurees. As usually assumed in IDS games, the adversary is considered to be an exogenous, persistent threat [20]. Thus, we do not model him as a strategic agent, but rather as probability $h(\cdot)$ of a successful breach in the targeted system. If a user decides to publicly disclose his SNPs online, the probability of a breach is equal to 1.

3 Genomic Privacy Games

The genomes of close family members are highly correlated. Thus, individuals' behaviors regarding their genomes will not only affect their personal genomic privacy, but also those of their relatives. Game theory enables us to model the

---

[3] See, e.g., https://genomeprivacy.org/ for an introduction to genomics.

[4] See, e.g., http://opensnp.wordpress.com/2011/11/17/first-results-of-the-survey-on-sharing-genetic-information/ to understand users' motivations for and fears about genome sharing.

interplay between users with dependent payoffs and potentially conflicting interests, and to predict their behaviors. We define two interdependent privacy games between family members: (i) the (storage-)security game G_s, and the disclosure game G_d. Both G_s and G_d are defined as a triplet $(\mathcal{P}, \mathcal{S}, \mathcal{U})$, where $\mathcal{P}$ is the set of players, $\mathcal{S}$ is the set of strategies, and $\mathcal{U}$ is the set of payoff functions.

- **Players:** The set of players $\mathcal{P} = \{P_1, ..., P_N\}$ corresponds to the set of N family members having their genomes sequenced, in both games G_s and G_d.
- **Strategies:** In game G_s, for each player P_i, the strategy $x_i \in \mathcal{S}$ represents the security investment for the storage of his genomic data. As differences between discrete and continuous models of investment appear only in some boundary cases [11,20], we consider here the discrete model, i.e., $x_i \in \{0,1\}$. $x_i = 1$ means "to invest in securing his own device", and $x_i = 0$ means "to not invest", by putting his data on his device or outsourced to an untrusted third party (that could be itself attacked). The strategy profile is then defined as $\boldsymbol{x} = [x_1, \cdots, x_N]^T$. In game G_d, the strategy is represented by the decision d_i to publicly share P_i's SNPs (e.g., on OpenSNP.org) or not. As the majority of genome-sharing people currently choose to disclose nothing or their whole set of SNPs, we consider here a discrete binary model, i.e., $d_i \in \{0,1\}$ (0 meaning "no disclosure" and 1 "full disclosure"). Note that a finer granularity of disclosure is studied in detail in a cooperative context in [16]. A player will choose $d_i = 1$ if and only if he perceives more utility by sharing than by protecting. The strategy profile is then represented by $\boldsymbol{d} = [d_1, \cdots, d_N]^T$.
- **Payoff Functions:** The utility of a player is, by definition, equal to the benefit minus the cost. In our setting, the first term of the benefit, b_i^g, represents the fact that a user's genome is sequenced and available for various benefits (e.g., personalized medicine). This generic benefit can be added to the benefit b_i^d that player P_i obtains by disclosing his genomic data online in game G_d. The cost comprises the (unit) cost of a security investment for protecting his genome, c_i, and the potential loss l_i of genomic privacy.[5] For instance, the cost c_i can represent the OS updates that can lead to a non-negligible cost (renewal of the equipment) once a device becomes too old to support them.

In our genomic context, the privacy loss l_i can be precisely quantified by relying upon the expected estimation error E_i between the SNP values inferred by the adversary $\hat{y}_i^k$'s and the actual values y_i^k's, $\forall g_k \in \Omega$ [14].[6] Defining Y_i^k as the random variable representing SNP g_k of player P_i, the genomic privacy of P_i is

$$E_i = \frac{1}{|\Omega|} \sum_{k:g_k \in \Omega} \sum_{\hat{y}_i^k \in \{0,1,2\}} P(Y_i^k = \hat{y}_i^k | Y_O = \boldsymbol{y_O}) \left\| y_i^k - \hat{y}_i^k \right\|_1, \qquad (1)$$

where Y_O represents the SNPs observed by the adversary. This set depends on the strategies of the players in G_s and G_d. We will denote $E_{i,0}$ to be

---

[5] Note that an expected monetary loss would be expressed as a non-decreasing function of l_i. This is left for future work.

[6] Note that a SNP value is encoded by the set $\{0,1,2\}$ whose elements represent the number of minor alleles in the SNP.

the genomic privacy when no SNP is observed, i.e., when $P(Y_i^k = \hat{y}_i^k | Y_O = \boldsymbol{y}_O) = P(Y_i^k = \hat{y}_i^k)$. This initial privacy level is computed by using the minor allele frequencies (MAFs) given by population statistics [14]. In general, as the observation depends on the strategy profile $\boldsymbol{x}$ (respectively $\boldsymbol{d}$), E_i will be a function of $\boldsymbol{x}$ (respectively $\boldsymbol{d}$) in game G_s (respectively G_d). As assumed in several IDS games (e.g., [19]), the probability of successful breach is set to zero when a player invests in security, i.e., $h(x_i = 1) = 0$. Otherwise, $h(x_i = 0) = p_a$ with $0 < p_a \leq 1$. For game G_d, $h(d_i = 1) = 1$ as discussed in Sect. 2, and $h(d_i = 0) = 0$.[7] In our genomic privacy game, contrarily to IDS games, the interdependence lies in the genomic-privacy loss and not in the breach probability $h(\cdot)$. The genomic-privacy loss l_i is defined as $E_{i,0} - E_i(\cdot)$, where $E_i(\cdot)$ is a function of the strategy profile $\boldsymbol{x} = (x_i, \boldsymbol{x}_{-i})$ or $\boldsymbol{d} = (d_i, \boldsymbol{d}_{-i})$. Note that the risk is non-additive: Either the adversary manages to know the player's genome directly (and the genomic privacy drops to zero), in which case the knowledge of another genome does not bring any extra information; or the adversary cannot access the player's genome and then there is only an indirect privacy loss. Defining $h(\boldsymbol{x}_{-i})$ as the probability of successful breaches into a subset of players' devices (other than P_i), the payoff function of a player P_i in G_s is

$$u_i(x_i, \boldsymbol{x}_{-i}) = b_i^g - (x_i c_i + h(x_i)E_{i,0} + (1 - h(x_i)) h(\boldsymbol{x}_{-i}) (E_{i,0} - E_i(\boldsymbol{x}_{-i}))), \tag{2}$$

and his payoff in game G_d is

$$u_i(d_i, \boldsymbol{d}_{-i}) = b_i^g + d_i b_i^d - ((1 - d_i)c_i + d_i E_{i,0} + (1 - d_i) (E_{i,0} - E_i(\boldsymbol{d}_{-i}))).^8 \tag{3}$$

- **Social Welfare:** We define the *social welfare* function as the sum of the payoffs of all players: $U(\boldsymbol{x}) = \sum_{i:P_i \in \mathcal{P}} u_i(\boldsymbol{x})$ for G_s, and $U(\boldsymbol{d}) = \sum_{i:P_i \in \mathcal{P}} u_i(\boldsymbol{d})$ for G_d.
- **Altruism:** Finally, we consider that family members are usually not purely selfish regarding their relatives, hence some altruistic factors play a role in their decisions. Following an idea introduced in [21] for social networks, we define a familial factor $\alpha \in [0, 1]$ that conveys the fact that relatives tend to be altruistic among themselves. We raise this factor to the power $k(i, j) \in \mathbb{N}^*$ that represents the degree of kinship between relatives i and j.[9] $\alpha = 0$ means that players are purely selfish, whereas $\alpha = 1$ implies that they are fully altruistic with their whole family. For instance, in G_s, the altruistic player P_i will maximize the following utility (instead of (2)):

$$u_i^a(x_i, \boldsymbol{x}_{-i}) = u_i(x_i, \boldsymbol{x}_{-i}) + \sum_{j:P_j \in \mathcal{P}, j \neq i} \alpha^{k(i,j)} u_j(x_i, \boldsymbol{x}_{-i}). \tag{4}$$

---

[7] In G_d, we assume that a player who does not share his SNPs will always invest in security. Note also that G_d is a special case deriving from G_s.

[8] In the following, we will use the more concise notation $E_{i|-i}$ to express the genomic privacy of P_i given a subset (that depends on $\boldsymbol{x}_{-i}$ or $\boldsymbol{d}_{-i}$) of other players' SNPs.

[9] $k = 1$ for first-degree relatives such as parent, child, sibling; $k = 2$ for second-degree relatives such as grandparent, grandchild, uncle, aunt, niece, and so on.

Table 1. Normal form of the two-player game G_s.

$P_1 \backslash P_2$	$x_2 = 1$	$x_2 = 0$
$x_1 = 1$	$(b_1^g - c_1, b_2^g - c_2)$	$(b_1^g - c_1 - p_a(E_{1,0} - E_{1|2}), b_2^g - p_a E_{2,0})$
$x_1 = 0$	$(b_1^g - p_a E_{1,0}, b_2^g - c_2 - p_a(E_{2,0} - E_{2|1}))$	$(b_1^g - p_a E_{1,0} - (1 - p_a)p_a(E_{1,0} - E_{1|2}),$ $b_2^g - p_a E_{2,0} - (1 - p_a)p_a(E_{2,0} - E_{2|1}))$

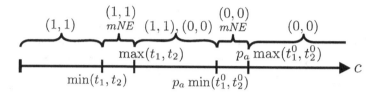

Fig. 1. Dependence of the NE of game G_s with respect to the investment cost c.

4   Two-Player Games

In this section, we study the interplay between two relatives who are, at first, selfish, and then become partially altruistic depending on their degree of kinship.

4.1   Selfish Players

We start our analysis with game G_s whose strategic representation is shown in Table 1. Assuming the cost of security investment to be the same for all players, i.e., $c_1 = c_2 = c$, we characterize all Nash equilibria.

Lemma 1. *For any value $c \in [0, \infty)$, there exists at least one pure Nash equilibrium (NE) in G_s. The NE are defined by the best responses (x_1^*, x_2^*):*

$$(x_1^*, x_2^*) = \begin{cases} (1,1) & if\, c < \min(t_1, t_2) \\ (1,1), mNE & if \min(t_1, t_2) < c < \max(t_1, t_2) \\ (1,1), (0,0) & if \max(t_1, t_2) < c < p_a \min(t_1^0, t_2^0) \\ (0,0), mNE & if\, p_a \min(t_1^0, t_2^0) < c < p_a \max(t_1^0, t_2^0) \\ (0,0) & if\, c > p_a \max(t_1^0, t_2^0) \end{cases} \tag{5}$$

if $\max(t_1, t_2) < p_a \min(t_1^0, t_2^0)$, where $t_i = p_a E_{i,0} - p_a^2(E_{i,0} - E_{i|j})$, $t_i^0 = E_{i,0}$, and mNE is a mixed-strategy Nash equilibrium. If $\max(t_1, t_2) > p_a \min(t_1^0, t_2^0)$, the third case NE in (5) become $(0,1)$ if $t_1^0 < t_2^0$ and $(1,0)$ if $t_1^0 > t_2^0$, and $\max(t_1, t_2)$ and $p_a \min(t_1^0, t_2^0)$ are swapped in the inequality bounds on c.

Due to space constraints, this proof is omitted and can be found in [15]. Figure 1 depicts how the NE evolves for different values of c. In order to obtain closed-formed Nash equilibria, we must analytically express the genomic privacy levels $E_{i,0}$ and $E_{i|j}$. In [14], the authors show that, in the general case, belief propagation on factor graphs can be used to compute the posterior marginal probability

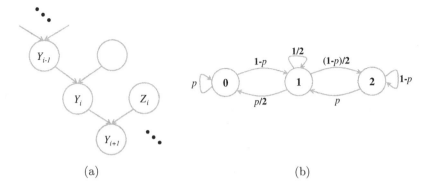

(a)   (b)

Fig. 2. Probabilistic models representing a SNP value evolution over multiple generations. (a) Bayesian network representation of a three-generation family, and (b) Markov chain representing the probabilities of moving from one SNP value (state) to another from generation i to $i+1$ or $i-1$. Probability p is the major allele frequency of the given SNP.

$P(Y_i^k|Y_O)$ given some observed genomic data, and thus to quantify genomic privacy. We now show that, if only two members are involved in the game, and no other familial genomic data is observed, we can derive a closed-form expression for $P(Y_i^k|Y_O)$, thus for $E_{i,0}$ and $E_{i|j}$. As we assume that all players have the same set of SNPs Ω sequenced and potentially exposed, and that the adversary can access either the whole sequence of SNPs or nothing (as he either successfully breaches the system or not), linkage disequilibrium (correlations) between the SNPs would not help the adversary very much, thus it is not used in the computation of genomic privacy here. Hence, when we want to compute the privacy at SNP g_k of player P_i, we consider only the observation at the same SNP g_k of player P_j. Each SNP can then be considered independently of other SNPs. In the following two lemmas, we focus on a single SNP, so drop the superscript k. Assuming Y_i is the random variable representing a SNP of an individual at generation i in a familial branch (see Fig. 2a), and p is the major allele frequency of the SNP, we have the following lemma.

Lemma 2. *The sequence $\{Y_n\}$ is a discrete stochastic process. Moreover, it is a first-order homogeneous Markov chain, i.e., the conditional probability of Y_{i+1} given (direct) ancestors in one of the parents' family branches is formally defined as $P(Y_{i+1} = y_{i+1}|Y_i = y_i, Y_{i-1} = y_{i-1}, \ldots) = P(Y_{i+1} = y_{i+1}|Y_i = y_i)$. Its transition matrix P is defined as follows:*

$$P = \begin{pmatrix} p & 1-p & 0 \\ p/2 & 1/2 & (1-p)/2 \\ 0 & p & 1-p \end{pmatrix},$$

where $p_{mn} = P(Y_{i+1} = n|Y_i = m)$, m and n belonging to the state space $\{0, 1, 2\}$.

This proof can be found in [15]. We have noticed that the reverse process, which is the conditional probability of Y_{i-1} given direct descendants Y_i, Y_{i+1}, $\ldots$, is also a first-order homogeneous Markov chain defined by the same matrix P where $p_{mn} = P(Y_{i-1} = n | Y_i = m)$. This means that going up or down the familial tree leads to the same conditional distributions. The corresponding Markov chain is shown in Fig. 2b.

Lemma 2 helps us determine the conditional probabilities of SNPs of direct ancestors or descendants given any relative's observed SNP. For instance, the conditional probability $P(Y_{i+k} | Y_i)$ of a relative k-degrees apart from another individual i whose SNP is observed and equal to m is, by definition of the Markov chain, given by $\boldsymbol{\pi}_{i+k} = \boldsymbol{\pi}_i P^k$, where $\boldsymbol{\pi}_i$ is a row vector that is equal to 1 in the mth coordinate and 0 elsewhere. Note also that the stationary distribution, defined as the vector $\boldsymbol{\pi}$ such that $\boldsymbol{\pi} = \boldsymbol{\pi} P$, is equal to the vector of prior probabilities $(P(Y_i))$, given by the major allele probability p:

$$\boldsymbol{\pi} = \begin{pmatrix} p^2 & 2p(1-p) & (1-p)^2 \end{pmatrix}. \tag{6}$$

This follows the intuition, as $\boldsymbol{\pi}$ is defined to be equal to any of the columns of P^k when k tends to infinity. When the observed relative j is far enough from the targeted individual i in the family tree, the genome of j has no influence on i's genome. The conditional probabilities are well-defined for *direct* relatives. However, if the individual whose SNP is observed is not a relative in direct line (e.g., an uncle or a niece), the transition matrix P cannot be applied alone and has to be combined with a matrix M whose elements m_{ab} represent the conditional probabilities $P(Y_{i_1} = b | Y_{i_2} = a)$ of i_1 given his sibling i_2. M is derived and expressed in [15]. Defining the 3×3 distance matrix D with elements $d_{ij} = |i - j|$ and the (column) vector $\boldsymbol{y}_i$ whose m^{th} coordinate is equal to 1 and others 0 (where m is the SNP value), we have the following lemma.

Lemma 3. *The genomic privacy E_i of individual i at any SNP is:*

$$\begin{cases} E_{i,0} = \boldsymbol{\pi} D \boldsymbol{y}_i & \textit{if no relative reveals the SNP} \\ E_{i|j} = \boldsymbol{\pi}_j P^k D \boldsymbol{y}_i & \textit{if } i \textit{ and } j \textit{ are direct relatives and } j's \textit{ SNP is revealed} \\ E_{i|j} = \boldsymbol{\pi}_j P^u M P^v D \boldsymbol{y}_i & \textit{if } i \textit{ and } j \textit{ are not direct relatives and } j's \textit{ SNP is revealed} \end{cases}$$

where k is the degree of kinship between i and j, u is the degree of kinship between j and his (direct) ancestor whose sibling is the (direct) ancestor of i, and v is the degree of kinship between i and his (direct) ancestor whose sibling is j's (direct) ancestor.

This proof can be found in [15]. To illustrate the third case of Lemma 3, let us take for example two close relatives, uncle and nephew. If j is the uncle of i, then the genomic privacy of i given j at a certain SNP is $E_{i|j} = \boldsymbol{\pi}_j P^1 M P^0 D \boldsymbol{y}_i = \boldsymbol{\pi}_j P M D \boldsymbol{y}_i$ whereas, if j is the nephew of i, the genomic privacy of i is $E_{i|j} = \boldsymbol{\pi}_j M P D \boldsymbol{y}_i$.

We can now quantify genomic privacy for a range of SNPs and get closed-form NE.

Theorem 1. *For any value* $c \in [0, \infty)$, *the pure Nash equilibrium is:*

$$(x_1^*, x_2^*) = \begin{cases} (1,1) & if \ c < \max(t_1, t_2) \\ (1,1), (0,0) & if \ \max(t_1, t_2) < c < p_a \min(t_1^0, t_2^0) \\ (0,0) & if \ c > p_a \min(t_1^0, t_2^0) \end{cases} \quad (7)$$

if $\max(t_1, t_2) < p_a \min(t_1^0, t_2^0)$, *where* $t_i^0 = \frac{1}{|\Omega|} \sum_{l:g_l \in \Omega} \pi^l D y_i^l$, $t_i = \frac{p_a}{|\Omega|} \left(\sum_{l:g_l \in \Omega} \right.$
$((1 - p_a)\pi^l + p_a \pi_j^l P_l^k) D y_i^l)$ *if* i *and* j *are direct* k^{th}-*degree relatives, and* $t_i = \frac{p_a}{|\Omega|} \left(\sum_{l:g_l \in \Omega} ((1 - p_a)\pi^l + p_a \pi_j^l P_l^u M P_l^v) D y_i^l \right)$ *if* i *and* j *are not in direct line,* u *and* v *as defined in Lemma 3. If* $\max(t_1, t_2) > p_a \min(t_1^0, t_2^0)$, *the second-case* NE $(1,1), (0,0)$ *becomes* $(0,1)$ *if* $t_1^0 < t_2^0$ *and* $(1,0)$ *if* $t_1^0 > t_2^0$, *and* $\max(t_1, t_2)$ *and* $p_a \min(t_1^0, t_2^0)$ *are swapped in the inequality bounds.*

The proof can be found in [15]. In order to make these NE more tangible, we quantify genomic privacy by relying upon real genomic data. We make use of the CEPH/Utah Pedigree 1463 that contains the partial DNA sequences of 4 grandparents, 2 parents, and 11 children [8]. We filter 8 of the 11 children out, thus keeping 9 relatives in total: GP1, GP2, GP3, GP4, P5, P6, C7, C8, and C9. We consider all the SNPs that are available on chromosome 1 (around 82,000). Note that, thanks to our closed-form expression of $E_{i|j}$, its computation on 82,000 SNPs takes less than one second. Figure 3 shows the thresholds separating the three different cases of NE in Theorem 1 with respect to p_a and c. $(1,1)$ stands below the two (dotted) red and green curves, and $(0,0)$ stands above these two curves. Thus, we note that for most values of c and p_a, either both relatives secure their genomes (if c is smaller than around half of p_a), or both do not secure them (if c is greater than around half of p_a). This shows that players, if they have similar cost c, have aligned incentives, leading to an efficient NE. However, there are some values of c and p_a for which two pure NE $(1,1)$ and $(0,0)$ co-exist. It is between the two curves, if the (dotted) red curve lies above the green one. If the green curve lies above the dotted one,[10] then we have either $(0,1)$ if $E_{1,0} < E_{2,0}$ or $(1,0)$ if $E_{1,0} > E_{2,0}$. The discrepancy between the two curves is the highest in Fig. 3c, as the difference between the initial privacy levels $E_{i,0}$'s and posterior levels $E_{i|j}$ is the most significant (see Table 2). On the contrary, in the game between C7 and GP1, the posterior levels $E_{i|j}$ are closer to the initial ones $E_{i,0}$ (because the two players are second-degree relatives), and the $E_{i,0}$'s differ between the two players, leading (for a tiny subset of values of p_a of c) to inefficient NE, such as $(0,1)$, as described above.

Discussion: We conclude that, for most security cost values and probabilities of successful breach, the players follow the same strategies, even though their genomic privacy levels are slightly different. They both either invest in security, or do not.

We now move to the disclosure game G_d. Table 3 shows the resulting payoffs for two players P_1 and P_2. The following theorem determines its NE.

---

[10] This happens for $p_a < 0.29$ in Fig. 3a and $p_a < 0.78$ in Fig. 3b.

Table 2. Genomic privacy levels of grandparent GP1, parent P5, children C7 and C8, from the CEPH/Utah pedigree 1463.

(P_1, P_2)	$E_{1,0}$	$E_{1\|2}$	$E_{2,0}$	$E_{2\|1}$
(P5,GP1)	0.4741	0.3579	0.4402	0.3179
(C7,GP1)	0.4788	0.4296	0.4402	0.3878
(C7,C8)	0.4788	0.3310	0.4803	0.3321

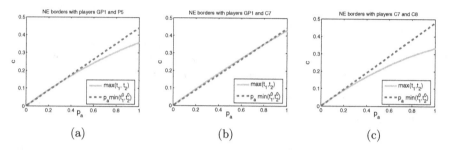

Fig. 3. Thresholds of Theorem 1 separating the three different pure NE cases of G_s. We show three different scenarios with two players: (a) Grandparent GP1 and parent P5, (b) GP1 and child C7, and (c) children C7 and C8 (Color figure online).

Table 3. Normal form of the two-player game G_d.

$P_1 \backslash P_2$	$d_2 = 0$	$d_2 = 1$
$d_1 = 0$	$(b_1^g - c_1, b_2^g - c_2)$	$(b_1^g - c_1 - (E_{1,0} - E_{1\|2}), b_2^g + b_2^d - E_{2,0})$
$d_1 = 1$	$(b_1^g + b_1^d - E_{1,0}, b_2^g - c_2 - (E_{2,0} - E_{2\|1}))$	$(b_1^g + b_1^d - E_{1,0}, b_2^g + b_2^d - E_{2,0})$

Theorem 2. *For any value $b_1^d \in [0, \infty)$, and $b_2^d \in [0, \infty)$, the pure Nash equilibrium is:*

$$(d_1^*, d_2^*) = \begin{cases} (0,0) & \text{if } ((b_1^d < E_{1,0} - c_1) \wedge (b_2^d < E_{2\|1} - c_2)) \vee \\ & ((b_1^d < E_{1\|2} - c_1) \wedge (b_2^d < E_{2,0} - c_2)) \\ (1,1), (0,0) & \text{if } (E_{1\|2} - c_1 < b_1^d < E_{1,0} - c_1) \wedge (E_{2\|1} - \\ & c_2 < b_2^d < E_{2,0} - c_2) \\ (1,1) & \text{if } ((b_1^d > E_{1,0} - c_1) \wedge (b_2^d > E_{2\|1} - c_2)) \vee \\ & (b_1^d > E_{1\|2} - c_1) \\ (0,1) & \text{if } (b_1^d < E_{1\|2} - c_1) \wedge (b_2^d > E_{2,0} - c_2) \\ (1,0) & \text{if } (b_1^d > E_{1,0} - c_1) \wedge (b_2^d < E_{2\|1} - c_2) \end{cases}$$

where $E_{i,0} = \frac{1}{|\Omega|} \sum_{l:g_l \in \Omega} \pi^l D y_i^l$, $E_{i\|j} = \frac{1}{|\Omega|} \sum_{l:g_l \in \Omega} \pi^l P_l^k D y_i^l$ *if i and j are direct k^{th}-degree relatives and, if i and j are not in direct line,* $E_{i\|j} = \frac{1}{|\Omega|} \sum_{l:g_l \in \Omega} \pi^l P_l^u D M P_l^v y_i^l$.

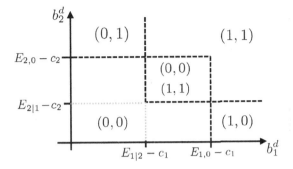

Fig. 4. Dependence of the NE w.r.t. the genome-sharing benefits b_1^d and b_2^d.

This proof can be found in [15]. Figure 4 illustrates the NE computed in Theorem 2. These NE depend essentially on the value of $b_i^d + c_i$ with respect to $E_{i,0}$ and $E_{i|j}$. A player P_i will disclose his genome, given that the other player discloses it as long as $b_i^d + c_i > E_{i|j}$. Whereas if the other player's best response is to not share, P_i will share only if $b_i^d + c_i > E_{i,0}$. Table 2 shows concrete values of genomic privacy $E_{1,0}$, $E_{2,0}$, $E_{1|2}$, and $E_{2|1}$, for first-degree direct relatives, second-degree direct relatives, and siblings.

Discussion: We conclude that, in G_d, if the discrepancy between the sharing benefits perceived by the players is high enough, these players follow opposite strategies, one putting the other's privacy at risk by sharing his genome.

4.2   Altruistic Players

In this subsection, we analyze how the equilibria evolve when the players are not purely selfish, but also consider their relatives' payoffs when making their decisions. Intuitively, by becoming more socially concerned, the players' decisions and their resulting NE should lead to higher social welfare. However, as we will see, social welfare does not always increase with altruism, unless some coordination between players happens.

To evaluate how the NE is affected by altruistic behavior, we focus on game G_d. Player P_1 considers the altruistic payoff $u_1^a(d_1, d_2) = u_1(d_1, d_2) + \alpha^{k(1,2)} u_2(d_1, d_2)$, instead of merely $u_1(d_1, d_2)$. The same applies symmetrically for P_2. We define the *familial Nash equilibrium* (FNE) as a strategy profile where, given the other player's strategy, no player can improve his altruistic payoff u^a by unilaterally changing his strategy. Defining $b_i = b_i^d + c_i$ for the ease of presentation, we have the following theorem.

Theorem 3. *For any value $b_1 \in [0, \infty)$, and $b_2 \in [0, \infty)$, the pure FNE is:*

$$(d_1^*, d_2^*) = \begin{cases} (0,0) & \text{if } ((b_1 < E_{1,0} + \alpha^k(E_{2,0} - E_{2|1})) \wedge (b_2 < E_{2|1})) \vee \\ & (b_1 < E_{1|2}) \wedge (b_2^d < E_{2,0} + \alpha^k(E_{1,0} - E_{1|2})) \\ (1,1),(0,0) & \text{if } (E_{1|2} < b_1 < E_{1,0} + \alpha^k(E_{2,0} - E_{2|1}) \wedge \\ & (E_{2|1} < b_2 < E_{2,0} + \alpha^k(E_{1,0} - E_{1|2}) \\ (1,1) & \text{if } ((b_1 > E_{1,0} + \alpha^k(E_{2,0} - E_{2|1})) \wedge (b_2 > E_{2|1})) \vee \\ & (b_1 > E_{1|2}) \wedge (b_2 > E_{2,0} + \alpha^k(E_{1,0} - E_{1|2}) \\ (1,0) & \text{if } (b_1 > E_{1,0} + \alpha^k(E_{2,0} - E_{2|1})) \wedge (b_2 < E_{2|1}) \\ (0,1) & \text{if } (b_1 < E_{1|2}) \wedge (b_2 > E_{2,0} + \alpha^k(E_{1,0} - E_{1|2})) \end{cases}$$

where $E_{i,0} = \frac{1}{|\Omega|} \sum_{l:g_l \in \Omega} \pi^l D y_i^l$, $E_{i|j} = \frac{1}{|\Omega|} \sum_{l:g_l \in \Omega} \pi^l P_l^k D y_i^l$ if i and j are direct k^{th}-degree relatives and, if i and j are not in direct line, $E_{i|j} = \frac{1}{|\Omega|} \sum_{l:g_l \in \Omega} \pi^l P_l^u D M P_l^v y_i^l$.

This proof can be found in [15]. These different NE are depicted in Fig. 5 by circled numbers separated by (thick) dotted lines. Note the shift upwards and to the right of the borders of the $(0,0)$ FNE, compared to the selfish NE (red dotted lines). This tells us that, by considering the other's player utility, the decision maker will choose to disclose his genome for a value of b_i higher than in the purely selfish scenario.

Discussion: We conclude that altruism, by internalizing externalities into players' payoffs, tends to reduce the privacy loss caused by the other player.

We now describe the strategies that a social planner would choose on behalf of the players in order to maximize social welfare, thus to attain the *social optimum* U^*.

Theorem 4. *For any value* $b_1 \in [0, \infty)$, *and* $b_2 \in [0, \infty)$, *the social optimum* U^* *is reached with the following strategies:*

$$(d_1^*, d_2^*) = \begin{cases} (0,0) & \text{if } (b_1 + b_2 < E_{1,0} + E_{2,0}) \wedge (b_1 < E_{1,0} + E_{2,0} - E_{2|1}) \wedge \\ & (b_2 < E_{1,0} + E_{2,0} - E_{1|2}) \\ (1,0) & \text{if } (b_1 > E_{1,0} + E_{2,0} - E_{2|1}) \wedge (b_2 < E_{2|1}) \\ (0,1) & \text{if } (b_2 > E_{1,0} + E_{2,0} - E_{1|2}) \wedge (b_1 < E_{1|2}) \\ (1,1) & \text{if } (b_1 + b_2 > E_{1,0} + E_{2,0}) \wedge (b_2 > E_{2|1}) \wedge (b_1 > E_{1|2}) \end{cases} \tag{8}$$

where $E_{i,0} = \frac{1}{|\Omega|} \sum_{l:g_l \in \Omega} \pi^l D y_i^l$, $E_{i|j} = \frac{1}{|\Omega|} \sum_{l:g_l \in \Omega} \pi^l P_l^k D y_i^l$ if i and j are direct k^{th}-degree relatives and, if i and j are not in direct line, $E_{i|j} = \frac{1}{|\Omega|} \sum_{l:g_l \in \Omega} \pi^l P_l^u D M P_l^v y_i^l$.

This proof can be found in [15]. The socially optimal strategies are represented schematically with respect to b_1 and b_2 by the texture of Fig. 5. Given this social optimum $U^*(s)$, the price of anarchy (PoA), which measures how the game efficiency decreases due to selfishness, is defined as $U^*(s)/\min_{NE} U(s)$ [18]. The price of stability (PoS) also measures this inefficiency but, assuming that players coordinate amongst themselves, considers the best NE instead of the worst one, i.e., is defined as $U^*(s)/\max_{NE} U(s)$ [4].

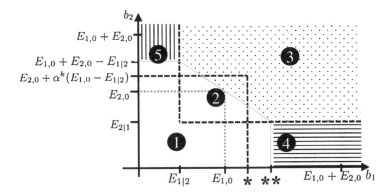

Fig. 5. Familial NE and social optima with respect to b_1 and b_2. Circled numbers represent the five different cases of Theorem 3, in order, separated by (thick) dotted lines in the figure. The red (small) dotted lines represent the borders of Fig. 4. The four different texture patterns represent the strategies of the social optimum, depicted in Theorem 4: white for $(0,0)$, vertical lines for $(1,0)$, horizontal lines for $(0,1)$, and dots for $(1,1)$. The single asterisk is $E_{1,0} + \alpha^k(E_{2,0} - E_{2|1})$, and the double asterisk is $E_{1,0} + E_{2,0} - E_{2|1}$ (Color figure online).

Following the notion of windfall of friendship (WoF) proposed in [21], we define the windfall of kinship (WoK) as the ratio between the social welfare of the worst FNE and the social welfare of the worst NE:

$$\kappa(\alpha, k) = \frac{\min_{FNE} U(\boldsymbol{s})}{\min_{NE} U(\boldsymbol{s})} \tag{9}$$

Given this definition, we can state the following theorem.

Theorem 5. *If b_1, b_2 are such that*

$$\begin{cases} b_1 + b_2 > E_{1,0} + E_{2,0} \\ b_1 < E_{1,0} + \alpha^k(E_{2,0} - E_{2|1}) \\ b_2 < E_{2,0} + \alpha^k(E_{1,0} - E_{1|2}), \end{cases} \tag{10}$$

then $\kappa(\alpha, k) < 1$ for any $k \geq 1$ and $0 < \alpha \leq 1$.

This proof can be found in [15]. This theorem tells us that, contrary to intuition, altruism in a family does not necessarily lead to higher social welfare, and induces a price of kinship rather than a windfall if the b_i's are in the range defined in (10). In this range, the social optimum is to disclose their genomes for both players, but there is the possibility to end up in a "non-disclose" $(0,0)$ FNE due to the altruistic factor, leading to an outcome worse than in the selfish NE. However, note that the WoK is always less than or equal to the PoA. Indeed, as for any $\alpha \in [0,1]$, $k \geq 1$, $\min_{FNE} U(\boldsymbol{s}) \leq U^*(\boldsymbol{s})$, it directly follows from (9) that $\kappa(\alpha, k) \leq \text{PoA}$.

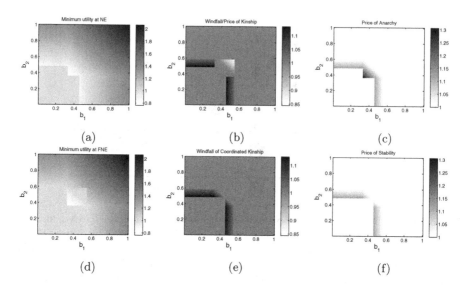

Fig. 6. Evaluation of the (in)efficiency of the NE and FNE with respect to b_1 and b_2. (a) Minimum social welfare at NE, (b) windfall/price of kinship, (c) price of anarchy, (d) minimum social welfare at FNE, (e) windfall of coordinated kinship, and (f) price of stability in G_d with GP1 and P5, $\alpha = 0.8$, and $b_1^g = b_2^g = 0.5$.

If we assume that some coordination can happen between the players, we can define the windfall of coordinated kinship (WoCK) as the ratio between the social welfare of the best FNE and the social welfare of the best NE:

$$\gamma(\alpha, k) = \frac{\max_{FNE} U(s)}{\max_{NE} U(s)} \tag{11}$$

This new definition enables us to state the following theorem.

Theorem 6. *For any* $b_1 \in [0, \infty)$, $b_2 \in [0, \infty)$, $k \geq 1$, *and* $\alpha \in [0, 1]$, *it holds that:*

$$1 \leq \gamma(\alpha, k) \leq PoS \leq PoA. \tag{12}$$

This proof can be found in [15]. In order to evaluate how the NE, FNE, WoK, WoCK, PoA, and PoS evolve in practice, we make use of the genomic data provided by the Utah family. We choose the two relatives GP1 and P5, and compute their genomic privacy based on their actual SNPs, as in Subsect. 4.1. We set $\alpha = 0.8$, $b_1^g = b_2^g = 0.5$ and compute results (NE, FNE, ...) for b_1 and b_2 varying between 0 and 1, with granularity 0.01. Figure 6 shows the resulting graphs. First, we notice the shift upwards and to the right of $(0,0)$ between NE and FNE; it follows the borders shown in Fig. 5. We also see that minimum social welfare is minimal in the squares standing in the middle of both Figs. 6a and 6d. Looking at Fig. 6b, we clearly notice that the WoK is smaller than 1 for the values of b_1 and b_2 close to 0.5, thus confirming Theorem 5. However, as soon as both players coordinate amongst themselves, the ratio between the social welfare of FNE and the social welfare of NE (WoCK) becomes always greater than or equal to 1, as illustrated in Fig. 6e. Finally, we note that PoA and PoS are always greater than or equal to 1, that PoS $\leq$ PoA, and that PoS $\geq$ WoCK, thus confirming Theorem 6.

Discussion: In conclusion, if players cannot coordinate amongst themselves, their altruistic prudence about the disclosure of their genomes can lead to a worse social outcome than in the purely selfish setting, as shown in Theorem 5 and in Fig. 6b.

5   N-Player Game

In this section, we extend the genomic privacy game to consider $N > 2$ relatives. Contrary to the two-player framework that allowed us to derive closed-form expressions, and thus compute all pure Nash equilibria very efficiently, we now face a more challenging problem. First, in general, all players (family members) can influence other players' payoffs, thus all other players' strategies have to be taken into account when a family member optimizes his own decision. Second, privacy levels $E_{i|-i}$ cannot be expressed in closed form if more than one other family member discloses their genomes.

In order to represent this complex game in a compact way and reduce its complexity, we rely upon *multi-agent influence diagrams* (MAIDs), introduced by Koller and Milch [17]. A MAID is an extension of the Bayesian network framework that embeds, in addition to random variables, decision and utility variables, and enables us to consider multiple strategic agents, thus represent games. We define a MAID $\mathcal{M}_d$ representing the N-player genomic-privacy game G_d. We show an example of $\mathcal{M}_d$ for a trio in Fig. 7. The chance[11] variable Y_i is defined as $P(Y_i = y_i) = 1$ (other values having probability 0) if $d_i = 1$, and $P(Y_i = \hat{y}_i | Y_O)$ if $d_i = 0$. Note that, we represent the chance variable Y_i for a single SNP, but in fact there are $|\Omega|$ chance variables that directly depend on d_i, and are independent of each other. A child's SNP is probabilistically determined by his parents' genomes, as explained in [14]. We also define two utility variables: $u_{i1} = b_i^g + d_i b_i^d - E_{i,0}$, which directly depends on d_i, and $u_{i2} = E_i$, which directly depends on the chance variable Y_i. Note that E_i is zero if $d_i = 1$ (genomic privacy drops to zero) and $E_i = E_{i|-i}$ if $d_i = 0$. Then, P_i's payoff u_i is $u_{i1} + u_{i2}$.

We assume that players move (decide) sequentially and with perfect information of previous decisions made by other players. Variables observed when a decision is made are depicted by dotted directed edges. For instance, in Fig. 7, the following decision ordering is shown: mother, father and then child. Under these assumptions, we can state the following lemma.

Lemma 4. *If a player $P_i \in \mathcal{P}$ moves, i.e., chooses his decision rule, at node D_i before P_j makes his own decision at node D_j, then D_i is not s-reachable from D_j.*

The proof directly follows from the concept of *s-reachability*, defined in Definition 5.3 of [17]. If D_i is s-reachable from D_j, then D_i is relevant to D_j or,

---

[11] In MAIDs, random variables are called chance variables.

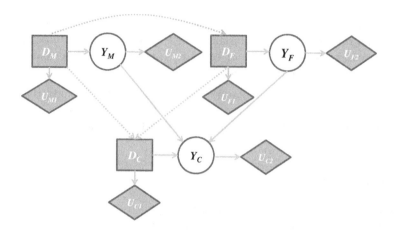

Fig. 7. Multi-agent influence diagram representing a trio (mother, father, child) with one decision variable (square), one chance variable (circle) representing the SNPs of the individual, and two utility variables (diamonds) per person. Full lines represent probabilistic or deterministic dependencies, whereas dotted lines represent the variables that an agent observes when he makes his decision. This figure illustrates a game with sequential moves, perfect information, and with purely selfish players.

in other words, D_j strategically relies on D_i. If a decision node D_i is observed by D_j (dotted edge in Fig. 7), it means that the decision rule $\delta(d_j)$ at D_j will be conditioned on the instantiations of D_i. The decision rule at D_j will be defined as $\delta(d_j|d_i), \forall d_i \in \{0, 1\}$, thus this decision will not be affected by a change in D_i. However, because D_j is not observed by P_i when he makes his decision, D_j will be relevant to D_i, thus s-reachable from D_i. Under perfect information, we can define, by using Lemma 4, for any sequence of strategic decision among players, an acyclic relevance graph[12]. From this acyclic relevance graph, we can construct a topological ordering of the decision nodes $D_1, ..., D_N$ such that if D_i is s-reachable from D_j, then $i < j$. In the example shown in Fig. 7, the topological ordering is D_C, D_F, D_M. In the general case, the topological ordering is such that, if P_i chooses his decision rule before P_j, then $j < i$. Hence, the topological ordering corresponds to the reverse decision order.

Theorem 7. *By iteratively deriving the optimal decision rule $\delta^*(d_i|\boldsymbol{pa}_{D_i})$ for each node D_i in topological order, and every instantiation $\boldsymbol{pa}_{D_i}$ of its parents in the MAID, we obtain a strategy profile $\boldsymbol{d}^*$ that is a Nash equilibrium of $\mathcal{M}_d$.*

This theorem essentially follows from Algorithm 6.1 and Theorem 6.1 of [17]. Note that, in our scenario, under the perfect information assumption, we do not need to define an arbitrary fully-mixed strategy profile at the beginning of the algorithm. The algorithm defined by Theorem 7 is similar to the one defined by backward induction in extensive-form games. However, the MAID approach enables us to run inference on $\mathcal{M}_d$ in order to compute the expected utilities given the decision rules of every player, and to eventually find a NE in $\mathcal{O}(|\Omega|2^N)$ instead of $\mathcal{O}(|\Omega|3^{2N})$ in the extensive-form game.

---

[12] See the definition of a relevance graph in Definition 5.4 of [17].

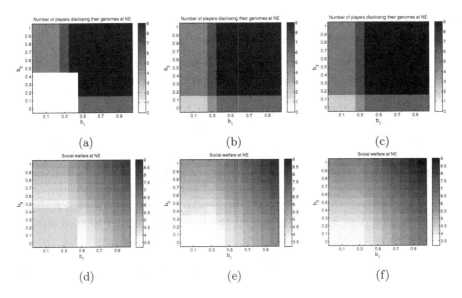

Fig. 8. Outcome of the N-player game. Number of players disclosing their genomes (first row) and social welfare (second row) at NE in the N-player game G_d. We set $b_2 = 0.4$ in (a) and (d), $b_2 = 0.6$ in (b) and (e), and $b_2 = 0.8$ in (c) and (f).

We numerically compute the NE of the N-player game G_d by using the Utah family dataset. We assume the sequence of decisions to be the following: GP1, GP2, GP3, GP4, P5, P6, C7, C8, and C9. We skip the details of the algorithm and inference, and we provide the main numerical results. We focus on 1,000 randomly chosen SNPs of chromosome 1,[13], and we compute the NE and resulting social welfare of the family for varying values of b_i's. We assume $b_i = b_1$ for all grandparents, $b_i = b_2$ for all parents, and $b_i = b_3$ for all children. We make b_1 and b_3 vary between 0 and 1 with granularity 0.1, and b_2 be equal to 0.4 (first column of Fig. 8), 0.6 (second column of Fig. 8) and 0.8 (third column of Fig. 8). In the first row of Fig. 8, we see the number of players who disclose their genomes at NE. In Fig. 8a, because b_2 is quite small (0.4), if b_1 and b_3 are also small (≤ 0.4), then nobody has the incentive to share his genome. If b_1 or b_3 are high enough for the grandparents and the children to share their genomes, this will automatically lead the parents to do the same because their genomic privacy will be reduced by their relatives' decision. We see this in the left strip where $b_3 \geq 0.5$ and $b_1 \leq 0.2$: Five relatives disclose their SNPs, the three children and the two parents. By increasing b_1 to 0.3, then two of the four grandparents have the incentive to share their SNPs, considering their privacy levels. We notice that when b_2 increases to 0.6 (Fig. 8b) and 0.8 (Fig. 8c), then even if b_1 and b_3 are very small, the parents' best responses are to disclose their SNPs. Then, if b_1 increases to 0.3 while $b_3 \leq 0.1$ (bottom strip), then two grandparents have

---

[13] As in Sect. 4, LD is not used as we assume the same set Ω of SNPs potentially shared by the players and targeted by the adversary.

the incentive to share their SNPs (4 players thus share them), and from $b_1 \geq 0.4$ all grandparents have the incentive to disclose their genomes.

Discussion: We conclude that, in some cases, when the perceived benefits do not clearly outweigh the genomic privacy losses, some people with the same perceived benefits might end up with different strategies at equilibrium.

Looking now at the social welfare values at NE, the most interesting finding is that the social welfare decreases between Fig. 8d and e for values of b_1 and b_3 smaller than 0.5, even though b_2 increases from 0.4 to 0.6. This is due to the privacy externalities created by the parents disclosing their SNPs, whereas grandparents and children have no incentives to do the same. Hence, misaligned incentives have a negative impact on the social welfare of a family. In future work, we intend to extend this model to altruistic players and see if this improves the global outcome. Our MAID $\mathcal{M}_d$ model can be easily adapted to take altruism into account.

We note that the proposed N-player game requires all family members to give their decisions sequentially but at a given time instant, which might not be feasible in real life, considering infants or even unborn family members. In future work, we plan to extend our current model in order to take into account the inherent dynamic nature of life.

6   Related Work

Interdependent risks in privacy have recently been demonstrated and explored in different settings. Due to their intrinsic social nature, online social networks (OSNs) are especially prone to indirect privacy risks. Mislove et al. evaluate the fraction of users in an OSN that would be sufficient in order to infer attributes of the remaining users [22]. Henne et al. study how OSN pictures uploaded by friends can reveal information about one's own location [13]. Dey et al. analyze the risk of age inference in OSNs, notably by relying on information posted by users' friends and friends-of-friends [7]. In the context of location privacy, Vratonjic et al. show how mobile users connecting to location-based services from the same IP address can indirectly compromise the location privacy of others [27]. Olteanu et al. study how users reporting co-locations with other users (e.g., on online social networks) can decrease others' location privacy [23]. In order to precisely quantify the effect of co-location information, they propose an optimal inference algorithm and two polynomial-time approximate inference algorithms. Humbert et al. propose a framework to quantify the damage to genomic privacy caused by relatives [14]. We extend this framework to study the interplay between rational agents with different motivations and utilities related to their genomic privacy, considering selfish and altruistic behaviors.

Acquisti et al. were among the first to propose an economic model for formalizing incentives and interactions between rational agents in the context of privacy [2]. More precisely, the authors rely on a game-theoretic approach in order to study the incentives and behaviors of participants in anonymity networks. Freudiger et al. analyze, by using game theory, the behavior of selfish mobile nodes that want to protect their location privacy at a minimum cost [10]. Biczók and Chia tackle, by using a game-theoretic framework, the issue of inter-dependent risks caused by agents with misaligned incentives regarding their privacy in online social networks [5]. They show how negative externalities can lead to inefficient equilibria in scenarios where two users decide about the adoption of an app. Pu and Grossklags go one step further by studying large groups of users who take others' preferences into account when making their own decisions [24]. These works build upon the literature on IDS games, surveyed in [20]. We follow a similar approach for genomic privacy. In addition, precisely quantify by using real data the possible direct and indirect privacy losses with a probabilistic framework. The non-linear dependencies between players in genomic privacy are also novel compared to previous work.

7 Conclusion and Future Work

In this work, focusing on the privacy of genomic data, we have studied the strategic decisions of family members about whether to disclose their genomes and how to secure their storage on personal devices. By using a game-theoretic approach, we have modeled the interplay between family members with different incentives and have predicted their behaviors at equilibrium. First, we extensively studied a two-player game between two either selfish or altruistic family members. Then, using multi-agent influence diagrams we have extended this to an N-player game. We believe that the proposed models can help the family members choose how to protect the privacy of their genomic data while still helping medical research and benefiting from the merits of genomics. In future work, we will study games with altruistic behaviors in the N-player game.

Acknowledgments. We would like to thank Kévin Huguenin and Alexandra-Mihaela Olteanu for their helpful comments and feedback.

References

1. http://www.vox.com/2014/9/9/5975653/with-genetic-testing-i-gave-my-parents-the-gift-of-divorce-23andme
2. Acquisti, A., Dingledine, R., Syverson, P.F.: On the economics of anonymity. In: Wright, R.N. (ed.) FC 2003. LNCS, vol. 2742, pp. 84–102. Springer, Heidelberg (2003)
3. Anderson, R., Moore, T.: The economics of information security. Science **314**(5799), 610–613 (2006)
4. Anshelevich, E., Dasgupta, A., Kleinberg, J., Tardos, E., Wexler, T., Roughgarden, T.: The price of stability for network design with fair cost allocation. SIAM J. Comput. **38**(4), 1602–1623 (2008)
5. Biczók, G., Chia, P.H.: Interdependent privacy: let me share your data. In: Sadeghi, A.-R. (ed.) FC 2013. LNCS, vol. 7859, pp. 338–353. Springer, Heidelberg (2013)
6. De Cristofaro, E., Faber, S., Gasti, P., Tsudik, G.: Genodroid: are privacy-preserving genomic tests ready for prime time? In: ACM WPES (2012)

7. Dey, R., Tang, C., Ross, K., Saxena, N.: Estimating age privacy leakage in online social networks. In: IEEE INFOCOM (2012)
8. Drmanac, R., Sparks, A.B., Callow, M.J., Halpern, A.L., Burns, N.L., Kermani, B.G., Carnevali, P., Nazarenko, I., Nilsen, G.B., Yeung, G., et al.: Human genome sequencing using unchained base reads on self-assembling dna nanoarrays. Science **327**(5961), 78–81 (2010)
9. Erlich, Y., Narayanan, A.: Routes for breaching and protecting genetic privacy. Nat. Rev. Genet. **15**(6), 409–421 (2014)
10. Freudiger, J., Manshaei, M.H., Hubaux, J.-P., Parkes, D.C.: On non-cooperative location privacy: a game-theoretic analysis. In: ACM CCS (2009)
11. Grossklags, J., Johnson, B., Christin, N.: The price of uncertainty in security games. In: Moore, T., Pym, D. (eds.) Economics of Information Security and Privacy, pp. 9–32. Springer, Heidelberg (2010)
12. Gymrek, M., McGuire, A.L., Golan, D., Halperin, E., Erlich, Y.: Identifying personal genomes by surname inference. Science **339**(6117), 321–324 (2013)
13. Henne, B., Szongott, C., Smith, M.: SnapMe if you can: privacy threats of other peoples' geo-tagged media and what we can do about it. In: ACM WiSec (2013)
14. Humbert, M., Ayday, E., Hubaux, J.P., Telenti, A.: Addressing the concerns of the lacks family: quantification of kin genomic privacy. In: ACM CCS (2013)
15. Humbert, M., Ayday, E., Hubaux, J.-P., Telenti, A.: Interdependent privacy games: the case of genomics. Technical report, EPFL-REPORT-203825 (2014)
16. Humbert, M., Ayday, E., Hubaux, J.-P.,Telenti, A.: Reconciling utility with privacy in genomics. In: ACM WPES (2014)
17. Koller, D., Milch, B.: Multi-agent influence diagrams for representing and solving games. Games Econ. Behav. **45**(1), 181–221 (2003)
18. Koutsoupias, E., Papadimitriou, C.: Worst-case equilibria. In: Meinel, C., Tison, S. (eds.) STACS 1999. LNCS, vol. 1563, p. 404. Springer, Heidelberg (1999)
19. Kunreuther, H., Heal, G.: Interdependent security. J. Risk Uncertainty **26**(2–3), 231–249 (2003)
20. Laszka, A., Felegyhazi, M., Buttyán, L.: A survey of interdependent security games. CrySyS Lab Technical report No. CRYSYS-TR-2012-11-15 (2012)
21. Meier, D., Oswald, Y. A., Schmid, S., Wattenhofer, R.: On the windfall of friendship: inoculation strategies on social networks. In: ACM EC (2008)
22. Mislove, A., Viswanath, B., Gummadi, K.P., Druschel, P.: You are who you know: Inferring user profiles in online social networks. In: ACM WSDM (2010)
23. Olteanu, A.-M., Huguenin, K., Shokri, R., Hubaux, J.-P.: Quantifying the effect of co-location information on location privacy. In: De Cristofaro, E., Murdoch, S.J. (eds.) PETS 2014. LNCS, vol. 8555, pp. 184–203. Springer, Heidelberg (2014)
24. Pu, Y., Grossklags, J.: An economic model and simulation results of app adoption decisions on networks with interdependent privacy consequences. In: Poovendran, R., Saad, W. (eds.) GameSec 2014. LNCS, vol. 8840, pp. 246–265. Springer, Heidelberg (2014)
25. Suarez-Tangil, G., Tapiador, J., Peris-Lopez, P., Ribagorda, A.: Evolution, detection and analysis of malware for smart devices. IEEE Commun. Surv. Tutorials **PP**(99), 1–27 (2013)
26. Sweeney, L., Abu, A., Winn, J.: Identifying participants in the personal genome project by name. SSRN **2257732** (2013)
27. Vratonjic, N., Huguenin, K., Bindschaedler, V., Hubaux, J.-P.: How others compromise your location privacy: the case of shared public ips at hotspots. In: De Cristofaro, E., Wright, M. (eds.) PETS 2013. LNCS, vol. 7981, pp. 123–142. Springer, Heidelberg (2013)

A Short Paper on the Incentives to Share Private Information for Population Estimates

Michela Chessa[1]($\boxtimes$), Jens Grossklags[2], and Patrick Loiseau[1]

[1] EURECOM, Biot, France
{michela.chessa,patrick.loiseau}@eurecom.fr
[2] The Pennsylvania State University, State College, USA
jensg@ist.psu.edu

Abstract. Consumers are often willing to contribute their personal data for analytics projects that may create new insights into societal problems. However, consumers also have justified privacy concerns about the release of their data.

We study the trade-off between privacy concerns related to data release and the incentives to contribute to the estimation of a population average of a private attribute. Consumers may decide whether to participate in the analytics project, and what level of data precision they are willing to provide. We show that setting a minimum precision level for participating users leads to a strict improvement of the estimation.

Keywords: Non-cooperative game theory · Privacy · Estimation cost · Data analytics · Incentives for participation

1 Introduction

Personal data has been heralded as the "New Oil" of the 21st Century [1]. The trend to economically utilize consumer data is facilitated by the growing importance and popularity of cloud computing services and social network sites.

On the one hand, the newly-won abundance of data allows for rigorous analytic treatment of many complex challenges related to social dynamics, public health considerations, market research, and political decision-making [2]. Many analytic results that are based on individuals' personal data can be interpreted as *public goods* with societal importance and consumers are willing to contribute their personal data for the purpose of creating new insights into societal problems. On the other hand, there are justified *privacy concerns* about the release of personal data, which may be used (or abused) for unsolicited advertisements, or social and economic discrimination (e.g., [3–5]). Individuals may also perceive the release and use of their data as an intrusion of their personal sphere [6,7], or as a violation of their dignity [8,9].

Understanding the trade-off between privacy, the quality of data analysis results, and willingness-to-participate in such projects is of current and growing importance [10]. Our research addresses this problem area. More precisely, we

© International Financial Cryptography Association 2015
R. Böhme and T. Okamoto (Eds.): FC 2015, LNCS 8975, pp. 427–436, 2015.
DOI: 10.1007/978-3-662-47854-7_25

are investigating individuals' incentives to participate in data analysis projects when they have (perceived or actual) privacy cost associated with their data release, but also derive (perceived or actual) benefits from the analysis' results.

Our research models, for example, a situation in which data about individuals is collected in a database (e.g., consumer data or clinical data). Control over the utilization of the data takes two forms: (1) individuals can authorize the access to their data at a self-chosen level of precision, and (2) individuals can decide whether they want to participate (or not), thereby authorizing (or declining) the release of their data irrespective of the level of precision. We further investigate the situation where the research analyst has flexibility to adjust requirements for data precision with the objectives that individuals are still willing to contribute to the project, and that the quality of the estimation improves.

We follow a game-theoretical approach to investigate this trade-off scenario. We conduct a rigorous analysis and derive concrete results about the precision of contributions, the quality of the population estimate, and the overall willingness to contribute to the project.

This paper is structured as follows. We review related work in Sect. 2. In Sect. 3, we develop and describe a canonical case of our model with homogeneous agents. We conduct our analysis in Sect. 4, and offer concluding remarks in Sect. 5.

2   Related Work

Research on the optimal design of experiments assumes that already the stage of data collection can be influenced by the analyst in order to improve the learning of a linear model [11,12]. In this paper, we allow the analyst to require data contributions at a certain level of precision to improve the computation of a population estimate, which is a related concept. Optimal design of experiments has been studied from the perspective of incentives [13], or with the scope of obtaining an unbiased estimator [14]. We propose to improve the design of experiments focusing on the privacy concerns of the agents.

Privacy-preserving techniques in the context of data analytics have a long history. Some recent papers propose new approaches, which allow users to protect their privacy selling aggregates of their data [15,16]. The more classical framework of ϵ-differential privacy [17,18], assumes that data are perturbed after an analysis has been conducted on unmodified inputs. That is, the analyst is considered trustworthy. In this framework, researchers have also studied the role of incentives [19–22]. Our work differs, as we assume agents to be releasing their data independently, and an untrusted data analyst which motivates perturbations of data before submission. The idea of affecting the level of precision of released personal data, adding noise in advance of data analysis has been studied in the context of privacy-preserving data-mining (see, e.g., [23,24]) and specific application scenarios such as building decision trees [25], clustering [26], and association rule mining [27]. From a mechanism design perspective, scenarios have been studied where survey subjects are assumed to potentially misreport their private values [28,29], or where buyers can access unbiased samples of private data by appropriately compensating the individuals to whom the data corresponds according to their privacy attitudes [30]. However, these works are not studied in the context of a strategic scenario. A non-cooperative approach is followed in [31], where an analyst performs a linear regression based on users' perturbed data (our starting point is a simplified version of this model). We continue this line of research by studying the benefits of restricting potential perturbation on the population estimate accuracy, and the incentives for participation in a game-theoretic framework.

Our research is also relevant to the context of the provisioning of public goods [32]. Our results show a new way of increasing the public good provision by restricting the agents' possible actions, as opposed to using monetary incentives.

3 Model Description

3.1 The Linear Model and the Estimation

Consider a set of n agents, denoted by $N = \{1, \ldots, n\}$. Each agent $i \in N$ is associated with a private variable $y_i \in \mathbb{R}$ which contains sensitive information. We suppose there exists $y_M \in \mathbb{R}$, s.t., the private variables are of the form

$$y_i = y_M + \epsilon_i, \quad \forall i \in N, \tag{1}$$

where ϵ_i are i.i.d., zero-mean random variables with finite variance $\sigma^2 < \infty$, which capture the inherent noise.

An analyst wishes to observe the private variables y_i and to estimate y_M (the mean of the y_i's). The agents, however, motivated by privacy concerns, do not allow the access to the actual values of their private variables, but to a perturbed value with added excess noise. More specifically, for each agent $i \in N$ the perturbed variable is given by $\tilde{y}_i = y_i + z_i$, where z_i is a zero-mean random variable with variance σ_i^2 chosen by her. We assume that the $\{z_i\}_{i \in N}$ are independent and are also independent of the inherent noise variables $\{\epsilon_i\}_{i \in N}$. The aggregate variance of the perturbed variable $\tilde{y}_i$ is $\sigma^2 + \sigma_i^2$. We define

$$\lambda_i = 1/(\sigma^2 + \sigma_i^2) \in [0, 1/\sigma^2], \quad \forall i \in N,$$

the *precision* of the perturbed variables $\tilde{y}_i$, i.e., the inverse of the aggregate variance. To simplify, we will assume that each agent chooses a level of precision $\lambda_i \in [0, 1/\sigma^2]$ (rather than its excess variance σ_i^2, as both are clearly equivalent, or even a more "user friendly" precision level normalized in $[0,100]$). If agent $i \in N$ has very high privacy concerns, she can choose a precision $\lambda_i = 0$. In our model, this corresponds to adding noise of infinite variance or, equivalently, this represents the fact that the agent can choose not to participate (i.e., not to allow the access to her data). Define $\boldsymbol{\lambda} = [\lambda_i]_{i \in N}$ the vector of the precisions.

The analyst has access to the perturbed variable $\tilde{y}_i$ as well as its precision λ_i, for each $i \in N$. Then, we assume that the analyst estimates the mean as

$$\hat{y}_M(\boldsymbol{\lambda}) = \frac{\sum_{i \in N} \lambda_i \tilde{y}_i}{\sum_{i \in N} \lambda_i}, \tag{2}$$

where observations with smaller variance receive a larger weight. This estimator is the standard generalized least square estimator. The estimator is unbiased, i.e., $\mathbb{E}[\hat{y}_M] = y_M$, and has variance

$$\sigma_M^2(\boldsymbol{\lambda}) = \mathbb{E}[(\hat{y}_M(\boldsymbol{\lambda}) - y_M)^2] = \frac{1}{\sum_{i \in N} \lambda_i} \in [\sigma^2/n, +\infty]. \tag{3}$$

Observe that, when $\lambda_i = 0$ for each $i \in N$, the variance (3) is infinite. This corresponds to the situation in which no agent decided to participate and then the analyst cannot estimate y_M. On the opposite end, when $\lambda_i = 1/\sigma^2$ for each $i \in N$, the analyst estimates y_M with variance σ^2/n, resulting only from the inherent noise. This corresponds to the situation in which each agent is giving data with maximum precision, i.e., no agent is perturbing her private variable. The set of precision vectors for which the estimator has a finite variance is $[0, 1/\sigma^2]^n \setminus \{(0, \ldots, 0)\}$.

3.2   The Game Γ *without* Minimal Precision Level

We next describe the interaction between the agents that results in their choices of precision levels. We assume that each agent $i \in N$ wishes to minimize a cost function $J_i : \mathbb{R}^n \to \bar{\mathbb{R}}$, s.t., for each $\boldsymbol{\lambda} \in [0, 1/\sigma^2]^n$,

$$J_i(\boldsymbol{\lambda}) = c\lambda_i^k + \sigma_M^2(\boldsymbol{\lambda}), \tag{4}$$

with $c > 0$ and $k \geq 2$. The first component is the *privacy cost*: $c\lambda_i^k$ is the cost that agent i incurs on account of the privacy violation sustained by revealing the perturbed variable. We assume it to be monomial and depending only on the precision λ_i, hence it is (strictly) convex. The second component, given by the variance of the estimation $\sigma_M^2(\boldsymbol{\lambda})$, is the *estimation cost*: it captures the cost of an inaccurate estimation of the mean. This cost translates the idea that agents benefit from an accurate estimate of the population average y_M. In that sense, the accuracy of the estimate can be seen as a public good to which each agent contributes by its choice of precision λ_i.

To describe the strategic interaction between the agents, we define the game $\Gamma = \langle N, [0, 1/\sigma^2]^n, (J_i)_{i \in N} \rangle$ with set of agents N, strategy space $[0, 1/\sigma^2]$ for each agent $i \in N$ and cost function J_i given by (4).

3.3   The Game $\Gamma(\eta)$ *with* Minimum Precision Level η

As we shall see (Sect. 4.1), the game Γ has a unique Nash equilibrium $\boldsymbol{\lambda}^*(n)$ for which the estimation cost $\sigma_M^2(\boldsymbol{\lambda}^*(n))$ is larger than the optimal cost σ^2/n due to the excess noise added by agents to protect their privacy. In this paper, we investigate a novel way in which the analyst can mitigate the effect of agents' privacy concerns and to improve the accuracy of the estimation obtained. Specifically, we propose to let the analyst fix a *minimum precision level* $\eta \in [0, 1/\sigma^2]$, which is equivalent to fixing a maximum variance for the noise agents can add to perturb their data. Obviously, it is not possible to force agents to reveal their data with a given precision (otherwise, the estimation problem would be trivial). Accordingly, we still assume that agents can choose not to participate, choosing a precision level zero. This idea of imposing a minimum precision level allows the analyst to improve the estimation using an adjustment of the initial scheme.

In the variant, we assume that agents are informed of the minimum precision level η and choose their precision λ_i in the range imposed by the analyst or decide not to participate, i.e., choose their precision in $\{0\} \cup [\eta, 1/\sigma^2]$. To analyze this variant, we define a modified game $\Gamma(\eta) = \langle N, [\{0\} \cup [\eta, 1/\sigma^2]]^n, (J_i)_{i \in N}\rangle$ (where the cost function J_i is still given by (4)), which is identical to Γ except for the restricted strategy space.

Observe that $\Gamma(0) = \Gamma$. For $\eta > 0$, the two games $\Gamma(\eta)$ and Γ differ as in the original one Γ, the agents can choose any precision, while in the variant $\Gamma(\eta)$, the participating agents have to respect a minimum precision level η. We analyze the two games Γ and $\Gamma(\eta)$ as *complete information games* between the agents, i.e., we assume that the set of agents, the action sets (in particular, when present, the value of the parameter η) and the costs are known by all the agents.

4 The Estimation

4.1 The Estimation in the Game Γ

We first analyze the estimation game Γ, in which the analyst allows the agents to choose any precision level between 0 and $1/\sigma^2$. A Nash equilibrium (in pure strategy) of this game is a strategy profile $\boldsymbol{\lambda}^* \in [0, 1/\sigma^2]^n$ satisfying

$$\lambda_i^* \in \underset{\lambda_i \in [0,1/\sigma^2]}{\arg\min} \; J_i(\lambda_i, \boldsymbol{\lambda}_{-i}^*), \quad \forall i \in N. \tag{5}$$

The game Γ with strategy space $[0, 1/\sigma^2]$ is a special case of the game in [31], where the existence of a unique Nash equilibrium is established. However, our specific assumptions allow us to characterize the equilibrium in more detail:

Theorem 1. *The game Γ has a unique Nash equilibrium $\boldsymbol{\lambda}^*(n)$ s.t. $\lambda_i^*(n) = \lambda^*(n) > 0$ for each $i \in N$, where $\lambda^*(n)$ is defined by*

$$\lambda^*(n) = \begin{cases} \left(\dfrac{1}{ckn^2}\right)^{\frac{1}{k+1}} & if \; \left(\dfrac{1}{ckn^2}\right)^{\frac{1}{k+1}} \leq 1/\sigma^2 \\ 1/\sigma^2 & otherwise . \end{cases} \tag{6}$$

Proof. Γ is a symmetric potential game, with potential function $\Phi : [0, 1/\sigma^2]^n \to \mathbb{R}$, s.t., for each $\boldsymbol{\lambda} \in [0, 1/\sigma^2]^n$

$$\Phi(\boldsymbol{\lambda}) = \sum_{j \in N} c\lambda_j^k + \sigma_M^2(\boldsymbol{\lambda}). \tag{7}$$

By the definition of a potential game, the set of Nash equilibria of Γ is contained in the set of local minima of function Φ. Function Φ has a unique local minimum

$\boldsymbol{\lambda}^* \in [0, 1/\sigma^2]^n$, which is also the unique Nash equilibrium of Γ. The optimum $\boldsymbol{\lambda}^*$ is such that for each $i \in N$, λ_i^* satisfies the following KKT conditions

$$
\begin{cases}
-\dfrac{1}{(\sum_{j \in N} \lambda_j^*)^2} + ck\lambda_i^{*k-1} - \psi_i^* + \phi_i^* = 0 \\
\psi_i^* \lambda_i^* = 0 \quad \phi_i^*(\lambda_i^* - 1/\sigma^2) = 0, \quad \psi_i^*, \phi_i^* \geq 0.
\end{cases}
\tag{8}
$$

Observe that, as a consequence of the assumption of monomial privacy cost, $\lambda_i^* > 0$ for each $i \in N$. Moreover, as Φ is a symmetric function on a symmetric domain, the only minimum has to be symmetric, i.e., $\lambda_i^* = \lambda^*$ for each $i \in N$. Then, solving the system in (8), we obtain that λ^* is given by (6). $\qquad\square$

Theorem 1 states that the unique equilibrium of Γ is symmetric and gives analytically the precision $\lambda^*(n)$ chosen by each agent at equilibrium. Remarkably, we observe that, for any n, $\lambda^*(n) > 0$, i.e., no agent decides not to participate. The equilibrium precision $\lambda^*(n)$ is a function of the number of agents n (unless n is so small that each agent provides data with maximum precision, i.e., no agent distorts her data). From (6), we derive the properties of $\lambda^*(n)$ which are summarized in the following corollary.

Corollary 1. *The equilibrium precision level $\lambda^*(n)$ satisfies*

(i) $\lambda^*(n)$ is a non-increasing function of the number of agents, and
(ii) $\lim_{n \to +\infty} \lambda^*(n) = 0$.

This corollary states that the equilibrium contribution of each agent decreases as the number of agents increases. This is a standard property in public good problems as agents choose their equilibrium contribution such that the marginal increase in the contribution cost equates the marginal decrease in the estimation cost, and the marginal effect of a single agent decreases when the number of agents increases. In the limit when n becomes very large, the contribution of each agent tends to zero (i.e., each agents adds a variance tending to infinity). The variance of the estimate of y_M obtained by the analyst at equilibrium is

$$
\sigma_M^2(\boldsymbol{\lambda}^*(n)) = \frac{1}{n\lambda^*(n)}.
\tag{9}
$$

The properties of the variance of the population estimate at equilibrium, as a function of the number of agents, are summarized in the following corollary.

Corollary 2. *The equilibrium variance of the estimate of y_M satisfies*

(i) $\sigma_M^2(\boldsymbol{\lambda}^*(n))$ is a non-increasing function of the number of agents n, and
(ii) $\sigma_M^2(\boldsymbol{\lambda}^*(n)) \sim_{n \to \infty} n^{\frac{2}{k+1}-1}$ and $\lim_{n \to +\infty} \sigma_M^2(\boldsymbol{\lambda}^*(n)) = 0$.

Proof. When $n_1 \geq n_2 > 0$, then $\lambda^*(n_1) \leq \lambda^*(n_2)$, because of Corollary 1. In particular, there exists $m > 0$ s.t., for each $n \geq m$, $\lambda^*(n) = \left(\frac{1}{ckn^2}\right)^{\frac{1}{k+1}}$, and we may write the estimation cost as

$$
\sigma_M^2(\boldsymbol{\lambda}^*(n)) = c^{\frac{1}{k+1}} k^{\frac{1}{k+1}} n^{\frac{2}{k+1}-1}.
$$

Then, $\sigma_M^2(\boldsymbol{\lambda}^*(n)) \sim_{n\to\infty} n^{\frac{2}{k+1}-1}$. For $k > 1$, this is a decreasing function which goes to zero when n goes to infinite. This proves (ii) and (i) in the case $n_1 \geq n_2 \geq m$. When $m \geq n_1 \geq n_2$, then

$$\sigma_M^2(\lambda^*(n_1)) = n_1^{-1}\sigma^2 \leq n_2^{-1}\sigma^2 \leq \sigma_M^2(\lambda^*(n_2)),$$

and when $n_1 \geq m \geq n_2$, then

$$\sigma_M^2(\lambda^*(n_1)) = n_1^{-1}\lambda^*(n_1)^{-1} \leq n_2^{-1}\left(\frac{1}{ckn_2^2}\right)^{\frac{1}{k+1}} \leq n_2^{-2}\sigma^2 = \sigma_M^2(\lambda^*(n_2)).$$

$\square$

Corollary 2-(i) shows that, for the analyst, it is always better to have a larger number of agents giving data despite the fact that, when the number of agents increases, each agent gives data with smaller precision (see Corollary 1). Part (ii) of Corollary 2 analyzes the case for a large number of agents n. Interestingly, when n gets large, the variance decreases at a rate smaller from the standard $1/n$. In particular, if k is small, the rate of decrease can be very slow. On the other end of the spectrum, if n is low (such that $\left(\frac{1}{ckn^2}\right)^{\frac{1}{k+1}} > 1/\sigma^2$), then at equilibrium every agent chooses the maximum precision level, and the estimation of y_M has minimum variance equal to σ^2/n.

4.2 The Estimation in the Game $\Gamma(\eta)$

We now move to the case where the analyst introduces a minimum precision level $\eta \in [0, 1/\sigma^2]$ with the goal of improving the accuracy of the estimate. We assume that $\lambda^*(n) \neq 1/\sigma^2$, since in that case, the estimation is already optimal with $\eta = 0$. A Nash equilibrium (in pure strategy) of the game $\Gamma(\eta)$ is a strategy profile $\boldsymbol{\lambda}^* \in \left[\{0\} \cup [\eta, 1/\sigma^2]\right]^n$ satisfying

$$\lambda_i^* \in \underset{\lambda_i \in \{0\} \cup [\eta, 1/\sigma^2]}{\arg\min} \; J_i(\lambda_i, \boldsymbol{\lambda}_{-i}^*), \quad \forall i \in N. \tag{10}$$

In the following lemma, we state that it is possible for the analyst to improve the estimation by setting a strictly positive minimum precision level.

Theorem 2. *Given Γ with equilibrium precision level $\lambda^*(n) \neq 1/\sigma^2$, there exists $\eta \in (\lambda^*(n), 1/\sigma^2]$ s.t. $\Gamma(\eta)$ has a unique Nash equilibrium $\lambda^*(n, \eta)$ and the estimation cost at equilibrium is strictly smaller, i.e., $\sigma_M^2(\lambda^*(n, \eta)) < \sigma_M^2(\lambda^*(n))$.*

Proof. The game $\Gamma(\eta)$ is a potential game, with potential function as in (7), but restricted to the smaller domain $\left[\{0\} \cup [\eta, 1/\sigma^2]\right]^n$. At first, we focus on the local minima in $[\eta, 1/\sigma^2]^n$. When $\eta = \lambda^*(n) + \epsilon$, with $\epsilon > 0$, the vector $\boldsymbol{\eta} = [\eta]_{i \in N}$ is the only local minimum of Φ on $[\eta, 1/\sigma^2]^n$. Because of the convexity of Φ, any deviation of agent $i \in N$ to a precision level in $(\eta, 1/\sigma^2]$ would make her cost function bigger. Moreover, if agent $i \in N$ deviates to 0, her cost function does not become smaller if $\lambda^*(n) \leq \left(\frac{1}{cn(n-1)}\right)^{\frac{1}{k+1}} - \epsilon$, and there always exists $\epsilon > 0$ s.t. this inequality holds and the corresponding η is a Nash equilibrium. We show that there exists ϵ s.t. $\Gamma(\eta)$ has unique equilibrium η. First, we state the following lemma.

Lemma 1. *Suppose that* $\boldsymbol{\lambda}' = (\lambda'_1, \ldots, \lambda'_n)$ *is a local minimum of the potential function* Φ *on* $\left[\{0\} \cup [\eta, 1/\sigma^2]\right]^n$, *with* $\eta \in (\lambda^*(n), \lambda^*(n-t)]$, $T = \{i \in N : \lambda'_i = 0\}$ *and* $t = |T|$. *Then,* $\boldsymbol{\lambda}'$ *is a local minimum on* $\{0\}^t \times [\eta, 1/\sigma^2]^{n-t}$ *and it is s.t.* $\lambda'_i = \lambda^*(n-t)$ *for each* $i \in N \setminus T$.

Let ϵ be s.t. $\eta = \lambda^*(n) + \epsilon \leq \lambda^*(n-t)$. Suppose that there exists a local minimum $\boldsymbol{\lambda}'$ s.t. calling $T = \{i \in N : \lambda'_i = 0\}$, then $t = |T| \geq 1$, i.e., the set of agents who are at a zero precision level is nonempty. Then, because of Lemma 1, $\lambda'_i = \lambda^*(n-t)$ for each $i \in N \setminus T$. This cannot be a Nash equilibrium. In fact,

$$\frac{1}{(n-t)\lambda^*(n-t)} > \frac{1}{(n-t+1)\lambda^*(n-t)} + c\lambda^*(n-t)^k,$$

when $k \geq 2$, meaning that if an agent in T deviates moving from the precision level 0 to the precision level $\lambda^*(n-t)$, she can strictly decrease her cost function. Then, η is the only Nash equilibrium and it is s.t. $\sigma_M^2(\boldsymbol{\lambda}^*(n, \eta)) = 1/(n\eta) < 1/(n\lambda^*(n)) = \sigma_M^2(\boldsymbol{\lambda}^*(n))$. $\qquad\square$

Theorem 1 shows that the analyst can indeed improve the quality of the estimation simply by setting a minimum precision level.

5   Concluding Remarks

In this paper, we investigated the problem of estimating population quantities with privacy-sensitive agents who add noise to their data before revealing it to the analyst. The agents choose the precision of the data they reveal to balance their privacy cost and the benefit they derive from a more accurate population estimate. We show that the analyst can improve the population estimate's accuracy by restricting the variance of the noise users can add while maintaining incentive compatibility (i.e., users are still willing to give their data with limited noise rather than dropping out). Our results posit a new way of increasing the provision of a public good (here, the population estimate's accuracy) beyond the level of voluntary contributions by restricting the agents' strategy space. This scheme is attractive by its simplicity, as it does not involve for instance transfers of money that are used in more classical schemes.

In this short paper, we proposed a first analysis of the model, making a number of restrictive assumptions. However, the interesting results we obtained make really appealing an extension of this work. In particular, we suggest three possible lines of future research. First, our model assumes a perfectly symmetric scenario. Understanding how our results can be extended to the heterogeneous agent case is, in our opinion, the first possible future work. See, for example, [33] for a distribution of privacy valuations across data types. Second, our system is very specific in the choice of the definition of the estimation cost and of the privacy cost. It would be interesting to investigate how the model behaves when assuming more abstract cost functions, to verify its applicability to more general scenarios. Third, we assumed that the analyst can collect data from n agents at no cost and we showed that the accuracy of the population estimate increases with n (although each individual contributes less). However, there could be a cost of collecting the data per agent (e.g., cost of asking for consent). A better understanding of this factor is of high practical relevance.

Acknowledgements. This work was funded by the French Government (National Research Agency, ANR) through the "Investments for the Future" Program reference # ANR-11-LABX-0031-01. We would like to thank the anonymous reviewers and Alvaro Cardenas for their helpful comments.

References

1. World Economic Forum: Personal Data: The Emergence of a New Asset Class (2011)
2. Varian, H.: Beyond big data. Business Econ. **49**(1), 27–31 (2014)
3. Acquisti, A., Fong, C.: An experiment in hiring discrimination via online social networks. Technical report SSRN: http://ssrn.com/abstract=2031979 (2013)
4. Mikians, J., Gyarmati, L., Erramilli, V., Laoutaris, N.: Crowd-assisted search for price discrimination in e-commerce: first results. In: Proceedings of the Conference on Emerging Networking Experiments and Technologies (CoNEXT), pp. 1–6 (2013)
5. Spiekermann, S., Grossklags, J., Berendt, B.: E-privacy in 2nd generation e-commerce: privacy preferences versus actual behavior. In: Proceedings of the 3rd ACM Conference on Electronic Commerce, pp. 38–47 (2001)
6. Altman, I.: The Environment and Social Behavior. Belmont. Plenum Press, New York (1975)
7. Warren, S., Brandeis, L.: The right to privacy. Harvard Law Rev. **4**, 193–220 (1890)
8. Acquisti, A., Grossklags, J.: Privacy and rationality in individual decision making. IEEE Secur. Priv. **3**(1), 26–33 (2005)
9. Westin, A.: Privacy and freedom. Atheneum, New York (1970)
10. Lane, J., Stodden, V., Bender, S., Nissenbaum, H.: Privacy, Big Data, and the Public Good: Frameworks for Engagement. Cambridge University Press, New York (2014)
11. Pukelsheim, F.: Optimal Design of Experiments, vol. 50. Society for Industrial Mathematics, Philadelphia (2006)
12. Atkinson, A., Donev, A., Tobias, R.: Optimum Experimental Designs, with SAS. Oxford University Press, New York (2007)
13. Horel, T., Ioannidis, S., Muthukrishnan, S.: Budget feasible mechanisms for experimental design. In: Pardo, A., Viola, A. (eds.) LATIN 2014. LNCS, vol. 8392, pp. 719–730. Springer, Heidelberg (2014)
14. Roth, A., Schoenebeck, G.: Conducting truthful surveys, cheaply. In: Proceedings of the 13th ACM Conference on Electronic Commerce, pp. 826–843 (2012)
15. Riederer, C., Erramilli, V., Chaintreau, A., Krishnamurthy, B., Rodriguez, P.: For sale : your data: by : you. In: Proceedings of the 10th ACM Workshop on Hot Topics in Networks, pp. 13:1–13:6 (2011)

16. Bilogrevic, I., Freudiger, J., De Cristofaro, E., Uzun, E.: What's the gist? privacy-preserving aggregation of user profiles. In: Kutyłowski, M., Vaidya, J. (eds.) ICAIS 2014, Part II. LNCS, vol. 8713, pp. 128–145. Springer, Heidelberg (2014)

17. Dwork, C.: Differential privacy. In: Bugliesi, M., Preneel, B., Sassone, V., Wegener, I. (eds.) ICALP 2006. LNCS, vol. 4052, pp. 1–12. Springer, Heidelberg (2006)

18. Kifer, D., Smith, A., Thakurta, A.: Private convex empirical risk minimization and high-dimensional regression. JMLR W&CP (Proceedings of COLT 2012) 23:25.1-25.40 (2012)

19. Ghosh, A., Roth, A.: Selling privacy at auction. In: Proceedings of the 12th ACM Conference on Electronic Commerce, pp. 199–208 (2011)

20. Nissim, K., Smorodinsky, R., Tennenholtz, M.: Approximately optimal mechanism design via differential privacy. In: Proceedings of the 3rd Innovations in Theoretical Computer Science Conference, pp. 203–213 (2012)

21. Ligett, K., Roth, A.: Take it or leave it: running a survey when privacy comes at a cost. In: Goldberg, P.W. (ed.) WINE 2012. LNCS, vol. 7695, pp. 378–391. Springer, Heidelberg (2012)

22. Ghosh, A., Ligett, K.: Privacy and coordination: computing on databases with endogenous participation. In: Proceedings of the 14th ACM Conference on Electronic Commerce, pp. 543–560 (2013)

23. Vaidya, J., Clifton, C., Zhu, Y.: Privacy Preserving Data Mining. Springer, New York (2006)

24. Domingo-Ferrer, J.: A survey of inference control methods for privacy-preserving data mining. In: Aggarwal, C., Yu, P. (eds.) Privacy-Preserving Data Mining. Advances in Database Systems, pp. 53–80. Springer, US (2008)

25. Agrawal, R., Srikant, R.: Privacy-preserving data mining. In: Proceedings of the 2000 ACM SIGMOD International Conference on Management of Data, pp. 439–450 (2000)

26. Oliveira, S., Zaiane, O.: Privacy preserving clustering by data transformation. In: Proceedings of the XVIII Simposio Brasileiro de Bancos de Dados, pp. 304–318 (2003)

27. Atallah, M., Bertino, E., Elmagarmid, A., Ibrahim, M., Verykios, V.: Disclosure limitation of sensitive rules. In: Proceedings of the Workshop on Knowledge and Data Engineering Exchange (KDEX 1999), pp. 45–52 (1999)

28. Dekel, O., Fischer, F., Procaccia, A.D.: Incentive compatible regression learning. J. Comput. Syst. Sci. **76**(8), 759–777 (2010)

29. Perote, J., Perote-Pena, J.: Strategy-proof estimators for simple regression. Math. Soc. Sci. **47**(2), 153–176 (2004)

30. Aperjis, C., Gkatzelis, V., Huberman, B.: Pricing private data. Electronic Markets (forthcoming)

31. Ioannidis, S., Loiseau, P.: Linear regression as a non-cooperative game. In: Chen, Y., Immorlica, N. (eds.) WINE 2013. LNCS, vol. 8289, pp. 277–290. Springer, Heidelberg (2013)

32. Morgan, J.: Financing public goods by means of lotteries. Rev. Econ. Stud. **67**(4), 761–784 (2000)

33. Acquisti, A., Grosslags, J.: An online survey experiment on ambiguity and privacy. Commun. Strat. **49**(4), 19–39 (2012)

Paying the Guard: An Entry-Guard-Based Payment System for Tor

Paolo Palmieri[(⊠)] and Johan Pouwelse

Parallel and Distributed Systems, Delft University of Technology,
Mekelweg 4, 2628 CD Delft, The Netherlands
p.palmieri@tudelft.nl, peer2peer@gmail.com

Abstract. When choosing the three relays that compose a circuit, Tor selects the first hop among a restricted number of relays called entry guards, pre-selected by the user himself. The reduced number of entry guards, that until recently was fixed to three, helps in mitigating the effects of several traffic analysis attacks. However, recent literature indicates that the number should be further reduced, and the time during which the user keeps the relays as guards increased. Therefore, developers of Tor recently proposed selecting only one entry guard, which is to be used by the user for all circuits and for a prolonged period of time (nine months). While this design choice was made to increase the security of the protocol, it also opens an unprecedented opportunity for a market mechanism where relays get paid for traffic by the users.

In this paper, we propose to use the entry guard as the point-of-sale: users subscribe to their entry guard of choice, and deposit an amount that will be used for paying for the circuits. From the entry guard, income is then distributed to the other relays included in circuits through an inter-relay accounting system. While the user may pay the entry guard using BitCoins, or any other anonymous payment system, the relays exchange I Owe You (IOU) certificates during communication, and settle their balances only at synchronized, later points in time. This novel deferred payment approach overcomes the weaknesses of the previously proposed Tor payment mechanisms: we separate the user's payment from the inter-relay payments, and we effectively unlink both from the chosen path, thus preserving the secrecy of the circuit.

Keywords: Tor · Anonymous payments · Economy of privacy enhancing technologies

1 Introduction

The demand for privacy and anonymity is increasing in today's Internet, and many tools of varying effectiveness are available to the users: from simple web proxies and virtual private networks (VPN), to mixnets and onion routing. These different solutions, however, share a common strategy: achieving privacy by relaying one's traffic through one or more intermediary hops, so that the

© International Financial Cryptography Association 2015
R. Böhme and T. Okamoto (Eds.): FC 2015, LNCS 8975, pp. 437–444, 2015.
DOI: 10.1007/978-3-662-47854-7_26

traffic origin is concealed, and censorship can be bypassed. A simple web proxy can hide an IP address to a casual observer and bypass trivial forms of Internet blockades, but more advanced privacy preserving technologies are needed when confronted to powerful adversaries. One such technology are anonymous routing networks, where the user's traffic is encrypted and bounced off a number of servers before reaching the intended destination, to provide both sender and receiver anonymity. While many similar designs have been proposed, such as Freenet [7] of Tarzan [13], the most widespread and popular network, currently counting millions of users, is Tor, the onion router [9]. Servers composing the Tor network are called *relays*, and the user selects among them a path (called *circuit*) through which his traffic will be relayed. A circuit is usually composed of three relays: an entry node, a middle node and an exit node, so that no single node can learn both the origin and the destination of the communication it relays. The communication itself is concealed by the user using three layers of encryption, and each relay peels off the most external layer before passing it on to the next hop, in a way similar to peeling off an onion (hence the name).

While the Tor design does not prescribe whether users should be also acting as relays, or relays should instead be powerful, dedicated server, the latter is the most common configuration [18]. With a high number of users and a relatively limited set of available relays, especially in the exit node role, the network is mostly sustained by high capacity nodes, that can cope with a high number of connections. However, the very nature of dedicated relays introduces the problem of providing the necessary incentives (whether monetary or not) to operate one. In fact, operating a relay is generally a risky and unprofitable business, and operators currently have to rely on external motivations, whether altruistic or malicious, to run one. Moreover, the high costs associated with running a good capacity node further discourage potential providers from operating a relay. This results in a low number of nodes, which adversely affects the performance and reduces the privacy properties of the network.

Despite an ongoing effort in designing an effective payment system to remunerate node operators, this still remains an open problem. The complexity of the task is due to two main factors: the need to preserve both user anonymity and circuit secrecy, which translates into the need for a privacy preserving payment mechanism; and the complex and distributed nature of the network, which requires payments from each single user to be spread through a number of different relays. In this paper, we propose a novel approach to this issue, which leverages the distributed nature of the payments between relays to provide privacy against actors not directly involved in the transactions (whether they are external observers or other relays). By doing so, we allow the use of anonymous but public record currencies such as BitCoins to be used for payments, although our design strives to remain currency-agnostic.

1.1 Contribution

We propose a system in which users pay for the Tor network by "subscribing" to an entry node. Each user deposits an amount that will be used for future traffic, and uses the entry node as starting hop in all circuits (which is consistent with the upcoming Tor protocol modifications as discussed in Sect. 2). During communication, the entry node and other relays in the circuits exchange I Owe You (IOU) certificates as promise of future payments, and all outstanding balances between relays are paid simultaneously at a later point in time, using an inter-relay payment mechanism. Both user-to-entry-node and relay-to-relay payments are currency-independent, and the payment mean can be agreed between the two parties. The novelty of our construction resides in the deferred and synchronized inter-relay payments, which enable a strong separation between the circuits used for communication and the related payments. At the same time, the user's advance payment prevents external observers from linking payments to generated traffic.

An open market for entry guards stimulates competition, and encourages operators to come out in the open and publicly advertise their services. This, in turn, enables users to make a more informed decision when selecting relays. A privacy-preserving payment mechanism provides economic sustainability to the Tor network and promotes the credibility of running Tor nodes as a legitimate business, thus leveling the playing field for operators not relying on external resources or motivations.

1.2   Related Works

The need for incentives to run relays in anonymous routing networks has been frequently discussed in the relevant literature, leading to different proposals.

The main challenge of remunerating the operators is to design a payment mechanisms that preserves the privacy properties of the underlying anonymous routing network [15]. The first payment schemes date back to the late nineties, and were proposed for the classical mix-nets [11,12]. More recently, Wendolsky proposed a volume-based accounting system for fixed-route mix cascade systems [19]. The first design to be proposed for Tor was PAR [1], in 2008. The scheme suffers, however, from a number of weaknesses [2]. A second payment mechanism is XPay [6], which aims at being a general privacy-preserving system for charging users of networked services. Similar systems have been proposed for BitTorrent [17], or designed for generic privacy enhancing technologies [5,14]. However, privacy-preserving payment schemes do not necessarily protect the user's privacy when associated to anonymous relaying networks, as demonstrated by the case of AN.ON [20].

2   Design

In the current Tor protocol, users select during the first connection a set of three relays, which will later be used as the entry nodes of all circuits created for communication for 30 to 60 days. These relays are called *entry guards*, and help mitigating several attacks, including the predecessor attack [21], selective denial of service [4], and statistical profiling. The entry guard design provides a degree of protection against attackers aiming at becoming the entry node of a particular user, and increases the start-up costs for such attackers by allowing only long-running and capable nodes to be selected as guards. However, a number of recent results indicate that the current design does not yet provide a sufficient level of protection, and may also introduce new vulnerabilities [3,10,16]. For these reasons, the Tor team recently proposed to switch to a single entry guard, to be used for a prolonged period of time (9 months) [8].

This design choice, primarily made to increase the security of the protocol, may also open the way for a payment mechanism for the Tor network. In fact, having a single point of entry to the network means that the user can pay directly the entry guard for all traffic. Our proposed mechanism takes advantage of this new setting, and relies on entry nodes as the interface to the users. Each user selects an entry node among the list of potential candidates (entry guards are a subset of the relays, based on larger bandwidth and higher reliability) and "subscribes" to it by making an initial deposit payment of an arbitrary amount. From then on, the entry node will be used as starting hop in all circuits, and will be responsible for indirectly paying the other relays used in the circuits created by the user. In order to deal with downtimes of single nodes, we assume users can connect to any node of the same *family* of the entry guard (families are publicly announced set of nodes run by the same operator). Since the entry node does not know the identity of the exit node, this happen through an inter-relay payment mechanism described in details in Sect. 2.1. The payment mechanism is based on promissory notes (a promise of future payment), called I Owe You (IOU) certificates. Relays pay to each other all the promissory notes issued during a time interval simultaneously, at a predetermined moment in time. We introduce therefore a risk element for relays holding IOUs, that we offset by introducing a reputation mechanism that affects the relays position in the public relay directory. Since we assume users to buy traffic in advance, the entry node will also keep a balance for the user.

2.1   Inter-Relay Accounting System

Once the user's payment has reached the entry node, and the circuit starts being used, non-entry relays in the circuit start relaying traffic for which they have not been paid yet. On the other hand, the entry node has availability of all funds paid by the user, including the amount owed to the following nodes in the circuit. Each node, starting from the entry node, issues to the following one the equivalent of promissory notes (or time bills), that we call I Owe You certificates. The certificates are relative to a specific interval in time, and are due to be paid at the next balance settlement deadline.

IOU Certificates. An *I Owe You certificate* (IOU) is a certificate signed by the issuing node containing information on the amount of traffic to be paid to the receiving node (the *value* of the IOU) and the date and time it was created (the IOU *timestamp*). IOUs are issued at regular intervals (agreed between the sending and receiving node), encrypted and attached to the traffic sent to the

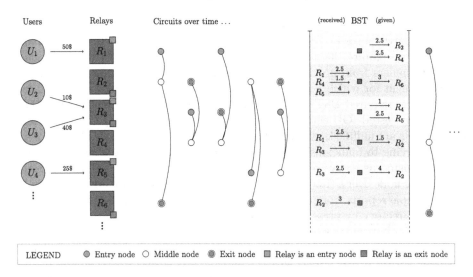

Fig. 1. The inter-relay payment mechanism. At the synchronized balance settlement (SBS) time, the relays settle their respective outstanding balances. This implies a reduced number of aggregated payments, where details of single transactions are lost. In the figure, for simplicity, we assume the same amount of traffic is exchanged in different circuits. Here, exit pricing is 1.5 times the regular traffic price.

receiving node. Each node in a circuit except the last issues IOUs to the following node, and each one except the first receives them from the previous one. As the position of a relay changes between different circuits, most relays will both issue and receive certificates during continued network operation.

Synchronized Balance Settlements. All relays participating in the network agree to predefined intervals of time during which IOUs are exchanged but not yet paid . After the end of a time interval, open balances (that is, unpaid IOUs) between relays are settled (paid) at a specific, predetermined moment in time, called *balance settlement time* (BST). The process is illustrated in Fig. 1. Aggregated, deferred payments are the pivotal property of the payment mechanism, contributing to enhance the privacy of the user and reduce risk-taking by relays. In fact, in a dynamic network, where relays are part of a significant number of circuits over a single time interval, most relays, taken two at a time, will both owe IOUs to each other. In fact, the duration of the interval itself can be calibrated to satisfy this assumption. This reduces the number of payments between relays (at most one of any two relays will pay the other), and obfuscates the actual amounts owed between relays to an external observer able to track payments.

Dealing with Fraudulent or Defaulting Nodes. A malicious entry node may perform a *hit-and-run attack* against other nodes by failing to pay to them the owed amounts at the following BST. We limit this risk by introducing a new requirement when flagging nodes as "entry guards" in Tor public relay directory. Tor already selects entry guards when a number of parameters are met:

uninterrupted up-time of the node and available bandwidth. This ensures that the node participates in a significant number of circuits for each time interval. Moreover, we require the node not to have any open (unpaid) or contested balance settlements from previous time intervals. A contested balance settlements is a settlement for which a node holding IOUs claims not to have been paid for them at the required BST. Such claim is sent to the relay directory, together with the contested IOU certificates, which are therefore publicly disclosed. Disclosed IOUs are nullified, and lose their value. Strategies to reduce the risk of an attacker trying to maliciously exclude honest nodes include allowing only nodes already trusted as entry to contest settlements, limiting the number of reports allowed per node over a time interval, and un-flagging a node already trusted only after multiple reports from different nodes. The accused node can also appeal to the relay directory by presenting proofs of payment for the contested IOUs: this is possible in particular when using public record currencies.

In order to avoid a situation in which the entry node receives a first user payment but drops the circuit without relaying any traffic, and therefore before issuing IOUs to the following node, we require nodes to issue a starting amount of IOUs to each other at circuit negotiation.

Traffic Pricing. For the purpose of this work, we assume traffic to be paid the same amount independently of the node relaying it, and we leave to future works the task of investigating a market in which relays can freely set their own price. However, the role of exit node in Tor is generally considered a risky one, and only a subset of nodes are willing to provide this service. This is due to the fact that, if a user visits questionable material behind the protection of a Tor circuit, the user himself will remain anonymous, but the material will appear to have been visited from the IP address of the exit node. For this reason, we introduce the possibility to pay a premium price to exit nodes. A potential strategy to do that is increasing the price paid to earlier nodes by the ratio of exit nodes against all nodes: if N is the set of all nodes, and $E \subset N$ is the subset composed only of nodes allowing exit traffic, we calculate the standard exit price p_E as $|N| / |E|$ times the standard price.

Time Interval Duration. The ability of the proposed system to hide the payments made for a single circuit by a single user relies on the aggregation of payments between relays imposed by the deferred balance settlements. The more relays owe to each other, the more difficult it is to reconstruct information on single transactions.

Based on the official Tor statistics[1], the average 2 million active users in the first 8 months of 2014 (number extracted from requests to the directories that clients perform periodically to update their list of relays) have been served by a number of relays that went up from more than 5000 in the first months of the year to more than 6000 in the month of August, with a slow but steady increase except for a downward movement in the month of May that reached 4500 as the lowest peak. The number of exit nodes has been stable over the same period

---

[1] https://metrics.torproject.org/.

to around 1000, while entry guards have been increasing from around 2000 to almost 2500. Considering the standard lifetime of a circuit, 10 min, we estimate that most entry and exit relays will have been in a circuit with most other relays after a time-frame of around 10 days. This estimate considers that the 10 % most popular relays are part of millions of circuits each day. We therefore suggest a conservative time interval duration of 15 to 20 days.

3   Conclusions

Anonymous routing networks are seeing an ever increasing interest, and the number of users went up from the few thousands early adopters of the first mix-nets to the millions of users of today's Tor network. Providing proper incentives to run relays is therefore crucial to ensure the sustenance and development of Tor. In this paper, we design a payment system that allows a relay to be remunerated by the users for the service provided. In particular, we propose users to select a single entry guard, and deposit to the selected node an amount that will be used for paying Tor traffic. In this system, inter-relay payments are strongly separated from both the user's payment and the circuits he creates, thanks to a mechanism based on I Owe You certificates and aggregated, deferred payments. Our design is currency-agnostic, and makes it possible to use anonymous but public-record currencies such as BitCoins while preserving the privacy properties of the system.

The market system we propose in this paper provides an effective platform for building an economy of Tor. Economic sustainability of relay operation will prompt more providers to run new relays or increase the capabilities of existing ones, which will positively impact the performance of the network. A better performing network will in turn increase the number of interested users, thus creating a virtuous circle that will allow anonymizing networks to thrive and prosper.

References

1. Androulaki, E., Raykova, M., Srivatsan, S., Stavrou, A., Bellovin, S.M.: PAR: payment for anonymous routing. In: Borisov, N., Goldberg, I. (eds.) PETS 2008. LNCS, vol. 5134, pp. 219–236. Springer, Heidelberg (2008)
2. Arnold, C., Jansen, R., Lin, Z., Parker, J.: On par for attack. Technical report, May 2009
3. Biryukov, A., Pustogarov, I., Weinmann, R.: Trawling for tor hidden services: Detection, measurement, deanonymization. In: 2013 IEEE Symposium on Security and Privacy, SP 2013. pp. 80–94. IEEE Computer Society (2013)
4. Borisov, N., Danezis, G., Mittal, P., Tabriz, P.: Denial of service or denial of security? In: Proceedings of the 2007 ACM Conference on Computer and Communications Security, CCS 2007. pp. 92–102. ACM (2007)
5. Carbunar, B., Chen, Y., Sion, R.: Tipping pennies? privately practical anonymous micropayments. IEEE Trans. Inf. Forensics Secur. 7(5), 1628–1637 (2012)
6. Chen, Y., Sion, R., Carbunar, B.: Xpay: practical anonymous payments for tor routing and other networked services. In: Al-Shaer, E., Paraboschi, S. (eds.) WPES, pp. 41–50. ACM, London (2009)

7. Clarke, I., Sandberg, O., Wiley, B., Hong, T.W.: Freenet: a distributed anonymous information storage and retrieval system. In: Federrath, H. (ed.) Designing Privacy Enhancing Technologies. LNCS, vol. 2009, pp. 46–66. Springer, Heidelberg (2001)

8. Dingledine, R., Kadianakis, N.H.A.G., Mathewson, N.: One fast guard for life (or 9 months). In: 7th Workshop on Hot Topics in Privacy Enhancing Technologies (HotPETs 2014) (2014)

9. Dingledine, R., Mathewson, N., Syverson, P.F.: Tor: The second-generation onion router. In: USENIX Security Symposium, pp. 303–320. USENIX (2004)

10. Elahi, T., Bauer, K.S., AlSabah, M., Dingledine, R., Goldberg, I.: Changing of the guards: a framework for understanding and improving entry guard selection in Tor. In: Yu, T., Borisov, N. (eds.) Proceedings of the 11th annual ACM Workshop on Privacy in the Electronic Society, WPES 2012, pp. 43–54. ACM (2012)

11. Franz, E., Jerichow, A.: A mix-mediated anonymity service and its payment. In: Quisquater, J.-J., Deswarte, Y., Meadows, C., Gollmann, D. (eds.) ESORICS 1998. LNCS, vol. 1485, pp. 313–327. Springer, Heidelberg (1998)

12. Franz, E., Jerichow, A., Wicke, G.: A payment scheme for mixes providing anonymity. In: Lamersdorf, W., Merz, M. (eds.) TREC 1998. LNCS, vol. 1402, pp. 94–108. Springer, Heidelberg (1998)

13. Freedman, M.J., Sit, E., Cates, J., Morris, R.: Introducing tarzan, a peer-to-peer anonymizing network layer. In: Druschel, P., Kaashoek, M.F., Rowstron, A. (eds.) IPTPS 2002. LNCS, vol. 2429, pp. 121–129. Springer, Heidelberg (2002)

14. Humbert, M., Manshaei, H., Hubaux, J.P.: One-to-n scrip systems for cooperative privacy-enhancing technologies. In: 2011 49th Annual Allerton Conference on Communication, Control, and Computing (Allerton), pp. 682–692 (2011)

15. Johnson, A., Jansen, R., Syverson, P.: Onions for sale: putting privacy on the market. In: Sadeghi, A.-R. (ed.) FC 2013. LNCS, vol. 7859, pp. 399–400. Springer, Heidelberg (2013)

16. Johnson, A., Wacek, C., Jansen, R., Sherr, M., Syverson, P.F.: Users get routed: traffic correlation on tor by realistic adversaries. In: Sadeghi, A., Gligor, V.D., Yung, M. (eds.) 2013 ACM SIGSAC Conference on Computer and Communications Security, CCS 2013, pp. 337–348. ACM, New York (2013)

17. Nielson, S.J., Wallach, D.S.: The bittorrent anonymity marketplace. CoRR abs/1108.2718

18. Palmieri, P., Pouwelse, J.: Key management for onion routing in a true peer to peer setting. In: Yoshida, M., Mouri, K. (eds.) IWSEC 2014. LNCS, vol. 8639, pp. 62–71. Springer, Heidelberg (2014)

19. Wendolsky, R.: A volume-based accounting system for fixed-route mix cascade systems. In: Second Privacy Enhancing Technologies Convention (PET-CON). pp. 26–33 (2008)

20. Westermann, B.: Security analysis of AN.ON's payment scheme. In: Jøsang, A., Maseng, T., Knapskog, S.J. (eds.) NordSec 2009. LNCS, vol. 5838, pp. 255–270. Springer, Heidelberg (2009)

21. Wright, M.K., Adler, M., Levine, B.N., Shields, C.: The predecessor attack: an analysis of a threat to anonymous communications systems. ACM Trans. Inf. Syst. Secur. 7(4), 489–522 (2004)

Proof-of-Work as Anonymous Micropayment: Rewarding a Tor Relay

Alex Biryukov and Ivan Pustogarov[⊠]

University of Luxembourg, Walferdange, Luxembourg
{alex.biryukov,ivan.pustogarov}@uni.lu

Abstract. In this paper we propose a new micropayments scheme which can be used to reward Tor relay operators. Tor clients do not pay Tor relays with electronic cash directly but submit proof of work shares which the relays can resubmit to a crypto-currency mining pool. Relays credit users who submit shares with tickets that can later be used to purchase improved service. Both shares and tickets when sent over Tor circuits are anonymous. The analysis of the crypto-currencies market prices shows that the proposed scheme can compensate significant part of Tor relay operator's expenses.

Keywords: Tor · Proof of work · Crypto-currency · Micropayment · Mining pools

1 Introduction

Many open peer-to-peer systems rely on volunteers donating their resources in order to achieve acceptable level of Quality of Service. E.g. in file-sharing applications, latency and failure rate depends on the number of users sharing their resources. In overlay routing systems packet latency depends on relays donating their bandwidth. Many of these systems suffer from free-riding: users consume resources without donating anything back. Obviously, this rational behavior is motivated by that users don't want to degrade their own performance. While not a P2P network in the traditional sense as there is a clear separation between clients and relays, Tor network suffers from the same free-riding problems: only limited number of relays provide decent bandwidth while the client base is rather large.

A number of incentive techniques were proposed to mitigate selfish behaviour of clients for traditional P2P systems. The bottom line of many of them is that a client is incentivized to donate the same type of resources to the network as he consumes. Unfortunately for Tor such incentives are hardly applicable: the majority of Tor users reside behind ISP NAT's and firewalls and thus cannot be checked by Tor authorities for reachability which prevents them from appearing in the Tor Consensus. In fact, for Tor it might be even undesirable to allow very

---

Full version is available at http://eprint.iacr.org/2014/1011.pdf.

© International Financial Cryptography Association 2015
R. Böhme and T. Okamoto (Eds.): FC 2015, LNCS 8975, pp. 445–455, 2015.
DOI: 10.1007/978-3-662-47854-7_27

low bandwidth nodes to become a part of the network [2] (and many clients can provide only limited bandwidth).

Another alternative would be to use a cryptocurrency and make direct payments to Tor relay operators. Many cryptocurrencies are not anonymous however which is in conflict with Tor goals. In this paper we propose a method to reward Tor relays. This method is based on crypto-currencies but does not have to involve direct payments; it rather adopts a mining-pool approach: a Tor relay implements mining pool functionality and provides Tor clients with mining jobs. When a client finds the job which meets requested difficulty, he submits the share to the Tor relay and gets priority tickets in exchange. Tor relays can either join a mining pool and delegate jobs to Tor clients or can do solo-mining and try to solve a block. The proposed approach does not require a central bank or a secure bandwidth measurement mechanism. The proposed approach may also help to solve scalability problem. The more users join the Tor network and use "paid" services, the more profitable it becomes to run a relay, and the more relays are expected to join the network.

The necessity of developing robust and secure incentives to participate in Tor was first mentioned in the Tor design paper [6]. Since then a lot of research has been done in the area [8,12,13,15,18], however in most cases they involve a central authority or require running a Tor relay. The idea described in [19] is close in spirit to our scheme (though not directly related) and suggests that a client offers a portion of his computation power in exchange for a service.

The rest of the paper is organized as follows. In Sect. 2 we describe the details of our approach. Analysis of the method is given is Sect. 3. Discussion in Sect. 4 concludes the paper.

2   Proof-of-Work as Payment for Service

2.1   Design Goals

The main objective of the proposed scheme is to compensate Tor relays for providing improved service and to encourage server operator's participation in the Tor network. In addition, we require the following properties. First, the scheme should not degrade the anonymity provided by Tor, i.e. it should not introduce new attack vectors. Second, it should not involve direct payments neither with fiat nor with crypto-currencies. The reason for this is that direct payment even with a digital currency like Bitcoin will reduce user privacy[1] and may become a strong psychological obstacle for adopting a scheme for ordinary users. Third, it should not rely on secure bandwidth measurement mechanisms. Fourth, it should not involve a central bank as in [12]. Sixth, the scheme should not require from users to run a Tor relay in order to get improved service. We analyse these properties in more detail in Sect. 3.

---

[1] An option of payment via anonymous crypto-currency like ZeroCoin [17] will be discussed in Sect. 4.

2.2   System Design

Tor users can get improved service from a Tor relay by producing proof-of-work and sending it to the relay over an anonymous Tor circuit. The relay can then forward this proof-of-work to a crypto-currency mining pool and earn coins. Users are rewarded by relay-specific *priority tickets* which can later be exchanged at the same relay for improved service (higher bandwidth or lower latencies). Tickets are issued by relays using blind signatures [3] and exchanged between users and relays over anonymous Tor circuits. Unlike [12] we do not use any bank entity and tickets are blind-signed by relays themselves.

Setup. In the setup phase a Tor relay first chooses a mining pool, the corresponding crypto-currencies and PoW algorithms (note that the relay can choose a pool which automatically switches to the most profitable currencies). Second, the relay generates a public/private key pair which will be used in generation of priority tickets (this key pair should be different from the relay's onion and identity keys). The relay then includes this information into its descriptor. A client which plans to obtain improved service chooses relays which announce compatible PoW algorithms.

Protocol 1. Ticket Purchase: Client C obtains a priority ticket from relay R

1: $C \rightarrow R$: SUBSCRIBE message.
2: $R \rightarrow C$: JOB message.
3: C : start mining a share.
4: C : If share w is found, generate random number x and its hash $H(x)$.
5: $C \rightarrow R$: w, $H(x)$.
6: R : check w, if correct pass it to the mining pool.
7: $R \leftrightarrow C$: Generate partially blind signature S over $\{H(x), d\}$, where d is an assigned by the relay timestamp, which specifies the current day.
8: C: Keeps the ticket $T_R = \{S, d, x, H(x)\}$.

Purchasing Priority Tickets. A relay will provide improved service for clients in exchange for priority tickets. Priority tickets are relay-specific which means that by default they can only be used to purchase service from the relay which issued them (see Protocol 2 if ticket exchange is required). The protocol for client C to obtain a ticket from relay R is described in Protocol 1. Prior to execution of the protocol, the client establishes an anonymous Tor circuit to the relay. All communications are carried over this circuit, including (optionally) the future client traffic. Client C registers for a new mining job with relay R and the relay sends a reply in which it specifies the PoW algorithm, difficulty per share, and data sufficient to construct a share (steps 1–2). At step 3, the client starts solving a new share. At steps 4–5 (given that the client solved the share), the client generates a random value x and its hash $H(x)$ and sends the share to R. The relay verifies the share and produces a partially blind signature S over $H(x)$ with timestamp d as an added factor according to [1]. The tuple

$T = \{S, d, x, H(x)\}$ is a priority ticket which the client can later exchange for the improved service. By reducing the granularity of the timestamp to just the current date makes all clients that got tickets on the same day undistinguishable.

Buying Improved Service. Every ticket that a client gets can be used to transmit cells with priority access during Δt seconds through the Tor relay which issued the ticket. In order to prevent double-spending, the relay should keep history of spent tickets. To limit the size of this database tickets should expire after e.g. 48 hours.

Priority Access. We suggest using Hierarchical Token Bucket Algorithm [14] to provide improved quality of service for users with priority tickets, however other options exist [7]. HTB is a simple algorithm and it is a logical step from the currently employed by Tor Token Bucket algorithm. The priority access scheme should allocate enough resources for "free" users so that people without funds to buy high-speed computers can still have reasonable QoS with Tor.

Ticket Exchange. So far in the proposed scheme a client gets tickets from the same relay R_1 for which he is working, and the tickets are valid at this relay only. Such scheme works best if the client provides proof-of-work simultaneously with sending his data over Tor. Assume now that a client pre-mined priority tickets with an intention to spend them later. He might become frustrated if at the time when he decides to spend them relay R_1 is off-line. In such a case relay R_1 may team with a backup relay R_2 and ask it to accept its priority tickets. R_2 can later request payment from R_1 in crypto-coins or by redirecting his clients to mine for R_2. Protocol 2 describes how priority tickets issued to client C by relay R_1 can be spent at relay R_2. When relays R_1 and R_2 are both online they synchronise their databases of spent tickets.

Protocol 2. Ticket Exchange: C gets improved service at R_2 by providing a ticket issued by R_1

Client C obtained ticket $T_{R_1} = \{S_1, d, x, H(x)\}$ from relay R_1. R_2 is a backup relay for R_1

1: $C \rightarrow R_2 : T_{R_1}$
2: R_2 : verify signature S_1 and timestamp d.
3: R_2: If correct, register T_{R_1} as spent (sync this with R_1).
4: R_2 : If T_{R_1} is correct, provide priority access.
5: $R_2 \rightarrow R_1$: PAYMENT_REQUEST (Once every N served tickets).

Assume that client C has ticket $T_{R_1} = \{S_1, d, x, H(x)\}$ issued by relay R_1. The objective of the Protocol 2 is for the client to be able to get improved service from relay R_2 while preserving the following properties: (1) A colluding client and relay should not produce "free" tickets which can later be used at other relays; (2) Double spending of the same ticket at two different relays should be prevented.

"Free" tickets created by colluding client C and relay R_1 are avoided by that R_2 requests payment for each batch of N served tickets (either in crypto-coins or by delegating new mining work). We can envision that in practice relays R_1, R_2 might be run by the same operator or by two operators, who trust each other. In the second case the amount of trust can be regulated by the size of N. In case R_1 stops paying, relay R_2 will stop accepting its tickets. In order to prevent double-spending of the same ticket at relays R_1 and R_2 they should regularly synchronise their databases of spent tickets.

Mining Strategies. The operator of a Tor relay which accepts PoW shares has two possibilities. First, he can decide to do solo-mining, by making his crypto-currency address a part of JOB messages sent to clients in the hope that one of the submitted shares will also solve a block. This strategy requires significant computational power at a large number of Tor clients. Second, the Tor relay operator may decide to ask for work from a large mining pool and then delegate this work to clients. The operator then resubmits the shares found by the clients to the mining pool. Note that the mining pool requests the relay to generate a share of difficulty lower than the current block's difficulty in the hope that one share will also solve the block. The Tor relay may use the same strategy towards Tor clients: it may request to generate PoW with difficulty lower than that indicated by the mining pool in the hope that a client's PoW will also solve the mining pool's share. With this approach the Tor relay may regulate how many tickets are issued to different clients, proportional to their mining power.

Donations. Clients that just want to support Tor relays without requesting any bandwidth can submit shares without requesting anything back.

3 Analysis

3.1 Profitability

Motivation. According to the performance statistics maintained by the Tor project[2] [21], it takes roughly between 10 and 15 s to download a 5 MB file over the Tor network on average (which results in 333 KB/s). While such speeds are likely to be enough for general Web-surfing they might be frustrating for bulk file downloads, watching videos, or having a video conference [11]. The later types of traffic could be the reason why Tor clients may decide to get improved service from Tor relays. This might be especially true for Bittorrent users. Bittorrent over Tor has been problematic for both Bittorrent users and Tor relay operators: users did not get enough speed, and Tor operators are concerned that bulk file downloads consume a lot of bandwidth and thus decrease Quality of Service (QoS) for Web-surfing users.

Another reason why a Tor client would want to have higher capacity/lower delays is to improve QoS for his hidden services. The current version of Tor

---

[2] For June – September 2014.

Hidden Services suffers from high delays and low speeds [10] which significantly reduces the number of users.

Choosing Crypto-currencies. There are more than 400 different crypto-currencies nowadays [5] (however only few of them achieved noticeable market capitalisation and are less susceptible to huge fluctuations in market value towards fiat currencies). According to [4,22] the following PoW algorithms are used in existing crypto-currencies: Blake-256, Groestl, HEFTY1, JHA, Keccak, NeoScrypt, Quark, Scrypt, Scrypt-Adaptive-Nfactor, Scrypt-Jane, SHA-256, X11, X13.

Profitability of mining a digital currency obviously depends on the miner's hash-rate, price of electricity, the currency's difficulty, and its current market price. The miner's hash-rate can vary significantly depending on hardware. Table 1 shows hash-rates achievable for different algorithms on Intel Core i7-2760QM (4 cores at 2.40 GHz). The table also includes maximum revenue[3] for each algorithm for the 1st of September 2014 according to [4] (averaged over multiple observations). Electricity costs are estimated to be 11 cents per day given that max power of the CPU is 45 W. During the day we also observed short periods of time when the revenue jumped to 11 cents per day. Also note that hash rates achievable on GPU's can be an order of magnitude higher. We assume that an average user of our protocol does not use ASICs.

Table 1. Hash rates of the proof-of-work algorithms on Intel Core i7-2760QM

Hashing algorithm	Rate on Intel Core i7-2760QM	Currency	Revenue per day
Blake-256	9,6 Mh/s	Blakecoin	n/a
Groestl	1 Mh/s	Diamond	2.1
HEFTY1	128 Kh/s	Heavycoin	n/a
JHA	308 Kh/s	Jackpotcoin	2.2 cents
Keccak	5.2 Mh/s	Maxcoin	0.7 cents
Quark	300 Kh/s	CNotes	3.8 cents
Scrypt	40 Kh/s	42	0.8 cents
		Litecoin	0.65 cents
		Dogecoin	0.26 cents
Scrypt-N	20 Kh/s	Vertcoin	2.3 cents
Scrypt-Jane	360 h/s	Yacoin	n/a
SHA-256d	9.6 Mh/s	Peercoin	0.01 cents
		Bitcoin	0.008 cents
X11	360 Kh/s	Smartcoin	3.8 cents
		Darkcoin	2.5 cents
X13	104 Kh/s	Marucoin	n/a

---

[3] Revenue can be smaller when trying to exchange due to small market size.

Profit Estimation. In order to estimate[4] how much a Tor relay can earn using the proposed scheme we first make the following assumptions:

- Among 2,000,000 daily Tor clients (according to the Tor statistics), only 500,000 are real users and the rest belong to botnets [16]. I.e. only 500,000 users can mine.
- Moreover we assume that each user's session takes about 1 hour and every user is willing to mine with a hash-rate similar to that from Table 1. The later implies that clients will spend 100 % of CPU on mining during 1 hour period. If clients decide to use less fraction of their CPU, the revenue of a Tor relay will decrease proportionally.

Income of a Tor relay obviously depends on the number of users which establish their circuits through this relay. This in turn depends on the relay's consensus bandwidth. We consider the case in which the scheme motivates running a Tor Exit node (currently there are only about 1,000 Exits out of 6,000 Tor relays). The green line in Fig. 1 shows the income of an Exit relay under the assumption that each client can mine an equivalent of 3.8 cents per 24 hours of which a fraction of 1/24 is received by the relay during a 1 h session. For such a case top Tor relays (with consensus bandwidth 200,000 KB/s) can earn about 500 USD per month. A middle-tier relay with consensus bandwidth 10,000 KB/s can earn about 25 USD. The green line in Fig. 2 shows monthly incomes assuming 11 cents per client per day (in which case a top Tor relay can earn up to 1,600 USD).

Running a high-bandwidth Tor relay obviously means high costs. In order to estimate the incurred costs we assume that the rental price is: 25 EUR per month for a relay with consensus weight less than 15,000; 40 EUR for weight between 15,000 and 50,000; 70 EUR for consensus weight larger than 50,000. In addition we assume that 10 TB of traffic is included into the server's price and one has to pay 2 EUR per additional 1 TB [9]. It is important to note that we consider costs which Tor relays already have regardless whether they use the proposed rewarding scheme or not. Note also that in order to compute traffic costs of a relay we take its consensus bandwidth (which represents the relay's speed in KB/s), and assume that the relay constantly transmits with such speed which results in upper bound of traffic costs.

Costs to run an Exit relay of specific bandwidth and corresponding profitability of running such a relay (given the income produced by mining clients) are shown in Figs. 1 and 2 with blue and red lines. A Tor relay partially compensates its costs in case of 3.8 cents per day per client; when clients mine an equivalent of 11 cents per day, the relay's costs are lower than its income. Additional income can be used for the server upgrade or to provide better free services.

---

[4] These are of course very rough estimates: it's not possible to learn the current hardware of Tor users, estimate the fraction of non-botnet Tor users, the number of Tor users which would be willing to mine, and the number of new (Bittorrent over Tor) users.

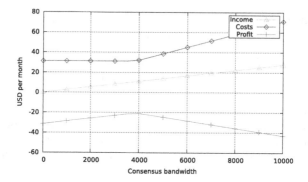

Fig. 1. Income, costs, and profit of an Exit relay in case of 3.8 cents per day per miner (Color figure online).

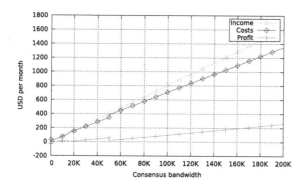

Fig. 2. Income, costs, and profit of an Exit relay in case of 11 cents per day per miner (Color figure online).

3.2 Anonymity

In this section we discuss anonymity of the proposed scheme. In Protocol 1, after client C mined a share he sends it to the corresponding Tor relay along with the hash of a random number (to be blindly signed). All communications are done over anonymous circuits, so that the Tor relay does not learn the originator of the messages (unless it is a Guard node). In addition blind signatures prevent the Tor relay from distinguishing client C from other clients. Finally shares generated by client C contain a Bitcoin address of either the Tor relay or a mining pool (the client is even not required to have a crypto-currency account), thus they don't reveal the identity of the client in spite of known attacks against Bitcoin (and hence Altcoins) anonymity [20].

A curious relay can however learn the hash rate of a client, thus it may recognize repeated connections from the same client. In order to mitigate such an attack a client is advised to randomize its hash rate. The same holds if a client decides to pre-mine bandwidth tickets from a relay.

We also note that a powerful miner can try to DoS the paid traffic of a relay, by taking all the paid traffic of a relay for itself. However such behavior is not rational, since it is economically more reasonable for such miner to just earn shares in the mining pool.

4   Conclusion and Discussion

Mining Bitcoins or Altcoins on consumer-grade hardware, GPUs or even first generation ASICs (for Bitcoin) is not profitable nowadays. This is due to the fact that the difference between the price of mined coins and the electricity costs is negative. Delegating mining (and thus electricity costs) to others while keeping the earned coins obviously makes it positive[5]. In this paper we propose a scheme to reward a Tor relay in which it subscribes for mining jobs at a crypto-currency mining pool and delegates these jobs to Tor clients (thus clients indirectly pay for electricity). The Tor relay then keeps all earned coins and in turn issues priority tickets and sends them to the clients. Priority tickets can be exchanged for the improved service at the same relay. The proposed scheme has four desirable properties: (1) it does not rely on a central bank; (2) it preserves user anonymity; (3) it removes a psychological barrier since clients do not pay directly (and thus the risk of their money being stolen is removed); (4) Tor relays are rewarded with crypto-currency coins which can be exchanged for fiat currencies and partially cover their operational expenses. A relay's income can vary significantly depending on crypto-currency exchange fluctuations, number of Tor clients willing to mine, hardware, etc. In a concrete example, assuming that clients mine for Exit relays only and if each client is able to mine an equivalent of 11 cents per day and mines 1 hour per day, an Exit relay with Consensus bandwidth 100,000 KB/s can earn 800 USD per month; such revenue should completely cover the relay's traffic costs and may allow the operator to upgrade to a more powerful server.

The proposed scheme does not decrease anonymity provided by the Tor network. All shares submitted by clients are anonymous and contain a Bitcoin address of either a Tor relay or a mining pool, thus attacks against Bitcoin anonymity become inapplicable. A curious relay can however learn a client's hash rate. Also in the case of pre-mining for later usage the relay will learn that the same user tries to go through it later on the same day.

Finally we would like to mention that if altcoins with strong anonymity (ex. Zerocoin [17]) become widely adopted it would be easy to integrate such payments into our scheme. A client will need to send together with the payment the blinded value for signing. The relay will need to broadcast a transaction with this value signed, from which the client will be able to derive the signature and thus the priority ticket.

---

[5] Our scheme thus also gives an interesting use case for the old mining gear which is otherwise obsolete. This might be the only way to buy lots of priority traffic on Tor relays.

Usages other than Tor. The proposed scheme can be used not only to reward Tor relays. The same approach can be adopted by entities which accept payments. We note, that for this scheme to be successful it may be useful to go for memory-hard proofs of work, which would have no advantage in GPU or ASICs. Scrypt function used in some alt-coins (ex. Litecoin) comes close to be adequate for this purpose, though more energy-optimal tradeoff-resistant proof-of-work functions can be designed for this task. We envisage that widespread use of such CPU mining in exchange for services may become a basis for a widely used micropayment system, which in turn becomes a strong alt-currency used by consumers (what is currently lacking in the Bitcoin universe, where the main activities are mining and hoarding of coins).

References

1. Abe, M., Okamoto, T.: Provably secure partially blind signatures. In: Bellare, M. (ed.) CRYPTO 2000. LNCS, vol. 1880, pp. 271–286. Springer, Heidelberg (2000)
2. AlSabah, M., Bauer, K., Elahi, T., Goldberg, I.: The path less travelled: overcoming Tor's Bottlenecks with traffic splitting. In: De Cristofaro, E., Wright, M. (eds.) PETS 2013. LNCS, vol. 7981, pp. 143–163. Springer, Heidelberg (2013)
3. Chaum, D.: Blind signatures for untraceable payments. In: Chaum, D., Rivest, R., Sherman, A. (eds.) Advances in Cryptology, pp. 199–203. Springer, US (1983)
4. CoinWars: Crypto Currencies (2014). http://www.coinwarz.com
5. Crypto-Currency Market Capitalizations (2014). http://coinmarketcap.com
6. Dingledine, R., Mathewson, N., Syverson, P.: Tor: the second-generation onion router. In: Proceedings of the 13th USENIX Security Symposium, August 2004
7. Evans, J.W., Filsfils, C.: Deploying IP and MPLS QoS for Multiservice Networks: Theory & Practice. Morgan Kaufmann Publishers Inc., San Francisco (2007)
8. From Onions to Shallots: Rewarding Tor Relays with TEARS (2014). http://dedis.cs.yale.edu/dissent/papers/hotpets14-tears.pdf
9. Hetzner Online Server Auction (2014). https://robot.your-server.de/order/market
10. Hidden Services need some love (2014). https://blog.torproject.org/blog/hidden-services-need-some-love
11. How much bandwidth does Skype need? (2014). https://support.skype.com/en/faq/FA1417/how-much-bandwidth-does-skype-need
12. Jansen, R., Hopper, N., Kim, Y.: Recruiting new Tor relays with BRAIDS. In: Keromytis, A.D., Shmatikov, V. (eds.) Proceedings of the 2010 ACM Conference on Computer and Communications Security (CCS 2010), ACM, October 2010
13. Jansen, R., Johnson, A., Syverson, P.: LIRA: lightweight incentivized routing for anonymity. In: Proceedings of the Network and Distributed System Security Symposium - NDSS 2013. Internet Society, February 2013
14. Linux HTB Home Page (2014). http://luxik.cdi.cz/devik/qos/htb/
15. Ghosh, M., Richardson, M., Ford, B., Jansen, R.: A TorPath to TorCoin: proof-of-bandwidth altcoins for compensating relays. In: 7th Workshop on Hot Topics in Privacy Enhancing Technologies (HotPETs), July 2014
16. Massive spike of Tor users caused by Mevade botnet (2014). http://www.net-security.org/secworld.php?id=15530
17. Miers, I., Garman, C., Green, M., Rubin, A.D.: Zerocoin: anonymous distributed e-cash from bitcoin. In: IEEE Symposium on Security and Privacy (2013)

18. "Johnny" Ngan, T.-W., Dingledine, R., Wallach, D.S.: Building incentives into Tor. In: Sion, R. (ed.) FC 2010. LNCS, vol. 6052, pp. 238–256. Springer, Heidelberg (2010)
19. Ostrovsky, R.: A proposal for internet computation commerce: how to tap the power of the web. In: Presentation at CRYPTO 1998 rump session (1998)
20. Ron, D., Shamir, A.: Quantitative analysis of the full bitcoin transaction graph. In: Sadeghi, A.-R. (ed.) FC 2013. LNCS, vol. 7859, pp. 6–24. Springer, Heidelberg (2013)
21. Tor Metrics: Performance (2014). https://metrics.torproject.org/performance.html
22. Windows GPU Miners for the More Commonly Used Crypto Algorithms (2014). http://cryptomining-blog.com/2595-windows-gpu-miners-for-the-more-commonly-used-crypto-algorithms/

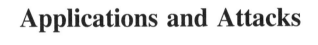

Applications and Attacks

Privacy Preserving Collaborative Filtering from Asymmetric Randomized Encoding

Yongjun Zhao$^{(\boxtimes)}$ and Sherman S.M. Chow$^{(\boxtimes)}$

Department of Information Engineering,
The Chinese University of Hong Kong,
Hong Kong, Hong Kong SAR
{zy113,sherman}@ie.cuhk.edu.hk

Abstract. Collaborative filtering is a famous technique in recommendation systems. Yet, it requires the users to reveal their preferences, which has undesirable privacy implications. Over the years, researchers have proposed many privacy-preserving collaborative filtering (PPCF) systems using very different techniques for different settings, ranging from adding noise to the data with centralized filtering, to performing secure multi-party computation. However, either privacy protection is unsatisfactory or the computation is prohibitively expensive.

In this work, we propose a decentralized PPCF system, which enables a group of users holding (cryptographically low-entropy) profile to identify other similar users in a privacy-preserving yet very efficient way, without the help of any central server. Its core component is a novel primitive which we named as *asymmetric randomized encoding* (ARE). Similar to the spirt of other cryptographic primitives, it is asymmetric in the sense that, honest party could enjoy performance boost (via precomputation) with the knowledge of a profile, whilst adversary aiming to recover the hidden profile can only launch dictionary attack against each encoded profile. Thanks to the simple design of ARE, our solution is very efficient, which is demonstrated by our performance evaluation. Besides PPCF, we believe that ARE will find further applications which require a balance between privacy and efficiency.

Keywords: Asymmetric randomized encoding · Privacy-preserving collaborative filtering · Recommendation system · Peer-to-peer network

1 Introduction

Collaborative filtering [42] (CF) is a widely used data mining technique in recommendation systems. People can obtain highly personalized and accurate recommendations for item of interest such as books, movies, *etc.* based on their past consumption activities (or *user-profile* in the rest of the paper), such as

Sherman Chow— is supported by the Early Career Scheme and the Early Career Award of the Research Grants Council, Hong Kong SAR (CUHK 439713), and Direct Grant (4055018) of the Chinese University of Hong Kong.

© International Financial Cryptography Association 2015
R. Böhme and T. Okamoto (Eds.): FC 2015, LNCS 8975, pp. 459–477, 2015.
DOI: 10.1007/978-3-662-47854-7_28

rating a movie or buying certain commodity. With the widespread of different online communities, and people's willingness to share experiences and opinions, CF is getting more popular. It also becomes increasingly important in our daily life as it brings better user-experience to customers and larger revenue to service providers.

However, the win-win benefits brought by CF come at the price of risking user privacy in various ways. For example, service providers might have the incentive to secretly sell user-profile to other parties, or they might unintentionally leak such information to public. The latter case actually happened, when Netflix released a dataset containing about 500,000 anonymous users' movie rating profile for more than 17,000 movies in an open competition for the best CF algorithm [43]. About two years later, Narayanan *et al.* [31] broke the anonymization of Netflix database by leveraging some limited auxiliary information of the users.

In the light of privacy breach [31], *privacy-preserving collaborative filtering* (PPCF) is moving towards untrusted server setting [32–34] or decentralized setting [4,8,9,29,30,37], to eliminate the trust assumption on a centralized server. Unfortunately, many randomization techniques [32–34] have been shown to be insufficient to preserve privacy. On the other hand, existing secure schemes either rely on heavy cryptographic tools or rely on additional network middleware (see Sect. 2 for a detailed discussion). It is fair to say designing a practical PPCF system without additional infrastructure remains an open problem.

In this paper, we tackle this challenge by formulating and proposing a novel primitive for the core functionality required in PPCF that only uses relatively lightweight cryptographic primitives. Most CF systems make use of user-to-user similarity for identification of similar users. Users can then exchange their profiles by themselves through a peer-to-peer (P2P) network and eventually generate recommendation themselves. The key insight of our design philosophy is that, an honest user comes with a user profile to search for similar users, while an adversary may not be motivated to just target a specific user. We thus put our attention to devise an encoding mechanism for the user profiles, such that honest users can efficiently identify similar users, while the best an adversary can do is to launch a dictionary attack per each participated user.

1.1   Our Contributions

Firstly, we design a specialized cryptographic tool called *asymmetric randomized encoding* (ARE) that enables highly efficient privacy-preserving filtering. An ARE scheme $\mathsf{ARE} = (\mathcal{P}, \mathcal{E}, \mathcal{T})$ is a tuple of three polynomial time algorithms, where $\mathcal{P}$ is the parameter generation algorithm, $\mathcal{E}$ is the encoding algorithm, and $\mathcal{T}$ is the test algorithm. Encoding algorithm $\mathcal{E}$ takes a binary string m and public parameter P as input and outputs a succinct representation $\mathcal{E}(P, m)$ of m that only leaks enough information for efficient filtering using the test algorithm $\mathcal{T}$. The "asymmetric" nature of ARE captures the property that, any honest user could efficiently run $\mathcal{T}$ algorithm with the knowledge of m, whilst adversaries without m could not due to the asymmetry in their goals and knowledge. Its "randomized" nature provides better security than any deterministic schemes.

We define appropriate security notions for ARE, propose a very efficient realization, and prove its security in the random oracle model.

While our proposed construction is very simple, we view the major novelty of our work is the identifications of 1) what can we rely on for security in a decentralized setting (without even a public-key infrastructure), where everyone could be an honest user or an adversary, and 2) the core functionality required in supporting PPCF. We believe ARE has a broader usage other than privacy-preserving collaborative filtering. For example, community detection [22], location-based services (checking if two users are nearby) and other applications which require a balance between efficiency and privacy in matching low-entropy (in a cryptographic sense) secrets.

We then show how to easily combine this "exact filtering" tool and *locality sensitive hashing* (LSH) to support "similar user filtering", which ultimately enables a very simple PPCF protocol: after a user has identified a few "similar" users securely, she simply exchanges actual user profile in a secure channel, and then runs a collaborative filtering algorithm locally to generate recommendations. Finally, we implement our scheme and evaluate its performance. We show that our solution is very efficient for practical use.

1.2   PAKE and Privacy-Preserving Matchmaking

After formulating the PPCF problem in this way, **password-based authenticated key exchange** (PAKE) [6] appears to be useful. It enables several parties holding a shared low-entropy password to securely establish a cryptographically strong session key. The major distinctive feature of PAKE is that it can withstand online dictionary attack, *i.e.*, one interaction of the protocol can only eliminate at most one possibility from the "passwords dictionary" (*i.e.*, one candidate in the password space). The security of a PAKE is usually established by upper bounding the probability of success by any adversary (under a certain formulation of security game between a challenger and an adversary) by something similar to $\frac{k_1}{2^\lambda} + \frac{k_2}{|\mathcal{M}|}$, where k_1 and k_2 are the number of attempts (modeled by "queries" either to the challenger or to the random oracle [7]) performed by the adversary, λ is a security parameter, and $\mathcal{M}$ is the password space. We will also formulate the security of our ARE in a similar vein.

Recently, Shin and Gligor [36] proposed a matchmaking protocol with enhanced privacy features. A matchmaking protocol enables two protocol participants holding the same "wish" (which may not have high entropy) to anonymously authenticate each other when their wishes match. Their protocol is based on PAKE [6,25,26]. To see how this protocol might be potentially useful in PPCF system, we start with the assumption that all users in the system are partitioned into well-defined "interest groups" according to their user-profiles. In order to identify similar users, one could run the matchmaking protocol using the identifier of "interest group" as the "wish".

The major drawback of this approach is that the protocol is inherently interactive, as the underlying primitive PAKE is interactive. To the best of our knowledge, there exists non-interactive AKE (which may be applicable on even weak mobile devices [44]), but not non-interactive PAKE. Even worse, this approach actually requires interaction between every pair of two parties, as that is the functionality supported by the underlying protocol of Shin and Gligor. Also, to maintain a certain level of authenticity (which is not a must in the PPCF setting), this matchmaking protocol requires the existence of a semi-trusted matchmaker, who is responsible for maintaining a list of pseudonyms of all valid users (and revoking misbehaved user's pseudonym if necessary). This semi-trusted matcher itself is a potential single-point of failure, which we tried to avoid. As a result, this approach is not that appropriate for our application.

2   Related Work

2.1   Privacy-Preserving Collaborative Filtering

Server Based PPCF. To the best of our knowledge, privacy-preserving collaborative filtering was first formulated in the centralized server setting [32–34]. A typical scenario would be the following: privacy-concerned end-users want to obtain useful personalized recommendations from an untrusted service provider, but they are unwilling to compromise too much of their privacy. The service provider collects private data from different end-users and runs a centralized CF calculator to generate user-specific recommendations.

In order to protect users' privacy, the general strategy adopted in the centralized setting [32–34] is to let users perturb their data before sending it to the service provider. Various perturbative techniques have been proposed. For example, actual ratings could be randomized by noise addition [33], fake ratings could be inserted [34], and actual sensitive ratings could be suppressed (deleted) [32]. The high level idea underlying all these is that the untrusted server could only know a vague user-profile, and the noise level serves as a tunable parameter trading off recommendation accuracy for user privacy. Unfortunately, various studies [23,24,48] have shown that the basic randomization techniques are not sufficient in many practical scenarios, where an adversary may possess some auxiliary information about the target user.

To better quantify the level of privacy that could be obtained using randomized techniques, McSherry *et al.* [28] also considered the notion of differential privacy [15]. Yet the security model is slightly different since it only protects end-users' privacy against other curious users as well as outsiders, meaning that the centralized server is still trusted. It remains an interesting question on how to enable differential privacy against an untrusted centralized server.

Decentralized PPCF. Early work of P2P collaborative filtering (date back to 2002 [11]) relies on secure multi-party computation and homomorphic encryption. The most significant limitation of it (and follow-up work [1,4]) is the high overhead due to the use of computationally expensive cryptographic tools.

Recently quite a few lightweight peer-to-peer protocols [8,9,29,30,37] have been proposed for identification of similar users with different level of privacy.

Earlier approaches [8,9] require the end-users to broadcast their obfuscated profile with noise injected to find out similar users and then ask them for recommendations. The limitation of these systems is that individual profiles are essentially exposed in plaintext. Shokri *et al.* [37] addressed this problem by classifying users' profiles into two types, namely, offline and online. An online profile, being only a subset of an offline one, is stored in an untrusted server to generate recommendations. Users keep their offline profile secretly but they will communicate with other users to aggregate offline profiles distributively. Online profiles are updated periodically by synchronizing with offline profiles. This can be seen as limiting the exposure by splitting the process into two stages. Nandi *et al.* [29,30] introduced the use of non-colluding decentralized middleware to enhance privacy. In a nutshell, these works either build on a weaker privacy model or rely on additional parties.

2.2 Cryptographic Approaches

The simplest approach to identify similar users is that, every participant broadcasts her profile in plaintext in a P2P network. Upon receiving other participant's profile, user privately decides whether this profile is similar to hers or not. Thus, users could generate recommendations using collected similar profiles. Each user might want to encrypt their profile for preserving their privacy. We have different options here. If symmetric key is used, the whole network needs to share the same key, which is clearly not a good solution. If the recipients' keys are used, a large amount of ciphertexts needs to be sent, or a large amount of computation (in the order of the size of the whole network) is needed to perform broadcast encryption (not to say most broadcast encryption schemes require a setup stage and is not possible in P2P setting.) The final option is to encrypt their profile using their own key. But it does not allow any comparison.

A few variants of public-key encryption may look potentially useful. However, they are not designed for our specific purpose, so they are not efficient enough and may exhibit shortcomings in our application. More importantly, they cannot enforce *asymmetry* in computation times between an honest test and a malicious dictionary attack. We will elaborate one by one below. To this end, we believe new ideas are needed to develop the "right" cryptographic primitive for PPCF.

Probabilistic Public-Key Encryption with Equality Test (PKEET). PKEET [46] allows anyone to test whether two ciphertexts c_1, c_2 (possibly generated using different public keys) are encrypting the same message. Although it is primarily targeted for searchable encryption and encrypted data partition, PKEET appears to satisfy our functional requirement. Specifically, every user waits for the PKEET-encrypted profiles from others for comparison.

There are two major drawbacks. First, the test algorithms of all existing PKEET schemes [38,39,46] are implemented using bilinear map, which is not that computationally efficient to process a large amount of ciphertexts. Second, PKEET allows *anyone* to test if two ciphertexts come from the same possibly *unknown* message. Public nature of the test means there is nothing differentiating an adversary from honest users. On the other hand, an adversary, without any knowledge of any profile, can just grab the ciphertexts from two different users and test if they correspond to the same profile.

Public-Key Encryption with Non-interactive Opening (PKENO). In PKENO [14,16], opening refers to the decryption. PKENO allows one holding the key pair (pk, sk) to provide non-interactively to *any third party* a "proof" about a ciphertext c. Then, anyone with this proof can verify if c is indeed an encryption of a certain plaintext m under pk. For PPCF, every user can broadcast an encryption of her own profile together with a proof, then run a verification procedure locally to see if the received profiles will be opened to their own profile.

PKENO suffers from drawbacks similar to those of PKEET. The most efficient instantiation of PKENO [16] still requires eight modular exponentiations plus some other computations for verification. The non-interactive proof can be used by both honest users and adversaries. Even worse, the proofs in many instantiations [16] can actually served as decryption keys, *i.e.*, attaching the proof simply reveals the message to everyone.

Plaintext-Checkable Encryption (PCE). PCE [10] is a randomized public-key encryption scheme that allows everyone to check its plaintext, *i.e.*, without the secret key, anyone can check if c is encrypting a plaintext m.

The original work of Canard *et al.* [10] showed how to transform any probabilistic public-key encryption scheme (and possibility its generalization like identity-based encryption) into a PCE, in the random oracle model. The basic idea is that the randomness ρ used in PKE to create a ciphertext c is derived from the message m and the random bit-string r ($\rho \leftarrow \mathcal{H}(m||r), r \leftarrow \{0,1\}^{\lambda}$, for a certain security parameter λ), and r is also sent along with the ciphertext c. Given $c||r$, anyone holding the message m could then reproduce the randomness ρ and re-encrypt m to get c' herself. The remaining plaintext-check procedure is a simple equality check of $c' \overset{?}{=} c$.

Recall that our design goal is to enable an honest user with the knowledge of the hidden message (*i.e.*, the profile) to be able to perform the checking procedure faster than an adversary without a specific candidate m in mind. That appears to be not possible for their generic construction when it is instantiated by existing efficient probabilistic public-key encryption schemes such as ElGamal. In more details, the most expensive operation will be modular exponentiation, yet the exponent is unknown without the knowledge of the randomness ρ in the ciphertext, *i.e.*, the knowledge of the m does not play an important role here for possible acceleration of the checking procedure. Another important difference is that we do not require the decryption functionality supported by PCE. As a result, we could design simpler and hopefully more efficient schemes.

Deterministic Encryption (DE). Deterministic public key encryption (or DE for short), formalized by Bellare, Boldyreva, and O'Neill [5], has been a hot topic recently, as it provides an alternative when randomized encryption [20] has inherent drawbacks. DE finds its application in fast searching on encrypted data, or in scenarios where length-preserving ciphertexts are desirable.

DE can be used to realize PPCF, but apparently an offline dictionary attack of preparing DE's of all possible profiles can be launched. Standard salting helps, yet that also hinders honest users as they need to use the different salt appended with the ciphertext for trail encryption and testing. Finally, as PCE, our PPCF application does not need decryption and a simpler scheme may suffice.

Fully Homomorphic Encryption (FHE). FHE is a powerful tool that allows secure evaluation over ciphertext. Secure instantiation of FHE is not known until 2009, when Gentry published his seminal work [17]. There are improvements in efficiency [18,41], but it is still a bit far from practical for many applications.

Secure Multi-party Computation (SMC). SMC was first formalized by Yao [47] and Goldreich et al. [19], as a method for a group of mutually distrustful parties to jointly compute a function f on their private inputs. Some early work of PPCF [1,11] used SMC as the underlying tool. They suffer from a high computational overhead, and they do not support dynamic user joining/leaving.

3   Preliminaries and Definitions

Here, we briefly review some basics about collaborative filtering and LSH, develop the notations for the rest of the paper, and lastly, define our new primitive.

3.1   Collaborative Filtering

In general, collaborative filtering (CF) algorithms can be broadly classified into two types: memory-based and model-based [42]. Our system only supports memory-based CF algorithms but we briefly mention model-based ones for completeness. We note that it is a challenging open question to support efficient privacy-preserving model-based CF, for the reason we will explain shortly.

Memory-based CF relies on pairwise statistical correlation. If two users have similar rating patterns according to existing records, they are likely to have similar opinion for some other items. We denote the rating from user u for an item i by r_{ui}, the set of all ratings of user u by a vector r_u, the set of items rated by user u by S_u. There are many ways to define similarity, such as cosine similarity and Jaccard similarity. The cosine similarity of two vectors r_1 and r_2 is defined by $\mathsf{SIM}(r_1, r_2)_{\mathsf{cos}} = \frac{r_1 \cdot r_2}{\|r_1\| \cdot \|r_2\|}$. Similarly, the Jaccard similarity of two sets S_1 and S_2 is defined by $\mathsf{SIM}(S_1, S_2)_{\mathsf{Jac}} = \frac{|S_1 \cap S_2|}{|S_1 \cup S_2|}$.

Let set N be the top-k users most similar to user u and who also rated item i. Using ratings from these users, we could predict user u's rating for item i in many ways. We list two possible predictions as follows:

$$r_{ui} = \frac{1}{k} \sum_{u' \in N} r_{u'i} \text{ or } r_{ui} = \sum_{u' \in N} \frac{\mathsf{SIM}(u, u')}{\sum_{u' \in N} |\mathsf{SIM}(u, u')|} r_{u'i}$$

where $\mathsf{SIM}(u, u')$ denotes some similarity metric like cosine similarity or Jaccard similarity defined above.

Model-based CF, as the name implies, performs filtering by modelling the global structures of users' ratings, instead of maintaining memory of users' rating. Important algorithms of this type include singular value decomposition (SVD), cluster analysis, Bayesian network, *etc.* Comparing with memory-based algorithms, model-based ones in general have better prediction performance but they are more computationally expensive. Yet, these algorithms require an overview of all users' ratings, which make it challenging to preserve privacy without using heavyweight cryptographic machineries, such as FHE and SMC.

3.2 Locality Sensitive Hashing

Our system relies on locality sensitive hashing (LSH) [2] to allow individual users to identify similar users locally, which we briefly review below.

A family $\mathcal{F}$ of LSH functions operates on a collection of objects. The most interesting and important property of an LSH function is that, similar objects are more likely to be hashed to the same bucket. Formally, let $\mathsf{SIM}(x, y)$ denote some similarity metric defined on the collection of objects, an LSH family satisfies:

$$\Pr_{h \in \mathcal{F}}[h(x) = h(y)] = \mathsf{SIM}(x, y).$$

Similar to the recent PPCF systems [13,30], we consider the following LSH of Charikar [12] that is defined over cosine similarity. First, pick k random vectors, with components drawn independently from a Gaussian distribution ($\mu = 0$, $\sigma = 1$). To calculate the LSH digest of a user-profile $\boldsymbol{r}$, we need to calculate the dot product of $\boldsymbol{r}$ with each random vector $\boldsymbol{v}_i$, namely $\boldsymbol{v}_i \cdot \boldsymbol{r}$. The ith bit of the LSH digest $L(\boldsymbol{r})[i]$ is set to 1 if $\boldsymbol{v}_i \cdot \boldsymbol{r} > 0$, 0 otherwise.

3.3 Cryptographic Notations

A binary string is represented using lower case letters like x, and $|x|$ denote its length. The ith bit of x is $x[i]$ and $x[i, j]$ denotes $x[i] \ldots x[j]$ for $1 \leq i \leq j \leq |x|$. If S is a finite set then $|S|$ denotes its size and $s \xleftarrow{\$} S$ denotes picking an element uniformly at random from the set S. For $i \in \mathbb{N}$, we let $[i] = \{1, \ldots, i\}$. We denote the security parameter by $\lambda \in \mathbb{N}$ and its unary representation by 1^λ.

Algorithms are polynomial time (PT) and randomized unless otherwise indicated. By $y \xleftarrow{\$} A(x_1, \ldots; R)$ we denote running algorithm A on input $x_1, \ldots$ using randomness R, and assigning the output to y. We may omit R for brevity.

Let $\mathbb{G}$ denote a group of order p, where p is a λ bit prime number, and g is a generator of $\mathbb{G}$. If m is a binary string of length less than or equal to λ, then we use *capital letter* M to denote some *efficient mapping* of m as a group element in $\mathbb{G}$. We do not expect any special property from this map. In particular, it does not need to be a cryptographic hash. We use $\mathcal{M}$ to denote the message space.

A family of hash functions $\mathsf{H} = (\mathcal{HK}, \mathcal{H})$ is a pair of PT algorithms, the second one is deterministic. The key generation algorithm $\mathcal{HK}$ takes input 1^λ and returns a hashing key K_h. The hashing algorithm $\mathcal{H}$ takes K_h and a message m, and returns its hash $H \leftarrow \mathcal{H}(K_h, m)$. In the security proof of our scheme, all the hash functions will be modelled as random oracles [7].

3.4 Asymmetric Randomized Encoding

An asymmetric randomized encoding scheme $\mathsf{ARE} = (\mathcal{P}, \mathcal{E}, \mathcal{T})$ is a tuple of three PT algorithms. The parameter generation algorithm $\mathcal{P}(\cdot)$ takes a security parameter 1^λ as input, and returns public parameter P. The encoding algorithm $\mathcal{E}(\cdot, \cdot)$ takes the public parameter P and a binary string m as input, returns $\mathcal{E}(P, m)$ as an encoding of m. $\mathcal{T}(\cdot, \cdot, \cdot)$ is the test algorithm that takes $P, m, \mathcal{E}(P, m')$ as input, outputs a boolean value T depending on the relation of m and m'.

Recall that the message uncertainty is the only thing differentiates an attacker from an honest user. We formalize test correctness and two security requirements for an ARE scheme as follows.

Test correctness requires that it is universally possible to check whether the preimage of $\mathcal{E}(P, m')$ equals to m with overwhelming probability. Formally,

$$\Pr[\mathcal{T}(P, \mathcal{E}(P, m'), m) = \text{`True'} \mid m = m'] > 1 - \delta,$$
$$\Pr[\mathcal{T}(P, \mathcal{E}(P, m'), m) = \text{`False'} \mid m \neq m'] > 1 - \delta,$$

where δ is negligible in λ.

Privacy requires that it is difficult to recover m only given $\mathcal{E}(P, m)$. Formally, we say that ARE satisfies *privacy* if the advantage of any adversary A against privacy satisfies

$$\mathbf{Adv}_{\mathsf{ARE}, A}^{\mathsf{Privacy}} = \Pr[m' = m | m' \xleftarrow{\$} A^{\mathcal{O}_H}(P, \mathcal{E}(P, m))] \leq \frac{k}{2^\lambda} + \frac{k}{|\mathcal{M}|}$$

where $\mathcal{M}$ denotes the set of all possible m, and A is any PT adversary who has access to random oracle(s) at most k times (in total, if there are multiple ones).

Unlinkability requires that it is difficult to guess whether two encodings come from the same message or not, when the messages are unknown. Formally, unlinkability is defined via the following game. The challenger chooses a pair of distinct messages m_0 and m_1, and a bit b, uniformly at random. The adversary A has polynomially-many access to encoding oracles $\mathcal{O}_{\mathcal{E}_0}(\cdot)$ and $\mathcal{O}_{\mathcal{E}_1}(\cdot)$, which returns encodings of m_0 and m_1 respectively. A is also given an encoding of m_b, i.e., $\mathcal{E}(m_b)$. Finally, A outputs a bit b'. We say that ARE is *unlinkable* if the advantage of an adversary breaking the Unlink game, denoted by $\mathbf{Adv}_{\mathsf{ARE}, A}^{\mathsf{Unlink}}$, satisfies

$$\mathbf{Adv}_{\mathsf{ARE}, A}^{\mathsf{Unlink}} = |\Pr[b' = b | b \xleftarrow{\$} \{0, 1\}, m_0 \xleftarrow{\$} \mathcal{M}, m_1 \xleftarrow{\$} \mathcal{M} \setminus \{m_0\},$$
$$b' \xleftarrow{\$} A^{\mathcal{O}_H, \mathcal{O}_{\mathcal{E}_0}, \mathcal{O}_{\mathcal{E}_1}}(P, \mathcal{E}(P, m_b))] - \frac{1}{2}| \leq \frac{2k}{2^\lambda} + \frac{2k}{|\mathcal{M}|}$$

where $\mathcal{M}$ denotes the message space, and A is any PT adversary who queries to random oracle(s) at most k times (in total, if there are multiple ones).

Note that encodings by PKEET, or any deterministic scheme like DE, would be insecure under this definition, due to the efficient algorithm for deciding if two ciphertexts are encrypting the same plaintext.

Remark 1. In this paper, we focus on construction in the random oracle model for the sake of efficiency. Thus, our security notions defined above assume random oracle in the first place. We could have proposed the following standard model security notion: removing the random oracle and the number k represents the number of invocation of $\mathcal{E}(P, \cdot)$ by the adversary. Unfortunately, currently we do not know any standard model instantiation of ARE, and thus the security definition "based on" the random oracle is also the best we can achieve currently. It will be interesting to see a construction provably secure in the random oracle model yet the adversary's winning probability does not grow with the number of queries to the random oracle.

Remark 2. One may consider it awkward to see a constant 2 in the numerators of the inequality $\mathbf{Adv}_{\mathsf{ARE},A}^{\mathsf{Unlink}} \leq \frac{2k}{2^{\lambda}} + \frac{2k}{|\mathcal{M}|}$. However, we claim that this constant is likely to be necessary by (somewhat informally) proving the following inequality $2\mathbf{Adv}_{\mathsf{ARE},A}^{\mathsf{Privacy}} - \epsilon \leq \mathbf{Adv}_{\mathsf{ARE},A}^{\mathsf{Unlink}}$. To see why the inequality holds, considering that in the Unlink game, the adversary is given polynomially-many access to encoding oracles $\mathcal{O}_{\mathcal{E}_0}(\cdot)$ and $\mathcal{O}_{\mathcal{E}_1}(\cdot)$. The adversary can break the Unlink game by trying to guess m_0 and m_1. If she succeeds in guessing any one of them, say m_0, she could then use the test algorithm $\mathcal{T}(P, m_0, m_b)$ to successfully learn the correct bit b. The probability of guessing either m_0 or m_1 is $\Pr[\text{guessing } m_0] + \Pr[\text{guessing } m_1] - \Pr[\text{guessing } m_0 \text{ and } m_1] = 2\mathbf{Adv}_{\mathsf{ARE},A}^{\mathsf{Privacy}} - \epsilon$, where $\epsilon = \Pr[\text{guessing } m_0 \text{ and } m_1]$. Thus, the adversary gains additional $2\mathbf{Adv}_{\mathsf{ARE},A}^{\mathsf{Privacy}} - \epsilon$ probability in breaking Unlink apart from the baseline random guessing probability $\frac{1}{2}$. That is to say, the adversary could break Unlink with probability at least $\frac{1}{2} + 2\mathbf{Adv}_{\mathsf{ARE},A}^{\mathsf{Privacy}} - \epsilon$, which implies $2\mathbf{Adv}_{\mathsf{ARE},A}^{\mathsf{Privacy}} - \epsilon \leq \mathbf{Adv}_{\mathsf{ARE},A}^{\mathsf{Unlink}}$.

4   System Model

We follow the system model of Berkovsky *et al.* [8]. We assume that users are organized in a purely P2P manner [11]. Within this P2P network, users could freely contact any other users who also joined the system. Such a system could be built using existing technologies (*e.g.*, [3]).

4.1   Profile Representation and Basic System Setup

Every end-user in the system is the holder of his or her own private user-profiles. Without loss of generality, we follow the existing representation [30] of user-profiles in the form of a list of ⟨key, value⟩ pairs, where keys could represent any commodity like books, movies, or other categories of goods, and values represent the interest level to the commodity corresponding to the key. Note that it is easy to transform this ⟨key, value⟩ pair representation into simple vector representation, as long as the size of possible key set is fixed and the positions of different keys are determined.

We assume that all participants have previously agreed on a consistent encoding of user-profile (e.g., the range of interest level). Also, they have agreed to use a selected LSH function, and a specific ARE scheme. In other words, the algorithms to use and their public system parameters are fixed for all users.

We emphasize that we do not assume any trusted or semi-trusted third party to support our system (although they could be easily added to our system to support more features). In particular, all the system parameters mentioned above can be generated without using any secret keys or trapdoor. Using this setting, we eliminate any trust issue of a single point in terms of privacy and availability.

4.2   Entities and Threat Model

End-users in the system want to obtain useful information from other participants. All users broadcast a short (comparing with the potentially long user-profile) randomized "identifier", in the form of encoded LSH digest, to their neighbourhood. Looking ahead, this "identifier" only leaks just enough information for other users to check whether the underlying LSH digest is similar to theirs or not, and no more information is leaked. We will also show how to identify similar users non-interactively in the following Sect. 6.

End-users in our system do not trust each other. In particular, they are only willing to expose their profile to those who are holding similar user-profile. That is to say, from an arbitrary user u's perspective, all other users are divided into two groups: similar users and dissimilar users, and these two groups are treated differently. Every dissimilar users and their coalition is treated as an adversary in our threat model, which is interested to gather global statistics of all users.

We further assume that users are honest-but-curious. That is to say, they will not deviate from the protocol specification but they want to gain more information by analyzing protocol transcript offline. Naturally, an adversary can always prepare a "fake" profile or even inject many such profiles to the system. Authenticity of profile and sybil-resistance are out of scope of this paper and can be dealt with additional measures (e.g., [40]). Our goal is to protect against unnecessary information leakage of users. In particular, the best an adversary can do is to launch a dictionary attack per each encoded profile obtained.

5   Instantiation of ARE

5.1   Proposed Construction

The **parameter generation algorithm** $\mathcal{P}(1^\lambda)$ randomly selects a λ-bit prime p, a prime order group $\mathbb{G}$ of order p, and two independent hash functions $H_1 : \{0,1\}^* \rightarrow \mathbb{Z}_p^*$ and $H_2 : \{0,1\}^\lambda \rightarrow \{0,1\}^\lambda$. Parameter $P = (p, \mathbb{G}, H_1, H_2)$ is generated as output. Here, $\mathbb{Z}_p^*$ is just $[p]$. All users joining our system are assumed to have agreed on a set of public parameters, thus we omit P below as input for brevity.

The **encoding algorithm** $\mathcal{E}$ takes input a λ-bit message m, selects a λ-bit random string r uniformly, returns $\mathcal{E}(m) = (c_1, c_2) = (M^{H_1(r)}, H_2(m) \oplus r)$ as output, where M is some efficient mapping of m to a group element in $\mathbb{G}$.

The **test algorithm** $\mathcal{T}$ takes input m and $\mathcal{E}(m')$. It first parses $\mathcal{E}(m')$ as (c_1, c_2), then compute $r = c_2 \oplus H_2(m)$, and finally return $M^{H_1(r)} \overset{?}{=} c_1$ as output.

Parameter Generation $\mathcal{P}(1^\lambda)$
Randomly select p, group $\mathbb{G}$ of order p, and hash functions $H_1 : \{0,1\}^* \to \mathbb{Z}_p^*, H_2 : \{0,1\}^\lambda \to \{0,1\}^\lambda$. Return $P = (p, \mathbb{G}, H_1, H_2)$.

Encoding $\mathcal{E}(m)$
Randomly select $r \overset{\$}{\leftarrow} \{0,1\}^\lambda$. Map m to $M \in \mathbb{G}$. Return $(c_1, c_2) = (M^{H_1(r)}, H_2(m) \oplus r)$.

Testing $\mathcal{T}(m, \mathcal{E}(m'))$
Parse $\mathcal{E}(m')$ as (c_1, c_2). Map m to $M \in \mathbb{G}$. Compute $r = c_2 \oplus H_2(m)$. Return $M^{H_1(r)} \overset{?}{=} c_1$.

Fig. 1. Our proposed construction

5.2 Pre-computation of Honest Users

It is trivial to see that our construction satisfies test correctness. Now we show the "asymmetry" of our construction. For an honest user holding M, she could perform some precomputation [27] by preparing $\hat{M}_i = M^{2^i}$ for $i = 0, 1, \ldots, |p|-1$. Upon receiving some encoding $\mathcal{E}(m') = (c_1, c_2)$, she first recovers r by $H_2(m) \oplus c_2$. Let $R \subset [|p|]$ be the set of indices such that $r[i] = 1$. Instead of computing exponentiation $M^{H_2(r)}$ directly, she only needs to compute a few multiplications, namely $\prod_{i \in R} \hat{M}_i$, which are quite minimal.

We would like to point out that this pre-computation step does not reduce the asymptotic complexity of modulo exponentiation. Suppose the base is n-bit and the exponent is λ-bit, using this pre-computation trick the overall complexity of modulo exponentiation remains $O(\lambda c(n))$, where $c(n)$ is the complexity of multiplication. But with proper implementation, this trick could still improve upon the standard repeated squaring algorithm by some constant factor, which could make a big difference when we are dealing with big data (of many candidate profiles). To see this, notice that an honest user is only interested in filtering out similar messages. Most of the computations are raising her M up to a certain power. With the above trick, each exponentiation requires only $\lambda/2$

multiplications on average instead of λ multiplications using the repeated squaring algorithm.

On the other hand, when the adversary's goal is recovering the hidden message from a *specific* encoding or see if any two encodings actually correspond to the same message, offline dictionary attack is needed to exhaust all possibilities in the message space $\mathcal{M}$, which we will show shortly afterwards. In other words, those without a specific m in mind cannot enjoy pre-computation.

5.3   Security Proofs

The following theorem asserts that our scheme satisfies our definition of privacy.

Theorem 1. *Our scheme in Fig. 1 satisfies privacy and unlinkability (defined in Sect. 3) in the random oracle model with H_1 and H_2 being random oracles.*

Proof. The adversary A is given $\mathcal{E}(m) = (c_1, c_2) = (M^{H_1(r)}, H_2(m) \oplus r)$ where m and r are both chosen uniformly at random. Since H_1 and H_2 are both random oracles, both $M^{H_1(r)}$ and $H_2(m) \oplus r$ should be totally random from adversary's point of view, leaking no information about r and M, unless either $H_1(r)$ or $H_2(m)$ has been queried by the adversary.

As $\mathcal{E}(m) = (c_1, c_2)$ leaks no information about r and M, an adversary could only make random queries to the two random oracles $H_1(\cdot)$ and $H_2(\cdot)$. Suppose the adversary is only given k_1 and k_2 accesses to the two random oracles respectively, where k_1 and k_2 are positive integers. Then the probability that such queries collide with r and m is $P_1 = \frac{k_1}{2^\lambda}$ and $P_2 = \frac{k_2}{|\mathcal{M}|}$ respectively. By union bound, the probability that collision happens on either random oracle (which equals $\mathbf{Adv}_{ARE,A}^{Privacy}$) is

$$\mathbf{Adv}_{ARE,A}^{Privacy} = P \leq P_1 + P_2 = \frac{k_1}{2^\lambda} + \frac{k_2}{|\mathcal{M}|} \leq \frac{k}{2^\lambda} + \frac{k}{|\mathcal{M}|} \tag{1}$$

where $k = k_1 + k_2$, concluding our proof for *privacy*.

The proof for *unlinkability* is in spirit very similar to the above proof. At the very beginning of the game, the challenger secretly picks $h_0, h_1 \xleftarrow{\$} \{0,1\}^\lambda$ and sets $H_2(m_0) = h_0, H_2(m_1) = h_1$ in its internal table. For every query to either encoding oracles, or for supplying $\mathcal{E}(m_b)$ to the adversary, the challenger always responds by returning a pair of strings randomly chosen from the appropriate domain. All these are valid responses unless collision occurs. With no collision, the adversary can only have $\frac{1}{2}$ chance in guessing the bit b correctly.

Notice that from adversary's point of view, for either case of m_0 or m_1, all received encodings can be interpreted in the correct encoding format as $(M^{r_1^*}, c_2) = (M^{H_1(c_2 \oplus H_2(m))}, c_2 \oplus H_2(m) \oplus H_2(m)) = (M^{H_1(r_2^*)}, r_2^* \oplus H_2(m))$, where $r_2^* = c_2 \oplus H_2(m)$, unless the adversary has queried $H_1(c_2 \oplus H_2(m))$ before. However, $c_2 \oplus H_2(m)$ is totally random because c_2 is chosen uniformly random and the adversary do not know $H_2(m)$. As a result, the adversary could only make random queries to $H_1(\cdot)$ and $H_2(\cdot)$. If it so happened that the adversary has queried $H_2(m_0)$ or $H_2(m_1)$, she could easily distinguish $\mathcal{E}(m_0)$ from $\mathcal{E}(m_1)$ by recovering r_2^* and further querying $H_1(r_2^*)$. This happens with probability at most $\frac{2k}{|\mathcal{M}|}$. On the other hand, if the adversary has queried $H_1(c_2 \oplus h_0)$ or $H_1(c_2 \oplus h_1)$ before, then the challenger has no freedom to set r_1^* to be the hash value. This happens with probability $\frac{2k}{2^\lambda}$, where k is the number of queries made by the adversary. To conclude, such unlikely event happens with probability at most $\frac{2k}{2^\lambda} + \frac{2k}{|\mathcal{M}|}$ by union bound. Thus we have $\mathbf{Adv}_{\mathsf{ARE},A}^{\mathsf{Unlink}} \leq \frac{2k}{2^\lambda} + \frac{2k}{|\mathcal{M}|}$, which concludes our unlinkability proof.   □

5.4   Discussion

One may ask why we chose to model security using one-wayness. We note that it is impossible to achieve any security against chosen-plaintext attack (CPA) or alike formulation because we mandate the "test correctness" requirement. If an adversary is given the ability to test whether a certain encoding corresponds to a certain message, he could trivially win any form of CPA game. Similar issues have been discussed in the literature of related cryptographic primitives like PKEET and PKENO [10, 46]. Also, there is no guarantee that m would have high entropy. Thus an adversary could always launch offline-dictionary attack. However, we insist that offline-dictionary attack should be the "best-possible" attack, namely there would not be any "smarter" algorithm. This fact is captured by the right hand side of our probability guarantee in Inequality (1). We believe that we have targeted for "best possible" security in our application.

6   Privacy-Preserving Filtering

We describe our system from the perspective of a user u, from joining the system to actually obtaining useful recommendations, via the following four stages.

Preparation of User's Own Profile. User u prepares her own profile, and applies the LSH function described in Sect. 3 to obtain a k-bit digest, where k is some multiple of λ. She then chops this digest into blocks of λ-bit long strings $m_1, m_2, \ldots$ and encodes these strings to $\mathcal{E}(m_1), \mathcal{E}(m_2), \ldots$ using our ARE scheme.

Broadcasting of Encoded Profile. Every user broadcasts the encodings to their neighbourhood. This procedure is repeated periodically for informing others about one's existence. It is easy to see that a new user can join the system freely. On the other hand, a time-to-live value can be attached to expire inactive users.

Identification of Matching Profiles. Other users in the system are also sending their profiles in the network periodically, so user u may receive such packets. Upon receiving encodings from others, user u decides locally which users are similar to her. This is done by running algorithm $\mathcal{T}$ of our ARE on each block of λ-bit string. Specifically, if there are at least t such blocks are equal to her own digest, then she considers this user to be similar to her. We call the parameter t as similarity threshold, and it is completely decided by user u herself. The more identical blocks, the more similar they are.

Actual Recommendation Stage. After some time, user u should be able to compile a list of similar users with their LSH-digest, and their similarity degree. User u contacts similar users in order to exchange user profile secretly. The policy of choosing whom to contact is again totally up to user u herself. For example, she might decide to choose the top 10 similar users, or she might decide to choose 20 random similar users in order to have better diversity. After collecting enough responses from other similar users, user u runs a memory based collaborative filtering algorithm (see Sect. 3) to generate recommendations herself.

How to Contact Users Securely. There are various ways to implement the required secure channel. They might just run a Diffie-Hellman key exchange protocol; or they might decide to run a PAKE protocol with the "password" being the common bits of their LSH digest which represents their wishes.

The exact information being exchanged between similar users are also up to their own choice. They can send an obfuscated version of their profile to others.

7   Evaluation

We implement ARE using Crypto++ v5.63. The system we use for performing our time analysis is Acer Aspire V5-473G, with 8 GB memory, and Intel Core i7-4500U 1.8 GHz with Turbo Boost up to 3.0 GHz. We use the standard SHA3 hash algorithm to instantiate hash functions H_1 and H_2[1].

We measure the performance in identifying matching profiles using various parameter settings listed below, where λ refers to the security parameter and k denotes the length of LSH digest. Thus $\frac{k}{\lambda}$ is the number of blocks. For each (k, λ) combination, a fixed m is randomly chosen, and $10,000$ encoded random profiles $\mathcal{E}(m_r)$ are generated to execute $\mathcal{T}(m, \mathcal{E}(m_r))$. All the obtained figures are the averaged result of $10,000$ such executions. The times are measured in milliseconds. Note that we run the experiment using a commodity laptop with not-yet optimized code. From these figures, it is clear that our scheme is very efficient and practical.

For the choice of parameters k, λ and t, intuitively, a larger λ enlarges the size of $\mathcal{M}$, which in turn means better privacy. On the other hand, according to the property of LSH, it becomes less likely to find an exact match. To overcome this, we could choose a bigger k to reduce the probability that none of the blocks matches, at the cost of computation cost and communication overhead. Thus, we can tune our parameters for different levels of privacy, efficiency, and usability (Fig. 2).

Our system computes a long LSH digest for each profile, chops the LSH digest into blocks, and uses the number of identical blocks to detect similar profiles. This approach is somewhat different from previous schemes [12,13,30] where

---

[1] We prepend dummy strings S_1 and S_2 to the input to instantiate two hash functions. The first λ-bit output of SHA3 is picked as output, *i.e.*, $H_i(m) = \text{SHA3}(S_i \| m)[0, \ldots, \lambda - 1]$ for $i \in [1, 2]$. For $H_1(m)$, there exists a small probability that the output is larger than $p - 1$. If that occurs, we re-hash the result until it fits.

Setting	Time (ms)	Setting	Time (ms)
$\lambda = 64, k = 256$	0.2293	$\lambda = 128, k = 256$	0.2254
$\lambda = 64, k = 512$	0.4603	$\lambda = 128, k = 512$	0.4566
$\lambda = 64, k = 1024$	0.9093	$\lambda = 128, k = 1024$	0.8633
$\lambda = 64, k = 2048$	1.8152	$\lambda = 128, k = 2048$	1.6962

Fig. 2. Performance evaluation for $10,000$ profiles

similarity is measured by the number of identical bits directly. To demonstrate that our modification works reasonably well, we conducted the following additional experiment. We constructed a random Netflix user profile p consisting of 200 ratings. Each rating is chosen from a Gaussian distribution with $\mu = 3.8$ and $\sigma = 1$ (according to the statistics of Netflix dataset [21]). Ratings are rounded to the nearest integers (and confined within $\{1, \cdots, 5\}$) to fit with the Netflix rating format. Then three other Netflix profiles r_1, r_2, r_3 are randomly constructed to represent "dissimilar profile", "similar profile" and "very similar profile" compared with p. These profiles are created by adding zero-mean Gaussian noise to p with different variances ($\sigma = 0.5, 0.4, 0.3$ respectively). An 1024-bit digest for each of these four profiles is computed using the LSH algorithm described in Sect. 3.2. We calculated the number of different bits and also the number of identical blocks compared with the digest of p (block length is 64-bit). The above experiment was repeated 500 times by choosing different LSH functions to obtain the following averaged numbers. The result is summarized in Fig. 3, from which we can conclude that, while the LSH digests of r_i's are all similar to those of p, there exists a clear distinction among "dissimilar profile", "similar profile" and "very similar profile" via our block-wise comparison (see the last row).

	Dissimilar Profile r_1	Similar Profile r_2	Very Similar Profile r_3
Noise Variance	0.5	0.4	0.3
# of Different Bits	44.672	32.042	18.592
# of Identical Blocks	1.08	2.13	5.04

Fig. 3. Performance evaluation of LSH algorithm based on ARE ($k = 1024, \lambda = 64$)

8   Conclusion and Future Work

In this paper, we present *asymmetric randomized encoding*, a simple yet novel cryptographic primitive that could be used for efficient privacy-preserving filtering. We define appropriate security notion for this primitive, and provide a simple and efficient construction. We prove the security of this construction in the random oracle model and evaluate its performance. We also describe how to use this primitive to build a practical peer-to-peer privacy-preserving collaborative filtering system.

Our security notion and construction are both proposed in the random oracle model. It is also of theoretical interest to propose ARE construction in the standard model. Last but not least, our system only supports memory-based filtering. We pose it as an open problem for efficient privacy-preserving model-based collaborative filtering.

References

1. Ahmad, W., Khokhar, A.A.: An architecture for privacy preserving collaborative filtering on web portals. In: IAS, pp. 273–278. IEEE Computer Society (2007)
2. Andoni, A., Indyk, P.: Near-optimal hashing algorithms for approximate nearest neighbor in high dimensions. Commun. ACM 51(1), 117–122 (2008)
3. Androutsellis-Theotokis, S., Spinellis, D.: A survey of peer-to-peer content distribution technologies. ACM Comput. Surv. 36(4), 335–371 (2004)
4. Basu, A., Vaidya, J., Kikuchi, H., Dimitrakos, T.: Privacy-preserving collaborative filtering for the cloud. In: Lambrinoudakis, C., Rizomiliotis, P., Wlodarczyk, T.W. (eds.) CloudCom, pp. 223–230. IEEE (2011)
5. Bellare, M., Boldyreva, A., O'Neill, A.: Deterministic and efficiently searchable encryption. In: Menezes, A. (ed.) CRYPTO 2007. LNCS, vol. 4622, pp. 535–552. Springer, Heidelberg (2007)
6. Bellare, M., Pointcheval, D., Rogaway, P.: Authenticated key exchange secure against dictionary attacks. In: Preneel, B. (ed.) EUROCRYPT 2000. LNCS, vol. 1807, pp. 139–155. Springer, Heidelberg (2000)
7. Bellare, M., Rogaway, P.: Random oracles are practical: a paradigm for designing efficient protocols. In: Denning, D.E., Pyle, R., Ganesan, R., Sandhu, R.S., Ashby, V. (eds.) ACM Conference on Computer and Communications Security, pp. 62–73. ACM (1993)
8. Berkovsky, S., Eytani, Y., Kuflik, T., Ricci, F.: Enhancing privacy and preserving accuracy of a distributed collaborative filtering. In: Konstan, J.A., Riedl, J., Smyth, B. (eds.) RecSys, pp. 9–16. ACM (2007)
9. Bertier, M., Frey, D., Guerraoui, R., Kermarrec, A.-M., Leroy, V.: The Gossple anonymous social network. In: Gupta, I., Mascolo, C. (eds.) Middleware 2010. LNCS, vol. 6452, pp. 191–211. Springer, Heidelberg (2010)
10. Canard, S., Fuchsbauer, G., Gouget, A., Laguillaumie, F.: Plaintext-Checkable Encryption. In: Dunkelman, O. (ed.) CT-RSA 2012. LNCS, vol. 7178, pp. 332–348. Springer, Heidelberg (2012)
11. Canny, J.F.: Collaborative filtering with privacy. In: IEEE Symposium on Security and Privacy, pp. 45–57. IEEE Computer Society (2002)
12. Charikar, M.: Similarity estimation techniques from rounding algorithms. In: Reif, J.H. (ed.) STOC, pp. 380–388. ACM (2002)
13. Chow, R., Pathak, M.A., Wang, C.: A practical system for privacy-preserving collaborative filtering. In: Vreeken, J., Ling, C., Zaki, M.J., Siebes, A., Yu, J.X., Goethals, B., Webb, G.I., Wu, X. (eds.) ICDM Workshops, pp. 547–554. IEEE Computer Society (2012)
14. Damgård, I., Hofheinz, D., Kiltz, E., Thorbek, R.: Public-key encryption with non-interactive opening. In: Malkin, T. (ed.) CT-RSA 2008. LNCS, vol. 4964, pp. 239–255. Springer, Heidelberg (2008)

15. Dwork, C.: Differential privacy: a survey of results. In: Agrawal, M., Du, D.-Z., Duan, Z., Li, A. (eds.) TAMC 2008. LNCS, vol. 4978, pp. 1–19. Springer, Heidelberg (2008)

16. Galindo, D., Libert, B., Fischlin, M., Fuchsbauer, G., Lehmann, A., Manulis, M., Schröder, D.: Public-key encryption with non-interactive opening: new constructions and stronger definitions. In: Bernstein, D.J., Lange, T. (eds.) AFRICACRYPT 2010. LNCS, vol. 6055, pp. 333–350. Springer, Heidelberg (2010)

17. Gentry, C.: Fully homomorphic encryption using ideal lattices. In: Mitzenmacher, M. (ed.) STOC, pp. 169–178. ACM (2009)

18. Gentry, C., Halevi, S., Smart, N.P.: Fully homomorphic encryption with polylog overhead. In: Pointcheval, D., Johansson, T. (eds.) EUROCRYPT 2012. LNCS, vol. 7237, pp. 465–482. Springer, Heidelberg (2012)

19. Goldreich, O., Micali, S., Wigderson, A.: How to play any mental game or a completeness theorem for protocols with honest majority. In: Aho, A.V. (ed.) STOC, pp. 218–229. ACM (1987)

20. Goldwasser, S., Micali, S.: Probabilistic encryption. J. Comput. Syst. Sci. **28**(2), 270–299 (1984)

21. Grigorik, I.: Dissecting the Netflix Dataset - igvita.com. Last accessed on 2014–09-12

22. Hu, P., Chow, S.S.M, Lau, W.C.: Secure friend discovery via privacy-preserving and decentralized community detection. In: ICML 2014 Workshop on Learning, Security and Privacy (2014). Full version appears at http://arxiv.org/abs/1405.4951

23. Huang, Z., Du, W., Chen, B.: Deriving private information from randomized data. In: Özcan, F. (ed.) SIGMOD Conference, pp. 37–48. ACM (2005)

24. Kargupta, H., Datta, S., Wang, Q., Sivakumar, K.: On the privacy preserving properties of random data perturbation techniques. In: [45], pp. 99–106

25. Katz, J., Ostrovsky, R., Yung, M.: Efficient password-authenticated key exchange using human-memorable passwords. In: Pfitzmann, B. (ed.) EUROCRYPT 2001. LNCS, vol. 2045, pp. 475–494. Springer, Heidelberg (2001)

26. Katz, J., Ostrovsky, R., Yung, M.: Efficient and secure authenticated key exchange using weak passwords. J. ACM, **57**(1) (2009)

27. Liu, J.K., Baek, J., Zhou, J., Yang, Y., Wong, J.W.: Efficient online/offline identity-based signature for wireless sensor network. Int. J. Inf. Sec. **9**(4), 287–296 (2010)

28. McSherry, F., Mironov, I.: Differentially private recommender systems: building privacy into the netflix prize contenders. In: IV, J.F.E., Fogelman-Soulié, F., Flach, P.A., Zaki, M.J. (eds.) KDD, pp. 627–636. ACM (2009)

29. Nandi, A., Aghasaryan, A., Bouzid, M.: P3: a privacy preserving personalization middleware for recommendation-based services. In: Hot Topics in Privacy Enhancing Technologies Symposium (2011)

30. Nandi, A., Aghasaryan, A., Chhabra, I.: On the use of decentralization to enable privacy in web-scale recommendation services. In: [35], pp. 25–36

31. Narayanan, A., Shmatikov, V.: Robust de-anonymization of large sparse datasets. In: IEEE Symposium on Security and Privacy, pp. 111–125. IEEE Computer Society (2008)

32. Parra-Arnau, J., Rebollo-Monedero, D., Forné, J.: A privacy-protecting architecture for collaborative filtering via forgery and suppression of ratings. In: Garcia-Alfaro, J., Navarro-Arribas, G., Cuppens-Boulahia, N., de Capitani di Vimercati, S. (eds.) DPM 2011 and SETOP 2011. LNCS, vol. 7122, pp. 42–57. Springer, Heidelberg (2012)

33. Polat, H., Du, W.: Privacy-preserving collaborative filtering using randomized perturbation techniques. In: [45], pp. 625–628

34. Polat, H., Du, W.: Achieving private recommendations using randomized response techniques. In: Ng, W.-K., Kitsuregawa, M., Li, J., Chang, K. (eds.) PAKDD 2006. LNCS (LNAI), vol. 3918, pp. 637–646. Springer, Heidelberg (2006)

35. Sadeghi, A., Foresti, S. (eds.) Proceedings of the 12th annual ACM Workshop on Privacy in the Electronic Society, WPES 2013, Berlin, Germany, November 4, 2013. ACM (2013)

36. Shin, J.S., Gligor, V.D.: A New Privacy-Enhanced Matchmaking Protocol. IEICE Trans. **96–B**(8), 2049–2059 (2013). Preliminary version appeared at NDSS 2008

37. Shokri, R., Pedarsani, P., Theodorakopoulos, G., Hubaux, J.-P.: Preserving privacy in collaborative filtering through distributed aggregation of offline profiles. In: Bergman, L.D., Tuzhilin, A., Burke, R.D., Felfernig, A., Schmidt-Thieme, L. (eds) RecSys, pp. 157–164. ACM (2009)

38. Tang, Q.: Public key encryption schemes supporting equality test with authorisation of different granularity. IJACT **2**(4), 304–321 (2012)

39. Tang, Q.: Public key encryption supporting plaintext equality test and user-specified authorization. Secur. Commun. Netw. **5**(12), 1351–1362 (2012)

40. Tran, D.N., Li, J., Subramanian, L., Chow, S.S.M.: Optimal sybil-resilient node admission control. In: INFOCOM, pp. 3218–3226. IEEE (2011)

41. van Dijk, M., Gentry, C., Halevi, S., Vaikuntanathan, V.: Fully homomorphic encryption over the integers. In: Gilbert, H. (ed.) EUROCRYPT 2010. LNCS, vol. 6110, pp. 24–43. Springer, Heidelberg (2010)

42. Wikipedia. Collaborative Filtering (2014). http://en.wikipedia.org/wiki/Collaborative_filtering. Last accessed on 2014–09-12

43. Wikipedia. Netflix Prize (2014). http://en.wikipedia.org/wiki/Netflix_Prize. Last accessed on 2014–09-12

44. Wu, T.-S., Lin, H.-Y.: Non-interactive authenticated key agreement over the mobile communication network. MONET **18**(5), 594–599 (2013)

45. Wu, X., Tuzhilin, A., Shavlik, J. (eds.) Proceedings of the 3rd IEEE International Conference on Data Mining (ICDM 2003), 19–22 December 2003, Melbourne, Florida, USA. IEEE Computer Society (2003)

46. Yang, G., Tan, C.H., Huang, Q., Wong, D.S.: Probabilistic public key encryption with equality test. In: Pieprzyk, J. (ed.) CT-RSA 2010. LNCS, vol. 5985, pp. 119–131. Springer, Heidelberg (2010)

47. Yao, A.C.-C.: How to generate and exchange secrets (Extended Abstract). In: FOCS, pp. 162–167. IEEE Computer Society (1986)

48. Zhang, S., Ford, J., Makedon, F.: Deriving private information from randomly perturbed ratings. In: Ghosh, J., Lambert, D., Skillicorn, D.B., Srivastava, J. (eds) SDM, pp. 59–69. SIAM (2006)

Anonymous and Publicly Linkable Reputation Systems

Johannes Blömer, Jakob Juhnke$^{(\boxtimes)}$, and Christina Kolb

Department of Computer Science, University of Paderborn, Paderborn, Germany
{bloemer,jakob.juhnke,christina.kolb}@uni-paderborn.de

Abstract. We consider reputation systems where users are allowed to rate products that they purchased previously. To obtain trustworthy reputations, they are allowed to rate these products only once. As long as they do so, the users stay anonymous. Everybody is able to detect users deviating from the rate-products-only-once policy and the anonymity of such dishonest users can be revoked by a system manager. In this paper we present formal models for such reputation systems and their security. Based on group signatures we design an efficient reputation system that meets all our requirements.

Keywords: Reputation · Trust · Group signatures · Anonymity · Linkability · Verifier-local revocation · Traceability · Strong-exculpability

1 Introduction

Reputation systems are an increasingly popular tool to give providers and customers valuable information about previous transactions. To provide trustworthy, reliable, and honest ratings there is a need for anonymous reputation systems that also guarantee that customers rate products only once. To further increase trust in the system, everyone - even outsiders - should be able to verify the validity of ratings. In this paper, we propose models for secure and anonymous reputation systems and give an efficient construction of such a system.

Some of the properties for reputation systems stated above have been studied in the context of group signatures, as defined in [3] for the static and in [4] for the dynamic case. However, the concept of group signatures does not meet all the requirements for reputation systems. In particular, reputation systems do not consist of a single group of users. Rather one can think of reputation systems as a family of group signature schemes - one for each product.

Moreover, we may have providers with several products. Hence, when looking at security and anonymity group signature schemes for different products can

---

J. Blömer and C. Kolb—Partially supported by the German Research Foundation (DFG) within the Collaborative Research Centre On-The-Fly Computing (SFB 901).
J. Juhnke—Supported by the International Graduate School "Dynamic Intelligent Systems".

R. Böhme and T. Okamoto (Eds.): FC 2015, LNCS 8975, pp. 478–488, 2015.
DOI: 10.1007/978-3-662-47854-7_29

not be considered in isolation. Finally, known constructions of group signatures do not provide all properties that we need for a secure and anonymous reputation system and do not provide them simultaneously.

Our Contribution. We define models for secure and anonymous reputation systems and give a first construction of such a system based on group signature schemes. We use the terms rating and message synonymously. Our construction provides anonymity, traceability, strong-exculpability, verifier-local revocation, and public linkability. Anonymity means that signatures of honest users are indistinguishable. Traceability means that it is impossible for any set of colluding users to create ratings that can not be traced back to a user of the system. Strong-exculpability means that nobody can produce signatures on behalf of honest users. A system has verifier-local revocation, if revocation messages only have to be sent to signature verifiers, but not to individual signers. Public linkability requires that anyone can decide whether or not two ratings for the same product were created by the same user, i.e. no secret key is required to link messages. Note that public linkability implies that users can only stay anonymous as long as they rate products just once. As a remark, it is well known how to realize the described properties in the context of group signatures, although not necessarily simultaneously.

Our construction of a reputation system is based on the group signature scheme by Boneh, Boyen, and Shacham [7] (BBS) and the dynamic version of the scheme presented by Delerablée and Pointcheval [11]. These schemes already give us anonymity, traceability, and strong-exculpability. To achieve verifier-local revocation we modify a technique by [25]. With the same technique we achieve public linkability. Note that anonymity of group signatures does not imply anonymity in our reputation system. This is due to the fact that providers control the groups corresponding to several products. Hence, they may combine information for different groups to violate anonymity. To prevent this, we need a system manager that contributes a trustworthy component to each group public key. In Sect. 2 we present a formal model for reputation systems. The security of our system can be shown in the random oracle model and is based on the same assumptions as the BBS scheme [7]. The formal security model and security proofs of our system are given in the full version of this paper [5].

Related Work. Reputation systems are a popular research topic in economics and computer science, see for example [1, 10, 12, 13, 18, 19]. Although privacy, i.e. anonymity and security, i.e. unforgeability, have been identified as key properties of reputation systems, no generally accepted privacy and security definitions for reputation systems have emerged. Definitions of anonymity based on differential privacy have been proposed in [10, 12, 26]. These are restricted to special reputation functions. In [1, 20, 24] cryptography has been proposed as a methodology to achieve anonymity in reputation systems, albeit without providing detailed definitions. In contrast to this, (anonymous) group signatures have been well studied in cryptography and formal security models exist. Important techniques to design group signature schemes were first described by Ateniese et al. [2].

For the case of static groups formal definitions of security were first given by
Bellare, Micciancio and Warinschi [3], for dynamic groups by Bellare, Shi and
Zhang [4]. Both works provide frameworks to construct group signature schemes.
One of the most efficient static schemes is that of Boneh, Boyen and Shacham
(BBS) [7]. Schemes with verifier-local revocation include [8,25], linkable, though
not publicly linkable, group signature schemes include [14,17,23]. In the context
of ring signatures different definitions of linkability have been considered before,
for example in [9,15,22,27]. Our definition of public linkability is based on the
definition given in [15].

2   A Model for Reputation Systems

Our model for reputation systems is based on the model for dynamic group
signature schemes by Bellare, Shi, and Zhang [4]. Therefore, we will use the
same notation for the authorities, algorithms and security properties as in [4].
From now on the system manager will be called group manager and providers
will be called key issuers, because these are their main roles in our reputation
system.

Algorithms. A reputation system consists of one authority called the group
manager, a set of authorities called the key issuers, and a set of users. The
group manager is assumed to be honest, provides the group manager's public
key $gmpk$, and is able to trace group members. Every key issuer provides *items*
with corresponding *item*-based public keys $ipk[item]$, which will be used by the
group members to rate/vote a specific *item*. Users have unique identities $i \in \mathbb{N}$
and may become group members by registering at the group manager.

The specification of a reputation system is a tuple of polynomial-time
algorithms $\mathcal{RS} = (\text{KeyGen}_{GM}, \text{KeyGen}_{KI}, \text{KeyGen}_{U}, \text{Register}_{GM}, \text{Register}_{U},$
Join, Issue, Revoke, Sign, Verify, Link, Open). Their functionality is described
as follows.

KeyGen$_{GM}$(): This randomized algorithm is run in the setup phase by the
group manager to create the public and secret key pair $(gmpk, gmsk)$. The secret
key $gmsk$ contains elements which allow tracing of group members and the
creation of revocation tokens.

KeyGen$_{KI}$(*item*): This randomized algorithm is run by a key issuer for every
item $\in \{0,1\}^*$ he provides to obtain an *item*-based public and secret key
pair $(ipk[item], isk[item])$. The tuple $(item, ipk[item])$ is added to the public
ItemList.

KeyGen$_{U}$(*i*): This randomized algorithm is run to create the user's public and
secret key pair $(upk[i], usk[i])$. The user's public key $upk[i]$ is used during the
registration to the group, the corresponding secret key $usk[i]$ is used to create
signatures.

Register$_{GM}$(St$_{GM}$, M_{GM}), Register$_{U}$(St$_{U}$, M_{U}): These randomized interactive algorithms are run by the group manager and a user $i \in \mathbb{N}$, who wants to

become a group member. If the group manager accepts, the tuple $(i, upk[i])$ is added to the registration table reg. The input parameters of the algorithms are some state information and a message, which was received from the communicating partner. It is assumed that the user starts the interaction.

$\mathbf{Join(St}_U, M_U), \mathbf{Issue(St}_{KI}, M_{KI})$: These randomized interactive algorithms are run by a user $i \in \mathbb{N}$ and a key issuer. The input parameters of the algorithms are some state information and a message, which was received from the communicating partner. It is assumed that the user starts the interaction. The first message of the user i must contain $upk[i]$ and an $item$. If Issue accepts, the key issuer sends a personal signing key for the given $item$ $gsk[i, item]$ to the user and saves the tuple $(upk[i], gsk[i, item])$ in the identification list IL_{item}.

$\mathbf{Revoke}(gmpk, gmsk, i)$: This deterministic algorithm is run by the group manager to revoke signers in case of misuse. Revoke computes the revocation token $grt[i]$ of user i and adds it to the public revocation list $\mathcal{RL}$.

$\mathbf{Sign}(item, gmpk, ipk[item], gsk[i, item], usk[i], M)$: This randomized algorithm is run by users to create signatures for specific $items$. Given the necessary keys and a message M, Sign computes and outputs a signature σ on M under the given keys.

$\mathbf{Verify}(item, gmpk, ipk[item], \mathcal{RL}, M, \sigma)$: This deterministic algorithm can be run by any user, even by an outsider, to obtain a bit v. We say that σ is a $valid$ signature of M with respect to the given keys, iff the bit v is 1.

$\mathbf{Link}(item, gmpk, ipk[item], (M', \sigma'), (M'', \sigma''))$: This deterministic algorithm can be run by any user, even by an outsider, to obtain a bit ℓ. We call σ' and σ'' $publicly\ linkable$ signatures, iff the bit ℓ is 1.

$\mathbf{Open}(gmpk, gmsk, M, \sigma)$: This deterministic algorithm is run by the group manager to $open$ signatures. Using $gmsk$, Open outputs the identity of the signer of σ or $\mathtt{failure}$.

Figure 1 illustrates the interaction of the described parties and the algorithms involved. It is not hard to see that the number of key issuers is not important in this model: a single key issuer has the same capabilities as a colluding set of key issuers. Therefore, in all formal definitions we will only consider the case that the number of key issuers is 1. Additionally, we assume that the signing keys from the key issuer given to a user are publicly verifiable, i.e. the correctness of keys can be checked using only public parameters.

Correctness. Informally, a reputation system must satisfy the following correctness requirements:

1. honestly created signatures of non-revoked users will be accepted by the Verify algorithm,
2. honestly created signatures can be traced back to the correct signer,
3. two different signatures for the same $item$ created by a single user will be detected by the Link algorithm.

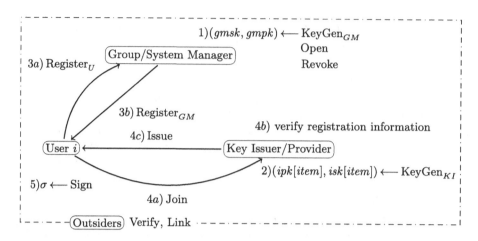

Fig. 1. Interaction of the parties within a reputation system.

Security Notions. To model the different attack capabilities of an adversary, we introduce oracles, which will be used in the definitions of security. We present only informal descriptions of these oracles, their formal definitions are given in the full version of this paper [5] and are based on [4,14]. We assume that a security experiment has run $\text{KeyGen}_{GM}()$ to obtain $(gmpk, gmsk)$, and manages the global sets $\mathcal{HU}, \mathcal{CU}, \mathcal{RU}, \mathcal{JIU}, \mathcal{GS}, reg$ and $ItemList$. Except $ItemList$ and reg all sets are only used within the formal definitions of the oracles and the security experiments. By $\mathcal{HU}$ we denote the set of honest users, by $\mathcal{CU}$ the set of corrupted users. The set $\mathcal{RU}$ contains all identities of users that currently engage in the registration protocol. The set $\mathcal{JIU}$ contains all identities of users that currently engage in the Join-Issue protocol. By $\mathcal{GS}$ we denote the set of queried signatures. All sets are assumed to be initially empty.

AddU(i): To add honest users to the group, the adversary can call this *add user* oracle. The oracle adds i to $\mathcal{HU}$ and executes the registration protocol by running Register_{GM} and Register_{U}. The oracle returns $upk[i]$ to the adversary.

AddItem($item$): An adversary can add *items* by using this *add item* oracle. The oracle then runs the KeyGen_{KI} algorithm and returns $ipk[item]$ to the adversary.

USK(i): To get the secret key $usk[i]$ of an honest user i, an adversary can call the *user secret key* oracle. Then the user i is added to $\mathcal{CU}$.

GSK($i, upk, item$): To get the secret signing key $gsk[i, item]$ of user i for a specified *item*, an adversary can call the *signing key* oracle.

RevU(i): To get the *revocation token* of user i, an adversary can call the *revoke user* oracle. The oracle runs the Revoke algorithm and returns $grt[i]$ to the adversary.

GSig($i, upk, item, M$): An adversary can use the *signing* oracle to obtain a valid signature for the message M with respect to the signing key of user i and the *item*-based public key $ipk[item]$. The queried signature is added to $\mathcal{GS}$.

SndToKI($i, item, upk[i], M_{KI}$): After corruption of user i, the adversary can use the *send to key issuer* oracle to engage in a join protocol with the key issuer. The oracle honestly runs the Issue algorithm and computes a response to M_{KI}.

SndToGM(i, M_{GM}): The *send to group manager* oracle can be used by an adversary to engage in a registration protocol with the honest group manager. The oracle honestly runs the Register$_{GM}$ algorithm and adds the user i to $\mathcal{CU}$.

WItemList($item, ipk$): An adversary can use the *write to item list* oracle to manipulate the *item* based public key of the specified *item*. If $ipk = \varepsilon$ the *item* is deleted from the list. Otherwise, the specified public key is set.

WIdentList($item, i, upk[i], gsk$): Using the *write to identification list* oracle an adversary can modify the secret signing keys of user $i \in \mathbb{N}$ for the specified *item*. If $gsk = \varepsilon$ the key information about user i is deleted from the list.

Open($item, M, \sigma$): The *opening* oracle can be used by the adversary to get the output of the Open algorithm, as long as σ was not produced by the GSig oracle.

In our reputation system we need anonymity, public linkability, traceability, and strong-exculpability. The anonymity and traceability experiments are based on [4], the public linkability experiment is based on [15], and the strong-exculpability experiment is based on [2,4,21]. Complete formal definitions of the oracles and the experiments are given in the full version of the paper [5].

The anonymity experiment $\text{Exp}_{\mathcal{A},\mathcal{RS}}^{\text{anon}-b}(k)$ asks an adversary to distinguish which of two group members signed a message for some *item*, where the identities, the message, and an *item* are chosen by the adversary. The adversary's attack capabilities are strong: it is possible to corrupt the key issuer and all but two users. These two users must be honest because otherwise the adversary could possibly link different signatures or use the revocation token of the users to determine their identities.

The public linkability experiment $\text{Exp}_{\mathcal{A},\mathcal{RS}}^{\text{publink}}(k)$ asks an adversary to output message-signature pairs for a single *item* chosen by the adversary, such that all pairs are valid and there are no two pairs that can be linked. The number of pairs must be one more than the number of users in the group. We allow the adversary to corrupt all users, but the key issuer has to be honest.

The traceability experiment $\text{Exp}_{\mathcal{A},\mathcal{RS}}^{\text{trace}}(k)$ asks an adversary to output a message-signature pair, for some *item* chosen by the adversary, which is valid but can not be traced back to a corrupted user. In this experiment the key issuer is assumed to be honest.

The strong-exculpability experiment $\text{Exp}_{\mathcal{A},\mathcal{RS}}^{\text{str}-\text{ex}}(k)$ asks an adversary to output a message-signature pair, for some *item* chosen by the adversary, which is valid and can be traced back to an honest user. We give an adversary the possibility to corrupt users and the key issuer. Because the key issuer can always generate signing keys for non-existing users, we force the adversary to output a signature on behalf of an honest user.

Discussion: The described experiments imply two different attack scenarios:

In the first scenario, for anonymity and strong-exculpability, we allow an adversary to corrupt key issuers and users. One could argue, that there is an oracle missing to allow an adversary to send corrupted data to honest users in the Join-Issue protocol. But this functionality is covered by the SndToGM, WItemList, and WIdentList oracles and by publicly verifiable signing keys. In the second scenario, for public linkability and traceability, key issuers are assumed to be honest, whereas users can be corrupted. In particular, this implies that users and key issuers are disjoint sets. The restriction to honest key issuers is necessary because a corrupted key issuer could generate secret keys for non-existing users. With an appropriate identity management this can be prevented and we could also allow corrupted key issuers in the experiments for public linkability and traceability.

An important issue is that of timing the operations. The key issuer may correlate transactions and ratings by their timing, thereby threatening the anonymity of users. Hence, our reputation systems needs a mechanism to prevent such attacks. In [10,16,20] different solutions to this problem are proposed, which can be incorporated into our construction.

3   Our Construction

In this section we describe our reputation system by giving formal definitions of all algorithms stated in Sect. 2. The reputation system is based on the group signature schemes [7,11,25]. An intuition for our system can be obtained from the honest-verifier zero-knowledge proof of knowledge for the so-called extended q-SDH problem explained in the full version of this paper [5].

We assume the communication between users and the group manager and between users and the key issuer to take place via secure channels. Furthermore, the user's public key $upk[i]$ is certified by the group manager, such that the key issuer can verify the integrity of the public keys during the Join-Issue protocol.

In the following definitions we consider bilinear groups $\mathbb{G}_1$ and $\mathbb{G}_2$, and two hash functions modeled as random oracles: $H\colon \{0,1\}^* \longrightarrow \mathbb{Z}_p$ and $H_1\colon \{0,1\}^* \longrightarrow \mathbb{G}_2$. Furthermore, as in [7], we use Linear Encryption - a CPA-secure Elgamal-like encryption scheme based on the Decision Linear Diffie-Hellman Assumption.

KeyGen$_{GM}$():

1. Select $w \xleftarrow{\$} \mathbb{G}_1$, $\hat{d} \xleftarrow{\$} \mathbb{G}_2$, $\xi_1, \xi_2, \zeta \xleftarrow{\$} \mathbb{Z}_p$ and compute $u := w^{\frac{1}{\xi_1}}$, $v := w^{\frac{1}{\xi_2}}$, $d := \psi(\hat{d})$, $h := d^{\zeta}$. The values (u, v, w) are the public key of the Linear Encryption, the values (ξ_1, ξ_2) are the corresponding secret key, $\hat{d}, d$ and h are the basis for public linkability and revocation.
2. Set $gmpk := (u, v, w, h, d, \hat{d})$ and $gmsk := (\xi_1, \xi_2, \zeta)$.

KeyGen$_{KI}$(item):

1. Select $g_{2_{item}} \xleftarrow{\$} \mathbb{G}_2$, $\gamma_{item} \xleftarrow{\$} \mathbb{Z}_p$, set $g_{1_{item}} := \psi(g_{2_{item}})$, $W_{item} := g_{2_{item}}^{\gamma_{item}}$.
2. Set $ipk[item] := (g_{1_{item}}, g_{2_{item}}, W_{item})$, add it to the *ItemList* and keep $isk[item] := \gamma_{item}$ secret.

KeyGen$_U$(i):

1. Select $y_i \xleftarrow{\$} \mathbb{Z}_p$, set $upk[i] := h^{y_i}$ and $usk[i] := y_i$.

Register$_{GM}$(St$_{GM}$, M_{GM}), Register$_U$(St$_U$, M_U):

1. The user sends his identity i to the group manager.
2. If $reg[i] = \varepsilon$, the group manager runs KeyGen$_U$ to obtain the tuple $(upk[i], usk[i])$, sets $reg[i] := (i, upk[i])$ and sends $(upk[i], usk[i])$ to the user i.

Join(St$_U$, M_U), Issue(St$_{KI}$, M_{KI}):

1. The user looks up $ipk[item] = (g_{1_{item}}, g_{2_{item}}, W_{item})$ in the *ItemList* and sends $(i, upk[i])$ to the key issuer.
2. The key issuer checks that there is no entry $(upk[i], \cdot)$ in the identification list IL_{item}, selects $x_{i_{item}} \xleftarrow{\$} \mathbb{Z}_p$, computes $A_{i_{item}} := (g_{1_{item}} \cdot upk[i])^{\frac{1}{x_{i_{item}} + \gamma_{item}}}$, gives $gsk[i, item] := (A_{i_{item}}, x_{i_{item}})$ to user i, and saves $(upk[i], gsk[i, item])$ in IL_{item}.

Revoke($gmpk$, $gmsk$, i):

1. Look up $upk[i]$ in $reg[i]$ and compute $D_i := upk[i]^{\frac{1}{\zeta}} = (h^{y_i})^{\frac{1}{\zeta}} = d^{y_i}$ using $gmsk$ and add the revocation token $grt[i] := D_i$ to the revocation list $\mathcal{RL}$.

Sign($item$, $gmpk$, $ipk[item]$, $gsk[i, item]$, $usk[i]$, M):

1. Obtain the value $\hat{f} \in \mathbb{G}_2$ by $\hat{f} := H_1(item)$, choose $\alpha, \beta, \mu \xleftarrow{\$} \mathbb{Z}_p$ and compute $T_1 := u^\alpha$, $T_2 := v^\beta$, $T_3 := A_{i_{item}} \cdot w^{\alpha+\beta}$, $T_4 := d^\mu$, $T_5 := \psi(\hat{f})^{\mu+y_i}$ and the helper values $\delta_1 := \alpha \cdot x_{i_{item}}$ and $\delta_2 := \beta \cdot x_{i_{item}}$.
2. Select $r_\alpha, r_\beta, r_x, r_y, r_\mu, r_{\delta_1}, r_{\delta_2} \xleftarrow{\$} \mathbb{Z}_p$ and compute $R_1 := u^{r_\alpha}$, $R_2 := v^{r_\beta}$, $R_3 := e(T_3, g_{2_{item}})^{r_x} \cdot e(w, W_{item})^{-r_\alpha - r_\beta} \cdot e(w, g_{2_{item}})^{-r_{\delta_1} - r_{\delta_2}} \cdot e(h, g_{2_{item}})^{-r_y}$ $R_4 := T_1^{r_x} \cdot u^{-r_{\delta_1}}$, $R_5 := T_2^{r_x} \cdot v^{-r_{\delta_2}}$, $R_6 := d^{r_\mu}$, $R_7 := \psi(\hat{f})^{r_\mu + r_y}$.
3. Compute $c := H(M, item, T_1, T_2, T_3, T_4, T_5, R_1, R_2, R_3, R_4, R_5, R_6, R_7)$ and $s_\alpha := r_\alpha + c \cdot \alpha$, $s_\beta := r_\beta + c \cdot \beta$, $s_x := r_x + c \cdot x_{i_{item}}$, $s_y := r_y + c \cdot y_i$, $s_\mu := r_\mu + c \cdot \mu$, $s_{\delta_1} := r_{\delta_1} + c \cdot \delta_1$, $s_{\delta_2} := r_{\delta_2} + c \cdot \delta_2$.
4. Output $\sigma := (item, T_1, T_2, T_3, T_4, T_5, c, s_\alpha, s_\beta, s_x, s_y, s_\mu, s_{\delta_1}, s_{\delta_2})$.

Verify$(item, gmpk, ipk[item], \mathcal{RL}, M, \sigma)$:

    1. Obtain the value $\hat{f} \in \mathbb{G}_2$ by $\hat{f} := H_1(item)$ and compute the values
       $R_1 := u^{s_\alpha} \cdot T_1^{-c}$, $R_2 := v^{s_\beta} \cdot T_2^{-c}$,

$$R_3 := \frac{\mathrm{e}(T_3, g_{2_{item}})^{s_x} \cdot \mathrm{e}(w, W_{item})^{-s_\alpha - s_\beta} \cdot \mathrm{e}(w, g_{2_{item}})^{-s_{\delta_1} - s_{\delta_2}}}{\mathrm{e}(T_3, W_{item})^{-c} \cdot \mathrm{e}(g_1, g_{2_{item}})^c \cdot \mathrm{e}(h, g_{2_{item}})^{s_y}},$$

       $R_4 := T_1^{s_x} \cdot u^{-s_{\delta_1}}$, $R_5 := T_2^{s_x} \cdot v^{-s_{\delta_2}}$, $R_6 := d^{s_\mu} \cdot T_4^{-c}$, $R_7 := \psi(\hat{f})^{s_\mu + s_y} \cdot T_5^{-c}$.

    2. Check that $c \overset{?}{=} H(M, item, T_1, T_2, T_3, T_4, T_5, R_1, R_2, R_3, R_4, R_5, R_6, R_7)$.
       If this holds, then accept, otherwise reject.
    3. For each element $D \in \mathcal{RL}$ check whether D is encoded in (T_4, T_5):
       $\mathrm{e}\left(T_5, \hat{d}\right) \overset{?}{=} \mathrm{e}(D \cdot T_4, \hat{f})$. If this is false for all $D \in \mathcal{RL}$, then the signer of
       σ has not been revoked and Sign accepts, otherwise rejects.
    4. If both checks accept, then output 1, otherwise 0.

Link$(item, gmpk, ipk[item], (M', \sigma'), (M'', \sigma''))$:

    1. Verify the signatures σ' and σ'' and compute the value $\hat{f} := H_1(item)$.
    2. Output 1, iff σ' and σ'' are valid and $\mathrm{e}\left(\frac{T_5'}{T_5''}, \hat{d}\right) \overset{?}{=} \mathrm{e}\left(\frac{T_4'}{T_4''}, \hat{f}\right)$ holds.

Open$(gmpk, gmsk, M, \sigma)$:

    1. Check that σ is a valid signature. If not, output `failure`.
    2. Compute $A_{i_{item}} := T_3 \cdot T_1^{-\xi_1} \cdot T_2^{-\xi_2}$ using $gmsk$ and look up the user index
       i from the identification list IL_{item}.
    3. If no entry for $A_{i_{item}}$ can be found in IL_{item} return `failure`, otherwise
       return i.

Theorem 1. *The above reputation system is* correct. *Furthermore, assuming the q-SDH Problem is hard in the bilinear groups* $(\mathbb{G}_1, \mathbb{G}_2)$ *and the Decision Linear Problem is hard in* $\mathbb{G}_1$, *the reputation system is* anonymous, publicly linkable, traceable, *and* strongly exculpable.

The q-SDH Problem and the Decision Linear Problem are standard problems in pairing-based cryptography and formal definitions can be found in [7]. Both problems are hard to solve in the Generic Group Model [6,7].

    Formal definitions of the security properties and proofs of security will be given in the full version of this paper [5].

References

1. Androulaki, E., Choi, S.G., Bellovin, S.M., Malkin, T.: Reputation systems for anonymous networks. In: Borisov, N., Goldberg, I. (eds.) PETS 2008. LNCS, vol. 5134, pp. 202–218. Springer, Heidelberg (2008)
2. Ateniese, G., Camenisch, J., Joye, M., Tsudik, G.: A practical and provably secure coalition-resistant group signature scheme. In: Bellare, M. (ed.) CRYPTO 2000. LNCS, vol. 1880, pp. 255–270. Springer, Heidelberg (2000)

3. Bellare, M., Micciancio, D., Warinschi, B.: Foundations of group signatures: formal definitions, simplified requirements, and a construction based on general assumptions. In: Biham, E. (ed.) EUROCRYPT 2003. LNCS, vol. 2656, pp. 614–629. Springer, Heidelberg (2003)

4. Bellare, M., Shi, H., Zhang, C.: Foundations of group signatures: the case of dynamic groups. In: Menezes, A. (ed.) CT-RSA 2005. LNCS, vol. 3376, pp. 136–153. Springer, Heidelberg (2005)

5. Blömer, J., Juhnke, J., Kolb, C.: Anonymous and publicly linkable reputation systems. Cryptology ePrint Archive: Report 2014/546 (2014). http://eprint.iacr.org/2014/546

6. Boneh, D., Boyen, X.: Short signatures without random oracles. In: Cachin, C., Camenisch, J.L. (eds.) EUROCRYPT 2004. LNCS, vol. 3027, pp. 56–73. Springer, Heidelberg (2004)

7. Boneh, D., Boyen, X., Shacham, H.: Short group signatures. In: Franklin, M. (ed.) CRYPTO 2004. LNCS, vol. 3152, pp. 41–55. Springer, Heidelberg (2004)

8. Boneh, D., Shacham, H.: Group signatures with verifier-local revocation. In: CCS 2004, pp. 168–177. ACM (2004)

9. Chow, S.S.M., Susilo, W., Yuen, T.H.: Escrowed linkability of ring signatures and its applications. In: Nguyên, P.Q. (ed.) VIETCRYPT 2006. LNCS, vol. 4341, pp. 175–192. Springer, Heidelberg (2006)

10. Clauß, S., Schiffner, S., Kerschbaum, F.: k-anonymous reputation. In: ASIA CCS 2013, pp. 359–368. ACM (2013)

11. Delerablée, C., Pointcheval, D.: Dynamic fully anonymous short group signatures. In: Nguyên, P.Q. (ed.) VIETCRYPT 2006. LNCS, vol. 4341, pp. 193–210. Springer, Heidelberg (2006)

12. Dellarocas, C.: Immunizing online reputation reporting systems against unfair ratings and discriminatory behavior. In: EC 2000, pp. 150–157. ACM (2000)

13. Dingledine, R., Mathewson, N., Syverson, P.: Reputation in P2P anonymity systems. In: Workshop on Economics of Peer-to-Peer Systems, vol. 92 (2003)

14. Franklin, M., Zhang, H.: Unique group signatures. In: Foresti, S., Yung, M., Martinelli, F. (eds.) ESORICS 2012. LNCS, vol. 7459, pp. 643–660. Springer, Heidelberg (2012)

15. Fujisaki, E., Suzuki, K.: Traceable ring signature. In: Okamoto, T., Wang, X. (eds.) PKC 2007. LNCS, vol. 4450, pp. 181–200. Springer, Heidelberg (2007)

16. Goodrich, M.T., Kerschbaum, F.: Privacy-enhanced reputation-feedback methods to reduce feedback extortion in online auctions. In: CODASPY 2011, pp. 273–282. ACM (2011)

17. Hwang, J.Y., Lee, S., Chung, B.-H., Cho, H.S., Nyang, D.: Group signatures with controllable linkability for dynamic membership. Inf. Sci. **222**, 761–778 (2013)

18. Jøsang, A., Ismail, R.: The beta reputation system. In: BLED 2002, pp. 41–55 (2002)

19. Kamvar, S.D., Schlosser, M.T., Garcia-Molina, H.: The eigentrust algorithm for reputation management in P2P networks. In: WWW 2003, pp. 640–651. ACM (2003)

20. Kerschbaum, F.: A verifiable, centralized, coercion-free reputation system. In: WPES 2009, pp. 61–70. ACM (2009)

21. Kiayias, A., Yung, M.: Group signatures: provable security, efficient constructions and anonymity from trapdoor-holders. Cryptology ePrint Archive: Report 2004/076 (2004). http://eprint.iacr.org/2004/076

22. Liu, J.K., Wei, V.K., Wong, D.S.: Linkable spontaneous anonymous group signature for ad hoc groups. In: Wang, H., Pieprzyk, J., Varadharajan, V. (eds.) ACISP 2004. LNCS, vol. 3108, pp. 325–335. Springer, Heidelberg (2004)

23. Manulis, M., Sadeghi, A.-R., Schwenk, J.: Linkable democratic group signatures. In: Chen, K., Deng, R., Lai, X., Zhou, J. (eds.) ISPEC 2006. LNCS, vol. 3903, pp. 187–201. Springer, Heidelberg (2006)

24. Michalas, A., Komninos, N.: The lord of the sense: a privacy preserving reputation system for participatory sensing applications. In: Computers and Communication. ISCC, vol. 23, pp. 1–6. IEEE (2014)

25. Nakanishi, T., Funabiki, N.: A short verifier-local revocation group signature scheme with backward unlinkability. In: Yoshiura, H., Sakurai, K., Rannenberg, K., Murayama, Y., Kawamura, S. (eds.) IWSEC 2006. LNCS, vol. 4266, pp. 17–32. Springer, Heidelberg (2006)

26. Steinbrecher, S.: Design options for privacy-respecting reputation systems within centralised internet communities. In: Fischer-Hübner, S., Rannenberg, K., Yngström, L., Lindskog, S. (eds.) Security and Privacy in Dynamic Environments. IFIP, vol. 201, pp. 123–134. Springer, Boston (2006)

27. Tsang, P.P., Wei, V.K.: Short linkable ring signatures for e-voting, e-cash and attestation. In: Deng, R.H., Bao, F., Pang, H.H., Zhou, J. (eds.) ISPEC 2005. LNCS, vol. 3439, pp. 48–60. Springer, Heidelberg (2005)

Hard Drive Side-Channel Attacks Using Smartphone Magnetic Field Sensors

Sebastian Biedermann[1]([✉]), Stefan Katzenbeisser[1], and Jakub Szefer[2]

[1] Security Engineering Group, Technische Universität Darmstadt
Darmstadt, Germany
{biedermann,katzenbeisser}@seceng.informatik.tu-darmstadt.de
[2] Computer Architecture and Security Laboratory, Yale University,
New Haven, USA
jakub.szefer@yale.edu

Abstract. In this paper we present a new class of side-channel attacks on computer hard drives. Hard drives contain one or more spinning disks made of a magnetic material. In addition, they contain different magnets which rapidly move the head to a target position on the disk to perform a write or a read. The magnetic fields from the disk's material and head are weak and well shielded. However, we show that the magnetic field due to the moving head can be picked up by sensors outside of the hard drive. With these measurements, we are able to deduce patterns about ongoing operations. For example, we can detect what type of the operating system is booting up or what application is being started. Most importantly, no special equipment is necessary. All attacks can be performed by using an unmodified smartphone placed in proximity of a hard drive.

1 Introduction

Hard drives are an integral part of almost any computer as they are the persistent storage medium for code and data. Operation of the hard drive is directly correlated with the type of workload being processed on the computer. The movement of the hard drive head is enabled by a magnetic field. This magnetic field can be picked up by sensors outside of the disk drive, and thus enables our new side-channel attacks. Whenever data is being written to, or read from, the head mechanism has to move, causing disturbance in the magnetic field which we can detect. Disk drives have previously been subject to research on covert timing channels, e.g. [3]. However, these attacks required direct access to the target computer. The magnetic side-channel, on the other hand, is a non-invasive attack which can be carried out without physical contact. This attack falls under the broad class of electromagnetic (EM) attacks. EM attacks have been carried out on various computer components, such as CMOS chips [5], or smart cards [1]. Disk drives, however, have not been subject to such attacks.

This work was supported by CASED (www.cased.de), EC-SPRIDE (www.ec-spride.de) and the the German Federal Ministry of Education and Research (BMBF) under grant no. 01C12S01V.

© International Financial Cryptography Association 2015
R. Böhme and T. Okamoto (Eds.): FC 2015, LNCS 8975, pp. 489–496, 2015.
DOI: 10.1007/978-3-662-47854-7_30

Our research was motivated by two trends in industry. First, there has been a great proliferation of smartphones with various sensors. The key sensor which we focus on is the digital compass, also called the magnetometer. Today's phones have sensors which can pick up magnetic fields having a strength of μT (micro Tesla, where Tesla is the unit of magnetic field strength or magnetic flux density). Second, the industry is constantly working on optimizing the size of the servers and computer equipment. This has led to smaller and thinner computers. The reduced size means there is less shielding and shorter distance from the disk drive to the outside of the computer chassis. This creates a situation where magnetic field fluctuations can be more easily detected using sensors such as those available on today's phones. Attacks are performed by using an application running on an unmodified smartphone. Our side-channel attacks allow us to:

- detect the operating system that is used;
- distinguish between known applications being started;
- distinguish Virtual Machine activity on a server;
- match ongoing network traffic to a server; and
- detect file caching based on disk activity.

2   Magnetic Field and Hard Drives

In this section we provide a short summary on magnetic fields and magnetic disk drives. More information is available in a variety of books, such as [7].

2.1   Magnetic Fields

Tesla (T) is the unit of magnetic field strength, often denoted as B. It can also be expressed in units of gauss (G), where 1 gauss equals 100 μT. As a point of reference, Earth's magnetic field ranges between 50 to 75 μT. The magnetic field strength in close proximity of a hard drive can vary due to the disk operation and the magnets inside the disk drive. In particular, the movement of mechanisms inside the hard drive when accessing data causes the magnetic field strength to fluctuate by about 3 μT when sensed next to hard drive ($d \approx 0$ cm). The field strength B decreases as a square of the distance d with $B \propto \frac{1}{d^2}$ from a point source. Given the magnetic field strength B_1 at distance d_1, the strength B_2 at distance d_2 can be inferred from $\frac{B_1}{B_2} \propto \frac{d_2^2}{d_1^2}$. Background magnetic field fluctuation (i.e. noise) always is about 0.1 μT in magnitude in our experiments. Thus, realistic maximum measurement distances d_i are constrained by the fact that the field changes need to be above the background noise, thus $B_i > 0.1$ μT.

2.2   Hard Drive Magnetic Fields

There are three sources of magnetic fields in a standard hard drive: (a) magnetic disk platters, (b) the disk drive head, and (c) the mechanisms for moving the disk drive head. Both (a) and (b) are too weak to be detected outside a disk drive chassis.

We show, however, that detecting the strength of (c) is feasible. In a hard drive, there are two magnets, one above and one below the head movement assembly. The head movement assembly includes a coil of wire. When current is passed through the wire, a magnetic field is generated, which causes the head assembly to displace. Depending on the direction of the current, the generated field interacts with the fixed magnets and causes the head movement assembly to move left or right from its rest position. At rest the head assembly is either all the way to the left or all the way to the right, depending on the particular disk in use. The strength of the field determines how far the head is displaced.

2.3   Magnetic Field Sensors on Mobile Devices

On a modern smartphone the magnetic field sensor measures the strength of the magnetic field along three axes. On Android-based devices, applications may access the *TYPE_MAGNETIC_FIELD* sensor to get the field readings. The sensor outputs data on the strength of magnetic field in units of μT along three axes. We experimentally verify that when placing the phone next to a drive, the z axis measurements give the least noisy readings. If the phone is placed on top of the drive, the x or y axis measurements provide best results assuming minimal curvature with the z axis perpendicular to both. Note, however, that the earth's magnetic field is parallel to most surfaces (x or y axis when the phone is laying flat on some surface) which can cause high noise along these axis. Thus, ideally the axis perpendicular to the earth's surface should be used for the measurements, which need not always be the z-axis.

2.4   Magnetic Field Measurements

In our experiments we use unmodified Samsung Galaxy S4 Mini and Samsung Galaxy S2 smartphones. We access their magnetometer using a custom application, however one which requires no special permissions (unlike applications that may require permissions to use camera or other sensors). Before any experiment is performed, the application measures the background magnetic field in order to calibrate subsequent measurements. This is done by taking 100 measurements along the x, y and z axis and computing the mean of all measurements. This way the average field strength ($\bar{x}$, $\bar{y}$, $\bar{z}$) of the background noise can be established. Once the background magnetic field strength is measured, the application records measurements M_i along the x, y and z axis which correspond to the difference between the newly measured value and the average background noise, $M_i = (timestamp_i, x_i - \bar{x}, y_i - \bar{y}, z_i - \bar{z})$.

3   Magnetic Side-Channel Attacks

This section presents a variety of magnetic side-channel attacks which we have explored. We focus on two targets. First, we launch attacks against a laptop in an office-type environment. Second, we launch attacks against a server co-located in a server rack with other running servers.

3.1   Attack Composition

The activity of the hard drive can be matched to changes in the magnetic field strength, since the head is moved each time files are written or read on different locations. Additionally, the magnitude of the magnetic field strength can be matched to different locations on a hard drive on which the head currently operates. These two different factors create characteristic fingerprints over time that can be matched to ongoing operations of a hard drive. The smartphone should be located closely, at best in a distance of $3-4$ cm to the target hard drive. In order to detect certain operations on an arbitrary target hard drive, we analyze correlations between measurements taken in an enrollment phase and attack measurements. During enrollment, we record several measurements of the same hard drive operation and compute the average of all measurements, which yields to a characteristic enrollment vector for one specific activity. Before computing the average, we synchronize all individual measurements. We do this by shifting the measured vectors by ±0.5 s; the shift which produces the best correlation with the previous measurements is taken. In the attack phase, we compute the correlation between a new measurement and all stored enrollment vectors. Again, in order to synchronize the new measurement with the enrollment vectors, we shift it by ±0.5 s. Finally, we classify the measurement to the enrollment class which achieves the highest correlation.

3.2   Example Attacks Against Laptop

The target laptop is an Acer Aspire 5733z with a Toshiba 320 GB disk drive with 5400 rpm. The attack setup is shown in Fig. 1. The smartphone is placed in front of the laptop, near where the disk drive is mounted.

Fig. 1. Laptop attack setup, shown with the Samsung Galaxy S4 Mini.

Fig. 2. Field strength while booting Linux and Win7 (average of 20 runs).

As one possible scenario, we envision a malware-infested smartphone. The malware, which the user downloaded when searching for a "digital compass" application, is running in the background on the phone and collecting magnetic sensor readings once it is triggered. The unsuspecting user may place the phone in close proximity to the laptop when working on the laptop in the office or in a cafe. In this position, the malware can launch a number of attacks, such as OS or application startup detection.

OS Boot-Up Detection: First, we use the measurements to investigate which operating system (OS) is booted on the laptop. Figure 2 shows recorded measurements during the boot-up of Ubuntu Linux 12.04 (64 Bit) and Windows 7 SP1 (64 Bit) on the same laptop, each taken for 20 s right after turning on the notebook. The first nine seconds are very similar in both curves, since first the BIOS is loaded and the hard drive is initialized. After nine seconds, the OS starts booting and differences in the course of the magnetic field can clearly be seen. These characteristic deviations are based on the different underlying file system as well as on different processes which are starting during boot-up. During enrollment we record vectors with 1000 measurements (ten seconds) starting nine seconds after the first change in the magnetic field could be detected. This way, we skip the BIOS and the firmware and only use the characteristic measurements of the operating system's boot-up. The enrollment vectors are averages over ten independent trials. Table 1 shows the average Pearson correlation between ten measurement vectors taken from different boot-ups of different OSs and enrollment vectors for Ubuntu Linux, Windows 7 and Windows Vista. In each case, the strongest correlation occurs between the measurement vector and the enrollment vector of the same OS. The correlation to other enrollment vectors of other OSs is small in comparison. We can use the correlation between attack measurements and enrollment measurements in order to decide which OS was booting. In this experiment, we use five measurements of each OS boot-up procedure for enrollment and ten new measurements which we classify to one of the three OS classes depending on their highest correlation. The results of this simple classification approach lead to an average error rate of 3 % across 20 enrollments and 20 attack measurements in each OS setup with which an attack vector was not correctly classified.

Application Start-Up Detection: In the next attack, we use the changes in the strength of the magnetic field to detect the start of some known applications. We use the same setup as before. The laptop runs Windows 7 SP1 (64 Bit) and has three different browsers, namely Microsoft Internet Explorer (ver. 8), Google Chrome (ver. 34) and Mozilla Firefox (ver. 28). Our attack goal is to determine

Table 1. Average correlation between new attack measurements recorded during booting different operating systems and the enrollment vectors.

Measurement	Enrollment vectors		
	Linux	Win7	WinVista
Linux	**0.40** ± 0.22	0.09 ± 0.08	0.12 ± 0.10
Win7	0.08 ± 0.04	**0.29** ± 0.10	0.14 ± 0.06
WinVista	0.04 ± 0.13	0.06 ± 0.12	**0.37** ± 0.22

Table 2. Average correlation between new attack measurements recorded during start of different browsers and the corresponding enrollment vectors.

Measurement	Enrollment vectors		
	IE	Chrome	Firefox
IE	**0.34** ± 0.11	0.23 ± 0.10	0.23 ± 0.08
Chrome	0.29 ± 0.14	**0.47** ± 0.11	0.07 ± 0.19
Firefox	0.22 ± 0.13	0.13 ± 0.15	**0.49** ± 0.16

which browser was started. Table 2 shows the average Pearson correlation between measurements and enrollment vectors recorded during the start of IE, Chrome and Firefox. In each case, the strongest correlation occurs between the measurements and the enrollment vectors of the same browser.

Based on the highest correlation, we can classify new samples to a browser class with an average error rate of 23 %. The results indicate that the start-up of different applications can be distinguished with a good accuracy.

3.3 Example Attacks Against Servers

In this section we present attacks against a server co-located in a server rack with other servers. The target server is a Dell R210 with a 2TB (7.2K RPM SATA) disk drive. The smartphone is placed on top of the server, near where the disk drive is mounted. In order to successfully mount the attack and to be able to place the smartphone, at least one rack above the target server needs to be empty. This also results in a distance of at least $1\frac{3}{4}$ inches (1 Rack Unit) between our target server and the next server. The distance greatly decreases the influence of other operating hard drives in the same server rack. As one possible attack scenario, we envision an unscrupulous data center employee who wants to gain information about processes running on the servers.

VM Activity Detection: In this example, an attacker tries to gather insights about virtual machines (VMs). Our server runs the Xen hypervisor 4.2 and different VMs, each having a storage of 128 GB. We measure the magnetic field during writing a file in different VMs vm01, vm02 and vm03. Figure 3 shows the average magnetic field measurements. The average strength can be used to estimate which VM is currently operating on the server's hard drive. Given an attack measurement, we again compute the average magnetic field strength and perform a classification based on the smallest difference to an enrollment measurement. Results showed that the activity of the server's hard drive can be assigned to vm01 or vm03 with an average error rate of 35 %. The differences between the magnetic field strengths of the VMs are small, but detectable.

Host Server Detection: As another example, the attacker may know that a website is hosted on a server in a data center and she wants to find out exactly which server actually hosts the site. To reach this goal, the attacker triggers downloads from the website with the smartphone while measuring the magnetic field radiated by servers in the rack in multiple trials. This way, the attacker can determine if a server created a magnetic field corresponding to a read operation of a data block having the appropriate size that matches the download. In order to test the effectiveness of our attack, we use ten enrollment measurements recorded during downloading a 32 MB file from our Web server and computed and average enrollment vector. We found that the attack and enrollment measurements correlate with 0.33 ± 0.11 if the file is downloaded from the server on which the smartphone is located, while the attack measurements correlate only with 0.12 ± 0.07 if the file is not downloaded from this server. Classifying 20 new attack measurements based on the highest correlation to the enrollment vector while only during 10 of the measurements the file is downloaded lead to an average error rate of 15 %. The correlation can be used to reveal the server that hosts the website which provides the download.

File Caching Detection: If a server caches files in memory, then host server detection attack can be prevented. However, detection of the caching behavior is also an interesting attack objective. Frequently accessed files can be distinguished from infrequently accessed ones – thus leaking information whether a file has recently been in use. Figure 4 shows disk activity (darker red regions show a larger change in the magnetic field over time) when several files of 16 MB are accessed, in this case downloaded from the Web server. Two of the files (namely 5 and 11) have been accessed before the test and became cached. To test the attack, we perform 10 enrollment measurements while downloading files and 10 enrollment measurements without downloading. Subsequently, we perform 20 attack measurements while downloading 20 different files, 10 of them were already downloaded before and are cached, 10 of them were never downloaded. We classify the attack measurements to one of the two classes "is read from hard drive" or "is not read from hard drive", the latter means the file was cached in memory. We do this by choosing the class that yields to the highest correlation. According to our results, an attacker can distinguish if a file has already been accessed or not on a Web server with an average error rate of 5 %.

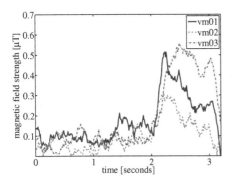

Fig. 3. Strength during writing data in vm01, vm02 and vm03 (50 runs).

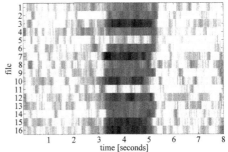

Fig. 4. Field while downloading files; 05 and 11 have already been accessed (Color figure online).

4   Related Work

There are a lot of other side-channel attacks, but usually they require access to the victim system or physical connection to measure the power usage, while our attack requires no physical connection, but only physical proximity. In 1984, Gold et al. [3] presented analysis of covert channels due to placement of the disk arm. While by 1991, Karger et al. [4] presented research on storage channels due to hard disk drive head movement. However, the majority of the past work on electromagnetic (EM) side-channels has focused on processors. Researchers used specialized magnetic sensors to sense emanations and recover a secret key [5]. Other work has shown that the electromagnetic attack on processors can obtain at least as much information as power consumption based side-channels [6]. Given the need for proximity when working with electromagnetic emanations, research has focused on smart cards where physical access and proximity are easy. Researchers have shown electromagnetic side-channel attacks on various smart cards with different hardware protections, and still were able to recover the encryption keys [2]. Others were even able to propose a model that completely and quantitatively expresses the information leaked from electromagnetic side-channel in CMOS devices, such as smart cards [1]. Purely using magnetic field measurements against hard drives has not been explored yet.

5   Conclusion

In this paper we presented a new class of side-channel attacks on computer hard drives. From measurements of the magnetic field, which carries information about the movement of the hard drive mechanisms, we are able to deduce patterns about ongoing operations. All experiments were performed using a modern, unmodified smartphone which was placed in proximity to a hard drive, even outside a laptop or a server chassis.

References

1. Agrawal, D., Archambeault, B., Rao, J., Rohatgi, P.: The em side channel(s). In: Kaliski, B.S., Koç, K., Paar, C. (eds.) CHES 2002. LNCS, vol. 2523, pp. 29–45. Springer, Heidelberg (2003)
2. Gandolfi, K., Mourtel, C., Olivier, F.: Electromagnetic analysis: concrete results. In: Koç, Ç.K., Naccache, D., Paar, C. (eds.) CHES 2001. LNCS, vol. 2162, pp. 251–261. Springer, Heidelberg (2001)
3. Gold, B.D., Linde, R., Cudney, P.F.: Kvm/37o in retrospect. In: IEEE Symposium on Security and Privacy, pp. 13–23 (1984)
4. Karger, P.A., Wray, J.C.: Storage channels in disk arm optimization. In: IEEE Symposium on Security and Privacy, pp. 52–63 (1991)
5. Mateos, E., Gebotys, C.: Side channel analysis using giant magneto-resistive (gmr) sensors. In: COSADE workshop Proceedings Published by CASED (2011)
6. Quisquater, J.-J., Samyde, D.: Electromagnetic analysis (EMA): measures and counter-measures for smart cards. In: Attali, S., Jensen, T. (eds.) E-smart 2001. LNCS, vol. 2140, pp. 200–210. Springer, Heidelberg (2001)
7. Rao, N.: Fundamentals of Electromagnetics for Electrical and Computer Engineering. Pearson Education, New Delhi (2011)

Hierarchical Deterministic Bitcoin Wallets that Tolerate Key Leakage

Gus Gutoski[1] and Douglas Stebila[2]([✉])

[1] Perimeter Institute for Theoretical Physics, Waterloo, Ontario, Canada
ggutoski@perimeterinstitute.ca
[2] School of Electrical Engineering and Computer Science and School of Mathematical
Sciences, Queensland University of Technology, Brisbane, Queensland, Australia
stebila@qut.edu.au

Abstract. A Bitcoin wallet is a set of private keys known to a user and
which allow that user to spend any Bitcoin associated with those keys. In
a *hierarchical deterministic (HD)* wallet, child private keys are generated
pseudorandomly from a master private key, and the corresponding child
public keys can be generated by anyone with knowledge of the master
public key. These wallets have several interesting applications including
Internet retail, trustless audit, and a treasurer allocating funds among
departments. A specification of HD wallets has even been accepted as
Bitcoin standard BIP32.

Unfortunately, in all existing HD wallets—including BIP32 wallets—
an attacker can easily recover the master private key given the master
public key and any child private key. This vulnerability precludes use
cases such as a combined treasurer-auditor, and some in the Bitcoin
community have suspected that this vulnerability cannot be avoided.

We propose a new HD wallet that is not subject to this vulnerability.
Our HD wallet can tolerate the leakage of up to m private keys with a
master public key size of $O(m)$. We prove that breaking our HD wallet is
at least as hard as the so-called "one more" discrete logarithm problem.

1 Introduction

Bitcoin [10] is a popular, decentralized cryptocurrency with monetary base worth
approximately USD 5 billion as of December 2014. Each stash of Bitcoin (technically, an *unspent transaction output*) is associated with a public key Q for
the Elliptic Curve Digital Signature Algorithm (ECDSA) [11]. A stash is spent
by presenting a new *transaction* with a valid digital signature under Q. Under
normal use, signatures are generated via knowledge of the private key d corresponding to Q. Ownership of a stash of Bitcoin is equated with knowledge of
the associated private key.

A Bitcoin *wallet* is a set of private keys known to a user. A single wallet
may contain hundreds or even thousands of distinct private keys. Wallets are
often stored in a database on a user's computer with appropriate backups to

© International Financial Cryptography Association 2015
R. Böhme and T. Okamoto (Eds.): FC 2015, LNCS 8975, pp. 497–504, 2015.
DOI: 10.1007/978-3-662-47854-7_31

guard against accidental loss. A typical Bitcoin user is constantly generating new, random private keys and so frequent (and burdensome) backups are essential.

Deterministic Wallets. *Deterministic wallets* alleviate much of the burden of wallet maintenance by generating a pseudorandom sequence of *child private keys* $d_1, d_2, \dots$ from a *master private key* $\hat{d}$ according to a formula such as

$$d_i = \text{hash}(i, \hat{d})$$

where hash$(\cdot)$ is a cryptographically secure hash function that is indistinguishable from a random function and which may or may not be publicly known.

These wallets are *hierarchical* in that each child key d_i could be viewed as a new master private key in its own right, from which a new sequence of child private keys $d_{i,1}, d_{i,2}, \dots$ could be generated and so on *ad infinitum*.

It is worth emphasizing that the entire hierarchy of private keys in the wallet can be recovered from knowledge of $\hat{d}$, making the wallet highly portable and easy to maintain. (Some Bitcoin users derive this master private key from the hash of a memorized password; the resulting wallet is called a *brain wallet*.)

The Master Public Key Property. Interestingly, the mathematics of any discrete logarithm system—including the ECDSA scheme used in Bitcoin—allow for deterministic wallets with the additional property that a user could create and publish a *master public key* $\hat{Q}$, from which anyone could compute the sequence $Q_1, Q_2, \dots$ of child public keys corresponding to the child private keys $d_1, d_2, \dots$ derived from $\hat{d}$, and yet knowledge of $\hat{Q}$ alone is insufficient to recover any of the private keys $\hat{d}, d_1, d_2, \dots$. (See Sect. 3 for details.) We refer to this property as the *master public key property*.

Deterministic wallets with the master public key property are confusingly called *hierarchical deterministic (HD) wallets* in the Bitcoin community. This label is something of a misnomer as the salient feature of HD wallets is not the hierarchy but rather the master public key property.

Credit for this concept is typically attributed to Maxwell [9]. The first widely available HD wallet software was the *Electrum* wallet, which appeared in November 2011 [1]. A specification of HD wallets was proposed in 2012 and subsequently accepted as Bitcoin standard BIP32 [12].

A Vulnerability in Existing HD Wallets. Unfortunately, all existing HD wallets—including BIP32-compliant wallets—admit an exploit whereby an attacker could easily recover the master private key $\hat{d}$ given the master public key $\hat{Q}$ and any child private key d_i. (Again, see Sect. 3 for details.)

This vulnerability was known to the author of the BIP32 standard [12]. Indeed, BIP32 compensates for this vulnerability by allowing for "hardened" child private keys that can be compromised without also compromising the master private key. Unfortunately, those hardened keys lack the master public key property: their public keys cannot be generated from the master public key.

Buterin calls attention to this vulnerability in his informative article, in which he announces open-source software that cracks BIP32 and Electrum wallets [5]. His pessimism is a challenge to the cryptography community:

[T]he obvious question is: can this [vulnerability] be fixed? The answer seems to be no; ... If this is indeed true, then raising awareness is the only solution, together with a change in BIP32 representation and in clients to make it clear that master public keys and hierarchical wallets do not mix.

Our Contribution. We present a new HD wallet that eliminates this vulnerability while retaining the master public key property (Sect. 4). For a chosen parameter m, our HD wallet can tolerate the leakage of up to m private keys with a master public key of size $O(m)$ and no blow-up whatsoever in the size of the master private key. We prove in Sect. 5 that breaking our HD wallet is at least as hard as the so-called "one-more" discrete logarithm problem.

We begin in Sect. 2 with a survey of several previously known use cases for HD wallets, including one—the combined treasurer-auditor—that is precluded by the vulnerability of existing HD wallets but not by our new HD wallet. Section 3 reviews the BIP32 vulnerability in detail.

2   Use Cases for HD Wallets

1. *Low-maintenance wallets, brain wallets.* As mentioned in Sect. 1, a rudimentary use of deterministic wallets is to allow the complete reconstruction of any Bitcoin wallet from a single master private key. These wallets are easier to maintain, more portable, and make brain wallets possible.

2. *A web merchant receiving payment from customers.* A motivating use case suggested by Maxwell [9] and described in the BIP32 standard [12] is that of a web merchant who generates fresh public keys for each sale. A deterministic wallet allows the merchant to easily generate and store only the *public* keys on a vulnerable online server while all the corresponding *private* keys are kept safe in offline storage.

   Moreover, the merchant can employ the hierarchical property of HD wallets to store only those public keys that are needed for receiving customer payments. This practice could enhance the merchant's privacy by eliminating the need to store *every* public key in his entire wallet on the vulnerable server.

3. *Detailed, trustless audits.* A user could reveal her master public key $\hat{Q}$ to third-party auditors, who could then use that key to view the full details of every subsequent transaction using Bitcoins from the stash associated with $\hat{Q}$. Such a user is assured that her funds are safe from theft by the auditor because the private keys associated with those funds are never revealed.

   One frequently suggested use case is a large company that reveals its master public key to regulators, thereby allowing an extremely detailed degree of oversight with near-negligible overhead costs. Another use case is that of a bank or online wallet service; revealing master public keys to depositors allows the bank to prove to those depositors that their funds are safe and that the bank is not operating a fractional reserve. *Coinkite* is a recent commercial example of such an online HD wallet [3].

4. *A treasurer allocating funds to departments.* The treasurer of a large company could create child key pairs for each department within the company. Department managers are given only the child private key for their department, so they cannot spend the funds allocated to other departments. Managers of large departments can employ the hierarchical property of HD wallets to create their own sub-tree of child keys and allocate funds among middle-managers in a similar fashion, and so on down the corporate hierarchy. Meanwhile, the treasurer, who knows the master private key, retains the full ability to move funds into and out of the different departments. This use case is suggested by, for example, the developers of the open-source *MoneyTree* HD wallet [2].

Treasurers and Auditors Don't Mix. An organization that simultaneously implements the treasurer (4) and auditor (3) use cases using current HD wallets leaves itself open a collusion between the auditor and a department manager, allowing them to run off with all the company's funds via the exploit mentioned in Sect. 1 and detailed in Sect. 3.

Enabling the Combined Treasurer-Auditor. Our HD wallet, presented in Sect. 4, is the first to facilitate the combined treasurer-auditor use case. Specifically, an organization with t dep artments is safe from a collusion between the auditor and all department managers if it uses our HD wallet with parameter $m > t$.

3   A Vulnerability in BIP32 Wallets

We now review the exploit in BIP32 Bitcoin HD wallets that allows an adversary to recover the master private key given the master public key and any child private key, thus precluding the combined treasurer-auditor use case discussed above. (This exploit appears to be folklore knowledge in the Bitcoin community.)

The key-generation formula employed by current HD wallets can be applied to any discrete logarithm system, such as the ECDSA used by Bitcoin. It is convenient to present the formula in simplified form using the familiar language of a generic additive group $\mathbb{G}$ of prime order p with generator $P \in \mathbb{G}$.

Recall that a private key d in a discrete logarithm system is an element of $\mathbb{Z}_p$ and the public key $Q \in \mathbb{G}$ corresponding to d is easily computed via $Q = dP$. Recall also that the task of recovering a private key d given only the public key Q and the generator P is the familiar *discrete logarithm problem (DLP)* for $\mathbb{G}$.

BIP32 Child Key Generation. Given a master key pair $(\hat{d}, \hat{Q})$ for a BIP32-compliant HD wallet, compute child private keys $d_1, d_2, \ldots$ and corresponding public keys $Q_1, Q_2, \ldots$ as

$$d_i = \hat{d} + \text{hash}(i, \hat{Q}) \pmod{p}$$
$$Q_i = \hat{Q} + \text{hash}(i, \hat{Q})P$$

for a strong, publicly known hash function hash $: \mathbb{Z} \times \mathbb{G} \to \mathbb{Z}_p$. It is easily seen that Q_i is indeed equal to $d_i P$ and thus the public key corresponding to d_i.

By contrast with the rudimentary deterministic wallet described in Sect. 1, child public keys Q_i can be computed using only knowledge of i, the master public key $\hat{Q}$, and the function hash$(\cdot)$. It is this fact that gives rise to the master public key feature of BIP32 HD wallets.

Exploit. Recovery of the master private key $\hat{d}$ given the master public key $\hat{Q}$, any child private key d_i, and corresponding index i is given by the formula

$$\hat{d} = d_i - \text{hash}(i, \hat{Q}) \pmod{p}.$$

4   A New HD Wallet that Tolerates Key Leakage

Master Key Generation. Instead of one master private key, our HD wallet uses m master private keys $\hat{d}_1, \ldots, \hat{d}_m$ for some reasonably-sized m to be determined by the requirements of the wallet. (For example, in the combined treasurer-auditor use case of Sect. 2, m must exceed the number t of departments in the organization.) To keep the master private key size down, these master private keys could be generated pseudorandomly with no loss of security using, say, the rudimentary deterministic wallet described in Sect. 1.

The master public keys $\hat{Q}_1, \ldots, \hat{Q}_m$ corresponding to master private keys $\hat{d}_1, \ldots, \hat{d}_m$ are given, as usual, by $\hat{Q}_i = \hat{d}_i P$. Whereas the master private keys could be generated pseudorandomly to save storage, one cannot simply publish a single "grand master" public key from which users could deduce the master public keys $\hat{Q}_1, \ldots, \hat{Q}_m$ as otherwise one would succeed only in pushing the original vulnerability up from child keys to master keys. Thus, these master public keys must be stored explicitly, incurring a $O(m)$ blow-up in public key size.

Child Key Generation. We now describe how child keys are derived from these m master keys. To this end let s be some publicly known master seed. This seed could be a universal constant such as 42—the Answer to the Ultimate Question of Life, The Universe, and Everything. Alternately, s might depend upon the wallet—say, a concatenation of the master public keys $\hat{Q}_1, \ldots, \hat{Q}_m$.

In what follows the hash function hash$(i, s) \mapsto (\alpha_1, \ldots, \alpha_m)$ produces an m-tuple of integers modulo p. As usual, we assume that hash$(\cdot)$ is publicly known and behaves as a random function. The ith child private key d_i and public key Q_i in our HD wallet are given by

$$d_i = \sum_{j=1}^{m} \alpha_j \hat{d}_j \quad \text{and} \quad Q_i = \sum_{j=1}^{m} \alpha_j \hat{Q}_j.$$

It is clear that child public keys can be computed from the master public keys $\hat{Q}_1, \ldots, \hat{Q}_m$, so that this HD wallet has the desired master public key property.

5   Security of Our HD Wallet Scheme

5.1   Security Definitions

If a child private key d_i is compromised then the adversary has learned only a random linear combination of the master private keys. Indeed, even if a *master* private key $\hat{d}_j$ is compromised then the adversary has learned only one out of the m keys needed to generate child keys. Intuitively speaking, in either case the breach is a linear constraint that reduces by at most one the dimension of the space of all possible master private key combinations; it seems that the adversary gains no useful information about any other master or child private key.

However, if m private keys are leaked then with overwhelming probability the adversary could recover all the master private keys by solving the corresponding linear system, in which case our HD wallet is completely broken. At best, then, our HD wallet is secure only if fewer than m private keys are leaked.

Within this context there is a wide spectrum of possible security definitions for an HD wallet. For example, a very strong definition of security might require that an adversary who obtains some combination of fewer than m master and child private keys cannot forge a signature for any uncompromised master or child key, even under an adaptive chosen-message attack. Since there is no known proof that the ECDSA (or finite field DSA) scheme is existentially unforgeable under chosen message attack, it is reasonable to consider somewhat weaker definitions.

Another security definition might require that an adversary who obtains fewer than m master and child private keys cannot recover any uncompromised master or child private key. We suspect that a security proof for our HD wallet could be obtained by reducing some variant of DLP to the task of breaking our HD wallet according to this security definition. However, it is likely that the variant of DLP in such a reduction would be new and contrived. (For a discussion of the dangers of basing the security of a cryptosystem upon the presumed intractability of contrived problems the reader is referred to Koblitz and Menezes [8] and references therein.)

For the purpose of this preliminary short paper, then, we content ourselves with a proof of security of our HD wallet against a *complete break*, in which an adversary who obtains fewer than m master and child private keys is able to recover *all* of the master private keys. Specifically, the problem of completely breaking our HD wallet is formalized as follows in Problem 1.

Problem 1. (Complete break of our HD wallet).

Input: (i) Master public keys $\hat{Q}_1, \ldots, \hat{Q}_m$, and (ii) an oracle that on input $\alpha_1, \ldots, \alpha_m \in \mathbb{Z}_p$ returns $k = \sum_{j=1}^m \alpha_j \hat{d}_j \pmod{p}$.

Restriction: The number of calls made to the oracle must be less than m.

Output: The master private keys $\hat{d}_1, \ldots, \hat{d}_m$.

5.2   Cryptographic Assumptions

We will prove that a complete break of our HD wallet is at least as hard as the so-called *one-more discrete logarithm problem (1MDLP)* defined as follows.

Problem 2. (One-more discrete logarithm (1MDLP) for generator $P \in \mathbb{G}$).

Input: (i) A *challenge* oracle that produces a random $Q_i \in \mathbb{G}$ when queried, and (ii) an oracle for DLP.

Restriction: Let m be the number of calls made to the challenge oracle. The number of calls made to the DLP oracle must be less than m.

Output: The discrete logarithms of all elements $Q_1, \ldots, Q_m$. That is, elements $d_1, \ldots, d_m$ of $\mathbb{Z}_p$ with $Q_i = d_i P$.

Although not as "natural" a problem as DLP, 1MDLP is arguably still a natural and clean mathematics problem. 1MDLP has appeared in prior literature—it was used, for example, by Bellare and Palacio to argue the security of the well known GQ and Schnorr identification schemes [4]. Indeed, 1MDLP has even been the subject of at least a bare minimum of scrutiny by the cryptographic community—again, see Koblitz and Menezes [8].

1MDLP is obviously no harder than DLP and there is some evidence suggesting that it is strictly easier, at least in some cases [7]. Nonetheless, it seems reasonable to assume that if DLP is intractable then so too is 1MDLP.

A Word of Caution. Although it may be reasonable to assume that 1MDLP is intractable in an asymptotic sense, it does not necessarily follow that an attacker could not efficiently solve 1MDLP for the specific choice of parameters used in real-world cryptosystems.

For example, the elliptic curve parameters in the secp256k1 standard used by Bitcoin are chosen so that the best known algorithms for DLP on the elliptic curve group take approximately 2^{128} steps [6]. However, it is conceivable that 1MDLP with these parameters could be solved in, say, only 2^{64} steps.

Such a solution to 1MDLP would not necessarily imply a complete break of our HD wallet because our security reduction is only unidirectional. Nevertheless, it would seriously call into question the security of our HD wallet with the secp256k1 parameters used by Bitcoin; a new security proof would be required.

5.3   Security Proof

Theorem 1. *A complete break of our HD wallet (Problem 1) is at least as hard as 1MDLP (Problem 2).*

Proof. Suppose we have an oracle that completely breaks our HD wallet for some number m of master private keys. This oracle can be used to solve 1MDLP with m queries to the challenge oracle as follows. First, query the challenge oracle m times to get m random group elements $\hat{Q}_1, \ldots, \hat{Q}_m$, which are passed as input to the oracle that completely breaks our HD wallet (Problem 1).

Calls by the oracle for Problem 1 to its input oracle on input $(\alpha_1, \ldots, \alpha_m)$ are simulated by querying the DLP oracle on $\alpha_1 \hat{Q}_1 + \cdots + \alpha_m \hat{Q}_m$ to obtain the required k. By assumption, the oracle for Problem 1 makes fewer than m such calls, so our reduction obeys the restriction of Problem 2. Also by assumption, the oracle for Problem 1 returns the master private keys $\hat{d}_1, \ldots, \hat{d}_m$, which is a correct solution to 1MDLP.   □

Remark 1. In Problem 1 the adversary is granted the luxury to *choose* the linear combination of master private keys revealed to him. In contrast, by compromising a child key in our HD wallet the adversary learns only a *random* linear combination of master private keys. Thus, our security proof holds even against adversaries who can somehow control the randomness used in deriving child private keys.

Acknowledgements. Research at the Perimeter Institute is supported by the Government of Canada through Industry Canada and by the Province of Ontario through the Ministry of Research and Innovation. GG also acknowledges support from CryptoWorks21. DS is supported by Australian Research Council (ARC) Discovery Project DP130104304.

References

1. Electrum lightweight Bitcoin wallet, November 2011. https://electrum.org/
2. Moneytree (2013). https://github.com/BitVault/money-tree, https://bitcointalk.org/index.php?topic=296139
3. Coinkite (2014). https://coinkite.com
4. Bellare, M., Palacio, A.: GQ and Schnorr identification schemes: proofs of security against impersonation under active and concurrent attacks. In: Yung, M. (ed.) CRYPTO 2002. LNCS, vol. 2442, pp. 162–177. Springer, Heidelberg (2002)
5. Buterin, V.: Deterministic wallets, their advantages and their understated flaws. Bitcoin Magazine, November 2013. http://bitcoinmagazine.com/8396/deterministic-wallets-advantages-flaw/
6. Certicom Research: SEC 2: Recommended Elliptic Curve Domain Parameters, v2.0 (2000). http://www.secg.org/
7. Koblitz, N., Menezes, A.: Another look at non-standard discrete log and Diffie-Hellman problems. J. Math. Cryptology **2**(4), 311–326 (2008)
8. Koblitz, N., Menezes, A.: Intractable problems in cryptography. In: Proceedings of the 9th Conference on Finite Fields and Their Applications, vol. 518, pp. 279–300. Contemporary Mathematics (2010)
9. Maxwell, G.: Deterministic wallets, June 2011. https://bitcointalk.org/index.php?topic=19137
10. Nakamoto, S.: Bitcoin: A peer-to-peer electronic cash system (2008). https://bitcoin.org/bitcoin.pdf
11. National Institute of Standards and Technology: FIPS-186-4: Digital Signature Standard (DSS), July 2013. http://nvlpubs.nist.gov/nistpubs/FIPS/NIST.FIPS.186-4.pdf
12. Wuille, P.: BIP32: Hierarchical Deterministic Wallets, February 2012. https://github.com/bitcoin/bips/blob/master/bip-0032.mediawiki

Authenticated Data Structures

Secure High-Rate Transaction Processing
in Bitcoin

Yonatan Sompolinsky[1]([✉]) and Aviv Zohar[1,2]

[1] School of Engineering and Computer Science,
The Hebrew University of Jerusalem, Jerusalem, Israel
{yoni_sompo,avivz}@cs.huji.ac.il
[2] Microsoft Research, Herzliya, Israel

Abstract. Bitcoin is a disruptive new crypto-currency based on a decentralized open-source protocol which has been gradually gaining momentum. Perhaps the most important question that will affect Bitcoin's success, is whether or not it will be able to scale to support the high volume of transactions required from a global currency system. We investigate the implications of having a higher transaction throughput on Bitcoin's security against double-spend attacks. We show that at high throughput, substantially weaker attackers are able to reverse payments they have made, even well after they were considered accepted by recipients. We address this security concern through the GHOST rule, a modification to the way Bitcoin nodes construct and re-organize the block chain, Bitcoin's core distributed data-structure. GHOST has been adopted and a variant of it has been implemented as part of the Ethereum project, a second generation distributed applications platform.

1   Introduction

Bitcoin is a disruptive protocol for distributed digital currency, which relies on cryptographic elements to secure its operation. Since its initial launch in 2009 by its mysterious creator Satoshi Nakamoto, general interest in the currency has been slowly increasing, and its uses have been slowly expanding.

While several obstacles such as regulatory uncertainty and an under-developed infrastructure still need to be overcome, the main challenges that must be faced from a computer science perspective are related to Bitcoin's ability to scale to higher transaction rates and to its ability to quickly process individual transactions. This paper aims to address both of these issues and the connections between them and Bitcoin's security against double-spend attacks.

The core idea behind the Bitcoin protocol is to replace the centralized control of money transmission ordinarily taken up by large organizations such as banks, credit card companies, and other money transmitters, by a large peer-to-peer network. The nodes of this network verify each other's work and thus ensure that no single entity is able to misbehave. Bitcoin achieves this by maintaining a complete and public record of all its transactions at each node in the network. This ledger, which is known as *the block chain*, is composed of a growing sequence

© International Financial Cryptography Association 2015
R. Böhme and T. Okamoto (Eds.): FC 2015, LNCS 8975, pp. 507–527, 2015.
DOI: 10.1007/978-3-662-47854-7_32

of *blocks*, each containing a set of approved transactions. The main challenge that Bitcoin overcomes is the synchronization of the ledger between the various nodes. Malicious parties may further try to interfere with this synchronization in order to double-spend—to redirect previously processed payments that will allow them to use the same money twice.

To help solve the double-spend problem blocks are required to contain a proof-of-work, which is computationally difficult to generate. The difficulty of this task is adaptively set so that a block is created approximately once every 10 min in the entire network. Once created, blocks are propagated through the network. The 10 min interval allows blocks to (usually) propagate to the vast majority of nodes before another block is created. If a node receives two conflicting blocks, which were created by distant nodes unaware of each other's work (or perhaps by a malicious attacker), it resolves the conflict by picking the block pertaining to the longest block chain and adopting it. Satoshi Nakamoto's original analysis of the protocol [12] shows that as long as any attacker holds less than 50 % of the computational power in the network, the probability that double-spend attacks succeed decreases exponentially with time, which essentially allows payments to be considered accepted and irreversible after some period. The analysis, however, assumes that blocks are sent across the network much faster than they are created, and so it is ill-fitted to a scenario in which many transactions are processed by the network (which necessitates the frequent creation of larger blocks, taking longer to transmit).

Indeed, capacity for additional transaction processing in Bitcoin is very much needed. As of December 2014, Bitcoin's network processes around 90 thousand transactions per day [2], a number which has been slowly growing, but still amounts to an average of roughly 1 transaction per second (TPS). In contrast, Visa's global payment system handled a reported 150 million transactions per day in 2010 (just under 2000 TPS), and has grown steadily since. If Bitcoin is not able to scale to appropriate rates that match demand, transaction fees will rise, and users will be driven to use other forms of payment.

Bitcoin's current low number of transactions is mainly due to its small userbase. Once adoption increases, the system will need to scale to process transactions at a higher rate, and previous security guarantees may no longer hold. We investigate how susceptible the protocol is to double-spend attacks when more transactions are processed per second. We note that larger block sizes or more frequent block creation events (which are required in order to increase the transaction throughput) result in more conflicts between blocks, which severely reduces the level of security from attacks.

To mitigate this, some methods for block compression were suggested by members in the Bitcoin community, e.g., transmitting only transaction hashes in blocks (an almost 16-fold reduction in size), or applying invertible Bloom lookup tables to communicate the differences between the subsets of transactions nodes are aware of [3]. Another approach is to use trustless off-chain transaction channels that slowly release money in minute portions to another party by updating a transaction that is only committed to the block chain once a reasonable sum of money has been transferred [1]. This approach has some downsides: money must be locked and is unusable for the duration of the channel's existence, it only allows the aggregation of transactions between two parties that maintain a channel, and finally, it is not always useful for other protocols built on top of block chains (such as Ethereum) where individual updates cannot be aggregated in a similar fashion.

We suggest an alternative to the longest-chain rule called GHOST, that changes the conflict-resolution procedure for the block chain. GHOST selects at each fork in the chain the heaviest subtree rooted at the fork. This protocol modification alleviates the above-mentioned security problem, and will help block-chain-based protocols grow further. A variant of GHOST has been adopted and implemented by the Ethereum project [4], a second generation distributed applications platform that has recently received a great deal of attention. To best utilize the capacity of the block chain all solutions should ideally be combined. Our own improvement, GHOST, can be seen as a modification which allows an increase in the protocol's block chain commitments, which in turn, will allow more transactions to take place at lower costs.

A second aspect of our work involves the time until the transaction is authorized. As blocks are currently created on average once every 10 min, a given transaction is only included in the chain after a relatively long amount of time. Several alternative currencies that have forked the Bitcoin source-code have modified this parameter and have set lower block creation rates (e.g., once every 12 seconds in the case of FastCoin). We explore and quantify the security implications of such choices, from lower resilience to attacks to the required waiting time for a transaction to be considered accepted.

It is important to note that in addition to the decreased difficulty of a double-spend attack, several other issues appear at high transaction rates: First, miners that are better connected to the network enjoy rewards slightly larger than their share of the hashing power, and second, the selfish mining strategy explored by Eyal and Sirer [8] can be employed by weaker miners. Both of these issues remain unsolved by the GHOST protocol alone. In a companion paper [10] we explore an additional modification (compatible with GHOST) that lowers the advantage of highly-connected miners, and provides an additional increase in throughput.

2   Basics of the Bitcoin Protocol

The Block Chain. Bitcoin uses a public ledger to record the entire transaction history, which essentially consists of a sequence of blocks, *the block chain*. New blocks are created from time to time and are added successively to the ledger. Each block contains the transactions that have occurred since the last block and a cryptographic hash of the previous block in the sequence, which identifies the predecessor uniquely.[1] A transaction is considered confirmed only once it is contained in some block which appears in this public log.[2]

---

[1] Hash collisions are so rare that this hash can be regarded as a unique identifier of the block.

[2] Merely being included in a block is not sufficient to fully guarantee the irreversibility of a transaction. Transactions become increasingly less likely to be reversed as more blocks are added on top of them to the chain.

The creation rate of blocks is set by requiring each block to contain a proof-of-work in its header, in the form of a solution to a computationally difficult problem (finding partial SHA-256 hash collisions). The problem depends on the most recent block, and is solved by randomly trying different inputs, thus ensuring some (random) time lag between successful block creation events. The reader is referred to [12] for a full explanation of the proof-of-work mechanism.

As the block chain, which represents the state of all "accounts", is kept locally at each node, it is imperative that any update to the state of accounts will be propagated to the entire network. Nodes which receive a transaction verify its validity, and send it, in turn, to all their neighbors. Similarly, nodes which receive a new block check its validity (i.e., its compatibility with all preceding blocks) and transmit it to their neighbors.

The Formation and Resolution of Forks. Successive blocks are not necessarily built atop one another, and thus they form a block tree rather than a single chain (Fig. 3 illustrates such a scenario). One reason for the existence of forks is the delay in the network: it is possible for two blocks to be created at (about) the same time by far-away nodes in the network, in which case neither will point at the other as its parent, and a fork occurs.

When faced with several (internally consistent) block chains each node in the network is required to adopt only one as the valid account of transactions, the "main chain". Bitcoin's rule is simple: pick the longest chain (or in case of ties, keep the one you received first). An important property of the longest-chain selection rule is that as time passes, all the nodes in the network will adopt the same main chain. Indeed, in order for a fork in the block tree to last, two fractions of the network need to successively create new blocks at about the same times, a series of events which becomes rarer as time develops.

In addition to delays, forks can also occur due to a malicious deviation of a node from the protocol. An attacker may choose to extend any arbitrary block, and generate forks. The protocol cannot and does not deal with these forks differently than with delay-induced ones; if the attacker manages to present a longer chain of blocks, this chain will be accepted by other nodes in the network, and the previous main chain will be abandoned.

Double-Spend Attacks. This method of overriding the main chain can be used by an attacker to reverse transactions, a scheme called a "double-spend attack". The attacker may pay some merchant and then secretly create a chain of blocks without this payment that is longer than the network's. By releasing his chain he can trigger the replacement in the ledger which effectively erases the transaction, or redirects the payment elsewhere (such an attack is illustrated in Fig. 3).

The computational effort required to create each block makes this attack a difficult undertaking, since the honest nodes usually have a great deal of computational power, and the attacker must get very lucky if he is to replace long chains.

However, if an attacker holds enough computational power he is able to generate blocks fast enough to bypass the main chain and override it, according to the longest-chain selection rule. This enables him to reverse any transaction that appears in the main chain at will. Specifically, if the attacker has more computational power than the rest of the network combined, he is able to generate blocks at a higher rate than the honest nodes and eventually to replace chains of arbitrary length. This stronger form of attack is known in Bitcoin jargon as "the 50 % attack".[3]

3   The Model

We model the Bitcoin network as a directed graph $G = (V, E)$. Each node v has some fraction $p_v \geq 0$ of the computational power of the entire network: $\sum_{v \in V} p_v = 1$. Each individual node v in the network generates blocks according to a Poisson process with a rate of $p_v \cdot \lambda$, so that the entire network combined generates blocks at a Poisson process with rate λ (the protocol's current value, $\lambda = \frac{1}{600}$, was chosen by Satoshi at Bitcoin's inception). We assume that each edge $e \in E$ has a delay d_e associated with it, which is simply the time it takes to send a block across it.

In the context of a network under attack, we will use $\lambda = \lambda_h$ as the honest network's block creation rate. The attacker's rate is denoted relative to the honest network by $q \cdot \lambda_h > 0$, for some $q > 0$. In contrast to the honest network, we assume that the attacker is creating long chains efficiently: its blocks are always built on top of one another.[4] See Appendix A for a more detailed consideration of the relation between the attacker and the network.

For every block B, we denote by $time(B)$ its (absolute) creation time. The blocks essentially form a time-developing tree structure that is rooted at the genesis block – the first block created at the moment of Bitcoin's inception; we denote the structure of this tree at time t by $tree(t)$, and by $subtree(B)$ the subtree rooted at B. Finally, the depth of block B in the tree will be denoted $depth(B)$.

The structure of the block tree is affected by the blocks that nodes point to as their parent, and extend. Formally, we model this choice as a function $s(\cdot)$ which maps a block tree $T = (V_T, E_T)$ to a block $B \in V_T$ that is to be the parent of the next block. Every node may posses a different view of the tree (it may not have heard of all created blocks) and thus applies s to its currently known tree.

The Bitcoin protocol currently requires nodes to build new blocks at the end of the longest chain that is known to them. Accordingly, we denote by $longest(t)$

---

[3] The 50 % attack owes its name to Satoshi's result showing that the main chain is secure (after sufficient waiting periods) as long as the attacker holds less than 50 % of the computational power. We show in this paper that in fact networks with delays are more vulnerable and can be attacked with less computational power.

[4] This essentially assumes that all computational assets held by the attacker are centralized and that blocks that it creates are transmitted instantly in its internal network.

the deepest leaf in $tree(t)$. Unless explicitly stated otherwise, we assume nodes follow this rule.

The term "main chain" will correspond to the path from the genesis block to the leaf that is selected for extension (usually $longest(t)$). The main chain is considered by nodes to be the single accepted version of transaction history. Its growth rate is therefore one of the core measures of the system's performance. Formally, the time it takes the main chain to advance from length $n-1$ to n is a random variable that we denote as τ_n. We denote $\tau = \lim_{n\to\infty} \frac{1}{n} \sum_{i=1}^{n} \tau_n$, and $\beta = \frac{1}{E[\tau]}$. β is the rate of block addition to the main chain, while λ is the rate of block addition to the block tree.[5]

Another parameter embedded in the protocol is the maximal block size (in KB), denoted by b. We assume throughout the paper that there is high demand for transaction processing and that blocks are always full to the limit.

Finally, we define the primary measure of Bitcoin's scalability as the number of transactions per second (TPS) the system adds to the history (the main chain), in expectation. We denote by K the average number of transactions per KB. The TPS is then: $TPS(\lambda, b) := \beta(\lambda, b) \cdot b \cdot K$.

4   Reduced Security at High Throughput

In this section we explain why the Bitcoin protocol becomes more susceptible to double-spend attacks when its throughput is increased. Assume an attacker creates blocks at a rate of $q \cdot \lambda_h$. If $q \cdot \lambda_h$ is greater than the growth rate of the network's main chain, β, the attack will always be successful (given enough time), regardless of the current length of the chain it aims to bypass and replace (by The Law of Large Numbers). Conversely, if $q < \frac{\beta}{\lambda_h}$, the probability of the attacker's chain bypassing the main chain decreases exponentially as the main chain grows in length (See Theorem 10 for the formal proof). We therefore think of the ratio $\frac{\beta}{\lambda_h}$ as the "security threshold" of the system.

The throughput of the protocol is affected by the two elementary parameters: the block creation rate λ, and the block size b. The difficulty of the computational problem which is required to create a valid block can be lowered in order to accelerate the block creation process. Similarly, larger blocks can be allowed to propagate if one wishes to increase the block size. A naïve attempt at increasing the throughput can be made by simply increasing both parameters. We argue that both of these modifications lead to an increased number of forks in the block tree, which in turn leads to a reduction of the security threshold of the system. In other words, *attackers can perform effective attacks with less computational power once the throughput is increased.* The qualitative tradeoffs between these parameters are depicted in Fig. 2.

---

[5] See Theorem 54, Chap. 2 in [17] for the compatibility of these two interpretations of β.

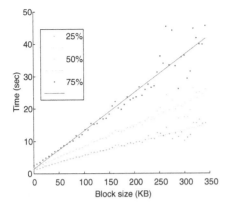

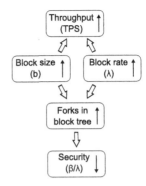

Fig. 1. The relation between the block size and the time it took to reach 25% (red), 50% (green), and 75% (blue) of monitored nodes, based on data provided by Decker and Wattenhofer [7] (Colour figure online).

Fig. 2. A general view of tradeoffs in the Bitcoin protocol. Increasing the block size or the block rate causes an increase in the TPS, but also decreases the security from double-spend attacks.

Larger Blocks. Indeed, while a node has not yet learned of the latest addition to the main chain, any block that it creates will not add to that chain, but rather contribute to a less updated alternative branch. Thus as the block size is increased, blocks naturally take longer to propagate through the network, hence more forks occur. This observation is well supported by a measurement study conducted by Decker and Wattenhofer [7] who have measured block propagation delays in the Bitcoin network. Figure 1, which is based on raw data that they have generously shared with us, depicts a clear linear relation between the block size and its propagation time.

Accelerated Block Creation. Similarly, if block creation is accelerated, more blocks are being created by the honest network (larger λ_h) while the most recent block in the main chain is propagated. Again, these blocks will often be created by nodes that are not fully up to date and will not extend the longest chain. The attacker on the other hand, also creates blocks faster (at a rate of $q \cdot \lambda_h$), but does not suffer from a loss of efficiency.

Reduced Security. In both cases described above, blocks that are created do not always contribute to the lengthening of the main chain, which makes it easier for an attacker to replace it.

Figure 3 illustrates a scenario in which a highly forked block tree was created by the honest network. The attacker secretly creates a chain of 6 blocks (denoted 1A, 2A, ..., 6A) which is clearly longer than the network's longest chain (ending in block 5B). If block propagation was faster (in relation to the creation rate),

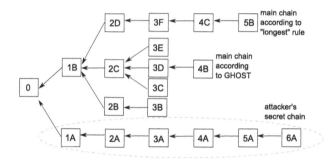

Fig. 3. A block tree in which the longest chain and the chain selected by GHOST differ. An attacker's chain is able to switch the longest chain, but not the one selected by GHOST.

all blocks in the honest network's tree would form a single long chain and would not be overtaken by the attacker.

5   The Greedy Heaviest-Observed Sub-Tree (GHOST)

In this section we present our main contribution to the protocol: a new policy for the selection of the main chain in the block tree. The advantage of this suggested change to the protocol is that it maintains the security threshold for successful 50 % attacks at 1 (rather than $\frac{\beta}{\lambda_h}$), even if the network suffers from extreme delays and the attacker does not. This allows the protocol designer to set high block creation rates and large block sizes without the fear of approaching the 50 %-attack cliff edge, which in turn implies that a high transaction throughput can be securely maintained.

The basic observation behind the protocol modification that we suggest, is that blocks that are off the main chain can still contribute to its weight. Consider, for example, the block tree in Fig. 3. Block 1B is supported by blocks 2B, 2C, and 2D that extend it directly, and include it in their chain. Similarly, blocks 3C, 3D, and 3E support both 1B and 2C as part of their chain. The heaviest subtree protocol we suggest makes use of this fact, and adds additional weight to blocks, helping to ensure that they will be part of the main chain.

Recall our definition from Sect. 3; any node chooses the parent of its next block according to a policy $s(T)$, that maps a tree T to a block in T which essentially represents the main chain. Formally, our new protocol is a new parent-selection policy. This new policy redefines the main chain, which is what should be regarded as the valid branch of transaction history.

For a block B in a block tree T, let $subtree(B)$ be the subtree rooted at B, and let $Children_T(B)$ be the set of blocks directly referencing B as their parent. Denote by $GHOST(T)$ the parent-selection policy we propose, defined as the output of the following algorithm.

Algorithm 1. *Greedy Heaviest-Observed Sub-Tree (GHOST)*
Input: Block tree T

1. *set B ← Genesis Block*
2. *if $Children_T(B) = \emptyset$ then return(B) and exit*
3. *else update $B \leftarrow \underset{C \in Children_T(B)}{\mathrm{argmax}} |subtree_T(C)|^6$*
4. *goto line 2*

The algorithm follows a path from the root of the tree (the genesis block) and chooses at each fork the block leading to the heaviest subtree. In the tree depicted in Fig. 3, for instance, the subtree of block 1B contains 12 blocks, whereas that of 1 A contains only 6. The algorithm will thus pick 1B as belonging to the main chain, and proceed to resolve the forks inside *subtree*(1B). This will result the choice of blocks 0, 1B, 2C, 3D, 4B as the main chain of the tree (and not the longest chain, ending in block 5B). This makes forks inside the subtree rooted at 1B of no consequence to the weight of block 1B itself — every addition of a block to *subtree*(1B) makes it harder to omit it from the main chain. In particular, when the attacker publishes its 6-blocks long secret chain, the same blocks as before remain in the main chain.

5.1   Basic Properties of GHOST

It is imperative to first show that all nodes eventually adopt the same history when following GHOST. For every block B define by ψ_B the earliest moment at which it was either abandoned by all nodes, or adopted by them all. We call the adoption of a block by all nodes the *collapse* of the fork.

Proposition 2 (The Convergence of History). $Pr(\psi_B < \infty) = 1$. *In other words, every block is eventually either fully abandoned or fully adopted. Moreover,* $E[\psi_B] < \infty$.

Proof. Let D be the delay diameter of the network. Assume that at time $t > time(B)$ block B is neither adopted by all nodes nor abandoned by all of them. Denote by $\mathcal{E}_t$ the event in which the next block creation in the system occurs between times $t + D$ and $t + 2D$, and then no other block is produced until time $t + 3D$. We argue that once such an event occurs, block B is either adopted or abandoned by all nodes. Indeed, between time t and $t + D$ all nodes learn of all existing blocks (as no new ones are manufactured), and therefore each pair of leaves (of the block tree) that have nodes actively trying to extend them must have equal weight subtrees rooted at some common ancestor. A single block is then created which breaks these ties, and another D time units allow it to propagate to all nodes, which causes them to switch to a single shared history. Notice that $Pr(\mathcal{E}_t)$ is uniformly (in t) lower bounded by a positive number, as it doesn't depend on t (as the exponential distribution is memoryless). Hence the

---

[6] We are in fact interested in the subtree with the hardest combined proof-of-work, but for the sake of conciseness, we write the size of the subtree instead.

expected waiting time for the first $\mathcal{E}_t$ event is finite (see "Awaiting the almost inevitable" in [18], Chap. 10.11). Finally, the stopping time ψ_B is upper bounded, by definition, by the waiting time for the first $\mathcal{E}_t$, implying $E[\psi_B] < \infty$. □

We now show the main advantage of the GHOST chain selection rule, namely, that it is resilient to 50 % attacks, even at high rates or with significant delays in the network: By waiting a sufficiently long period of time τ after the block's creation, the probability that its status will change from "accepted" to "abandoned" can be made arbitrarily small.

Proposition 3 (Resilience to 50 % Attacks). *Assume the attacker's block creation rate is $q \cdot \lambda_h$, and $0 \le q < 1$. The probability that a block B will be off the main chain sometime after $time(B) + \tau$, given that it was in the main chain at $time(B) + \tau$, goes to zero as τ goes to infinity.*

Contrast the statement above with the security threshold introduced in Sect. 4, where $q < \frac{\beta}{\lambda_h}$ was required to guarantee resilience against 50 % attacks. This proposition suggests that in any network following the GHOST rule, the security threshold is 1.

Proof (of Proposition 3). The event in which B is eventually discarded from the main chain is contained in the event that a collapse has yet to occur (i.e., $\psi_B \ge time(B) + \tau$). Relying again on the finiteness of $E[\psi_B]$ (Proposition 2), and applying Markov's inequality, it follows that the probability that by $time(B) + \tau$, B was either already abandoned or already adopted by all (honest) nodes goes to 1, as τ goes to infinity. In the former case, the proposition holds trivially. In the latter case, blocks are now built in B's subtree at the rate of λ_h, which is higher than $q\lambda_h$. Thus, as τ grows, the gap between the size of $subtree(B)$ and the attacker's chain grows, making the probability of the attack succeeding sometime in the future arbitrarily low (The Law of Large Numbers). □

The Rate of Collapse in GHOST. In Subsect. 5.1 we have discussed the collapse time ψ_B for any block B and its implications to the growth and convergence of the main chain in GHOST. Long living forks imply longer waiting times until the entire network contributes confirmations to a block, and further implies long waiting times for transaction authorization. It can prove useful to further investigate how fast the collapse at B occurs. We do this for a simple model including only two forks, each with equal contributing computational power. Even this seemingly simple case proves to be non-trivial.

Theorem 4. *Consider a network with two nodes, u and v, that equally create blocks at a rate of $\lambda/2$, which are connected by a single link with delay d. For any block B, $E[n_B] \le \dfrac{(d\lambda)^2}{8} + \dfrac{d\lambda}{2}$, where $n_B := |subtree_T(B)|$ for $T = tree(\psi_B)$.*

The theorem gives an upper bound for the special configuration of two nodes; we conjecture, however, that it is the worst case, and that in general setups collapses occur even faster. See the online full version for its proof.

6   Main Chain Growth in GHOST and in Longest-Chain

In this section we begin to systematically compare the two chain selection rules. Central to this comparison is an analysis of the growth rate of the main chain (β) under each one. Since this growth rate is highly dependent on the exact topology of the network which is both unknown and extremely difficult to measure, we take a dual approach: First we bound the rates analytically from above and below. Second, we simulate networks with randomly sampled overlay topologies and measure the resulting block-trees. We then go on to discuss the implications of these results in terms of security, throughput, and resource use of each rule.

6.1   A Lower Bound

We begin our analysis with the following approach: suppose that a cluster of relatively well connected nodes (with delay diameter D) contains a fraction $0 \leq \alpha \leq 1$ of the computational power of the entire network. In this case, blocks created within this sub-network propagate internally relatively quickly, and we can bound the rate of growth of the main chain from below. The bounds are tight, both for longest-chain and for GHOST, and thus form a good basis for comparison.

Lemma 5 (Longest-Chain and Bounded Delay). *Let $G=(V,E)$ be a network graph (a sub-graph of the entire network) which generates blocks at a rate $\lambda' = \alpha \cdot \lambda$ with delay diameter D. Then under the longest-chain rule, the rate at which the longest chain grows $\beta(\lambda) \geq \frac{\lambda'}{1+\lambda' \cdot D}$.*

Lemma 6 (GHOST and Bounded Delay). *Let $G=(V,E)$ be a network graph (a sub-graph of the entire network) which generates blocks at a rate $\lambda' = \alpha \cdot \lambda$ with delay diameter D. Then under the GHOST rule, the rate at which the longest chain grows $\beta(\lambda) \geq \frac{\lambda'}{1+2\lambda' \cdot D}$.*

Both Lemmas 5 and 6 can be shown to be tight. The bound is achieved in a complete graph with n nodes, $n \to \infty$, where the delay on all edges is exactly D, and each node has $1/n$'th of the computational power. This lower bound can thus be thought of as approximating the ideal decentralized network, where the computational power is well distributed among many equidistant nodes.

Lemma 5 follows, intuitively, from the fact that after some block U at depth n was created and sent to all nodes (D seconds), it takes in expectation $\frac{1}{\lambda}$ seconds for the next block U' to be created. As the creator of U' was certainly aware of the creation of U, its depth must be at least $n + 1$. The rate is thus lower bounded by $\frac{1}{D+\frac{1}{\lambda'}} = \frac{\lambda'}{1+\lambda' \cdot D}$. Refer to Appendix B for a formal proof.

As GHOST does not select the longest chain, it can be expected that the rate of growth of its main chain will be somewhat lower than in the longest-chain rule. This is indeed the case. The loss in growth rate, however, is relatively minor, and unlike in the longest-chain rule, has no bearing on the security of GHOST. Lemma 6 follows as an immediate consequence of the following claim, which is proven in Appendix C.

Claim 7. *Let B be a block in tree T in a network as in Lemma 6, then regardless of history, the expected waiting time for the creation of the last child of B is upper bounded by $2D + \frac{1}{\lambda'}$.*

Application to Throughput (Under Longest-Chain). What recommendations should we give the designer of the system who wishes to set the protocol's parameters, given that the network's topology is unknown? We now show how some rather limited knowledge of the network's topology could be used by the designer to guarantee a certain measure of security.

Assume we have managed to measure the delay diameter of some fraction of the network, namely, the maximal time $D(b)$ it takes a block of size b to arrive at some fraction α of the network. Following the results depicted in Fig. 1, we adopt a linear model of the delays; we thus assume that $D(b)$ is of the form $D(b) = D_{prop} + D_{bw} \cdot b$. Notice that D_{prop} is a measure of aggregate propagation delay, and D_{bw} is an aggregate measure of bandwidth in units of seconds per KB.

Lemma 8. *Assume there exists a sub-network with a block creation rate of $\alpha\lambda$ and delay diameter $D(b)$, in a network following the longest-chain rule. Then for any $x \in \left(0, \frac{K}{D_{bw}}\right)$, the protocol is able to achieve both a throughput of at least x TPS and a security threshold of at least $\alpha \cdot \left(1 - \frac{x \cdot D_{bw}}{K}\right)$, through a right choice of the parameters b and λ.*

Proof. By Lemma 5, the main chain grows at a rate of at least $\frac{1}{\frac{1}{\alpha\lambda} + D(b)}$. By the definition of the throughput, $TPS = b \cdot K \cdot \beta \geq \frac{K}{\frac{\frac{1}{\alpha\lambda} + D_{prop}}{b} + D_{bw}}$. For any $x \in \left(0, \frac{K}{D_{bw}}\right)$, there exists a large enough $b = b_x$ such that the RHS equals x (fixing λ), thereby guaranteeing $TPS \geq x$. The lower bound on β then implies:

$$\frac{\beta}{\alpha\lambda} \geq \frac{1}{1 + \alpha\lambda\left(D_{prop} + b_x \cdot D_{bw}\right)} = 1 - \frac{1}{\frac{1}{\alpha\lambda \cdot b_x \cdot D_{bw}} + \frac{D_{prop}}{b_x \cdot D_{bw}} + 1} = 1 - \frac{x \cdot D_{bw}}{K}.$$

$\square$

Any evaluation of the real Bitcoin network's behavior under higher throughput requires full knowledge of the topology of the network. Unfortunately, the structure is both unknown (partly because it is hard to measure, but also because miners attempt to keep their connections secret) and keeps shifting as nodes connect and disconnect. To obtain an order of magnitude estimation we apply Decker and Watenhoffer's measurements of Bitcoin's network to the bound from Lemma 8.

The best linear fit to the results, for $\alpha = 0.5$, yields a slope of $D_{bw} = 0.066$. This implies, for instance, an achievable throughput of 15.15 TPS, coupled with resilience to attackers with q up to 0.25 computational power.

Application of the Bound to GHOST (Efficiency). We have shown in Proposition 3 that the security threshold in a network following GHOST is always 1. While this means there is no limiting security constraint (contrary to the longest-chain case), the throughput cannot grow limitlessly: the transmission of many blocks (only a fraction of which contribute to the main chain) consumes bandwidth. Therefore, the ratio $\frac{\beta}{\lambda}$ is still of interest, not in a security context, but rather as a measure of the network's efficiency in its resource utilization.

Following the same method as previously, one can apply the linear delays model to Lemma 6 and show that the network's efficiency under a given throughput is at least $\alpha \cdot \left(1 - \frac{TPS \cdot 2 \cdot D_{bw}}{K}\right)$. E.g., the network is able to process 9.09 transactions per second, while maintaining an efficiency of at least 0.2.

6.2   An Upper Bound

We proceed now to give upper bounds on the main chain's growth rate. The idea of the upper bound is to locate a partition of the network graph, such that blocks take at least d time units to cross the partition (i.e., all links crossing the cut have delay at least d). Given such a partition the network is inherently inefficient to some degree, as the communication delay between the two parts may cause forks. The following theorem formalizes this:

Theorem 9. *Let $G=(V,E)$ be the network graph. Let $S,T \subset V$ be a partition of the nodes such that $\forall s \in S, \forall t \in T$ we have $d_{\{s,t\}} \geq d$, and let $p_S, p_T (p_S \neq p_T)$ be the fraction of computational power owned by nodes in S,T correspondingly. Then both under longest-chain and under GHOST, the main chain's growth rate is bounded from above as follows: $\beta(\lambda) \leq \frac{(p_S\lambda)^2 e^{p_S\lambda 2d} - (p_T\lambda)^2 e^{p_T\lambda 2d}}{p_S\lambda e^{p_S\lambda 2d} - p_T\lambda e^{p_T\lambda 2d}}$.*

The theorem is tight – networks consisting of only two nodes add blocks to the main chain at *exactly* this rate. We defer the rather involved proof to the online full version.

6.3   Simulation Results

We simulated the growth of the main chain in networks roughly emulating the topologies of Bitcoin's P2P overlay network for nodes adhering either to longest-chain or to GHOST. Following a behavior similar to the default in Bitcoin's reference client, each node initiates links to 8 uniformly selected neighbors (and accepts all links others initiated). We simulate a network with 1000 nodes, and assign computational power uniformly at random. The propagation delays on the links were sampled from a normal distribution ($\mu = \sigma = 100$ milliseconds). Similarly, the bandwidth of each node was drawn from a normal distribution ($\mu = 1, \sigma = 0.2$ MB). Both values were redrawn for negative results. The system was later allowed to evolve as blocks were propagated by nodes. Figure 5 depicts the security threshold measured in the system as a function of the block creation rate. Figure 4 illustrates the resulting TPS in both cases, and shows that the loss

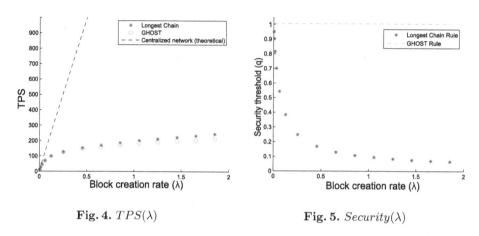

Fig. 4. $TPS(\lambda)$ **Fig. 5.** $Security(\lambda)$

in efficiency of network resources caused by following the GHOST rule is indeed relatively small. See further discussion in Subsect. 6.1.

7   Security Against Weak Attackers

We have so far considered only the effect that delayed block propagation has on the 50 % attack. Even attackers with a modest block creation rate can still succeed in a double-spend attack if they are lucky enough to generate many blocks in a quick burst; Satoshi, in his original paper, analyzes this threat. His analysis does not apply, however, to networks with non-negligible delay, and so we revisit this question.

The Acceptance Policy in Longest-Chain. The process of transaction authorization is defined by an acceptance policy chosen by the recipient of funds. Formally, the policy can be described as a function $n(t, r, q)$, where r is the risk the recipient is willing to tolerate, q the upper bound on the attacker's fraction of computational power, and t the time that elapsed since the transaction was broadcast to the network. If the transaction receiver observes n blocks ("confirmations") atop his transaction by time t, he approves it only if $n \geq n(t, r, q)$, and otherwise waits for n to increase.[7] The policies for the GHOST and longest-chain rules differ. Notice however, that in both cases, if t seconds have passed since the transaction was received, the probability that the attacker has completed k blocks is $\zeta_k := e^{-q\lambda_h t} \frac{(q\lambda_h t)^k}{k!}$. Thus, given some n, t we have a probability distribution on the initial gap between the attacker and the honest network. The following theorem bounds the probability that an attacker will close this gap.

---

[7] Previous work, such as [12,16], considered simpler policies that did not take elapsed time into account.

Theorem 10. *Consider a network G with delays. Let $1/\beta_1$ be an upper-bound on the expected waiting time for the next lengthening of the main chain, for all possible states of the system. Let $q\lambda_h < \beta_1$ be the creation rate of the attacker (according to a Poisson process), and suppose the gap between the network's longest chain and that of the attacker is X_0 blocks. Then the probability that the attacker will succeed in extending its chain to be longer than the network's is at most $\left(\frac{q\lambda_h}{\beta_1}\right)^{X_0+1}$.*

The theorem is proved in the online full version. This result justifies the following acceptance policy:

$$n(t,r,q) := \min_n \left\{ \sum_{k=0}^{n} \zeta_k \cdot \left(\frac{q\lambda_h}{\beta_1}\right)^{n-k+1} + \sum_{k=n+1}^{\infty} \zeta_k \leq r \right\}$$

The first term inside the parenthesis corresponds to the chance of the attacker closing the gap (at some future time) given that at time t he is behind by $n-k$ blocks. The second term aggregates the probability that its chain is long enough at the moment of acceptance.

The Acceptance Policy in GHOST. In GHOST, a block B gains confirmations from all blocks in its subtree. Once a collapse to a single subtree occurs, further confirmations are added at a full rate of λ_h. This justifies the following policy:

$$n(t,r,q) := \min_n \left\{ (1-\eta_B^t) \cdot \left(\sum_{k=0}^{n} \zeta_k \cdot \left(\frac{q\lambda_h}{\lambda_h}\right)^{n-k+1} + \sum_{k=n+1}^{\infty} \zeta_k \right) + \eta_B^t \leq r \right\}$$

where η_B^t is the probability that at time t, block B has yet to be included in the main chain of the entire honest network. The formulation given above includes the event of a collapse. Subject to that occurrence, block B gains confirmations at a faster pace.

8   GHOST Implementation Details

Below we outline some additional details about the use and implementation of the GHOST chain selection rule.

Links to Multiple Parents. As our protocol requires knowledge of off-chain blocks by all nodes, we propose that their headers (but not necessarily their entire contents) be propagated to all nodes. Information about off-chain blocks can then be embedded inside each block by simply listing the hashes of other childless blocks it is aware of.

Deployment. At low block creation rates, and with small block sizes, both GHOST and the conventional longest-chain rule behave the same: all blocks will simply be on a single long chain. Differences between the two rules appear only at high throughputs. The adoption of GHOST can therefore be gradual at low transaction rates–nodes will be partially compatible with the longest-chain version as long as transaction rates do not increase (additional references to block headers can be placed inside fields that the regular protocol currently ignores, and so backward compatibility can be maintained). This point, however, is of little importance. Increasing Bitcoin's block size or the block creation rate will require a hard fork in the protocol. Consequently, for these changes to take place a majority of the mining power needs to accept them.

Retargeting (Difficulty Adjustment). Given potentially complex relations between the growth rate of the main chain and the rate of created blocks, and the fact that GHOST depends more on the total rate of block creation, we suggest a change in the way automatic difficulty adjustments to the proof-of-work are done. Instead of targeting a certain rate of growth for the longest chain, i.e., β (which is Bitcoin's current strategy), we suggest that the total rate of block creation be kept constant (λ), which can be done, as the information on the entire block tree is available following the links to all ancestor blocks. Notice that the relation between β and the difficulty is highly complex, and so Bitcoin's current targeting mechanism will malfunction at high rates.

Fees and Minted Coins. While GHOST does make use of off-chain blocks to secure the protocol, we believe it is best to allocate minted coins only to the creators of blocks that are on the main chain, similarly to how the longest chain rule works today. The rate of minting can be adjusted independently from the block creation rate (but in a very similar way) by adjusting the amount of minted coins per block given the measured number of blocks in the recent past (e.g., in a 2 week window). A companion paper on *Inclusive protocols* [10] discusses the inclusion of transactions from blocks that are off the main chain (and the allocation of related fees).

Preventing Amplified Denial of Service Attacks. As each block in Bitcoin is sent to the entire network by the nodes themselves, any burst of blocks may disrupt the network. Attackers are naturally limited in their ability to create *recent* blocks due to the proof-of-work requirement, but may try to create blocks off-chain that are built upon blocks in the distant past (when the difficulty level was low). This issue is handled by the current implementation using checkpoints (points in the chain before which no additional off-chain blocks are accepted). Other mechanisms that involve probabilistic proofs of combined difficulty (for large chains that go back too far in the past) have also been suggested. Both solutions can be adapted to GHOST as well.

9   Additional Related Work

The original security analysis done by Satoshi [12] has been improved in a whitepaper published by Meni Rosenfeld [16]. Several papers have looked at incentive concerns related to the operation of the protocol, examining issues related to transaction propagation [6], selfish mining [8], and the distribution of rewards within mining-pools [15]. Other works on Bitcoin have looked at its privacy aspects [5,13], including analysis of its transaction graph [14] which allows to de-anonymize some of its users. The Zerocoin protocol has been offered as a way to improve anonymity [11].

Our work deals, among other issues, with enabling fast confirmations for transactions in the network. A paper by Karame *et. al.* discusses similar issues, that relate to possible attacks on nodes that accept zero-confirmation transactions [9]. They suggest several countermeasures that may help avoid such attacks. Their work does not deal with an attack by an adversary with a significant block creation rate, which can compute alternative chains on its own.

A paper closely related to ours is one that was published by Decker and Wattenhofer, in which they present a measurement study of message propagation times in the Bitcoin network. They associate delays with the creation of forks in the block-tree, and with an increased vulnerability to the 50 % attack [7]. As far as we are aware, no other work addresses the issue of Bitcoin's scalability, or its security in a network with delayed block propagation.

10   Conclusion

This paper has focused primarily on the effect network delays have on Bitcoin's security from double-spend attacks. In this context we presented GHOST, our suggestion for the modification of the protocol, which helps secure Bitcoin when processing transactions at high rates. Regarding the current state of the protocol, we have given some theoretical security guarantees that can be applicable even if limited information is known about the network topology. Our results underscore the importance of the health of the network to Bitcoin's security and scalability.

Many additional research questions should be addressed in light of our results: How should the block creation rate and block size dynamically adjust to changing network conditions? Additionally, in Bitcoin so-called Simplified Protocol Verification nodes can operate without downloading the entire block chain. If we are to increase the number of blocks per second, their job becomes harder. It is therefore of great interest to create light nodes that can, for example, verify the block chain probabilistically, without needing to download all headers. Finally, it can be shown that in networks with delay that operate at high rates, large miners get more than their fair share of the blocks, an effect that skews rewards in favor of large miners and slowly pushes the system towards a more centralized one. One way to mitigate the problem, which can be applied to GHOST as well, is presented in a companion paper on *Inclusive protocols* [10].

Acknowledgements. The authors were supported in part by the Israel Science Foundation (Grants 616/13, and 1773/13), and by the Israel Smart Grid (ISG) Consortium.

A Where Is the Attacker in Longest Chain?

From a practical perspective, we must remember that a node listening to the Bitcoin network does not really know the amount of computational power the honest nodes in the network possess. In particular, the attacker may be building blocks along with the network up until the time of the attack, or he may not. Therefore, all that is observed is some amount of computational power which triggers the reported block creation rate λ_{rep}. We now ask ourselves what is the worst case when using the longest-chain rule? An attacker who participates or one that does not? Also, what is the right security threshold in terms of λ_{rep} (rather than λ_h which is unknown)?

We begin with the assumption that the attacker has a fraction q of the computational power of the honest network. Denote by λ_a, λ_h the block creation rate of the attacker and the honest nodes respectively, and by $\lambda = \lambda_a + \lambda_h$ their joint rate. Our assumption is $\lambda_a = q\lambda_h$ as before. λ_{rep} is the observed rate of block creation in the system (before the attack), which is in the range $[\lambda_h, \lambda_h + \lambda_a]$. The following proposition shows that for a given threshold q it is enough to use λ_{rep} as a measure of the honest network's creation rate, as the attacker would only make it harder on itself if it joined the rest of the network and generated blocks before the attack. This is quite counter-intuitive, as the attacker that adds to the rate before the attack fools the network into thinking it is stronger. In reality, it increases the number of its blocks but lowers the network's efficiency, which is the true measure of resilience to attacks.

Proposition 11. *If the network's observed block rate is λ_{rep}, for a given block size, and $\beta(\lambda_{rep}) \geq q\lambda_{rep}$, then the network is secure against an attacker with computational power lower than $q\lambda_h$. Furthermore, an attacker is most effective if it does not participate in block mining before the attack.*

Proof. If a fraction f of the attacker's blocks were included in λ_{rep} prior to the attack, then $\lambda_{rep} = \lambda_h + f \cdot \lambda_a$. I.e., $\lambda_h = \lambda_{rep} - f \cdot \lambda_a = \lambda_{rep} - fq\lambda_h$. This implies that $\lambda_h = \frac{\lambda_{rep}}{1+f \cdot q}$. Hence,

$$\beta(\lambda_h) = \beta\left(\frac{\lambda_{rep}}{1 + f \cdot q}\right) \geq^1 \beta(\lambda_{rep}) \geq^2 q\lambda_{rep} \geq^3 q\lambda_h =^4 \lambda_a,$$

meaning that the longest chain of the honest network alone outgrows the block creation rate of the attacker, and thus gives resilience to attacks after some time. In the above, inequality 1 follows from β's monotonicity, 2 follows from the proposition's assumption, 3 from the fact that λ_{rep} includes the honest network's rate, and 4 from the initial assumption on the attacker's block creation rate.

The attacker's chain thus grows slower than the longest chain in the honest network's tree.

The lower f is, the tighter the first inequality, and the smaller the gap between the rate of network and that of the attacker — making the attack easier to carry out. Therefore, an attacker is most effective when $f = 0$.   □

B   Proof of Lemma 5

Lemma 5:
Let $G=(V,E)$ be a network graph (a sub-graph of the entire network) which generates blocks at a rate $\lambda' = \alpha \cdot \lambda$ with delay diameter D. Then under the longest-chain rule, the rate at which the longest chain grows $\beta(\lambda) \geq \frac{\lambda'}{1+\lambda' \cdot D}$.

Proof. We follow a sequence of block creation events for blocks $U_0, U_1, U_2, \ldots$ such that each block U_{i+1} is the first block to be created after D seconds have passed from the creation of the previous block U_i (so that there has been sufficient time to send U_i to all nodes in the network), i.e., the first block B for which $time(B) - D > time(U_i)$. Let us now make the following claim.

Claim 12. *Let $U_0, U_1, U_2, \ldots$ be a series of blocks that were created at least D time units apart. Then for all $n \in \mathbb{N}$: $Depth(U_n) - Depth(U_0) \geq n$.*

The claim can be proven by induction, and we defer its proof to the online full version.
    Denote by $X_i = time(U_i) - time(U_{i-1})$ the random variable representing the time between block creations. Notice that the X_i's are i.i.d. random variables (because the time interval they denote is exactly D time units for the block to spread plus an exponentially distributed waiting time for the next block's creation somewhere in the network). Also note that $\beta \geq E[\frac{1}{n}\sum_{i=1}^{n} X_i]^{-1}$, as the chain grows by at least n during the time $\sum_{i=1}^{n} X_i$. We therefore have $\beta \geq \frac{1}{E[X_1]}$. Additionally, we know that $E[X_1] = D + E[Y]$, where Y is a random variable with an exponential distribution with parameter λ'. As $E[Y] = \frac{1}{\lambda'}$ we have:
$\beta \geq \frac{1}{D+\frac{1}{\lambda'}} = \frac{\lambda'}{1+\lambda' \cdot D}$.   □

C   Proof of Claim 7

Claim 7:
Let B be a block in tree T in a network as in Lemma 6, then regardless of history, the expected waiting time for the creation of the last child of B is upper bounded by $2D + \frac{1}{\lambda'}$.

Proof. Let C be the first block created after D seconds have passed from B's creation. Denote by τ the time from B's creation until C has been created and yet another D seconds elapsed. We argue that $E[\tau] \leq 2D + 1/\lambda'$. This is easy to see: It takes $1/\lambda'$ seconds in expectation to create block C, an event which can only occur after D seconds have passed from B's creation. Then, we deterministically wait another D seconds to propagate C to the entire network.

We claim that after τ seconds from B's creation, B will have no more children. Let us examine the two possible cases:

Case I: C is a descendant of B. Once C has been propagated to all nodes, no node considers B a leaf, and the GHOST chain selection rule only extends leaves (in the subtree known to the extending node).

Case II: C is not a descendant of B. Because B was propagated to all nodes before C was created, the node that extended C was well aware of B, but did not extend it. It therefore had a strictly heavier subtree than B is part of after the creation of C. D seconds later, block C is known to all other nodes, along with its entire supporting subtree. In this case, B will not be extended directly either – nodes have switched away from B if no other children extend it, or have switched to its descendants if it does have children. □

References

1. https://bitcoinj.github.io/working-with-micropayments
2. https://blockchain.info/charts/n-transactions
3. https://gist.github.com/gavinandresen/e20c3b5a1d4b97f79ac2
4. https://www.ethereum.org/
5. Androulaki, E., Karame, G.O., Roeschlin, M., Scherer, T., Capkun, S.: Evaluating user privacy in bitcoin. In: Sadeghi, A.-R. (ed.) FC 2013. LNCS, vol. 7859, pp. 34–51. Springer, Heidelberg (2013)
6. Babaioff, M., Dobzinski, S., Oren, S., Zohar, A.: On bitcoin and red balloons. In: The 13th ACM Conference on Electronic Commerce, pp. 56–73. ACM (2012)
7. Decker, C., Wattenhofer, R.: Information propagation in the bitcoin network. In: 13th IEEE International Conference on Peer-to-Peer Computing (P2P), Trento, Italy (2013)
8. Eyal, I., Sirer, E.G.: Majority is not enough: bitcoin mining is vulnerable. In: Christin, N., Safavi-Naini, R. (eds.) FC 2014. LNCS, vol. 8437, pp. 431–449. Springer, Heidelberg (2014)
9. Karame, G.O., Androulaki, E., Capkun, S.: Double-spending fast payments in bitcoin. In: The 2012 ACM conference on Computer and communications security, pp. 906–917. ACM (2012)
10. Lewenberg, Y., Sompolinsky, Y., Zohar, A.: Inclusive block chain protocols. In: Böhme, R., Okamoto, T., (eds.) FC 2015. LNCS, 8975, pp. xx–yy. Springer, Heidelberg (2015)
11. Miers, I., Garman, C., Green, M., Rubin, A.D.: Zerocoin: Anonymous distributed e-cash from bitcoin. In: IEEE Symposium on Security and Privacy (2013)
12. Nakamoto, S.: Bitcoin: A peer-to-peer electronic cash system (2008)
13. Reid, F., Harrigan, M.: An analysis of anonymity in the bitcoin system. In: Altshule, Y., Elovici, Y., Cremers, A.B., Cremers, N., Pentland, A. (eds.) Security and Privacy in Social Networks, pp. 197–223. Springer, New York (2013)
14. Ron, D., Shamir, A.: Quantitative analysis of the full bitcoin transaction graph. In: Sadeghi, A.-R. (ed.) FC 2013. LNCS, vol. 7859, pp. 6–24. Springer, Heidelberg (2013)
15. Rosenfeld, M.: Analysis of bitcoin pooled mining reward systems (2011). arXiv preprint arXiv:1112.4980

16. Rosenfeld, M.: Analysis of hashrate-based double spending (2014). arXiv preprint arXiv:1402.2009
17. Serfozo, R.: Basics of applied stochastic processes. Springer, Heidelberg (2009)
18. Williams, D.: Probability with martingales. Cambridge University Press, Cambridge (1991)

Inclusive Block Chain Protocols

Yoad Lewenberg[1], Yonatan Sompolinsky[1(✉)], and Aviv Zohar[1,2]

[1] The School of Engineering and Computer Science,
The Hebrew University of Jerusalem, Jerusalem, Israel
{yoadlew,yoni_sompo,avivz}@cs.huji.ac.il
[2] Microsoft Research, Herzliya, Israel

Abstract. Distributed cryptographic protocols such as Bitcoin and Ethereum use a data structure known as the block chain to synchronize a global log of events between nodes in their network. Blocks, which are batches of updates to the log, reference the parent they are extending, and thus form the structure of a chain. Previous research has shown that the mechanics of the block chain and block propagation are constrained: if blocks are created at a high rate compared to their propagation time in the network, many conflicting blocks are created and performance suffers greatly. As a result of the low block creation rate required to keep the system within safe parameters, transactions take long to securely confirm, and their throughput is greatly limited.

We propose an alternative structure to the chain that allows for operation at much higher rates. Our structure consists of a directed acyclic graph of blocks (the block DAG). The DAG structure is created by allowing blocks to reference multiple predecessors, and allows for more "forgiving" transaction acceptance rules that incorporate transactions even from seemingly conflicting blocks. Thus, larger blocks that take longer to propagate can be tolerated by the system, and transaction volumes can be increased.

Another deficiency of block chain protocols is that they favor more connected nodes that spread their blocks faster—fewer of their blocks conflict. We show that with our system the advantage of such highly connected miners is greatly reduced. On the negative side, attackers that attempt to maliciously reverse transactions can try to use the forgiving nature of the DAG structure to lower the costs of their attacks. We provide a security analysis of the protocol and show that such attempts can be easily countered.

1   Introduction

Bitcoin, a decentralized digital currency system [9], uses at its core a distributed data structure known as the block chain—a log containing all transactions conducted with the currency. Several other distributed systems, such as Ethereum, a general distributed applications platform, have extended Bitcoin's functionality, yet still rely on a similar block chain to synchronize information between nodes.

As Bitcoin, Ethereum, and their likes gain wider acceptance, it is expected that pressure to include more data in their blocks will increase as well. Due to

© International Financial Cryptography Association 2015
R. Böhme and T. Okamoto (Eds.): FC 2015, LNCS 8975, pp. 528–547, 2015.
DOI: 10.1007/978-3-662-47854-7_33

bandwidth constraints, larger blocks propagate through the network less efficiently, and may thus result in suboptimal performance if too many transactions are included. This is mainly due to the uncoordinated creation of blocks by different nodes which results in conflicts. The current protocols dictate that whenever conflicts occur, only a single block is adopted, and the others are discarded.

This paper explores an alternative mechanism for the formation of the block chain that is better suited for such protocols when block sizes are large, or when blocks are created often. Our modification allows the inclusion of transactions from conflicting blocks. We thus create an incentive for nodes to attempt and include *different* transactions, and thereby increase throughput.

Conflicts, and the Structure of the Block Chain. The block chain in each protocol is replicated at every node and assists nodes in reaching a consensus on the state of all "accounts". Blocks, which make up the chain, contain an identifier (a cryptographic hash) of their predecessor in the chain, as well as a set of transactions that are consistent according to the state of the ledger represented by the chain they extend. To avoid creating a monopoly on the approval of transactions, all nodes have the ability to create blocks. To create a block, a node (also known as a miner) has to solve a computationally intense proof of work problem (the proof of work computation essentially consists of guessing inputs to a cryptographic hash function which succeeds only probabilistically). Once a block is created, it is distributed to the rest of the network. Blocks may be created by different nodes at roughly the same time, and may thus extend the same parent block. Such blocks may include different subsets of transactions, some possibly conflicting (conflicting transactions are those that move the same money to different destinations – they cannot be allowed to co-occur). The protocol therefore includes a mechanism for choosing which block survives to extend the chain, while the other conflicting ones are effectively ignored. The mechanism used by Bitcoin is this: given several extensions of the current chain, pick the longest chain as the version to adopt. Ethereum on the other hand uses a different selection strategy which is a variant of GHOST [12] (readers unfamiliar with the basic Bitcoin protocol are referred to [9]).

The chain selection rule can be exploited by a malicious node to reverse a payment, an attack known as *double-spend*. The attacker can attempt to build a secret chain of blocks which does not contain the transaction and later, if its chain is long enough, replace the main chain, thereby reversing the payment.

Previous work [6,12] has shown that with increasing block sizes (or equivalently with increasing block creation rates), more stale (off-chain) blocks are created. This, in turn, leads to several problems: First, the security of the protocol against malicious attacks suffers. Second, increases in block size do not translate to linear increases in throughput (as the contents of off-chain blocks are not included in the ledger). Finally, the situation in which blocks conflict puts smaller less connected miners at a disadvantage: They earn less than their respective share of the rewards, and may be slowly pushed out of the system due to competition with larger miners, a fact which endangers the decentralization of Bitcoin.

The problems mentioned above form barriers to the scalability of block chain protocols. If block sizes are not increased, competition between transactions that attempt to enter the block chain will raise fees to high levels that discourage use of the protocol.

Indeed, Ethereum's adopted chain selection protocol was specifically designed to provide stronger security guarantees exactly in these high throughput settings [13], but other issues such as the skewed reward distribution at high rates, or the loss of throughput due to excluded blocks have not been improved. Our suggested modification aims to provide an additional improvement, and works well with GHOST, with its variant used by Ethereum, with the standard longest-chain protocol, and in fact, with any protocol that selects a "main" chain.[1]

The Block DAG, and Inclusive Protocols. We propose to restructure the block chain into a directed acyclic graph (DAG) structure, that allows transactions from *all* blocks to be included in the log. We achieve this using an "inclusive" rule which selects a main chain from within the DAG, and then selectively incorporates contents of off-chain blocks into the log, provided they do not conflict with previously included content. An important aspect of the Inclusive protocol is that it awards fees of accepted transactions to the creator of the block that contains them—even if the block itself is not part of the main chain. Such payments are granted only if the transaction was not previously included in the chain, and are decreased for blocks that were published too slowly.

Analysis of such strategies is far from simple. We employ several game theoretic tools and consider several solution concepts making different assumptions on the nodes (that they are profit maximizers, cooperative, greedy-myopic, or even paranoid and play safety-level strategies). In all solution concepts one clear trend emerges: nodes play probabilistically to minimize collisions, and do not choose only the highest fee transactions that would fit into their block.

One potential negative aspect of our suggestion is that attackers that try to double-spend may publish the blocks that were generated in failed attempts and still collect fees for these blocks. We show that this strategy, which lowers the costs of double-spend attacks, can be easily mitigated with slightly longer waiting times for final transaction approval, as the costs of an attacker grow significantly with the waiting time.[2] We additionally consider a new attack scenario (which has not been analyzed in previous work) in which an attacker creates a public fork in the chain in order to delay transaction acceptance by nodes.

Another issue that arises as many conflicting blocks are generated by the protocol, is the problem of selfish mining [7], in which miners deviate from Bitcoin's proposed strategy to increase their gains. Inclusive protocols remain susceptible to this form of deviation as well, and do not solve this issue.

---

[1] For the sake of brevity, we do not go into the details of GHOST or of its Ethereum-variant, except where specifically relevant.

[2] This is guaranteed only if the attacker has less than 50 % of the computational power in the network.

To summarize, our main contributions are:

1. We utilize a directed acyclic structure for the block graph in which blocks reference several predecessors to incorporate contents from all blocks into the log (similar structures have already been proposed in the past, but not to include the contents of off-chain blocks).
2. We provide a game theoretic model of the competition for fees between the nodes under the new protocol.
3. We analyze the game under several game theoretic solution concepts and assumptions, and show that in each case nodes randomize transaction selection from a wider range of transactions. This is the key to the improved performance of the protocol.
4. We demonstrate that Inclusive protocols obtain higher throughput, more proportional outcomes that less discriminate smaller, less-connected players, and that they suffer very little in their security in comparison to non-inclusive protocols. We consider both security against double-spend attempts, as well as attackers that are trying to delay transaction acceptance in the network.

2   From Trees to Directed Acyclic Graphs (DAGs)

We now begin to describe our proposed changes to the protocol. We start with a structural change to the blocks that will enable further modifications. In the current Bitcoin protocol, every block points at a single parent (via the parent's hash), and due to natural (or malicious) forks in the network, the blocks form a tree.

We propose, instead, the node creating the block would list *all* childless blocks that it was aware of. Surely, this added information does not hurt; it is simple to trace each of the references and see which one leads, for example, to the longest chain. We thus obtain a directed acyclic graph (DAG) in which each block references a subset of previous blocks. We assume that when block C references B, C's creator knows all of B's predecessors (it can request them). The information that can be extracted from a block's reference list is sufficient to simulate the underlying chain selection rule: we can follow the longest-chain rule, for example, by recursively selecting in each block a single link—the one leading to the longest chain.

The provision of this additional information amounts to a "direct revelation mechanism": Instead of instructing nodes to select the chain they extend, we simply ask them to report all possible choices, and other nodes can simulate their choice, just as they would have made it (the term *direct revelation* is borrowed from economics where it is widely used in mechanism design [10]).

In fact, any chain selection protocol can be applied in this manner, as the references provide all information needed to determine the choice that the block creator would have made when extending the chain. The only issue that needs to be handled is tie breaking (as in the case of conflicting chains of equal length). To do so, we ask nodes to list references to other blocks in some order, which is then used to break ties. Note that nodes are only required to list the childless nodes in the DAG; there is no need to list other nodes, as they are already reachable by simply following the links.[3]

Formally, we denote by $BDAG$ the set of all directed acyclic block graphs $G = (V, E)$ with vertices V (blocks) and directed edges E, where each $B \in V$ has in addition an order $\prec_B$ over all its outgoing edges. In our setup, an edge goes from a block to its parent, thus childless vertices ("leaves") are those with no *incoming* edges. Graphs in $BDAG$ are required to have a unique maximal vertex, "the genesis block". We further denote by $sub(B, G)$ the subgraph that includes all blocks in G reachable from B.

An underlying chain selection rule F is used to decide on the main chain in the DAG (e.g., longest-chain or GHOST). The rule F is a mapping from block DAGs to block chains such that for any $G \in BDAG$, $F(G)$ is a maximal (i.e., non-extendable) chain in G. The order $\prec_B$ is assumed to agree with F, in the sense that if A is one of B's parents and $A \in F(sub(B, G))$, then A is first in the order $\prec_B$.

2.1   Exploiting the DAG Structure—The Inclusive Protocol

We define Inclusive-F, the "Inclusive" version of the chain selection rule F, which incorporates non-conflicting off-chain transactions into a given blocks accepted transaction set. Intuitively, a block B uses a postorder traversal on the block DAG to form a linear order on all blocks. If two conflicting transactions appear, the one that appeared earlier according to this order is considered to be the one that has taken place (given that all previous transactions it depends on have also occurred). Thus, we use the order on links that blocks provide to define an order on blocks, which we then use to order transactions that appear in those blocks, and finally, we confirm transactions according to this order.

To make the Inclusive algorithm formal, we need to provide a method to decide precisely the set of accepted transactions. Bitcoin transactions are composed of inputs (sources of funds) and outputs (the targets of funds). Outputs are, in turn, spent by inputs that redirect the funds further. We define the consistency of a transaction set, and its maximality as follows:

Definition 1. *Given a set of transactions T, a transaction tx is consistent with T if all its inputs are outputs of transactions in T, and no other transaction in T uses them as inputs. We say that T is consistent, if every transaction $tx \in T$ is consistent with $T \setminus \{tx\}$.*

Definition 2. *We say that a consistent set of transactions T from a block DAG G is maximal, if no other consistent set T' of transactions from G contains T.*

---

[3] DAGs are already required by GHOST (although for different reasons), and Ethereum's blocks currently reference parent blocks as well as "uncles" (blocks that share the same parent as their parent). Thus, this modification is quite natural.

The algorithm below performs a postorder traversal of the DAG $sub(B, G)$. Along its run it confirms any transaction that is consistent with those accepted thus far. The traversal backtracks if it visits the same block twice.[4]

The algorithm is to be called with arguments Inclusive-$F(G, B, \emptyset)$, initially setting $visited(\cdot)$ as False for all blocks. Its output is the set of transactions it approves.

Algorithm 1. *Inclusive-$F(G, B, T)$*
Input: a DAG G, a block B with pointers to predecessors $(B_1, ..., B_m)$ (ordered according to $\prec_B$),[5] and a set of previously confirmed transactions T.

1. IF $visited(B)$ RETURN T
2. SET $visited(B) := True$
3. FOR $i = 1$ TO m:
4. $T = $ Inclusive-$F(G, B_i, T)$
5. FOR EACH $tx \in B$
6.   IF (tx is consistent with T) THEN $T = T \cup \{tx\}$
7. RETURN T

We say that B is a *valid* block if at the end of the run on $sub(B, G)$ we have $B \subseteq T$.[6] The algorithm's run extends $\prec_B$ to a linear order on $sub(B, G)$, defined by: $A \prec_B A'$ if Inclusive-$F(G, B, \emptyset)$ visited A before it visited A'. The following proposition states that the algorithm provides consistent and maximal transaction sets:

Proposition 1. *Let T be the set returned by Inclusive-$F(G, B, \emptyset)$. Then T is both consistent and maximal in $sub(B, G)$.*

The proof is immediate from the algorithm.

An important property of this protocol is that once a transaction has been approved by some main chain block B of G, it will remain in the approved set of any extending block as long as B remains in G's main chain. This is because transactions confirmed by main chain blocks are first to be included in the accepted transaction sets of future main chain blocks. Since both in longest-chain and GHOST blocks that are buried deep in the main chain become increasingly less likely to be replaced, the same security guarantees hold for transactions included in their Inclusive versions.

Fees and Rewards. Each transaction awards a fee to the creator of the first block that included it in the set T. Formally, let A be some block in $sub(B, G)$. Denote by $T(A)$ the set of transactions which block A was the first to contain,

---

[4] It is important to note that the algorithm below describes a full traversal. More efficient implementations are possible if a previously traversed DAG is merely being updated (with methods similar to the unspent transaction set used in Bitcoin).

[5] If B is the genesis block, which has no predecessors, $m = 0$.

[6] The Inclusive algorithm can also handle blocks that have some of their transactions rejected.

according to the order $\prec_B$. Then (according to B's world view) A's creator is awarded *a fraction* of the fee from every $tx \in T(A)$. Although naïvely we would want to grant A all of $T(A)$'s fees, security objectives cannot always permit it. This is one of the main tradeoffs in the protocol: On the one hand, we wish to award fees to anyone that included a new transaction. This implies that poorly connected miners that were slow to publish their block will still receive rewards. On the other hand, off-chain blocks may also be the result of malicious action, including published blocks from a failed double-spend attack. In this case we would prefer no payoff would be received. We therefore allow for a somewhat tolerant payment mechanism that grants a block A a fraction of the reward which depends on how quickly the block was referenced by the main chain. The analysis that will follow (in Sect. 3) will justify the need for lower payments.

Formally, for any block $A \in G$ define by $pre(A)$ the latest *main chain* block which is reachable from A, and by $post(A)$ the earliest *main chain* block from which A is reachable; if no such block exists, regard $post(A)$ as a "virtual block" with height infinity; if A is in the main chain then $pre(A) = post(A) = A$. Denote $c(A) := post(A).height - pre(A).height$; $c(\cdot)$ is a measure of the delay in a block's publication (with respect to the main chain).

In order to penalize a block according to its gap parameter $c(\cdot)$ we make use of a generic discount function, denoted γ, which satisfies: $\gamma : \mathbb{N} \cup \{0\} \to [0,1]$, it is weakly decreasing, and $\gamma(0) = 1$. The payment for (the creator of) block A is defined by:

$$\gamma(c(A)) \cdot \sum_{w \in T(A)} v(w),$$

where $v(w)$ is the fee of transaction w. In other words, A gains only a fraction $\gamma(c(A))$ of its original rewards. By way of illustration, consider the following discount function:

Example 1.

$$\gamma_0(c) = \begin{cases} 1 & 0 \leq c \leq 3 \\ \frac{10-c}{7} & 3 < c < 10 \\ 0 & c \geq 10 \end{cases} \tag{1}$$

γ_0 grants a full reward to blocks which are adequately synchronized with the main chain ($\gamma_0(c) = 1$ for $c \leq 3$), on the one hand, and pays no reward at all to blocks that were left "unseen" by the main chain for too long, on the other hand ($\gamma_0(c) = 0$ for $c \geq 10$); in the mid-range, a block is given some fraction of the transaction rewards ($\gamma_0(c) = \frac{10-c}{7}$ for $3 < c < 10$).

Money Creation. In addition to fees, Bitcoin and other cryptocurrencies use the block creation process to create and distribute new coins. Newly minted coins can also be awarded to off-chain blocks in a similar fashion to transaction fees, i.e., in amounts that decrease for blocks that were not quickly included in the main chain. A block's reward can therefore be set as a fraction $\gamma(c(A))$ of the full reward on the chain.[7] As our primary focus is on the choice of transactions to include in the block, we assume for simplicity from this point on, that no money creation takes place (i.e., that money creation has decayed to negligible amounts—as will eventually occur for Bitcoin).

Now that we have defined the Inclusive protocol, we begin to analyze its implications.

3   Security

The original security analysis of Satoshi [9], as well as analysis done by others [11,12], has considered the *probability* of a successful double-spend attack under the regular non-inclusive scheme. An alternative analysis may instead measure the cost of the attack rather than their success probability (both have been analyzed in [11]).

Below we prove that the Inclusive version of the protocol is at least as secure as the non-inclusive one, in terms of the probability of successful attacks. In addition, we show that the cost of an attack under Inclusive can be made high, by properly modifying the acceptance policy.

3.1   Acceptance Policy

The recipient of a given transaction observes the network's published blocks, and needs to decide when to consider the payment "accepted", that is, when it is safe to release the goods or services paid for by the transaction. He does so by making sure his transaction is included and confirmed by the main chain, and calculating the probability that it would be later excluded from it.

Probability of Successful Attacks. We now compare the probability of a successful attack under the regular longest-chain protocol to the one under its Inclusive version. Our method applies to other main chain rules as well (e.g., GHOST). Recall that under Inclusive the blocks form a DAG, whereas when Inclusive is not implemented they form a tree (see Sect. 2). Notice that if $G(t)$ is the block DAG at time t, then if the network would have followed the non-inclusive setup, its block tree $T(t)$ would be precisely the subgraph of $G(t)$ obtained by removing all edges in blocks' reference list apart from the main edges (i.e., the first pointer in every block). For any DAG G let $F(G)$ be its main chain according to the underlying selection rule F (G can also be a tree).

Theorem 2. *Let $G(t)$ be the block DAG at time t, and let $T(t)$ be the block tree that is obtained from $G(t)$ by discarding the non-main edges. For any block $B \in F(G(t))$,*

$$\forall s > t : \Pr(B \notin F(G(s))) = \Pr(B \notin F(T(s))) \tag{2}$$

---

[7] The total reward can be automatically adjusted to maintain a desired rate of money creation by a process similar to the re-targeting done for difficulty adjustments.

Proof. This is immediate from the fact that Inclusive does not change the way the main chain is selected, therefore, for all s: $F(G(s)) = F(T(s))$.   □

As a corollary, the probability that a transaction would be excluded from the main chain does not become higher under Inclusive, as the security guarantees of main chain blocks apply to individual transactions as well (see the discussion succeeding Algorithm 1). In particular, any acceptance policy employed by a recipient of funds in a network following a non-inclusive protocol (see, e.g., [9, 11,12]) can be safely carried out when Inclusive is implemented.

Cost of Attacks. As mentioned at the beginning of this section, one may be interested in measuring the cost of a double-spend attack rather than its success probability. A potential drawback of including transactions from off-chain blocks is that it mitigates the cost of a failed double-spend attack. Double spend attacks consist typically of chains constructed by the attacker that are initially kept secret. The construction of blocks requires computational resources. Under the non-inclusive setup, when the attacker withdraws from the attack (usually after failing to build blocks faster than the network), its blocks are discarded. In contrast, under the Inclusive protocol, the attacker may still publish its secret chain and gain some value from transactions contained inside.

However, the recipient of funds can cancel this effect by waiting longer before accepting the payment. Indeed, if the attacker is forced to create long secret chains, its blocks suffer some loss due to the lower reward implied by the function $\gamma(\cdot)$.

To formalize this we provide first some definitions and notations. Denote by $G(t)$ the *published* developing block DAG at time t, and assume some main chain block B_{tx} confirms the transaction tx (that is, $tx \in$ Inclusive-$F(G(t), B_{tx}, \emptyset)$). Let $H(t) \subseteq G(t)$ be the set of blocks from which B_{tx} is reachable, and denote the main chain atop B_{tx} (including itself) by $H_{main}(t) \subseteq H(t)$. Let $A(t) \subseteq G(t) \setminus H(t)$ be the set of blocks which satisfy $post(\cdot) \succ B_{tx}$; these are blocks which can be used by the attacker to reverse the transaction (even though the attacker did not necessarily create all of them), and the requirement on their $post(\cdot)$ block is to exclude from this set blocks earlier than B_{tx}, under the order of G (which do not affect the resolution of future conflicts).

Denote by *val* the expected reward from a block, under the Inclusive reward-scheme. *val* is equal, in equilibrium, to the expected cost of creating a block. We will simplify our analysis by assuming that *val* is constant. Finally, for convenience, we analyze the case where the underlying chain selection rule (F) is GHOST; the results apply to the longest-chain rule as well, after some slight changes.

Lemma 3. *Assume the attacker holds a fraction of at most q of the computational power. If $|H_{main}(t)| = n$, $|A(t)| = m$, and the attacker has created k secret blocks, then the cost of a failed attack satisfies*

$$cost \geq \sum_{h=m+1}^{m+k} (1 - \gamma(n + 2 - h)) \cdot val \qquad (3)$$

Proof. In the best case for the attacker, its blocks form a chain which is built atop $A(t)$. If A_h is its hth block ($1 \leq h \leq k$) then $pre(A_h).height < B_{tx}.height - 1 + m + h$, or otherwise A_h necessarily references a block in H_{main} as its main parent (recall that a block's ordered reference list is forced to agree with F), and in particular it supports tx and does not participate in the attack.

In addition, the attacker's secret blocks are not published before the acceptance, hence their $post(\cdot)$ block height is at least $B_{tx}.height + n$. We conclude that the discount parameter on A_h is at most

$$\gamma \left((B_{tx}.height + n) - (B_{tx}.height - 1 + m + h - 1) \right),$$

hence its cost is at least $(1 - \gamma(n + 2 - m - h)) \cdot val$. After a change of parameter we arrive at (3). □

We now make use of this result to show that a payee that follows the acceptance policy introduced in [12] can make the attack cost arbitrarily high by waiting sufficiently before acceptance.

Corollary 4. *Let tx be a transaction in $G(t)$, and assume an attacker builds a secret chain that does not confirm tx, and that it persists with its attack as long as the payee has not approved the transaction. Then the minimal value of the* double-spend *needed for the attack to be profitable in expectation grows exponentially with t.*

Proof. Let $|H_{main}(t)| = n$, $|H(t)| = N$, and $|A(t)| = m$. The probability that an attacker with a fraction $q < 0.5$ of the computational power has managed to create k secret blocks is at most $e^{-q\lambda(t-t_0)} \frac{(q\lambda(t-t_0))^k}{k!}$, where t_0 is the time it began its attack. Following the dynamics of GHOST, the payee can wait for a collapse to occur, i.e., for B_{tx} to be included in the main chain of all honest nodes. Consequently, the probability that the attack will be successful is upper bounded by $\left(\frac{q}{1-q} \right)^{(N+1-m-k)^+}$. Here we used a worst-case assumption, according to which the attacker is able to exploit all of the blocks in $A(t)$ for its attack.

In case of a successful attack the attacker profits the amount double-spent, which we denote DS, while the profit from its blocks is offset by their creation costs. On the other hand, the cost of a failed attack is given by (3). Calculating the attack cost, we arrive at:

$$\text{attack-cost} \geq \sum_{k=0}^{\infty} e^{-q\lambda(t-t_0)} \frac{(q\lambda(t-t_0))^k}{k!} \cdot \left(-DS \cdot \left(\frac{q}{1-q} \right)^{(N+1-m-k)^+} \right. \tag{4}$$

$$\left. + \left(1 - \left(\frac{q}{1-q} \right)^{(N+1-m-k)^+} \right) \cdot \sum_{h=m+1}^{m+k} (1 - \gamma(n + 2 - h)) \cdot val \right)$$

For a given time t, there is a probability distribution over DAGs that will be created by the network. This induces random variables for $N = N(t)$, $n = n(t)$, and $m = m(t)$. As t grows these become arbitrarily close to their expected values (by the Law of Large Numbers). We can thus replace N with its expectation $(1-q)\lambda \cdot t$, and notice that $\mathbb{E}[n]$ grows with time and $\mathbb{E}[m]$ approaches a constant. Isolating DS shows that its minimal value in order for $\mathbb{E}$ [attack-cost] to be non-positive grows exponentially with t (assuming γ is non-trivial, that is, $\gamma \neq 1$).
□

To illustrate the growth of the attack cost, we show in Table 1 the minimal double-spend needed in order for an attack to be profitable in expectation. The table entries admit to the minimal DS making the attack profitable; here we fixed N and averaged over t (in contrast to the previous corollary). In addition, for simplicity we assumed $m = 0$ and $n = N$, corresponding to the case where the honest network suffers no delays. The penalty function γ_0 was selected as the one from Example 1, and the expected reward from a block were normalized so that $val = 1$. Notice that waiting for only one or two blocks is not safe at all, as the attacker can easily afford to try and create longer chains under the function γ_0 that we have chosen.

Table 1. The minimal double-spend (normalized by blocks' expected rewards, val) needed in order for an attack to be profitable in expectation, as a function of the number of confirmations and the attacker's computational power.

q	1	2	3	4	5	6	7	8	9	10
2 %	0	0	$9.3 \cdot 10^2$	$1.2 \cdot 10^5$	$1.1 \cdot 10^7$	$8.3 \cdot 10^8$	$5.8 \cdot 10^{10}$	$3.8 \cdot 10^{12}$	$2.4 \cdot 10^{14}$	$1.3 \cdot 10^{16}$
6 %	0	0	79	$3.1 \cdot 10^3$	$8.7 \cdot 10^4$	$2.1 \cdot 10^6$	$4.5 \cdot 10^7$	$9.1 \cdot 10^8$	$1.8 \cdot 10^{10}$	$2.9 \cdot 10^{11}$
10 %	0	0	22	$4.8 \cdot 10^2$	$7.5 \cdot 10^3$	$9.9 \cdot 10^4$	$1.2 \cdot 10^6$	$1.4 \cdot 10^7$	$1.5 \cdot 10^8$	$1.4 \cdot 10^9$
14 %	0	0	8.5	$1.3 \cdot 10^2$	$1.3 \cdot 10^3$	$1.2 \cdot 10^4$	$9.4 \cdot 10^4$	$7.1 \cdot 10^5$	$5.1 \cdot 10^6$	$3.2 \cdot 10^7$
18 %	0	0	4.0	44	$3.3 \cdot 10^2$	$2.1 \cdot 10^3$	$1.2 \cdot 10^4$	$6.8 \cdot 10^4$	$3.6 \cdot 10^5$	$1.6 \cdot 10^6$
22 %	0	0	2.0	18	$1.0 \cdot 10^2$	$5.1 \cdot 10^2$	$2.3 \cdot 10^3$	$9.7 \cdot 10^3$	$3.9 \cdot 10^4$	$1.4 \cdot 10^5$
26 %	0	0	1.1	7.9	37	$1.5 \cdot 10^2$	$5.3 \cdot 10^2$	$1.8 \cdot 10^3$	$5.7 \cdot 10^3$	$1.6 \cdot 10^4$
30 %	0	0	0.63	3.8	15	49	$1.4 \cdot 10^2$	$4.0 \cdot 10^2$	$1.0 \cdot 10^3$	$2.4 \cdot 10^3$
34 %	0	0	0.36	1.9	6.4	18	45	$1.0 \cdot 10^2$	$2.3 \cdot 10^2$	$4.6 \cdot 10^2$
38 %	0	0	0.20	0.92	2.8	6.9	15	30	58	$1.0 \cdot 10^2$
42 %	0	0	0.10	0.43	1.2	2.6	5.2	9.3	16	25
46 %	0	0	04	0.16	0.40	0.82	1.5	2.5	3.9	5.6
50 %	0	0	0	0	0	0	0	0	0	0

The results above are not quite satisfying, as they demonstrate only the costs of an attack from a specific class: We assumed the attacker does not withdraw before the payee's acceptance. One could consider more sophisticated attack policies in which the attacker might withdraw earlier in order to reduce costs. The main obstacle here, is that there exist selfish mining strategies in which a miner profits from withholding some of his blocks, even under the non-inclusive setup [7]. We point out that a malicious miner can execute double-spend attacks while employing selfish mining strategies, thereby guaranteeing itself an expected positive profit. While Inclusive protocols reduce the cost of a failed attack, we conjecture that adequate acceptance policies cancel this effect (as we have shown in Corollary 4 for one attack profile).

3.2 Delayed Service Attack

Another possible form of an attack is that of delayed service. The acceptance policy described above implies that if a recipient of a payment observes many blocks in the DAG that have the potential to form a competing main chain that will not accept his transaction, it must delay acceptance. Consequently, an attacker may decide to create its blocks deliberately off-chain, in attempt to increase the waiting time for transaction authorization in the network.

Notice that the attacker can never profit from a delayed service attack, say by reversing a previous payment, as its attack blocks are immediately published and are therefore transparent to any transaction authorizer. Moreover, the longer the attack goes on the greater its cost, as the gap between the $post(\cdot)$ and $pre(\cdot)$ of the participating blocks grows larger.

Assume the attacker wishes to delay the confirmation of transactions that lie in some block B. This can be done by increasing $|A(t)| = m$, that is, by publishing blocks from which B is not reachable. Despite the threat from $A(t)$, the honest network may add enough blocks to $H(t)$ for these transactions to be accepted.

We simulated this attack on a network with 100 equal miners, a delay of 2 seconds between each two, and a creation rate of 1 block per second. Figure 1 depicts the (fraction of) computational power needed by an attacker as a function of the increase in waiting time it aims to induce. The payees are assumed to use the policy induced by (4), with $q = 0.2$, and DS at most $1000 \cdot val$.

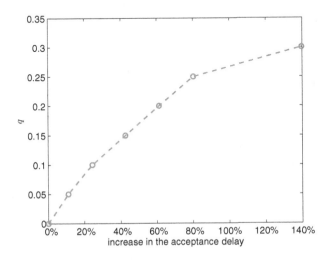

Fig. 1. The fraction of computational power an attacker needs to hold as a function of the increase in waiting time it aims to induce.

4 Transaction Selection Under Inclusive Protocols

Up until now, we have not considered the effect of the Inclusive protocol on how participants choose the transactions they will include in their blocks. In fact, these choices are quite important: If all nodes choose the same subset of transactions for inclusion in their blocks, any two blocks that are created in parallel are likely to have many collisions, and throughput will not be high.

In this section we model transaction selection as a game, and show that nodes are actually incentivized to avoid collisions. They choose transactions with high fees, but will also compromise for lower fees with transactions that will have fewer collisions.

4.1 The Game Model

We model the process of embedding transactions in blocks as an infinite-horizon extensive form game, with N players (the miners), with imperfect information, i.e., players may be only partially aware of other players' moves (as they do not immediately see all the blocks that have been created; this is the main non-trivial aspect of the game). The game develops at discrete time steps $t = (1, 2, ...)$, with the gap between consecutive steps denoted Δ (where Δ is small).

We denote a transaction by w_i (or simply w) and ignore any property apart from its fee, which is assumed to fall into one of n discrete values, $v_1 > v_2 > ... > v_n > 0$ (fees in Bitcoin, for example, are specified in whole units of Satoshis). We write $v(w)$ to denote w's fee.

At every time step "nature" adds the same transactions simultaneously to all players' memory buffers (also known as *memory pools*). The number of new transactions is an independent random variable with mean $\eta\Delta$, for some $\eta > 0$. The fee of each new transaction is v_l with probability r_l, for some probability vector $\boldsymbol{r}$. If the size of the memory buffer of some player exceeds its limit $L > 0$, the transactions with lowest fees are dropped. Effectively, this means that nature's action space at every time step is finite, and can be mapped into $[n]^L$. Nature additionally chooses a (possibly empty) subset of players which will create a block at this time step. The probability that at a certain step player i will create a block is $\lambda_i\Delta$, with $\sum_{i=1}^{N} \lambda_i = \lambda$ being the network's block creation rate.

Player i observes only a partial signal of the actions of nature. He sees all new transactions,[8] and whether or not he was chosen to create a block. If so, he chooses a subset of his memory buffer of size at most b, where b is a positive integer constant representing the number of transactions per block. The chosen transactions are deleted from i's action space immediately, and from player j's action space after $t + d_{i,j}$ time steps, for some $N \times N$ integer matrix $(d_{i,j})_{i,j=1}^{N}$ (effectively deleting them from i and j's memory buffers). This simulates the delay in block propagation.

---

[8] This assumption approximates well the situation in the real Bitcoin network, in which transactions propagate quickly relative to blocks.

We are particularly interested in the case where the incoming rate of transactions exceeds the rate at which they are accepted into blocks (without this assumption, there is no scalability problem, and block sizes can be decreased).

A player may choose to use mixed strategies, namely, to select a distribution over the subsets of size b from his buffer. Instead of using distributions over a possibly exponential number of such subsets, it is more convenient to assign a probability (between 0 and 1) to every individual transaction in the buffer, such that the probabilities sum up to b. This scheme can be translated to probabilities over subsets (we show this in the full version of this paper). We adopt the latter approach, for its simplicity.

The Payoff Function. Denote by $T(B)$ the set of transactions which block B was the first to contain, according to the order on blocks induced by Algorithm 1's run, denoted "$\prec$".[9] Then B's creator is awarded a fraction of $\sum_{w \in T(B)} v(w)$, as defined by $\gamma(c(B))$.

Finally, as is usually customary in infinite horizon games, a discount factor $0 < \beta < 1$ is applied to all rewards, such that if a player has created blocks $B_1, B_2, \ldots$ at time steps $t_1, t_2, \ldots$, his reward from the game is $\sum_j \beta^{t_j} \cdot \gamma(c(B_j)) \cdot \sum_{w \in T(B_j)} v(w)$.

4.2   Rationality in the Inclusive-F Game

The solution concept that best matches our scenario (in which players have partial information about the recent actions of others) is the *sequential equilibrium* which was developed by Kreps and Wilson [8]. This concept explicitly considers the beliefs of players about the history and current state of the game. Intuitively, the sequential equilibrium concept ensures that a single player does not expect to benefit from deviating (given these beliefs). Threats are additionally "credible" and behaviors are temporally consistent (this is similar to sub-game perfection). Finally, players' beliefs about the state of the game are required to be "consistent".

We extend the result in [5] to the infinite horizon setting and show the existence, for all $\epsilon > 0$, of an ϵ-perfect sequential equilibrium in our game (in which players who deviate may gain, but no more than ϵ).

Lemma 5. *For every $\epsilon > 0$ there is an ϵ-perfect sequential equilibrium in the Inclusive-F game.*

---

[9] To make this formal some work is needed: Let $G(t)$ be the block DAG which consist of all blocks created up to time t. We require that the underlying chain selection rule F break ties between equally weighted leaves, in some predetermined perhaps arbitrary way. Denote by B_t the leaf of the main chain $F(G(t))$. Assume F converges, in the sense that a block in the main chain becomes less likely to be replaced, as time grows: $B \in F(G(t)) \implies \lim_{s \to \infty} \Pr(B \notin F(G(s))) = 0$ (longest-chain and GHOST, for instance, satisfy this property). We can thus speak of the eventual- or limit-order "$\prec$" on all blocks in the history of the game, defined by $A \prec A'$ if $\exists t_0, \forall t > t_0 : A \prec_{B_t} A'$ (see the discussion succeeding Algorithm 1 for the definition of $\prec_{B_t}$).

We prove this in the full version of this paper.

Note that several equilibria may (and do) exist, and worse yet, while the proof of existence is constructive, it requires the exploration of an exponentially large state space (essentially enumerating all possible subsets of transactions that will enter the buffer in the future). We therefore desire an efficient algorithm that will preform well in practice.

4.3 Myopic Strategies

We restrict the discussion in this subsection to a simplified version of the game, namely, the single shot game. In this setup, when a player chooses transactions for his current block, he disregards the effect this choice may have on which transactions will be available for his next block. In addition, we assume all players have identical buffers of transactions to choose from. Finally, we assume that a block's position within the block DAG does not depend on its creator's identity.

This simplified model can be seen as a good approximation to an adequately distributed network, in which individual players hold a small fraction of the total computational power. A small player does not create blocks often, and thus his current block has very little effect on his future rewards.

A Myopic Equilibrium. For any block B let $pconf(B)$ denote the set of blocks which precede B in the order "$\prec$" but are not reachable from it. Assume that all players include transaction w in their block (if the block is indeed created) with a marginal probability p_w; then B's expected reward from selecting w is $w \cdot (1 - p_w)^{|pconf(B)|} \cdot \mathbb{E}[\gamma(c(B)) \mid |pconf(B)|]$. We define,

$$f(p_w) := \sum_{l=0}^{\infty} \Pr(|pconf(B)| = l) \cdot (1 - p_w)^l \cdot \mathbb{E}[\gamma(c(B)) \mid l].$$

One could verify that $w \cdot f(p_w)$ is the player's expected reward from embedding w in B. Note that f is strictly decreasing in p_w, and so its inverse f^{-1} exists.

Theorem 6. *Suppose the memory buffer consists of k_l transactions with fee v_l ($1 \le l \le n$). Denote the individual transactions by $w_1, \ldots, w_m$, which are sorted in descending order of their fees. Denote the index of $v(w_i)$ by $l(w_i)$. The marginal probability $p_i := \frac{q_{l(w_i)}}{k_{l(w_i)}}$ ($1 \le i \le m$) defines a symmetric equilibrium in the single-shot inclusive-F game, where:*

- $q_l = \begin{cases} k_l \cdot \min\left(f^{-1}\left(\frac{c_{kmax}}{v_l}\right), 1\right) & 1 \le l \le k_{max} \\ 0 & k_{max} < l \le n \end{cases}$
- $\forall 1 \le l \le n\colon G_l(z) := \sum_{h=1}^{l} k_h \cdot \min\left(f^{-1}\left(\frac{z}{v_h}\right), 1\right) - b$
- $k_{max} := \max\{k \le n \mid \forall l \le k : G_l(v_l) \le 0\}$
- c_{kmax} *is the root of* G_{kmax}.[10]

---

[10] Note that $k_{max} \ge b$, and that the existence of a root for G_{kmax} follows from the fact that f's domain is $[0, 1]$ hence this is also f^{-1}'s image.

The proof is deferred to the full version of this paper. In Sect. 5 we show that this strategy performs well, in terms of throughput and utility, despite the simplifying assumptions used to derive it.

In addition to the analysis above, we also explored other solution concepts, namely, safety-level strategies and cooperative strategies that maximize the social welfare. They are discussed in Appendix A. In all cases, players use randomized strategies to select transactions for their blocks in a way that results in an increase in throughput.

5   Implications of Inclusive Protocols

5.1   Throughput

The throughput of the system, when the Inclusive protocol is implemented, depends on the behavior of the players. We demonstrate Inclusive's ability to achieve significantly higher results by checking the throughput when the players act according to the myopic strategy defined above.

We simulated a network with 100 identical players. The distance between each pair of players was a constant $d = 1$ second. We examined different block creation rates λ varying from 0 to 10 blocks per second. Block sizes were set to $b = 50$ transactions per block. The transaction arrival rate was 65 transactions per second, and their fees drawn uniformly from $[0,1]$. In each simulation we compared the performance of the myopic strategy to the non-inclusive outcome. We compare the resulting throughput to the optimal achievable rate, which is achieved in centralized networks with no delays. Figure 2 depicts the results, showing substantial gains over the non-inclusive protocol.

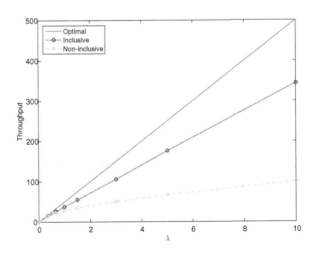

Fig. 2. The fraction of optimal throughput achieved in Inclusive and non-inclusive longest-chain protocols.

5.2   Fairness

While a miner with computational power $q\lambda$ owns a fraction q of blocks in the block DAG (in expectation), highly connected miners will have more of their blocks in the main chain compared to poorly connected ones. This phenomenon lowers the profitability of weak players that are unable to match the return on investment enjoyed by larger ones, and slowly pushes Bitcoin towards an increased concentration of mining power. Given two miners with equal connectivity, but differing hash rates, the larger miner of the two also enjoys an advantage as he immediately begins to extend his own block using more computational power than his weaker opponent.

Inclusive protocols significantly mitigate this effect. Off-chain blocks reward their owners with some fees, so weak or poorly connected miners, who have a higher proportion of off-chain blocks, suffer fewer losses.

Consider, for instance, a network with two strong miners each owning a fraction 0.45 of the total computational power, and a weak miner owning 0.1. We simulated this scenario, and examined the revenue of the small miner. The results are given as a fraction of the social welfare, in Fig. 3, and show a significant mitigation of the nonlinearity phenomenon.

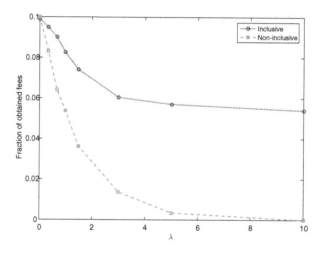

Fig. 3. The fraction of rewards obtained by a weak (10 %) miner under delays.

6   Related Work

The Bitcoin protocol was published by Satoshi Nakamoto in a white paper in 2008 [9]. The security analysis in the paper was later improved in [11]. The propagation of large blocks in the network was first studied in [6], where empirical measurements and analysis have shown that larger blocks conflict more often, and some economic implications such as the desire of miners to create smaller blocks was considered. Additional analysis of phenomena related to larger block sizes was given in [12]. The incentives of miners to propagate transactions was studied in [2]. A recent work by Eyal and Sirer has shown that large miners may choose not to follow the exact protocol and may delay the propagation of their own blocks in order to increase their revenue [7]. These effects still persist in our own version of the protocol, and so we assume that honest nodes follow the protocol without such manipulations.[11]

Additional techniques to mitigate the effects of an increased number of transactions on the network include the proposal for micro-transactions channels (see, e.g., [4]). These channels effectively allow two transacting parties to open a micro-payment channel by freezing some sum of money and transmitting it in small quantities, effectively updating a transaction that includes the total transfer thus far. The aggregating transaction is committed to the block chain after some time has passed. Micro-transaction channels are not as useful in second generation protocols, as they are not suitable to updates that cannot be easily aggregated. In addition, the costs of locking money in advance and the limitation to channels between pairs of nodes further restrict the use of this approach. Other discussions in the Bitcoin community include the use of invertible Bloom filters to reduce the amount of information transmitted between nodes [1].

As our work considers structural changes to the block chain structure, it is also worthwhile to mention proposals such as Side Chains [3] that are currently being discussed in the Bitcoin community.

7 Conclusion

We presented the Inclusive protocol that integrates the contents of off-chain blocks into the ledger. Our modification results in incentives for behavior changes by the nodes that lead to an increased throughput, and a better payoff for weak miners. Our plans for future work include additional analysis of transaction authorization policies and waiting times as well as evaluations of the protocol under selfish mining.

Acknowledgements. The authors were supported in part by the Israel Science Foundation (Grants 616/13, 1773/13 and 1227/12), by the Israel Ministry of Science and Technology (Grant 3-6797), and by the Israel Smart Grid (ISG) Consortium.

A Additional Game Theoretic Analysis

A.1 Safety Level

As the players' behavior is unknown and can take different courses, one may be interested in the player's *safety level*, namely, the minimal utility he can

---

[11] Successful manipulations require strong attackers that are either highly connected, or have massive amounts of computational power.

guarantee himself. In the worst case for the player, the rest of the players choose a strategy which minimizes his utility, and the safety level is his best response to such a scenario.

Formally, player i's safety level is the solution to the zero-sum game, where i is the max-player while the rest of the network acts as his united adversary min-player. The following theorem provides the player with a marginal probability over his memory buffer, which serves as his maxmin strategy for the single-shot game at time t.

Theorem 7. *Denote player i's memory buffer by $w_1, \ldots, w_m$ (sorted in descending order of their fees) at a time in which it was able to create a block. Denote $\delta := 2 \cdot \max_j\{d_{i,j}\} \cdot (\lambda - \lambda_i)$, and for all $q \in [0,1]^m$ define $f(q) := \sum_{k=1}^{m} q_k \cdot \left(w_k e^{-\delta} \sum_{l=0}^{\lceil \frac{k}{b} \rceil - 1} \frac{\delta^l}{l!} \right)$. Let q^* be the solution of the next linear program:*
$$\max f(q) \text{ s.t. } \forall k < m : q_k w_k \geq q_{k+1} w_{k+1} ; \forall k : 0 \leq q_k \leq 1 ; \sum_{k=1}^{m} q_k = b.$$
Then i's utility from q^* is at least $f(q^*)$, regardless of the strategy profile of the other players.

The idea behind the proof is to construct a game in which player i chooses transactions for his blocks, while the rest attempt to choose the very same transactions. In the worst case scenario for the player, his rivals correlate their blocks' contents so as to maximize collisions with i's blocks. Another worst case assumption is that the delay between the players and i is maximal. Refer to the full version of the paper for a formal construction and proof of the theorem.

A.2   An Optimal Strategy

The performance of any solution of the game, including those considered thus far, should be compared to the optimal setup. If players would play cooperatively, so as to try and maximize the system's performance, then all blocks would contain unique transactions, with the top most fees available. Formally, if n blocks were created by the network during some long time period T, then the system's hypothetical optimal performance, $OPT(T)$, is defined as the sum of the top $n \cdot b$ transactions created within T (this is not necessarily feasible, as high transactions may not be available to early blocks).

Recall that transactions arrive at a rate of η. Their values are drawn according to some probability vector r, and we denote by R the corresponding CDF. The rate at which transactions are embedded in the DAG is denoted $\lambda_{out} := b \cdot \lambda$ (it is the hypothetical optimal throughput).

We define a threshold below which transactions are totally ignored by the players: $v_{thresh} = R^{-1}(1 - \frac{\lambda_{out}}{\eta})$. This threshold defines a cutoff, $\theta := \{j : v_j > v_{thresh}\}$. We claim that if players choose transactions above this cutoff, *uniformly*, then the resulting social welfare, which is the throughput weighed according to fees, would coincide with $OPT(T)$, as T goes to infinity. We denote the described strategy by UCO (Uniform above CutOff), and by $UCO(T)$ the total weighed throughput achieved by applying UCO up to T.

Proposition 8. *Assume nodes have an unlimited memory buffer. Let T be some time window, and denote by $n(T)$ the number of blocks that were created by that time. Then, $\lim\limits_{T \to \infty} \frac{1}{n(T)} \cdot \mathbb{E}[OPT(T)] = \lim\limits_{T \to \infty} \frac{1}{n(T)} \cdot \mathbb{E}[UCO(T)]$, where the expectation is taken over all random events in the network and in the realization of UCO.*

The intuition behind the result is that choosing a cutoff as we have prescribed implies that the incoming and outgoing rates of transactions to the buffer are equal. Thus, results from queueing theory show that the expected size of the buffer is infinite, and miners always have enough transactions above the cutoff to include in blocks. In particular, for large enough memory buffers, there are effectively no collisions between different blocks, and the transactions in blocks are unique. This surprising result is achieved at a cost: transactions have long expected waiting times for their authorization.

References

1. Andresen, G.: O(1) block propagation. https://gist.github.com/gavinandresen/e20c3b5a1d4b97f79ac2
2. Babaioff, M., Dobzinski, S., Oren, S., Zohar, A.: On bitcoin and red balloons. In: The 13th ACM Conference on Electronic Commerce, pp. 56–73. ACM (2012)
3. Back, A., Corallo, M., Dashjr, L., Friedenbach, M., Maxwell, G., Miller, A., Poelstra, A., Timón, J., Wuille, P.: Enabling blockchain innovations with pegged sidechains (2014)
4. Bitcoinj: Working with micropayment channels. https://bitcoinj.github.io/working-with-micropayments
5. Chakrabarti, S., Topolyan, I.: A direct proof of the existence of sequential equilibrium and a backward induction characterization (2010)
6. Decker, C., Wattenhofer, R.: Information propagation in the bitcoin network. In: 13th IEEE International Conference on Peer-to-Peer Computing (P2P), Trento, Italy, September 2013
7. Eyal, Ittay, Sirer, Emin Gün: Majority is not enough: bitcoin mining is vulnerable. In: Christin, Nicolas, Safavi-Naini, Reihaneh (eds.) FC 2014. LNCS, vol. 8437, pp. 431–449. Springer, Heidelberg (2014)
8. Kreps, D.M., Wilson, R.: Sequential equilibria. Econometrica: J. Econometric Soc. **50**, 863–894 (1982)
9. Nakamoto, S.: Bitcoin: a peer-to-peer electronic cash system (2008)
10. Nisan, N., Roughgarden, T., Tardos, E., Vazirani, V.V.: Algorithmic Game Theory, Chap. 9. Cambridge University Press, Cambridge (2007)
11. Rosenfeld, M.: Analysis of hashrate-based double spending. arXiv preprint arXiv:1402.2009 (2014)
12. Sompolinsky, Y., Zohar, A.: Secure high-rate transaction processing in bitcoin. In: Böhme, R., Okamoto, T. (eds.) FC 2015. LNCS, vol 8975, pp. 507–527. Springer, Heidelberg (2015)
13. Wood, G.: Ethereum: a secure decentralised generalised transaction ledger (2014)

VeriStream – A Framework for Verifiable Data Streaming

Dominique Schöder and Mark Simkin[⊠]

Saarland University, Saarbrücken, Germany
`schroeder@me.com, simkin@ca.cs.uni-saarland.de`

Abstract. In a Verifiable Data Streaming (VDS) protocol a computationally weak client outsources his storage to an untrusted storage provider. Later, the client can efficiently append and update data elements in the already outsourced and authenticated data set. Other users can stream arbitrary subsets of the authenticated data and verify their integrity on-the-fly, using the data owner's public verification key. In this work, we present VeriStream, a fully-fledged framework for verifiable data streaming with integration into Dropbox. At its core, our framework is based upon a novel construction of an authenticated data structure, which is the first one that allows verifiable data streams of unbounded length and at the same time outperforms the best known constructions in terms of bandwidth and computational overhead. We provide a detailed performance evaluation, showing that VeriStreamonly incurs a small bandwidth overhead, while providing various security guarantees, such as freshness, integrity, authenticity, and public verifiability, at the same time.

1 Introduction

Cloud storage providers like Dropbox, Amazon Cloud Drive, and Google Drive are on the rise and constantly gain popularity. Users are able to outsource their storage into the "cloud" of some dedicated provider and access or share their data with others later on. The advantages of cloud storage are manifold. Among many, users are no longer bound to specific devices or locations when accessing their data and users can share or collaborate on their data with others easily. Many of these providers allow their users to retrieve, i.e. stream, smaller subsets of the initially outsourced data set. In the case of multimedia content, prominent examples are YouTube and SoundCloud. They allow users to upload their audio and video files and share them with others. A different user can stream the whole uploaded file or just smaller parts of it. This streaming scenario is not solely limited to multimedia content. Another interesting example can be found in the stock market. Here, stock brokers base their purchasing decisions on the latest published stock quotes. These stock quotes are published by trusted stock managers and distributed through web services like Yahoo Finance or quote.com Brokers use these services to stream the latest published stock quotes and buy or sell stocks accordingly.

© International Financial Cryptography Association 2015
R. Böhme and T. Okamoto (Eds.): FC 2015, LNCS 8975, pp. 548–566, 2015.
DOI: 10.1007/978-3-662-47854-7_34

All these scenarios have in common that the users have to trust the storage provider that streams the content back to the requesting user. Currently, there are little or no mechanisms in place to protect and ensure the integrity of such dynamic streamed content. A first step towards solving this problem was done in [22], where the problem of Verifiable Data Streaming (VDS) was defined on a theoretical level. The authors provided a first solution based on generalized Merkle-Trees, so called Chameleon Authentication Trees (CATs), that allow a data owner, having a secret signing and a public verification key, to upload his content in a unidirectional fashion. That is, the owner can upload and append data to the existing data set by sending one message per chunk to the server, without needing to update his public verification key after each transmitted data chunk. In addition, the CAT allows the data owner to efficiently update arbitrary subsets of the authenticated outsourced data set, without the need to re-upload or re-authenticate any of the elements that are not updated. After an update, the verification key is updated to invalidate the stale data elements, however all other data elements remain authenticated under the new verification key.

1.1 Our Contribution

On the practical side, we present VeriStream, the first fully-fledged framework for providing streaming applications with security guarantees, such as stream authenticity, integrity, correct ordering of the streamed elements, public verifiability, and efficient updates simultaneously. The VeriStreamstandalone client can be used upload, update, and stream content from personal web servers. In addition, VeriStreamallows its users to use their Dropbox account as the underlying storage layer. Apart from up- and downloading arbitrary files in an authenticated fashion, our framework also supports video and audio streaming with on-the-fly verification. In Sect. 5 we provide a detailed performance evaluation of VeriStreamand compare its performance to the construction from [22].

On the theoretical side we improve upon the state-of-the-art for verifiable data streaming [22]. Their construction is upper bounded during the initialization by some parameter N, meaning that it can authenticate up to N elements. Their construction incurs a computational and bandwidth overhead of $\mathcal{O}(\log N)$

Table 1. Comparison of existing and proposed CAT constructions. N is the upper bound of elements that can be authenticated, whereas M is the number of already authenticated elements. Security proof indicates whether the construction's proof of security is given in the standard model or whether it requires the random oracle model.

	Proof size	Client's state	Upload time/space	Update time/space	Streaming time/space	Unbounded	Security proof
[22]	$\mathcal{O}(\log N)$	$\mathcal{O}(\log N)$	$\mathcal{O}(\log N)$	$\mathcal{O}(\log N)$	$\mathcal{O}(\log N)$	✗	Standard
Dynamic	$\mathcal{O}(\log M)$	$\mathcal{O}(1)$	$\mathcal{O}(\log M)$	$\mathcal{O}(\log M)$	$\mathcal{O}(\log M)$	✓	ROM
δ-bounded	$\mathcal{O}(\log M)$	$\mathcal{O}(1)$	$\mathcal{O}(\log M)$	$\mathcal{O}(\log M)$	$\mathcal{O}(\log M)$	✗	Standard

for each outsourced, updated, or streamed element. The size of their client's state is $\mathcal{O}(\log N)$. In particular this means, either N is chosen large, e.g. polynomial, to be able to authenticate a quasi unbounded amount of elements, which incurs a prohibitively large overhead, or N is chosen small, which in turn means that the resulting construction can only authenticate a limited number of elements.

We propose two novel constructions. The first one, the fully-dynamic CAT, is the first scheme that can authenticate an *unbounded* number of elements and is secure in the random oracle model. The second one, the δ-bounded CAT, has an upper bound on the number of elements it can authenticate, and we prove its security in the standard model. Both of our constructions only incur a computational and bandwidth overhead of $\mathcal{O}(\log M)$ for each outsourced, updated, or streamed element, where M is the number of authenticated elements so far. Note that in general the number of outsourced elements M is significantly smaller than the upper bound N. The size of our client's state is $\mathcal{O}(1)$. For a concise comparison of the existing and our proposed constructions see Table 1.

1.2   System Overview

In this section we outline the high-level workflow and usage of VeriStreambased on the classic task of outsourcing and sharing data. An overview is given in Fig. 1. The major entities are the data owner, other clients that may read data uploaded by the data owner, and the untrusted server storing the data. To allow an easy integration of our framework into already deployed systems, we designed VeriStreamto coexist with the existing system. This means that our framework does not directly alter or modify any of the transmitted data, but only appends and strips its own additional data to and from the trans-

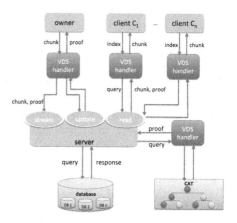

Fig. 1. High-level overview of VeriStream.

mitted data chunks. All involved entities use VDS handlers to authenticate or verify transmitted data. When the data owner wants to upload some data to the server, he initializes his local VDS handler with his secret key. Rather than transmitting all data chunks directly to the server, they are passed through the VDS handler, which authenticates them on-the-fly by appending a proof of correctness to the data chunk. The retrieving server uses his VDS handler to strip the proof from each data chunk. The data itself is stored in a database and the proofs are stored in a CAT. It should be noted, that uploading data to the server does not require the owner to update his verification key after each chunk, which would put an unrealistic burden on the public directory or PKI that handles the keys.

A client can request data chunks by transmitting their indices. The server fetches the data chunks from the database and computes the corresponding proofs of correctness using his VDS handler, which has access to the CAT. The data and the appended proofs are sent to the client, who can verify the correctness and authenticity of each received data chunk separately on-the-fly, using the VDS handler and the data owner's public verification key.

When the data owner wants to update some data chunk in the database, he first receives the element the same way other clients do. After verifying the authenticity of the retrieved chunk, he uses his VDS handler in combination with the retrieved data chunk, its proof of correctness, and the new data chunk to compute a new proof of correctness for the new chunk. The new data chunk with the appended proof is then sent to the server. The owner updates his public verification key at the PKI or the public directory. This is necessary to invalidate the now stale chunk and protect other users from retrieving old data from the server. However, even though the owner only requested and modified the updated chunk, all other outsourced data chunks remain valid under the new verification key.

1.3   Related Work

Verifiable data streaming (VDS) protocols have been introduced by Schröder and Schröder [22]. The authors formalized the problem on a theoretical level and gave a first construction for a bounded number of elements. Their shortcomings in comparison to our constructions are already discussed in Sect. 1.1. A related line of research investigates verifiable databases (VDBs). VDBs have been extensively investigated in the context of accumulators [5,6,16] and authenticated data structures [14,15,19,26]. These approaches, however, often rely on non-constant assumptions, such as the q-Strong Diffie-Hellman assumption, as observed in [4]. More recent works, such as [4] or [8], only support a polynomial number of values instead of exponentially many, and the scheme of [4] is not publicly verifiable. Furthermore, the VDB schemes require the data owner to update his verification key after each newly uploaded element. In contrast, in a VDS protocol, data can be added non-interactively and without updating the verification key by sending a single message to the server. VDS can be seen as a generalization of VDBs.

Another line of research deals with (dynamic) proofs of retrievability (PoR). Here, the client uploads his data to some untrusted server. A PoR protocol allows the user to efficiently verify, whether all of his data is still stored on the server [7, 10,23,24]. A weaker form of PoR are so called proofs of data possession [9]. They only ensure that the server stores most of the data. In these scenarios the protocols only ensure that all or most of the data is stored, but they do not provide any security guarantees w.r.t. the authenticity of streamed content.

Recently, the notion of streaming authenticated data structures was introduced by Papamanthou, Shi, Tamassia and Yi [18], where a computationally weak client and a server observe a stream of data independently. Afterwards the client can perform range queries and verify the results from the server against a verification value it computed while observing the stream. However both notions differ in the following aspects: The verification token of their scheme changes after each streamed/uploaded element, while ours does not. In their scheme, no secret key is involved, which means that a client can only verify responses if he has either seen the seen stream, or if he obtained the verification token from a trusted party. Furthermore, since the key changes after each new element, all elements that are transmitted after receiving the verification token cannot be verified. Our proofs are logarithmic in the size of the uploaded dataset, while theirs are logarithmic in the size of the universe from which the elements are drawn. Finally, we provide comprehensive benchmark results, while their work only provides a asymptotical run time analysis.

Another successful line of research consider "pure" streaming protocols between a sender and possibly multiple clients, such as TESLA and their variants such e.g., [20,21]. In contrast to our setting, the TESLA protocols assume that the sender and the receiver are loosely synchronized and these protocols do not offer public verifiability. The signature based solution of [21] is also different, because the protocol does not support efficient updates, which is a necessary property for our applications, such as e.g., verifiable cloud storage.

NAÏVE APPROACHES: There are a few seemingly simple solutions to the described problem, which do not work. In this paragraph we would like to discuss the shortcomings of some of them. The first idea might be to use a simple Merkle Tree. In a Merkle tree the data is stored in the leaves and the value of each internal node is defined as the hash of the concatenation of its children's values. The verification key is the value of the root node and a proof of correctness for some data chunk consists of all nodes that are required to compute the root node's value starting from the leaf, where the data chunk is stored. This solution would recompute the tree after each uploaded element. This means, that whenever we upload some new data chunk, the verification key is updated, which puts an infeasible burden on the public directory or PKI that stores the public keys. A different approach would be to use signature chains, i.e. for all two adjacent data chunks we compute one signature. Here, the problem is that efficient updates are not possible. When updating a data chunk, we need to invalidate its old version, but here the verification key is just the signature's public key and does not depend on the uploaded data itself. The data owner would need to update the signature's public key and recompute all signature in the chain, which is clearly infeasible. The same argument also holds for forward-secure signature schemes [13], where the secret key is updated from time to time. Since the public key remains the same, freshness cannot be ensured, i.e. a user is not able to distinguish the fresh data chunk from a stale version thereof.

2   Chameleon Authentication Trees

Our formal definition of CATs differs slightly from [22], since we directly model updates as a property of the CATs. This allows us to build VDS protocols in a black-box way from CATs, while [22] needed to make specific *non*black-box assumptions about the proof that might not hold in general. The second difference is that we do not put an upper bound on the number of leaves. Thus, the only input of catGen is the security parameter. The formal definition of VDS from [22] can easily be adapted.

Definition 1. *A* chameleon authentication tree *is a tuple of efficient algorithms* $\Pi_{CAT} = (\mathsf{catGen}, \mathsf{catAdd}, \mathsf{catUpdate}, \mathsf{catVerify})$, *which are defined as follows:*

$\mathsf{catGen}(1^\lambda)$: *The key generation algorithm takes the security parameter λ and outputs a key pair* $(\mathsf{vp}, \mathsf{sp})$. *For simplicity we always assume that* vp *is contained in* sp.

$\mathsf{catAdd}(\mathsf{sp}, \ell)$: *The insertion algorithm takes a secret key* sp, *and a datum ℓ from some data space $\mathcal{L}$. It outputs a new secret key* sp', *a position i at which ℓ was inserted and a proof π_i, which is a publicly verifiable proof showing that ℓ is indeed stored at position i.*

$\mathsf{catUpdate}(\mathsf{sp}, i, \ell)$: *The update algorithm takes the secret key* sp, *a position i at which we want to perform the update, and the new datum $\ell \in \mathcal{L}$ as input. It replaces the current datum at i with ℓ and outputs a new key pair* $(\mathsf{vp}', \mathsf{sp}')$ *as well as a proof π_i for the new datum.*

$\mathsf{catVerify}(\mathsf{vp}, i, \ell, \pi_i)$: *The verification algorithm takes the public key* vp, *a position i, a datum ℓ and a proof π_i as input and outputs 1 iff ℓ is stored at position i. It outputs 0 otherwise.*

SECURITY OF CATS: Our security definition deviates from the one given in [22], by taking update queries of the adversary into account. We present a single definition that covers both, structure-preservation and one-wayness. Intuitively, we say that a CAT is *secure* if no efficient adversary can modify the tree by changing the sequence of the data stored in it, substituting any datum, or by adding further data to it. In particular, the definition also prevents the adversary from returning stale to clients. The game is defined as follows:

Setup: The challenger generates a key-pair $(\mathsf{sp}, \mathsf{vp}) \leftarrow \mathsf{catGen}(1^\lambda)$ and hands vp over to the adversary $\mathcal{A}$.

Uploading: Proceeding adaptively, the attacker $\mathcal{A}$ uploads a datum $\ell \in \mathcal{L}$ to the challenger. The challenger adds ℓ to the database, computes $(\mathsf{sp}', i, \hat{\pi}) \leftarrow \mathsf{catAdd}(\mathsf{sp}, \ell)$, and returns $(i, \hat{\pi})$ to $\mathcal{A}$. Alternatively, the adversary may update any element in the outsourced database by sending an index i, a datum ℓ' to the challenger. The challenger then runs the update algorithm with $\mathcal{A}$ updating ℓ_i to ℓ'. At the end of the update protocol the challenger returns the updated proof π_i' and the updated public-key vp' to $\mathcal{A}$. Denote by $Q := \{(\ell_1, 1, \hat{\pi}_1), \ldots, (\ell_{q(\lambda)}, q(\lambda), \hat{\pi}_{q(\lambda)})\}$ the ordered sequence of the latest versions of all uploaded elements and let vp^* be the corresponding public key.

Output: Eventually, $\mathcal{A}$ outputs $(\ell^*, i^*, \hat{\pi}^*)$. The attacker $\mathcal{A}$ is said to win the game if one of the following two conditions is true:

  a) If $1 \leq i^* \leq q(\lambda)$ and $(\ell^*, i^*, \hat{\pi}^*) \notin Q$ and $\mathsf{catVerify}(\mathsf{vp}^*, i^*, \ell^*, \hat{\pi}^*) = 1$.
  b) If $i^* > q(\lambda)$ and $\mathsf{catVerify}(\mathsf{vp}^*, i^*, \ell^*, \hat{\pi}^*) = 1$.

We define $\mathbf{Adv}_{\mathcal{A}}^{sec}$ to be the probability that the adversary $\mathcal{A}$ wins in the above game.

Definition 2. *A chameleon authentication tree* Π_{CAT} = (catGen, catAdd, catUpdate, catVerify) *is* secure *if for any* $q \in \mathbb{N}$, *and for any efficient algorithm* $\mathcal{A}$, *the probability* $\mathbf{Adv}_{\mathcal{A}}^{sec}$ *evaluates to 1 is negligible (as a function of λ).*

3   Constructing Fully Dynamic CATs

We now present our fully dynamic CAT construction, which is the first construction that is able to authenticate an unbounded number of data elements and improves upon the state-of-the-art in terms of computational and bandwidth overhead. In the following we first recall the definition of chameleon hash functions and then present our construction.

3.1   Chameleon Hash Functions

A chameleon hash function is a randomized hash function that is collision-resistant but provides a trapdoor to efficiently compute collisions. It is defined through the tuple $\mathcal{CH}$ = (chGen, ch, col) [12], where the key generation algorithm chGen(1^λ) returns a key pair (csk, cpk). We set ch($\cdot$) := ch($cpk, \cdot$) for the remainder of this paper. The function ch($x; r$) produces a hash value $h \in \{0,1\}^{out}$ for a message $m \in \{0,1\}^{in}$ and a randomness $r \in \{0,1\}^\lambda$. The function is collision-resistant meaning that given cpk it is computationally difficult to compute a tuple $(m, r), (m', r')$ such that $(m, r) \neq (m', r')$ and ch(m, r) = ch(m', r'). However, using the trapdoor csk and the collision-finding algorithm col(csk, x, r, x') we can break the collision-resistance property and find a value r' such that both, (x, r) and (x', r') map to the same hash value.

We call $\mathcal{CH}$ invertible if it is surjective and there exists an efficient algorithm scol(csk, x, y) that outputs an r for any input x and y such that y = ch($x; r$). This property has previously been defined by Shamir and Tauman [25].

Chameleon hash functions can be instantiated from the discrete-logarithm assumption [2,12], the factoring assumption [25], the RSA assumption [2,11], or in a generic way from certain Σ-protocols [3].

3.2   Intuition

The main idea of our construction is to build a binary tree, which stores the data elements in its leaves and grows dynamically from bottom up. Whenever the tree of a certain depth d is full, the data owner can increase the tree's depth by one using his secret trapdoor. The resulting tree is of depth $d + 1$ and can therefore store another 2^d elements. The previous full tree becomes the left child under the new root and the right child serves as a place holder for an empty subtree, which can be used to store new data.

This new approach of dynamically increasing the depth of the tree means that we cannot simply store the root node's value in the public key, since it changes whenever the depth is extended. Instead, our idea is to define the new root through a deterministic function that is applied to a fixed value in the public key and depends on the current depth of the tree. More precisely, let ρ be the value in the public key pk and assume that the depth of the tree is d. Then, the root node is defined as $H^d(\rho)$, where H is a collision-resistant hash function and by $H^d(\rho)$ we denote the d-fold application of H to ρ.

Our binary tree is structured as follows: Each node value is computed as the output of a function of the concatenated values of its children. For nodes which are left children themselves we use a collision-resistant hash function. For right children we use a chameleon hash function. The only exception to this rule are all nodes, that have been a root at some point, i.e., all nodes at the very left of each level. We insert the data elements into the trees starting from the leftmost leaf moving to the right. Whenever we insert some data element into a leaf we have to ensure that, roughly speaking, the root node's value computed from that leaf remains the same as before the insertion. Therefore, we search for a node computed by a chameleon hash function on the path from the inserted leaf to the root and compute an appropriate collision using our secret trapdoor.

In the following, we exemplify basic idea of our construction with a small example, where we will refer to a node v at height h and index i by $v_{h,i}$. Please note, even though we will be including two leaves at the same time, this should not be seen as a restriction or a problem. It is done for the sake of clarity and the construction can be easily extended to insert one leaf at a time, as it is done in our framework.

<u>SETUP:</u> We compute $(cpk, csk) \leftarrow \mathsf{chGen}(1^\lambda)$ using the key generation algorithm of the chameleon hash function. The setup algorithm stores the trapdoor csk of the chameleon hash function in the private key sk; the corresponding public verification key pk contains cpk and a randomly chosen value ρ. At the beginning of the streaming protocol, the tree is empty.

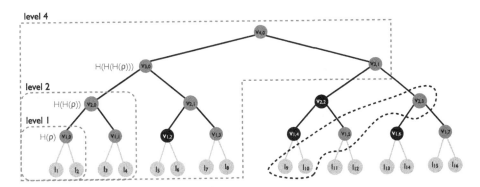

Fig. 2. The fully dynamic CAT. Green nodes are computed using the chameleon and black nodes using the collision-resistant hash functions. The tree stores 2^i elements at level i (Color figure online).

APPENDING THE ELEMENTS ℓ_1, ℓ_2: In the first step, we append the elements ℓ_1 and ℓ_2 to the tree. Since the tree is empty, i.e. it has depth 0, it is necessary to increase its depth by one. In order to add ℓ_1 and ℓ_2 to the tree without changing the root, the data owner uses his secret trapdoor to compute $r_{1,0} \leftarrow \mathsf{scol}(csk, \ell_1 \| \ell_2, H^1(\rho))$. Hence $\mathsf{ch}(\ell_1 \| \ell_2; r_{1,0}) = H(\rho)$. Recall that scol outputs some randomness r when given (y, x) and the secret key csk such that $y = \mathsf{ch}(x; r)$. At this stage the entire tree consists only of two leaves and one root node as depicted in Fig. 2 (level 1). To verify that the leaves (ℓ_1, ℓ_2) are in the tree, the verification algorithm checks whether $H^1(\rho) = \mathsf{ch}(\ell_1 \| \ell_2; r_{1,0})$ holds.

APPENDING THE ELEMENTS ℓ_3, ℓ_4: Next, we add ℓ_3 and ℓ_4 to the tree. Since the current tree is full, we need to extend its height to obtain new free leaf positions. Therefore, we pick a random $x_{1,1}$ and $r_{1,1}$ and we compute the dummy node $v_{1,1} \leftarrow \mathsf{ch}(x_{1,1}; r_{1,1})$. The randomly chosen pre-images are stored by the client in his secret local state. To ensure the integrity of the tree, we need to find a randomness $r_{2,0}$ for the new root $v_{2,0}$ such that $\mathsf{ch}(H^1(\rho) \| v_{1,1}; r_{2,0}) = H^2(\rho)$. Again, this is achieved by exploiting the inversion property of the chameleon hash function to compute $r_{2,0} \leftarrow \mathsf{scol}(csk, H^1(\rho) \| v_{1,1}, H^2(\rho))$. We can now add our leaves ℓ_3 and ℓ_4 to the tree by appending them to the lowest free right child, which is $v_{1,1}$. Thus, we compute $r'_{1,1} \leftarrow \mathsf{col}(csk, x_{1,1}, r_{1,1}, \ell_3 \| \ell_4)$. The resulting proof for ℓ_3, ℓ_4 would therefore contain $(v_{1,0}, r_{2,0}, r_{1,1})$. The corresponding tree is shown in Fig. 2 (level 2).

APPENDING THE ELEMENTS ℓ_5, ℓ_6 AND ℓ_7, ℓ_8: Since the tree is full again, we need to increase its depth the same way we did before. Afterwards, we search for the lowest right child, which does not have any children yet. In this case the node is $v_{2,1}$ that has been computed by $\mathsf{ch}(x_{2,1}; r_{2,1})$. The dummy values $(x_{2,1}, r_{2,1})$ can be retrieved from the local client state. In order to append ℓ_5 and ℓ_6, we generate an empty subtree below $v_{2,1}$. This subtree consists of a dummy node $v_{1,3}$ and the leaves ℓ_5 and ℓ_6. After appending ℓ_5 and ℓ_6 below $v_{1,2}$, we compute $r'_{2,1} \leftarrow \mathsf{col}(csk, x_{2,1}, r_{2,1}, v_{1,2} \| v_{1,3})$. The proof for these elements contains $(r'_{2,1}, v_{1,3}, v_{2,0})$. Next, ℓ_7 and ℓ_8 can authenticated by appending them to $v_{1,3}$ and computing a collision in the same fashion as in the previous steps.

VERIFICATION: The verification algorithm works analogously to the one of a Merkle tree. One might get the impression that the size of the proofs grows with the number of leaves *for all leaves*. This, however, is not the case. For instance, the node $v_{1,0}$ verifies the leaves ℓ_1 and ℓ_2 even if 2^{50} elements are stored in the tree. The verification algorithm still simply checks whether $H(\rho) = \mathsf{ch}(\ell_0 \| \ell_1; r_{1,0})$.

UPDATING THE TREE: Whenever we wish to update the i-th element in the database to some element ℓ'_i, we simply replace the element, recompute the values on the path from ℓ'_i to the corresponding root node, pick a fresh value ρ', and update all sub-roots w.r.t. ρ'. Updating the sub-roots means that the client has to compute logarithmically many collisions.

CONSTANT STATE: In the intuitive description of our construction, the client's state is logarithmic in the depth of the tree, since all created dummy nodes $y \leftarrow \mathsf{ch}(x; r)$ are stored by the client. To reduce the client's state to $\mathcal{O}(1)$ we use a pseudorandom function PRF to compute the dummy elements on the fly. That is, for each dummy node $v_{h,i}$, the clients computes the pair $(x_{h,i}, r_{h,i}) \leftarrow \mathsf{PRF}(k, h\|i)$, rather than choosing it randomly. This allows us to recompute the dummy nodes we need on-the-fly without storing them.

The secret seed of the PRF is stored as part of the secret key. Therefore, the final secret key in our construction consists of the trapdoor csk of the chameleon hash function, the seed k of the PRF, and a counter c that keeps track of the next free leaf index. In practice and in our framework, one can instantiate the PRF using a symmetric encryption scheme, such as AES.

3.3 Formal Construction

We now provide a detailed description of all algorithms, that have been sketched in the previous section. We avoid using the PRF in this description for the sake of clarity, but the modification is absolutely straightforward as described above.

Construction 1. *Let $H : \{0,1\}^* \mapsto \{0,1\}^{len}$ be a hash function and $\mathcal{CH} = (\mathsf{chGen}, \mathsf{ch}, \mathsf{col}, \mathsf{scol})$ an invertible chameleon hash function that maps strings of length $\{0,1\}^*$ to $\{0,1\}^{len}$. The fully-dynamic chameleon authentication tree $\Pi_{\mathsf{CAT}} = (\mathsf{catGen}, \mathsf{catAdd}, \mathsf{catUpdate}, \mathsf{catVerify})$ consists of the following efficient algorithms:*

$\mathsf{catGen}(1^\lambda)$*: The setup algorithm generates a key-pair of the chameleon hash $(cpk, csk) \leftarrow \mathsf{chGen}(1^\lambda)$, it picks a uniformly random value $\rho \leftarrow \{0,1\}^\lambda$, and denote by st the private state. This state stores the next free leaf index c, a set of pre-images of unused dummy nodes and the last computed proof. Initially we set $c \leftarrow 0$, while the set of pre-images and the last computed proof are both empty. It returns the public verification key $\mathsf{vp} = (cpk, \rho)$ and the private key $\mathsf{sp} = (csk, \mathsf{st}, \mathsf{vp})$.*

$\mathsf{catAdd}(\mathsf{sp}, \ell)$*: Parse sp as $(csk, \mathsf{st}, \mathsf{vp})$ and check whether the current tree is full, i.e., whether c is a power of two:*

THE COUNTER c IS A POWER OF TWO: *In this case the current tree is full, we need to increase its current depth by one to obtain a tree of depth d, which has free leaves again. To do so, we store the old root node $H^{d-1}(\rho)$ as the left child of the new root node $H^d(\rho)$ and we create a dummy node $v_{d-1,1}$ for the right child as follows: First, we pick the values $x_{d-1,1}$ and $r_{d-1,1}$ uniformly at random and we compute the dummy node $v_{d-1,1} \leftarrow \mathsf{ch}(x_{d-1,1}; r_{d-1,1})$. Second, we exploit the inversion property of the chameleon hash function in order to compute $r_{d,0} \leftarrow \mathsf{scol}(csk, H^{d-1}(\rho)\|v_{d-1,1}, H^d(\rho))$. Next, we add $(x_{d-1,1}, r_{d-1,1})$ to the set of pre-images and $v_{d-1,1}$ to the proof in st and proceed as in the case where c is not a power of two.*

THE COUNTER c IS NOT A POWER OF TWO: *Since the tree is not full, we search for the lowest right child $v_{i,j}$, which has no children, in the proof that was stored in st during the last run of catAdd. Then, we generate a skeleton subtree below $v_{i,j}$ the following way. First, we descend from $v_{i,j}$ along the left edge until we reach height 1. Then we create one adjacent dummy node at each height, i.e., we create dummy nodes at $v_{i-k,2^k \cdot j+1}$ for $k = 1 \dots i-1$. The pre-image of each created dummy node is added to st. Now, we append the given leaf ℓ as the left most child to the newly generated subtree at height 0. Given the leaf and the dummy nodes, the value of $v_{i,j}$ can now be determined recursively by computing $v_{i,j} \leftarrow v_{i-1,2\cdot j} \| v_{i-1,2\cdot j+1}$. We re-establish the tree's integrity by computing a randomness $r'_{i,j} \leftarrow \mathsf{col}(csk, x_{i,j}, r_{i,j}, v_{i,j})$. We create a proof π for ℓ, which contains all newly created dummy nodes, $r'_{i,j}$, the node adjacent to $v_{i,j}$ and all nodes from the old proof, which were above $v_{i,j}$. Finally, we increase the next free leaf index c in the client state by one, replace the proof in st with the newly generated one, and return it.*

catVerify($\mathsf{vp}, i, \ell, \pi$): *Parse vp as (cpk, ρ). In order to verify, whether π authenticates ℓ we compute, starting from the bottom, each node as the hash or the chameleon hash of the concatenation of its two children until we compute a node with index 0. All nodes and randomnesses that are needed are taken from the given π. In case the node we want to compute has a odd index, we use the chameleon hash function. Otherwise we use the hash function. Let $v_{d,0}$ be the node at which we terminated. We return 1 iff $v_{d,0} = H^d(\rho)$, and 0 otherwise.*

catUpdate(sp, i, ℓ'): *Parse sp as $(csk, \mathsf{st}, \mathsf{vp})$ and vp as (cpk, ρ). Request ℓ_i, with its proof of correctness π_i. Request ℓ_0 with its proof of correctness π_0. Compute catVerify($\mathsf{vp}, i, \ell_i, \pi_i$) and catVerify($\mathsf{vp}, 0, \ell_0, \pi_0$) and abort if one of them outputs 0. Let $\pi = \pi_i \cup \pi_0$ denote the total set of nodes and randomnesses obtained by the client at this point. Replace ℓ_i with ℓ' and recompute all values that are on the path from ℓ' to the root recessively. Pick a new $\rho' \leftarrow \{0,1\}^\lambda$ and replace ρ with ρ' in vp. This means that at each height h we now have to ensure again that $H^h(\rho') = \mathsf{ch}(v_{h-1,0} \| v_{h-1,1})$. Therefore, we compute $r'_{h,0} \leftarrow \mathsf{scol}(csk, v_{h-1,0} \| v_{h-1,1}, H^h(\rho'))$ at each height h and add all newly computed $r'_{h,0}$ to π and return π.*

Theorem 1. *If $\mathcal{CH}$ is an invertible one-way collision-resistant chameleon hash function and H is a collision-resistant hash function modeled as a random oracle, then Construction 1 is a secure unbounded verifiable data streaming protocol.*

Due to space constraints the security proof will be available in the full version.

4   Implementation

VeriStreamis written in Java and it contains all protocols described in this paper as well as a separate library for chameleon hash functions, which contains implementations of the Krawczyk-Rabin [12], the Ateniese and de Medeiros chameleon hash [2], and its elliptic curve equivalent. For the elliptic curve operations we used the Bouncy Castle Cryptographic API (Release 1.49) [1]. In addition we provide a generic interface for transforming Σ-protocols, that fulfil certain properties into chameleon hash functions [3]. Using this interface we instantiated a chameleon hash function from the Fiat-Shamir protocol [3]. Many chameleon hash functions only take input from certain message spaces, e.g., Krawczyk-Rabin expects messages from $\mathbb{Z}_q^*$. We provide a simple wrapper that transforms them into functions that take arbitrary large inputs, by first hashing the input with a common collision-resistant hash function, like SHA-256, before passing it to the chameleon hash function. The remaining algorithms of the chameleon hash functions are adapted accordingly by the wrapper.

We developed a platform independent standalone client that uses VeriStream (see Fig. 3). It allows its users to manage, upload, download, or share files of an arbitrary format in an authenticated fashion. Users can choose whether they want to upload their data to a private web storage or whether they want to use their Dropbox account as the underlying storage layer. The client is able to stream audio and video content with on-the-fly-verification, even if Dropbox is the underlying storage layer.

For developers, VeriStreamoffers a simple to use interface by the means of so called VDS handlers. This handler is parameterized by the VDS protocol type and chameleon hash function that shall be deployed. It offers methods for creating, verifying, updating, and obtaining proofs from CATs. Since network bandwidth is an important issue, we transform the proofs into compact byte sequences representations before sending them over the network, rather than relying on bloated formats like JSON. We implemented a server, based on a common thread-pool architecture, that receives from and streams data to clients, where both parties deploy a VDS handler to secure the transmitted content.

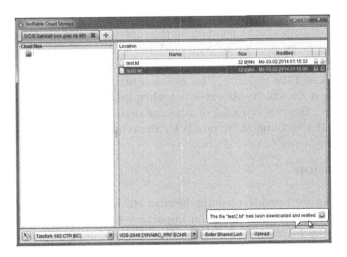

Fig. 3. Screenshot of the VeriStreamstandalone client.

Efficiency Optimizations. For performance and bandwidth reasons, our framework differs from the theoretical description in several points that we discuss in the following.

SHORT PROOFS: When uploading data to the server it is not necessary to always send the whole proof. Instead, it is sufficient to only send all nodes that are below the chameleon hash node that was extended. One can think of this optimization as transmitting only the delta between the previous proof(s) and the current one.

PARALLELIZING THE CAT: Recall that the insertion algorithm always generates a certain amount of chameleon dummy nodes by picking random pre-images and storing them in the client state. Later on, when we insert elements below one such dummy node, we use the pre-images from the state to compute a collision in that dummy accordingly. Now, instead of picking these pre-images completely at random, we provide the possibility to pick them using a pseudorandom function, which takes the dummy nodes position as input. This way, we reduce the client state to constant size, since we do not need to store the pre-images anymore. Furthermore, being able to compute the values of dummy nodes independent of the actual existing tree allows us to obtain concurrent versions of all protocols. The position of an element in the data stream while uploading uniquely defines its position in the CAT. Having the element, and using the pseudorandom function to obtain the dummy value to which that element will be appended, we can compute the short proof independent of the remaining tree. We believe that it is not straightforward to see that the parallelization of the CAT indeed works, because almost half of the nodes are computed using a collision-resistant hash functions and these nodes cannot be pre-computed without knowing the pre-images. However, a closer look at our construction shows that all these values belong to the left part of the tree and these elements have all been pre-computed before.

CONTINUOUS REQUESTS: Depending on the concrete scenario, a single or multiple elements in succession can be requested. In the case, where multiple adjacent elements are requested, we exploit the following observation: Given the proof π_i for some leaf i and the proof π_{i+1} for its successor $i + 1$, all nodes in π_{i+1}, that are above the node which was extended when inserting the leaf $i + 1$ are also contained in π_i. Hence when a set of adjacent elements is requested, we send the full proof for the first and short proofs for the remaining elements.

5   Evaluation

In this section, we provide a comprehensive efficiency analysis of VeriStream. In this analysis, the chunk size is an important variable, because we compute one proof for each chunk and we therefore test our implementation with different chunk sized to obtain detailed insights into the protocols performance. In addition, we conduct several different benchmarks highlighting all possible operations for all discussed protocols. Our experimental analysis was conducted

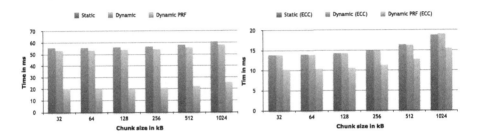

Fig. 4. Average time for authenticating one data chunk. On the left all computations were performed on cyclic groups. On the right on elliptic curves.

on a Intel Core i3-2120 CPU with 8 GB of RAM running Ubuntu 12.04 with Java 1.6.0.

EVALUATION OF OUR FRAMEWORK: We analyzed the performances of all protocols by uploading and streaming 2 GB of data with different chunk sizes, such as 32 kB, 64 kB, ..., 1024 kB. Smaller chunk sizes result in more chunks and therefore bigger CATs. In addition, we were interested in the performance impact of utilizing a pseudorandom function for computing the dummy nodes and therefore we conducted experiments with the fully dynamic CAT that used a pseudorandom function. As the underlying chameleon hash function we used the scheme due to Ateniese and de Medeiros. For a performance comparison of different chameleon hash functions see Appendix B. As the underlying group we used both elliptic curves and regular cyclic groups with a security parameter of 112 bits. The CAT from [22] was initialized with a depth of 30, which results in a tree that can authenticate 2^{30} data chunks. In the following we will refer to their construction in the figures as *static*. To obtain meaningful and detailed performance results, we computed the averages of the following measurements:

– Time for hashing a chunk and authenticating it.
– Time for obtaining and verifying a proof from the CAT.
– Bandwidth overhead produced by a proof retrieved from the CAT.

EVALUATION RESULTS: When authenticating and uploading data chunks to the server, the data owner only sends short proofs to the server as described in Sect. 4. A comparison of the computational overhead incurred by this authentication step in the different constructions is depicted in Fig. 4. One can see that our constructions outperform the construction from [22]. In particular, this is interesting, since our fully dynamic CAT also provides a better functionality, i.e. it allows uploading and streaming an unbounded amount of data. One somewhat surprising result is, that combining our construction with a pseudorandom function not only reduces the size of the client's state, but also significantly increases its performance. In practice, the computation of the client's state after each uploaded chunk is far more expensive than the evaluation of the pseudorandom function. All protocols perform better by more than a factor of two, when using the elliptic curve chameleon hash function.

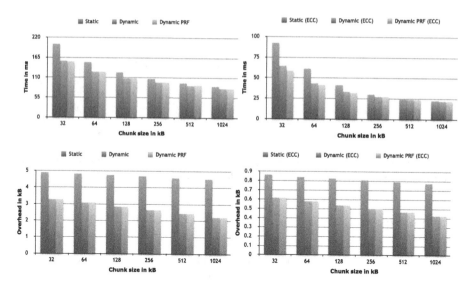

Fig. 5. The two plots at the top depict the average full proof computation and verification time per data chunk. The two plots at the bottom show the average bandwidth overhead for one data chunk.

In the next step we analyzed the computational and bandwidth overhead of the retrieval operation. We measured the time it took to compute the proof from the CAT upon a client request for a certain element and verify the returned proof. More precisely we created a CAT that contained proofs for a 2 GB large data set and requested all chunks from it, such that each proof in the CAT had to be computed once. For each received proof the verification algorithm was executed once. We stress that we did not use the efficent method for retrieving sequential parts of the uploaded data, but purposely requested each chunk on its own with its full proof. The results of this experiment can be seen in Fig. 5. At the top one can see the average time it took to obtain a proof from the CAT and verify it. At the bottom one can see the average size of such a retrieved proof. The protocol from [22] performs worst w.r.t. to computational and bandwidth overhead, what confirms our expectation, since, in contrast to the dynamically growing trees, all elements in their construction verify against the very top level root value. This requires, on average, much more bandwidth and more computational power. Our two constructions perform roughly equally well as expected. Using the elliptic curve variant of the Ateniese and de Medeiros chameleon hash results in a improvement of roughly factor 5 with regards to the size of the proofs and a speed up of about factor 3.

Acknowledgements. Dominique Schröder and Mark Simkin were supported by the German Federal Ministry of Education and Research (BMBF) through funding for the Center for IT-Security, Privacy, and Accountability (CISPA; see www.cispa-security.org). Dominique Schröder is also supported by an Intel Early Career Faculty Honor Program Award.

A δ-bounded CATs

The fully dynamic CAT is more efficient than previous constructions [22] and allows the data owner to upload an unbounded amount of data. However, the proof is only given in the random oracle model and the construction requires the additional inversion property of chameleon hash functions. Although two of the three chameleon hash functions we consider, namely the Fiat-Shamir [3] and the Ateniese and de Medeiros [2] construction have this property, it is still desirable to find a solution based on weaker assumptions, which can be proven in the standard model. Therefore we propose the δ-bounded CAT, which is upper bounded by the depth δ, but is provably secure in the standard model and has roughly the same computational and bandwidth overhead as the fully dynamic construction.

A.1 Intuition

Let us reconsider our first construction. There, we exploited the inversion property of our chameleon hash function to find randomnesses that mapped to certain root values. To provide a proof in the standard model we have to refrain from using this property. Instead, we pre-compute δ dummy root values $\rho_{h,0}$ where $h = 1 \ldots \delta$, publish them in the public key pk, and keep their pre-images secret in our state st. An authentication path with depth i is then verified against $\rho_{i,0}$. Since we keep all pre-images in our state, we can use col rather than scol to find collisions.

Note, again we can make use of a pseudorandom function to make the client's state constant.

A.2 Construction

We now provide the formal description of all algorithms of the δ-bounded CAT construction.

Construction 2. *Let $H : \{0,1\}^* \mapsto \{0,1\}^{len}$ be a hash function and $\mathcal{CH} = $ (chGen, ch, col) a chameleon hash function. The δ-bounded chameleon authentication tree $\Pi_{\mathsf{CAT}} = $ (catGen, catAdd, catUpdate, catVerify) is defined as follows:*

catGen($1^\lambda, \delta$): *The algorithm computes $(cpk, csk) \leftarrow$ chGen(1^λ) and sets $c \leftarrow 0$. For $i = 1, \ldots, \delta$ it generates dummy nodes $\rho_{i,0}$ and stores their pre-images in st. It returns the private key sp $= (csk, \mathsf{st}, \mathsf{vp})$ and the public key vp $= (cpk, (\rho_{1,0}, \ldots, \rho_{\delta,0}))$*

catAdd(sp, s): *Parse sp as $(csk, \mathsf{st}, \mathsf{vp})$ and check whether the current tree is full, i.e., whether c is a power of two:*

THE COUNTER c IS A POWER OF TWO: *In this case the tree is full again. We need to extend its height by one to create a tree which has free leaves. Let d be its depth before increasing it by one. If $d = \delta$ we abort, since the tree* has reached its maximum capacity. Otherwise, we compute a dummy node $v_{d-1,1}$, and store its pre-images in st. Next, we need to compute $r'_{d,0}$ such that $\mathsf{ch}(\rho_{d-1,0}\|v_{d-1,1}, r'_{d,0}) = \rho_d$. We use the stored pre-image $(x_{d,0}, r_{d,0})$ of $\rho_{d,0}$ from st and compute $r_{d,0} \leftarrow \mathsf{col}(csk, x_{d,0}, r_{d,0}, \rho_{d-1,0}\|v_{d-1,1})$. Now we add $v_{d-1,1}$, $r'_{d,0}$ to π in st and proceed as in the case where c is not a power of two.

THE COUNTER c IS NOT A POWER OF TWO: In this case the tree is not full. The algorithms behaviour here is identical to the one in the fully dynamic version as defined in Construction 1.

catVerify(vp, i, ℓ, π): Parse vp as $(cpk, (\rho_{1,0}, \ldots, \rho_{\delta,0}))$. In order to verify, whether π authenticates ℓ we compute, starting from the bottom, each node as the hash or the chameleon hash of its two children until we compute a node with index 0. If the a nodes index is odd, we compute it using the chameleon hash function, and we use the hash function otherwise. All required nodes and randomnesses are taken from π. Let $v_{d,0}$ be the node at which we terminated. Return 1 iff $v_{d,0} = \rho_{d,0}$, and 0 otherwise.

catUpdate(sp, i, ℓ'): Parse sp as $(csk, \mathsf{st}, \mathsf{vp})$. Request ℓ_i, with its proof of correctness π_i, and compute catVerify(vp, i, ℓ_i, π_i); abort if it outputs 0. Otherwise, replace ℓ with ℓ' and recompute the new value of the corresponding root $v_{d,0}$. Update the root node's value at that height in the public key vp' accordingly. Recompute all root node values above $v_{d,0}$ update the vp' accordingly.

Regarding security, we obtain the following theorem.

Theorem 2. Suppose that $\mathcal{CH}$ is a one-way collision-resistant chameleon hash function and H is a collision-resistant hash function, then Construction 2 is a secure δ-bounded chameleon authentication tree.

The proofs is similar to the previous one, with the difference that we do not need to program the random oracle anymore, and can easily be deduced.

B   Evaluation of Chameleon Hash Functions

We discuss the performance of chameleon hash functions on their own, since they represent the most expensive building block in our protocols. In particular, we examine the hashing and collision finding performances of the Fiat-Shamir, the Ateniese and de Medeiros, its elliptic curve equivalent, and the Krawczyk-Rabin chameleon hash.

To evaluate their performances, we used each of them to compute 2000 hashes for randomly generated 160 bit long messages and then computed the average time it took. We used a security parameter of 2048 and chose all sizes in the underlying primitives according to the NIST Recommendations 2012 [17]. For the elliptic curve variation of the Ateniese and de Medeiros hash we used the P-224 curve.

The collision finding performances were measured by running the experiment above with the difference that we additionally computed a collision for another

Table 2. Chameleon hash function benchmarks in milliseconds.

	Hash	Hash and Coll
Fiat-Shamir	6.501	21423.046
Krawczyk-Rabin	10.213	10.2305
Ateniese and de Medeiros	26.617	54.1225
Ateniese and de Medeiros (EC)	7.637	12.134

randomly generated message after each hash operation. The average times for computing one hash, or one hash and one collision respectively are depicted in Table 2.

One can see that when only performing the hash operation, the Fiat-Shamir construction is the fastest one. Unfortunately its performance for computing collisions is very poor, which renders it infeasible for applications that require high throughput. Quiet interestingly Ateniese and de Medeiros is slower than its elliptic curve pendant. Further tests with a smaller security parameter like 1024 showed that the elliptic curve variant is slower at first, but scales much better, when the security parameter increases. As expected from the mathematical description of the Krawczyk-Rabin chameleon hash, it performs very well and its collision finding algorithm is extremely efficient. However, it is not invertible and therefore it cannot be used in the dynamic constructions.

References

1. Bouncy Castle Crypto APIs
2. Ateniese, G., de Medeiros, B.: On the key exposure problem in chameleon hashes. In: Blundo, C., Cimato, S. (eds.) SCN 2004. LNCS, vol. 3352, pp. 165–179. Springer, Heidelberg (2005)
3. Bellare, M., Ristov, T.: Hash functions from sigma protocols and improvements to VSH. In: Pieprzyk, J. (ed.) ASIACRYPT 2008. LNCS, vol. 5350, pp. 125–142. Springer, Heidelberg (2008)
4. Benabbas, S., Gennaro, R., Vahlis, Y.: Verifiable delegation of computation over large datasets. In: Rogaway, P. (ed.) CRYPTO 2011. LNCS, vol. 6841, pp. 111–131. Springer, Heidelberg (2011)
5. Camenisch, J., Kohlweiss, M., Soriente, C.: An accumulator based on bilinear maps and efficient revocation for anonymous credentials. In: Jarecki, S., Tsudik, G. (eds.) PKC 2009. LNCS, vol. 5443, pp. 481–500. Springer, Heidelberg (2009)
6. Mironov, I.: (Not so) random shuffles of RC4. In: Yung, M. (ed.) CRYPTO 2002. LNCS, vol. 2442, p. 304. Springer, Heidelberg (2002)
7. Cash, D., Küpçü, A., Wichs, D.: Dynamic proofs of retrievability via oblivious RAM. In: Johansson, T., Nguyen, P.Q. (eds.) EUROCRYPT 2013. LNCS, vol. 7881, pp. 279–295. Springer, Heidelberg (2013)
8. Catalano, D., Fiore, D.: Vector Commitments and Their Applications. In: Kurosawa, K., Hanaoka, G. (eds.) PKC 2013. LNCS, vol. 7778, pp. 55–72. Springer, Heidelberg (2013)

9. Erway, C.C., Küpçü, A., Papamanthou, C., Tamassia, R.: Dynamic provable data possession. In: Al-Shaer, E., Jha, S., Keromytis, A.D. (eds.), 16th Conference on Computer and Communications Security, ACM CCS 2009, pp. 213–222. ACM Press, Chicago, Illinois, USA, 9–13 November 2009

10. Gazzoni Filho, D.L., Barreto, P.S.L.M.: Demonstrating data possession and uncheatable data transfer. Cryptology ePrint Archive, Report 2006/150 (2006). http://eprint.iacr.org/

11. Hohenberger, S., Waters, B.: Realizing hash-and-sign signatures under standard assumptions. In: Joux, A. (ed.) EUROCRYPT 2009. LNCS, vol. 5479, pp. 333–350. Springer, Heidelberg (2009)

12. Krawczyk, H., Rabin, T.: Chameleon signatures. In: ISOC Network and Distributed System Security Symposium - NDSS 2000. The Internet Society, San Diego, California, USA, 2–4 February 2000

13. Black, J.A., Rogaway, P.: A block-cipher mode of operation for parallelizable message authentication. In: Knudsen, L.R. (ed.) EUROCRYPT 2002. LNCS, vol. 2332, p. 384. Springer, Heidelberg (2002)

14. Martel, C., Nuckolls, G., Devanbu, P., Gertz, M., Kwong, A., Stubblebine, S.G.: A general model for authenticated data structures. Algorithmica 39, 2004 (2001)

15. Naor, M., Nissim, K.: Certificate revocation and certificate update. IEEE J. Sel. Areas Commun. 18(4), 561–570 (2000)

16. Nguyen, L.: Accumulators from bilinear pairings and applications. In: Menezes, A. (ed.) CT-RSA 2005. LNCS, vol. 3376, pp. 275–292. Springer, Heidelberg (2005)

17. National Institute of Standards and Technology. Recommendation for key management. Special Publication 800–57 Part 1 Rev. 3, NIST (2012). http://www.keylength.com/

18. Papamanthou, C., Shi, E., Tamassia, R., Yi, K.: Streaming authenticated data structures. In: Johansson, T., Nguyen, P.Q. (eds.) EUROCRYPT 2013. LNCS, vol. 7881, pp. 353–370. Springer, Heidelberg (2013)

19. Papamanthou, C., Tamassia, R.: Time and space efficient algorithms for two-party authenticated data structures. In: Qing, S., Imai, H., Wang, G. (eds.) ICICS 2007. LNCS, vol. 4861, pp. 1–15. Springer, Heidelberg (2007)

20. Perrig, A., Canetti, R., Song, D.X., Tygar, J.D.: Efficient and secure source authentication for multicast. In: ISOC Network and Distributed System Security Symposium - NDSS 2001, pp. 35–46. The Internet Society, San Diego, California, USA, 7–9 February 2001

21. Perrig, A., Canetti, R., Tygar, J.D., Song, D.X.: Efficient authentication and signing of multicast streams over lossy channels. In: 2000 IEEE Symposium on Security and Privacy, pp. 56–73. IEEE Computer Society Press, Oakland, California, USA (2000)

22. Schröder, D., Schröder, H.: Verifiable data streaming. In: Yu, T., Danezis, G., Gligor, V.D. (eds.) 19th Conference on Computer and Communications Security, ACM CCS 2012, pp. 953–964. ACM Press, Raleigh, NC, USA, 16–18 October 2012

23. Schwarz, T., Miller, E.L.: Store, forget, and check: using algebraic signatures to check remotely administered storage. In: Proceedings of the IEEE International Conference on Distributed Computing Systems (ICDCS 2006), July 2006

24. Shacham, H., Waters, B.: Compact proofs of retrievability. In: Pieprzyk, J. (ed.) ASIACRYPT 2008. LNCS, vol. 5350, pp. 90–107. Springer, Heidelberg (2008)

25. Manger, J.: A chosen ciphertext attack on RSA Optimal Asymmetric Encryption Padding (OAEP) as standardized in PKCS #1 v2.0. In: Kilian, J. (ed.) CRYPTO 2001. LNCS, vol. 2139, p. 230. Springer, Heidelberg (2001)

26. Roberto Tamassia and Nikos Triandopoulos. Certification and authentication of data structures. In: AMW (2010)

Poster Abstracts

Cryptanalysis of a Protocol from FC'10 (Poster Abstract)

Mohsen Toorani

Department of Informatics,
University of Bergen, Bergen, Norway
mohsen.toorani@ii.uib.no

Abstract. We show that the YAK protocol does not provide the key control attribute, and is vulnerable to some attacks. We also propose some improvements.

The YAK protocol [1,2] is a variant of the two-pass HMQV protocol [3], but uses zero-knowledge proofs for proving knowledge of ephemeral secret keys. It is based on public keys, certified by certificate authorities. Although the YAK protocol is claimed to be an authenticated key exchange (AKE) protocol [1,2], the authentication is just zero-knowledge verification of a random number, generated by the other party. There is no binding between entity identifiers and the session key derivation function. Any AKE protocol should provide several security attributes, and it should withstand well-known attacks [4].

There are claims for security and efficiency of the YAK protocol [1,2], but we show that it does not provide the *key control* attribute which is a requirement for key exchange protocols. We also show that the YAK protocol is vulnerable to an *unknown key-share attack* and a *key-replication attack*. The key confirmation is left optional in the YAK protocol, but it is crucial to have it in order to avoid an *impersonation attack*. In case of having the key confirmation, it is crucial to verify that public keys are of prime order. Otherwise, the protocol will be vulnerable to a *small subgroup attack*. In the YAK protocol, it is assumed that such verification is part of any zero-knowledge proof technique.

The YAK protocol is not secure in any security model that allows the above attacks. This includes the HMQV [3] and eCK [5] security models.

References

1. Hao, F.: On robust key agreement based on public key authentication. In: Sion, R. (ed.) FC 2010. LNCS, vol. 6052, pp. 383–390. Springer, Heidelberg (2010)
2. Hao, F.: On robust key agreement based on public key authentication. Secur. Commun. Netw. **7**(1), 77–87 (2014)
3. Krawczyk, H.: HMQV: a high-performance secure Diffie-Hellman protocol. In: Shoup, V. (ed.) CRYPTO 2005. LNCS, vol. 3621, pp. 546–566. Springer, Heidelberg (2005)
4. Toorani, M.: Cryptanalysis of a new protocol of wide use for email with perfect forward secrecy. Secur. Commun. Netw. 8(4), 694–701 (2015)
5. LaMacchia, B., Lauter, K., Mityagin, A.: Stronger security of authenticated key exchange. In: Susilo, W., Liu, J.K., Mu, Y. (ed.) ProvSec 2007. LNCS, vol. 4784, pp. 1–16. Springer, Heidelberg (2007)

© International Financial Cryptography Association 2015
R. Böhme and T. Okamoto (Eds.): FC 2015, LNCS 8975, pp. 569, 2015.
DOI: 10.1007/978-3-662-47854-7

Web Application Security with Contactless Identity Cards Using Near Field Communication (Poster Abstract)

Arvo Sulakatko and Alex Norta

Information and Communication Technology,
Tallinn University of Technology,
Ehitajate tee 5, Tallinn, Estonia
arvo.sulakatko@jsc-solutions.net, alex.norta.phd@ieee.org

Abstract. For over a decade, web servers have been able to encrypt their communication with the client by using Secure Socket Layer Protocol [1]. While this option only prevents casual eavesdropping for generic web sites and applications, for other applications the server must know who the client is. The client operating systems and web browsers may install a client-side certificate in their keystore that awaits selection. An essential requirements for identity services is to prevent identity theft. With the advancement of cost effective contactless cards, such a solution is with reach. Currently, only contact cards have been used to serve as client certificate keystores. Since all new android devices are equipped with NFC [3] reader chips, the research opportunity arises how to store on contactless cards an identity for web applications. Such cards with a set of secret PIN codes can not be copied and must be in physical posession of the user. Until recently, a web application was neither able to interact with the certificates used to secure the connection, nor was a web application able to sign any data. With the availability of implemented W3C WebCrypto API [2], a possible solution is within reach. We propose an architecture to extend Google Chrome for Android and use PIN1-protected client certificates from Contactless Identity Cards that use Near Field Communication to perform an SSL handshake. After loading a web application, it inspects the Contactless Identity Card and performs additional tasks such as signing data by prompting a request for PIN2.

Keywords: Web Applications · Secure Hardware · NFC

References

1. Davis, M., Gray, S., Kuehr-McLaren, D., Morrison, I., Shoriak, T.: Systems, methods and computer program products for authenticating client requests withclient certificate information. uS Patent 6,088,805, 11 Jul 2000. http://www.google.com/patents/US6088805
2. Hofstede, N., Van den Bleeken, N.: Using the w3c webcrypto api for document signing. In: WASH, pp. 10–16 (2013)
3. Yadav, A., Sharma, A.: Near field communication (2014). http://jiaats.cyberoot.org/Journals-Pdf/JEEE/jeee-3.pdf

© International Financial Cryptography Association 2015
R. Böhme and T. Okamoto (Eds.): FC 2015, LNCS 8975, pp. 570, 2015.
DOI: 10.1007/978-3-662-47854-7

OpenCard (Poster Abstract)

Pascal Paillier and Tancrède Lepoint

CryptoExperts, Paris, France
contact@cryptoexperts.com

Smart cards are an opaque technology. Programmable smart cards (JavaCard, MultOS, BasicCard) do not allow access to the (fast!) cryptographic primitive operations on the cryptographic co-processors, and use slow virtual machines. Worse, to access manufactured cards (and their complex software development tools), one has to order high volumes and sign non-disclosure agreements with chip manufacturers.

Introducing OpenCard. OpenCard is a truly, fully *open* smart card that supports user-defined applications developed in native code (C and/or assembly). Its purpose is to provide a simple smart card environment that can serve as a support for instrumenting and testing on-card applications without facing the limitations of cards based on virtual machines. It features a versatile operating system on top of which sets of APDU commands or software extensions containing native APIs, non-volatile data objects and various user-defined customizations are easily installed. Contrarily to other smart card platforms, OpenCard is programmable at a low, close-to-the-hardware level and is 100 % user-definable.

Features. OpenCard embeds a 32-bit ARM core (ARM SecurCore SC100), 512kB of flash memory and 18kB of RAM. The operating system provides native access to DES/3DES, AES and RSA co-processors. It also provides an advanced *on-card debugging*: no additional hardware such as emulation boards is required for development. Software development tools are free, open-source and run under Windows, OS X and Unix environments.

Extensions and OpenCard Market. OpenCard makes it easy to program your own cryptographic algorithms and applications making use of co-processors, and even to share your extensions within the OpenCard developers community. An online OpenCard Market displays pre-defined extensions and third-party code that can be easily downloaded into an OpenCard to build up a complete on-card application. OpenCard is ideal for smart card based hardware wallets for crypto-currencies such as Bitcoin.

CryptoExperts. CryptoExperts is a young start-up company founded by internationally recognized industrial and academic researchers in cryptography. Driven by more than 16 years of experience in smart cards development, we are proud to introduce OpenCard. With OpenCard, developers now have deeper access and high flexibility to build innovative, fast and secure smart card applications.

OpenCard will be available by mid 2015, with no minimum order, on
https://www.cryptoexperts.com/opencard

© International Financial Cryptography Association 2015
R. Böhme and T. Okamoto (Eds.): FC 2015, LNCS 8975, pp. 571, 2015.
DOI: 10.1007/978-3-662-47854-7_1

Author Index

Printed in the United States
By Bookmasters